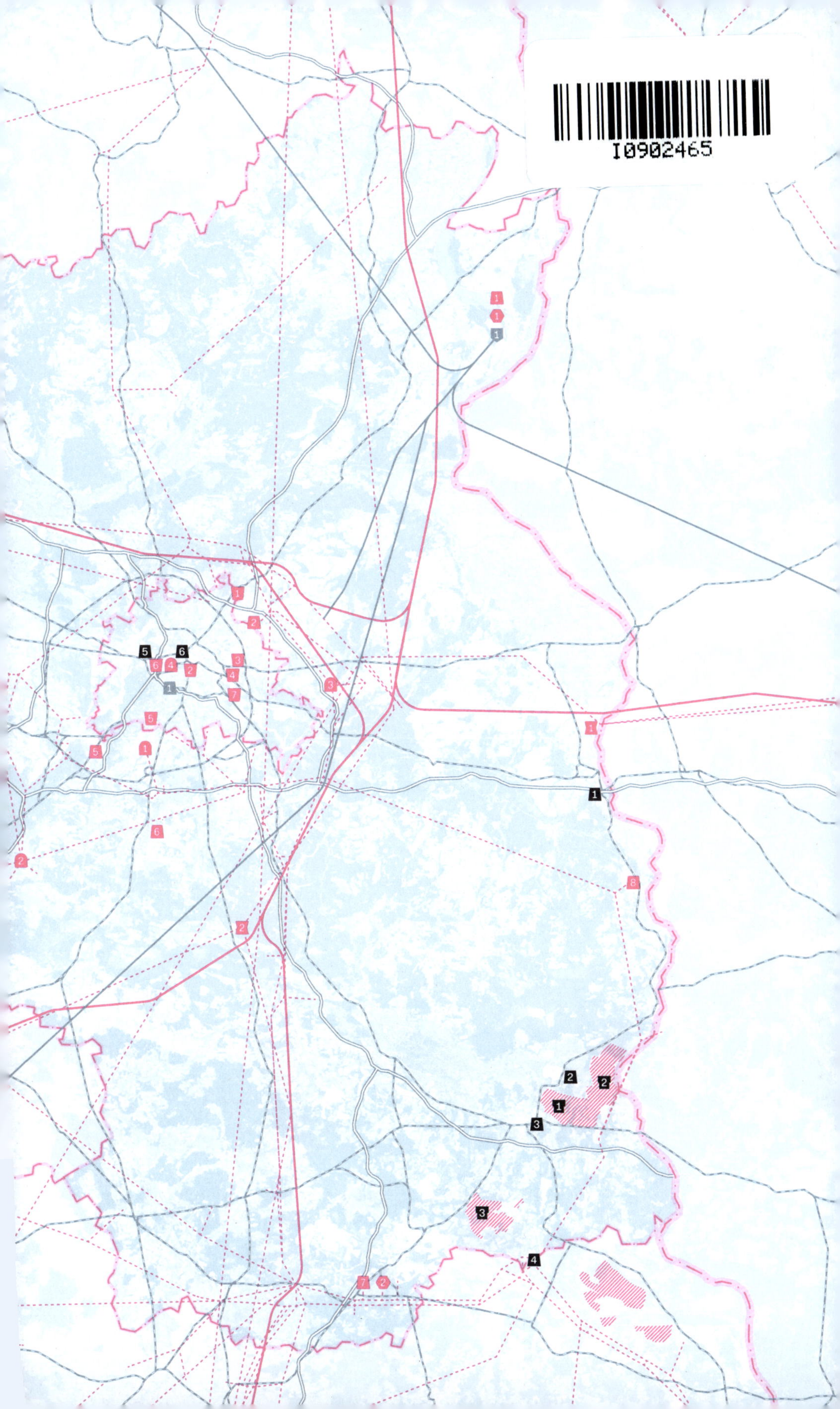

Abbreviations

AC	Alternating current
AD	Anno Domini
AEG	Allgemeine Electricitäts-Gesellschaft
Agip	Azienda Generale Italiana Petroli [Italian General Petroleum Corporation]
BASF	Badische Anilin- und Sodafabrik
BauGB	Baugesetzbuch [German Building Code]
BC	Before Christ
BEWAG	Berliner Städtische Elektrizitätswerke Aktien-Gesellschaft [see StEW]
BGR	Bundesanstalt für Geowissenschaften und Rohstoffe [Federal Institute for Geosciences and Natural Resources]
BNetzA	Bundesnetzagentur [Federal Network Agency]
BRD	Bundesrepublik Deutschland [Federal Republic of Germany]
CdS	Cadium sulphide
CdTe	Cadmium telluride
CFRP	Carbon-fibre reinforced plastic
CHP	Combined heat and power
CIGS	Copper indium gallium diselenide
CMEA	Council for Mutual Economic Assistance
CO_2	Carbon dioxide
CPC	Caspian Pipeline Consortium
CPT-MIX S	EU's Climate Target Plan Mix Scenario
DC	Direct current
DDR	Deutsche Demokratische Republik [German Democratic Republic]
DIY	Do it yourself
EEG	Erneuerbare-Energien-Gesetz [Renewable Energy Sources Act]
EV	Electric vehicle
EnBW	Energie Baden-Württemberg AG
ENI	Ente Nazionale Idrocarburi [Italian National Hydrocarbons Board]
ENTSO-E	European Network of Transmission System Operators for Electricity
EVW	Erdölverarbeitungswerk [crude oil processing plant]
FEC	Final Energy Consumption
FPSA	Final Production Sharing Agreement
FSRU	Floating storage and regasification units
GAE	Gross available energy
GDP	Gross domestic product
GHG	Greenhouse gas
GRP	Glass-reinforced plastic
HKW	Heizkraftwerk [Combined heat and power station]
IBA	Internationale Bauausstellung [International Building Exhibition]
ICE	German Intercity Express
ICGA	Imperial Continental Gas Association
ISE	Fraunhofer-Institut für Solare Energiesysteme
IEA	International Energy Agency
KATS	Karachaganak Atyrau Transportation System
KOTS	Karachaganak Orenburg Transportation System
KPC	Karachaganak Processing Complex
KPO	Karachaganak Petroleum Operating
LEAG	Lausitz Energie Bergbau AG
LMBV	Lausitzer und Mitteldeutsche Bergbau-Verwaltungsgesellschaft mbH
LNG	Liquefied natural gas
LTS	Large technical systems
LUKOIL	Langepas, Uray, and, Kogalym Oil [Russian multinational energy corporation]
MEGAL	Mittel-Europäische Gasleitung
MVL	Mineralölverbundleitung GmbH Schwedt
MWAE	Ministerium für Wirtschaft, Arbeit, und Energie, Brandenburg
NATO	North Atlantic Treaty Organization
NECP	National Energy and Climate Plan "Net Zero 2045"
PEC	Primary Energy Consumption
PCK	Petrolchemisches Kombinat
PETS	PCK & elf Tanklagerbetrieb Seefeld GbR
PPA	Power Purchase Agreement
PV	Photovoltaics
REE	Rare-earth elements
RWE	Rheinisch-Westfälisches Elektrizitätswerk AG
SPZ	Sanitary Protection Zone
StEW	Berliner Städtische Elektrizitätswerke [see BEWAG]
StrEG	Stromeinspeisungsgesetz [Electricity Feed-In Act of 1991]
TAG	Trans Austria Gasleitung
UCPTE	Union for the Co-ordination of Transmission of Electricity [Western European power grid]
UGSS	Russian Unified Gas Supply System
UN COP21	21st Conference of Parties, 2015 United Nations Climate Change Conference
VES	Vereinigte Energie Systeme [Eastern European power grid]
WBS 70	Wohnungsbauserie 70
YNAO	Yamalo-Nenets Autonomous Okrug

Power, Flows, and Transformation

Portraits of Berlin-Brandenburg Energy Spaces

David Bauer
Santiago Martínez Murillo
Philipp Misselwitz
Yuliya Navatskaya
Joseph Smithard (eds.)

jovis

Contributors

Edouard Barthen
Elke Beyer
Simon Breth
Philipp Deilmann
Felix Frankowiak
Anke Hagemann
Patrick Martin
Amelia Mega
Bui Luu Quynh Nguyen
Cordelia Polinna
Elif Soylu
Paul Strobel

Heartfelt thanks to

Theodora Karachatzi
Christian Gäth
Rosa Catalina Hanhausen
Martin Pohl
Katerina Tzouvala
Dilara Uçar
Oded Yatzkan

Content

1 Introduction

1.1

About this Book

Accounting for nearly three-quarters of annual global greenhouse gas GHG emissions, the transformation of energy networks is a pivotal step towards planetary sustainability[1]. In order to transition our current operating systems and work within planetary boundaries, various decarbonisation strategies will need to be implemented over the next two decades. This process will reshape territories, towns, and streets worldwide.

Energy supply is a driving force of urbanisation. Energy availability has shaped and defined economic, cultural, and social activities, mediated through complex and geographically-distributed infrastructural assemblages. Urban structures and landscapes depend largely on the way we produce, distribute, and consume energy, including its diverse carrier systems and sources. Energy is in everything from the procurement of materials, food, and shelter, to the facilitation of medical care, transportation, communication, education, recreation, and logistics (as well as the production of nearly every consumer good available). Energy is everywhere, and so are the collateral effects of its exuberant and on-demand consumption, which extend far beyond the limits of sustainability. At this critical juncture, it is imperative to think about the future of urbanisation, especially in view of the energy transition that is already underway. The future formula of this brave new energy world is indeed as simple and powerful as kWh/m^2.[2]

The book at hand is a modest attempt to explore energy supply and transition as a spatial and material phenomenon. It portrays a select number of spaces connected to German energy procurement in the capital region of Berlin-Brandenburg. The assembled pages result from one-and-a-half years of teaching and research into energy spaces past, present, and future, focusing specifically on the infrastructural assemblages that connect them. Undertaken at the Habitat Unit within the Institute of Architecture, TU Berlin, the research comprised various pedagogical formats that purposefully expand beyond the boundary of mere architectural production. The final assembly and major revision of the collected fragments was undertaken by a small team of teaching fellows and students, supported by the chair and its resources. Their devotion has resulted in a rather complex, experimental book design that comprises a multi-layered journey through various formats, regions, and timeframes.

It was created under the umbrella of BB2040.de, a collaborative online platform exploring #transformation processes in #BerlinBrandenburg from the perspective of #infrastructures. Both projects were made possible by the generosity and financial support of Robert Bosch Stiftung, to whom we are very grateful.

What to Expect and How to Read this Book

In order to meet the steep heating, energy, and lighting demands of our cities, industries, and homes, most urban agglomerations rely on extensive territories. The infrastructure networks responsible for mediating and transforming the flow of energy between global production sites and their centres of consumption are largely hidden from everyday observers, as they span great distances beyond the immediate confines of the visible footprint.

The central premise of this volume revolves around a basic yet complex question: where does the region of Berlin-Brandenburg source its energy from, and by what means? In an effort to address this inquiry, the authors have compiled a collection of maps, drawings, texts, and photographs. These resources are employed to unveil various aspects of the vast systems of urban energy accumulation and to illustrate the intricate elements and interconnections that link the seemingly disparate regions involved in energy production, distribution, and consumption. Being firm believers in the need to decarbonise, the authors also address potential strategies for the future transformation of some of these systems. [p. 305]

The book is divided into three distinct parts, each differing in length and scope. The initial section serves as a brief general introduction, acquainting the reader with the state of energy affairs, emergent transition pathways, and the prevailing trends within the context of Europe, Germany, and Berlin-Brandenburg. [p. 17] Furthermore, beyond simply reflecting upon the transformation needed within these systems, this introductory section relates this study to the role of education and teaching concepts that foster a multi-disciplinary approach towards the spatial planning disciplines. [p. 30]

The subsequent section comprises three concise narratives that shed light on the historical transformation of energy regimes and their spatial implications. Within this section, typologies of consumption, production, and transmission are examined across three different scales. The first narrative focuses on households, aiming to investigate the extent to which changes in energy utilisation have influenced the redefinition of dwelling typologies. [p. 53] The following narrative then expands this scope to encompass larger, citywide configurations, specifically analysing the evolutionary trajectory of Berlin's waterways as critical conduits for energy production and transportation. [p. 64] Finally, attention is directed towards developments within the Berlin power grid, which serves as a representative example of a large technical system that has undergone significant transformation over time. [p. 74]

The longest part of the book will cover a selection of specific energy carriers and technologies that are constitutive for sustaining the region. Given the scope of the project and the specificity of its focus, both the selection of carriers as well as the selection of sites are necessarily limited. The book does not cover all the energy resources employed in national and regional energy procurement, nor does it cover all the sites that would be vital to retrace a seamless flow from the sources of extraction through various transport routes and places of consumption. However, by focusing on coal [p. 100], oil [p. 140], gas [p. 176], solar [p. 230], and wind energy [p. 268], the authors have chosen a representative overview of some of the most vital and long-lasting material resources and technologies that can be interlinked within the localised framework of the book. The chapter is divided into two main sections, namely fossil fuel carriers [p. 89] and renewable or inexhaustible technologies [p. 213].

Within this there are five sub-chapters, each following a clear structure that allows for a comparative reading of respective energy carriers. After giving a short general introduction, the sub-chapters will discuss each carrier's physical properties as well as the multi-scalar supply networks that are essential to their extraction, transport, and consumption. Thereafter, the reader is introduced to the wider context of Germany, as well as the specific region of Berlin-Brandenburg, followed by case studies illustrating select sites that lie along the carrier's path from source to sink. Sometimes, these five sub-chapters are juxtaposed with additional essays contributed by guest writers. Given this fluid structure, the book can easily be read in a non-linear fashion.

These chapters are bookended by two photo essays from the Berlin-based photographer Bui Luu Quynh Nguyen, each lending colour and complexity to the (sometimes very reduced) graphical representation.

Given the extensive possibilities of what can be said about energy in the past, present, and future, reduction has been the key to coping with the project and successfully bringing it between two covers.

A whole library of excellent books on the topic in its regional context is accessible to the willing scholar, and a short selection of further reading is attached at the end of each chapter as well as at the back of the book. Notably, this work has been partially assembled during a period marked by colossal shifts in stagnant and decades-old energy supply patterns, occurring in the wake of the Russian invasion of Ukraine. During the year 2022, information about supply patterns was shifting on a weekly basis and was often hard to pin down.

With the acceleration of climate change and related events unfurling across large stretches of the globe, the daily newspapers are beginning to read like a prequel to Kim Stanley Robinson's *Ministry of the Future*. As one of the most relevant sectors in the quest for global decarbonisation, energy is now majorly in focus and is consequently in a continual state of flux—something which, on occasion, made the authors' lives quite difficult. Moreover, as one of the most capital and investment-intensive markets, the process of tracing energy sources is a complex endeavour, often yielding ambiguous results—sometimes providing an excess of information and, at other times, leaving the authors with nothing at all.

Ultimately, this volume should be regarded as a source of inspiration for readers, aiming to challenge the commonplace assumption that electricity simply comes from a socket or that heat emanates solely from a radiator.

With all that said, we hope the reader will enjoy these little stories we have put together.

The editors

1.2

Power, Flows, and Transformation

David Bauer

We Need to Talk about Energy Dependencies

In 2021, the European Union had an average energy import dependency of 55 %, meaning that its production and stocks only met less than half of its actual needs.[3] This figure reflects the extent to which an economy depends on other countries to fulfil its own energy demands. Besides Norway, which is a massive exporter of oil and gas, no other nation in Europe today can sustain itself solely through domestic resources. Some member states—such as the energy poster child Iceland, with its subterranean heat and rich tidal movement, or the small Baltic nation of Estonia—have reduced to remarkably low numbers. Overall, however, there remains a strong need for massive material inflows from external providers.[4]

Fig. 1 Energy import dependency / Rate of fossil fuel dependency in European countries, 2021 in %

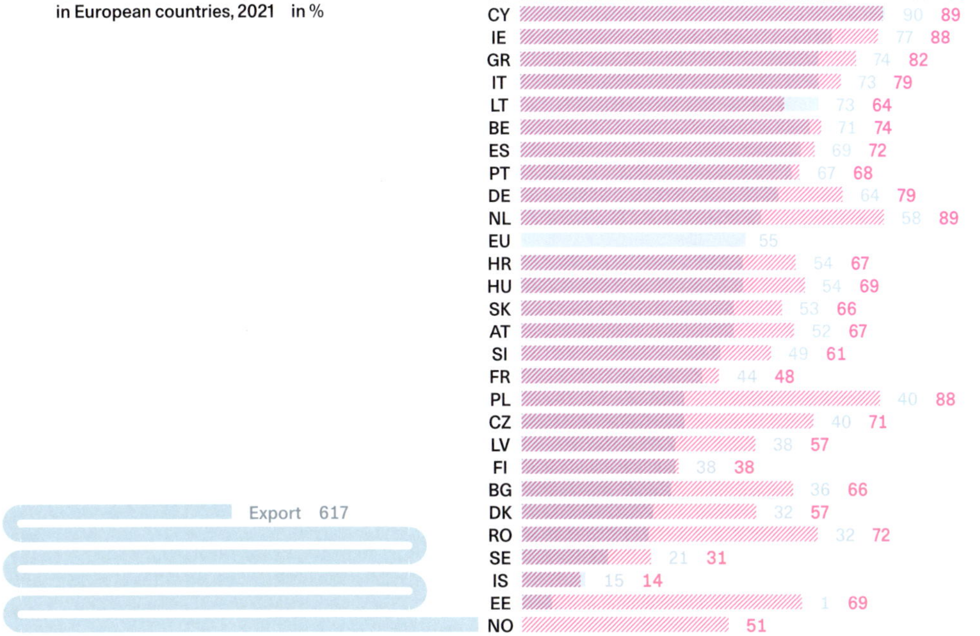

This phenomenon is largely tied to the fact that the gross available energy GAE in the EU—an essential aggregate in energy balances that represents the quantity of energy necessary to satisfy all demands—is made up of around 70 % fossil fuels, transported from a handful of resource-rich countries through an intricate system of pipelines, barges, trains, containers, roads, sea ports, and rivers. In the highly industrialised and urbanised world of the 21st century, energy import dependency has become a normal—and in many cases unavoidable—phenomenon.

However, the resources utilised to fuel the unprecedented industrial and economic transformations experienced by many nations over the last century are not evenly distributed across the globe. In terms of energy, our world is divided into a few "haves" and many "have-nots": as long as we continue to extract fossil fuels from below ground, this is unlikely to change.

However, the percentage of fossil fuel dependency is startlingly high given that the commitment to the UN COP21 Paris Agreement, adopted in 2015, requires the rapid disentanglement from hydrocarbons within less than three short decades.[5] As political and economic elites gradually implement carbon pushback through national and international policies, as well as economic incentives for markets to engage on a continental scope, a glimpse into the EU's energy balance sheets may not inspire too much hope. Since 1990, the first year for which EU statistical data is available, the dependency on fossil fuels has dropped by a mere 13 % on average.[6]

Fig. 2 Rate of fossil fuel dependency, European Union, 1990–2021 in %

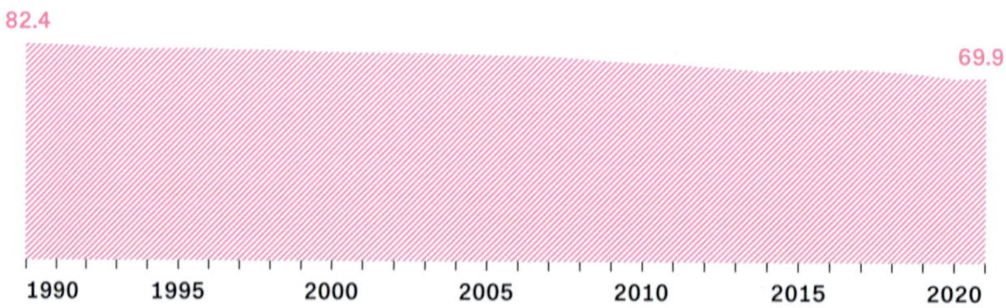

With the European Green Deal launched in 2019, the European Commission has established the ambitious objective of evolving into the world's inaugural climate-neutral continent by 2050. This necessitates implementing an array of policies to cut net GHG emissions by a minimum of 55 % by 2030, compared to the levels in 1990.[7] In this make-or-break decade, each member state must play its part to reach the EU-level target through individual National Energy and Climate Plans NECP.

The overarching strategy to achieve decarbonisation is threefold. Firstly, conserving energy is paramount. Secondly, there is a need to transition energy consumption towards renewable sources. Lastly, a concerted effort to electrify various sectors is crucial, given that these technologies are primarily geared towards electricity production.

Enter Germany

Given its status as the EU's most populous country and its largest industrial producer,[8] the energy transformation in Germany is of paramount significance. Its role as the principal net importer and consumer of energy in absolute terms[9] means that the strategies pursued at the national level will not only wield substantial influence on CO_2 reduction but will also stand as an exemplar of how to achieve decarbonisation in one of the world's leading global producers. [Fig. 3]

In 2023, Germany had a Primary Energy Consumption PEC of around 10,735 PJ or around 2,982,500 GWh.[10] To make this number more accessible, consider that 1 PJ — which is equivalent to 1 million billion (10^{15}) joules or 278 GWh — amounts to the electricity consumption of approximately 79,000 German households with a national average consumption of around 3,500 kWh per year.[11]

Hence, the total PEC corresponded to an equivalent of electricity consumed by more than 853,000,000 households, representing a total capacity of approximately 2,000 % compared to the number of households in Germany in the year 2023.[12] The difficulty here is that we do not only consume electricity, but divide this PEC among various carriers, applications, and transmutation systems to generate different forms of energy usage across different sectors. [Fig. 10]

The term "Primary Energy Consumption" refers to the total energy content of all domestically utilised energy sources, including fossil and non-fossil fuels.[13] In order to fit industrial and domestic purposes, PEC—often coming in the form of crude resources—needs to be converted into more readily usable forms of energy with considerable losses. When it reaches the consumer, it is called "Final Energy Consumption" FEC. Technological infrastructures, such as refineries or power stations, are some of the very visible components in this transmutation. Several examples of final energy include electricity, heating oil, biogas, and district heating, as well as fuels such as gasoline, diesel, and kerosene.

Fig. 3 Primary Energy Consumption, European countries, 2022 in TWh

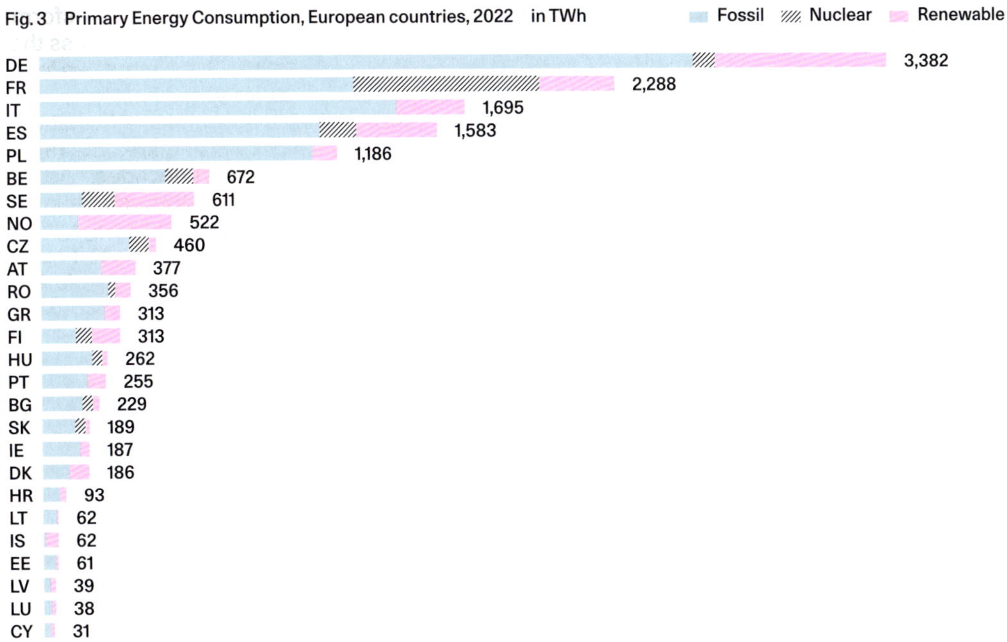

Typically, the reliance on specific energy sources varies across different sectors. [Fig. 5] The industrial sector accounts for the most significant proportion of domestic FEC, constituting nearly 30 % annually. Following this, the transportation of goods and people claims the next substantial share. More than a quarter of the total FEC is apportioned to this sector, with a pronounced emphasis on use in combustion engines. This distribution is reflected in private household consumption, which is mainly attributed to indoor heating using fossil fuels. The service sector represents the most minor fraction within the overall distribution.[14]

Fig. 4 Share of Germany's Primary Energy Consumption by source in PJ

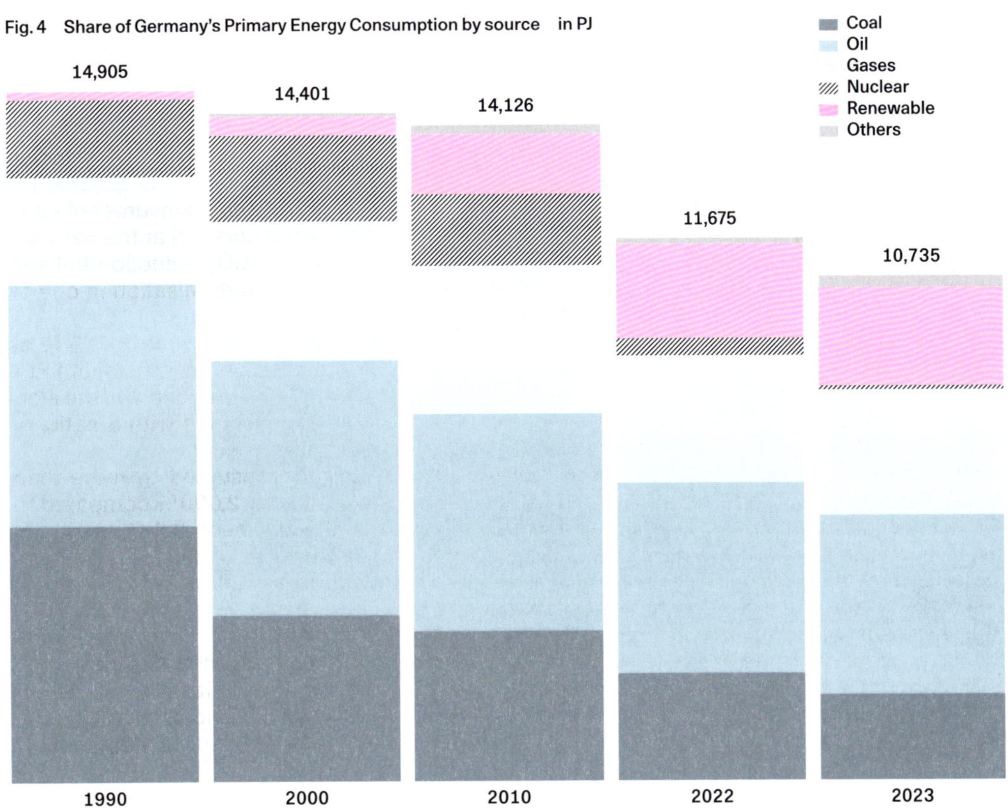

Looking ahead to the established targets, it is crucial to acknowledge that despite a decline of approximately 28 % in PEC between 1990 and 2023, the FEC in Germany has only decreased by about 11 %, just like in many other countries around the globe, showing only moderate reduction.[15] Although there is a trend towards increasingly efficient energy utilisation and conservation, economic growth and heightened consumer demands impede the much-needed substantial decline in overall consumption. Despite demand reduction having been emphasised by several studies as a pivotal aspect of the energy transition, the discursive approaches of post-growth scenarios—as well as the prospect of intentional and permanent self-limitation on the part of consumers—is generally not well received in political debate. Hence, there appears to be a prevalent inclination towards reliance on technological solutions and a tendency towards escalating efficiencies, which are increasingly perceived as the most viable routes within a contentious political discourse.

As outlined in the German NECP from October 2019, the objective is to attain a decrease of nearly one-third in primary energy consumption by 2030, relative to the levels recorded in 2008.[16] In order to fulfil the climate targets, the plan envisages the share of renewable energies rising to 80 % of the existing electricity supply within the next seven years.[17] In 2023, approximately 52% had been achieved, indicating a substantial increase. However, this figure does not yet account for the growing demand for expanded electricity production needed to decarbonise other sectors.[18]

Unfortunately, electricity comes with the incredible disadvantage that, unlike many of the physical energy carriers used by humanity throughout the ages, it cannot be efficiently stored without being tangibly embodied through some or other technological means. Whether in the form of batteries, water-pumping stations, gas, or the long-anticipated rollout of hydrogen technology, electricity is a fleeting charge that must be captured and maintained.

Fig. 5 Final Energy Consumption by sector and carrier in Germany, 2022 in TWh

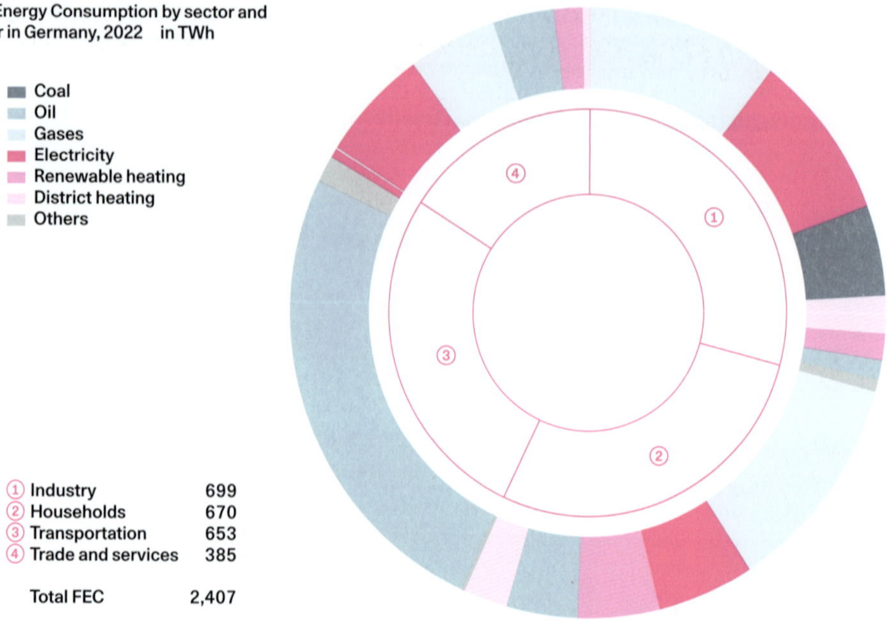

①	Industry	699
②	Households	670
③	Transportation	653
④	Trade and services	385
	Total FEC	2,407

While specific sectors have already begun to diversify or switch to different sources, others remain notoriously resistant. If you observe a disproportionate number of Tesla vehicles in your vicinity, you probably live in a particularly affluent part of an affluent city or town. However, this observation may not accurately represent the actual share of electric vehicles EVs in the overall mobility landscape, which currently remains in the low single digits.[19] The mobility sector continues to be overwhelmingly dominated by fossil fuels, as does the domestic heating sector: more than three-quarters of home energy supply is still obtained from gas, oil, and coal. Over 50 % of FEC is attributed to the requirement for diverse forms of heat, catering to applications ranging from the 20-year-old boiler in Berlin and Brandenburg basements all the way to the building-sized steam cracker furnaces at BASF Ludwigshafen. A substantial portion of this consumption is solely attributed to various gas sources.[20]

Back on the Trail

Although Germany embarked on the path towards purposefully decarbonising its primary energy provision over two decades ago by introducing the Renewable Energy Sources Act EEG in the year 2000,[21] the reality remains stark: 80 % of Germany's PEC is still under the sway of carbon-emitting technologies, namely fossil fuels. [Fig. 4] This ongoing and considerable reliance has not only undermined the credibility of the *Energiewende,*[22] once considered the most ambitious global effort to strategically reshape the energy landscape, but it has also strengthened a range of critical interdependencies.

At its inception, the EEG presented itself as an ambitious and forward-looking legislative framework that served as a model for several other countries, paving the way towards cutting renewable energy generation costs by almost 95 % in 20 years.[23] Predominantly driven by private individuals—through community energy initiatives as well as municipal and city utilities—wind parks, solar fields, and biogas storage proliferated across the landscape, seamlessly integrating into the national grid and underscoring the viability of these novel energy sources and their numerous advantages. Differing from neighbouring countries like France and Poland, which respectively hold steadfast to their respective nuclear and coal power plants, Germany's strategy unveiled a pathway for a grand but gradual transition that was unfurling *in media res*.

While individuals and communities propelled a remarkable boom in renewable technology, the German industry, being incrementally relieved from the mandatory plans of the EEG, began to tune and revise its production strategy: importing cheap energy and converting it into high-value and premium goods, predominantly for export to the burgeoning consumer power of China. Amidst a deepening European financial crisis that adversely affected many countries, German companies experienced an exceptional decade of expansion and prosperity. This period, spanning from 2010 to 2020, was characterised by significant increases in GDP, exports, and stock market performance.[24]

Fig. 6 Import dependency of selected sources in Germany in PJ

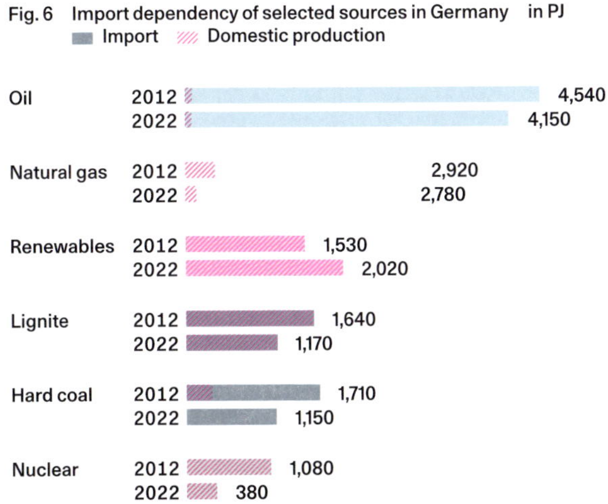

Despite this apparent success story, domestic industry was hindered by a culture of conservatism that limited the widespread adoption of renewable technologies. Unlike carmakers, chemical, and steel manufacturers, the handful of large energy utilities in the country showed even less ambition for transformation. Despite ten years of implementation since the beginning of the millennium, Germany's largest electricity producer — RWE — sourced only 2.6 % of its energy from renewable sources in 2011,[25] a negligence that comes at a considerable price in the volatile energy markets the world is currently entangled in.

Aside from its significant coal reserves, Germany has a dependancy on fossil resources that it simply does not possess. [Fig. 6] With a comprehensive import dependency rate of roughly two-thirds, [Fig. 1] it surpasses the European average.[26] Nearly all utilised oil, gas, and hard coal is primarily sourced from foreign states.

Shifting Energy Geography

Due to the geographical distribution of Germany's industries, and the location of its most densely populated areas, energy consumption and production are not evenly dispersed across the country. Energetically speaking, this has led to a distinct divide that can be seen in the patterns of individual states within the BRD, with a large population and industrial output normally equalling heavier fuel consumption and thus greater reliance on energy imports.

According to many decarbonisation scenarios, Germany[27] is compelled to shift the bulk of its energy production towards renewable sources through widespread electrification, which will unify all sectors under a common currency. [p. 219] The pathway to this development was forged in the 1990s through a series of legislations that restructured the energy market, mandating electricity supply companies to purchase electrical energy from renewable sources and offer adequate compensation for it.[28]

Historically, electricity production happened solely through a comparatively small number of conventional or nuclear power stations which were situated close to industrial and populous centres or, in the case of coal, often in direct proximity to the mines themselves. Given that transportation and transmission incurred significant costs, the delivery of power over long distances often resulted in substantial financial losses. Therefore, locating facilities in balance with resources, convenient transport infrastructure, and end consumers became imperative.

The power stations were frequently situated alongside major railway systems, rivers, and inland ports to facilitate the sourcing of cooling water and the transportation of coal. [pp. 64, 77, and 136] The distribution of electricity followed a relatively linear and static system, designed to ensure a predictable generation capacity accessible to both small-scale and large-scale consumers.

Fig. 7 Land-use of energy carriers per unit of electricity, 2021 in m²/MWh

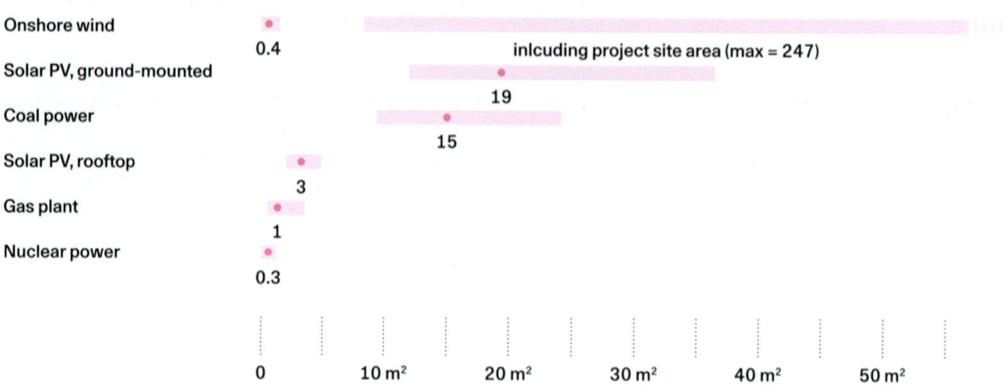

The geographical distribution of renewable technologies, however—whether deriving energy from wind, solar, hydropower, geothermal sources, or biofuels—adheres to a different set of geographical and even geological principles. From an economic perspective, the feasibility of renewable power generation facilities requires them to be situated in regions abundant with a different set of energy resources compared to before. Wind turbines are impractical in areas with no wind, solar panels are inefficient without sunlight, and hydropower stations lose their viability without an adequate water supply.

Another aspect to consider is that, compared to their fossil counterparts, these technologies require a larger physical footprint for the same energy output volume.[29] [Fig. 7] Consequently, their deployment often necessitates expansive, undeveloped areas, leading to the establishment of facilities in predominantly rural regions, often at a considerable distance from densely populated and industrially intensive areas with high energy demand.[30] In urban areas, meanwhile, this is complemented by the rising number of smaller PV systems installed on the rooftops of single-family and multi-family houses. Nevertheless, despite their growing numbers, experts argue that these systems are more inclined to play a subsidiary role in the broader energy production landscape, which will in the future mainly rely on large-scale facilities.[31] [p. 243]

Consequently, faced with the impending absence of fossil and nuclear fuels, Germany must adjust to a new paradigm in which significant industrial production hubs no longer align with energy producers in the conventional sense. Instead, it must contend with a considerable decentralisation of small energy inputs that is reshaping the landscape and overruling the concept of compact energy-generating facilities. One outcome of this is the emergence of entirely new sceneries characterised by prominent and visible energy production sites, in many cases spanning greater distances than their traditional counterparts.

This distribution pattern is coupled with challenges like network limitations, which hinder efficient power transmission, as well as grid expansion delays owing to (public) resistance towards the massive clustering of high-voltage transmission lines. Additionally, the presence of a single bidding zone that tries to keep uniform prices—despite significant regional differences in renewable power production across the entire country—has already led to a complex and patchy energy system that is subject to much dispute.[32]

Contrary to the prevailing notion that the emerging energy landscape will primarily be regional, the actual scenario suggests a trend towards large scale interconnectedness spanning across Germany and Europe. In turn, this is leading to the emergence of new major energy districts and regions that sell and bid across one unified European energy market.[33]

Massive monitoring will be needed since the direct associations between specific types of power stations and their respective load categories (base, intermediate, and peak load power stations) as they were previously understood will no longer apply in the future. Instead, there will be a greater demand for dynamic controllability that will facilitate inter-regional exchanges and for flexible power stations with rapid start-up and shutdown times. Whereas today, each major city has historically had various types of large-scale power stations [p. 77, p. 131] in its immediate conurbation or in its slightly more distant hinterlands, the future will bring greater reliance on partnerships between energy-producing fields and farms and dense urban centres.

Berlin-Brandenburg

The capital region of Berlin-Brandenburg can be seen as an attractive case study and, according to its own description, as a model region for transformation and exchanges.[34] Although Berlin is Germany's biggest city, it is simultaneously its third smallest state. Due to its location within the larger territory of Brandenburg, Berlin has historically depended on its infrastructural connections to outside regions. This reliance has persisted, despite the abnormal and costly period of self-sufficiency imposed upon West Berlin during the Cold War.[35] [p. 80]

Berlin encompasses an area of 891 km^2 and had a population of 3,850,000 in at the end of 2022, yielding a population density of roughly 4,200 inhabitants per km^2.[36] In contrast, Brandenburg, one of the least densely populated states in the BRD, spans an area of around 29,600 km^2 with a population of 2,540,000 inhabitants, resulting in a mere 86 inhabitants per km^2.[37] Berlin is approximately 48 times more densely populated than Brandenburg. Given its confined perimeter and the absence of domestic resources, the city finds itself in the position of being a significant energy importer. The bulk of its power influx arrives through Brandenburg's gas, oil, and electricity grids.

Conversely, Brandenburg has historically served as a notable energy producer and relevant transit space. The state features critical entry points for transcontinental pipeline networks which supply oil and gas to significant sections of the country. Brandenburg's underground not only functions as a distributor of oil and gas, but also serves as the location for one of the country's most significant subterranean gas storage facilities. [p. 196] With one of the major national refineries [p. 158] situated within its borders, it further assumes a pivotal role in providing fuel for roughly nine out of ten vehicles in Berlin.[38] Moreover, Brandenburg is among the four German states that persist in the extraction and conversion of domestic coal into electricity for export. [p. 113] This traditional energy landscape is now complemented by significant renewable energy development. As of 2023, Brandenburg led Germany's renewable energy deployment with approximately 4,000 wind turbines, 61,500 photovoltaic installations and 454 biogas facilities, achieving the nation's highest renewable capacity per capita.[39] [pp. 241, 272, and 280]

Fig. 8 Berlin and Brandenburg's Primary Energy Consumption by source, 1990–2020 in PJ

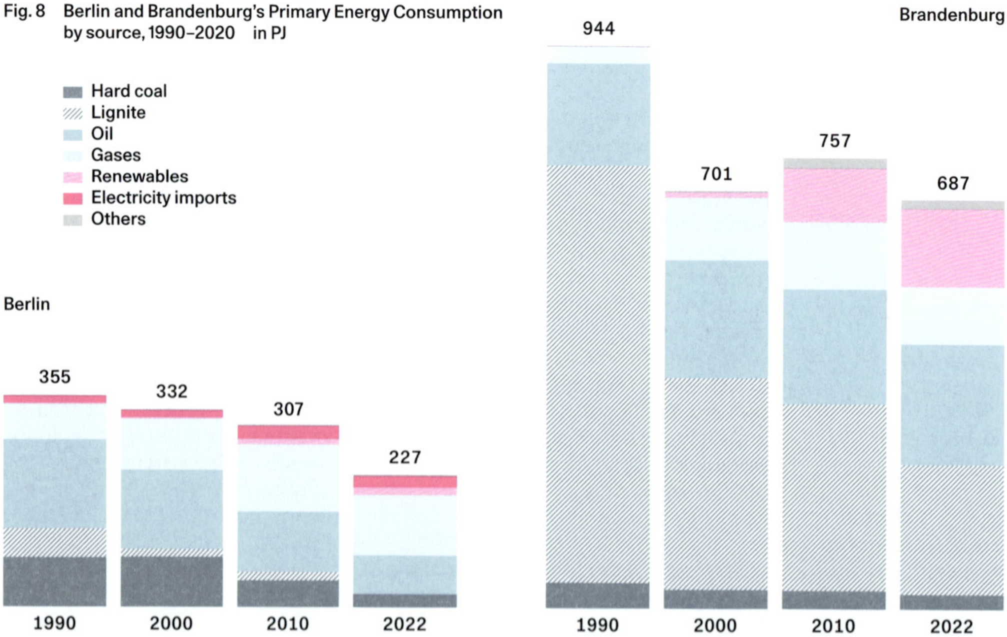

Inevitably, the close interaction between these two parties will only be amplified by the profound transformations currently occurring in the German energy system. Given the demand for substantial land area, not only Berlin but other populous hubs will need help to identify domestic terrains suitable for accommodating renewable technologies of varying sizes and scales, while also adhering to standards of social and ecological acceptability.

Using wind energy as a critical example, the state of Berlin is required to allocate an area equivalent to 0.25 % of its land mass to wind production by the end of 2026, and to increase this to 0.5 % by the end of 2032 for the installation of large turbines.[40] Given the limited available space, Berlin has already begun utilising extraterritorial city-owned lands[41] in the surrounding Brandenburg region, specifically on the former *Rieselfelder*—holdovers from the 19th-century sewage farms that were employed to process inner-city manure during the city's industrialisation.[42] [p. 283]

Having embarked on renewable energy production at an early juncture, the self-proclaimed "Energieland Brandenburg" (Energy State Brandenburg)[43] has now positioned itself as one of the leading states and, by extension, one of the pioneering regions globally, proffering new insight into potential models for how the "future normal" might look on various scales. [p. 287] However, as a forerunner, the region contends with a rising number of inherent conflicts and challenges. Already approaching the upper limit of wind turbine capacity mandated at the federal level, several regional projects are encountering stern opposition to further implementation, and face significant public dissent. Solar parks sprout quickly on the relatively spacious and (at least when compared to areas in other German regions) still moderately priced parcels of land. [p. 241] While the state possesses considerable spatial potential, there is an increasing need to restrain and strike a balance with other emerging goals that are imperative in the wider transformation towards sustainability, including landscape preservation, agricultural considerations, and the mounting demands placed on wooded areas. Forests cover more than one-third of Brandenburg, and with 10 % of its surface consisting of mostly drained lowland moors, it is considered one of the marshiest areas in the BRD.[44]

Moreover, as the region seeks to retain its energy-intensive industrial activities—spanning sectors such as steel and cement production, paper and plastic manufacturing, and timber processing, among others—it must also develop comprehensive strategies to align with its predetermined objectives. This includes achieving a 23 % reduction in PEC by 2030, followed by a more ambitious 39 % reduction by 2040. To achieve this, the proposed strategy aims to develop a domestic hydrogen economy utilising its dense infrastructural network and growing renewable production capacities. In terms of overall primary energy consumption, the target range for renewable energy is currently set between 42 % and 55 % by 2030 and a more substantial range of between 68 % and 85 % by 2040.[45]

As we will see throughout the book, Brandenburg already possesses the necessary land area, coupled with a relatively low population, to foster and create a robust renewable energy economy, ready to export beyond its own boundaries. On the other hand, Berlin's options to increase its own production are less abundant, and its primary strategies for decarbonisation focus on restructuring its infrastructure to incorporate efficient low-carbon technology and reduce overall energy consumption, despite projected growth and a rising population. The current objectives for achieving these goals include phasing out coal-based energy generation in its remaining domestic power stations [pp. 74 and 136], increasing solar capacity through rooftop integration, implementing storage technologies on all scales, and gradually transitioning towards a multi-sourced carbon neutral district heating supply.[46] To reduce GHG emissions by 95 % compared to 1990 levels—effectively resulting in emissions of only 1,462 Mt of CO_2 equivalent[47]—it is paramount that the city significantly and rapidly reduces its energy consumption. However, to put the difficulty of this task into perspective, to meet the emissions target by 2045, the entire city of Berlin must discharge less CO_2 in total than the emissions from roughly 300,000 vehicles, each releasing about 4.6 t annually.

Fig. 9 Total emissions in Germany 1990–2022 and emission targets 2030 and 2045 in Mt CO_2e

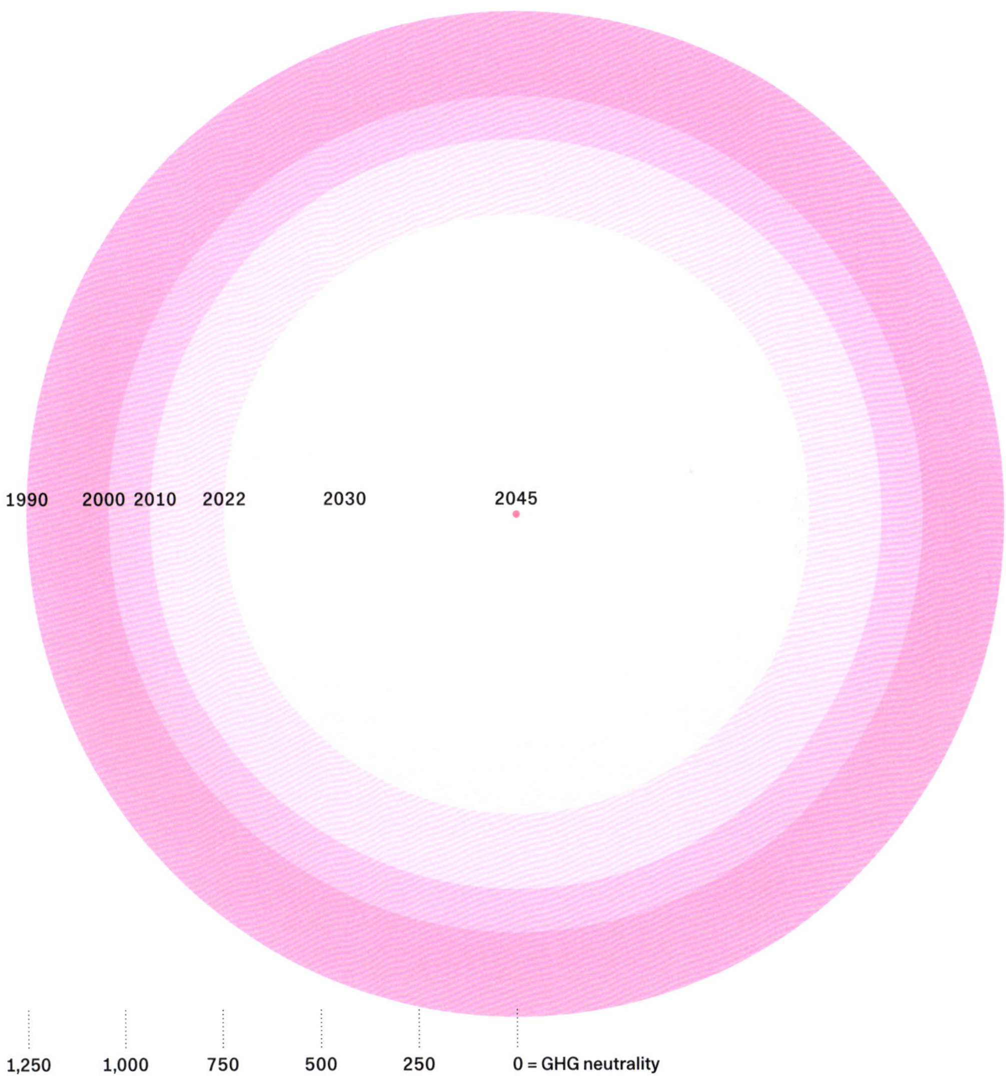

Besides improving energy efficiency in a growing city, a major relief strategy is to partially outsource certain functional aspects such as manufacturing, waste management, and infrastructure development to external entities, whether regional or international. This approach has historical roots in the modern Western city, where concerns about health and the high costs of urban land led to the de-functionalisation of cities. This prompted the expansion of larger-scale production and infrastructure beyond city limits.[48]

When considering the future of energy production, especially concerning large-scale combined heat and power CHP stations, which have a rich historical legacy in Berlin, various functional adaptations will be necessary to adequately serve district heating. At this stage, the majority of these stations implement said functional adaptations by utilising natural gas, which has significantly lower CO_2 emissions than coal. Gas supply presents an intriguing historical parallel, particularly in the context of Berlin's urban development. Historically, gas provision infrastructure and its production centres have played a dominant and visible role in the city's energy metabolism. [p. 70] Derived from the carbonisation of coal, at its peak there were 33 gasworks emitting massive quantities of smoke and soot throughout the conurbation, some of them even operating until 1991.[49] However, with the reunification of Germany, this production landscape underwent a significant transformation as Berlin transitioned towards solely importing remote natural gas sources, leading to the abandonment of large areas within the city. Today, only a few of these once-vital installations are preserved. Of the more than 150 large storage tanks—in some cases measuring up to 100 m—only a handful remain, having mostly been transformed into upscale residences or office spaces. However, in the wake of the Russian invasion of Ukraine in 2022, gas storage facilities, which had fallen out of favour due to the consistent supply provided by pipeline systems, experienced an unexpected resurgence in public interest and strategic importance, as the reader will see in the course of this book. [pp. 196 and 210]

However, it is not solely the energy infrastructure that has been outsourced. Over the past three decades, logistics centres and industrial areas catering to the expanding city have progressively relocated to strategically positioned, more cost-effective locations beyond the state's borders.[50]

Both the airports in Tempelhof and Tegel that existed in 1991 have been shuttered, making way for urban residents and upmarket real estate development. Airborne traffic is now solely managed through the shared airport in Schönefeld, effectively shifting the previously incurred GHG emissions to Brandenburg. Even though the city-state is taking action to provide some of its own resources in the renewable future, achieving sustainability will continue to necessitate leveraging resources from nearby and distant locations. Therefore, despite their diverging profiles, thinking about "the city" and "the region" as distinct or separate entities may not be helpful in supporting the wider energy transition.

The relationship between Berlin and Brandenburg offers a fertile ground for remodelling future energy supply systems that can be applied elsewhere, providing valuable insights into the trade-offs and blind spots involved in power distribution within urban–rural networks. As the imperative towards decarbonisation grows, it becomes crucial to ensure a fair distribution of responsibilities—not only between urban areas and immediate rural regions but also considering the extensive externalisation beyond visible boundaries.

Fig. 10 Energy balance flow in Germany, 2023 in TWh

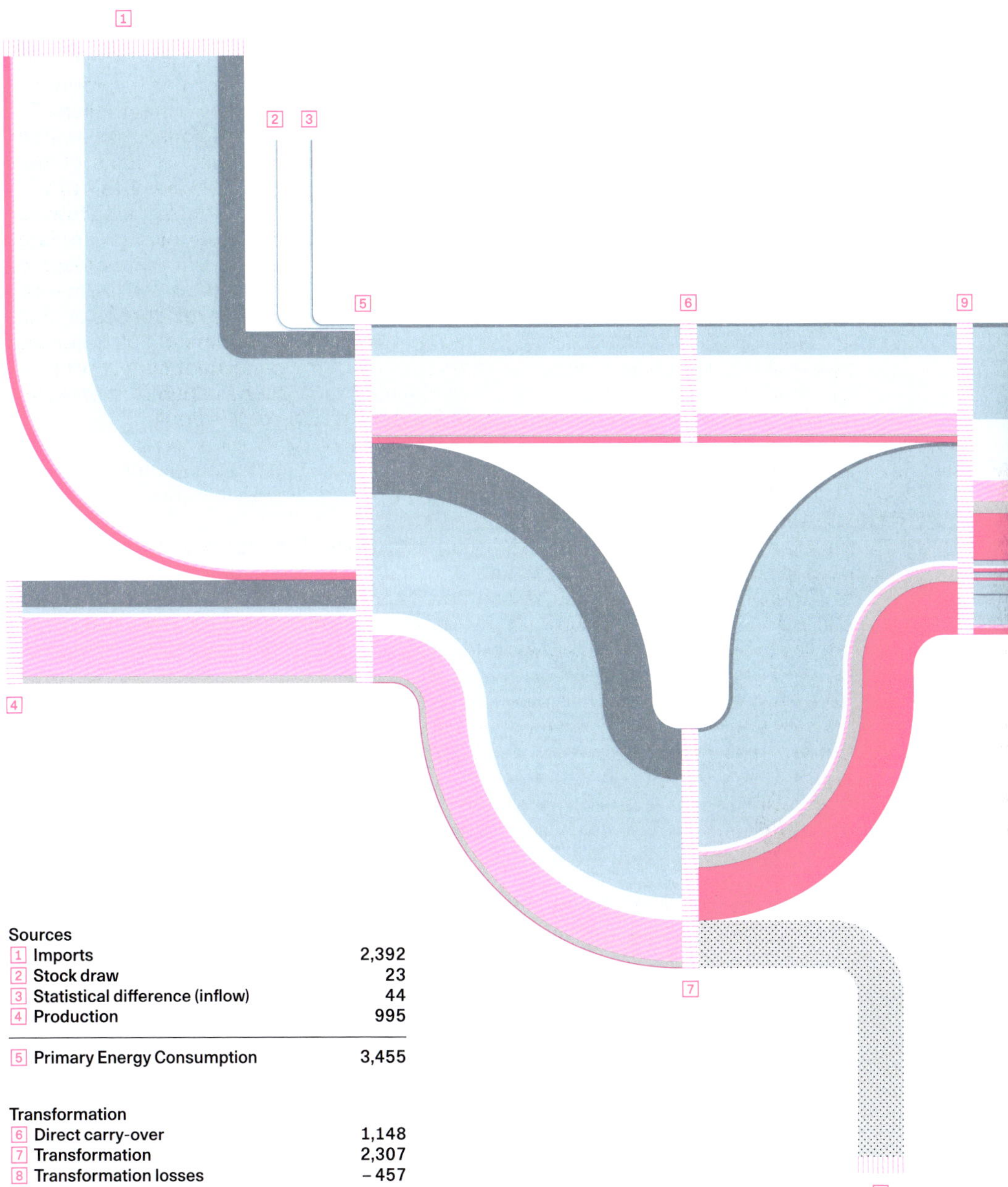

Sources	
1 Imports	2,392
2 Stock draw	23
3 Statistical difference (inflow)	44
4 Production	995
5 Primary Energy Consumption	3,455
Transformation	
6 Direct carry-over	1,148
7 Transformation	2,307
8 Transformation losses	– 457
9 Available after transformation	2,998

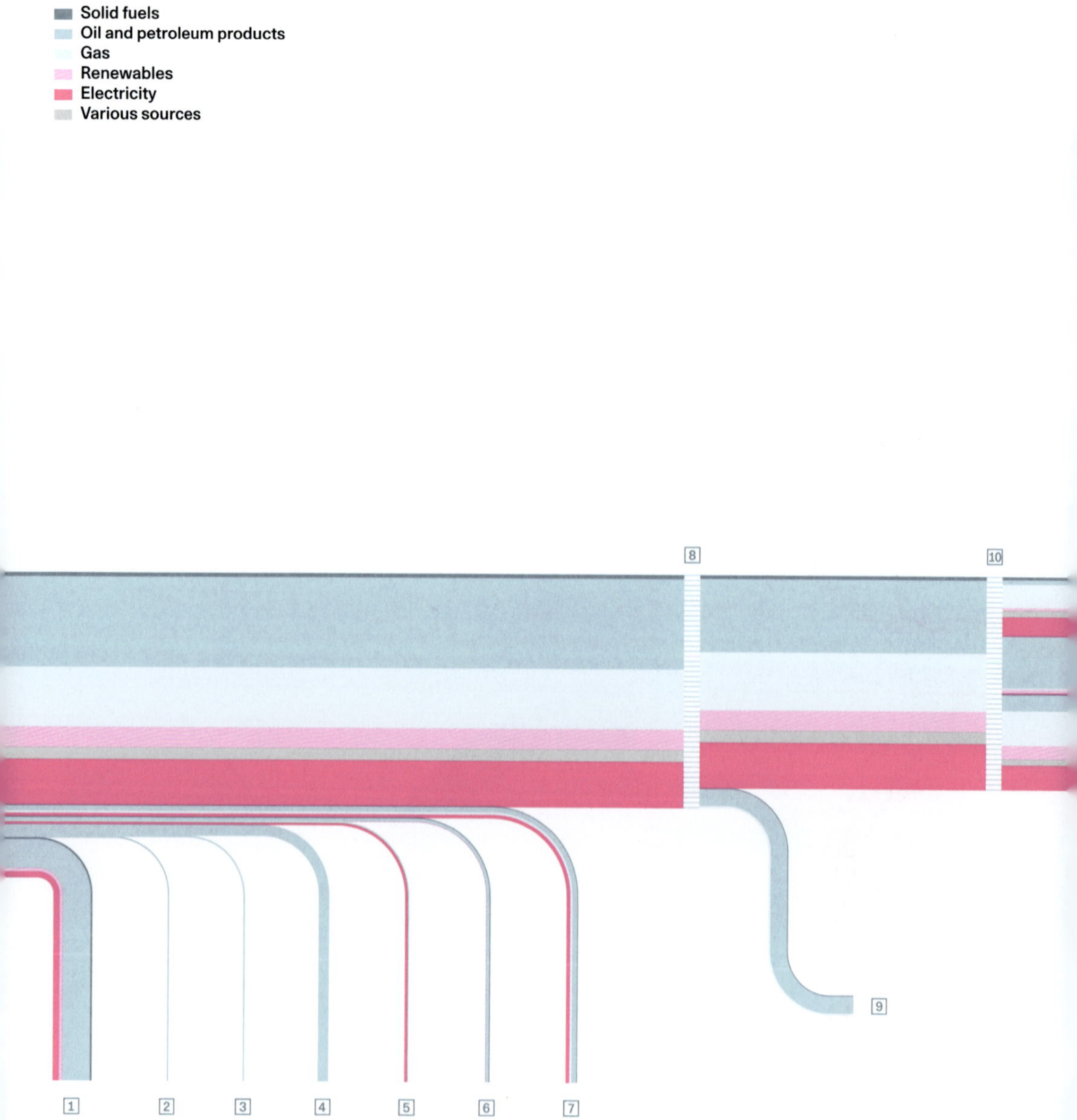

9 Available after transformation	2,998
Transmission	
1 Exports	-393
2 Stock build	-6
3 Marine bunkers	-15
4 International aviation	-109
5 Transmission losses	-41
6 Statistical difference (outflow)	-38
7 Consumption of energy branch	-112
8 Final consumption	2,284
9 Final non-energy consumption	-194
10 Final Energy Consumption	2,090

Consumption by 1 Industry	582
1 Iron and steel production	78
2 Chemical and petrochemical	139
3 Non-metallic minerals	68
4 Machinery	54
Consumption by 2 Transportation	569
5 Road traffic	540
Consumption by 3 Other sectors	939
6 Commercial and public services	278
7 Households	617

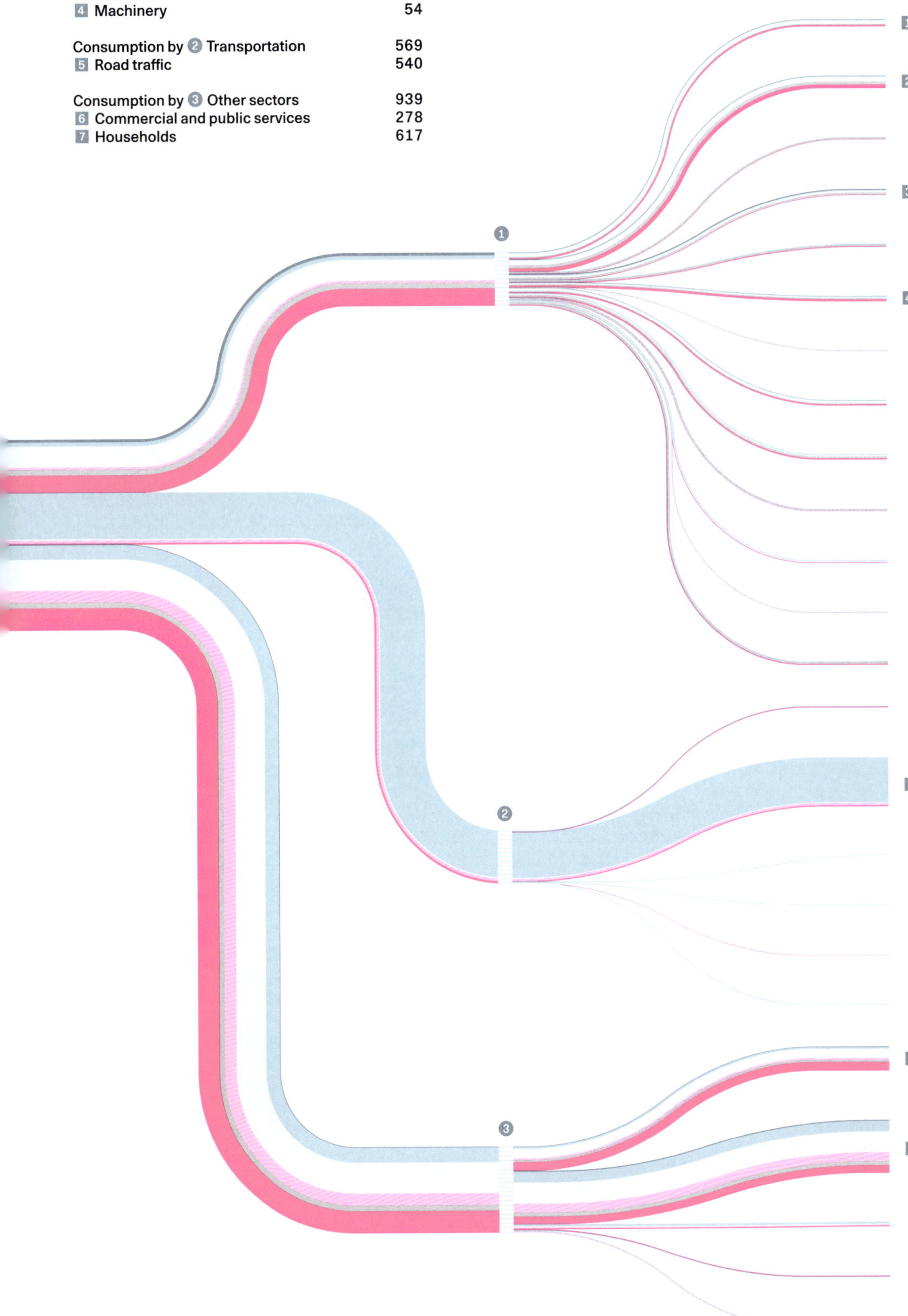

1.3

Urban Energy Landscapes

A Multi-Scalar and Relational Perspective

Anke Hagemann
Elke Beyer

The supply of energy in Berlin-Brandenburg is organised in complex trans-local networks, which are in some respects similar to the production systems of many other commodities within globalised "supply chain capitalism".[51] However, depending on the properties of particular energy carriers as well as the historically specific material cultures of energy use, these networks operate highly specialised infrastructure systems within architectural and territorial sociotechnical regimes, constituting "urban energy landscapes"[52] which extend far beyond the traditional imaginary of bounded urban regions. Planetary urbanisation and architectural production as we know it have been shaped and configured by energy flows or, more precisely, by the intra- and inter-urban circulations of energy carriers or intermediaries: by the ways they are produced, distributed, consumed, and put to use, not least in building construction and operation.[53] These processes have created intricate interdependencies and power asymmetries ranging across geographic scales and regions, generating multiple collateral effects and by-products that affect different localities and ecologies all along the networks. And similar to other commodities, in the context of architecture and urban design practise and education, buildings or entire urban areas are far too often studied in "dissociation"[54] from the energy landscapes—or geographies of trans-local energy supply networks—they not only tap into, but co-constitute: as interfaces, outlets, and points of convergence in different urban systems, sociotechnical assemblages, and metabolic processes.

How can spatial practitioners such as architects and urban designers come to terms with the immense complexity of the trans-local production systems of energy provisioning? And what kinds of agency can they aspire to in the transition towards more sustainable, just, and resilient energy regimes? In our view, a multi-scalar, relational, and trans-local understanding of urban energy landscapes—one informed by cross-disciplinary research and theorisations of infrastructure systems and commodity production networks (as well as material culture and urban political ecology)—offers a useful and necessary approach for research, learning, design, and spatial practise in the fields of architecture and urbanism. Such a conceptual framework fosters a more adequate understanding of how individual buildings and urban areas are not only embedded in but form constitutive elements of the territorial systems and regimes of energy consumption. Additionally, it allows us to venture closer towards thinking and designing the scenarios and tools of spatial intervention that will productively disrupt present-day paradigms.

The exploration of current energy systems presented in this book builds on a research framework developed to analyse the dynamic interplay between global commodity production networks and urban spaces on different scales.[55] It combines the topological perspectives of large-scale, trans-local production systems or supply chains, actor constellations, and networked infrastructures with fine-grain analyses of the materiality of energy carriers, and of the diverse architectural or engineering technologies configuring the environment of urban energy landscapes. Multi-scalar mappings and analytical drawings capture the physical assets necessary to operate energy production networks or supply chains and render the sites functioning as critical nodes or multipliers within the urbanised territories of large-scale energy landscapes. These range from sites of extraction to those of conversion and distribution, to commodification, consumption, and disposal of exhausted materials. This multi-scalar and relational perspective on energy systems in the city of Berlin and the surrounding federal state of Brandenburg not only reveals intense interrelations and land-based conflicts in this urban region, but also manifold trans-local planetary connections and repercussions. Both ranges of interdependence are of immense relevance for future urban transformation scenarios related to energy infrastructure and decarbonisation.

The findings assembled in the following chapters have evolved from research and learning formats—urban design studios and research seminars—which we have co-taught since 2019. In these formats, the conceptual and methodological approach of our research on the multi-scalar, trans-local spatial arrangements and material circulations of global commodity production in different sectors (including the clothing industry,[56] food supply,[57] transport infrastructure, and construction materials)[58] was applied and elaborated by bringing it together with an urban design methodology based on interdisciplinary knowledge, speculations about the future, and scenario planning.[59] Through the polyphonic, tenacious research and urban design work of participants— to whom we gratefully acknowledge our indebtedness—the projects developed have contributed planetary and regional perspectives on extractivism (or, the extractive regimes that energy supplies have been based on since the dawn of the fossil fuel age), as well as perspectives on the collateral effects and externalities of "green" or "renewable" energy carriers. Others have exposed the short-sightedness of notions like "energy autonomy" or "self-sufficiency" based on current wind or solar power technology once the focus is widened to include the globalised production networks and supply chains of the machinery and essential raw materials required. Impressively, these projects teased out the interdependency of systemic transformations occurring at the architectural and urban scale, correlating them with those taking place in landscapes at much larger scales—whether geographically close or remote.

Many wicked problems[60] have emerged through the collaborative research and learning processes, on the one hand exposing the trouble with applying technological fixes to technological fixes, and on the other the extraordinary challenges of strategic design and decision making in the face of conflicting options. At the same time, important conclusions can be drawn regarding the potential agency of architectural and urban research and design practise. Energy systems are not only crucial vectors for urban development, but they express the larger urban footprint and metabolism—namely the actual extent of urbanisation on a planetary scale. Analysing the extended urban landscapes of energy systems—much like food and other commodity supply systems—illuminates the complexity of urbanisation processes as well as the scale of the challenges we currently face. It sheds light on manifold stakeholders and sociotechnical arrangements, not to mention environmental and historical layers of material culture, which provide the context for reflecting on the positionality of architectural and urban design practise in the face of ongoing political and ecological complexity. This requires a broad and cross-disciplinary knowledge base, indispensable in the varied toolbox that is needed to build knowledge for urban design interventions and strategies that are capable of engaging with the built environment at multiple scales, both in relational and metabolic perspective. At the same time, the competencies of architects and urban designers in conducting spatial analyses across different scales and eloquently visualising their findings can serve as valuable counterstrategies to understand, to map, and to expose the blind spots and missing links within habitual "geographies of dissociation"[61] as they are built into urban material cultures. Tracing and mapping the interactions between large-scale transformations of landscapes and climate, the shrouded "black boxes" of infrastructural systems, and the immediate physical environment of everyday lifestyles of consumption (constituted by the architectures of residential, work, and leisure spaces) offers powerful communication strategies to literally "bring home" an agenda of energy transition and decarbonisation, and the disputes and conflicts associated with it. Architectural and urban spatial practise, design, and education ought to claim their potential for critical agency to address and mediate the inevitable challenges and conflicts and, most importantly, to implement the sociotechnical changes needed to adapt and equip urban environments for more sustainable, socially, and environmentally just ways of living. The transition towards sustainable, just, and resilient energy provisioning will have fundamental impacts on urbanisation and reconfigure existing rural-urban linkages. The regional implementation and adaptation of green technologies and more sustainable ways of living will be a crucial challenge—and will come with dispute. Design and education strategies are critical to implement these changes; and infrastructure-oriented (urban) design could provide much needed tools and levers to address upcoming challenges and mediate conflicts.

1 Ritchie, Hannah, and Max Roser. 2023. "Sector by Sector: Where Do Global Greenhouse Gas Emissions Come From?".
2 See: Sijmons, Hugtenburg, van Hoorn, and Feddes, "Landscape and Energy: Designing Transition"
3 Eurostat, "Energy import dependency by products".
4 Numerous pertinent EU policies are interconnected with this indicator. The Energy Security Strategy underscores the necessity of bolstering domestic energy production, which emphasises boosting local renewable energy generation, enhancing energy efficiency, and addressing infrastructural gaps. Furthermore, the EU's cohesion policy funds spanning the period 2021 to 2027 (and including the restorative "Next Generation EU" recovery initiative) allocate resources for investments in renewable energy endeavours. A notable strategic blueprint, "REPowerEU", has been conceived with the objective of diminishing the EU's reliance on energy imports, particularly from Russia, driven by concerns of vulnerability and escalated prices ensuing from Russia's incursion into Ukraine. Additionally, the revised Directives on Energy Efficiency and Renewable Energy establish ambitious EU targets slated for achievement by 2030.
5 United Nations, "The Paris Agreement | UNFCCC".
6 Eurostat, "Share of fossil fuels in gross available energy".
7 European Commission, "A European Green Deal".
8 Eurostat, "Industrial Production Statistics".
9 On a global scale, Germany stands as the largest importer of gas, the sixth-largest importer of oil, and the sixth-largest importer of hard coal. Within Europe, it holds the top position in all these categories. See: Energy Institute, "Statistical Review of World Energy".
10 The numbers vary, depending on the source. For conservative estimates see: AG Energiebilanzen e. V., "Energy Consumption in Germany in 2023".
11 Destatis, "Electricity Consumption of Households by Household Size".
12 Author's own calculation. In 2023 there were 41,330,000 households in Germany. Based on: Destatis, "Households, by Type of Household".
13 In other words, primary energy sources are those that provide energy directly without undergoing conversion. Examples include hard coal, lignite, oil, natural gas, as well as solar energy, wind power, hydropower, geothermal energy, and tidal energy.
14 Umweltbundesamt, "Energieverbrauch nach Energieträgern und Sektoren".
15 AG Energiebilanzen e. V., "Auswertungstabellen zur Energiebilanz Deutschland Daten für die Jahre von 1990 bis 2023"
16 Bundesministerium für Wirtschaft und Energie, "Integrated National Energy and Climate Plan", 11.
17 The numbers vary, depending on the source. For conservative estimates see: AG Energiebilanzen e. V., "Energy Consumption in Germany in 2023", 33.
18 In 2021, the German Federal Ministry for Economic Affairs and Energy (BMWi) issued a statement projecting that the national electricity demand would increase to approximately 658 terawatt-hours (TWh) by 2030. This projection was based on various factors, including the growing adoption of e-mobility (+68 TWh), the utilisation of electric heat pumps in buildings and heating grids (+35 TWh), the production of hydrogen (+20 TWh), battery production, and the expansion of data centres. In sum, this results in a 13 TWh increase in electricity consumption compared to the levels observed in 2018. See: Bundesministerium für Wirtschaft und Energie, Prognos Institut, und Öko-Institut, "Entwicklung des Bruttostromverbrauchs bis 2030".
19 Statista, "Electric Vehicle Market Share in Germany".
20 AG Energiebilanzen e. V., "Auswertungstabellen zur Energiebilanz Deutschland Daten für die Jahre von 1990 bis 2021".
21 Law for the Priority of Renewable Energies (Renewable Energy Sources Act – E.E.G.) and the Amendment of the Energy Industry Act and the Mineral Oil Tax Act, 2000.
22 The *Energiewende* (German for energy turnaround) is the ongoing energy transition by Germany to a low carbon, environmentally sound, reliable, and affordable energy supply.
23 Kost, "Studie zu Stromgestehungskosten".
24 For economic indicators, see: World Bank, "World Development Indicators".
25 Berkel and Bundeszentrale für Politische Bildung, "Die Grossen Vier".
26 Eurostat, "Energy import dependency by products".
27 See: Prognos Institut, Öko-Institut, und Wuppertal-Institut, "Klimaneutrales Deutschland 2045 Wie Deutschland seine Klimaziele schon vor 2050 erreichen kann, Zusammenfassung"; Sterchele et al., Studie: Wege zu einem klimaneutralen Energiesystem – Die deutsche Energiewende im Kontext gesellschaftlicher Verhaltensweisen.
28 These legislations, in chronological order, included the Electricity Feed-In Act (Stromeinspeisungsgesetz or StromEinspG) of 1990, the Energy Industry Act (Energiewirtschaftsgesetz or EnWG) amendment of 1998, and the Renewable Energy Sources Act (Erneuerbare-Energien-Gesetz or EEG) of 2000.
29 The Berliner Stadtgüter GmbH is managing approximately 16,600 ha of land in Brandenburg, an area that accumulates to nearly the size of Berlin's largest district, Treptow-Köpenick.
30 For a concise illustration of the decentralisation of electricity grids in Germany, see: Graebig et al., Strom, Netz, Fluss, 51–52.
31 Luczak, "Forschungbericht zum Energiesystem x.0 — Nr. 1: Intelligente und effiziente Vernetzung von Energieerzeugern und -verbrauchern auf Quartiersebene", 136–39.
32 Eriksen and Clean Energy Wire, "Grid Operators Consider Splitting Germany's Single Power Market Zone".
33 European Commission, "New Rules for Europe's Electricity Market".
34 "Hauptstadtregion Berlin-Brandenburg".
35 For a more in-depth exploration of this historic experiment, please refer to: Moss, Remaking Berlin, 217 ff.
36 Amt für Statistik Berlin-Brandenburg 2024, 6.
37 Amt für Statistik Berlin-Brandenburg 2023, 4.
38 PCK Schwedt, "PCK – Wir bewegen Berlin und Brandenburg!"
39 IKEM, "Region of the future: Economic potential of renewable energies in Brandenburg".
40 Senatsverwaltung für Mobilität, Verkehr, Klimaschutz und Umwelt, "Bericht zur Umsetzung des Berliner Energie- und Klimaschutzprogramms (BEK 2030) – Berichtjahr 2022", 22.
41 Senatsverwaltung für Mobilität, Verkehr, Klimaschutz und Umwelt, "Berliner Energie- Und Klimaschutzprogramm 2030, Umsetzungskonzept Für Den Zeitraum Bis 2021", 2023, 22.
42 Senatsverwaltung für Umwelt, Verkehr und Klimaschutz, "Berliner Energie- und Klimaschutzprogramm 2030 Umsetzungskonzept für den Zeitraum bis 2021", 22.
43 Ministerium für Wirtschaft, Arbeit und Energie, "Energiestrategie 2040", 6.
44 Ministerium für Infrastruktur und Landwirtschaft des Landes Brandenburg, "Facts on Forests and Forestry in Brandenburg", 2–3.
45 Ministerium für Wirtschaft, Arbeit und Energie, "Energiestrategie 2040", 3.
46 Senatsverwaltung für Mobilität, Verkehr, Klimaschutz und Umwelt, "Bericht zur Umsetzung des Berliner Energie- und Klimaschutzprogramms (BEK 2030) – Berichtjahr 2022", 17.
47 Senatsverwaltung für Mobilität, Verkehr, Klimaschutz und Umwelt, 14.
48 Waterhouse, Boundaries of the City, 300.
49 See: Bärthel and GASAG AG, Die Geschichte der Gasversorgung in Berlin.
50 Beyer et al., "Die globale Fabrik, Räume der Logistik und die letzte Meile in Berlin-Brandenburg".
51 Ibid.
52 Castán Broto, Urban Energy Landscapes; Roesler, City, Climate, and Architecture.
53 Calder, Architecture; Förster et al., Environmental Histories of Architecture.
54 Ibert et al., "Geographies of Dissociation".
55 Hagemann and Beyer, "Globalizing urban research, grounding global production networks".
56 Hagemann and Beyer.
57 Hagemann and Quintero González, Feeding the city: Lebensmittelkreisläufe und die Produktion städtischer Räume.
58 Beyer et al., "Industrial Infrastructure".
59 Bauer, "Unboxing Urban Infrastructure".
60 For expansion on the concept of wicked problems, please refer to: Rittel and Webber, "Dilemmas in a General Theory of Planning".
61 Ibert et al., "Geographies of Dissociation".

Currentscapes

Bui Luu Quynh Nguyen

Power Stations in Berlin and Brandenburg

KPMG

VATTENFALL

LOVE

AMANO

2

Transmission, Transition, Transformation

2.1

Energy Spaces in Transformation

David Bauer

People living through the 20th century have seen a level of change and rapid, often tumultuous, transformation that surpasses any prior generation throughout history.[1] The 21st century, as it is anticipated, will witness an even more accelerated pace of change. One of the most monumental undertakings in this era is the decarbonisation of entire energy systems. At its core, this transformation embodies a significant paradigm shift, moving away from a reliance on the continuous consumption of energy carriers towards the production and development of technology with the capacity to harness energy from atmospheric sources.

This chapter embarks on a brief exploration to elucidate how changes and transformations in energy procurement have unfolded over the course of the last few centuries. It does this by portraying and dissecting architectural and urban phenomena across three scales.

The first visual essay in this chapter delves into the domain of households, examining housing typologies and the inherent co-evolution of energy consumption and availability in relation to spatial arrangements. Throughout time, the interplay between changing energy sources and their users is mirrored in the architectural structure of residences and the behaviours of their occupants. The primary focus here will be on five prevalent typologies, disregarding extravagant experimental designs that were often found in highly affluent and aristocratic households. The section explores these shifts through the lens of historical case studies taken from the Berlin-Brandenburg region, which serve as partial generalisations—with appropriate abstraction—for broader trends within this cultural sphere.

The second visual essay surveys the expansion of water systems as a pivotal form of infrastructure, facilitating the dissemination of new energy paradigms. It examines how, over four distinct temporal junctures, the post-medieval city of Berlin became an extensive, multifaceted conglomeration of functionalities and technologies, shaped by watercourses and the emerging patterns of energy supply they enabled. Mills, fuel markets, gasworks, and power stations are employed as exemplars to illustrate this interrelation.

The final part of the chapter directs the focus towards one of the central technical systems on which substantial portions of our decarbonised futures rely: the electricity grid. Spanning nearly 140 years of development in the city of Berlin, it unveils, on the one hand, how a small, decentralised network of cables together with a handful of machines evolved into an integrated, transcontinental superstructure that sustains the livelihoods of hundreds of millions of individuals. On the other, it shows that, contrary to a gradual upward trend, the expansion of electricity mirrors the city's tumultuous history and politics.[2]

In order to afford the reader an initial orientation, a series of overarching trends can be encapsulated as follows:

Firstly, the shift from traditional fire-based energy supply to novel technologies was accompanied by changes in house layouts. While most common dwellings, even well into the 19th century, were assembled both functionally and spatially around an open hearth, the dissolution of light, warmth, and heat into different technologies also dispersed the role of this central space into new functional units.

Secondly, in tandem with the rise of expansive large technical systems LTS [3] and piped infrastructure[4], residences evolved into nodes within intricate networks of interdependent elements, on which they relied for sustenance. With the waning of self-sufficiency that characterised the firepit, energy provision systems underwent a process of centralisation that also reflected the intricate nature of their operations and administration. Consequently, procurement methods had incremental and progressive externalisation: spanning spaces both within and beyond the city limits and yielding significant, unpredicted outcomes, including massive pollution. However, as time went on and this externalisation was consolidated, the complex processes facilitating the influx of energy into domestic residences became increasingly opaque and abstracted. As such, these energy systems operated largely outside the public eye, detached from popular understanding.

Thirdly, the issue of energy storage has consistently held paramount importance. Whether in the form of wood stacks, coal boxes, basements, oil tanks, or gasholders, the tangible existence of energy carriers within households and cities has been crucial throughout history. The advent of globalised fuel markets and long-distance transmission led to a phase of reduced reliance on these local storages through externalisation. However, with the collective transition towards electricity sourced from renewables, storage will again assume a central role, even within private households.

Lastly, despite the proliferation of novel energy sources such as gas and electricity, energy scarcity dominated the 19th and early 20th centuries and made the daily use of these resources only partially accessible to the broader populace. Cold parlours and chambers—once brimming with the entire family, enveloped in the glow of candles and petroleum lights—continued to be a fundamental constant of the domestic environment until two generations ago. With the phase-out of general combustion, we are entering historically uncharted territory and must ascertain whether the frameworks that emerged due to a brief period of energy abundance can remain unchanged.[5]

2.2

Household Typologies in Transition

David Bauer
Amelia Mega

Fig. 1 View into a kitchen in a *Berliner Mietskaserne,* circa 1910

1 All Around the Firepit: the Medieval Household[6]

Since the inception of human habitation and extending well into the medieval era, people predominantly harnessed energy by means of open fire, both within and outside the dwelling. Some theories even propose that the inclusion of a fireplace might be one of the earliest motivations for constructing shelters.[7] Unlike the contemporary kitchen, which constituted a distinct economic space within the *oikos,* the early medieval firepit symbolised the foundational unity of all energy requirements. Positioned centrally, it radiated light, warmth, and cooking heat, while simultaneously dispersing smoke and soot into every nook and cranny.

The household itself was confined to a single interior where all essential and productive activities concerning daily sustenance occurred, particularly during colder seasons. The entire life of the *ménages,* which was bound not so much by blood ties but rather by collaborative labour and the joint management of the resources it produced, unfolded in this room. Even livestock were sheltered by the large, thatched roofs. In addition to the open hearth, which accommodated a suspended cooking cauldron, an arched baking oven was typically situated in the courtyard or in a bake-house serving the entire village. For fuel, people generally collected wood, primarily in the form of branches, supplemented with peat and—in some cases—charcoal, where available.

❶ Sleeping area
❷ Stable
❸ Storage

Related utilities
① Firepit

Fig. 1 Schematic representation of a 12th-century house in Düppel, Brandenburg

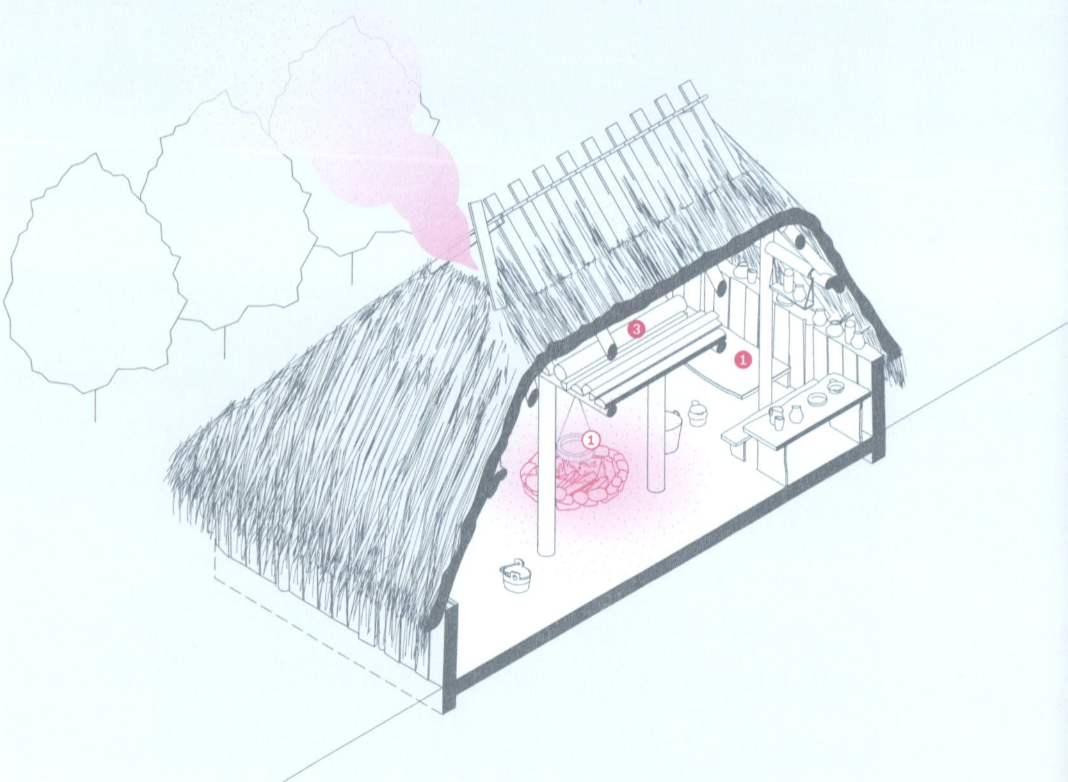

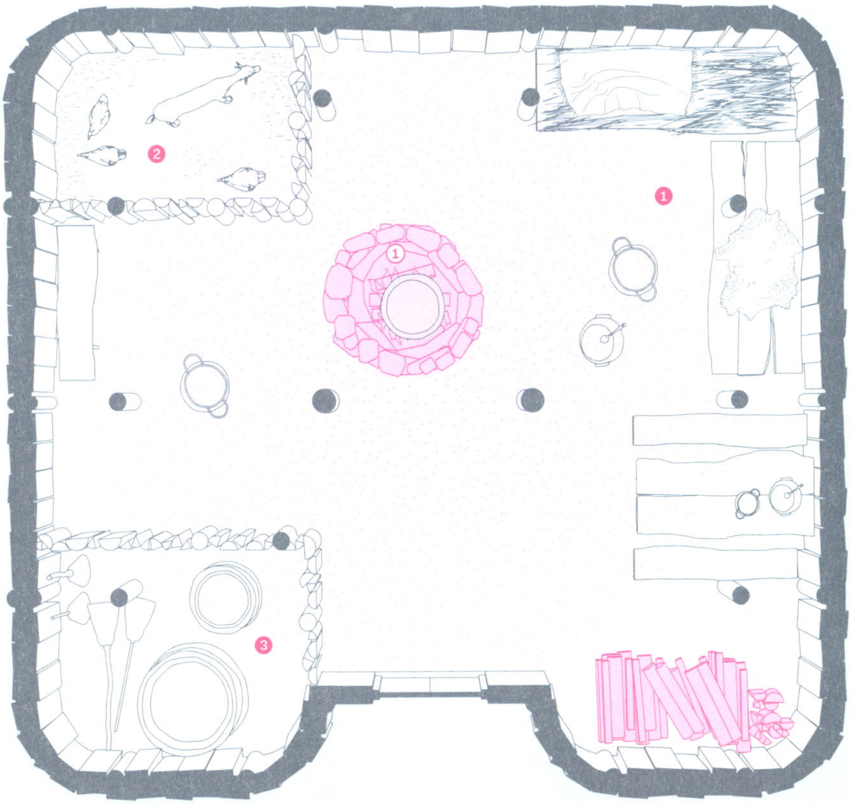

1
2
1
3

2 The "Black Kitchen" and the Division of Space around the Hearth[8]

In the subsequent centuries, as people began to compartmentalise their households into distinct functional spaces, the ancient firepits transformed into a sort of house within the house, known as the "Black Kitchen". In the case of this 18th-century house-barn from Oderbruch, it was characterised by a masonry dome fortified with thick plaster walls and featured a sculptural mantel chimney which protruded through the spacious hay loft and roof. The kitchen, stained black from soot and fumes, had no access to any of the outer walls, thus receiving no daylight, and earning its distinctive name. Despite the evolution of separate kitchen spaces for daily meal preparation, the kitchen remained a central area where various forms of production, especially among the less affluent peasantry, took place. Due to its central position, other rooms—including the stables—were often interconnected with or accessed through it. The thick walls stored the heat from the kitchen to warm the adjacent parlour and chambers. They were equipped with built-in alcoves designed for storing heart pine or fatwood, valued for their flammability and utilised as a source of illumination in holders.

Wood continued to serve as the primary fire source, with room separation designed to direct stifling smoke and soot away from the hearth. By the 18th century, charcoal gained popularity as a less smoke-emitting alternative, produced by the peasantry in forested areas through the carbonisation of fast-growing trees. Some wealthier households installed additional stove hearths in other parlours, allowing them to be independently heated. In a time before mechanisation, the house-barn included planned spaces for energy storage, beyond just energy carriers. Muscular energy, provided by the interaction of bodies and nutrients, played a vital role in sustaining human culture. Meeting basic energy needs meant that food, hay, and grains were stored separately, often on a dedicated upper storey, while the beasts of burden that harvested these goods were sheltered under the same roof.

1 Porch
2 Hallway
3 Black kitchen
4 Kitchen
5 Bedroom
6 Living room
7 Barn
8 Storage

Related utilities
(1) Wood oven
(2) Wood stove
(3) Masonry stove/ *Kachelofen*
(4) Candlestick / candelabra
(5) Chimney

Fig. 2 Schematic representation of an 18th-century house-barn in Oderbruch

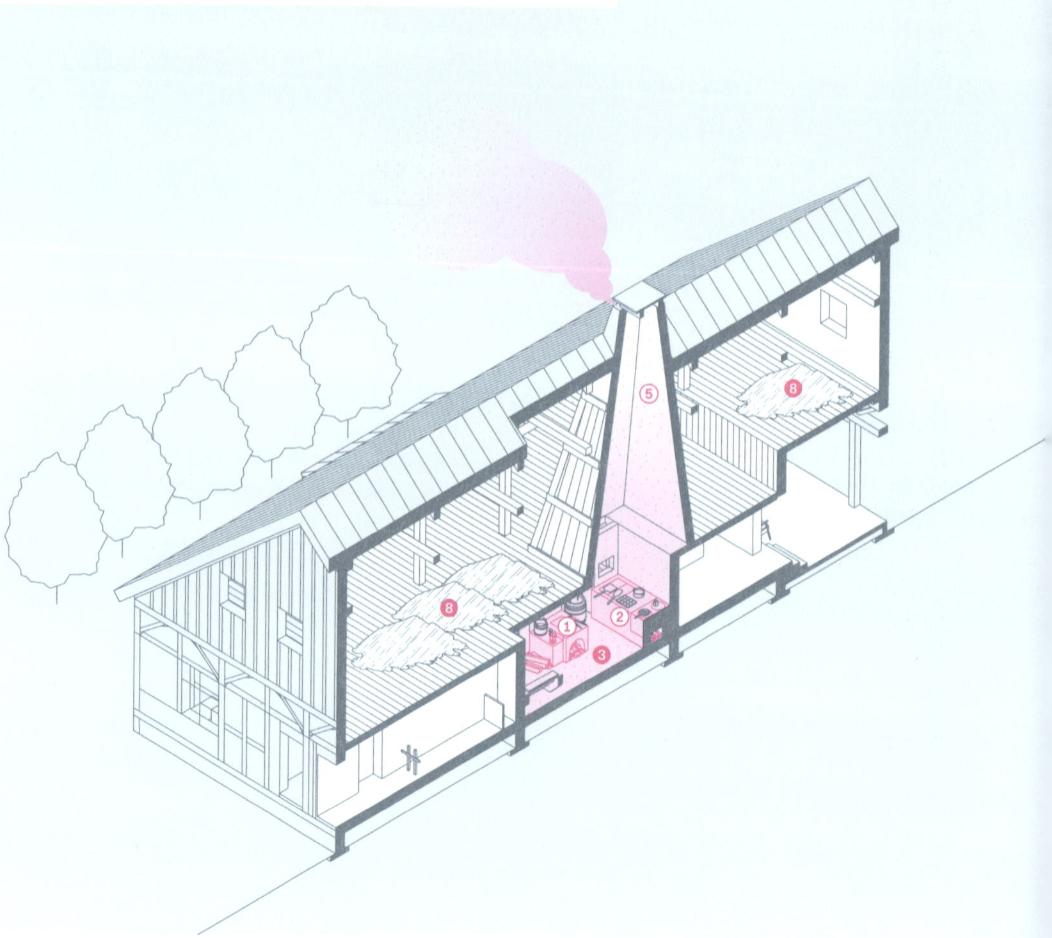

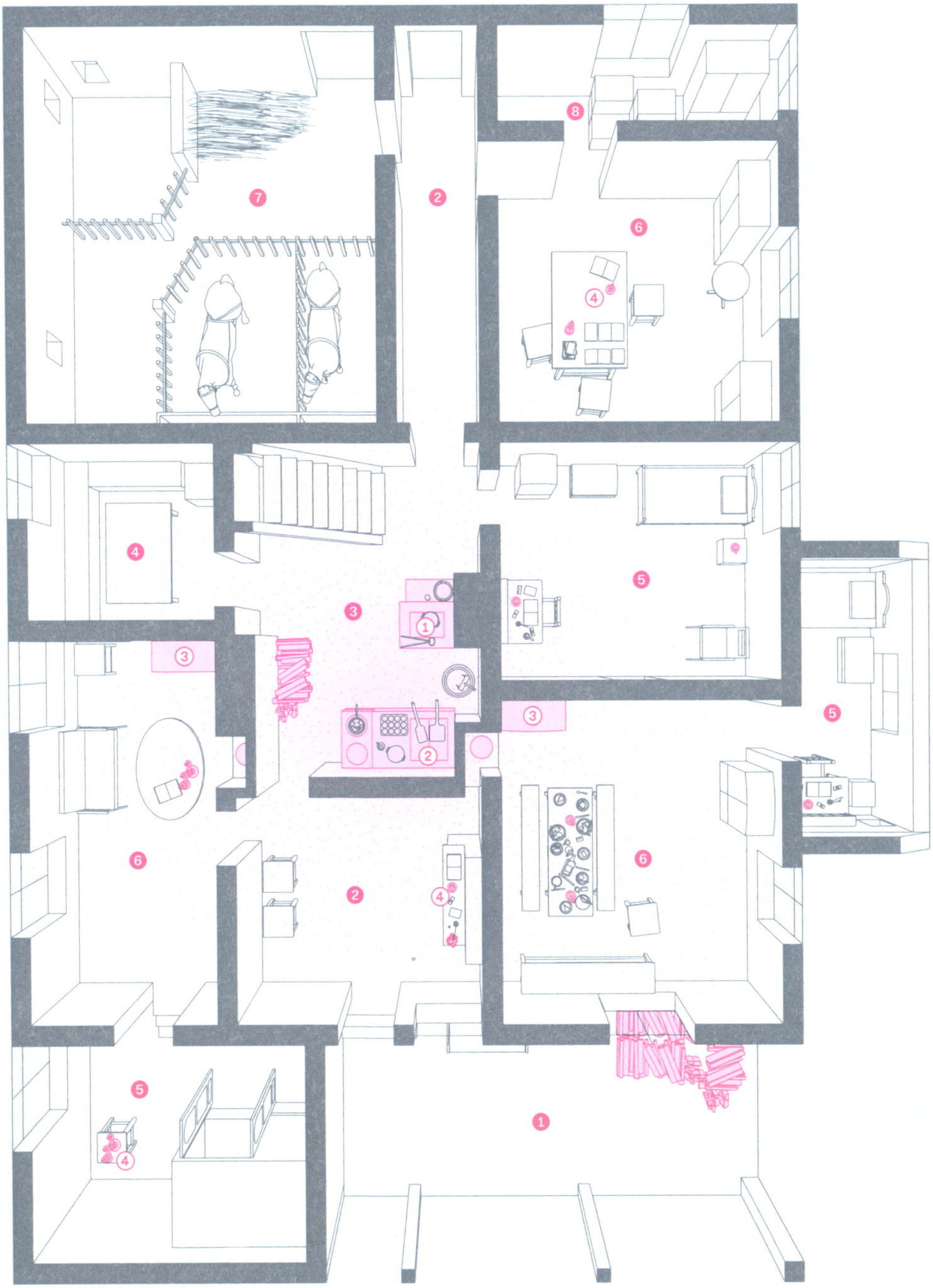
7
2
8
6
4
4
5
3
1
3
3
2
5
6
6
2
4
5
4
1

3 New Housing for the Working Class: the Emergence of Large Systems and the Absence of Immediate Improvement[9]

The burgeoning industrial extraction of mineral energy fuels impacted urban and rural environments earlier than it demonstrably affected individual households. From the second half of the 19th century on, economic conditions in the predominantly rural areas of central Prussia began to change and worsen due to the increasing influence of mechanisation and the breakdown of the medieval social structure after the Napoleonic Wars. Hundreds of thousands of uprooted and impoverished peasants streamed into Berlin's sprawling conurbation, seeking work in the expanding industrial areas. This phenomenon coincided with the emergence of rampant land speculation and financialisation. In response, the *Berliner Mietskaserne,* a novel and extremely compact housing typology, began to organise a wide array of inhabitants and activities within a comparatively small footprint. Coupled with the accessibility of new fuel sources, the vertical densification—with blocks extending up to six storeys—required not only a methodical approach to housing design but also the arrangement of its metabolic requirements. Additionally, it called for innovative urban supply infrastructure and governance, particularly concerning fire service regulations.

Until the outbreak of the First World War, the constrained living conditions of the working class who formed the majority of Berlin's populace were defined by destitution and scarcity. Much like before, the kitchen—accommodating the now-enclosed fires of the metal stove—persisted as the primary source of warmth in most instances, serving as the hub for various activities and as the primary living space. Despite having tiled stoves in other rooms, heating with coal sourced from specific vendors or markets was expensive, highlighting the continued importance of wood and kindling. With the emergence of underground pipe systems pumping town gas to those who could afford it for cooking, the houses began to grow into nodes within broader energy production cycles of urban technology. This phenomenon was consolidated by the introduction of electricity at the end of the century, which enabled the physical detachment of production sources from consumption sites, often separating them by many kilometres.

— Gas pipe

1 Hallway
2 Kitchen
3 Bathroom
4 Bedroom
5 Storage

Related utilities
(1) Coal-powered stove
(2) Small gas stove
(3) Heater
(4) Chimney
(5) Coal storage
(6) Coal delivery
(7) Coal shop
(8) Underground gas system

Fig. 3 Schematic representation of a *Berliner Mietskaserne* around 1880

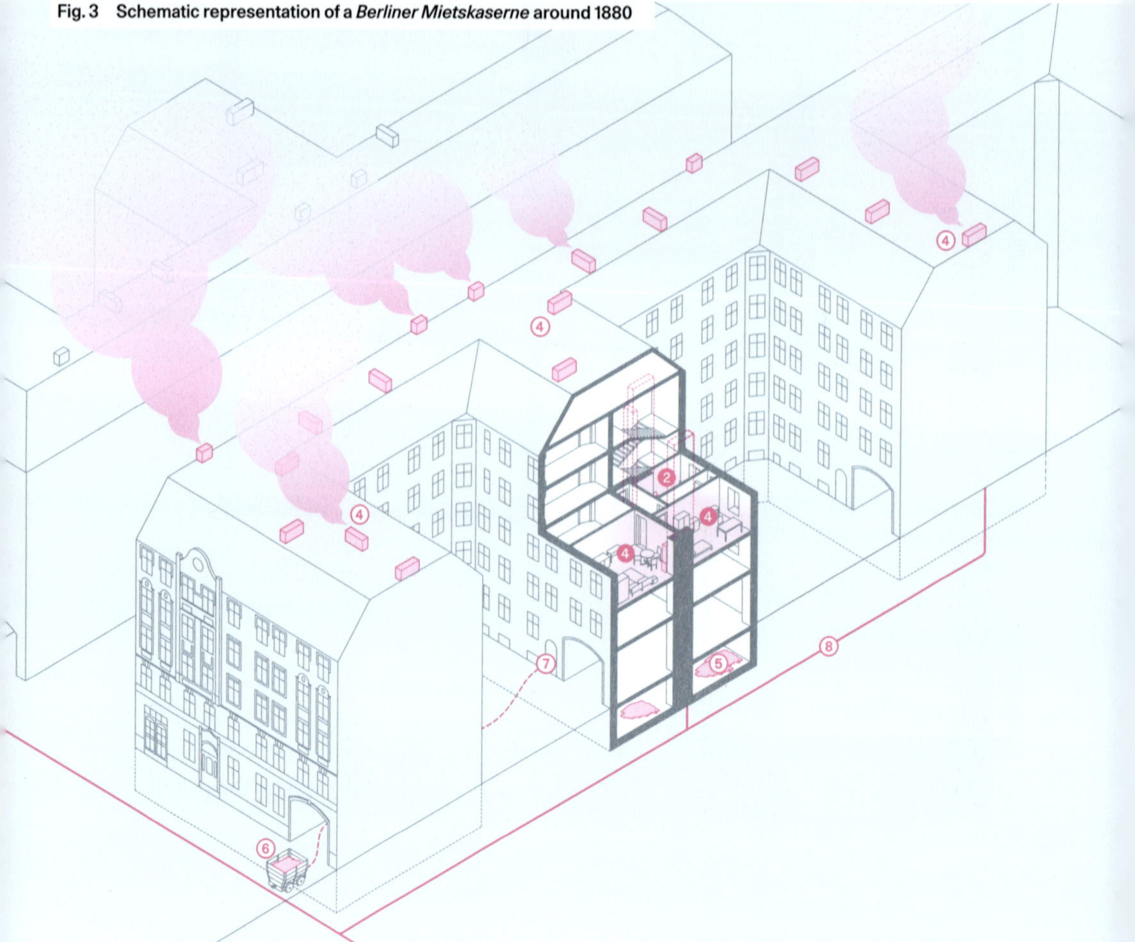

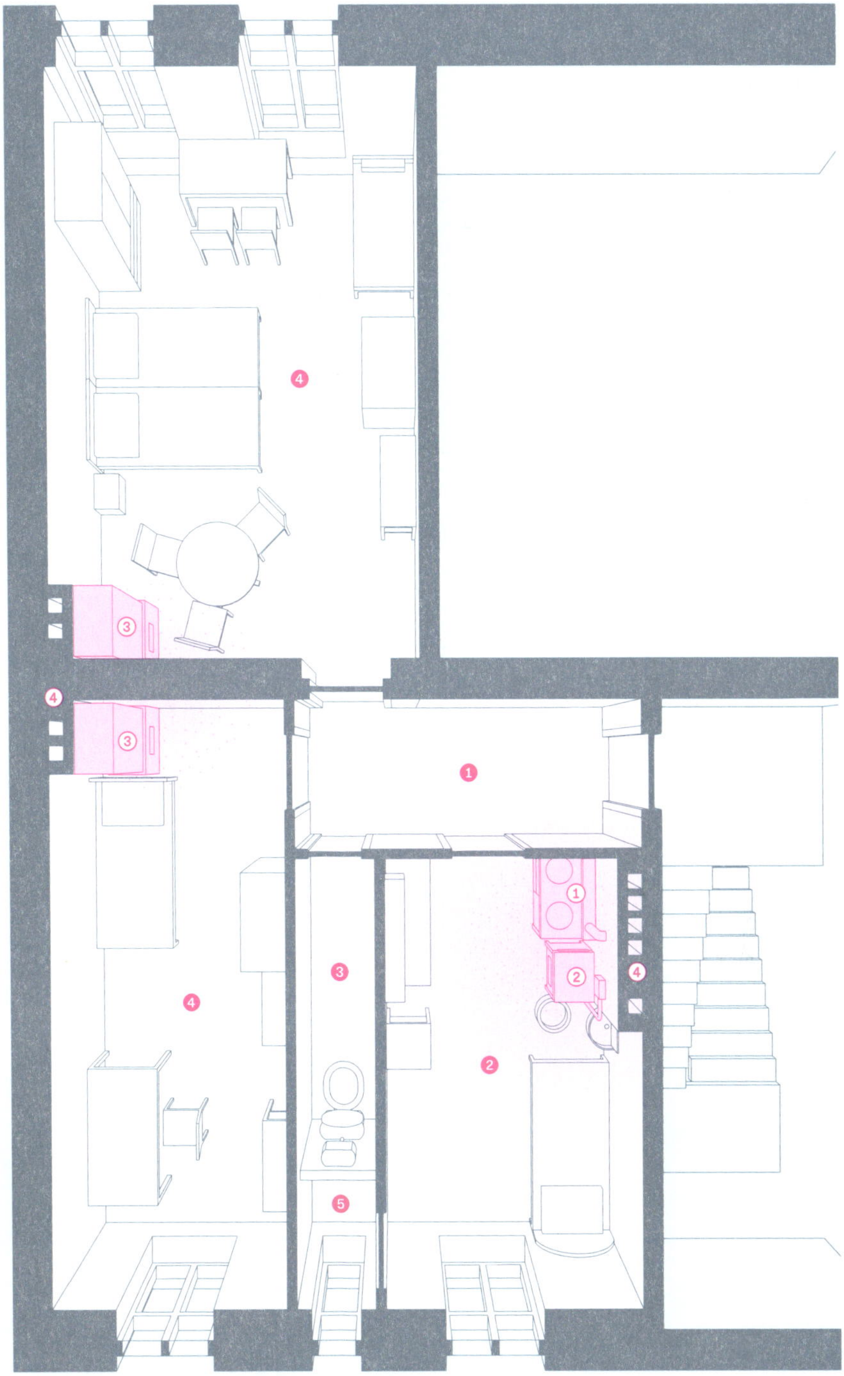
4
3
4
3
1
1
4
3
2
4
2
5

4 Thoroughly New, Entirely Modern: externalising Energy Requirements in Prefabricated Housing[10]

The gradual disappearance of the open fire, coupled with the increasing diversity and abundance of energy sources, liberated households from the traditional reliance on a single, versatile central living space. With the distribution of warmth (now facilitated through steel pipes from basement boiler rooms), illumination (primarily supplied by electricity), and heat for food preparation (whether from gas or electric stoves), the floorplans of post-war modern mass housing initiatives offered numerous novel functionalities.

In the streamlined prefab slabs of the Deutsche Demokratische Republik DDR, warm water became readily accessible from wall taps, now installed in both kitchens and bathrooms, with the latter expanding its role beyond its core function as a toilet area. Heat came from wall-mounted radiators in each room, increasingly fostering living spaces that were equipped with leisure furnishings and entertainment amenities. Over millennia, storytelling and manual craftsmanship had offered solace during long, dark winter nights. Now, electricity breathed vitality into television screens, reproducing images from the local neighbourhood to the vastness of space. The availability of affordable voltage led to the emergence of newfangled household appliances—small aides that elevated and enhanced people's lifestyles, much like the items only affordable to bourgeois households in previous decades.

Even more revolutionary was the fact that everything entered homes discreetly, from centralised hubs operating on a grand scale.[11] Repurposed waste, heat, and electricity from nearby power stations connected apartments to one vital source, facilitating thousands of domestic units simultaneously. Integrating these hubs into the burgeoning network of transcontinental gas pipelines emerging from the east signified a significant expansion of the household's already integrated system.

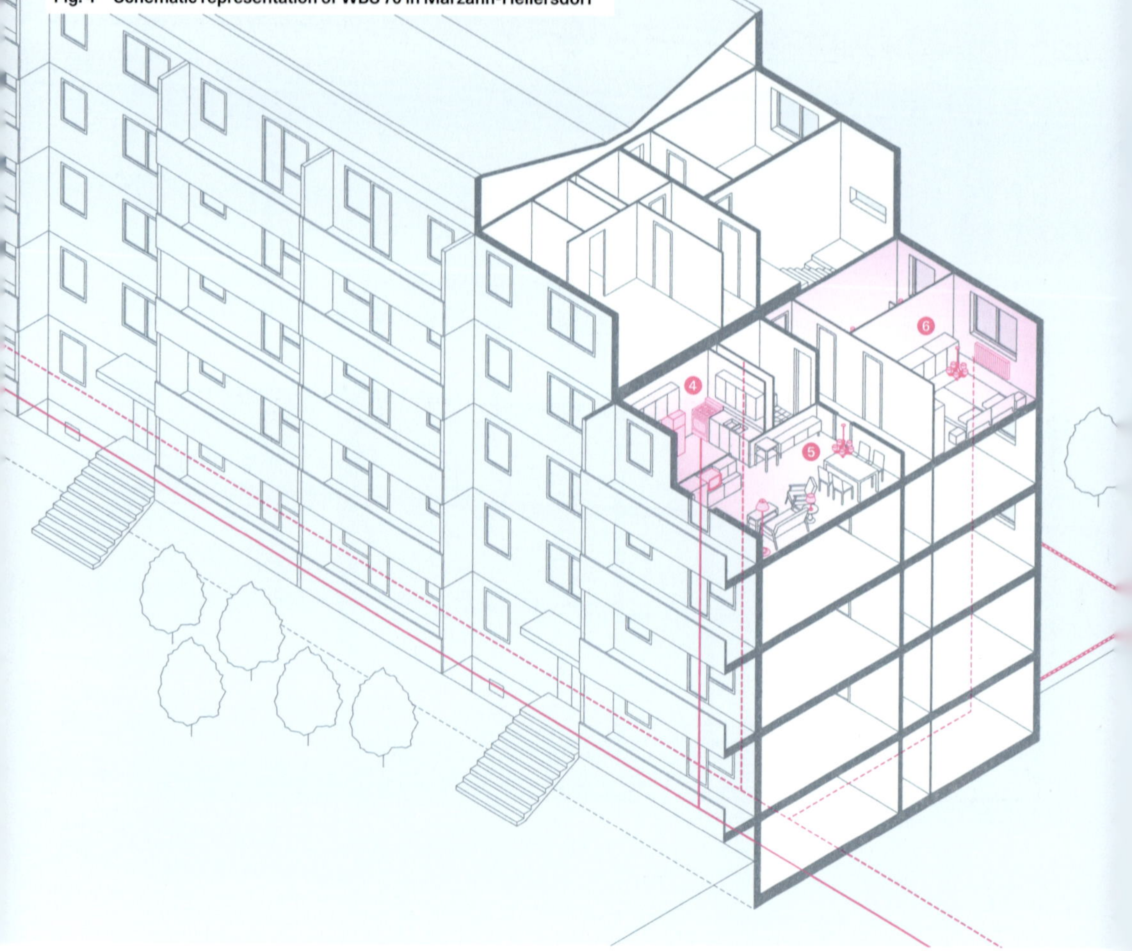

Fig. 4 Schematic representation of WBS 70 in Marzahn-Hellersdorf

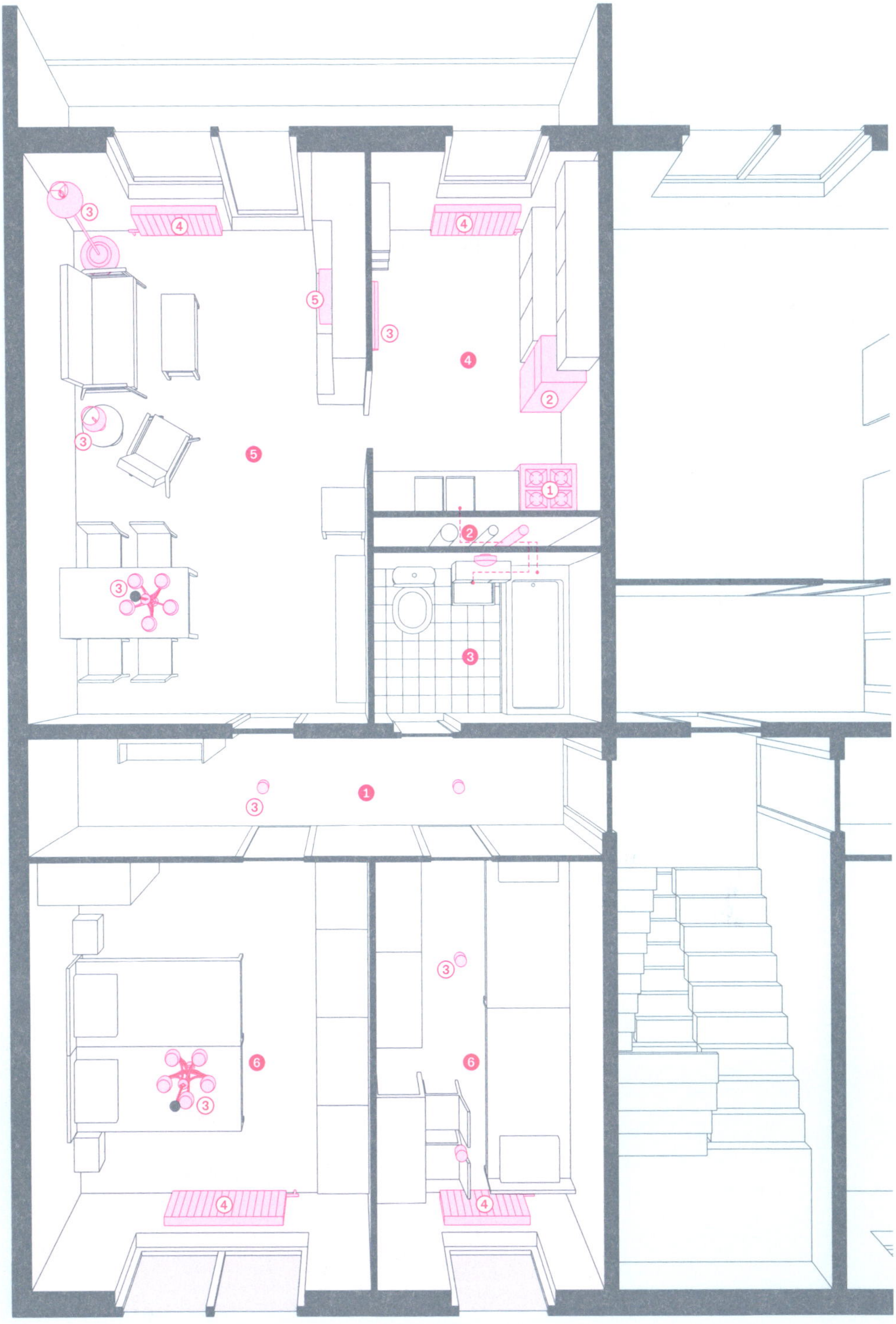
3
4
5
3
4
3
2
3
5
1
2
3
3
1
3
3
6
3
6
3
4
4

5 Fully-Electric: the (Future) House of the Decarbonised Prosumer Class[12]

The quest to decarbonise the household is an attempt to find ways to ensure the emission-free production and storage of one unifying currency: electricity. The all-encompassing rewiring of daily activities must entail a complete shift away from all combustible energy sources. For the children of 2045, the familiar image of a house topped with a smoking chimney will be considered a picturesque symbol of a bygone era. Instead, they will associate home with the black shimmer of solar-panelled roofs and the silent whir of air conditioning or heat pumps.

Feeding into an energy grid that efficiently manages bi-directional streams and buffers energy loads, the dwelling will be a cog in a vast system. However, it won't merely serve as the endpoint for energy flows. Instead, it will function as an energy generator, primarily through its exterior surfaces; concurrently, it will serve as an energy reservoir, predominantly through the sophisticated array of appliances and devices housed under its roof. From cars to toothbrushes, technology will be everywhere: required to efficiently store electricity during times of abundance and emit it in times of need.

The extent to which energy scarcity—a persistent but often overlooked threat for humans in some parts of the globe—will intermittently resurface, and impact the daily lives of its inhabitants, remains to be seen. As living space *per capita* continues to increase worldwide, particularly outside densely populated urban centres, an ageing population will face the challenge of reconfiguring extensive living areas, some of which were built over 40 years ago, to suit an entirely different era.

— Refrigerant line
— Cable
--- Hot water pipe
-x- Powerline

1. Entrance
2. Laundry room
3. Bathroom
4. Garage
5. Storage/wardrobe
6. Bedroom
7. Study
8. Living and dining area
9. Kitchen

Related utilities
(1) Solar PV panels
(2) Home storage battery
(3) Electric vehicle
(4) EV charger
(5) Heat pump for space heating and cooling
(6) Centralised home system
(7) Appliances: lamps, TV, computer, stove, refrigerator, washing, and drying machines
(8) Electric heater
(9) Heat pump water heater
(10) Floor heating

Fig. 5 Schematic representation of a potential single-family house in the future

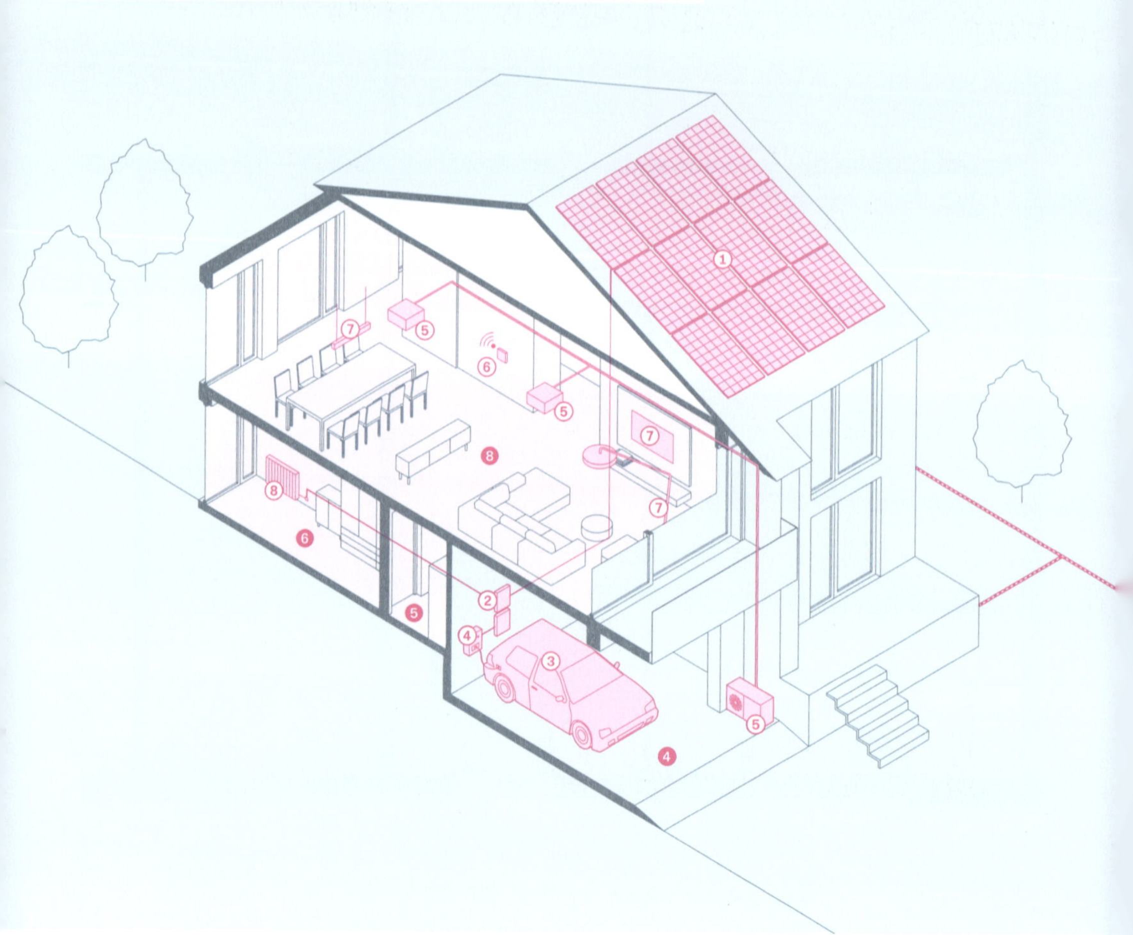

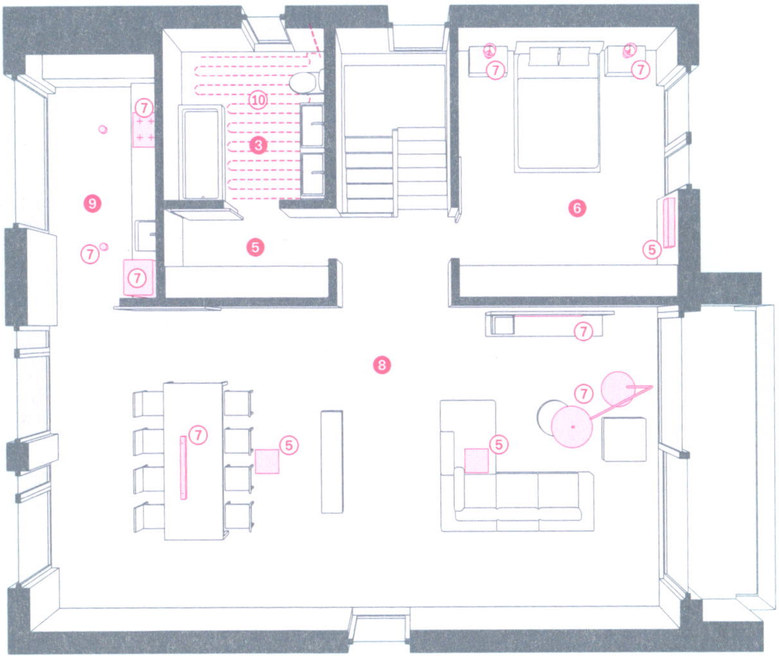
7
10
3
9
7
7
5
7
7
6
5
8
7
7
5
7
5

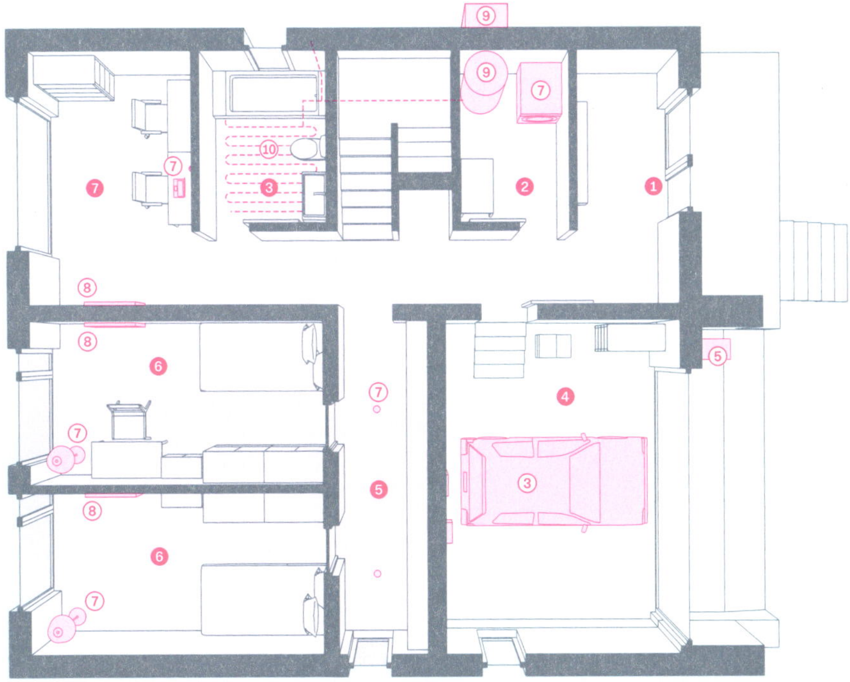
9
9
7
10
7
7
3
2
1
8
8
6
7
7
5
4
3
5
8
6
7

Urban Energy Tributaries

Paul Strobel

The volume of goods transported on Berlin's waterways has been in decline for years. Between 2020 and 2021, however, the trend saw a reversal as the amount of coal and crude oil transported on Berlin's rivers and canals almost doubled.[13] How did this statistical shift occur? The answer is clear: the winter was, on average, 2 °C colder than the previous year. Consequently, the energy demand increased. This cause-effect relationship underlines the pivotal role of waterborne transportation—and the infrastructure enabling it—in maintaining Berlin's thermal energy supply. Most probably, this is not the first association that comes to mind when looking at the recreational use of urban canals, including the Spree, Dahme, or Havel. And yet, this is a nexus that has shaped urban energy supply and its spatial logic for many centuries, well into the present day.

The history of Berlin's energy landscapes cannot be told without also telling the story of its waterways. Before the construction of the power stations that still prevail along the city's waterfronts today, numerous gasworks lined urban canals and rivers during the 19th and 20th centuries. Over the years, vessels brought immeasurable quantities of coal to Berlin via water routes—from Schlesien, the Ruhr-Region, and Great Britain. Prior to the industrial dominance of fossil energy sources, the waterways also proved indispensable in feeding the ever-hungry urban appetite: thousands of barges served peat- and wood-handling sites, and the old city centre was organised around the Mühlendamm (mill dam). Here, the Spree's currents were converted into mechanical energy. The ever-grinding mills were some of the first powerhouses in the city.

The flow of water spatially orchestrated the emergence of urban facilities for energy production. The development of the city's energy systems was, likewise, one of the defining reasons for the development of urban and regional waterways, a process which necessitates the straightening of rivers, the laying of new canals, and the construction of new locks. Despite its functional obsolescence, this infrastructural network is still formative for the urban fabric today. Waterfront power stations, gasworks, as well as coal- and wood markets interface with local energy landscapes and ex-local extraction sites in the urban hinterlands. As such, the waterways have become the mediators between different points in sprawling energy systems, tying together seemingly disconnected, distant locations. In the following pages, we will take a closer look at some of the aspects mentioned by mapping out the evolution of urban energy systems in relation to the emergence of Berlin's waterway network.

Fig. 6 Amount of goods transported on Berlin's waterways in t

	2020	2021
① Coal, crude oil, and natural gas	605,359	309,475
② Ores, stones, and rare earths	373,863	611,753
③ Mineral products	230,214	236,225
④ Wood products, paper, cardboard	206,212	195,100
⑤ Secondary raw materials, waste	183,901	195,482
⑥ Other products	25,813	45,099

As Lewis Mumford notes, waterways proved to be the first reliable infrastructural system in most ancient cities.[14] Besides Havel and Dahme, the Spree ③ was a crucial locational factor in Berlin's founding. The once untamed river was subject to engineered modifications early in the city's history. Strikingly, the most significant interference with its natural course was not related to shipping or fishing, but instead involved harnessing it as an energy source.

The Mühlendamm, the city's first "power station", was located between Berlin and Cölln. As the geographical and functional centre of the young town, it was neatly integrated into the urban fabric. The two economic hubs of the city, Molkenmarkt and Cöllnischer Fischmarkt, neighboured the agglomeration north and south. After damming the Spree, six mills were established which could convert water movement into mechanical energy. Tanning, fulling, saw, and grain mills were clustered around the embankment.[15]

Despite initial bourgeois governance, the Prussian elector took absolute control of these critical facilities in 1448. Consolidating a milling monopoly, the Amt Mühlenhof was established, comprising various farmsteads and villages in the region. Peasants were compelled to grind agricultural goods at the urban mills, subject to the regular payment of fees—revenue that was, in turn, fundamental to financing the life of the royal court.[16] Further mills operating under royal power were located south of the *Stadtschloss* (city palace). The Werdersche Mühlen were dedicated to processing lumber, which was stored in the adjacent wood yards.

Beyond their effect on defining royal power, urban nutrition, and production, the mills also motivated the extension of the waterway network. Berlin's first canal—Kupfergraben ①—was mainly erected to circumvent the blocked Spree. River energy remained a crucial force until the rise of the steam engine. Until then, the mills at Mühlendamm were steadily extended, technically updated, and—in the case of fire (e.g. in 1838)—entirely rebuilt.[17] The last mills at Mühlendamm were demolished in 1892 and replaced by a sluice, which allowed continuous navigation for the first time in 500 years. The Werdersche Mühlen disappeared from the cityscape slightly earlier; they were dismantled in 1876.[18]

Mühlendamm
1 Cöllnische Mühle
2 Walkmühle
3 Mittelmühle
4 Klippmühle
5 Säge-, Loh-, Ledermühle
6 Berliner Mühle

Werdersche Mühlen
7 Walkmühle
8 Schneidemühle

Royal wood markets
Urban ports

Waterways
① Kupfergraben
② Fortress moat
③ Spree

Fig. 7 Berlin, 1700

Fig. 8 Mühlendamm

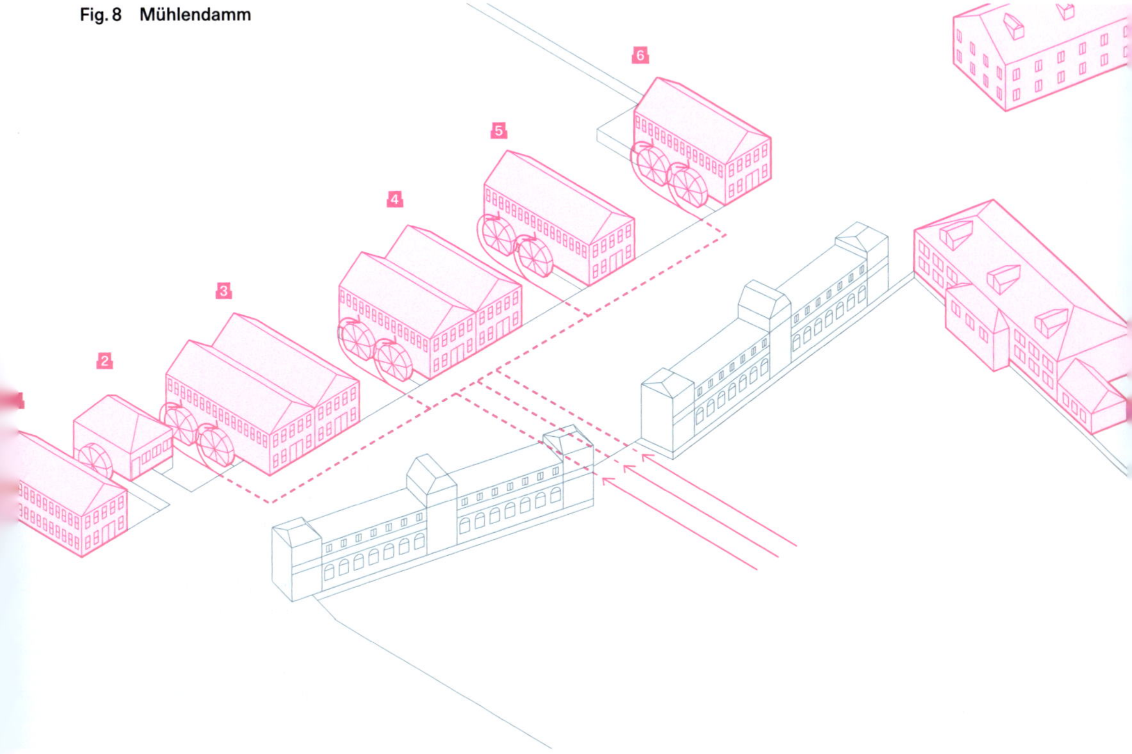

Pre-dating industrial times, the main carriers for thermal energy were wood, peat, and charcoal. Usually regionally sourced, these materials were shipped to Berlin if rivers and canals would allow it. Since no central facilities for thermal energy production existed (which happened directly in people's homes and in the city's first factories), large swathes of the city's watersides were dedicated to distributing energy carriers. Wood markets and trans-shipment points for peat and coal proliferated on the banks of canals and rivers in patterns analogous to urban growth. The necessity of their accessibility also guided the extension of urban waterways: incrementally, the old Landwehrgraben ❶ (moat) south of the city was expanded to become a Floßgraben (raft canal) and finally consolidated as today's well-known Landwehrkanal. A second connection to the Spree was then provided by constructing the Luisenstädtischer Kanal ❷.[19] Both canals were integral parts of a series of integrated urban plans developed by the general director and principal landscape architect of the Royal Prussian Gardens, Joseph Peter Lenné.

The shipment and sale of fuels that powered the rising metropolis had been heavily restricted, and either royal- or guild-privileged for a long time. However, this situation changed in the early 19th century with the abolishment of the Skippers' Guild and serfdom, as well as the liberalisation of domestic trade in Prussia (1818), which gave rise to new occupations.[20]

Shipping merchants, the so-called *Schiffsvolk,* ensured the city's energy supply. At resource extraction sites, families specialised in transporting all kinds of goods, including agricultural products and, most importantly, bricks.[21] Wood was felled and brought to the city from Schorfheide, Uckermark, Spreewald, Fläming, and Havelland. Peat-cutting, meanwhile, took place in varied locations including Linum, the forests of Schorfheide, the Eberswald glacial valley, and the Niederlausitz and Storkow moors. With the gradual shift towards coal, the mining areas were increasingly concentrated in the city's south.

For the shippable summer season, the *Schiffsvolk* lived on their barges in order to complete as many trips as possible to the city.[22] Their economic ventures, distinct waterborne lifestyles, and diverse forms of internal organisation (e.g. the shipping cooperative) underline the social interconnectedness of energy landscapes and infrastructure space.

Freight rails

Wood markets
Urban ports
Mills
Gasworks

Urban Ports
1 Alter Packhof
2 Engelbecken
3 Schöneberger Hafen

Waterways
❶ Landwehrkanal
❷ Luisenstädtischer Kanal

Fig. 9 Berlin, 1856

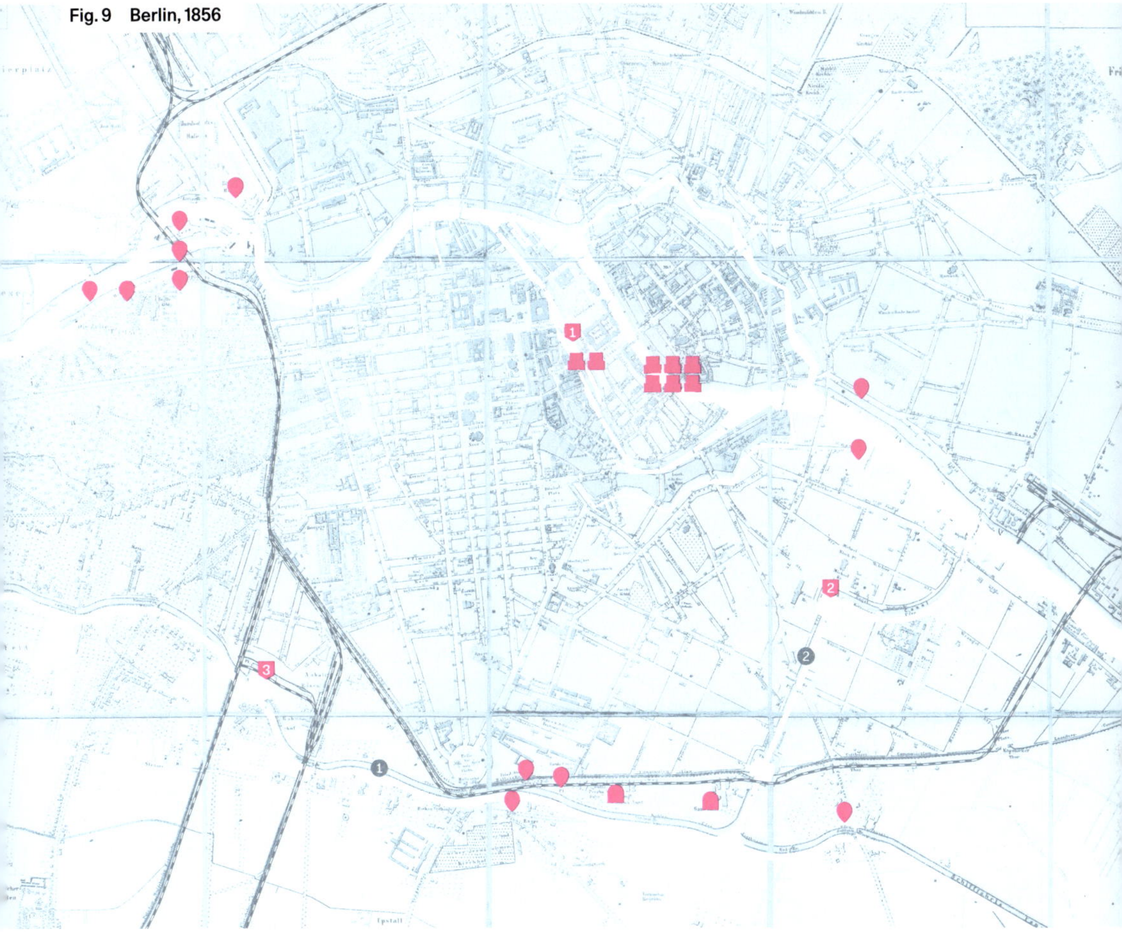

Fig. 10 Engelbecken

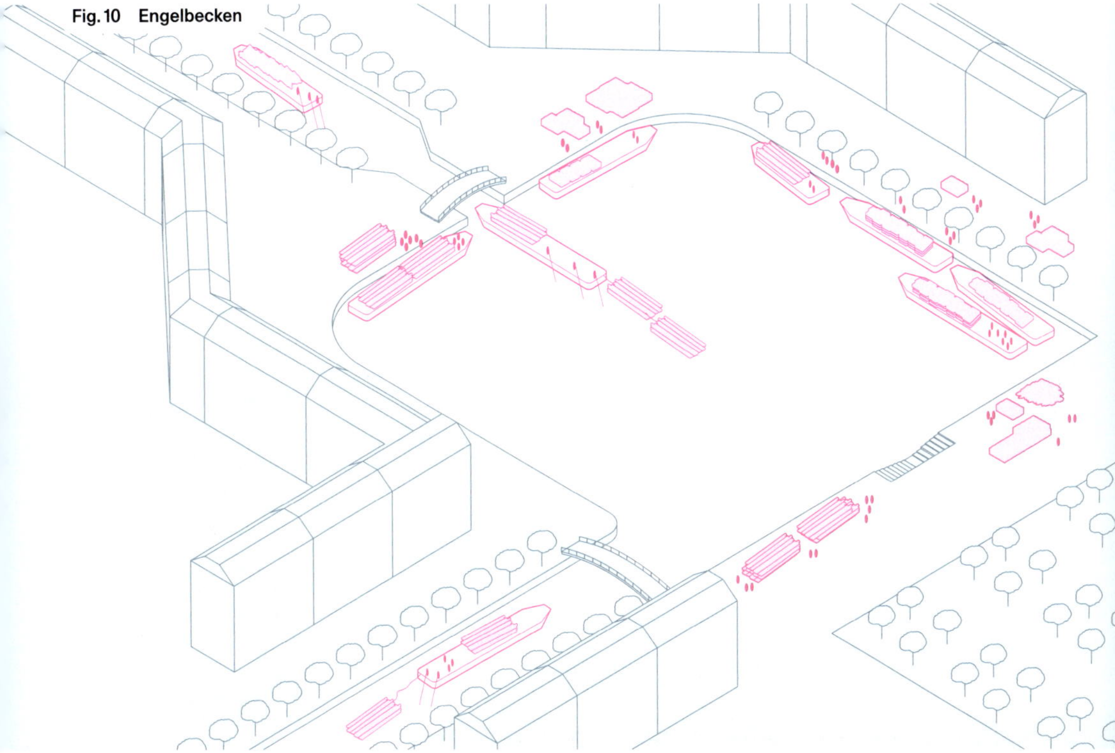

In the second half of the 1800s, Berlin's energy and waterway infrastructure underwent rapid transformation. With urban growth peaking, the demand for fuels skyrocketed. The Prussian state and the municipality of Berlin put forward a series of major engineering interventions.[23] The extension of the Landwehrkanal ①, the construction of Berlin-Spandauer Schifffahrtskanal ②, the Charlottenburger Kanal ③, and the Berliner Schifffahrtsweg provided a powerful circulatory system for the transmission of a new energy carrier: coal. Thousands and thousands of years-old organic deposits were brought to Berlin by shipping companies, excavated from the depths of Schlesien and Lausitz and Great Britain's coal regions.

In addition to earlier modes of distribution, new logics of energy supply unfolded in novel spatial logics. Gasworks proliferated along the canals. On-site coal was transformed into town gas, which was then used to light and heat the city. The gasworks incorporated landings, unloading, and storage facilities on the banks of the canals to handle the solid fuels, which were burnt in large combustion chambers. The gas produced was then stored in cylindrical tanks for further distribution. Starting from the gas stations, an underground network was developed, which delivered the carrier, at least in some parts of the city, directly to the households.

With the expansion of these facilities, new actors also gained relevance. Initially, the expansion of gas stations and the associated pipeline network was driven by private companies. The Imperial Continental Gas Association ICGA was the first company to engage in the profitable business. However, in the coming decades, municipal stakeholders shaped the extension of the gas infrastructure.[24] As gasworks proliferated, small-scale fuel transport gradually vanished. Energy production and transmission together with local energy landscapes were scaled-up, rationalised, and centralised.

Gas service area
Freight rails

Wood markets
Urban ports
Mills

Gasworks
1 ICGA I, 1826
2 ICGA II, 1838
3 Berlin I, 1847
4 Berlin II, 1847
5 Berlin III, 1859
6 Charlottenburg, 1861
7 Schöneberg, 1870
8 Berlin IV, 1872

Waterways
① Landwehrkanal
② Berlin-Spandauer Schifffahrtskanal
③ Charlottenburger Verbindungskanal

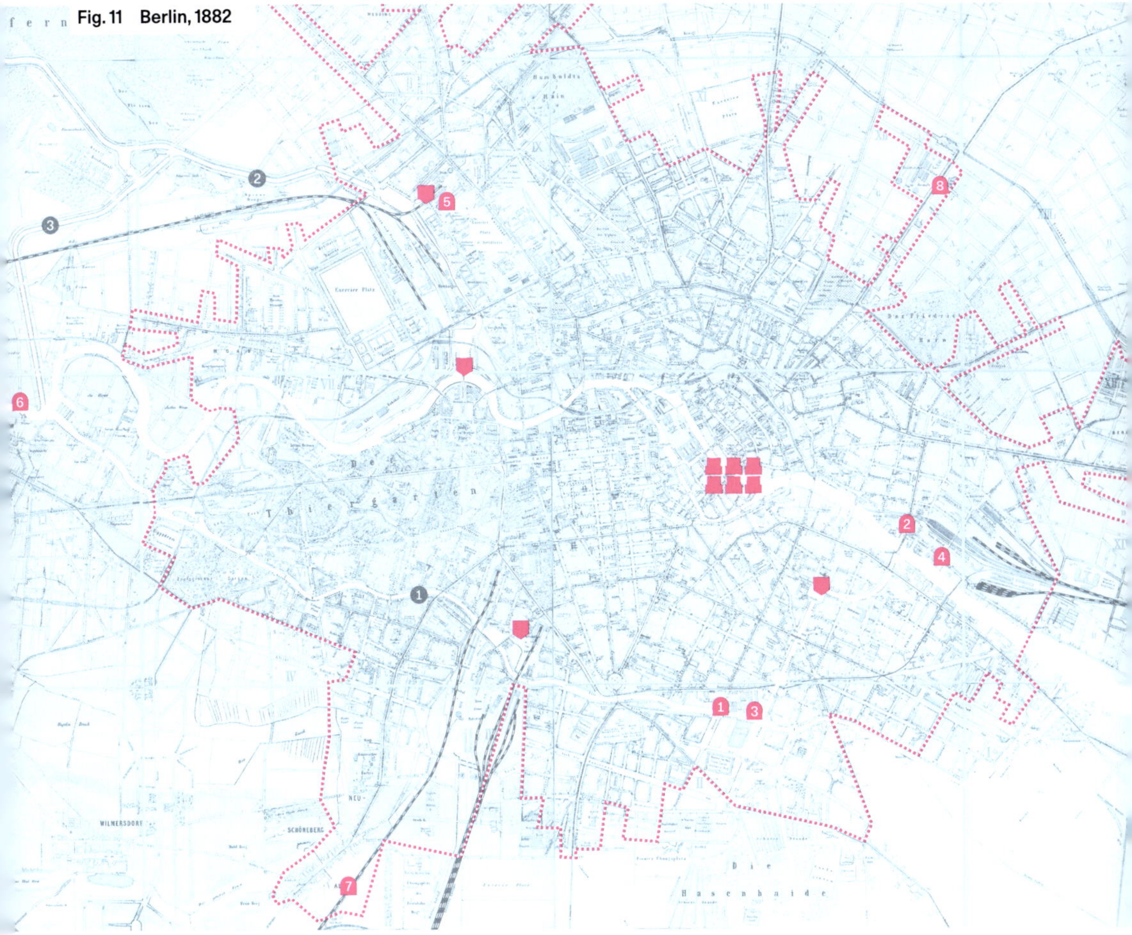

Fig. 11 Berlin, 1882

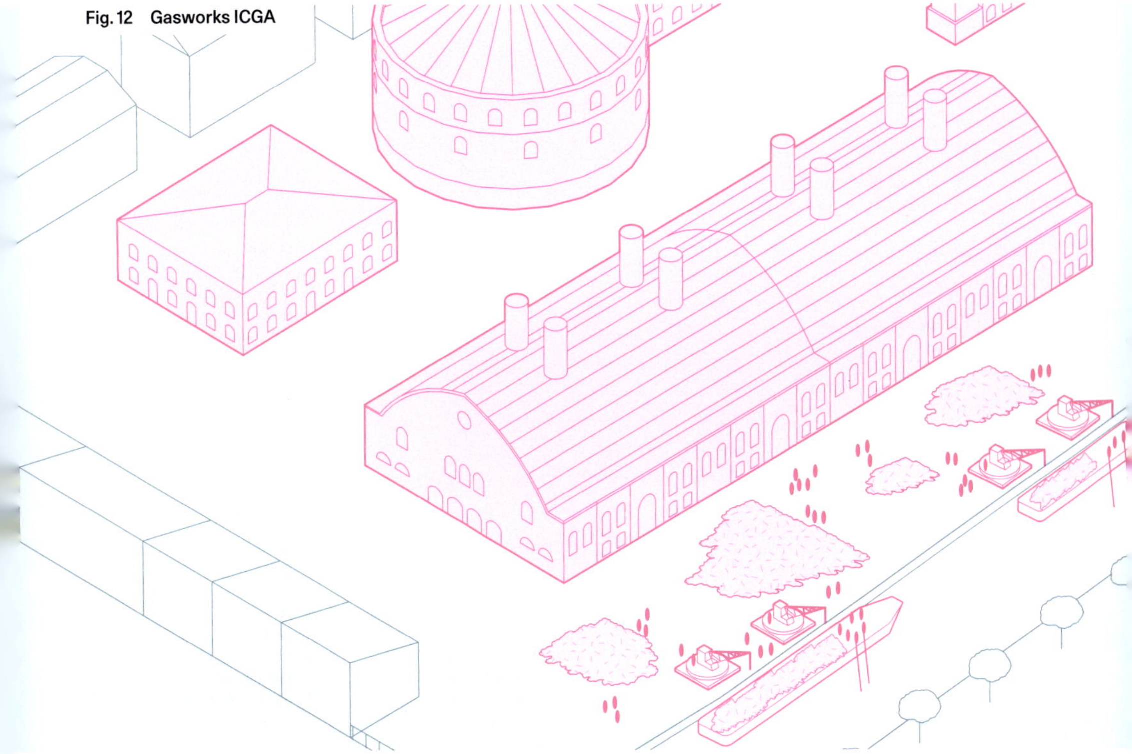

Fig. 12 Gasworks ICGA

In line with the sociotechnical innovations of the Industrial Revolution, Berlin turned into an "Electropolis", with electric current setting the pace of the city. Its provision was part of the new municipal self-image. Berlin financed and constructed numerous public power stations to facilitate industrial growth.[25] Between 1897 and 1931, eight power stations were built on the banks of the city's canals and rivers. In 1928 Berlin's municipal enterprises consumed 1,900,000 t of black coal.[26] The largest share was transported along the waterways. The origins of the solid fuel, arriving at canal- and riverside power stations and industrial facilities, are a key example of the role played by waterways in expanding the city's catchment area. Coal was imported from mines as far away as Great Britain, with supplemental import routes connecting Berlin with coalfields in Schlesien and the Rhein-Ruhr Region.

The Klingenberg Power Station 6 on the Spree waterfront became the city's flagship. It was owned and operated by the municipal electricity provider Berliner Städtische Elektrizitätswerke Aktien-Gesellschaft BEWAG. The monumental station featured an automated crane system, allowing for direct coal transfer from vessels and cargo trains to the combustion chambers. Additionally, the coal-fired power generation necessitated large amounts of cooling water, which were obtained from the river via underground in- and outlet channels.[27]

This direct link made canals and rivers a critical locational factor for power stations, despite the rise of the railways, which offered much faster and smoother circulation.[28] Consequently, the close bonds between waterways and energy infrastructure remained. This strong link was one of many reasons why another canal was built on Berlin's municipal territory—as well as factors such as drainage, wastewater treatment, and settlement of industry. The most extensive canal project—and the last one to date—is the Teltowkanal 1, connecting Spree and Havel south of the city.[29] The German Kaiser ceremonially opened the canal in 1906, symbolically celebrating its role in the industrial growth of the German capital with a ride on his steamboat.

With the rise of electricity, the trends towards local centralisation, geographical expansion of hinterlands, and rationalisation of energy landscapes' operations continued. Consequentially, over centuries, Berlin's energy infrastructure developed into a highly technical and largely automatised system.

Gasworks
1 ICGA I, 1826
2 Gaswerk Schöneberg, 1873
3 Gaswerk Berlin IV, 1873
4 Gaswerk Charlottenburg II, 1889
5 Gaswerk Niederschöneweide, 1899
6 Gasanstalt Rixdorf II, 1903
7 Gaswerk Mariendorf, 1912
8 Gaswerk Berlin VI, 1916

Power stations
1 Kraftwerk Charlottenburg, 1900
2 Kraftwerk Steglitz, 1911
3 Elektrizitätswerke Südwest, 1912
4 Kraftwerk Oberhavel, 1913
5 Kraftwerk Rummelsburg, 1913
6 Kraftwerk Klingenberg, 1926
7 Kraftwerk West, 1930

Urban ports
Gasworks

Waterways
1 Teltowkanal
2 Britzer Kanal
3 Neuköllner Kanal
4 Hohenzollernkanal

Fig. 13 Berlin, 1937

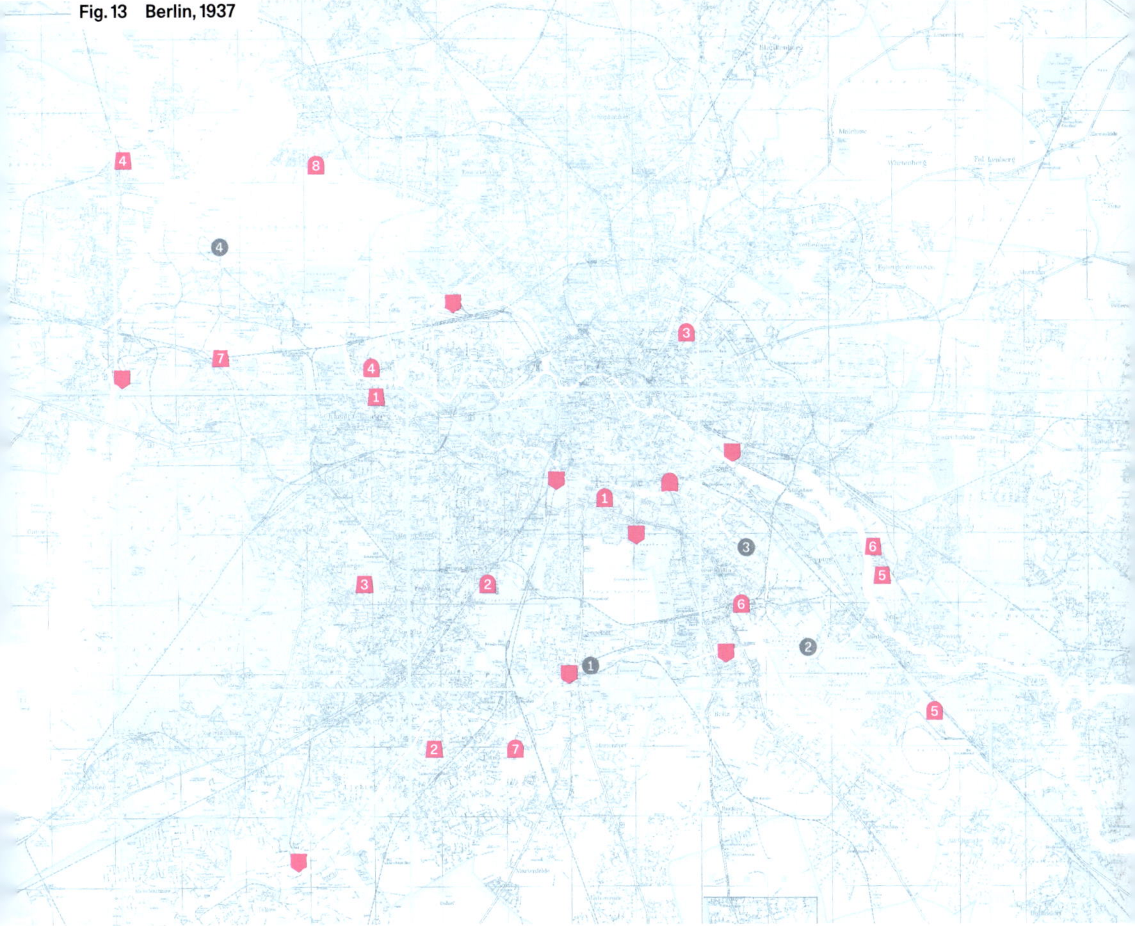

Fig. 14 Kraftwerk Klingenberg

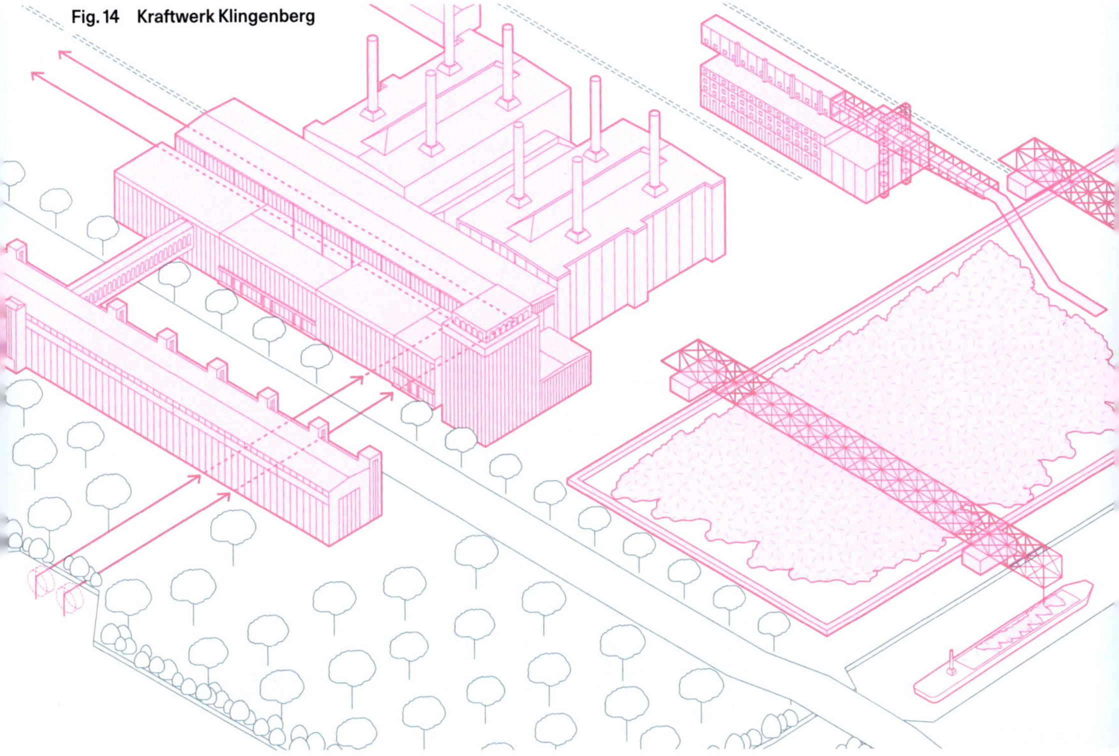

2.4

From the Basement to All Over Europe

David Bauer
Felix Frankowiak

Fig. 15 The Centralstation at Markgrafenstraße 2

Fig. 16 Early public electricity supply, 1886

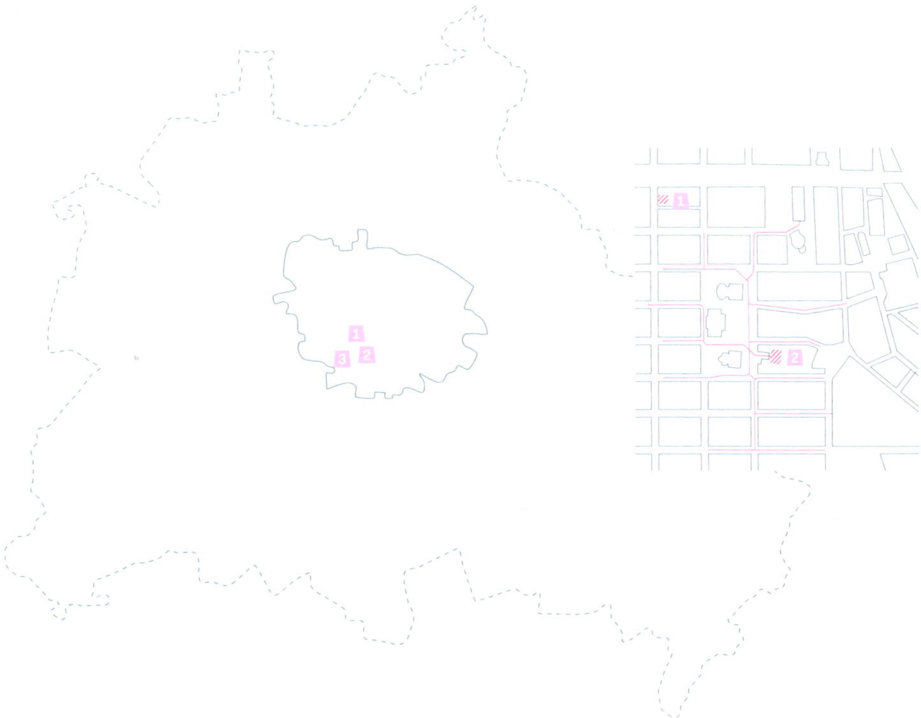

1 1886: the Basement of Electric Entrepreneurs

Power stations
1 Friedrichstraße
2 Markgrafenstraße
3 Mauerstraße

City boundary
1861
1920

Power cables
100 V

Berlin's initial power network had its humble origins in a basement on the corner of today's Unter den Linden and Friedrichstraße. Developed by a group of entrepreneurs and industrialists with visionary aspirations to advance the field of electricity production beyond the confinements of experimentation, this predecessor to the power station was developed to commercially illuminate one of the most prestigious cafés in town with hundreds of flickering light bulbs.

Under constant surveillance and perpetual coal-feeding, the *souterrain* machine room generated around 100 kW of power, driven by four steam engines which moved seven dynamos. It operated at a direct voltage DC of merely 100 V—the equivalent of eight contemporary car batteries.[30] However, due to its low-voltage capacity, it could only supply customers in the immediate vicinity, typically all residing within one block of houses. This earned it the name "Blockstation".

A year later and a few streets further south, Berlin's first public power station, known as a Centralstation at Markgrafenstraße 2, was inaugurated to extend electric power supply to a larger area. It consisted of a newly built machine hall that housed six compound steam engines and twelve DC generators that now operated at 110 V, with five times as much output as their predecessor.[31] At this time, just 28 consumers were connected via overhead power lines, including major customers like the Königliches Schauspielhaus and the Reichsbank.[32] Despite increased productivity, the grid's supply area was remained limited to an 800 m radius in the city centre due to significant power losses in DC transmission, making an extension of the grid impractical. The Centralstation was thus likewise restricted to serving a very limited number of consumers.[33] One year after the inauguration of the Centralstation, a second public power station was erected in Mauerstraße 3 at the behest of the city. In this location, a small two-storey building was directly integrated into the inner courtyard of the block.

		1884	1885	1886	1889
DC power stations	100 V	1 Friedrichstraße	2 Markgrafenstraße	3 Mauerstraße	4 Spandauer Straße

Fig. 17 Competing power grid development, 1900

2 1900: the Electric Breakthrough

The development of alternating current AC alongside the invention of electrical transformers in the late 1890s led to a new era in electricity supply. From then on, electricity could be enforced and transmitted over large distances at high voltages and reduced currents. This, in turn, minimised energy losses caused by physical resistance during transmission, a problem that had troubled the young industry for over a decade. To make this electricity usable for customers in public buildings, factories, and private households, it had to first be converted from high-voltage AC into low-voltage DC. This conversion took place at substations which operate at the grid interface between different voltage levels.[34]

With the growing demand for electricity usage, a new generation of larger coal-fired power stations began to emerge, mainly along the existing waterways of different municipalities and cities in the conurbation of Residenzstadt Berlin.[35] In 1900, Oberspree 1 and the newly built power station Moabit 3 began to deliver electricity to northern and western regions through the first 6 kV three-phase overhead power lines.[36] Due to advantages regarding higher voltage and improved power transmission, AC prevailed over DC. The innovative three-phase system gradually replaced the existing power stations, which were repurposed as substations.[37] By the turn of the century, Berlin had different kinds of networks and grids operating side by side.

Power stations (DC)
2 Markgrafenstraße
3 Mauerstraße
4 Spandauer Straße
5 Schiffbauerdamm

Power stations (AC)
1 Oberspree
2 Charlottenburg
3 Moabit

Substations
1 Mariannenstraße
2 Nalepastraße
3 Palisadenstraße
4 Reichpietschufer
5 Voltastraße

Municipal border
— 1861
···· 1920

Power cables
— 3 kV
— 6 kV

1890 1891 1895 1900 1907 1908

▸ 3 kV
5 Schiffbauerdamm

AC power stations ▸ 6 kV 1 Oberspree 2 Charlottenburg [p. 77] 3 Moabit [p. 78] 4 Rummelsburg Moa

Fig. 18 HKW Charlottenburg, 2023

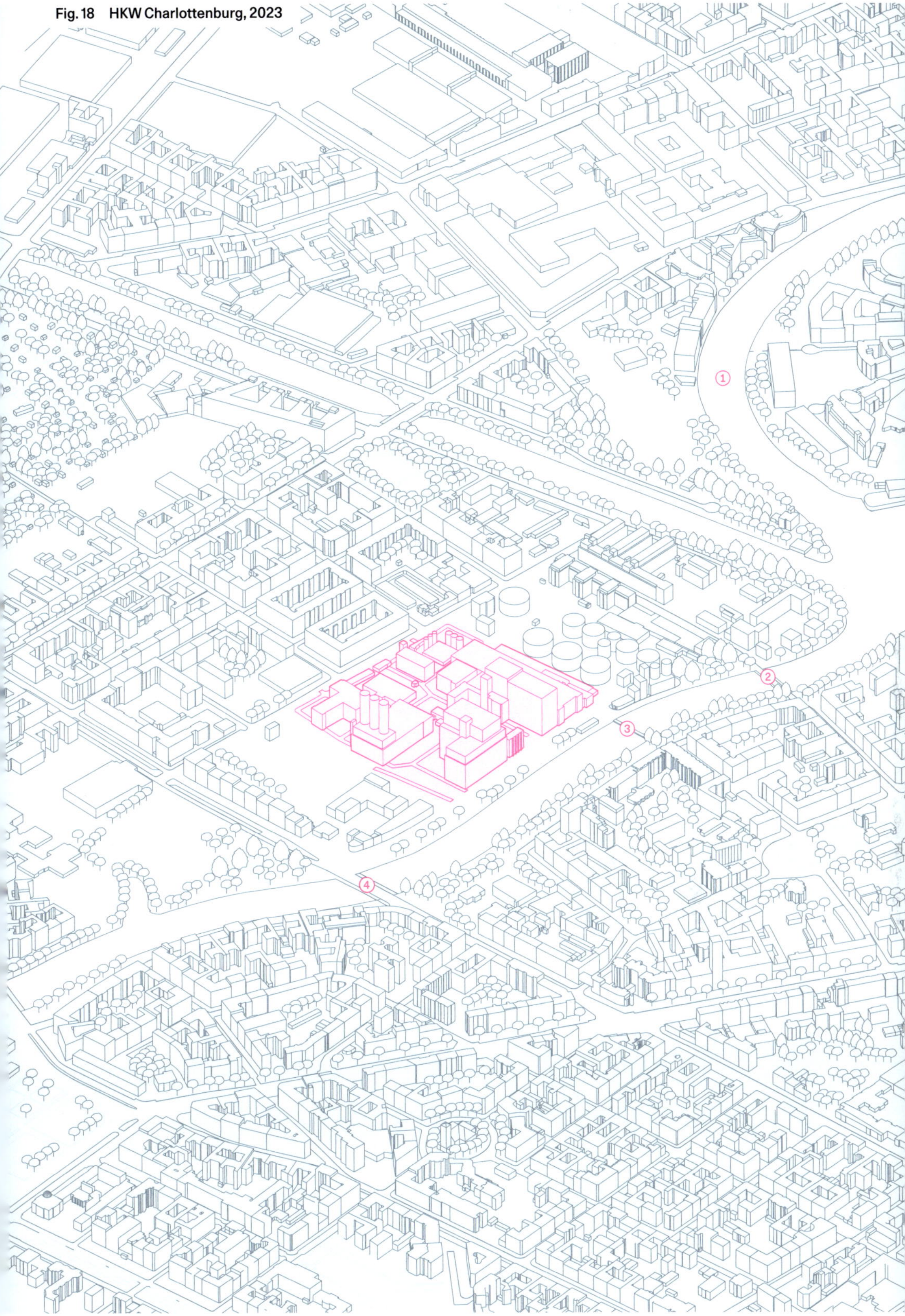

① Spree
② Röntgenbrücke
③ Siemenssteg
④ Caprivibrücke

Fig. 19 HKW Moabit, 2023

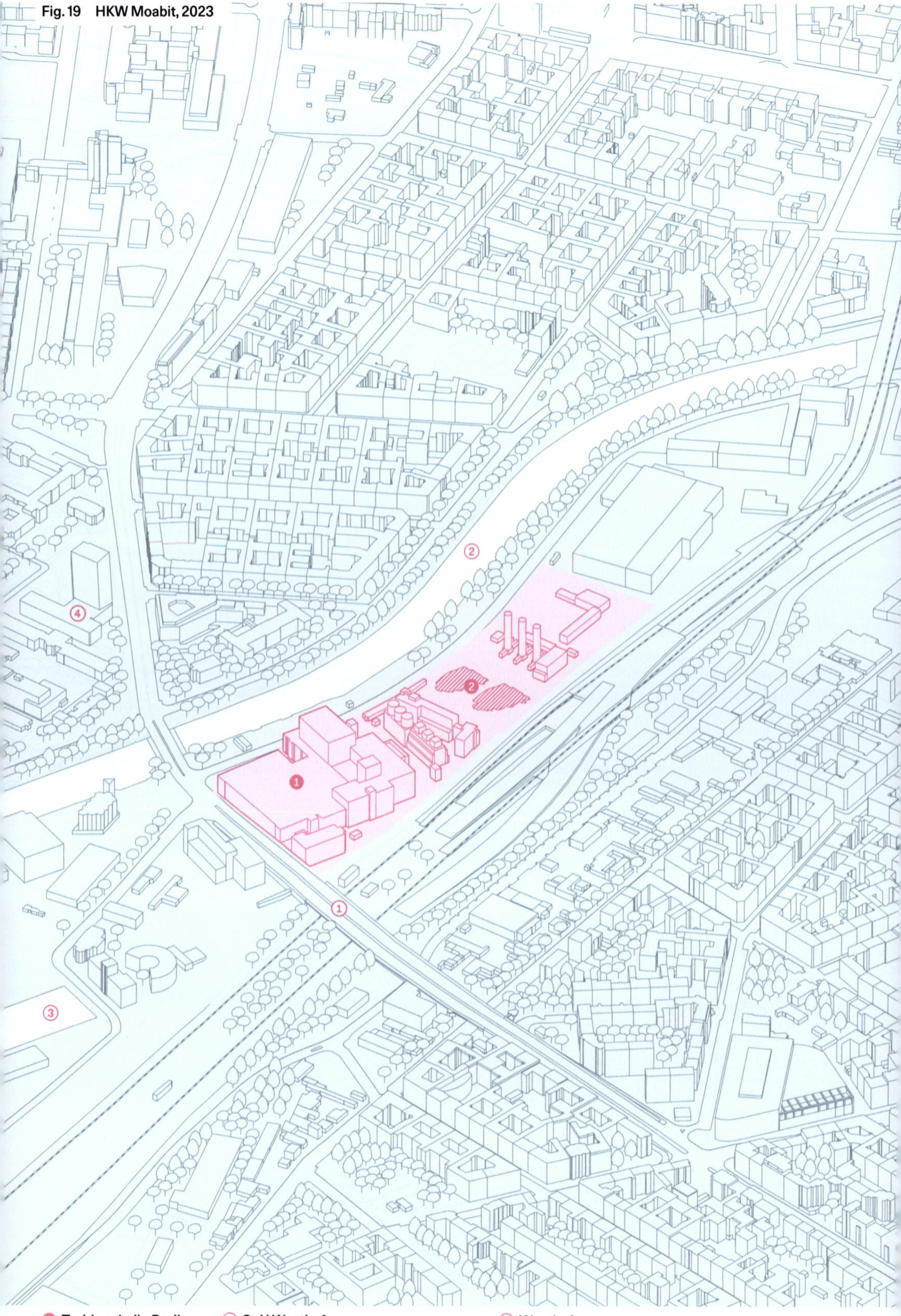

❶ Turbinenhalle Berlin
❷ Coal storage
① S+U Westhafen
② Berlin-Spandauer Schifffahrtskanal
③ Westhafen
④ Charité Campus Virchow-Klinikum

Fig. 20 High-voltage power grid with long-distance overhead transmission lines, 1934

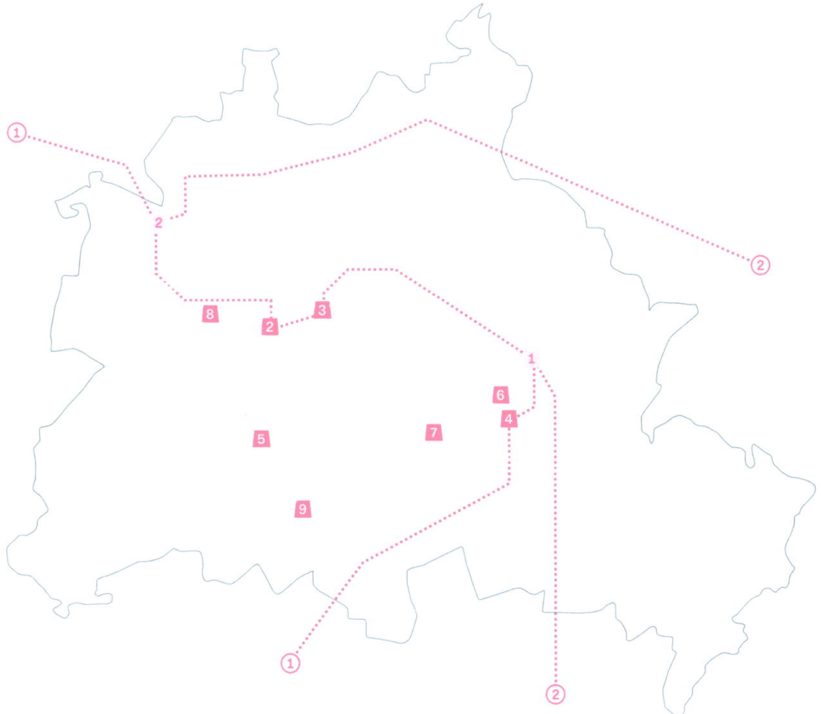

3 1934: Groß-Berlin and Beyond

With the social acceptance and widespread adoption of new technologies, particularly in the domain of public transport, the demand for electricity rapidly surged, placing consistent pressure on the need to expand production and transmission capacities. With the commissioning of the Rummelsburg power station 4 in 1907 and the extension of the Moabit power station one year later, Berlin achieved electric generation in the megawatt range for the first time before the turn of the decade.[38]

However, these efforts to effectively quench consumer thirst for electricity proved continuously insufficient as new demand rapidly emerged. The escalating consumption of the expanding armaments industry, which fuelled the slaughter on the Western Front during the First World War, surpassed the existing infrastructural capacity. The city began sourcing electricity from regions beyond its boundaries in response to this pressing need. In 1917, efforts were initiated to tap into the potential of the emerging lignite districts in the state of Sachsen-Anhalt and in Lausitz [p. 116] through the establishment of 110 kV long-distance overhead transmission lines, linking the Rummelsburg power station to a newly established lignite-fired facility at Zschornewitz and Trattendorf.

With the foundation of Groß-Berlin in 1920, unifying the power grid became a central project for the democratic government of the now much larger city. Over the years, the electricity services in the conurbation had developed into a haphazard patchwork of 12 utilities, which operated 16 power stations with independent grids and varying voltage systems.[39] Most of these utilities were incorporated into the municipally-owned Berliner Städtische Elektrizitätswerke StEW and later BEWAG, with the exception of wealthier south-western parts of the city which persisted in retaining their existing suppliers 5. In the pursuit of fairly distributing access to electricity to the broader public, the municipality initiated a dual approach. On the one hand, they constructed power stations of heretofore unseen sizes, such as the Klingenberg station 6; on the other, they sought to extend the interregional grid to import greater quantities of electrical power.[40] Since the end of the 1920s, Berlin covered its energy base load exclusively from this external supply, only using its own systems to provide cover for seasonal and temporary peak loads.[41]

Power stations
2 Charlottenburg
3 Moabit
4 Rummelsburg
5 Elektrizitätswerk Südwest
6 Klingenberg
7 Neukölln
8 Reuter
9 Steglitz

Substations
1 Friedrichsfelde
2 Teufelsbruch

Direction towards
① Zschornewitz
② Trattendorf

Municipal border
— 1920

Overhead power lines
⋯ 110 kV

1911 1918 1921 1925 1928

▸ 30 kV — Rummelsburg—Zschornewitz ▸ 110 kV — Friedrichsfelde—Trattendorf — Teufelsbruch—Trattendorf

5 Elektrizitätswerk Südwest [p. 83]

Teufelsbruch—Zschornewitz

Fig. 21 Berlin's divided power grid, 1955

4 1955: Divided Berlin and the Electric Island

The massive bombing raids on Berlin during the last years of the Second World War caused considerable devastation and disruption to the city's physical infrastructure. The political events that followed the division of Berlin by the Allied Forces fundamentally recomposed electricity supplies. Following the Berlin Blockade, the separation of power connections between the Eastern and Western zones was implemented on 5 March 1952. Severed from direct access to resource-rich rural areas and the possibility of long-distance transmission, West Berlin emerged as an energetic exclave of the BRD, and needed to rebuild its energy infrastructure in an attempt to sustain itself through autonomous conditions, known as the "island operation".[42] Initially, this meant flying in thousands of tons of coal through the Tempelhof Airport to keep the power stations running. The dependence on this single carrier was diversified in the coming four decades. Still, stockpile management and load-balancing energy storage became an essential feature of the half-city's metabolism due to its inability to fall back on an external grid.[43] Expanding its power production with gigantic facilities, the city had already reached self-reliance by the late 1950s. At the time, West Berlin focused on overlaying the existing 30 kV lines with a 110 kV high-voltage grid. For this purpose, 110, 30, and 6 kV substations were built.[44]

While West Berlin had to focus on developing an autonomous power grid, East Berlin's electric utilities underwent a comprehensive restructuring, shifting from largely self-reliant municipal entities to state-run socialist organisations that adhered to national and party directives rather than urban policies.[45] The existing infrastructure was gradually integrated into the supraregional supply structure of the DDR, which was now severed from hard coal supplies in the Ruhr region and began to massively expand its lignite reserves in Lausitz and Central Germany. With this came a gradually increasing dependency on energy imports for households and industry via long-distance transmission. The division of the DDR and BRD power grids in 1954 had repercussions that extended far beyond the city limits of Berlin, since both states formed part of the foundation for the independent development of the Eastern European (Vereinigte Energiesysteme or VES) and Western European (Union for the Coordination of Production and Transmission of Electricity UCPTE) power grids.[46]

Power stations
- 2 Charlottenburg
- 3 Moabit
- 4 Rummelsburg
- 5 Elektrizitätswerk Südwest
- 6 Klingenberg
- 7 Neukölln
- 8 Reuter
- 9 Steglitz

Substation
- 1 Neuenhagen
- 2 Teufelsbruch

Municipal border
- 1920
- Berlin Division (1949–89)

Power cables
- 110 kV

Overhead power lines
- 110 kV

1952 1954 1958 1962 1964 1978

UCPTE power grid ▸ 380 kV

Isolated operation of West Berlin's power grid

VES power grid 6 HKW Mitte [p. 82]

Fig. 22 HKW Wilmersdorf, decommissioned in 2021

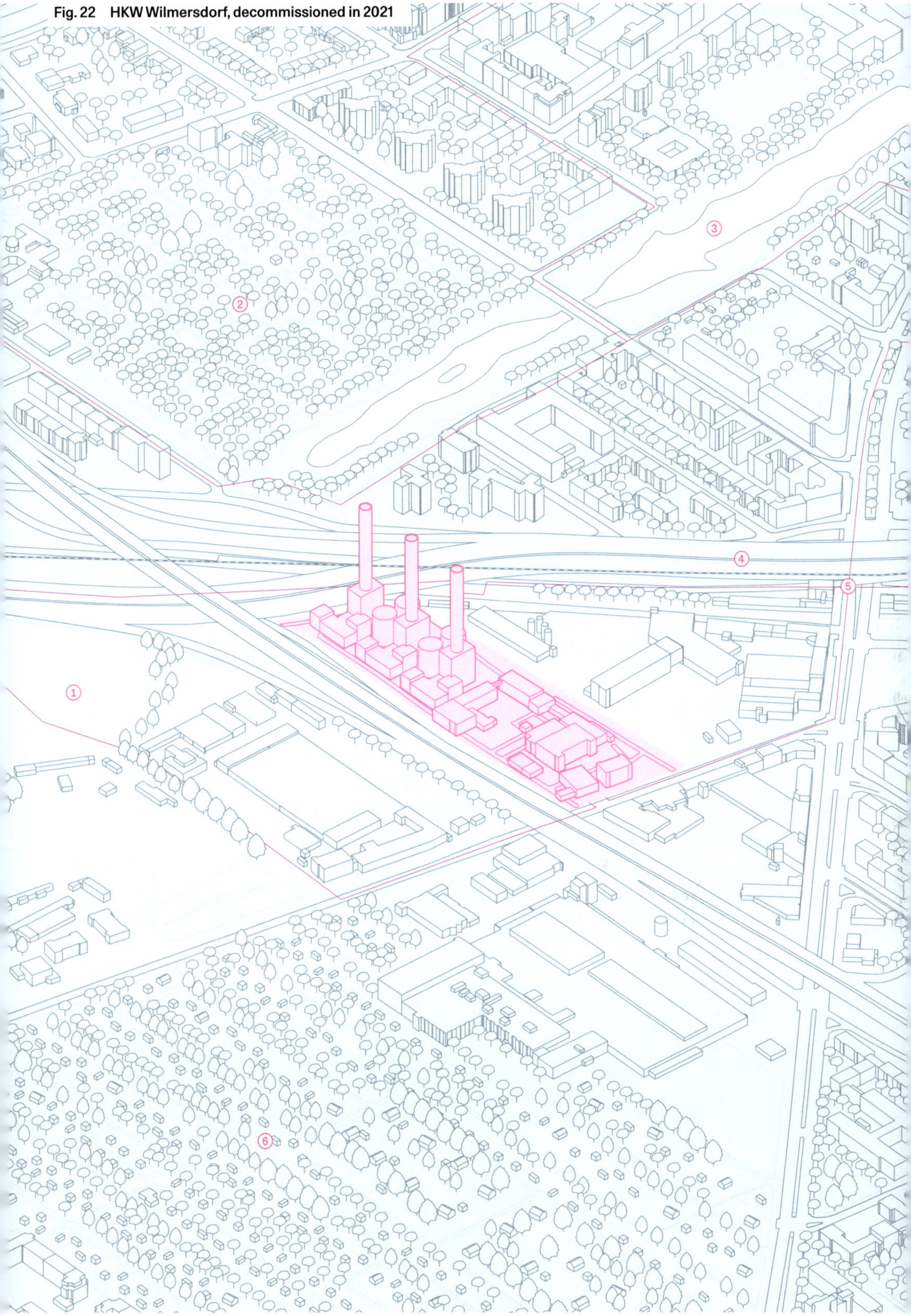

(1) Wilmersdorf Stadium
(2) Wilmersdorf Cemetery
(3) Fennsee
(4) Motorway A100
(5) S+U Heidelberger Platz
(6) Allotment garden colony “Alt Rheingau”
— High-voltage lines

Fig. 23 HKW Mitte, 2023

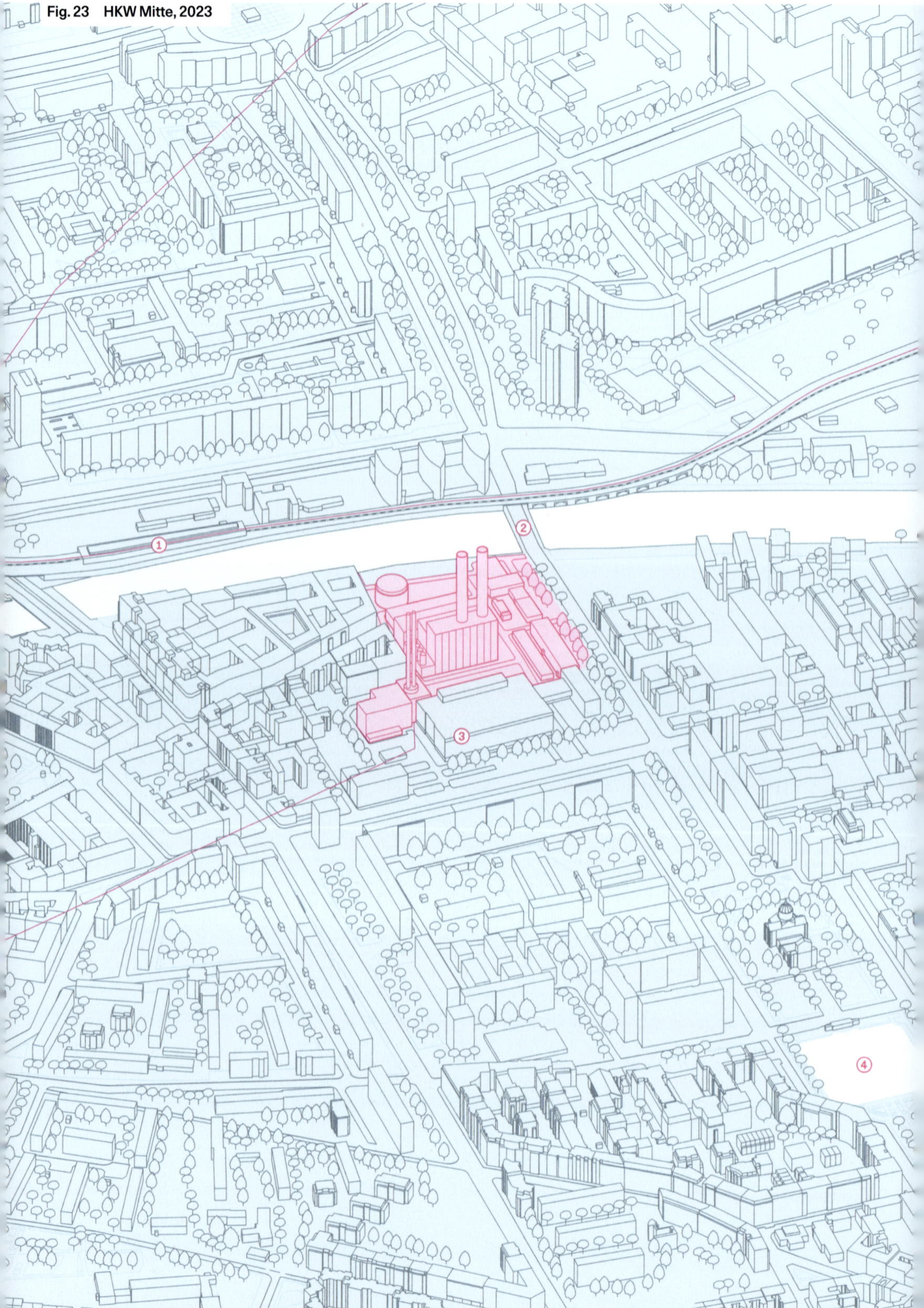

① S+U Jannowitzbrücke
② Michaelbrücke
③ Tresor / Kraftwerk Berlin
④ Engelbecken

High-voltage lines

Fig. 24 Divided high-voltage power grid, 1991

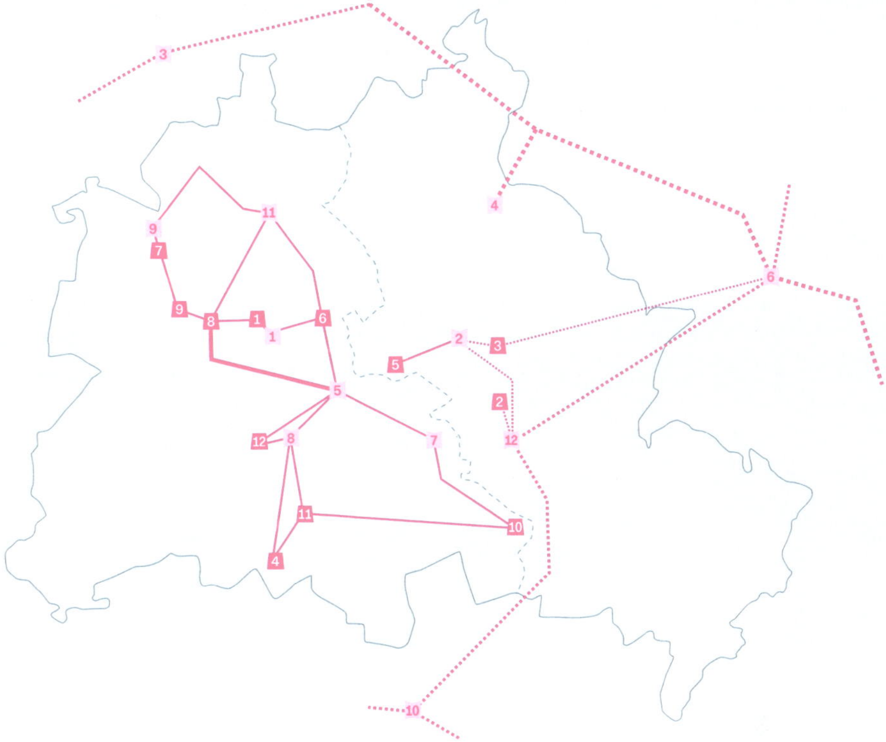

5 1991: Electric Reunification

Following political reunification, the previously divided power grids were gradually unified. During the years of separation, West Berlin operated a total of nine power stations with various fuel types, responsible for the annual distribution of 10 billion kWh.[47] At the time of constructing the Reuter 8 and, later, the Lichterfelde 4 station, the city possessed some of the most potent power stations in the entire BRD. The increasing production capacities of the modernising power stations and the spatially limited option of underground routes for cables made it increasingly uneconomical to rely on 110 kV systems. From the 1970s onwards, the old grid was overlaid by a 380 kV extra-high-voltage grid, which initially linked the Reuter power station to the Mitte substation 5. Maintaining this electric independence came at high economic and environmental costs. The grid had to accommodate inefficient redundancies and produced massive inner-city air pollution, while monopolising large areas of precious surface-space for storage and generation capacities.[48]

The eastern part of Berlin meanwhile struggled with a consistent rise in demand which more than tripled during a 40-year span.[49] Three power stations were used to fulfil this increased electrical consumption, primarily from the household sector and the increasing adoption incurred by the construction of modern large-scale settlements. This ran alongside the continuous outsourcing of energy production due to the spatial separation and rationalisation of the state-planned systems. Whereas East Berlin had been providing electricity to other parts of the DDR in 1950 this reliance was now inverted, reaching a low point of merely 6 % self-sufficiency by 1980.[50]

In 1992, the "island" status of West Berlin was terminated by establishing a 100 kV emergency line connecting it to the East Berlin grid. The construction of a supraregional 380 kV extra-high-voltage line two years later integrated the reunited city into the Western European UCPTE network.[51] Finally, on 13 September 1995, the VES and UCPTE were partially synchronised and continue to exist as one Continental European power grid.[52]

Power stations
1 Charlottenburg
2 Klingenberg
3 Lichtenberg
4 Lichterfelde
5 Mitte
6 Moabit
7 Oberhavel
8 Reuter
9 Reuter West
10 Rudow
11 Steglitz
12 Wilmersdorf

Substation
1 Charlottenburg
2 Friedrichshain
3 Hennigsdorf
4 Malchow
5 Mitte
6 Neuenhagen
7 Neukölln
8 Prinzregentenstraße
9 Teufelsbruch
10 Thyrow
11 Wittenau
12 Wuhlheide

Municipal border
1920
Former division

Overhead power lines
110 kV
220 kV
380 kV

1992 — Power grid reconnected — ▸ 380 kV

1994 — Berlin becomes part of UCPTE

1995 — UCPTE and VES connect

Fig. 25 Current high-voltage power grid, 2023

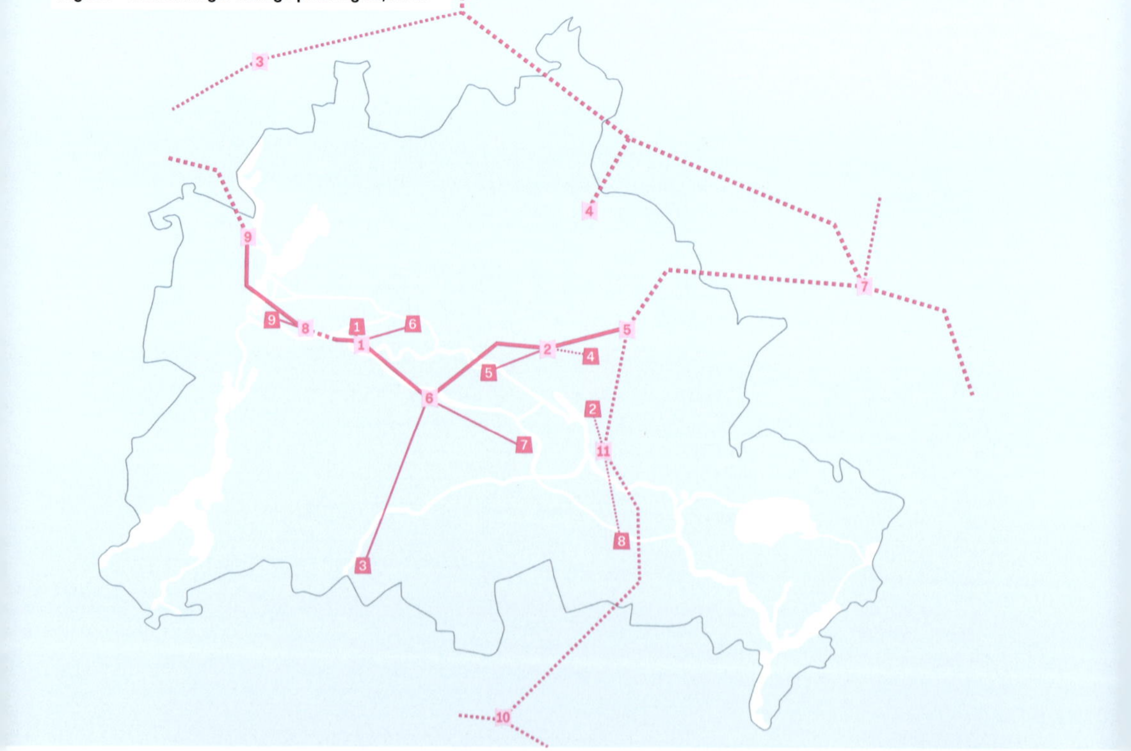

6 2023: the Future Grid

Throughout the last 20 years, Berlin's electricity infrastructure has undergone several transitions, with more changes to come in the future. Nine of the large power stations, which represented the prowess of various political regimes throughout history, still persist. However, they are now predominantly producing district heat rather than electricity, and—except for Reuter West 9 and Moabit 6—do so through the incineration of gas instead of coal. Despite its inherited and proven potential for production, the united Berlin has become a solid net importer of power.[53] Integrated into the synchronous grid of Continental Europe, it fulfils more than half of its requirements through a transnational network of high and extra-high-voltage lines.[54]

In 2022, Berlin's distribution complex comprised 35,000 km of underground cables, a mere 5,000 km short of the equator.[55] As the transformation towards sustainability necessitates further moves towards decarbonisation, demands on the distribution grids are changing. Previously designed for a one-directional flow of energy from a few large producers to millions of consumers, the grid will now have to be adapted to accommodate a more heterogeneous and decentralised form of power generation. The integration of renewable energy technologies diversifies the flow, general structure, and quantity of production facilities. Besides a relatively small number of eight wind turbines, the city has registered 45 biomass power stations and more than 11,000 PV systems.[56] From private balcony power stations to solar roof farms, a growing number of dispersed power generators with somewhat unpredictable inflows will require a new form of "smart" grid that can coordinate highly volatile energy in and outflows. To achieve this, information and communication technologies play a crucial role in facilitating the seamless integration of energy producers, energy storage facilities, and energy consumers. With the "Masterplan SolarCity", Berlin's Senate proclaimed the ambitious goal that 25 % of Berlin's future electricity should be generated via solar power by 2035 or 2050. By the end of 2022, the total installed capacity amounted to a mere 4.4 % of the envisioned target.[57] Despite these aspirations of total self-reliance through renewable sources, given both its restricted size and the significant rate of consumption, future Berlin will still be highly reliant on external inputs—and on an intercontinental power grid that expands from Great Britain and Scandinavia to Turkey and Northern Africa.

Power stations
1 Charlottenburg
2 Klingenberg
3 Lichterfelde
4 Marzahn
5 Mitte
6 Moabit
7 Neukölln
8 Gropiusstadt
9 Reuter West

Substation
1 Charlottenburg
2 Friedrichshain
3 Hennigsdorf
4 Malchow
5 Marzahn
6 Mitte
7 Neuenhagen
8 Reuter
9 Teufelsbruch
10 Thyrow
11 Wuhlheide

Municipal border
1920

Power cables
110 kV
380 kV

Overhead power lines
110 kV
220 kV
380 kV

2000 Diagonal power grid through Berlin
2009 ENTSO-E: interconnected power grid of the European Union
2021 Decommissioning of HKW Wilmersdorf
2023 Smart grids

Fig. 26 Common regional transmission tower typologies

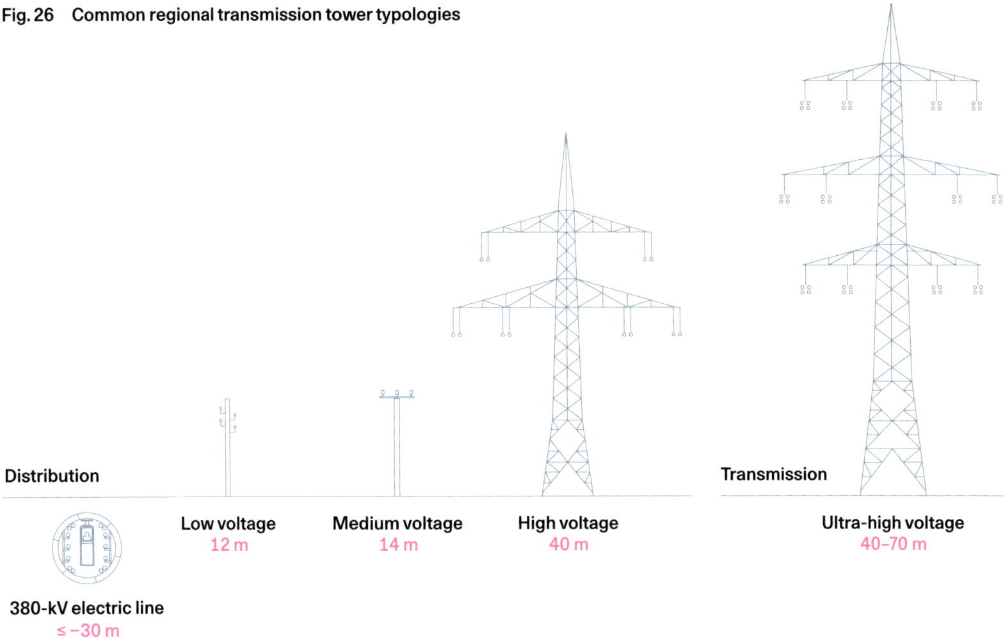

Fig. 27 Length comparison of Berlin's power grid

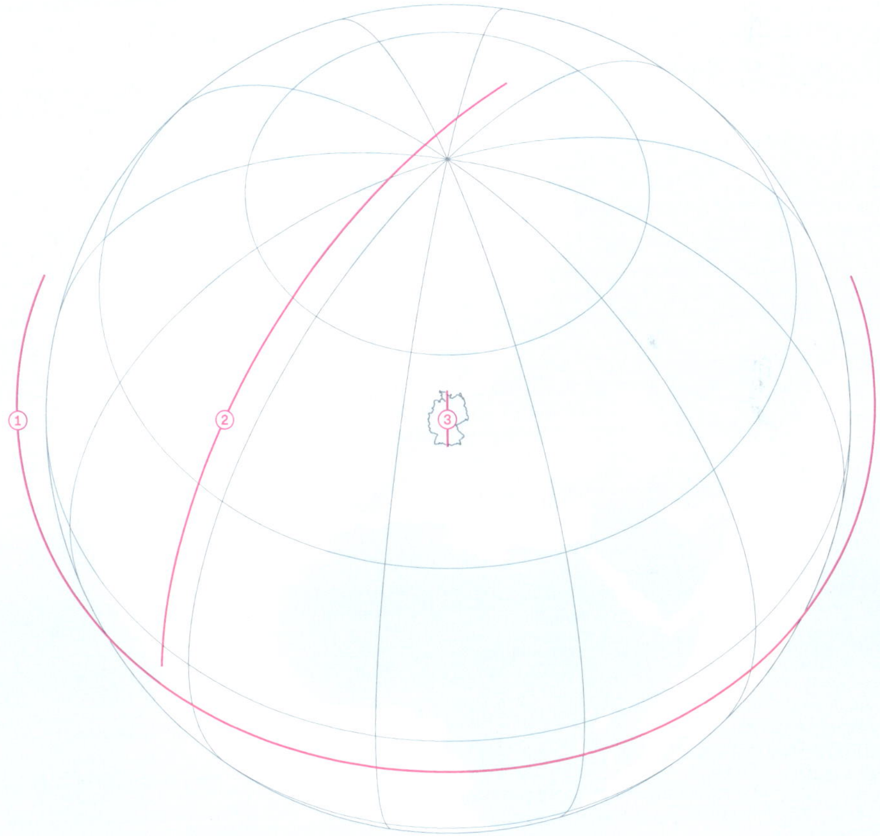

① Low-voltage grid	23,900 km
② Medium-voltage grid	10,900 km
③ High-voltage grid	850 km

Fig. 28 Overview of currently used transmission cables

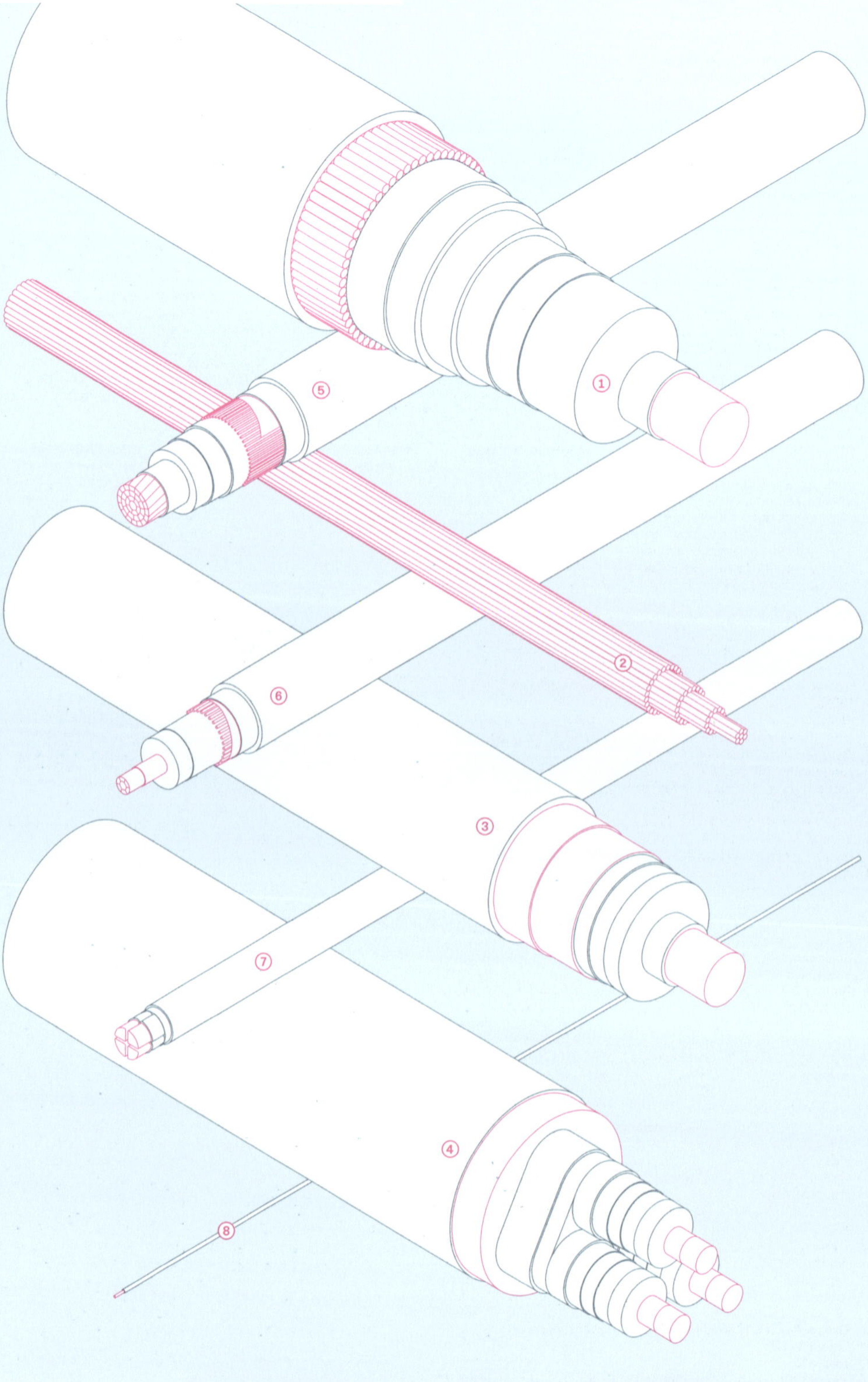

— Conductor
— Insulator

① Single-core submarine cable	420 kV	⑤ Medium-voltage	18/30 kV
② Bare overhead conductor	400 kV	⑥ Medium-voltage	6/10 kV
③ Single-core cable	220 kV	⑦ Low-voltage	600/1,000 V
④ Three-core cable	64/110 kV	⑧ Building wires	300/500 V

Endnotes

1 For a comprehensive overview of the monumental transitions over the past two centuries, please refer to: Smil, *Grand Transitions.*
2 For a comprehensive exposition on the intertwined dynamics between infrastructural development and its sociotechnical implications, please see: Moss, *Remaking Berlin.*
3 In reference to the term, please see: Hughes, "The evolution of large technological systems".
4 In reference to the term, please see: Moss, *Remaking Berlin,* 21.
5 See: Smil, *How the world really works.* The central thesis of Smil's book is that the transition to clean energy, which people desire, will take a long time and that unrealistic assumptions about how quickly it can be achieved—based on flawed understandings of our energy system and its role in modern life—could exacerbate matters.
6 Floorplans and descriptions have been compiled through site visits to Museumsdorf Düppel and the following source: Müller, *Museumsdorf Düppel.* The Düppel Museum Village recreates a medieval village on a 40-acre site, dating back to around 1200 AD. It was established in 1975 and is located on the original site where peasants lived 800 years ago. The houses in this village likely had a similar appearance to those in Berlin-Cölln during the late 12th century.
7 For a comprehensive discussion, please refer to: Marot, "Fireplace".
8 Floor plans and descriptions have been compiled using the following source: Laudel, "Der Typenwandel des ländlichen Wohnhauses im Oderbruch zwischen 1753 zwischen 1850—Der Einfluss von friderizianischer Kolonisation und preussischer Obrigkeit auf die Hausformen der ländlichen Untertanen", 34.
9 Floor plans and descriptions have been compiled using the following sources: Geist and Kürvers, *Das Berliner Mietshaus Teil 2. 1862–1945,* 536.
10 Floor plans and descriptions have been compiled using the following sources: Bundesministerium für Raumordnung, Bauwesen und Städtebau, *Leitfaden für die Instandsetzung und Modernisierung von Wohngebäuden in der Plattenbauweise.*
11 Bundesministerium für Raumordnung, Bauwesen und Städtebau, 105ff.
12 Floorplans and descriptions have been compiled using the following sources: Rosenberg, *Electrify Everything in Your Home—A Guide to Comfy, Healthy, Carbon-Free Living.*
13 Amt für Statistik Berlin-Brandenburg, "Güterbeförderung auf Binnenwasserstraßen in Berlin nach Güterabteilungen".
14 Mumford, *The City in History,* 88.
15 Herzberg and Rieseberg, *Mühlen und Müller in Berlin,* 50 ff.
16 Escher, *Berlin und sein Umland,* 66ff.
17 Herzberg and Rieseberg, *Mühlen und Müller in Berlin,* 57ff.
18 Ibid., 89.
19 Natzschka, *Berlin und seine Wasserstraßen,* 67ff.
20 Ibid., 56f.
21 The *Schiffsvolk* also transported agricultural products and bricks.
22 Köstering and Schleicher, "Berlins ist keine Hafenstadt. Kleinschiffahrt 1850–1920", 18 ff.
23 Kloos, "Der Wasserverkehr", 218ff.
24 Bärthel and GASAG AG, *Die Geschichte der Gasversorgung in Berlin,* 24ff.
25 Dame, *Elektropolis Berlin.*
26 Moss, *Remaking Berlin,* 75.
27 Röck and Bärthel, *Berlin und seine Bauten.* 10, A,2, Teil X, Bd. A Anlagen und Bauten für Versorgung; Teil 2, Stadttechnik, 204ff.
28 Peters, "Rail City Berlin", 61.
29 Natzschka, *Berlin und seine Wasserstraßen,* 97ff.
30 Tepasse, *Stadttechnik im Städtebau Berlins—19. Jahrhundert: Kompendium Stadttechnikgeschichte: Wasser und Abwasser, Gas und Strom,* 215.
31 Oswald, "Vorlesung Elektrische Energieversorgung—Vorlesungsskript".
32 Bahde, Bürgel, and Hahn, "100 Jahre Stromverteilung in Berlin", 49.
33 Oswald, "Vorlesung Elektrische Energieversorgung—Vorlesungsskript", 8.
34 Tepasse, *Stadttechnik im Städtebau Berlins—19. Jahrhundert: Kompendium Stadttechnikgeschichte: Wasser und Abwasser, Gas und Strom,* 216.
35 Oberhollenzer, "Öffentliche Elektrizitätsversorgung", 208.
36 Tepasse, 216.
37 Ibid., 216.
38 Bahde, Bürgel, and Hahn, "100 Jahre Stromverteilung in Berlin", 51.
39 Moss, *Remaking Berlin,* 54f.
40 VDE Verband der Elektrotechnik Elektronik Informationstechnik e.V, "Hochspannungsleitung Teufelsbruch—Werderstrasse".
41 Oberhollenzer, "Öffentliche Elektrizitätsversorgung", 213.
42 Ibid., 215.
43 In 1932, the first storage facility, known as a "Ruth-Storage" or steam accumulator, was constructed on the premises of Charlottenburg Power Station to produce steam and act as a buffer for peak load coverage. In 1986, the world's largest battery storage facility was inaugurated in a substation in Steglitz. It consisted of 1416 interconnected battery blocks designed to rapidly stabilise volatilities in the island energy grid for a quarter of an hour within seconds.
44 Bahde, Bürgel, and Hahn, "100 Jahre Stromverteilung in Berlin", 56, 61.
45 Moss, *Remaking Berlin,* 144.
46 Tillmann, "Die Entwicklung des Verbundbetriebes in Deutschland und in Europa. 25 Jahre elektrische Wiedervereinigung Deutschlands", 5, 7.
47 Moss, *Remaking Berlin,* 178.
48 Ibid. 178,
49 Ibid. 149.
50 Ibid. 149.
51 Porsch and Schossig, "Die Wiedervereinigung der Netze in Europa, Deutschland und Thüringen (Strom, Bahn, Gas und Telekommunikation)", 28.
52 Porsch and Schossig, 29.
53 Amt für Statistik Berlin-Brandenburg 2022.
54 Amt für Statistik Berlin-Brandenburg, "Statistischer Bericht: Energie- und CO_2-Bilanz in Berlin 2020", 3.5 Strombilanzen Berlin 2021–2020.
55 "Zahlen, Daten, Fakten—Stromnetz Berlin".
56 Senatsverwaltung für Wirtschaft, Energie und Betriebe, "Berlin—Länderbericht zum Stand des Ausbaus der erneuerbaren Energien sowie zu Flächen, Planungen und Genehmigungen für die Windenergienutzung an Land", 7.
57 Senatsverwaltung für Wirtschaft, Energie und Betriebe, "Masterplan Solarcity Berlin Monitoringbericht 2022", 9.

3 Fossil Energy Carriers

120 g

0.1 ℓ

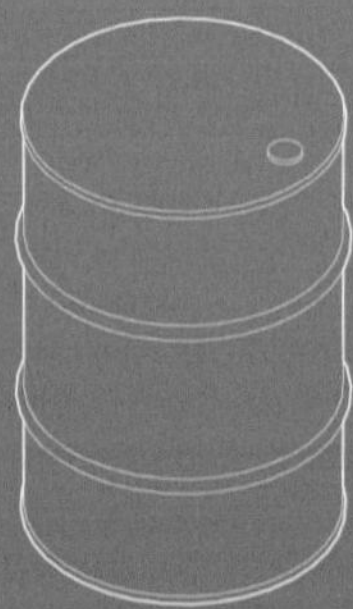

$0.1\ m^3$

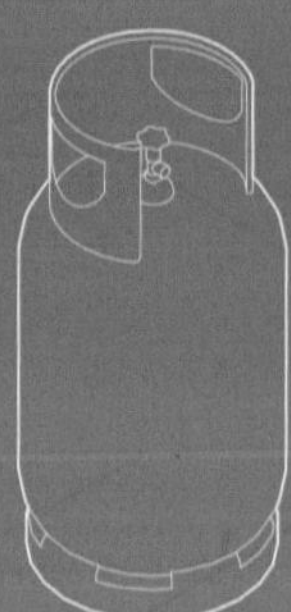

Each of these produce 1 kWh of power.

3.1

Spatial Ramifications of Fossil Fuel Utilisation

David Bauer
Joseph Smithard

The term "fossil fuel" encompasses a category of hydrocarbon-containing substances of biological origin which are found in the Earth's crust, and primarily harnessed to extract energy. Given this rather technical definition, one could say that fossil fuel can be described as something ancient and lifeless, entombed deep beneath the Earth's surface, which is then extracted, ignited, and blown into the air to release energy. Fossil fuels represent extensive spans of space and time, compacted into concentrated energy in the form of matter. They emerge from the complex interplay between geological forces and the passage of deep time,[1] in which vast expanses of ancient paleo flora and fauna were compressed and condensed into portable solids and liquids. Hence, fossil fuels act not only as primary carriers of energy across geological eras, but also function as substantial reservoirs of stored energy.

Though considerably ancient in origin, the use of hydrocarbons to generate light, heat, and power is a relatively brief chapter within the wider chronicle of human cultural evolution. For context, envision the inception of the Upper Palaeolithic stone tool tradition[2] (chiefly among Neanderthals and early *Homo sapiens*) as the starting point on a 1 m scale stretching to the year 2025. Within this temporal framework, the epoch of fossil fuel dominance would be encapsulated within a minuscule 6 mm span.

Fig. 1 The adoption of fossil fuels in the human evolutionary timeline ■ intensive use of fossil fuels

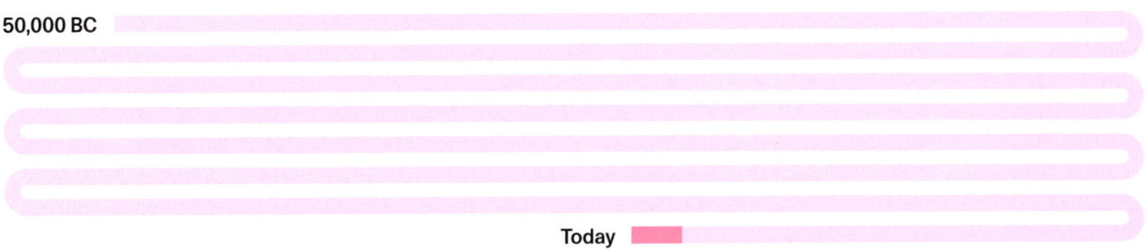

This minute line may represent the most influential and impactful 6 mm imaginable, ushering in a time when a single generation would witness a more profound transformation in—and experience a still greater sense of alienation from—their immediate surroundings than all the cumulative generations that preceded them. Considering the even shorter time elapsed since 1945—a period distinguished by a unique and unparalleled surge in rapid growth and human-induced modifications to the Earth's surface, often termed the "Great Acceleration"—the scope of these transformations is undeniably breath-taking.[3] [Fig. 3]

Although premodern societies observed cultural shifts and weathered diverse events, including plagues, wars, and global climate shifts, their distinguishing feature was a remarkable degree of inertia and pattern persistence in fundamental facets of human existence.[4] In particular, energy production served as a pivotal cornerstone that endured in an essentially unchanged form for millennia. Generations diligently collected wood and twigs to tend to their hearths, nurtured crops and vegetables to sustain their households, and cared for animals that they relied on to engage in demanding manual tasks. This cyclical rhythm continued from one generation to the next. Where feasible, primitive machines harnessed water and, later, wind to power basic mechanisms for tasks such as grinding, lifting, pumping, and threshing. The overwhelming majority of necessities required by communities, however, were sourced from their immediate environment, predominantly in the form of plants and plant-derived materials.

The transition from reliance on phytomass (the biomass of living plants) to fossil fuels (essentially the energy locked within dead matter) can be likened to accessing an exuberant source of steroid-energy whose potency was akin to that of the agrarian revolution, albeit operating at an entirely different speed.[5] This shift facilitated the transition from depending on living beings as a power source to harnessing the immense potential of inanimate prime movers. It also marked the transformation from artisanal manufacturing methods that had endured for millennia to the sweeping wave of full-scale industrialisation.

Today, the production of energy has become synonymous with the burning of fossil fuels. Constituting nearly three-quarters of global primary energy consumption in 2022, the world has become significantly reliant on the conventional coalition of coal, oil, and gas.[6]

Fig. 2 Global energy transitions, 1800–2020 in %

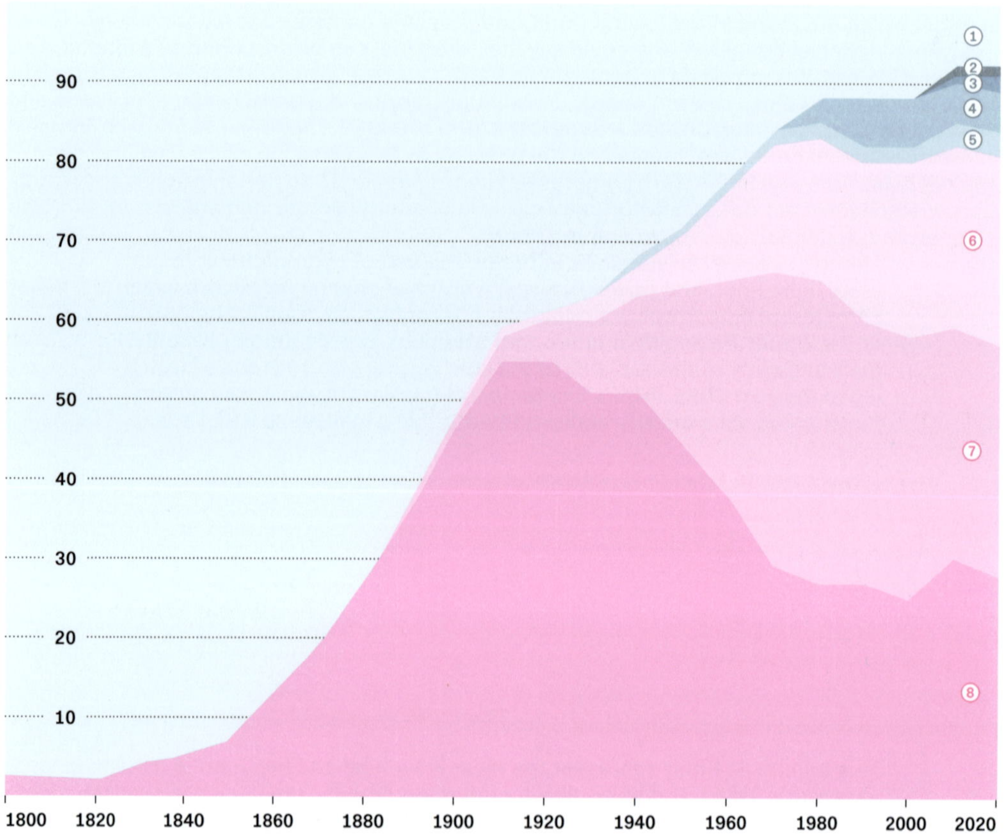

Non-fossil sources
1 Traditional biofuels (e.g. wood)
2 Modern biofuels
3 Wind and solar power
4 Nuclear power
5 Hydropower

Fossil sources
6 Natural gas
7 Crude oil
8 Coal

The sheer availability of incredible amounts of cheap energy[7] has instigated a diverse array of environmental transformation and degradation. Further, the rollout of fossil fuels into world-shaping commodities has brought about significant alterations in the utilisation and perception of space, landscapes, and the environment. Six of these facets will be further examined in the forthcoming paragraphs and subsequent chapters.

Fig.3 The Great Acceleration, 1750–2010

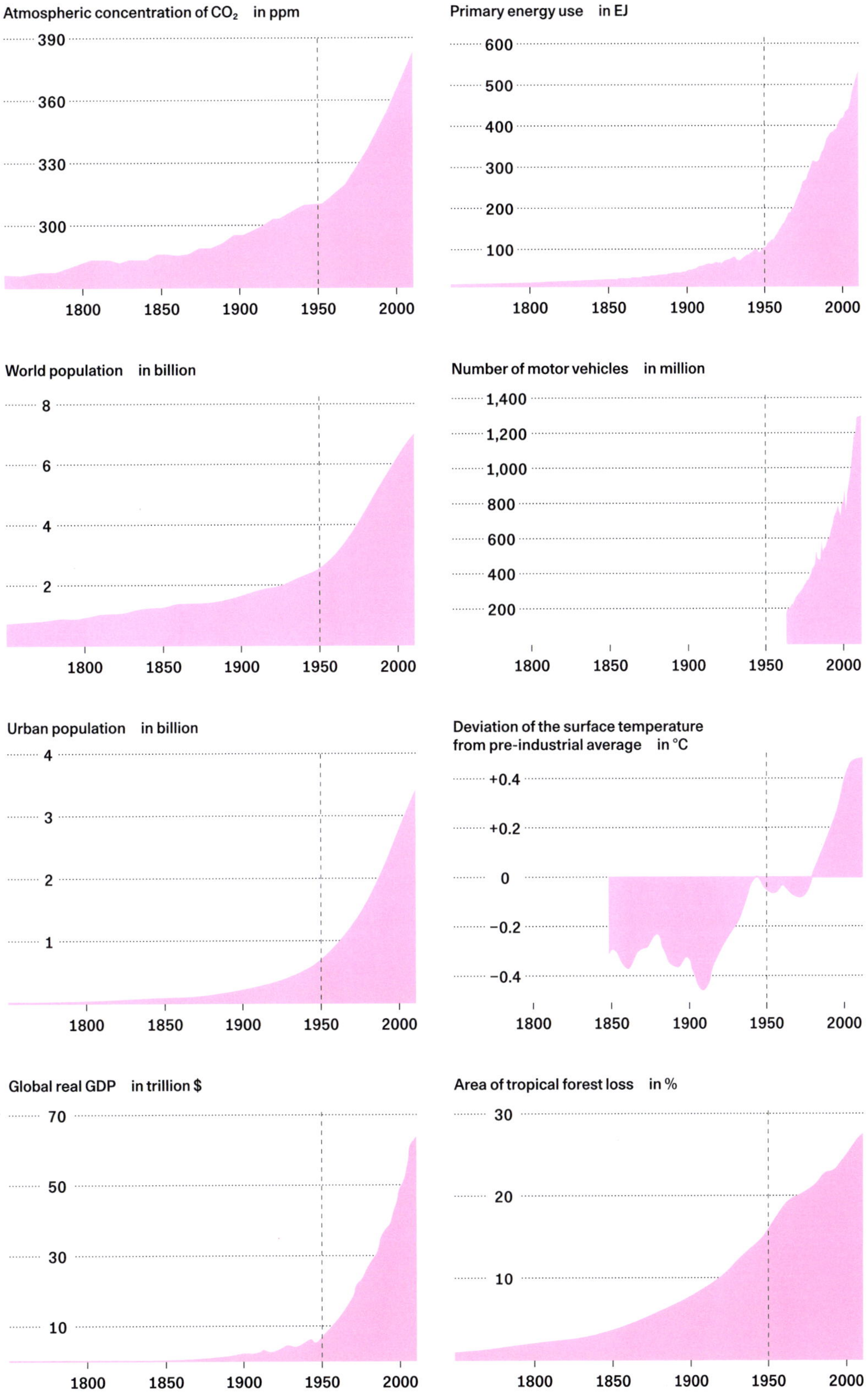

The use of fossil fuels has changed how humans perceive and interact with the Earth's surface and subsurface.

Throughout history, the subterranean world has had pan-cultural associations with death and darkness, enveloped in enigmatic and forbidden domains overseen by otherworldly entities. The entrances to subsoil caves were frequently intertwined with religious rituals, rendering the underground a realm to be avoided by the ordinary masses. The industrial extraction of natural reserves, whether minerals or energy carriers, fundamentally altered collective understandings of the underground as a site for receiving the dead, reframing it instead as vital for human sustenance. On the one hand fossil consumption made active exploration and engagement with the underground not only lucrative but indispensable.[8] On the other hand, apart from serving as the cradle of raw energy materials, the Earth's subsurface evolved as a valuable site for the secure (and rather convenient) storage of transmission and circulatory systems, giving rise to many of the urban technology complexes the modern world is so dependent upon today. Consequently, perceptions of the underground have shifted in the cultural imaginary: it is no longer a sacred and uncanny realm, but a highly technological sphere dominated and shaped by scientific and managerial expertise.

Fig. 4 Catacombs in Paris in the 1860s

Furthermore, the ownership of subterranean domains and their fossil reservoirs has long been a subject of contention and conflict, leading to varying legal interpretations of possession rights across different historical and geographical contexts. These disputes have, in turn, reshaped economic perspectives, creating a more nuanced understanding of the relationship between the above and below.[9]

Historically, the earliest subsurface property rights adhered to the principle of *cuius est solum eius est usque ad coelum et ad inferos,* which translates to "whoever's is the soil, it is theirs all the way to Heaven and all the way to Hell". This principle originated from Roman law and was adopted by many legal systems of the early modern period, including common law in England and the United States, which defined the absolute and exclusive rights of landowners to exploit any minerals—or, later, fossil fuels—found beneath their own holdings.[10]

However, with the sudden rise in value, this basic and archaic principle was challenged and modified by several legal doctrines and statutes. Some of the most crucial questions revolved around the volatility and difficulty of controlling oil and gas reserves. Often extending over vast areas and various plots, the depletion of common sources by individuals created large disputes. Certain US states harbouring early pioneers in oil and gas field development embraced the "rule of capture". This principle permitted individuals who drilled wells on their own land to simply extract any oil or gas that flowed into it, irrespective of its origin within the subsurface of neighbouring landowners. This "first come, first served" mentality led not only to violent conflicts but also resulted in incredibly wasteful extraction practices.

Over the years, the interests of individual landowners and the wider public in conserving natural resources became more and more relevant, leading to alternative legislation. The doctrine of correlative rights, for instance, limited the "rule of capture" by requiring that each landowner had a fair opportunity to produce their share of oil or gas from a common reservoir. In some jurisdictions, the ability to exploit mineral rights—as a subset of subsurface rights beyond a specified depth—was and still is completely separate from the property title. Here, the rights are often owned permanently by the state and are only leased from it for a fixed time. Some countries went even further, nationalising their fossil fuel resources and declaring them public property.

Dark Matter

Fossil fuels comprise enormous volumes of ancient biomass, thus representing extensive and historic spatial dimensions. The overwhelming majority of sources trace their origins to the Palaeozoic Era, also known as the epoch of ancient life when the Earth experienced the proliferation of lifeforms both on land and in the sea. Coal, being the eldest of the fossil fuel triad, had its beginnings in the preserved remnants of higher terrestrial plant species, predominantly accumulating within the expansive tropical rainforest belt of the Pangean supercontinent that emerged during the Carboniferous epoch.[11] The very name "Carboniferous", derived from the amalgamation of the Latin terms *carbō* (indicating "coal") and *ferō* (conveying "to bear" or "carry"), alludes to this historical association with coal formation. Not only was the planet densely forested with trees, but the atmospheric conditions were remarkably different from the present day. Characterised by a very oxygen-rich atmosphere, the Earth fostered ecosystems of immensely potent megafauna, conditions that are neither replicable nor comparable to today's world. Each piece of coal, in essence, encapsulates a condensed fragment of these prehistoric forests, transporting compressed amounts of photosynthetic energy across millions of years. The folding of space throughout time is so remarkably efficient that, in fact, the total energy contained within the current global phytomass is approximately 100,000,000,000,000,000,000,000 J (10^{22} J), roughly equivalent to the energy capacity of all recognised fossil fuel reserves combined.[12]

Fig. 5 Geological epochs and the origins of ■ coal ■ oil and natural gas in million years

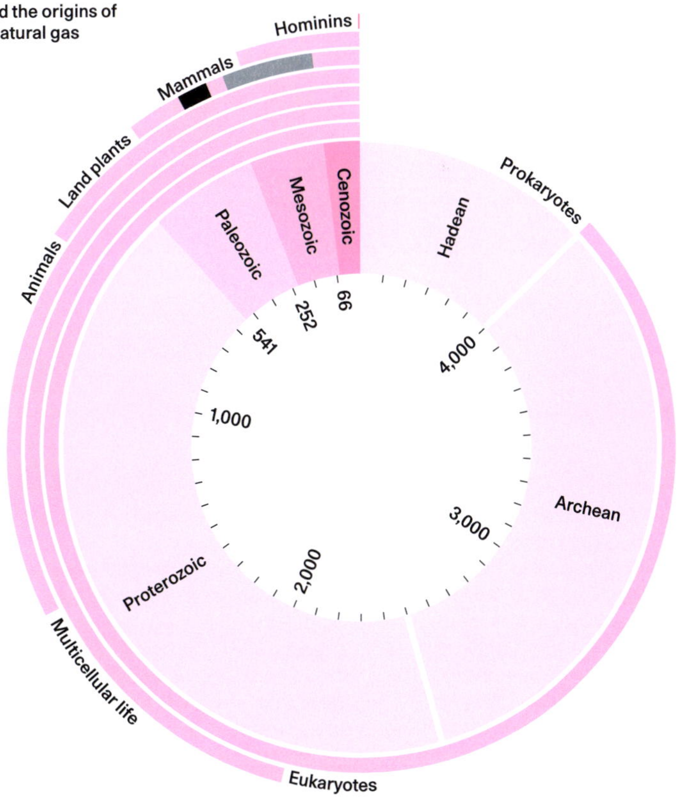

(Paleo-)Geography

Understanding the world through the lens of territorial availability of fossil fuels has introduced novel hegemonic dynamics and restructured the interrelation between central and peripheral regions worldwide. It reshaped energy production, moving it away from its traditional ties to the egalitarian Cartesian concepts that governed land-use patterns in a more balanced, equitable, and logical manner. Instead, energy provisioning became deeply rooted in paleogeography, namely the conditions of a world that no longer exist.

While retrieving energy from biomass was—in some form or another—possible in many climatic zones through the application of cultural ingenuity and labour, attaining fossil fuels also required enough luck to stumble upon on them in the first place. For *aeons,* the deformation and reformation of the world's surface have bestowed certain locations with abundant subterranean storerooms, while others have had no access to such resources within their territories.

Deep time exerted its influence in a somewhat paradoxical manner, as a significant portion of the major reserves, particularly those of oil and gas, are concentrated in some of the world's most hostile and unforgiving regions. Large swathes of these areas previously had limited economic significance due to their harsh climates and barren conditions, making them unsuitable for supporting urban populations and larger communities. However, since the middle of the last century, landscapes ranging from the open sea to the High North and the deserts of the Middle East have emerged as the most significant producers and suppliers of energy resources, disseminating their reserves well beyond their immediate surroundings with multitudinous effects. Through them, various other landscapes hitherto unsuitable for sustaining civilisational infrastructure could now be kept alive and even thrive, which led to an unprecedented and extensive expansion of human activity across the globe.

Fig. 6 Aerial view of Dubai

This expansion is even more acute in the case of the Middle East, where the wealth beneath the seemingly-barren desert surface has catalysed some of the most eccentric urbanism in human history, driven by oil and gas money as well as by transformative technology designed to mediate the adverse conditions.

However, the proliferation of human culture, driven by the search for fossil fuels in previously untouched landscapes, went far beyond the desert. This phenomenon is exemplified by the establishment of industrial monotowns in the sub-zero expanses of the post-Soviet Extreme North. With approximately 12,000 oil rigs scattered across international waters, the open sea has not only emerged as a paramount energy source but also serves as the backdrop for thousands of workers inhabiting artificial techno-islands which are constructed and sustained for the sole purpose of extraction.[13]

Concentration and Urbanisation

Cities are the result of socio-spatial concentration.[14] The occurrence of large urban centres is documented throughout history, even before the widespread use of fossil fuels. However, the growth and development of places like Uruk, Babylon, Istanbul, Hangzhou, Edo, and Beijing were singularities made possible through powerful organisations as well as concentrations in agriculture, trade, military power, and governance. Fossil fuels have not only facilitated the expansion of cities to dimensions that dwarf even the grandest of ancient empires, but they have also—through lavish consumption and the adoption of markedly inefficient land utilisation practices—enabled a prevailing way of life that fosters disconnection from the natural environment. At the centre of the world's first fossil empire, London counted around 1,000,000 inhabitants at the start of the 19th century. With the proliferation of coal, the next hundred years saw an uncontrolled and unplanned expansion, with a total population surpassing 6,500,000 people in Greater London in 1901.[15] Within the century, the conurbations of Berlin, Paris, New York, and Chicago expanded beyond the historical limits of growth, concentrating resources, economic capacities, and populations unlike anything seen before.

In 2018, our global energy systems more or less successfully sustained over 548 cities, each harbouring more than 1,000,000 residents. Among them, over sixty cities share a magnitude comparable to that of London in the year 1900. Notably, 18 of these urban centres have expanded to surpass 15,000,000 inhabitants.[16] To provide context, each of these urban centres is effectively hosting a population equivalent to the entire dispersed human community around 5000 BC.[17] The ability to support such dense populations is underpinned by extensive mobility and interconnectedness with remote areas.

Moreover, modern urban structures have demonstrated a remarkable ability to disengage from their immediate surroundings in terms of resource dependency, available land for production, and even climatic conditions.

Infrastructural Spaces

The rise of fossil fuels is closely linked to the emergence of vast global infrastructure systems, that have not only redefined the world through their function, but have also physically transformed it through their existence as interconnected and contiguous spatial entities of transcontinental scale.

In order to mediate energy and energy carrier flows, regions with abundant reservoirs must address the challenges of long-distance transport, commodification, and standardisation to cater to their respective markets. Layers of extractive, productive, and circulatory systems form gargantuan networks and corridors of territorial contiguity around trans-, extra-, and national locales across the globe. Within this framework, railroads, waterways, pipelines, highways, and overland lines emerge

Fig. 7 Tender platform rig. Offshore, Louisiana (undated)

as essential protagonists in facilitating the transmission of these material—and, at times, hazardous—substances. This infrastructure, which constitutes in large part systems of circulation, has enjoyed a reciprocal evolution with fossil fuels, each one shaping the other's development.[18] On the one hand, these complex assamblages function as underlying and sometimes literally invisible facilitators, built for very specific purposes and held under the strict control of authoritative technology. On the other hand, over time, they have gained extreme rigidity, resilience, and inbuilt power that constitute the basis for most of the vital operational structures on which modern society rests.[19]

Fig. 8 Technical landscape of Russian gas extraction

These systems are not only vulnerable to drastic repercussions in the event of failure, disasters, or haphazard integration. They are also often regarded as enigmatic black boxes, characterised by incomprehensible and byzantine complexity. While the peasantry in the past could simply burn sticks in their hearths or even create charcoal in their yards, the intricate process of designing, implementing, administering, provisioning, operating, and maintaining fossil fuel infrastructure is primarily managed by a range of highly specialised experts. Their up-, mid-, and downstream processes are kept exclusive through meticulously managed advanced technologies at mining sites, refineries, ports, pipelines, and storage facilities. The increasing complexity of the financing, construction, and administration of these intricate structures further empowers this detachment.

Monofunctional, Technological, and Deteriorated Spaces

While urban centres often stand at one end of infrastructural development, operational landscapes and technological non-city spaces tend to stand at the other.[20] They are both the source and the sink, simultaneously generating essential metabolic inputs and receiving unwanted by-products. The extraction, production, and transmission landscapes of fossil fuel streams can thus be considered quasi-exemplary for such spatial configurations, with several very direct as well as extended impacts.[21] The exploitation and processing of fossil fuels transform land into unusable landscapes. Owing to the monumental footprint and substantial scope of extractive activities, they exhibit a predominantly monofunctional pattern of occupation, interspersed with immense technostructure that is primed for highly automated industrial production. Specialised security protocols render extensive tracts of land largely inaccessible and unsuitable for other purposes. The predominantly ecocidal nature of exploitive industries like oil, gas, and coal extraction leads to massive environmental degradation and irreversible eco-systemic disruption. It is perhaps hard to imagine any plausible "healthy" means of co-existing with the gas field next door. Yet, finding new patterns and restorative techniques for repurposing thousands of square metres of exploited mining sites represents a technological, as well as ecological, headache that haunts entire states. The effects of transportation and midstream operations manifest across the spectrum, spanning from relatively minor incidents like accidents involving coal trains and barges, to catastrophic events such as pipeline leaks or large-scale marine oil spills.

Navigating the growing intricacies of metabolic exchanges between urban centres (agglomeration landscapes) and resource-producing regions (operational landscapes) in the 21st century requires a nuanced understanding of nonlinear processes. This complexity is especially relevant when examining the dynamics of fossil fuels where, given the immense vulnerability and exposure of its infrastructure, the potential for disaster is a looming concern. In addition to their direct effects, oil, gas, and coal have spurred a swift worldwide proliferation of human-driven land-use. Road construction, for instance, currently stands as one of the foremost catalysts for ecosystem degradation and biodiversity decline across the globe. Beyond tarmac, nearly half of the maritime cargo tonnage consists of oil shipments and, staggeringly, there are more kilometres of pipeline than there are railroads in the world.[22]

Fig. 9 Flooded open-cast mine in the Lausitz region

Endnotes

1 The concept of "deep time"—introduced and utilised by John McPhee, a writer and geology professor—serves to elucidate the immense scale and duration of geological events, often beyond human perception, while also providing a contrasting perspective between human history and culture and the broader context of natural history and the environment. See: McPhee, *Basin, and Range*.
2 Reference timeframe around 50,000 BC.
3 For a good introduction to the term, see: McNeill and Engelke, *The Great Acceleration*.
4 Smil, *Grand Transitions*, 1f.
5 Jared Diamond describes the uptake of settled farming culture as a centuries-long (and partly millennia-long) process, depending on the geographical location. See: Diamond, *Guns, Germs, and Steel*, 104.
6 British Petroleum, Statistical Review of World Energy, 2021.
7 In this context, the term "cheap energy" pertains to: Patel and Moore, *A History of the World in Seven Cheap Things*.
8 To obtain a comprehensive introduction to the subject of sub-surface developments in energy infrastructure, please refer to: Zillman et al., *The Law of Energy Underground*.
9 For an introduction, see: Omorogbe and Oniemola, "Property Rights in Oil and Gas under Domanial Regimes".
10 Zillman et al., *The Law of Energy Underground*, 22.
11 McGhee, *Carboniferous Giants and Mass Extinction*, 24.
12 Nentwig, Bacher, and Brandl, *Ökologie kompakt*, 235.
13 Alexander et al., "Using environmental DNA to better inform decision making around decommissioning alternatives for offshore oil and gas infrastructure".
14 Brenner and Katsikis, "Operational Landscapes".
15 London Online. "London Population".
16 The previously mentioned numbers are sourced from: UN Department of Economic and Social Affairs, "The World Cities in 2018 – Data Booklet", 6, 10–29.
17 Goldewijk, Beusen, and Janssen, "Long-Term Dynamic Modelling of Global Population and Built-up Area in a Spatially Explicit Way: HYDE 3.1".
18 One good example for this is the evolution of the coalmine-railway complex in 18th and 19th century England, as represented in: Rhodes, *Energy*.
19 For a comprehensive introduction to the origin and evolution of the term infrastructure, please refer to: Carse, "Keyword: infrastructure: How a humble French engineering term shaped the modern world"; Moss, *Remaking Berlin*, 16–33.
20 Brenner and Katsikis, "Operational Landscapes".
21 A comprehensive list of factors can be found in: Butt et al., "Biodiversity Risks from Fossil Fuel Extraction".
22 O'Rourke and Connolly, "Just Oil? The Distribution of Environmental and Social Impacts of Oil Production and Consumption", 589.

Fossil Energy Carriers

Coal

3.2

3.2.1

Introduction to Coal

David Bauer
Joseph Smithard

Coal is nothing less than the substance that freed society from the cold, millennia-long grip of energetic austerity. Its rise spanning nearly 200 years marked the arrival of cheap automated power and electricity—as well as soot and air pollution—to nearly every city, street, and factory on Earth. It fired the hearts and bellies of the rapidly industrialising nations, harnessing the power of steam to generate mechanical energy; in turn, these contraptions served as reliable converters, transforming concentrated reservoirs of buried prehistoric solar energy into a source of unstoppable motion that propelled humanity's leap from antiquity to modernity.[1]

Fig. 1 Wood collectors in Central Europe, 1716

A Wooden Society

Throughout 99.9 % of *Homo sapiens'* existence, the energy required for survival and progress came predominantly from renewable and regenerating sources, harnessed primarily from the powerful heat of the sun. Solar radiation was skilfully converted into nourishment, providing energy to people and animals for sustenance and labour. It fuelled the growth of woodlands and forests, offering sources of fire and heat. Other elements like wind and waterpower also became essential for transportation, driving early machinery.[2]

In pre-industrial societies, much like today, the need for energy was a paramount cornerstone of daily experience. However, the relationship to time and space was distinct from modern times. On the one hand, the inefficient conversion of solar radiation into bio-based matter led to the need for dwellings that had access to vast landscapes and extensive provision areas. On the other, it also required sufficient time for nature's forces to replenish grazing lands and timber resources through photosynthesis.[3] In Central Europe, communities were essentially "wooden cultures",[4] heavily reliant on access to the forest for their daily needs. Uncontrolled depletion and clearcutting often resulted in the swift decline of entire populations.[5] As a result, notwithstanding a few exceptional cases, dwellings in pre-industrial societies were typically contained and dispersed entities, often strategically positioned near rivers, pasturelands, and vast wooded areas designated for a reliable fuel supply. Siting was crucial as the dependence on replenishable biological resources, which posed critical transportation challenges.

Wood gathering involved various practices, commonly including collecting fallen branches, deadwood, and small trees either by foot or cart. However, significant gathering beyond volumes that would serve individual needs required clustering and aggregation prior to being transported to cities, resulting in substantial energy expenditures at the outset. Critically, land transport was limited to short distances to ensure a positive energy yield.[6] Where waterways were accessible, importing logs from distant regions beyond municipal control could mitigate the absence of locally owned forests. This approach often represented the sole economically viable option for transporting wood over larger territories. Municipalities recognised the importance of this method and invested substantial funds in ensuring that even small rivers or creeks could be adapted for efficient log transportation.

Moreover, they took active measures to regulate and govern the numerous participants involved in the intricate rafting and log-driving systems.[7] The fact that transportation was the single factor that made wood as a fuel source expensive or even inaccessible resulted in the placement of energy-intensive trades deep into the forest. This led to remote colonies entirely devoted to certain professions of the forest economy, typically populated by woodcutters, raftsmen, resin workers, and glassmakers. Charcoal burner settlements were also crucial in providing high-caloric fuel, partly for domestic use but especially for industrial purposes such as ore smelting and glass production.[8]

Tapping the Subterranean Forest

From the 18th century onwards, dependence on the immediate intake and conversion of caloric value changed. During this transformative period, coal emerged as the main protagonist, marking the end of the long-standing dominance of wood, wind, and waterpower that had prevailed for millennia. In north-western Europe, the epicentre of this change, the transition to fossil fuels was relatively gradual until the 19th century.[9] This shift took place against a backdrop of broad, sweeping transitions in socioeconomic conditions, as well as advances in technical innovation, manifesting in the accelerated interaction of pioneering technologies with developments in mechanical power. In turn, these forces collided in a new type of working environment—the factory.[10]

Fig. 2 "ILSE" (Borsig 4473/1895) was constructed for Ilse Bergbau AG in the Lausitz region to facilitate the transportation of lignite from the mining pits

Fig. 3 Three-phase alternator by Allgemeine Electricitäts-Gesellschaft, ca. 1906

Both phenomena relied on new forms of energy. While the workshops were fuelled by a new class of wage labourers—streaming in their masses from impoverished rural areas to equally destitute, densely-populated urban centres—the technical transition was grounded in the self-sustaining interplay of coal, steam, and iron.[11] [Fig. 2] Coal fuelled the industrial blast furnaces that created the iron necessary for building machines and rail tracks, revolutionising fuel transport and extraction. As a result, coal's own energy was employed in its own generation, a cycle that was occurring at a rapidly accelerating rate.

Within decades, the black rock became the lifeblood of the economic metabolism, as the appetite for energy escalated to levels that surpassed any previous benchmarks. In turn, this expansion began to restructure cities and landscapes, forming new and extraordinary configurations. Expansive factory complexes began to sprout along the fringes of pre-modern cities, continually expanding with each passing decade. Gasworks spawned along the canals, giving rise to the first closed systems of urban technology dedicated to illuminating the streets at night. Coal-laden barges—arriving from distant fields and mines onto riverbanks and into town ports—instigated a profound shift, shattering the age-old bonds between settlements and their immediate hinterlands, severing the millennia-long reliance on local resources for sustenance. Coal collapsed space and time. Steamboats defied the forces of tides and winds, while trains swiftly transported their cargo across vast distances that once required months or even years to traverse. Giant machines, possessing enormous strength, revolutionised labour, replacing beasts of burden and augmenting the capabilities of workers. Beyond their superhuman force, coal-fired engines offered a distinct advantage that set them apart from the inexhaustible energy supply of the forests or the sun: the uncanny ability for precise and minute control. While natural resources required adapting to the rhythms of wind and water to harness mechanical energy, tapping into the subterranean "forest" of coal introduced the irresistible potential of accessing vast quantities of energy on demand.[12]

By the end of the 19th century, industrialising regions were intricately connected by an expansive network of water- and railways, with remote yet concentrated carbon stores. This vast hard-wired system included thousands of miners and machines toiling tirelessly to extract coal from belowground and transport it to the surface. Massive quantities now surged across continents, travelling from mines to ports, cities, and factories. Along this system of conduits and channels, specialised work-forces diligently oversaw a seamless energy flow.[13]

Trans-localisation was exacerbated with the advent of steam-powered electrical turbines at the end of the 19th century, which enabled the transmission and utilisation of power at distances far removed from the fires and soot that had long-defined energy production. Centralisation of electricity became possible as large stations, fuelled by coal, were established to generate electricity on a massive scale. [Fig. 3] The otherworldly effects of this energy shocked contemporary society, lighting streets and powering factories beyond the habitual veil of darkness. However, this shift was not without its challenges. The once quaint townscapes and their pastoral surroundings gave way to sprawling metropolises, juxtaposing economic and technological progress with massive ecological deterioration.

The End of Coal?

Until the end of the Second World War, coal reigned as the primary fuel source. However, in the post-war era, its dominance started to wane as rapid technological advancements and breakthroughs in physical and chemical research opened the way for using alternative energy sources. Oil, nuclear energy, and later natural gas emerged as promising contenders, pointing towards a future characterised by cleaner, more efficient, and more controllable energy options. This shift coincided with significant geopolitical restructures, enabling access to alternative fuel sources that proved to be more versatile and potent when harnessed correctly. In 1950, coal accounted for nearly 44.5 % of the global primary energy consumption, contributing significantly to the post-war economy and global reconstruction efforts. Nevertheless, this percentage experienced roughly a 10 % decline over the course of a decade, soon approaching parity with the rapidly expanding oil industry. Within an additional five-year period, oil had emerged as the dominant energy source worldwide.[14]

Despite playing a diminished role in most high-income economies, coal remains a central focal point in the climate and energy discourse. This is due to the paradoxical fact that, while its overall share in the global energy mix has gradually decreased over time, both extraction and consumption of coal have steadily increased. In 2021, coal-fired generation reached an all-time high, with approximately 8,500 coal power stations operating worldwide. These stations accounted for over one-third of global electricity generation, accounting for 20 % of global GHG emissions per annum.[15] Even more concerning, the global power station inventory is on average still relatively young. If these stations continue to operate according to their current predicted lifespan and utilisation rates, they are projected toaccumulate up to 330 Gt of CO_2, therefore more than doubling the historical emissions of all coal power stations that have been operational up to this point.[16]

Fig. 4 National coal consumption of ····· CN -·-· US ═ IN — DE in TWh and coal phase-out targets

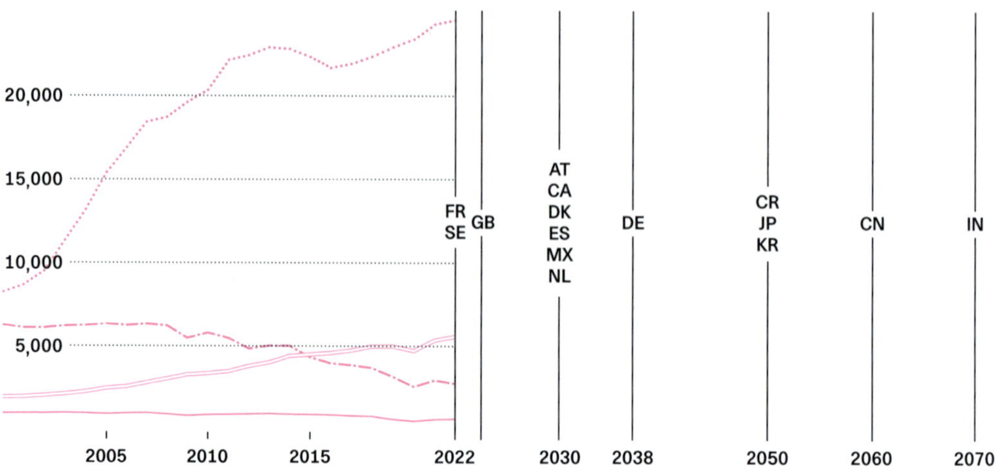

The use of coal is distinguished from other fuels by its geographic concentration. China alone represents more than half of the global demand, and emerging markets and developing economies account for over 80 % of its usage share. Faced with this trajectory, mounting pressure (from transnational organisations, the wider public, and the private sector) has compelled governments, particularly in the northern hemisphere, to develop strategic and binding phase-out plans. [Fig. 4] Every pathway towards avoiding severe climate change impacts involves an early and substantial reduction in coal-related emissions. Notably, the International Energy Agency's IEA "Net Zero Emissions by 2050" scenario sets forth the global requirement for the complete cessation of unabated coal generation by 2040.[17] To align with this trajectory, a yearly average reduction of approximately 8 % in emissions from coal-fired power stations is imperative until 2030.[18]

The challenge of phasing out is multifaceted, encompassing concerns related to energy security, labour markets, and identity shifts. Countries face considerable resistance when transitioning away from coal fuel in part because mining plays a substantial role in their economies, adding significantly to employment and accounting for a substantial portion of their GDP.

In 2022, coal markets experienced severe disruptions, with traditional trade flows shaken, prices surging, and demand surpassing 8,000,000,000 t for the first time.[19] Global energy security was further complicated by high oil and natural gas prices resulting from Russia's invasion of Ukraine, as well as extreme weather events, leading some regions to revert to domestic sources to secure electricity supplies. Although this recent surge in coal-fired generation is likely to be a temporary glitch, it highlights the precariousness of the global energy landscape, where geopolitical events can easily swing the course back towards an unwanted energy veteran.

Fig. 5 Coal consumption by income category, 1965–2023 in TWh

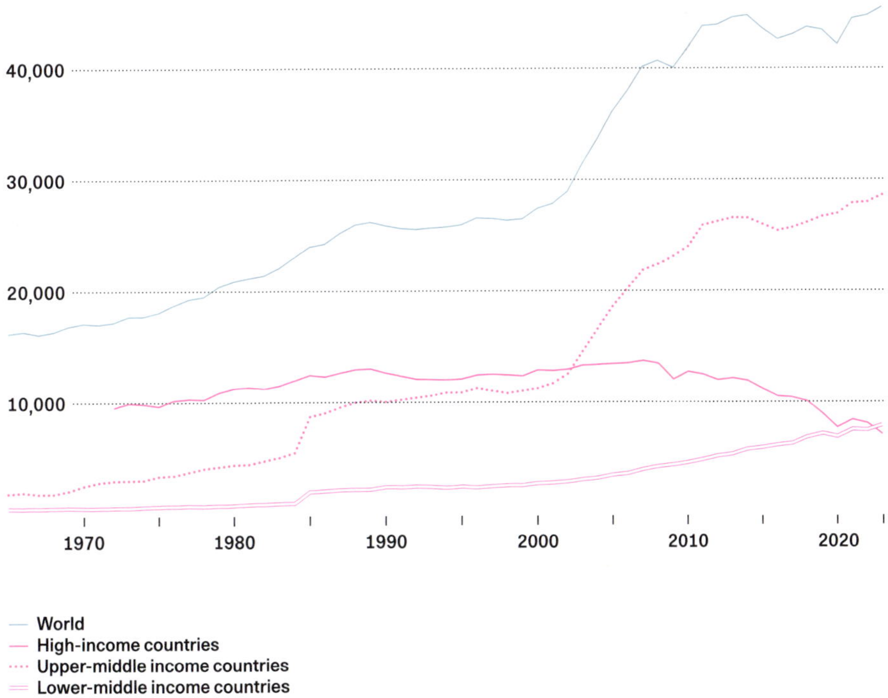

Properties, Production, and Supply

David Bauer
Joseph Smithard

Coal is an umbrella term for a group of heterogeneous, combustible rock types that—owing to their large amount of embodied carbon—are almost exclusively used for energy provision and by-product materials. Compared with oil and gas, coal is the oldest fossil resource. The overwhelming majority of its formations can be traced back to a geological epoch traversing the Carboniferous Period and the Permian Era, characterised by a global tropical and subtropical climate. During this period, plants extended their geographic range and grew to monstrous sizes. Remarkably, around 90 % of current coal deposits originated during this geologically fleeting timeframe, which represents just the blink of an eye in the vast timescale of our planet's existence.[20]

All life feeds on itself under a natural cycle of decomposition and regeneration. Plants die, decompose, and are broken down into chemical and organic compounds that nourish new plant life, creating a perpetual rotation of growth and sustenance. However, since the emergence of terrestrial plant life, the dynamic interplay of cataclysmic geological processes, global extinctions, and fluctuations in sea levels has consistently reshaped the morphology, topography, and climates of continental land masses. These pivotal reformations of the Earth's surface, combined with a general absence of wood-consuming organisms in the early stages of these evolving ecosystems, periodically disrupted the cycle of growth and decay. Subsequently, organic matter was preserved and left partially intact for a very long time.[21] These were the distinct conditions under which coal formation occurred.

A very simplified model of its genesis involves two distinct processes: peatification and coalification. Peatification, a bio-chemical process, encompasses the gradual accumulation, compaction, and partial decomposition of plant material, spanning a timeframe of 10,000 to 15,000 years.[22] The result is a soft, brown, and fibrous material used for energy by various cultures due to its simple harvesting methods.

Fig. 6 Peat harvesting in Germany, 1905

Coalification is a geological and chemical process that unfolds over millions of years following swamp peat formation. During this process, layers of sediment envelop the peat deposits. Weight from the overlying strata increases, exerting pressure and generating elevated temperatures. These conditions drive off volatile components and gradually increase carbon content. The diverse geographical contexts, influenced by environmental and geological factors, give rise to different grades or ranks of coal. [Fig. 7]

Low-ranks, known as brown coals, tend to be soft and crumbly, with a dull, earthy appearance and greater oxygen and moisture levels than the higher ranks. Bituminous coal and anthracite, or hard coal, are more robust and possess a black, glass-like shine due to their higher carbon content. As coal's rank increases, both its carbon and energy contents rise while its moisture and oxygen levels decrease.

Coal is the world's dirtiest and deadliest fuel, not only because it emits the most carbon dioxide per unit but because it has severe health impacts through air pollution. These effects are intricately linked to coal's rank and its content heterogeneity. Lower-rank coals produce more detrimental by-products than matured hard coal, exacerbating the consequences associated with combustion.[23]

Despite its well-documented and substantial environmental impact, coal remains dominant due to its abundance. In 2021, with 59%, it continued to be the primary resource for electricity generation and plays a crucial role in fuelling industrial processes.[24] Its importance in the global energy landscape is evident across all coal ranks, and extraction is carried out through three primary methods: surface mining, underground mining, and in situ mining.[25]

Fig. 7 Typical composition of coal by weight in % and heating value in MJ/kg

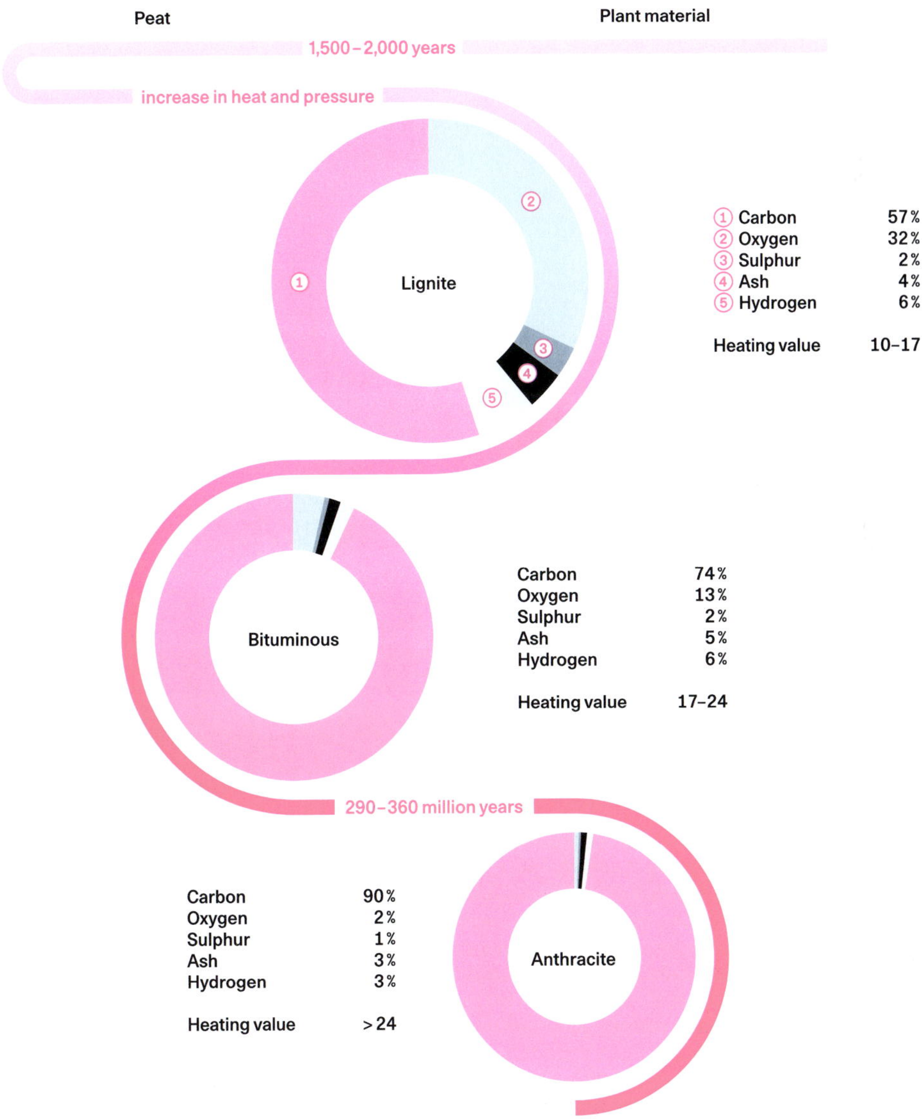

Surface Mining

Brown coal is primarily extracted through surface mining methods, which represent a highly engineered, ecocidal approach characterised by the systematic ploughing of vast land areas. [Fig. 8]

Extraction typically targets coal deposits at depths exceeding 100 m below the surface. This process involves three primary stages: overburden removal, seam extraction, and subsequent land reclamation.[26] To access the beds, the overlying rock and strata, referred to as the "overburden", are fragmented using explosives. Subsequently, this fractured material is excavated and disposed of in previous mines or disposal areas. Once unsurfaced, the exposed "coal seam"[27] is extracted through towering bucket-wheel excavators. [Fig. 27] Equipped with rotating buckets, the machinery penetrates the coalbed, scooping up the coal-rich material. The excavated lignite is then transported via colossal conveyor systems to railroads or overland trucks for further processing, distribution to coal markets, or, in many instances, direct delivery to regional power stations for incineration.

Fig. 8 Welzow-Süd open-cast mine, 2024

On-site, the final step involves land reclamation, wherein the excavated hole is refilled with the overburden. During mining, the upper soil layers, including the fertile topsoil, are removed to access the deposit. This process disrupts the soil structure and depletes the organic matter essential for plant growth. The outcome is lunar-like landscapes, which require significant financial resources to be restored to a state suitable for plant growth. To aid in land restoration, the area is covered with stockpiled topsoil, and vegetation is reintroduced. Mining also leads to substantial disruption of local water cycles, with extraction fields needing to be drained as a result. The term "reclamation" can thus be considered misleading, since fully restoring the original local water cycles and ecosystems—even in those few cases where it is done correctly—is often unachievable.

Underground Mining

The objective of underground mining is to access coal seams located at considerable depths, where the continuous displacement of the upper strata becomes uneconomical. While these operations entail higher costs and labour requirements compared to surface mining, they are often employed to extract high-rank coal varieties, which hold greater value in the energy market. Mining operations and technologies encompass a range of strategies but can generally be classified into two main approaches: full and partial extraction. Both methods access coal seams by driving vertical shafts or angled tunnels close to the deposits. Subsequently, the main reserve is divided into panels to facilitate systematic and organised extraction.

In partial extraction methods, the coal seam is fragmented using explosives at the mining face. Continuous miner machines are used to cut into the coal seam and transport the extracted resource via shuttle cars and an extensive haulage infrastructure to the surface. During this mining process, certain pillars or blocks of coal are intentionally left behind strategically to prevent roof collapses within the deposit.

By contrast, full-extraction mining employs methods that aim to retrieve such significant volumes of coal that the roof rock is intentionally allowed to collapse in a controlled manner.

Fig. 9 Historic section drawing of a bituminous coal mine

Coal Shipments

As Lignite is heavy, and has a comparatively low energy yield, it is primarily utilised in close proximity to the deposit, forming a network of opencast mines and power stations that ensure immediate and secure supply. As a result, there is no significant international market for its derivates, and only a fraction of production is processed into solid or pulverised fuels (such as briquettes, dust, and coke) for commercial and residential purposes.

Hard coal, on the other hand, is a globally traded product. [Fig. 17+18] Once it reaches the surface, it is crushed, washed, and screened to remove impurities such as rocks, clay, and sulphur. It is then transported to export terminals for shipment by means of rail, barge, or—when the mine and terminal are in close proximity to one another—through large-scale conveyor systems.

In all major coal-producing countries, mining operations are primarily controlled by a small number of very large corporations. These companies possess their own export capacities at a limited selection of loading ports, indicating the absence of complex market structures.[28] Ports, coal carriers, and bulkers are specifically designed for the transport. They have spacious cargo holds with specialised equipment such as conveyor systems, grabs, or loaders to enable efficient haulage operations. Once loaded, ships embark on journeys along established shipping routes to reach their destinations. Upon arrival at ports, cranes and conveyors unload coal for transportation to nearby storage yards, close to power stations and steel factories. Intermediate storage near ports ensures a steady supply before further transit. [Fig. 29]

Incineration

Coal's primary usage is in three sectors: electricity production, heat generation, and metallurgical processes. The largest application is in power generation by electric utilities, which accounts for approximately 36% of global resource utilisation.[29] In the modern context, electricity can be viewed as the cleaner end of a dirty supply chain, where the exchange of dust, soot, and physical labour is replaced by the convenience of plugging into a socket. Despite technological advancements, the basic principle of generating electricity through incineration remains similar to that of early power stations. Coal is crushed and dried before being blown into a specialised combustion chamber or furnace to boil water. The resulting high-pressure steam is channelled and used to drive turbines connected to electric power generators.[30] [Fig. 28]

Due to the constant production of residual high-temperature steam, electricity production can be combined with heat generation and temperature control. Cogeneration, also known as combined heat and power CHP production, operates similarly to coal-based electric power production. However, in these specific stations, the low-pressure steam discharged from the turbines is first directed to an industrial plant or building, where it is utilised for various purposes before being condensed and returned to the boiler. This results in extensive networks of district heating for industrial facilities, public buildings, large campuses, or residential blocks.

Metallurgical or met coal is a specific type of coal used in steel production. It is characterised by its high carbon content and low instance of impurities. Initially, the fuel is heated without air to drive off volatile components and convert them into a solid form of carbon called coke. The coke is then combined with iron ore and limestone in a blast furnace, heated to temperatures ranging from 1,300 to 1,500 °C. This process melts the ore, reducing it to metallic iron, while limestone helps to remove impurities.

3.2.3

Coal in the Local Context

David Bauer
Joseph Smithard

In 2022, coal ranked as Germany's third-largest source of primary energy.[31] [p. 19] Despite being surpassed by combined renewable technologies as the dominant source of electricity in 2020, the first year of the pandemic, the country's demand experienced significant repercussions thereafter.[32] To accommodate for 19 % of its domestic energy needs in 2021, Germany burned 40,400,000 t of hard coal and about 126,300,000 t of lignite.[33] To contextualise this, in terms of weight, domestic lignite production alone is equivalent to nearly one-quarter of global rice production in 2022 and 2023, a staple food that sustains more than half of the world's population.[34]

Despite significant reductions since the 1990s, with lignite witnessing a decline of 63 % and hard coal seeing a decrease of 51 %, both sources continue to play a significant role in providing energy and stimulating political debate.[35]

Fig. 10 Production of hard coal and lignite in Germany in Mt

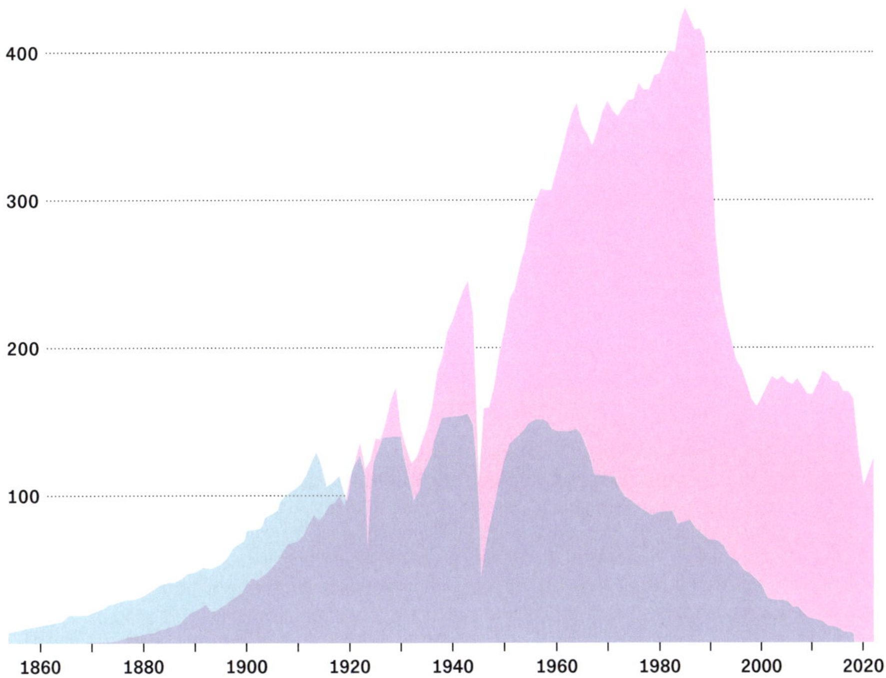

Across Germany, most coal is utilised as fine powdered dust and incinerated in electric or CHP stations nationwide. In 2022, these stations accounted for one-third of the 509,000,000,000 kWh of electricity produced and fed into the grid, indicating an alarming 8.4 % increase in coal-based electricity generation compared to the previous year.[36] The unanticipated resurgence was triggered by a massive surge in natural gas prices, precipitating a profound upheaval in energy markets and, consequently, a marked reduction in the production of electricity derived from gas. To underscore the volatility of the energy economy in this transitioning decade, in 2023, Germany witnessed a substantial decline in lignite and hard coal power production, reaching levels not observed since the 1960s and 1950s, respectively. This decline, amounting to nearly one-third of coal-fired power production, reduced its share of total net power generation to 26 %, while renewables, comprising almost 60 % of net power production, saw a 7 % increase, primarily propelled by a notable rise in wind turbine output.[37]

The Coal Home Depot

Coal is Germany's only domestically abundant energy resource, and throughout the country's history, it has been extracting and managing gargantuan quantities of untapped fossil energy. Following the phase-out of hard coal extraction in 2018, lignite has emerged as Germany's primary raw fossil fuel. Around 1,250,000,000 t are accessible through already developed and planned surface mines.[38] When considering subterranean reserves,[39] the BRD is harbouring an astonishing 34,150,000,000 t of extractable brown coal. To put this into perspective, the country's largest lake, Bodensee, holds approximately 50,000,000,000 t of water. Accordingly, Germany's lignite reserves alone could fill the lake up to three-quarters of its total capacity.[40] If extracted, this would yield enough energy to satisfy Germany's electricity consumption for roughly the next 150 years.[41] When considering, however, the economic and ecological costs of implementing and restoring degraded landscapes, as well as the undeniable and considerable acceleration of climate change, any reliance on the short-term comfort or safety-net these fossil assets provide must be prevented.

With nearly one-tenth of the world's reserves and an equivalent share of globally estimated resources, the unified Germany has historically held the title of the world's largest lignite producer. However, in recent times, China's expansion into surface mining has surpassed even Germany's accumulated production, incurring a shift in the global landscape of lignite mining.[42] In the context of the EU, however, Germany remains the elephant in the room, accounting for 46 % of the total coal production among all member states.[43]

Fig. 11 Leading producers of lignite in 2022 in Mt

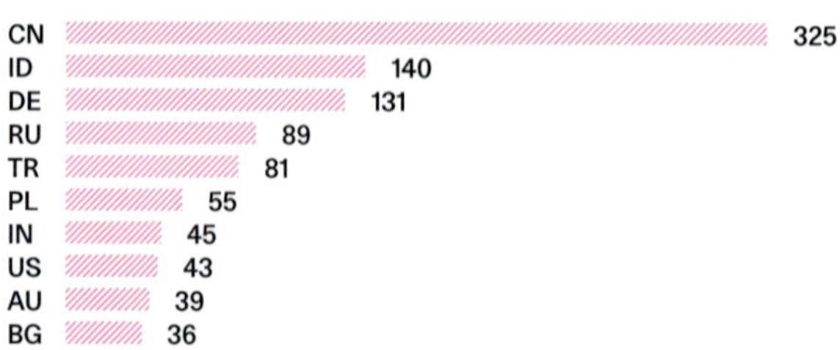

Due to the challenging economics of export logistics, only 1 % of this domestic product is shipped from the extraction sites to distant locations.[44] When it does, lignite travels within Europe via railways, water networks, and in most cases indirectly through electricity exchange within the synchronous grid of Continental Europe.

Besides brown coal, Germany's subterranean reservoir encompasses more than 82,000,000 t of hard coal resources. Unlike reserves, which are economically and technically viable for extraction, the term "resources" refers to quantities of raw material that have been identified but are not recoverable due to technical and economic constraints.[45] The discontinuation of federal subsidies for hard coal extraction led to the closure of Germany's last remaining domestic mine in 2018. Consequently, deposits no longer qualify as reserves, resulting in the country importing 100 % of its fuel from seven major national producers and several smaller ones, with in 2023 Australia, the United States, the Netherlands, Colombia, and South Africa being the primary suppliers in order of rank.[46] These reach the country through 13 domestic and several European coal ports, and are transported either by ship or rail to their respective processing stations. [p. 126]

Coal Geography

Germany's coal deposits are found in a corridor that traverses from east to west, extending from France into Poland. Domestic hard coal is concentrated in West Germany, with the two largest mining regions in the Ruhr area and the Saarland. Lignite has a broader distribution and is currently exclusively mined in open-cast mines within three coalfields across districts in the Rheinland, Central Germany, and the Lausitz.

Fig. 12 Active and former coal-mining districts in Germany

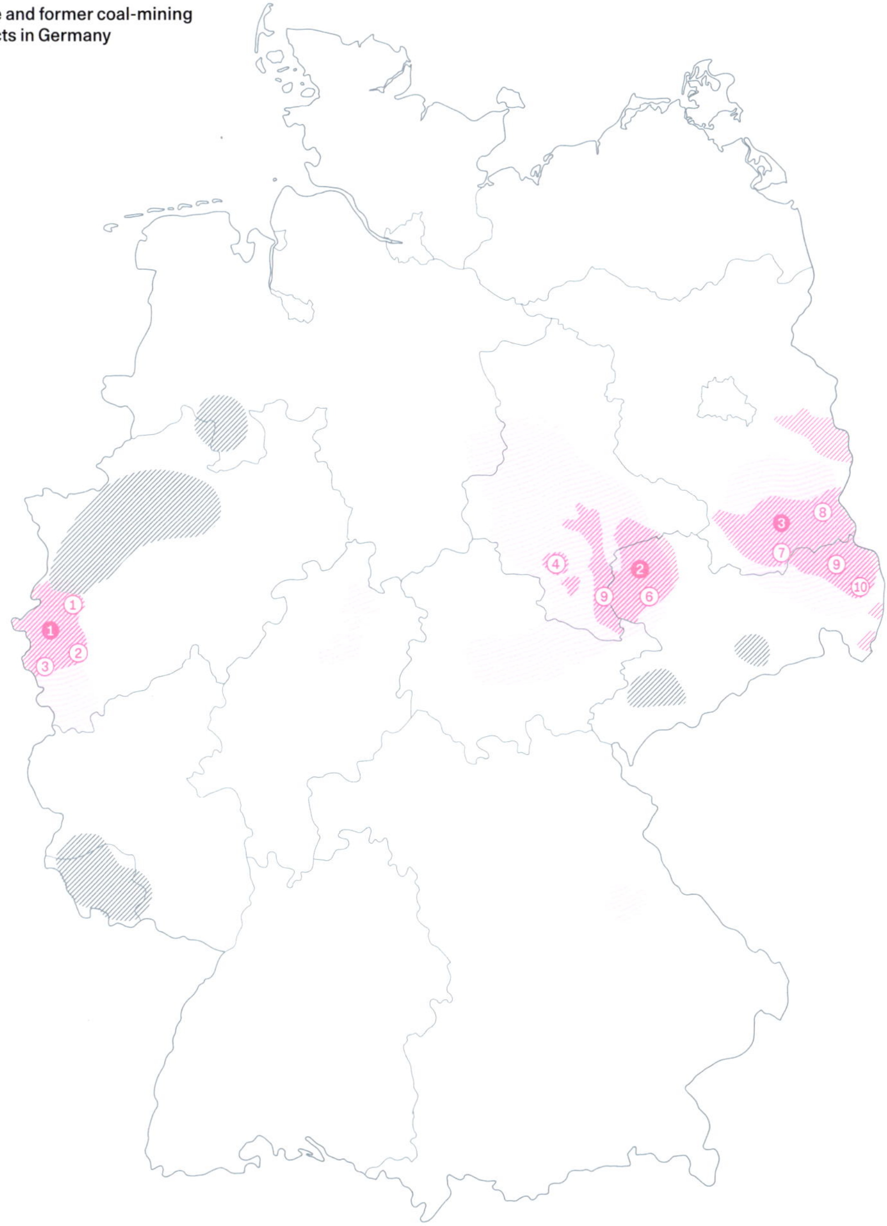

1 Rhein district
2 Central German district
3 Lusatian district

Lignite districts with active extraction
Lignite districts with former extraction
Hard coal districts with former extraction

Active lignite mines	Start of operation	End of operation	Mined amount (Mt/a)
1 Garzweiler II	2006	2045	35.0
2 Inden	1982	2030	19.0
3 Hambach	1978	2045	40.0
4 Amsdorf	1959	2025–30	0.3
5 Profen	1941	2030–35	8.0
6 Vereinigtes Schleenhain	1949	2040	11.0
7 Welzow-Süd	1959	2027–30	20.0
8 Jänschwalde	1974	2023	9.0
9 Nochten	1968	2045	18.5
10 Reichwalde	1985	2045	13.2

Phase-out 203(8)

The exit of coal-fired energy production and the end of domestic lignite extraction are on the horizon. However, with the official announcement of the phase-out in 2038, this goal remains a distant and abstract future.[47] Despite the resounding warnings and protests from the scientific community and the public sphere, both urging for a swifter exit, detaching Germany from its only abundant domestic fossil fuel source remains an arduous and gruelling process. This is partly due to the deep entanglement of regional job markets, economic dependencies, and the adopted identities rooted in decades-long mining traditions. Looking at the demographics of its staff, it appears that the coal industry's closure will coincide with the natural exit of its workforce, as approximately two-thirds of personnel in the lignite mining industry are set to retire by 2030. While the entire sector currently employs around 20,000 people, this number is projected to decrease to 8,000 by the decade's end.[48] As the end of coal approaches, it also marks the end of one of the most transformative and impactful extractions on German soil, leaving behind a startling legacy. Over the decades, some 313 settlements have been lost to open-cast mining, encompassing a vast expanse of 179,490 ha.[49]

Berlin-Brandenburg

Considering its turbulent history, Berlin is a city with an unusually high number of power stations within its conurbation. [p. 74] While the final operational lignite-fired CHP plant, Klingenberg, received its last shipment of Lausitz resources in 2017, the city still hosts nine active power and heat stations running on hard coal.[50] [pastedown front] However, despite the presence of historically coal-fired stations, only one-third of the electricity and one-fifth of the combined heat generated derive from coal, with a significant portion sourced from gas.[51] The shift in supply due to the 2022 reduction in Russian gas may have impacted this balance, but figures are not yet available. Nonetheless, the trajectory for Germany's future is clear. Berlin is emerging as a post-coal city: with plans to divest by 2030, the city is leading the charge towards an alternative future.[52] This vision aligns with a broader transition across the Ruhr region of West Germany, while the rest of the nation aims to bid farewell to coal by 2038. However, the dichotomy between Berlin and Brandenburg is intriguing, since the latter remains a major lignite producer and exporter of electricity, with vast open-cast mine landscapes in the Lausitz having long been a cornerstone of the region's identity.

3.2.4

Lausitz

David Bauer
Joseph Smithard

The Lausitz district, situated along the Polish border in the south-eastern part of Brandenburg, is one of Germany's last three operational coal mining regions. Only four sites remain from a once sprawling network of 31 open-pit mines, a legacy spanning 160 years of continuous lignite extraction. [Fig. 21] Jänschwalde and Welzow-Süd are both situated in Brandenburg, while the mines of Nochten and Reichwalde are in Sachsen. The production in the region is equally shared between both states.[53] The mines primarily supply lignite to three power stations—Jänschwalde, Schwarze Pumpe, and Boxberg—which are interconnected by a dedicated *Kohlenverbindungsbahn* (coal railway). The region holds a substantial total coal reserve of 11,300,000,000 t, with 2,800,000,000 t considered commercially extractible.[54] In 2022, the Lausitz Energie Bergbau AG LEAG extracted 48,500,000 t of lignite, with 94 % of this production used for electricity and heat generation.[55]

Fortuitous Findings

Local legend has it that God made the Lausitz region, but the Devil created the coal deposits beneath it. While this proverb may have universal application to many mining regions worldwide, it also shows the ambivalent relation between local communities and these subterranean riches. The history of the province has been shaped by a series of significant transformations, which have been accompanied by massive structural challenges. It began with arbitrary discoveries of coal seams near the surface, dating back to the late 18th century.[56] The frequency of these findings sparked small-scale extractions that operated using a series of rudimentary open pits.[57] However, it took until the 1850s before lignite was considered a viable energy source.[58] The early mining entrepreneurs often owned energy-intensive industrial establishments such as brick and glassworks, distilleries, or textile factories, which began to spread across the region. As wealth accumulated, several landholders, merchants, and industrialists united to develop a more comprehensive exploitation of the coal seams. They set up deep underground shafts and focused on supplying coal primarily to local businesses.[59]

The realisation of immense coal reserves beneath the primarily agricultural landscape sparked significant growth in the region and in the late 19th century Lausitz became a major lignite extraction hub. The first catalyst for this transformation was the improvement in connectivity to fuel markets in rapidly industrialising cities like Berlin, Frankfurt Oder, and Dresden. This was achieved through the extensive expansion of the railway network and the introduction of compact briquette production, which effectively abolished the longstanding transportation constraints within a matter of years.[60] This progress was complemented by significant technological advancements in coal-fired pumping, enabling large-scale groundwater lowering. Within decades, the once-regional coal moguls began to operate trans-regional mining empires of national importance.

The economic boom was as lucrative as it was labour-intensive, and therefore impossible to materialise with entrepreneurial-expansionist visions and technological fixes alone. Instead, it depended on thousands of workers who flowed into the region searching for work. Faced with the challenge of accommodating a growing population, mining companies took matters into their own hands and began constructing their own *Werksiedlungen* (workers' settlements) that often mushroomed close to the pits themselves.[61]

Becoming an Energy District

The construction of the first regional lignite-fired power station in 1894 marked another significant milestone in the region's transformation.[62] Although it took another two decades to be fully realised, it provided a new avenue for converting and transporting energy resources beyond the limitations of the local area, which had not been pursued until the end of the First World War. [pp. 74–85] Before 1919, lignite had a diminished role in electricity generation. Its low calorific value, poor transportability, and the lack of suitable heating and transmission technology made it unfeasible. Following the capitulation of the First World War, the German Empire relinquished control of some of its most productive hard coal mining regions —in Oberschlesien, the Saar Basin, and Eupen-Malmedy—as part of territorial concessions. Consequently, lignite emerged as a crucial component of inter-war autarky aspirations in the Weimar Republic and, later, in Nazi Germany's electricity production, with its share increasing to nearly 60 %. In 1934, the Nazi government seized control of the largest private company in the region, expropriating it on the grounds of Jewish descent and thus gaining control over 75 % of the regional lignite industry.[63]

Fig. 13 Historical postcard of an open-pit mine, Senftenberg

Following Germany's partition, the new DDR found itself cut off from the hard coal reserves. In response, the leadership adopted a national energy-autarky strategy, turning to lignite as a crucial resource for the young republic.[64] In 1957, the implementation of a planned coal and energy strategy marked a significant consolidation of material resources and labour in the sector. New mines were established and Lausitz was designated as a specific energy and coal district. Given its new identity, the region saw a massive influx and concentration of heavy industry and energy production, including the establishment of gasworks, coking and briquette factories, power stations, and a massive expansion of open-cast extraction sites. In certain areas, the population increased ten-fold, incentivising rapid prefabricated housing programmes that created tens of thousands of apartments to cope with the steep population growth.

During the early 1980s, rising Soviet crude oil prices further drove the DDR's increased focus on lignite for energy self-sufficiency. Consequently, brown coal extraction in Lausitz increased from 134,000,000 t in 1970 to 162,000,000 t in 1980, reaching its peak in 1988 with over 200,000,000 t.[65] Concurrently, the number of employees in the mining sector also surged to almost 80,000 people.[66] With an annual production of over 300,000,000 t of lignite at its peak, the DDR emerged as the largest lignite producer in the world, accounting for one-fourth of the global annual production.[67]

As lignite extraction became both the predominant narrative and economic identity of the Lausitz region, it also brought considerable damage to the landscape. Open-cast mining devastated not only surface ecosystems but also disturbed the water balance far beyond Lausitz itself. Air pollution caused by incineration, ash, and dust plagued many districts. Around 135 settlements were fully or partially demolished due to the expansion of open pits, resulting in tens of thousands of people being relocated, often against their will, which was met with strong resistance.[68] [Fig. 21] Unlike today, the displaced communities received little to no compensation and were resettled in prefabricated mass housing complexes with no regard for the region's rural vernacular.

Fig. 14 Flooded and renaturalised open-cast mine, Annahütte

Pits and Voids

German reunification marked a steep turning point for the lignite industry, leading to a sudden loss of momentum. From 1989 to 1995, the Lausitz region—especially those areas heavily reliant on mining and energy generation—experienced significant transformation processes that were mutually intertwined. With the sudden dismantling of the DDR's industry, the main coal consumers collapsed within a few years. This abrupt change led to the cessation of operations in numerous open-pit mines and left many of the almost 80,000 miners in the Lausitz region unemployed.[69] Many mines and power stations were permanently closed, and the remaining operations were divided into two sectors: privatised ongoing mining operations and state-led remediation efforts. To transition the resources of the planned economy into the capitalist market logic of the BRD, mining sites, power stations, and other parts of the infrastructure initially became part of the Treuhand, a state-owned trust responsible for privatising state-owned assets. Subsequently, they were sold off to a consortium of various West German and, eventually, international energy companies.[70]

After German reunification, approximately 35,000 ha in the Lausitz region remained un-reclaimed, comprising residual pits and landfills. These mines and associated power stations and facilities presented a significant challenge for future remediation prospects. Over 200 holes of varying sizes needed to be secured to prevent dangerous voids dominating the now purposeless moon landscape. Some of them covered expansive areas, reaching up to 90 km² and depths of up to 80 m. As the proprietor of the lignite business, the legal responsibilities that could or would not be privatised fell to the state.

Brave New Worlds

As the pumping systems that once kept the mines dry have ceased operation, groundwater levels have risen, transforming the area into lakes and dramatically altering the landscape. Regional revitalisation processes prioritised strategies to restore a balanced water regime with regulated quality, covering an overall surface area of approximately 120,000 ha across all districts of what was formerly East Germany.[71] Over the course of 30 years, immense re-naturalisation and recultivation efforts transformed the abandoned mines into a designated tourism area with 21 lakes and planned water areas.[72] The start of the International Building Exhibition IBA in 2000 supported this new vision for the former mining region. Through urban and regional planning tools, it promoted "soft locational factors", creating alternative identities and prospects for both the people and the region.

3.2.5

Thoughts on a Resilient Relationship Between Berlin and Lausitz

Cordelia Polinna
Simon Breth

There is probably no other region in Europe where growth and shrinkage are as close to each other as in Berlin and Brandenburg—and especially in Lausitz. Berlin has developed very dynamically in recent years. The city was suddenly seen as a creative powerhouse, a start-up metropolis, a tourist magnet. However, the Lausitz region, despite "Reconstruction East" and an unprecedented transformation—from one of the largest open-cast coal mining regions in the world to a gigantic local recreation area, now known as the "Lausitz Lakeland"—has shrunk considerably at the same time. Three factors for decline overlap here, reinforcing each other: the change in the political system, which brought about new possibilities in terms of shaping one's own life; deindustrialisation, which many people perceived as a radical "structural break";[73] and demographic change, a development that was perceived as broadly negative, accompanied by feelings of emptiness and resentment on the part of "losers" who were "left behind" in the declining region.[74] This opposing development of Berlin and the Lausitz region exposes a host of potential conflicts. Historically, there are already close ties between the two regions, which will only increase in the future due to the energy transition, plus the need to strengthen regional value chains and the lack of available housing in the metropolises. Too little thought is given, however, to the relationship between these two areas, particularly in the case of spatial planning, for example. Both socially and politically, the polarisation of urban and rural areas increasingly generates a lack of understanding and even disdainful attitudes, which is cause for concern.[75] To be a resilient, sustainable region, the joint development of Berlin and the Lausitz must be based on mutual appreciation. However, questions remain as to how this can be achieved.

What does shrinkage do to a region, and why does no one move to the Lausitz?

Population decrease in the Lausitz region since 1990 has had various effects: technical and social infrastructures are oversized; the excess of prefabricated housing has been capped in many places by the "Urban Redevelopment East" funding programme;[76] and migration is often selective. Young, educated, capable people—and especially women—tend to escape the region, leaving older people and a surplus of males behind.[77] The negative consequences of shrinkage could be summarised as the loss of soft location factors. It is hardly surprising therefore that the shortage of skilled workers is now being felt in the region as a limiting factor for positive economic development.[78]

The growing Berlin and shrinking Lausitz could resolve many of their problems cooperatively in a way that benefits both regions. But those who move from Berlin to Lausitz often experience the dramatic effects of moving away from an urban society, especially when confronted with the limitations of a dwindling environment. Those hoping to snuggle into a quiet life of rural romance after years in the hectic city are disappointed in the face of limited mobility options and the need for self-reliance, faced with a lack of access to restaurants, cafés, and other services. Instead, in the Lausitz region, it is a matter of taking over medical practices, businesses, and political offices which suffer from a lack of skilled workers. Commitment and a high level of dedication are required. This development also has many exciting aspects: Lausitz is full of voluntary initiatives and community associations that maintain and operate swimming pools, zoos and other cultural sites, as well as providing fire protection and disaster prevention. These strengthen the social fabric, leading to subjective satisfaction.

Why is Lausitz so interesting as a region of the future?

What would a debate about the future of the Lausitz region look like? One that is not conducted as a debate about emptiness and deficits, but about future-oriented opportunities? One that conveys a realistic picture of this region, and not a false romantic idea of life in the countryside? One that prevents the pendulum from swinging towards an unhealthy degree of growth—with negative consequences such as overheated real estate markets and resentment between old residents and newcomers? A development model geared towards maximum growth can no longer be the goal for Lausitz—especially in view of the impacts of growth on planetary boundaries. Perhaps it is possible to develop a resilient model that triggers just as much influx as the region needs, creating a balanced age and education average. The following theses can be the first parameters for such a development model:

Thesis 1 Think Lausitz and Berlin together!

Historically, today and in the future, there are major interdependencies between Berlin and the Lausitz region. Berlin is dependent on the large areas of Lausitz for many needs, including production and renewable energy, as well as housing. Lausitz, on the other hand, is not populated densely enough to be able to offer complex cultural, medical, and educational services. People who live in Lausitz derive their culture from the big city. This can stay that way, it works very well! Metropolis and countryside—each area has its talents and its roles to play.[79] However, we need a "pact" between Lausitz and Berlin: for climate neutrality and resource turnaround, for mutual appreciation, for an acceptance of different lifestyles, so that we can meet the challenges of the future together. Derived from this, we need a common spatial vision, a spatial image.[80]

Thesis 2 Lausitz is already the energy region of the future, this is where the energy transition is being made!

The Lausitz is already a "Reallabor" of the energy transition, and the region is extremely open to innovation. At 300 m, the world's tallest wind measurement tower has been erected in Klettwitz, in the district of Oberspreewald-Lausitz. Elsewhere, huge areas of photovoltaics are being built in the Lausitz Energy Park and a hydrogen storage power station will be built in Schwarze Pumpe.[81] However, these positive developments—many of which were initiated in the 1990s—tend to go unnoticed in an often-political discourse. The many groundbreaking developments that can be observed in Lausitz go far beyond the truncated demand for more wind turbines, but continue on in the technology-oriented and innovative tradition of the wider energy region.

Thesis 3 Lausitz is an important location for local value creation and re-localisation.

Important technology sectors are already located in Lausitz, for example, at BASF in Schwarzheide, Dekra at the Lausitzring, or Altech in Schwarze Pumpe. The Lausitz is a transformation-experienced region of the future. It is far ahead of other, more saturated regions in thinking through how to deal with change processes, and it demonstrates that innovation can emerge from crises. In the future, not only will we need more land to produce renewable energies, but also for local food production and other value chains. Even in rural areas, we cannot afford to leave land lying fallow or to occupy it with only one use. The Lausitz offers good conditions for the re-localisation of industry. Supply chains for everyday products can also become local again here, based on Lausitz's industrial tradition. Due to its history, Lausitz still has many empty buildings and brownfields that can be redeveloped and converted for future needs.

Thesis 4: Spaces of opportunity.

The Lausitz region is a space of opportunity for personal development. Countless companies in almost all sectors have problems with succession planning—from craft trades to engineering firms—and there are many opportunities here to test one's abilities. Those who want to reorient themselves professionally should urgently consider a change of location. One's career development may take an unforeseen turn. At the same time, there is still a lot of spatial potential—vacancies that need to be activated, brownfields on which things can grow—and free spaces that are unlikely to be affordable for many in the large metropolises.

Thesis 5: Lausitz offers opportunities for resilient living with attractive local recreation.

The countryside is perceived by some as more resilient because personal provision in the event of a crisis is easier. Since there is often more private space available, the possibilities for stockpiling—as well as various independent ways of heating and generating energy—are different (though not necessarily easier) in a country house than in a city dwelling. Neighbourly help and active engagement in associations and social clubs are issues that can go hand in hand with an increased sense of security. As an after-effect of the pandemic, and in view of increasing global warming, local recreation is an important factor somewhere like Lausitz. A house near the lake is still possible here. However, these positive aspects are quickly offset by a lack of certain "soft factors", as described above. Those who moved to the countryside, motivated by how nice it was on holiday, will be bitterly disappointed after the first winter.

Thesis 6: Lausitz benefits from civil society involvement.

Many activities and services in Lausitz and other rural regions are based on a strong voluntary commitment. Only with civil society, voluntary work, and intensive cooperation between a wide range of actors can the many challenges that lie ahead be mastered. This is an important aspect of resilient development. In view of diminishing financial resources, the state cannot absorb all these tasks alone. It is therefore all the more important that it provides a good, enabling infrastructure to support voluntary work. In the case of the volunteer fire brigades, this means modern emergency vehicles and good fire service buildings that are also suitable as meeting places and training venues. Self-organised educational, sporting, and cultural activities also need rooms and equipment—kitchens, sound systems, computers—that can be used if you are involved in activities that strengthen the regional spirit. With diverse civil initiatives already running village shops and swimming pools cooperatively, alongside organising cultural events and strengthening feelings of self-efficacy, the Lausitz region is a pioneering template for a resilient future.

Endnotes

1 Smil, *Grand Transitions*, 235.
2 See: Sieferle, *The Subterranean Forest*.
3 Mitchell, *Carbon Democracy*, 11ff.
4 A term taken from: Ennos, *The Age of Wood*.
5 To delve further into the imperative of regulating woodcutting, please refer to: Diamond, *Collapse*; Radkau, "Wood and Forestry in German History".
6 Sieferle, *The Subterranean Forest*, 57.
7 Schott, "Energizing European Cities: From Wood Provision to Solar Panels – Providing Energy for Urban Demand, 1800–2000", 137.
8 Schwarz, *Die Ländlichen Siedlungen, Die Zwischen Land Und Stadt Stehenden Siedlungen*, 313.
9 Schott, "Energizing European Cities: From Wood Provision to Solar Panels – Providing Energy for Urban Demand, 1800–2000", 137.
10 Lewis and Maslin, *The Human Planet*, 192.
11 For a concise and insightful overview of the profound impacts of the Industrial Revolution in Germany, please consult: Hahn, *Die Industrielle Revolution in Deutschland*, Chapter 3, 6, and 7.
12 Lewis and Maslin, *The Human Planet*, 199.
13 Mitchell, *Carbon Democracy*, 18ff.
14 Author's calculations taken from British Petroleum, *Statistical Review of World Energy 2021*.
15 Birol and Malpass, "It's Critical to Tackle Coal Emissions".
16 International Energy Agency, *Coal in Net Zero Transitions*, 13–15.
17 International Energy Agency, "Global Energy and Climate Model".
18 Birol and Malpass, "It's Critical to Tackle Coal Emissions".
19 IEA, "Coal 2022", 11.
20 McGhee, *Carboniferous Giants and Mass Extinction*, 98.
21 Shaw, *Planet of the Bugs*, 75.
22 Malvadkar, Forbes, and McGurl, "Coal Resources, Formation Of", 530.
23 Ritchie and Roser, "What Are the Safest and Cleanest Sources of Energy?".
24 International Energy Agency, "World Energy Outlook 2022—Analysis", 280.
25 For an extensive examination of mining techniques, refer to: Lien, "Advances in Coal Mining Technology"; Schissler, "Coal Mining, Design and Methods Of".
26 Jenkins, *Energy Systems: A Very Short Introduction*, 24.
27 A coal seam is a dark brown or black banded deposit of coal that is visible within layers of rock.
28 Ganswindt, Rötters, and Heffa, "Bitter Coal – Ein Dossier über Deutschlands Steinkohleimporte", 9.
29 Ritchie, Roser, and Rosado, "Energy".
30 Paul, "Coal, Fuel and Non-Fuel Uses", 438.
31 Umweltbundesamt, "Primärenergieverbrauch".
32 AG Energiebilanzen e. V., "Energieverbrauch fällt 2022 auf niedrigsten Stand seit der Wiedervereinigung".
33 Bundesanstalt für Geowissenschaften und Rohstoffe, "BGR Energiedaten 2022 – Daten und Entwicklungen der deutschen und globalen Energieversorgung" Table A33, A26.
34 Fukagawa and Ziska, "Rice", 2.
35 Umweltbundesamt, "Primärenergieverbrauch".
36 Destatis, "Stromerzeugung 2022".
37 Fraunhofer-Institut für Solare Energiesysteme, "Nettostromerzeugung in Deutschland Im Jahr 2023".
38 Bundesanstalt für Geowissenschaften und Rohstoffe: "BGR Energiestudie 2023 – Daten und Entwicklungen der deutschen und globalen Energieversorgung", 32.
39 In the context of natural resources, a reserve refers to a subset of a resource that has been identified, quantified, and is considered economically and technically feasible to extract with current technology and under present economic conditions.
40 Author's calculation: Due to lignite's lower density (0.9 t/m^3) compared to water (1 t/m^3), the 34.15 billion tons of lignite would occupy approximately 37.9 billion m^3, or about 76% of the Bodensee's 50 billion m^3 volume.
41 Deutschlandfunk, "Erdgas, Erdöl, Kohle und Uran – Welche Rohstoffe hat Deutschland?".
42 Bundesanstalt für Geowissenschaften und Rohstoffe, "BGR Energiedaten 2022 – Daten und Entwicklungen der deutschen und globalen Energieversorgung", A-32.
43 Eurostat, "Coal Production and Consumption up in 2022 – Products Eurostat News".
44 Statistik der Kohlewirtschaft e. V., "Ausfuhr von Braunkohle nach Empfängerländern ab 1979".
45 Bundesanstalt für Geowissenschaften und Rohstoffe, "BGR Energiedaten 2022 – Daten und Entwicklungen der deutschen und globalen Energieversorgung", A-23.
46 Destatis, "Einfuhr von Steinkohle für die Jahre 2018 bis 2022".
47 Bundesregierung, Gesetz zur Reduzierung und zur Beendigung der Kohleverstromung und zur Änderung weiterer Gesetze (Kohleausstiegsgesetz).
48 Hermann et al., "Beschäftigungsentwicklung in der Braunkohleindustrie: Status quo und Projektion".
49 Bundesministerium für Wirtschaft und Klimaschutz, "Kohle".
50 LEAG, "Letzte Lausitzer Kohle für Kraftwerk Klingenberg in Berlin".
51 Amt für Statistik Berlin-Brandenburg, "Statistischer Bericht: Energie- und CO_2-Bilanz in Berlin 2020".
52 Senatsverwaltung für Wirtschaft, Energie und Betriebe, "Voller Energie zur solaren Stadt: Infobroschüre zum Masterplan Solarcity Berlin".
53 Öko-Institut, Die deutsche Braunkohlenwirtschaft 2021, 54.
54 Bundesverband Braunkohle, "Braunkohle in Deutschland – Daten und Fakten 2022".
55 Lausitz Energie Bergbau AG, "Tagebau Lausitz | Geschäftsfeld Bergbau | LEAG".
56 Steinhuber, "Einhundert Jahre bergbauliche Rekultivierung in der Lausitz. Ein historischer Abriss der Rekultivierung, Wiederurbarmachung und Sanierung im Lausitzer Braunkohlenrevier", 48f.
57 Baxmann, Schirmer, and Internationale Bauausstellung Fürst-Pückler-Land, *Zeitmaschine Lausitz – vom "Pfützenland" zum Energiebezirk*, 63f.
58 Kabus, "The History of an Industrial Region", 39ff.
59 Steinhuber, "Einhundert Jahre bergbauliche Rekultivierung in der Lausitz. Ein historischer Abriss der Rekultivierung, Wiederurbarmachung und Sanierung im Lausitzer Braunkohlenrevier", 60f.
60 Lausitzer und Mitteldeutsche Bergbau-Verwaltungsgesellschaft mbH, "Werkbahnen im Lausitzer Braunkohlenbergbau"; Steinhuber, "Einhundert Jahre bergbauliche Rekultivierung in der Lausitz. Ein historischer Abriss der Rekultivierung, Wiederurbarmachung und Sanierung im Lausitzer Braunkohlenrevier", 66.
61 Kil et al., *Zeitmaschine Lausitz – Werksiedlungen*, 19ff.
62 Steinhuber, "Einhundert Jahre bergbauliche Rekultivierung in der Lausitz. Ein historischer Abriss der Rekultivierung, Wiederurbarmachung und Sanierung im Lausitzer Braunkohlenrevier", 115.
63 Kabus, "The History of an Industrial Region", 41.
64 Lintz and Wirth, "Sanierung Alter Industrieregionen in Ostdeutschland", 470.
65 Statistik der Kohlewirtschaft e. V., "Ausfuhr von Braunkohle nach Empfängerländern ab 1979".
66 Statistik der Kohlewirtschaft e. V., "Beschäftigte nach Revieren ab 1929".
67 Kahlert, *Die Energiepolitik der DDR*, 10.
68 Vereingung Deutscher Wirtschaftsarchivare e.V. et al., "Entstehung, Entwicklung und Bedeutung der Lausitzer und Mitteldeutschen Braunkohlenindustrie im Spiegel ihrer Überlieferung im Bergarchiv Freiberg", 15; "Archiv Verschwundener Orte – Verschwundene Orte".
69 Statistik der Kohlewirtschaft e. V., "Beschäftigte nach Revieren ab 1929".
70 After being sold by Vattenfall in 2016, the operations are now facilitated by LEAG, a consortium of the Czech energy provider Energetický a Průmyslový Holding (EPH) and the investment firm PPF Investments.
71 Lintz and Wirth, "Sanierung Alter Industrieregionen in Ostdeutschland", 470.
72 Tourismusverband Lausitzer Seenland e. V., "Lausitzer Seenland".
73 Hannemann, "Schrumpfende Städte in Ostdeutschland". See also: "(Der) Begriff der Deindustrialisierung (erfasst) Ausmass, Inhalt und Resultat des wirtschaftlichen Strukturwandels und der daraus resultierenden hohen Arbeitslosigkeit, der demografischen Entwicklung und der urbanen Rückbildungsprozesse in den ostdeutschen Bundesländern nur unzureichend: 'De-LPGsierung' (Dekollektivierung der Landwirtschaft), 'De-Administrierung' und 'De-Militarisierung' sind gleichermassen Prozesse mit erheblichen Auswirkungen auf die wirtschaftliche Situation der Städte in Ostdeutschland".
74 Müller and Steinberg, "Region Im Wandel".
75 Stroms and Siedentop, *Stadt und Land*.
76 Hannemann, "Schrumpfende Städte in Ostdeutschland".
77 Umweltbundesamt, *Analyse des historischen Strukturwandels in der Lausitz (Fallstudie)*.
78 Industrie- und Handelskammer Cottbus, "Konjunkturreport Lausitz".
79 Priebs, *Stadt-Umland-Beziehungen*.
80 Urban Catalyst, Studio Amore, and brethdelacalle Architekten, "Von der Lausitz uur WOWsitz: Planungslabor Raumbild 2050".
81 Bundesministerium für Wirtschaft und Klimaschutz, "Habeck besichtigt Projekte der Energiewende in der Lausitz".

Fig. 15 Total hard coal production and exports by country, 2022 in Mt

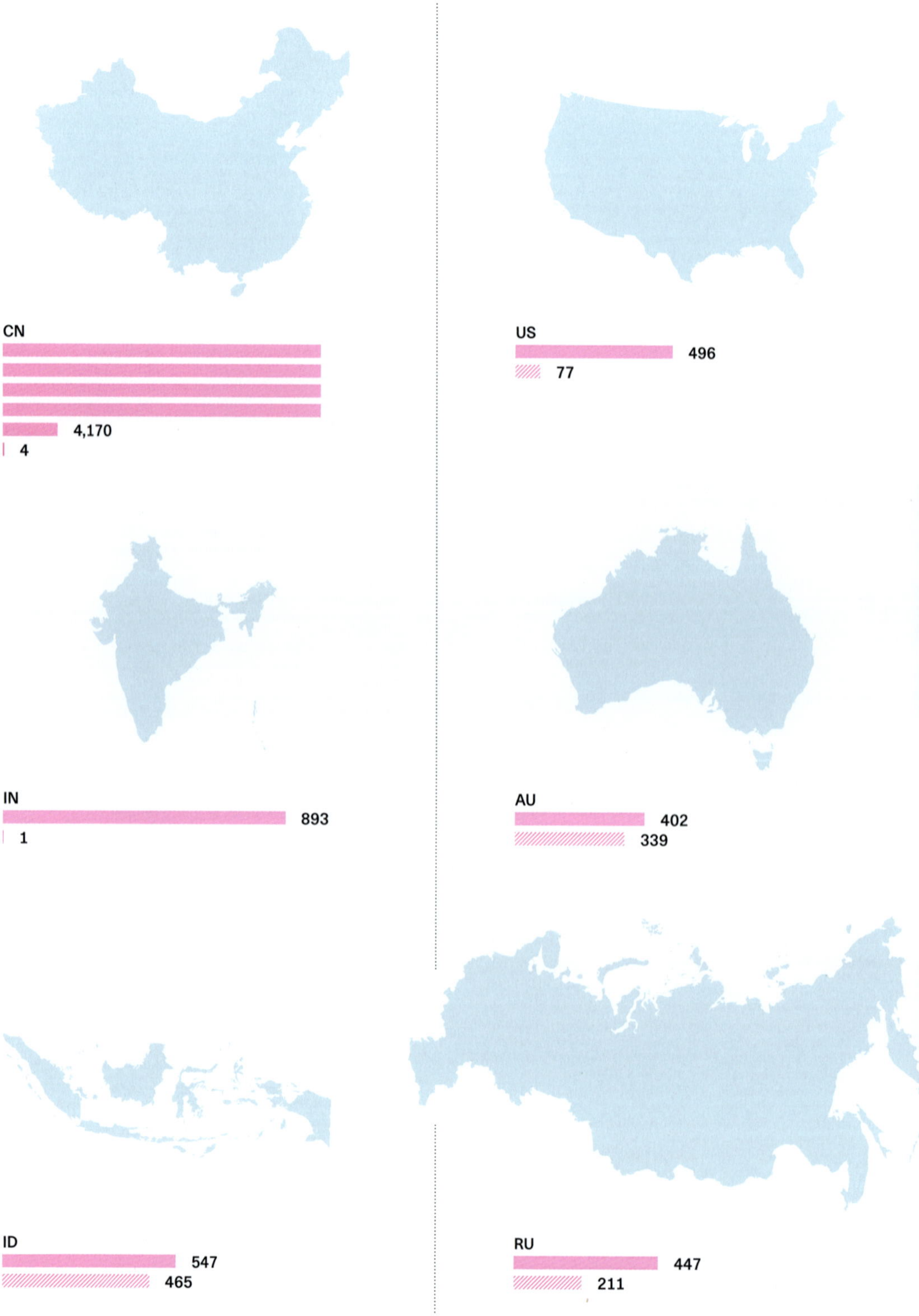

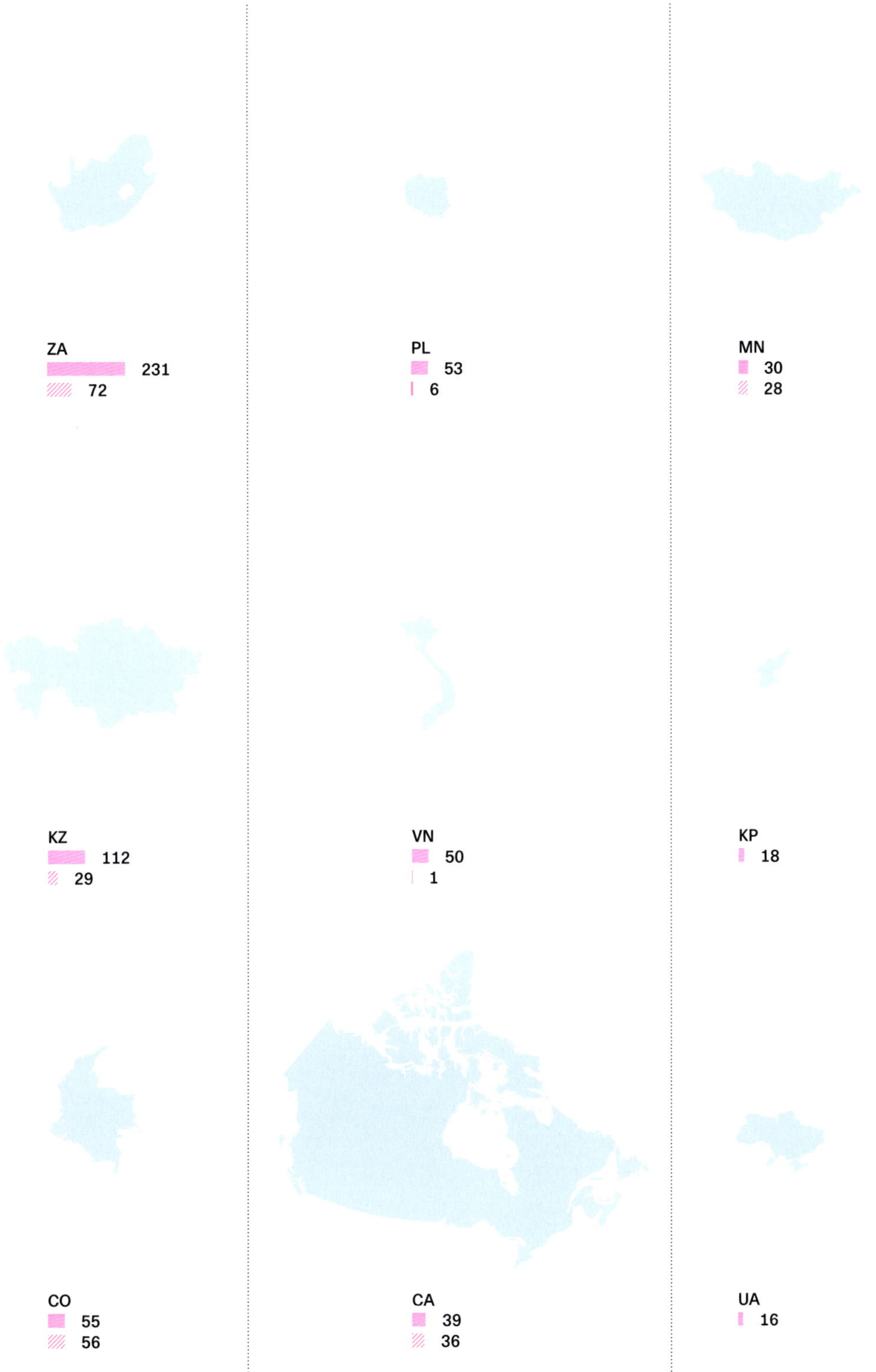
ZA
231
72
PL
53
6
MN
30
28
KZ
112
29
VN
50
1
KP
18
CO
55
56
CA
39
36
UA
16

Fig. 16 Coal supply chain

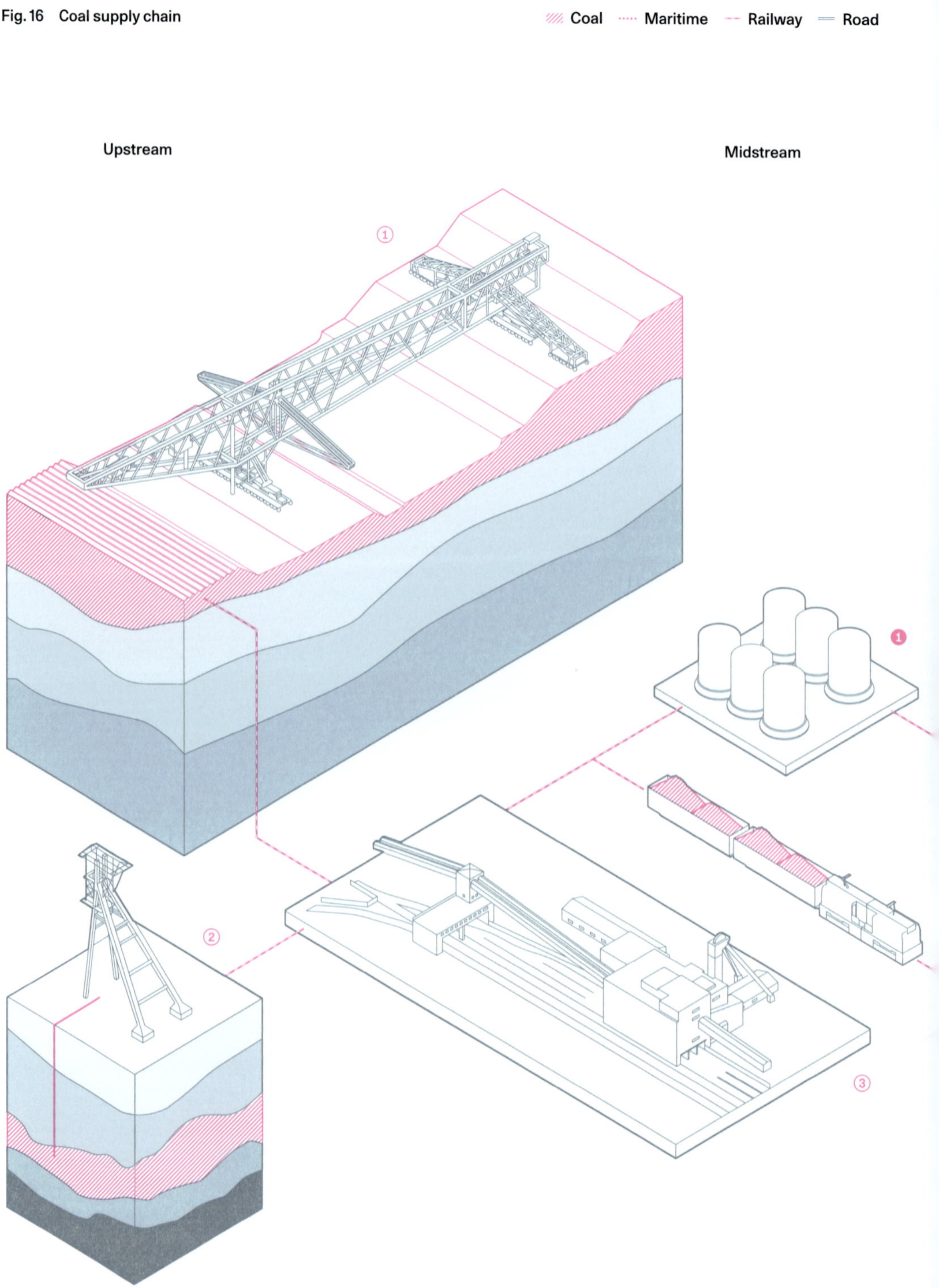

Production (DE)

① Open-pit mine
② Underground mine
③ Enrichment plant

Transmission (DE)

❶ Stockpile
❷ Coal terminal

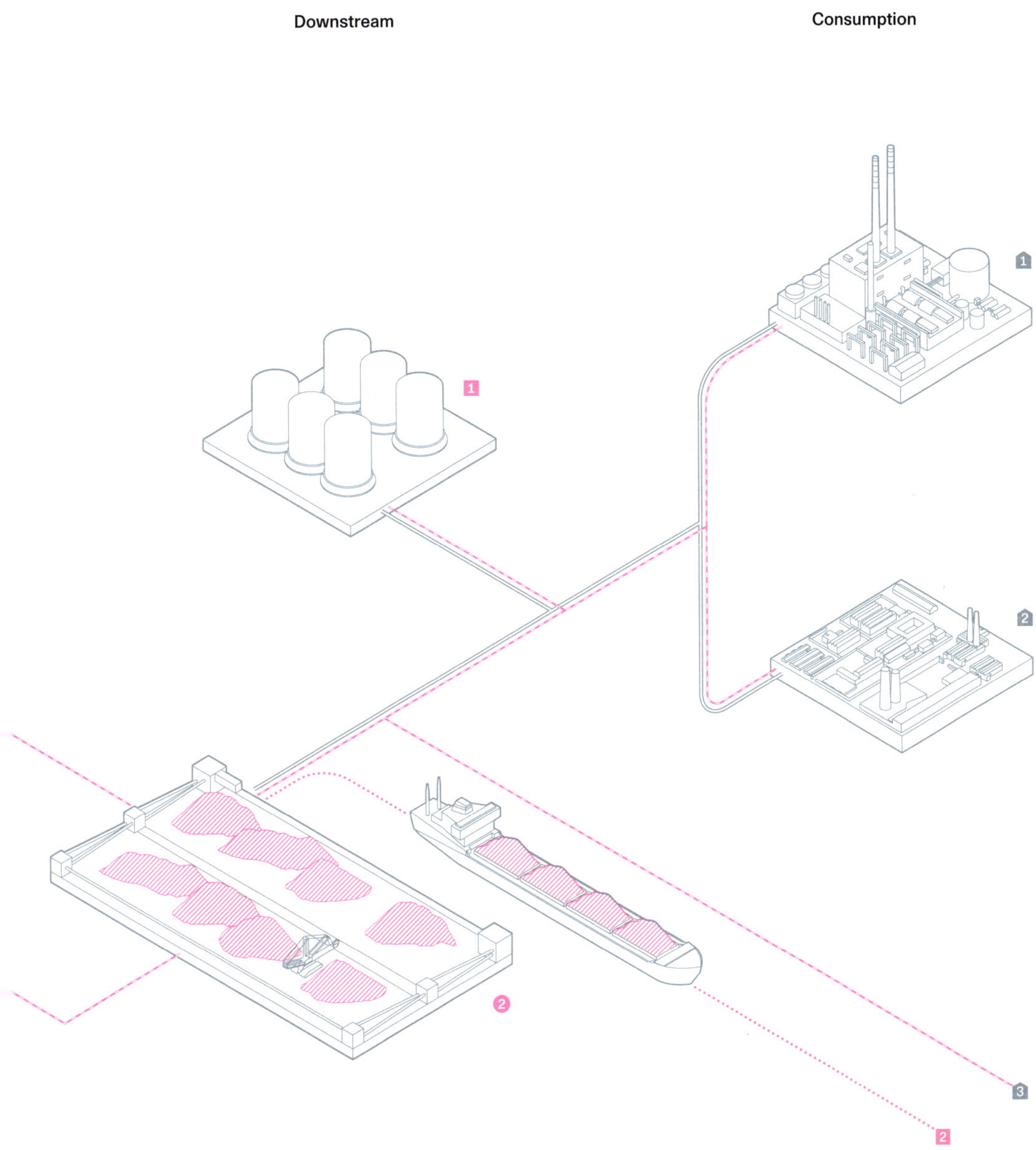

Distribution (DE)

1 Stockpile
2 Merchant wholesale

Final Consumption

1 Electricity and heat
2 Industry
3 Secondary consumers

Fig. 17 Global hard coal import routes to Germany

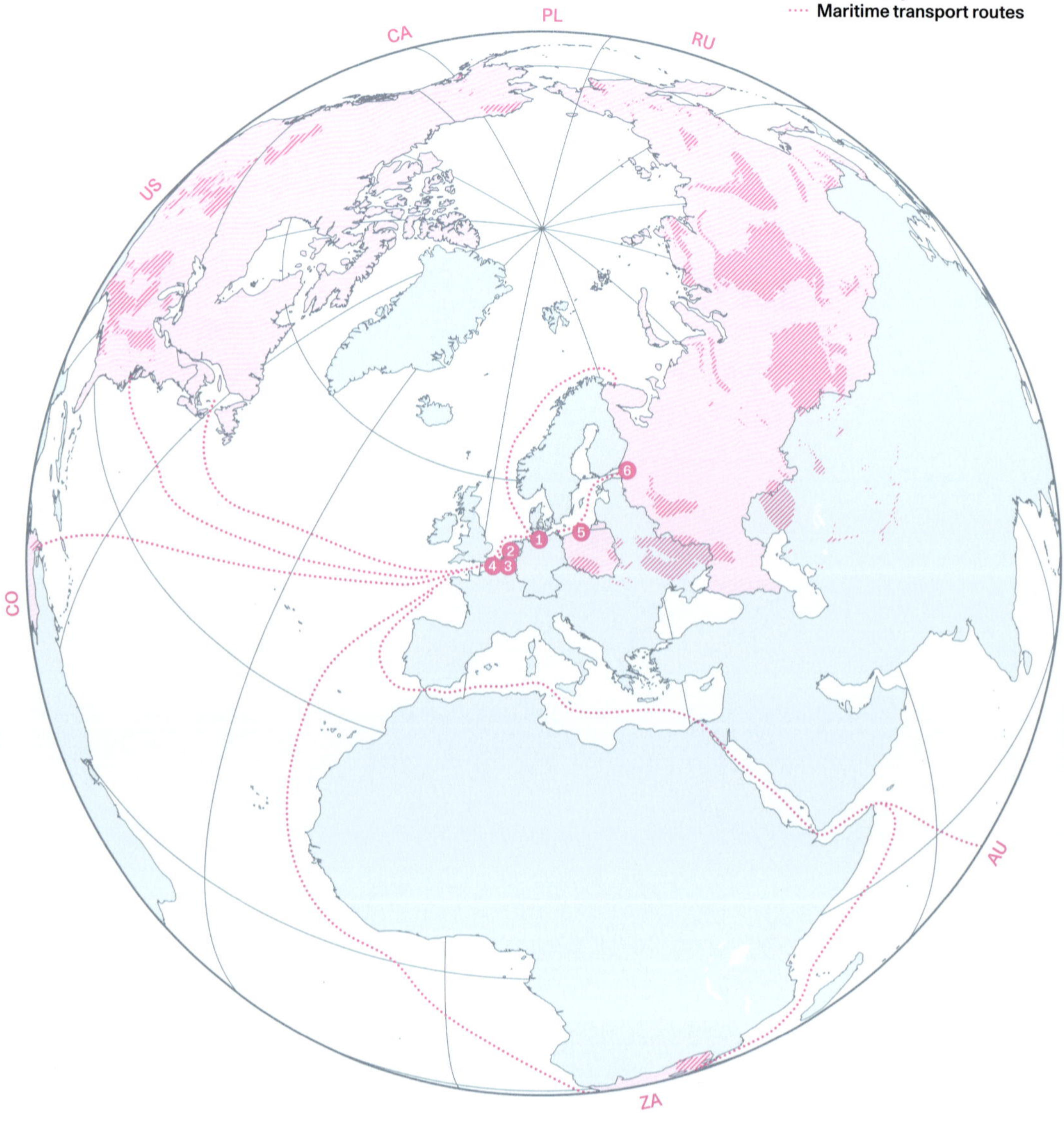

1 Coal terminals in Germany: Stralsund, Rostock, Wismar, Kiel, Rendsburg, Flensburg, Brunsbüttel, Glückstadt, Stade, Hamburg, Wilhelmshaven, Nordenham, Bremen, Mukran
2 Coal terminals in the Netherlands: Amsterdam, Rotterdam, Eemshaven, Vlissengen, Terneuzen
3 Coal terminals in Belgium: Antwerp, Ghent
4 Coal terminals in France: Dunkirk
5 Coal terminals in Poland: Gdynia, Szczecin-Świnoujście, Gdansk
6 Coal terminals in Russia: Ust-Luga, Vysotsk

Fig. 18 Imports of hard coal by supplying country, 2021 and 2022 in kt

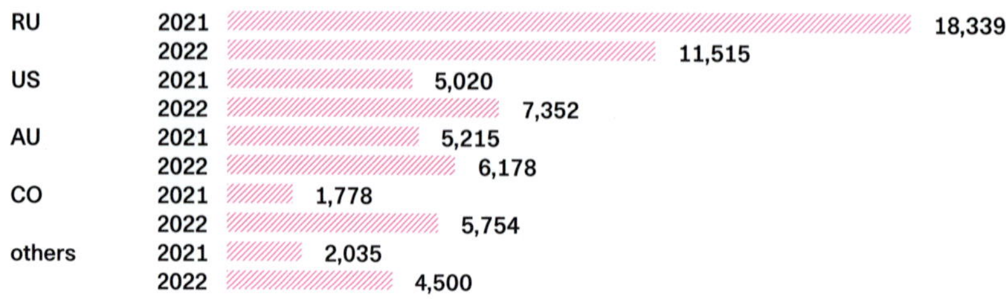

Fig. 19 Domestic coal resources and European transportation network

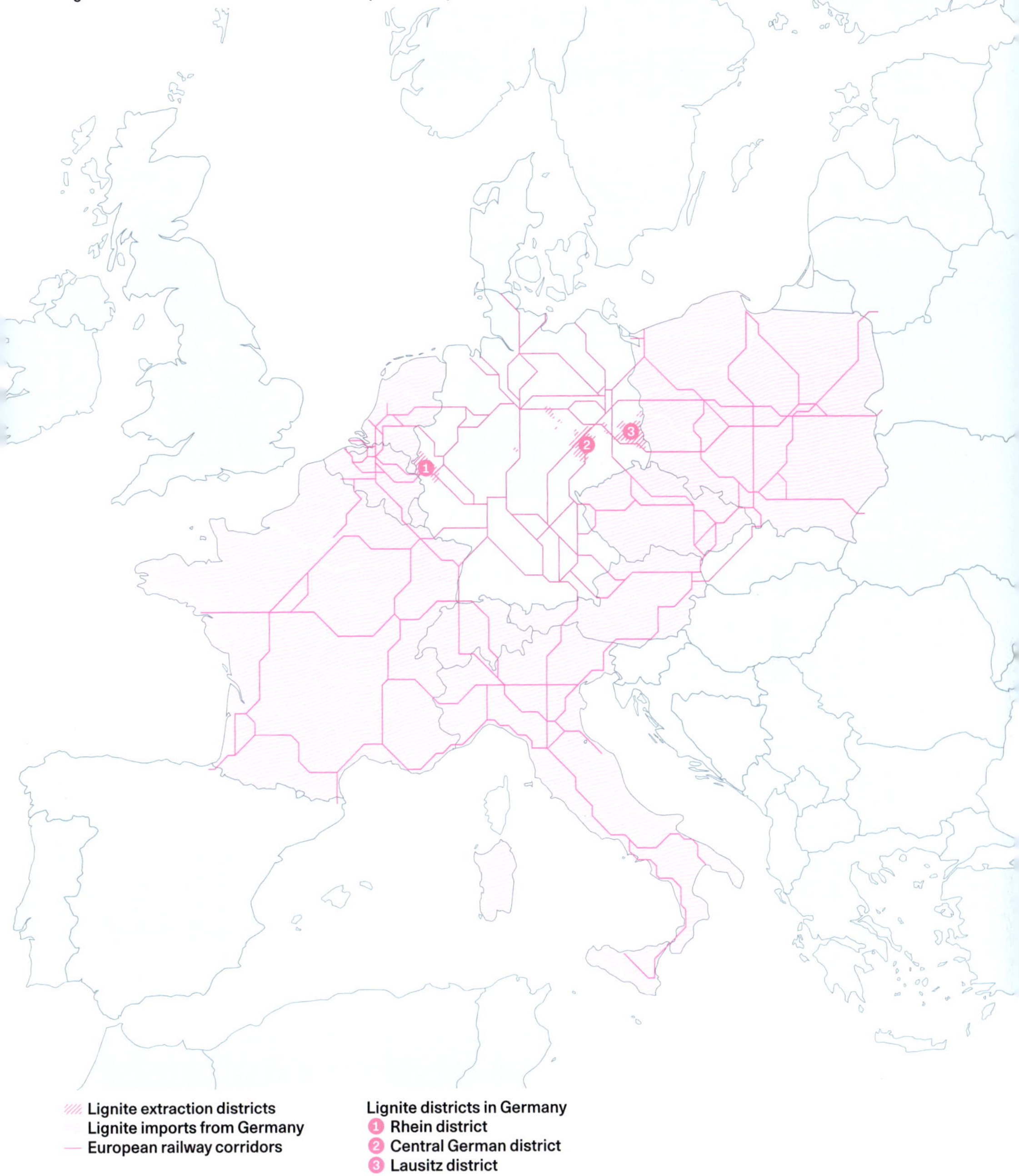

Fig. 20 Exports of domestic lignite to recipient countries, 2021 and 2022 in kt

Fig. 21 Lausitz open-cast mines

Open-cast mines
1 Jänschwalde
2 Welzow-Süd
3 Nochen

Power stations
1 Kraftwerk Jänschwalde
2 HKW Cottbus
3 Kraftwerk Schwarze Pumpe

Locations
1 Cottbus
2 Spremberg
Devastated towns

Mines in operation
Closed mines
Urban areas
Roads
Power lines
Regional borders
National borders

1
2
3
1
2
3
5 km

Fig. 22 Jänschwalde and Cottbus Nord coal mines, 2023

- 1 Jänschwalde mine
- 2 Cottbus Nord mine
- 1 Kraftwerk Jänschwalde
- 1 Cottbus Nord wind park
- 2 Forst-Briesnig wind park
- 3 Deponie Jänschwalde I solar park (in planning)
- 4 Bohrau energy park (in planning)
- 5 Floating PV system

Locations
- ① Cottbus
- ② Cottbuser Ostsee (under development)
- ③ Forst (Lausitz)

- Railways
- Power line
- Recultivated area
- Proposed artificial lake
- Solar park area
- Energy industry
- Wind turbine
- Wind turbine (in planning)

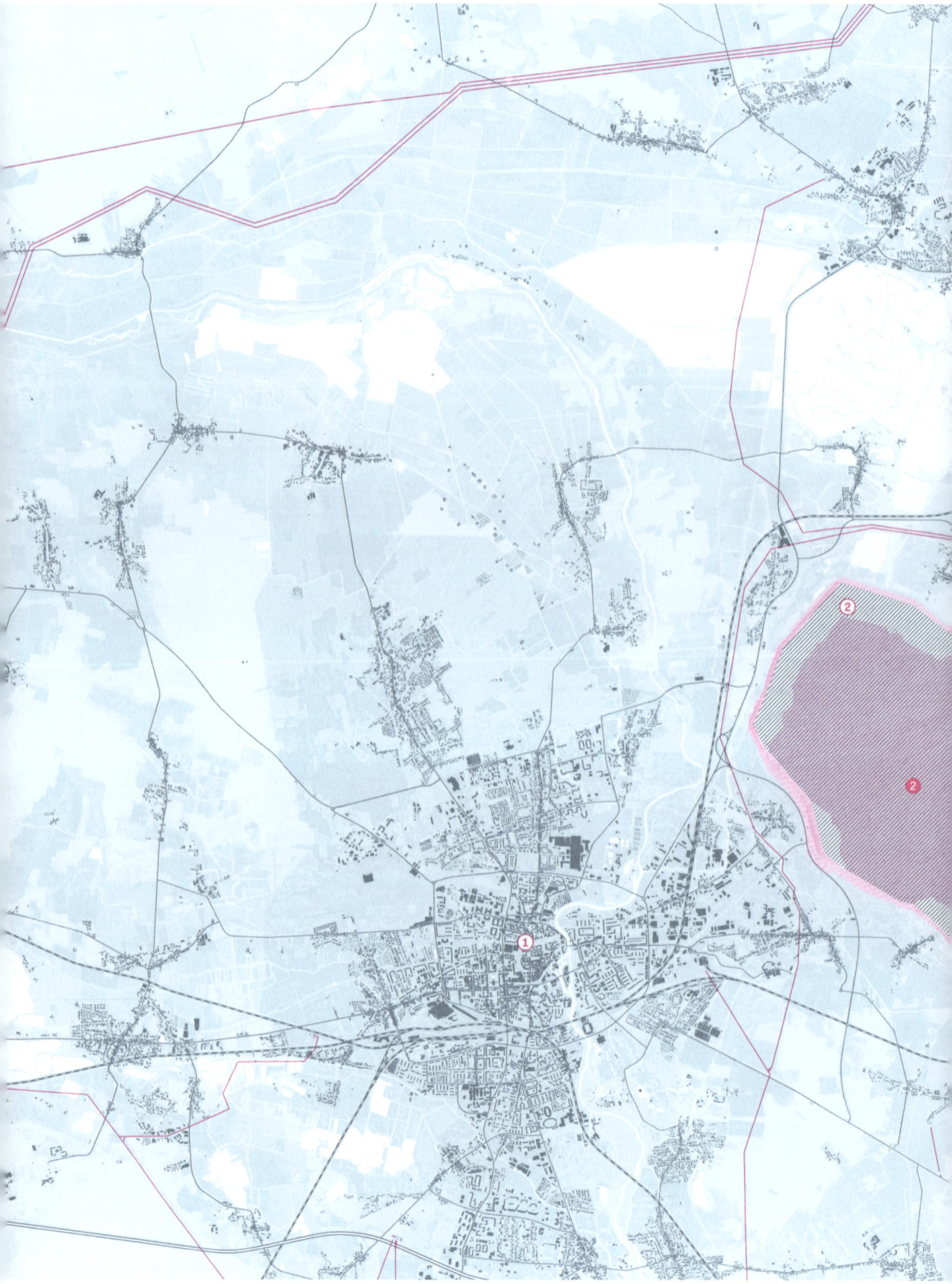

1
1
2
1
3
4
3
2 km

Fig. 23 Cottbus district, 1985

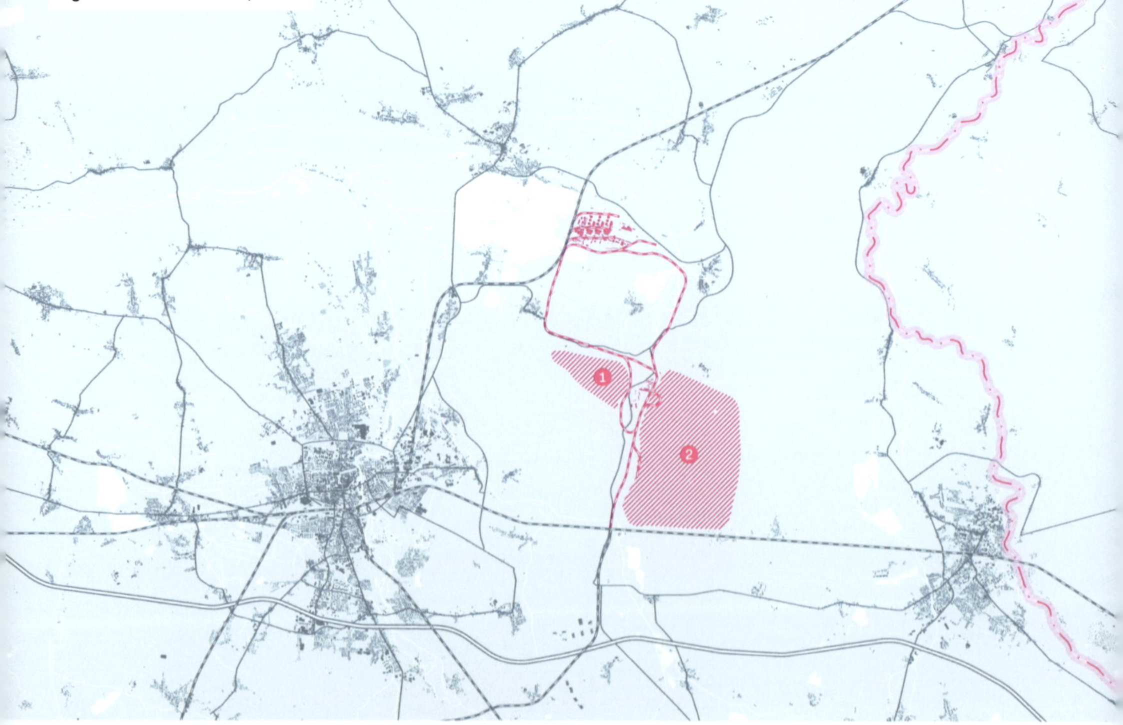

1974–81 The Cottbus Nord ❶ and Jänschwalde ❷ open pits start operations.
1976 The foundation of Jänschwalde power station is laid.
1981–89 Six power station blocks (A–F) generate electricity and provide heat for Jänschwalde, Cottbus, and Peitz.

Fig. 24 Cottbus district, 1998

1994 LMBV starts recultivating over-excavated areas that were the outcome of activity at the Jänschwalde open-pit mine between 1974 and 1990.

Active mining area
Exhausted mining area

Fig. 25 Cottbus district, 2010

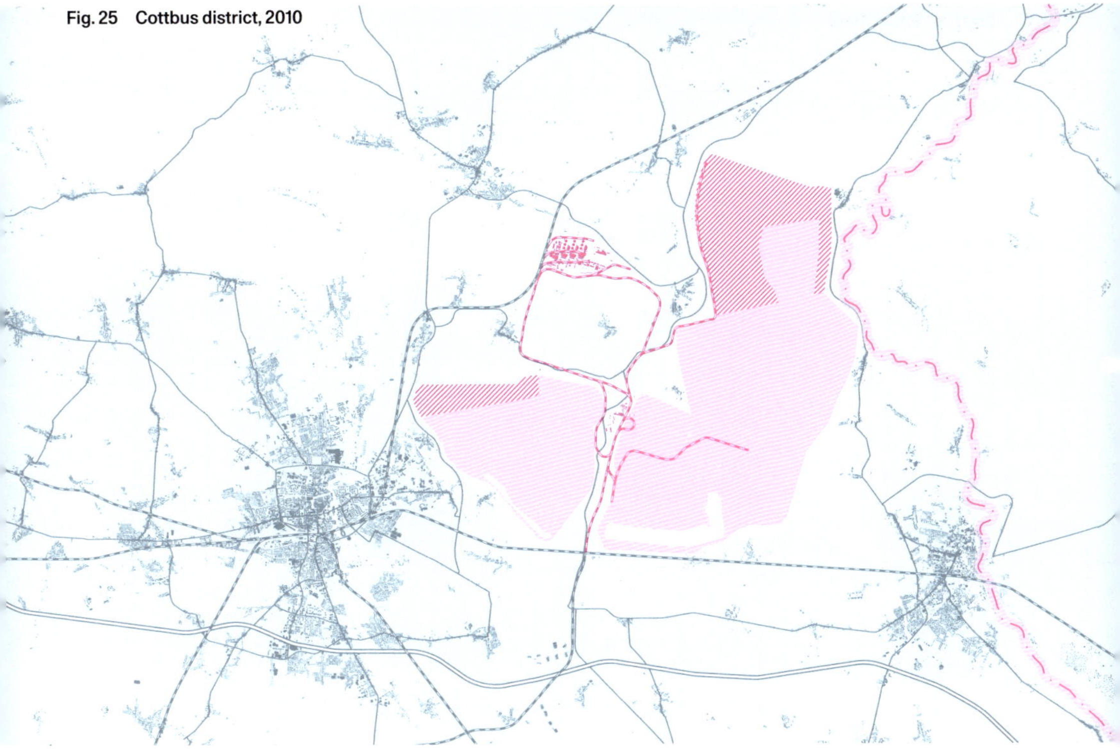

2010 The towns of Groß Lieskow, Klein Lieskow, Lakoma, and Tranitz are completely dredged.

Fig. 26 Cottbus district, 2023

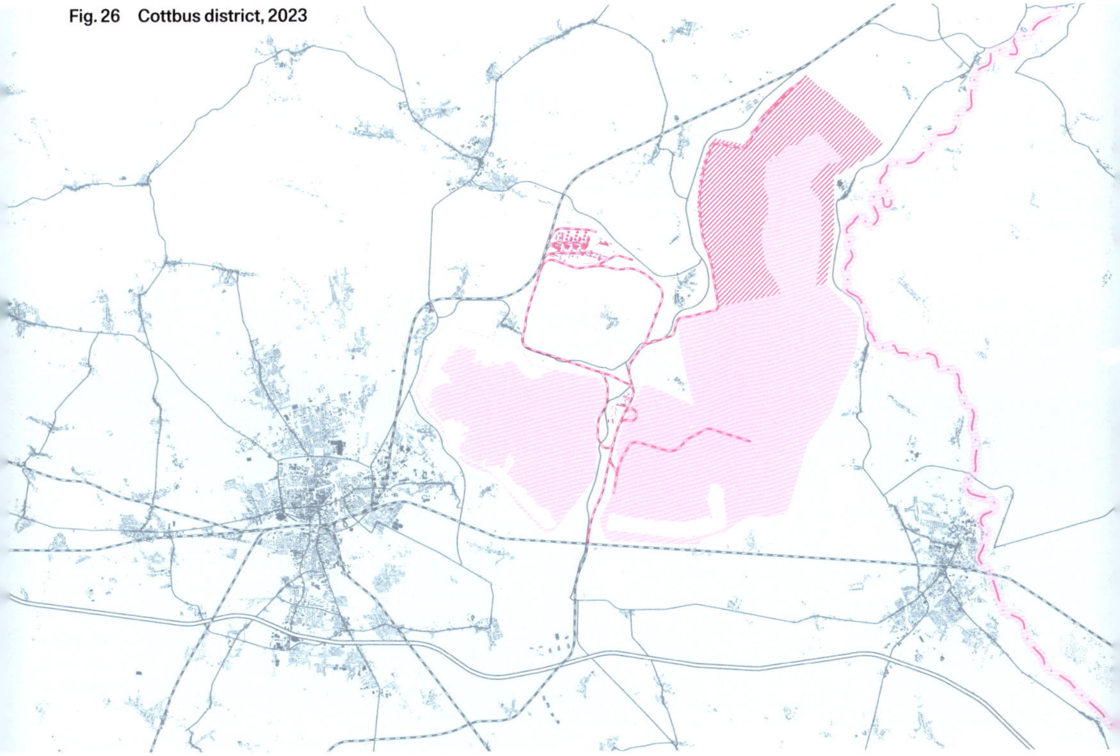

2015 The Cottbus Nord pit is shut to be recultivated.
2023 The approved reserves of raw materials in Jänschwalde are expected to be exhausted.

10 km

Fig. 27 Schematic drawing of open-cast mine in Welzow-Süd

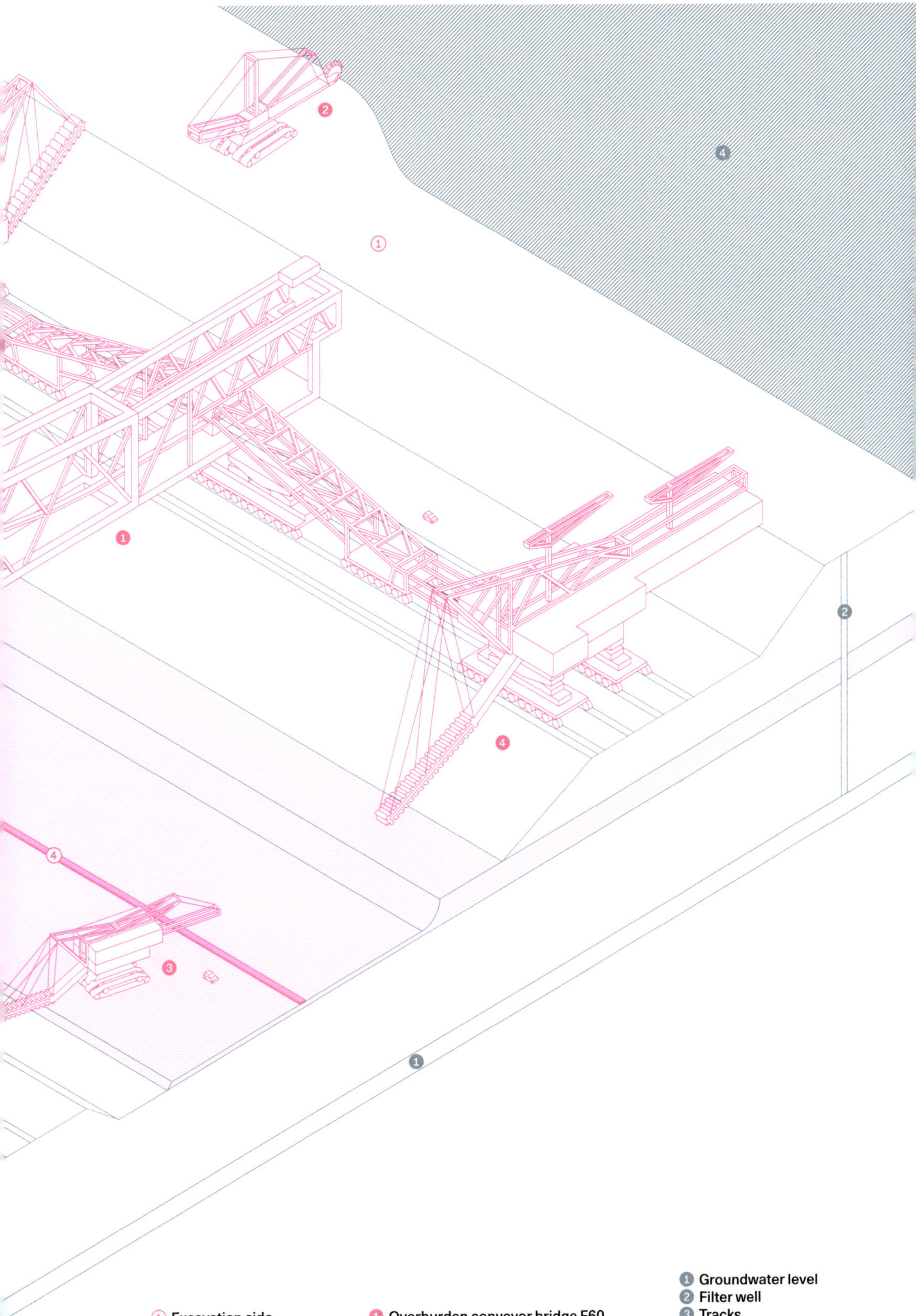

1. Excavation side
2. Dumping side
3. Lignite
4. Lignite conveyor belt

1. Overburden conveyor bridge F60
2. Open-cast mine forefield excavators
3. Coal excavators
4. Overburden excavators

1. Groundwater level
2. Filter well
3. Tracks
4. Forefield
5. Dump
6. Recultivation

Fig. 28 Reuter West power station

1. Harbour
2. Coal bunker
3. Conveyor belt
4. Boiler house
5. Machine house
6. Central heating system
7. Electric generators
8. Filter
9. Denitrification system
10. De-sulphurisation area
11. Ash silo
12. Cooling tower
13. Multi-purpose building
14. Pump station
15. Workshop
16. Storage
17. Thermal energy storage
18. Heavy oil tanks
19. Gypsum storage
20. Unloading station
21. District heating distributor
22. Coal silo
23. Substation
24. Three-cell cooling tower
25. Recycling plant
26. Waste-to-energy plant

❶ Sewage treatment plant
❷ Material processing and disposal plant

① Spree
② Alte Spree
③ U Ruhleben
④ Allotment site

Railways
Power line
Pipeline
Power station boundaries
Coal
Solar panels

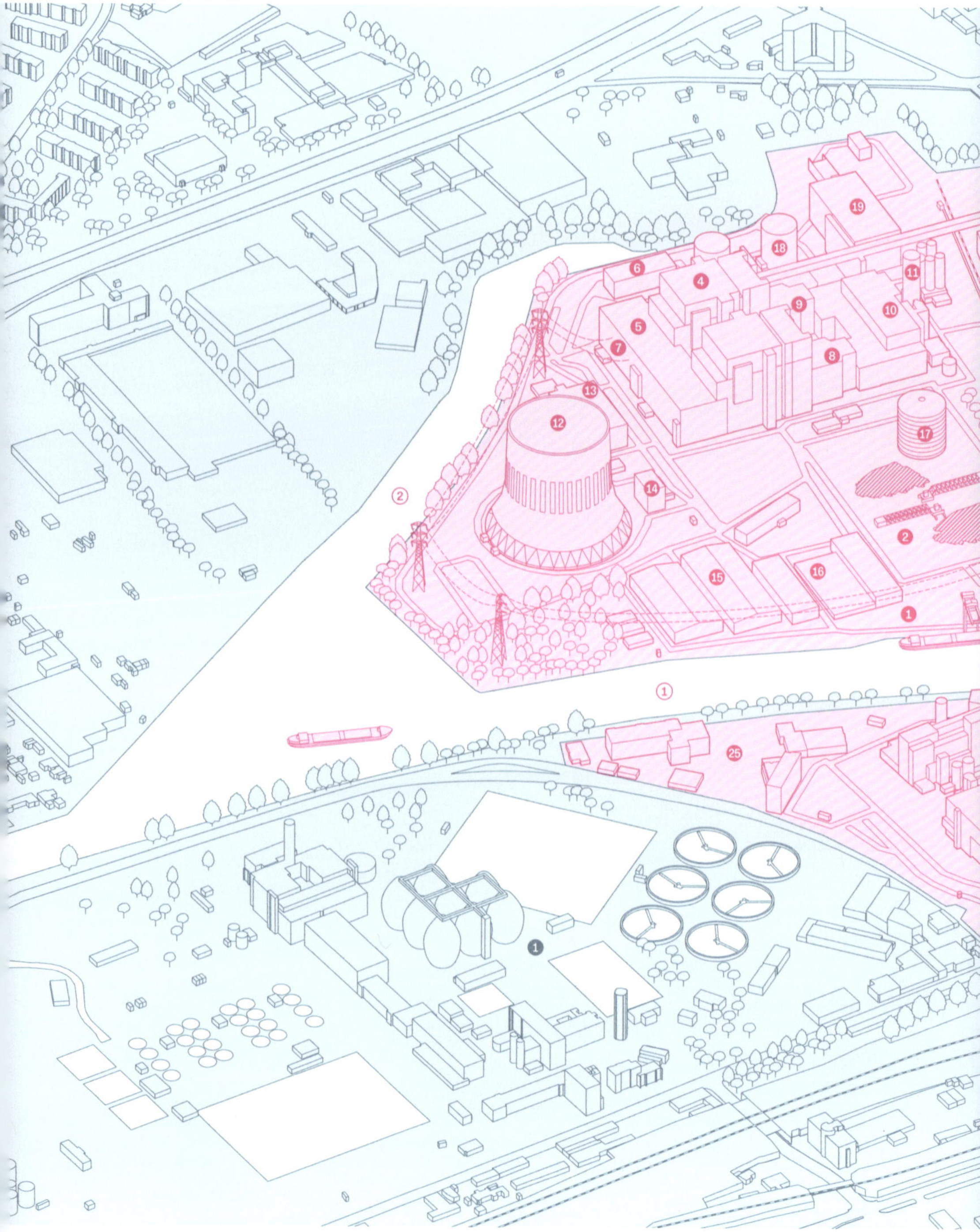

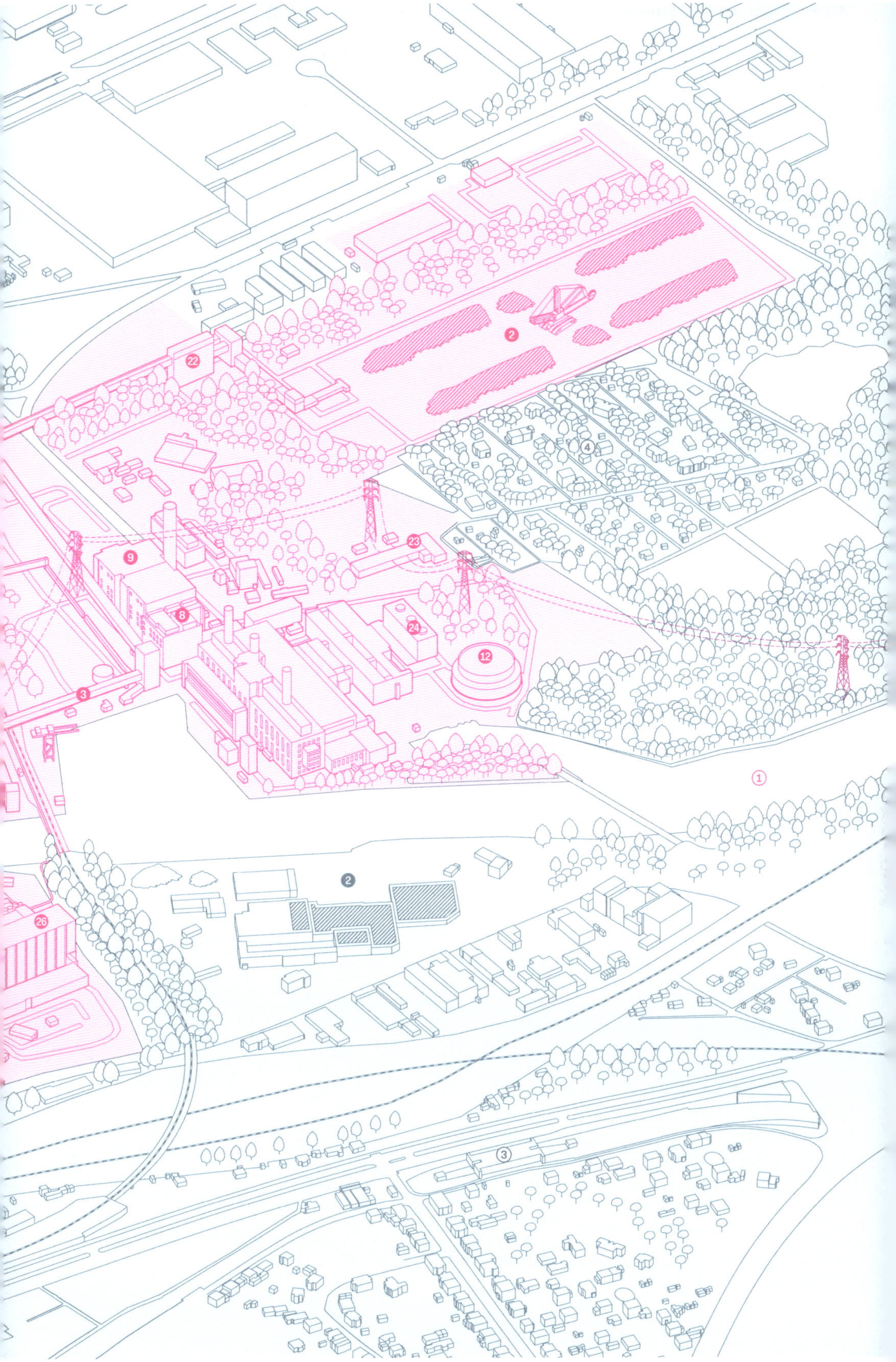
2
22
4
9
23
8
24
12
3
1
2
26
3

Fig. 29 Rostock coal terminal

1 Grain terminal
2 Bulk terminal
3 General cargo
4 Oil terminal
5 Customs office
6 Liebherr Rostock

1 Rostock power station
2 Loading station
3 Reclaimer
4 Gantry crane

Railways
Conveyor belts
Coal-related areas
Coal

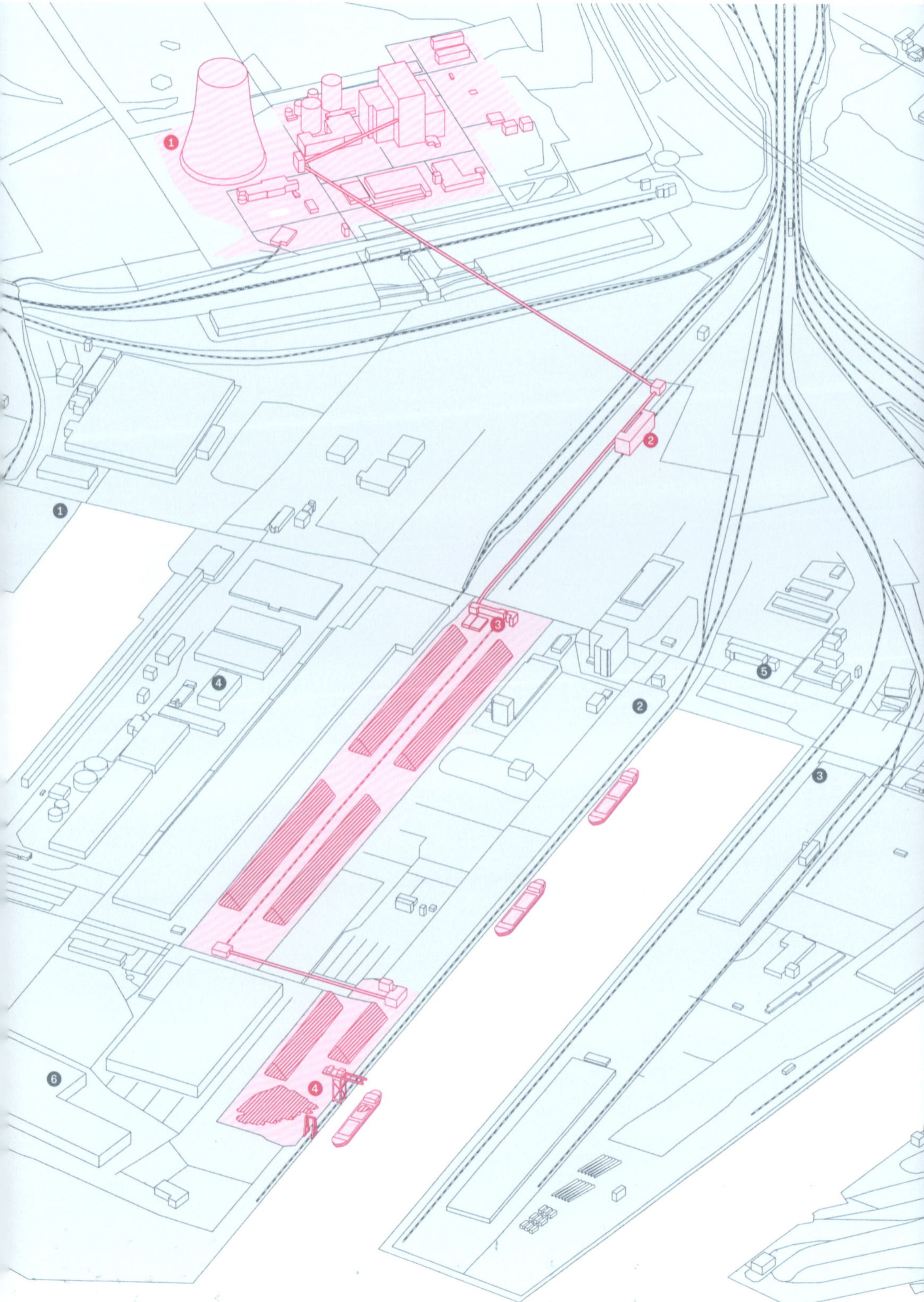

Oil

3.3

3.3.1

Introduction to Oil

David Bauer
Joseph Smithard

Oil, unlike any other substance, has drastically transformed the globe. The influence of its refined products can be traced everywhere. Oil is in the clothes we wear, the food we eat, the cosmetics we use, the air we breathe, the streets and houses that we live in, and in the Great Garbage Patch floating in the oceans.[1] Without oil, the global landscape would would look entirely unrecognisable. Without it, the ability to capture imagery of our world as we currently recognise it would have remained an unattainable feat. The snapshots of the "Blue Marble", captured from the vantage point of outer space, underscore the profound influence that oil has exerted in shaping our collective perception of the Earth. Dethroning "King Coal" as the world's primary energy source after the Second World War, oil rose to prominence as the pivotal player in global politics and economics, powering the world's machinery. According to the annual energy statistics published by British Petroleum, over the last 56 years, the world has consumed around 186,286,000 t of crude oil, and despite several significant discontinuities, multiple crises, and predicted peaks in global production, overall consumption has continuously increased.[2] As a result, the profound impact of this rise on the spatial configuration of the Earth's surface cannot be overstated.

Fig. 1 World oil consumption, 1965–2023 in TWh

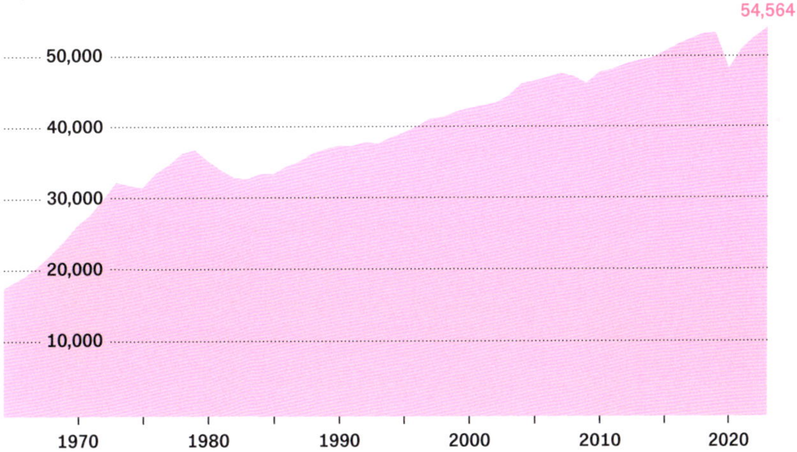

Oil has fundamentally reshaped mobility and transportation, connecting distant locations through intricate infrastructural frameworks that facilitate the circulation of resources, goods, and people within a globally interconnected network. Through this, it has accelerated the trends of global urbanisation, arguably causing the most significant changes in land-use and land coverage observed in the past millennium. Primarily spearheaded by the evolution of the combustion engine used in automobiles and ships, petroleum derivatives have established themselves as the primary fuel source for virtually all vehicles worldwide. The desire for permanent—and, moreover, permanently cheap—mobility fuelled the modernist architectural imagination, emphasising a new world where the boundaries between city and country would blur and unify manmade environments.[3] Today, the global reach of oil distribution networks and infrastructures has led to an extended form of urbanisation which encompasses the entire planet, erasing any meaningful distinction between the urban and non-urban.[4] Unrestricted mobility, whether in the form of daily commutes over long distances or annual holidays in far-reaching tourist destinations, has cemented itself as a paradigm of personal necessity—a necessity largely formulated as the Western imperative of progress and wealth. Fuelled by oil, the global supply and commodity chain keeps the world's economies rumbling. Oil is not just moving us; more importantly, it moves the world around us, as unchallenged as gravity itself.

Fig. 2 Petroleum products obtained from crude oil

1	Gasoline	43%
2	Heating oil / diesel fuel	23%
3	Kerosene-type jet fuel	9%
4	Coke	5%
5	Heavy fuel oil	4%
6	Still gas	4%
7	Liquefied refinery gases	3%
8	Asphalt	3%
9	Petrochemical feedstock	2%
10	Lubricants	2%
11	Kerosene	1%
12	Other	1%

The landscapes involved in oil's production and distribution encompass a vast array of physical spaces—ranging from extraction fields, mega refineries, floating supertankers, and continental pipelines to company HQs located in sky-high tower blocks.[5] These spaces are often unevenly concentrated, with some regions bearing the brunt of the most harmful environmental and social impacts. Besides the ongoing wars that destabilise entire regions, the most adverse effects that coincide with the rise of oil include a long and frequent series of uncontrolled spills, severe and irreparable pollution of entire ecosystems, as well as the displacement of local and Indigenous communities.

Consequently, whatever evolves in tandem with oil is likely to stay entangled with it. The case of petrochemical extraction and refinement is much like that of other extraction sites. It has given economic boosts to regions, cities, and towns that are characterised primarily by their remoteness, with low levels of sectoral diversification within the local employment population and a high dependency on one trade. Industrial oil hubs, meanwhile, are literally on the needle and, in most instances, do not have the investment power to reimagine, or even to speculate about, remodelling themselves into an alternative and sustainable future beyond petroleum. Today, the massive wealth generated by oil gives face to many urban and financial centres, and is integral in developing some of the most prestigious and daring projects built within the last century. However, beyond football stadiums, fantastic façades, and entire new desert cities, oil has driven the expansion of some of the most common high street typologies found in any urban setting.

Due to its material properties and the processes involved in its extraction, production, and distribution, oil is incredibly dependent on its technical infrastructure setup, with vast spatial and political dimensions operating simultaneously and at multiple scales.[6] Along its path of commodification from a crude resource to a refined product, oil crosses various geographical and political boundaries while continuing to be dominated by a small number of cartels, as well as the foreign investment of transnational players and financial institutions. However, its network is contingent on both small and large businesses as well as national governments with differing degrees of control over land and funds. While “big oil” predominantly operates on an “extra-state” scale, governments are nonetheless needed to provide access to sites and resources, meaning exporters are reliant on national infrastructures, policies, legal frameworks and, most importantly, on citizens as consumers.[7]

Fig. 3 Largest oil and gas companies by revenue, 2022 in billion $

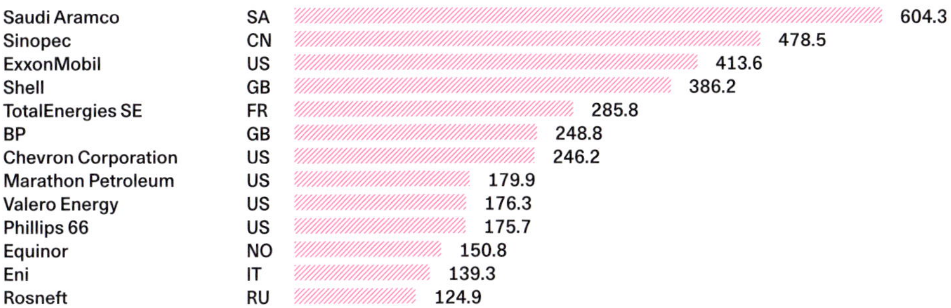

The rise of “big oil” presented a unique opportunity to unite economic, political, and symbolic power to such a degree that it has proved highly robust in accelerating its output and controls. Powerful industry operators, supported by politically powerful nations, have successfully consolidated the sector, investing in advanced technical innovations and professional knowledge. At the same time, oil companies are, in all probability, the most unyielding enablers of global pollution in the history of mankind, with a colossal share in the acceleration of irreversible climate change and ecosystem degradation on an unprecedented scale.

Although investments in the oil sector have fallen sharply worldwide since 2014, the thirst for petrochemicals has suddenly resurfaced at a time of global precarity. In 2022, capital expenditures in the oil and gas upstream sector surged by 39 %, marking the highest level observed in eight years and representing the most substantial year-on-year gain on record.[8] However heavy the backlash may be, just as with coal, oil production has to cease eventually, and this sooner rather than later. According to a forecast by the IEA, global oil demand is projected to decelerate notably between 2022 and 2028 as the energy transition advances. Despite the prospect of an imminent peak in oil demand before the end of the decade, the continued growth in petrochemical feedstock and air travel is expected to drive overall consumption from 102,000,000 in 2023 to 105,700,000 barrels per day by 2028, after which it will gradually decline. This decline is attributed to the shift towards lower-emission energy sources, the focus on energy efficiency enhancements, and the rapid proliferation of electric vehicle EV sales.[9]

3.3.2

Properties, Production, and Supply

David Bauer
Joseph Smithard

Crude oil, also known as petroleum, is a naturally occurring liquid commonly found in the upper layer of the Earth's crust. It is composed largely of a complex mixture of different hydrocarbons and a group of organic compounds which, as their name implies, consist of long chains of hydrogen and carbon atoms. While these chains store a significant amount of energy and make crude oil a potent fuel, it is the broad mixture of different hydrocarbons—ranging from small, simple molecules like methane to large, complex molecules like heavy oils and tars—that give petroleum a wide range of applications in chemical production.[10] Crude oils are categorised by density and sulphur content. High density oils are "heavy", and low-density oils are "light". Low sulphur oils are referred to as "sweet", and high sulphur oils are referred to as "sour".

Debate among the scientific community about the origins of oil is divided between two major camps.[11] A predominant part of the scientific community endorses the biogenic theory, which suggests that oil resulted from the accumulation of decomposed remains of marine and terrestrial paleofauna and botany that piled up in oxygen-deprived environments such as swamps, river deltas, and ocean basins. Over an inordinate amount of time, these organic materials were buried deeper and deeper, and were exposed to heat and pressure that caused them to undergo chemical changes and eventually transform into liquid hydrocarbons.[12] The theory suggests that all oil available on earth to this day would have been created between the Mesozoic, Palaeozoic, and Cenozoic Era, rendering it a finite commodity with geologically defined, fixed locations. [p. 95] While the biogenic theory has garnered considerable support, another more controversial hypothesis posits an abiogenic origin, proposing that oil arises from chemical reactions occurring among inorganic materials lurking in the depths of the Earth's mantle and crust. Though it does not discount the planetary forces at play, and the colossal timescales involved, the abiogenic theory contends that oil is constantly being generated deep within the Earth, with hydrocarbons migrating upward and amassing in subterranean reservoirs.[13]

What Makes Oil?

Oil is what it is because of how it is.[14] Many factors have contributed to its rise, but none more so than its molecular makeup. It has become one of the most valuable commodities in the world and its chemistry holds the key to its supremacy.

Firstly, oil has a comparably high energy density, resulting from its chemical structure. In comparison to other fossil fuels, such as coal and natural gas, it contains a higher proportion of hydrogen within its molecules. As a result, it possesses a significant energy density, allowing for the storage or transportation of a greater quantity of energy within a given volume.[15] [Fig. 4]

Secondly, the fluid nature of oil renders it highly amenable to transportation across long distances. This means that it can be facilitated by a broad and complementary range of infrastructural means. Furthermore, this attribute allows for the storage of significant quantities, in diverse containers and tanks, over long periods and with little maintenance.

Thirdly, the complexity of oil's chemical composition lends itself as an accompaniment to its versatility. Besides being the industry standard for energy conversion, many of its integrated substances are used to produce basic materials and primary commodities. Oil is not just a fuel that stills our hunger for energy, it likewise fuels our addiction to plastics, as well as countless other materials, since it embodies thousands of varieties of products and goods. Nonetheless, on average over two thirds of a barrel of oil is converted into gasoline, diesel, and kerosene.[16] [Fig. 6]

Fig. 4 Typical composition of crude oil by weight in %

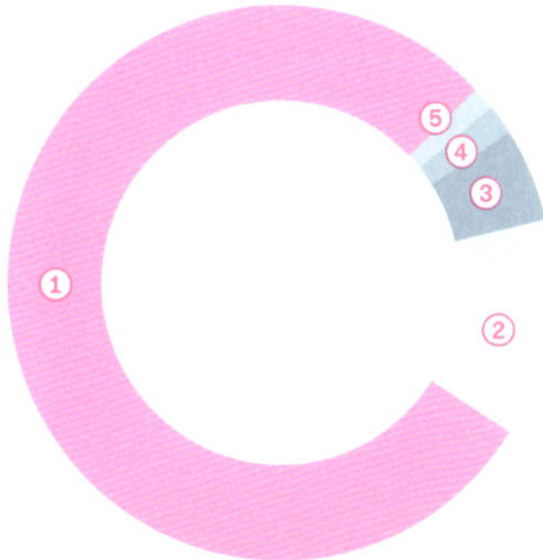

1	Carbon	83–87 %
2	Hydrogen	10–14 %
3	Sulphur	0.1–6 %
4	Nitrogen	0.1–2 %
5	Oxygen	0.1–2 %

A final noteworthy property is its geography. Oil reserves are found in concentrated deposits in specific regions around the world, such as the Middle East and the Americas. This is in stark comparison to coal, the primary energy source throughout the 19th century, which was widely available in many regions. Historically, coal's distribution was highly decentralised. The technology for its extraction and use was relatively simple and facilitated the possibility of coal production being organised around locally owned mines and mills. Consequently, operation was often controlled by a diverse array of actors, including small businesses and municipalities. In contrast, and due to its relative geographical sparsity, oil has from its very beginning been in the hands of single, sizeable players that exert control over large regions. The technology required to extract and refine oil is more complex and more capital-intensive, requiring large-scale, centralised operations that are controlled by a network with significant financial and political power.[17]

Processing

Oil doesn't have much worth at the wellhead. To extract it from the darkness of the underground, and turn it into something "useful", is a capital-intensive process requiring complex methods of transmutation.[18] Resultantly, the global petroleum industry is structured into distinct sectors specialising in exploration, production, refining, transportation, and the marketing of crude oil. The bulk of these procedures take place in the mid- and downstream stages of production, shifting refinement processes and their facilities closer to the consumer. Furthermore, oil differs from both gas and electricity in terms of storage, transmission, and distribution since it can be transported via a broader range of infrastructures that include sea shipping, inland waterways and pipelines, as well as by rail and road. [Fig. 21]

Upstream

The upstream phase involves exploration, drilling, and separating oil from gas and mud. Exploration begins with aircraft or satellite surveys, followed by seismic surveys that provide geological detail. If recoverable oil is a likely prospect, exploration wells are drilled. The eventual fields are then operated by a consortium that holds the rights to land and state power. The extraction processes are categorised into two types based on the location of the fields: onshore and offshore.[19]

Onshore drilling facilities consist of a group of wells located in a field. The wellheads are connected by "gathering pipelines" which transport the oil and gas to a production and processing facility within the field. [Fig. 5]

Offshore drilling is applied in the marine context. It typically involves the use of a single platform that is either bottom-supported and fixed to the ocean floor, or mobile and floating, secured with anchors.

Many diverse methods of setting up a well have been established, but all include the stable construction of an outlet that allows for the extraction of oil through pressure or mechanical force. Crude oil is typically found in reservoirs of porous source rock and impermeable caprock. A conventional well is drilled vertically, and mud is injected to keep the hole open and counteract the pressure of any gas or fluid encountered. When a well is established for production, a casing is inserted and a "Christmas tree" valve is installed to control the flow of oil and gas. Once the oil is out, it undergoes treatments for standardisation. These processes occur close to the fields and include separating the oil and gas from water and contaminants, removing impurities, and adjusting the viscosity, ready for transportation and use. Stripping oil of unwanted substances is a persistent source of environmental pollution and degradation, not to mention considerable health concerns.

Fig. 5 Pump jack used to mechanically lift liquid out of the well, California, US

Midstream

Once extracted from the fields, crude oil enters the midstream sector, which covers the transportation, storage, and trading of unprocessed oil. In this context, there are two primary transportation methods: either through tankers and barges navigating interregional water routes or via transcontinental pipeline systems. The predominant mode of international trade relies on open-sea transportation, whereas pipelines are primarily utilised for domestic and intracontinental distribution.[20] Despite the efficiency of pipelines, the use of tank trucks and railroads remains prevalent due to the challenges of transporting oil to certain markets, particularly in remote areas. Due to its immense scale, the oil transport infrastructure serves not only as a network for oil dispersal but also as an interim storage facility, thereby increasing the overall capacity for storing oil beyond its natural reservoirs.

Oil storage is crucial in balancing out supply and demand. During price slumps, companies tend to increase their storage to prepare for increased demand, and these stored resources are then withdrawn when prices reach a peak. Aboveground tanks are utilised for crude and refined oil, as well as finished oil products. At times, the deployment of supplementary tanker ships in harbours is utilised, albeit this represents the costliest alternative for provisional storage. While at petrol stations, tanks are typically stored underground to reduce the risk of explosion.

Downstream

The downstream sector pertains to the final stages of commodification, encompassing refining and marketing. Refineries are typically located near urban areas or major industrial clusters to enhance the efficiency of product distribution and sales. Crude oil in its natural state goes through several distillation processes to be turned into petroleum products. The fundamental framework encompasses the processes of separation, conversion, and treatment.

To separate oil, it is heated to around 400 °C and passed through a distillation column. The lighter hydrocarbon gases are condensed to form gasoline, while medium-weight fuels, such as diesel, are drawn off at different levels of the column. Heavy molecules, such as fuel oil, condense at the bottom of the column. Within one barrel of crude oil, approximately 43 % is refined into gasoline, 23 % into heating oil and diesel fuel, and around 9 % into kerosene and jet fuel.[21]

Marketing oil products involves the distribution of refined products. Suppliers of crude oil and petroleum commodities direct their goods towards valuable markets, often meaning those that are closest. However, refining configurations, product demand, and geopolitical conflicts all have heavy influences on trade.

Fig. 6 Crude oil refinement process

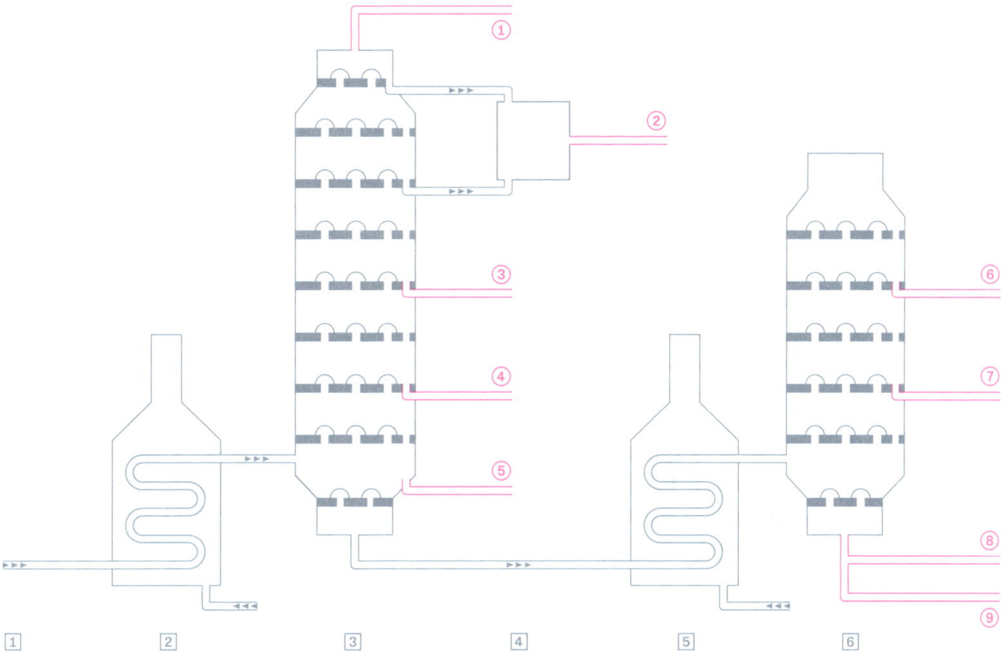

Processes
1 Crude oil intake
2 Furnace heating
3 Atmospheric distillation
4 Transfer of atmospheric bottoms
5 Furnace heating
6 Vacuum distillation

Final products
1 Liquefied petroleum gases
2 Gasoline
3 Kerosene / jet fuel
4 Heating oil / diesel fuel
5 Atmospheric gas oil
6 Heavy fuel oil
7 Heavy vacuum gases
8 Petroleum coke
9 Asphalt

Oil in the Local Context

David Bauer
Joseph Smithard

During the years 2022 and 2023, respectively, oil accounted for 35 % of Germany's energy usage, establishing it as the country's major energy carrier.[22] Only a small percentage of this, however, was utilised for power production and heating. The lion's share derives from the nationwide demand for mobility, namely oil's popularity as a transportation fuel.

Germany's reliance on oil and its derivatives is substantial, yet its domestic production is constrained, sourced from around 43 oilfields concentrated in the North Sea, with the majority (nearly 90 %) coming from just ten fields. The single largest one of them contributes 950,000 t/a, accounting for 56% of the total production.[23] Although this figure may seem high, it amounts to less than 2 % of Germany's yearly need. Indeed, the Federal Institute for Geosciences and Natural Resources BGR reports that Germany imported approximately 98 % of its primary mineral oil consumption.[24] This statistic emphasises that despite being one of the world's most notorious petroleum consumers, the nation is nevertheless desperately reliant on oil deliveries from around the world.

Fig. 7 Domestic oil reserves vs. annual consumption in Mt

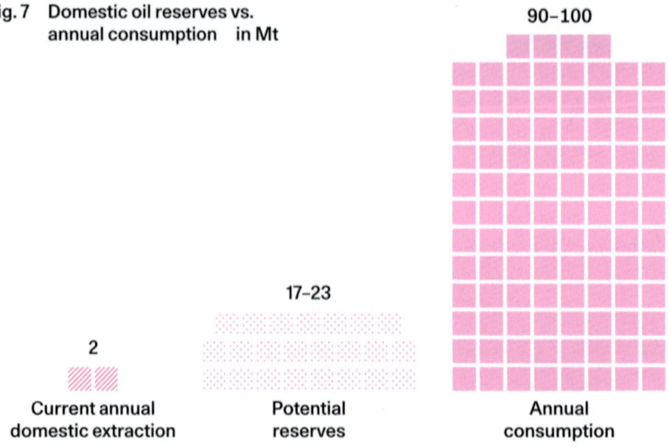

In 2022, Germany imported 88,000,000 t of crude oil through cross-border oil pipelines and ports.[25] The following year saw a decrease in imports by nearly 15,000 t, largely due to the significant impact of the Russian invasion of Ukraine on international energy markets and domestic industries. If all imports were to stop, the existing accumulation of oil within the national territory would—in a best-case scenario—sustain the state for a quarter of a year.[26] Since Germany is so heavily dependent on imports, mandatory oil reserves equating to at least ninety days of net imports are stored in caverns, tanks, and refineries around the country. Amounting to approximately 23,000,000 t, the reserves are primarily located in significant cavern storage fields and facilities in north-western Germany.[27]

Crude oil reaches the country through four transnational primary pipelines, as well as via the ports of Hamburg, Wilhelmshaven, Brunsbüttel, and Rostock. [Fig. 22] The national pipeline system is owned by the petroleum-refining industry and operates as the joint venture of several petroleum companies. An internal network of pipelines connects harbours, refineries, and storage containers.

The import and movement of oil into and within Germany operates across three primary sectoral systems. Oil from Rotterdam is distributed along the western backbone that spans Hamburg in the north and Ludwigshafen in the south. Oil from Trieste enters through Bayern and is transported via a southern cluster in the west to Germany's largest refinery in Karlsruhe, and to Burghausen in the east. Oil from Russia is sent via the Druzhba pipeline to the Petrolchemisches Kombinat PCK refinery, close to the town of Schwedt in Brandenburg [p. 158], with this later going on to connect with industrial hubs in the town of Leuna, Sachsen-Anhalt.

Germany's divided past has led to a peculiar infrastructural arrangement of oil and gas distribution that persists in the present. Besides the evidence of separation being traceable in pipeline clusters, the geopolitical scars of partition are still recognisable through the origins and supply routes of its oil carriers.

Prior to 2021, a significant share of BRD's oil supply relied on four major producers: the Russian Federation, the United Kingdom, the United States, and Norway. Of these, Russia held a prominent position, contributing nearly one-third of the total supply. This share, while diminishing after the onset of its military invasion of Ukraine, remained high at around 28 % at the end of 2022. However, in response to international censure and the European Union's imposition of an embargo on Russian oil, Germany announced the termination of its imports. In January 2023, only 3.5 kt of officially declared Russian oil reached the country, indicating a reduction of 99.9 % compared to the figures recorded in January 2022.[28] To counteract this decline, supplementary deliveries were arranged, primarily by increasing imports from Norway and the United Kingdom and by initiating the receipt of shipments from Kazakhstan through the existing infrastructure of eastern pipelines.[29] As per data from the German Federal Statistical Office, in May 2023, more than 875 kt of crude oil from Kazakhstan was imported, representing an increase of approximately 30 % compared to the corresponding month in the previous year.[30] Ensuring the continuous inflow of oil from the east is of geographic importance, as it sustains the operations of a hard-wired refinery and other facilities in East Germany, intricately linked to the complex and unalterable technical transport systems which have been in place for more than five decades.

Fig. 8 Monthly oil imports by selected country in kt/m

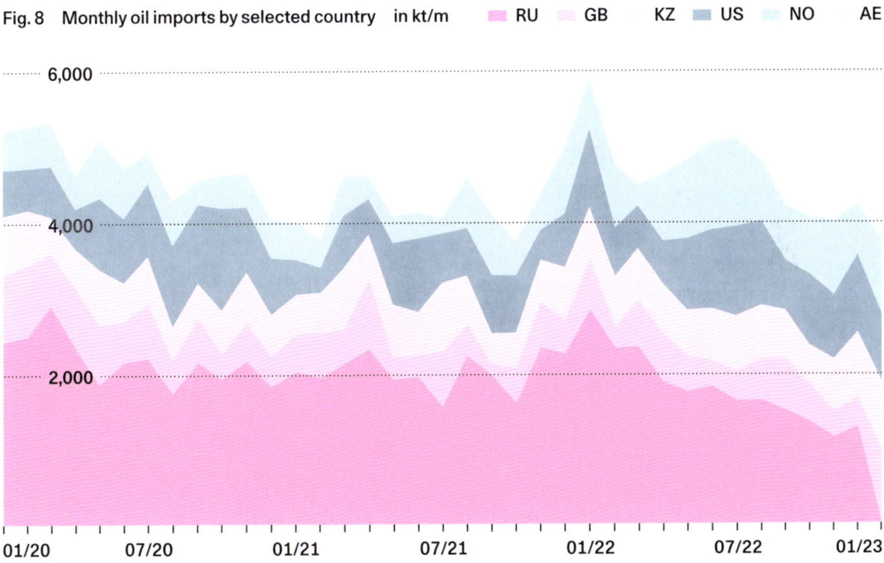

Berlin-Brandenburg

The state of Brandenburg is home to one of the epicentres of a major transcontinental oil network. The PCK refinery in Schwedt acts as a crucial node with two distinct functions. On the one hand, it is the traditional entry point for filtering Russian oil into the German market, thereby comprising a central hub for petroleum refining in East Germany. On the other, it simultaneously marks the end of one of the largest oil distribution systems in the world, the Druzhba pipeline.

The pipeline—which starts in Ufa, Russia—collects oil from Western Siberia, the Urals, and the Caspian Sea Region, before splitting into northern and southern branches. The PCK refinery is also connected to the seaport of Rostock, which delivers tanker oil through a specific line that they themselves own. The Schwedt refinery converts almost 12 % of all German oil imports, supplying an overwhelming majority of transportation fuels in the Berlin-Brandenburg region.

Fig. 9 Largest crude oil refineries by capacity in Germany, 2020 in Mt/a

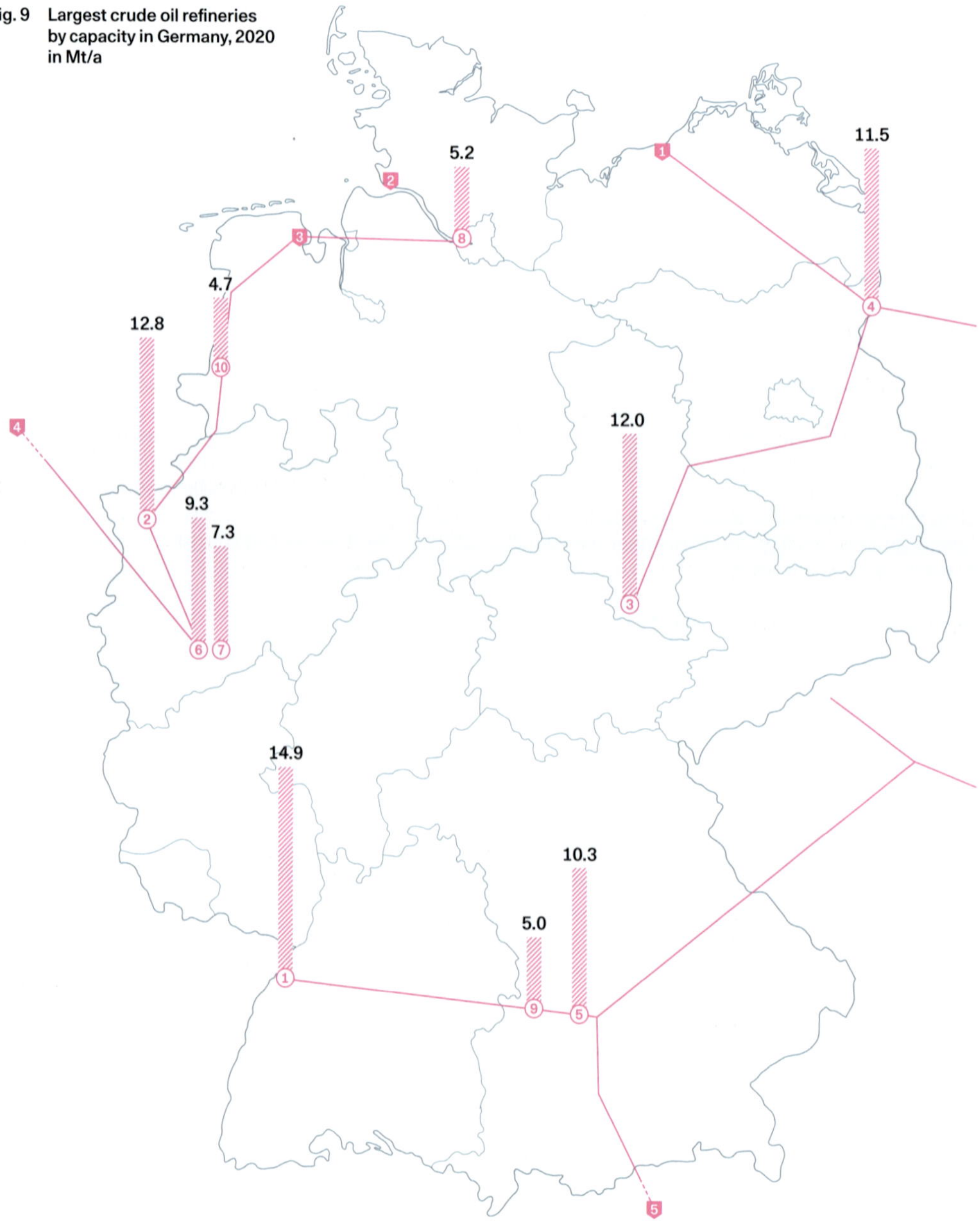

Refineries
① Mineralölraffinerie Oberrhein (Phillips 66, Esso, Rosneft, Shell)
② Ruhr Öl (BP)
③ Total Mitteldeutschland (Total)
④ PCK Schwedt (Rosneft, Shell, Eni)
⑤ Bayernoil (Varo, Rosneft, Eni, BP)
⑥ Rheinland Godorf (Shell)
⑦ Rheinland Wesseling (Shell)
⑧ Holborn Europa (Deutsche Tamoil)
⑨ Gunvor Ingolstadt (Gunvor Group)
⑩ Emsland (BP)

Sea ports
1 Rostock
2 Brunsbüttel
3 Wilhelmshaven
4 Rotterdam
5 Trieste

3.3.4

The Druzhba Pipeline

Joseph Smithard

The "Druzhba", or "Friendship Pipeline",[31] is one of the world's largest crude oil networks, crossing 45 major rivers, over 200 rail- and highways, and multiple neighbouring countries—with conflicting agendas. Spanning over 5,000 km, the pipeline begins at the purpose-built Russian city of Almetyevsk, where the oil from the largest arteries of Siberia, the Urals, and the Caspian Sea come together.[32] From Almetyevsk, the line travels to Mozyr in Belarus, where it splits into two branches going north and south. The northern section, Druzhba-1, runs through Belarus, Poland, and Germany, while the southern section, Druzhba-2, transports fuel to Ukraine, Slovakia, Hungary, the Czech Republic, and Austria. Through the collaboration of 20 transnational pump stations, the Druzhba has the capacity to pump more than 2,000,000 b/d.[33] In Berlin and Brandenburg alone, nine out of ten cars are powered by refined fuels imported through the Druzhba pipeline.[34] However, what began as a policy of rapprochement between the Soviet Union and its rapidly industrialising allies has evolved over the last three decades into an infrastructural instrument of aggression between once-trusted partners.

Fig. 10 Ownership of Druzhba pipeline and technical capacity in Mt

Oil for the Bloc

Rapid industrialisation after the Second World War and the death of Stalin in 1953 led to an unexpected phenomenon. The combination of the Soviet Union's skyrocketing energy needs and the desire of Stalin's successor, Nikita Khrushchev, to moderate the exploitation of the economies he controlled led to the Eastern Bloc satellite states becoming increasingly bold in expressing their energy interests and needs.[35] This led to a realisation: coal, the former carrier of choice, could no longer cut it. However, emerging from the test fields of the Second World War was oil, a promising commodity with high energy density, versatility across industries, and relative ease of transport. Out with coal and in with oil was officially agreed upon by senior officials of the Soviet Union and its satellite states during a session of the Council for Mutual Economic Assistance CMEA held in Prague in 1958. By 1959, the DDR announced the "chemicalisation of the national economy"[36], and this subsequently transformed into a bloc-wide policy, leading to the construction of refineries in Schwedt, Bratislava, Płock, Százhalombatta, and Novopolotsk.

Soviet energy played a crucial role in maintaining cohesion within the bloc. But, while the Soviet Union possessed vast oil reserves, the rest of the bloc was resource-poor. Unlike coal, which was abundant across the regions and required relatively short haulage distances, the challenge lay in transporting oil across a union of countries that occupied nearly one-sixth of the Earth's land surface.[37] In the late 1950s, the highlighted fundamental infrastructure deficiencies across the bloc. Transporting oil along the existing rail and road network was simply too expensive. Feasibility studies into a pipeline alternative calculated that transporting 1 t of crude oil would cost 1.00 ĸ on a northern route and 0.91 ĸ on the southern route, compared to 3.2 to 3.5 ĸ by rail. In essence, pipeline transport proved to be three times cheaper than rail.[38] Consequently, the CMEA approved the Druzhba pipeline, which served as an infrastructural showcase for Soviet technology and signalled a return to harmonious relations across the member states.

Fig. 11 DDR stamp celebrating the Druzhba pipeline, 1966

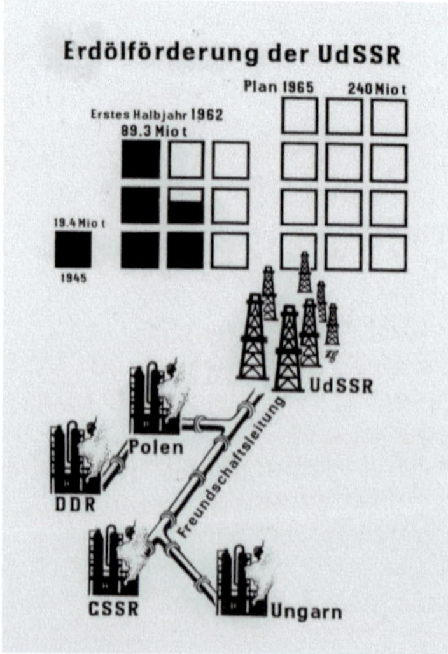

Fig. 12 Soviet oil production, exports and future projection, 1962

How Was it Made?

The construction of the pipeline was one of the first major international projects of its kind. In order to reduce construction costs, each participant was responsible for supplying certain parts of the required materials and machinery to all the other nations involved. The pipes for the pipeline were manufactured in the Soviet Union and Poland, while valves and fittings were sourced from the Czech Republic, pumps from Germany, and communication equipment and automation systems from Hungary. During construction, over 15,000,000 m^3 of earth were excavated along the entire route, and a total of 730,000 t of pipes were laid.[39]

Construction, however, faced significant challenges. In 1960, during the planning phase, poor steel production audits in the Soviet Union resulted in pipes with an inadequate diameter. The DDR was tasked with filling the production gap, but by 1962, it also faced its own steel shortage. Embarrassingly, to keep the Bitterfeld pipe factory operational, the DDR was forced to purchase 7000 t of steel from the BRD.[40] To compound the issue, later that year, the Berlin-Cuba missile crisis led NATO to ban pipe exports from member states to the Soviet Union. This move had a massive impact on the project, as over 80 % of imports came from the BRD.

Nonetheless, the first pipeline became fully operational in 1964, albeit one year behind schedule. Gradually, it reached capacity by 1966, leading to the proposal and construction of Druzhba-2. By 1973, the pipeline finally connected to the edge of the iron curtain with the DDR's refinery in Schwedt receiving oil.[41]

Cracks in the Friendship

After the collapse of the Soviet Union, the pipeline has remained a significant legacy of the Soviet energy system. However, this legacy presents both opportunities and constraints for Russia and the post-Soviet states as a political tool. Russia's position as a mono-supplier of oil has created a largely hub-and-spoke system, where oil-poor republics like Ukraine and Belarus have limited access to supplies from other oil-rich countries besides Russia, such as Turkmenistan, Uzbekistan, and Azerbaijan. Consequently, Russia has maintained a disproportionate level of power since 1991, not only as a supplier to these states but also as a gatekeeper for supplies.

Embargoes on oil, like the one imposed by Russia on Ukraine in the winter of 1994, have shown themselves to be an incredibly effective means of exerting influence. In retaliation, attempts by Belarus in 2007 and Ukraine in 2009 to raise the price of transit fees for Russian oil travelling west resulted in Transneft blocking the Pipeline, affecting the flow of oil to Germany, Poland, the Czech Republic, and Hungary.[42] Until this point, Germany's almost 40-year addiction to pipeline oil had never come into question. As a result, in an attempt to reduce its reliance on Russian oil, the German government openly sought alternatives to diversify its energy supply, actively investing in renewable and more autonomous technologies, such as offshore wind.[43]

In 2019, the pipeline was forced to cease operation for over two weeks due to contamination. Levels of organochlorine compounds, dozens of times over the acceptable limit, caused severe damage to the Mozyr refinery in Belarus. Despite not receiving any contaminated oil in Germany, the refineries in Schwedt and Leuna were forced to reduce production by 30 %.[44] The blame for the contamination remains unknown. However, the damage had an estimated impact of billions of dollars, with up to 5,000,000 t[45] (ca. 37,000,000 barrels[46]) of oil tainted, as well as the reputation of what was once a reliable distributor.[47]

The EU's 2023 embargo on Russian oil prompted Germany to pursue oil agreements with Kazakhstan, the United States and the Middle East.[48] Nevertheless, bypassing oil transport without fully utilising the pipeline remains a challenge. On the one hand, oil now arrives via the seaport in Rostock, but the pipeline from this terminal, with a capacity of 9,000,000 t, is insufficient to meet the needs of the refineries in Schwedt and Leuna.[49] On the other hand, Kazakhstan's authorisation to transport oil to Germany via the northern route of the Druzhba pipeline remains uncertain, as oil travelling west must flow through Transneft-controlled Russian territory.

Fig. 13 Construction of the Druzhba pipeline, 1972

3.3.5

Karachaganak and Monotown Aksay

Joseph Smithard

With confirmed hydrocarbon reserves across 300 oil fields and over 60 gas condensate fields[50], the Republic of Kazakhstan is among the top oil and gas-producing countries worldwide, behind only a few Middle Eastern and Latin American countries, Russia and the United States.[51] At the heart of its production is the Karachaganak field, [Fig. 25] one of the largest oil and gas fields in the world. Located in northwest Kazakhstan on the lower banks of the Ural River, it extends over more than 280 km^2 into the grasslands and steppe of the pre-Caspian Basin. Over millions of years, this once-massive Permian and Carboniferous reef complex has transformed into a vast deposit, estimated to contain 1,200,000,000,000 m^3 of gas and 1,000,000,000 t of crude oil.[52] Fast forward to the present day, and the Karachaganak Field serves as a key upstream reservoir, essentially the starting point of the pipeline(s), for oil destined for affluent economies across Europe, Asia, and the Middle East. It is so key, in fact, that Karachaganak accounts for 13,400,000 t/a of oil—roughly 15 % of the country's total production—and more than 19,000,000,000 m^3/a of gas—over 50 % of the country's production.[53] However, Kazakhstan's position as a gross exporter, with approximately 80 % of its oil and 60 % of its gas going to, or through, Russia and China,[54] means that negotiating a field such as Karachaganak comes with complex agreements, intricate infrastructural connections—spanning multiple countries, and meticulously planned monotowns built solely to extract oil and gas.

The Production Sharing Agreement

The Karachaganak field was discovered in 1979 when regional drilling operations revealed significant hydrocarbon reserves. The field's discovery resulted from exploratory drilling efforts conducted by the Soviet Ministry of Geology.[55] These drilling activities were part of broader exploration campaigns aimed at identifying and delineating hydrocarbon reserves in various regions of the Soviet Union. Within five years, under the operatorship of Karachaganakgazprom, "Unit 3"—a facility for separating and partially stabilising oil and gas—was built, meaning the field could begin supplying the Union with crude oil and gas derivates via the Karachaganak Orenburg Transportation System KOTS to the Russian industrial hub in Orenburg.[56] By 1990, around 200 vertical wells had been drilled, reaching a peak production plateau of 12,000,000 m^3/d of gas and 100,000 b/d of oil.[57] Unit 3 fed the field's demands of the Soviet Union until its dissolution in 1991, which marked a distinct change in the outlook for the Kazakhstani government and the Karachaganak field itself. In the immediate post-Soviet period in Kazakhstan, no environmental legislation existed.[58] Well blowouts, improper well abandonment, inadequate disposal of cuttings, absence of wastewater treatment systems, and a lack of general maintenance caused the field to seriously deteriorate, leading to a significant drop in production.[59] Kazakhoil, the new state-owned oil company, had inherited a facility it could not handle. To remedy the situation, in 1995 Kazakhoil – with its newfound market freedom – signed a Production Sharing Principles Agreement PSPA with British Gas, the Italian General Petroleum Corporation (Agip now ENI), and Russian state-owned Gazprom (now LUKOIL). BP, Agip, and Gazprom began to rectify the situation by decommissioning 32 wells, beginning soil remediation practises, and reducing gas flares.[60] By 1997, a Final Production Sharing Agreement FPSA was signed with the existing partners and the US corporation Chevron.

Karachaganak Petroleum Operating

Under the name Karachaganak Petroleum Operating B.V KPO, a 40-year production-sharing agreement within the consortium led to a multi-stage construction process, establishing multiple connections across international pipelines and transport networks.[61] Alongside the renovation of Unit 3, the Karachaganak Processing Complex KPC was constructed in 2001, which also included a 120 MW power station on the site. [Fig. 26] With the construction of the KPC and the need for a larger workforce, KPO built a 28 km rail link to the purpose-built Soviet Monotown Aksay, where they also established their headquarters.[62] Streamlining the industry led to a significant increase in production. However, consequently, the existing five-pipeline, 140 km KOTS system to Orenburg could not meet the rising requirements of increased production.

Fig. 14 Karachaganak Processing Complex

In 1992, the Republic of Kazakhstan and the Sultanate of Oman signed an agreement to establish the Caspian Pipeline Consortium CPC, a 1,500 km pipeline transporting Caspian oil from the Tengiz field—Kazakhstan's largest oil field—to the Novorossiysk-2 Marine Terminal at the Russian Black Sea.[63] As with the Karachaganak field, this project was unachievable without foreign support. Later, in 1996, the Russian Federation joined the two existing states, along with a consortium of eight private shareholders representing the interests of seven major oil-producing companies.[64] The states and companies involved practically mirrored those already signed to the Field's existing FPSA. As a result, it became paramount that the Karachaganak field would connect to the CPC in the south and the Druzhba in the north. [p. 167] Coinciding with the competition of the KPC, a 650 km pipeline corridor, known as the Karachaganak Atyrau Transportation System KATS, was connected in 2003, establishing two new major distribution points. Atyrau in the south now pipes oil to the Black Sea via the CPC, and the Bolshoi Chagan pumping station near the Urals now sends oil to the Druzhba. To complement this process in the early 2010s, a second processing facility, known as Unit 2, was also built.[65]

How is it Made?

Under the current system, oil is extracted from 118 production wells. Karachaganak is known for its high content of naturally occurring hydrogen sulphide, referred to as sour gas, which must be removed. This sour gas is pumped to the facilities at Unit 2, where it is separated and processed. The pressurised gas is then distributed back into injection wells. This process causes the gas to expand laterally through porous rock, exerting pressure on underground reservoirs and pushing up further oil reserves. Additionally, due to its quality, the oil extracted from the wells undergoes a stabilisation process. This involves partially distilling "live" crude oil into a "dead" or stabilised crude oil by removing light hydrocarbon components and reducing vapour pressure. Stabilisation renders the oil suitable for storage in atmospheric tanks and transportation through pipelines. Unit 3 and the KPC then serve as the main production hubs, channelling hydrocarbons into different production lines designated for onsite power production and transport to domestic and international markets.[66]

Fig. 15 Kazakhstan oil trade, 1990–2023 in Mt

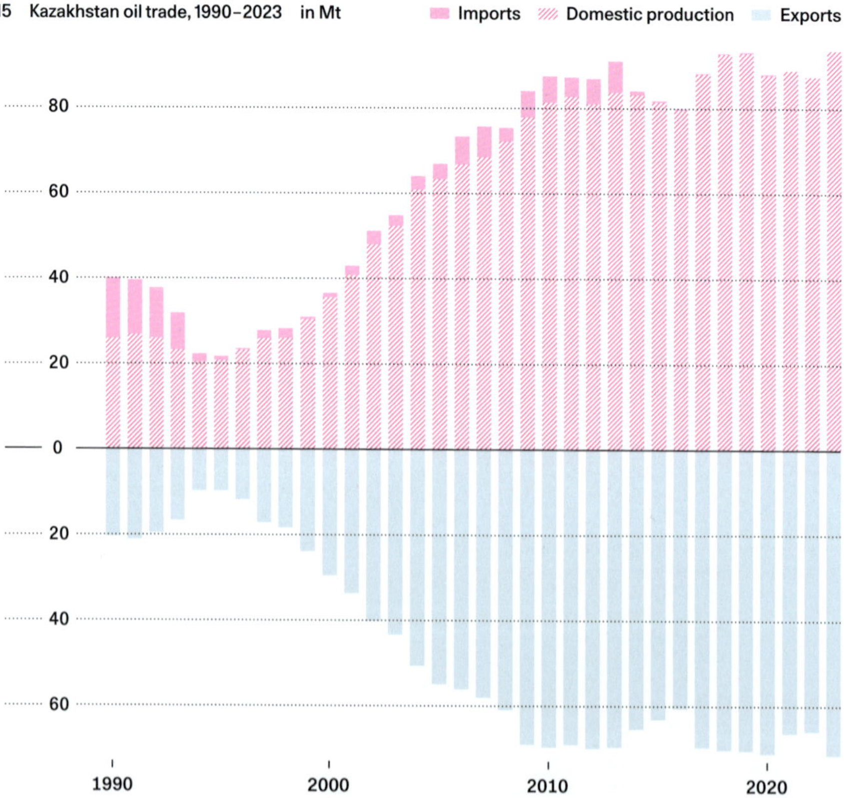

Monotown Aksay

Oil and gas extraction demands a highly specialised and trained workforce. Additionally, since these resources are frequently located in remote and harsh environments, a unique form of urbanisation has emerged, centred around extraction and extraction alone. Monotowns represent an extreme case of specialised settlements, where socio-economic development heavily relies, if not entirely, on the performance of one key enterprise that defines the town's identity. Many of these towns, particularly in the former Soviet Union, were established to process raw materials and metals.[67] Workers were enticed to unthinkable locations by attractive wage arrangements and state support measures. This resulted in the formation of large urban communities centred around factories, mines, and pits. Consequently, residents either worked directly in the town's main industries or provided services to support those who did.

Aksay is a monotown, and without the Karachaganak field, there wouldn't be much of Aksay. Situated approximately 15 km southwest of the field, Aksay's growth since the discovery of oil and gas in the late 1970s has been closely tied to the fortunes of this single extractive industry, both in the past, present, and likely in the future. There was life before oil. Initially founded in 1936, the settlement sprung up around a train station along the Uralsk to Sol-Ilietsk railway line, strategically located close to the Russian border. Originally named "Kazakhstan", the town subsisted almost entirely on local farming and the maintenance of the rail network.[68] However, with the discovery of oil and gas in 1979, Aksay changed in an instant. No longer just a stop along a remote railway line, it became the natural choice for housing the incoming workforce of the Karachaganak field. Accordingly, the town's population tripled throughout the 1980s.[69] [Fig. 16] Engineers and professionals from Soviet bloc countries, including Czechoslovakia, Bulgaria, Hungary, and the DDR, were brought to the region. Their task was not only to establish the technological infrastructure required for oil extraction but also to expedite the much-needed expansion of the city.

Several micro-districts with multi-storey residential buildings began to develop. These were complemented by a comprehensive social and municipal infrastructure, including schools, kindergartens, shopping and entertainment centres, sewage treatment plants, and advanced road networks.[70] A large portion of this infrastructure was built by a foreign workforce, who often applied the construction standards of their own countries. This led to the implementation of nation-specific typologies of prefabricated housing systems. Some of these typologies remain intact today, giving rise to districts in Aksay known as the "DDR housing" or the "Czech town".[71] [Fig. 27]

Despite the wealth brought about by the extraction industry, producing chemicals and processing hydrocarbons in the nearby field drastically heightened water and air pollution. The absence of environmental legislation in Kazakhstan, which persisted well into the aftermath of the Soviet period, resulted in a series of large-scale accidents in the field. This, in turn, spread increased levels of airborne chemicals to neighbouring areas like Aksay in the 1990s, primarily due to the low efficiency of gas-cleaning devices.[72] In the region, decisions such as shrinking the Sanitary Protection Zone SPZ to only 3 km left the inhabitants of the Berezovka and Bestau villages [Fig. 25], situated between the field and Aksay, exposed to constant and severe health hazards—while also depriving them of any legal basis for resettlement. Confrontation arose between residents and non-governmental organisations on the one hand, and the authorities and leadership of KPO on the other, eventually leading to the extension of the SPZ and the clearance of these two settlements. As a result, residents were relocated to Aksay or other neighbouring monotowns around the field.[73]

Fig. 16 Population growth in Aksay

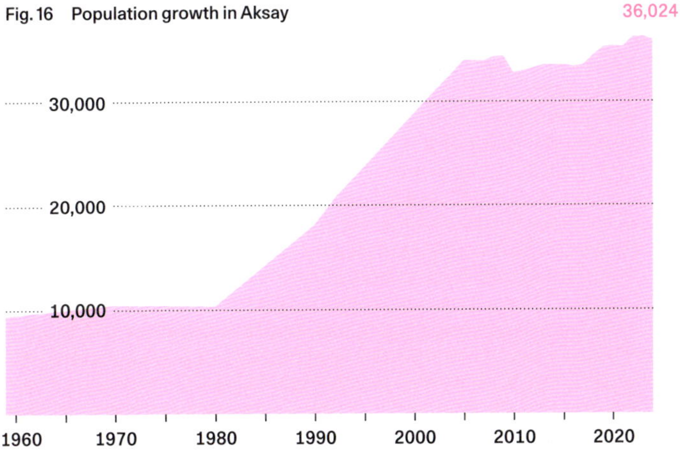

Ending Oil

As with so many other petroscapes, the city's growth and its inhabitants' outlook largely depend on the functionality of a single enterprise, and this balance will henceforth determine the level of its socioeconomic development. Looking towards the future, the combination of its relative remoteness and the global shift away from oil and gas leaves mono-production petroscapes like the Karachaganak field and Aksay particularly vulnerable to the changes that may be yet to come.[74] However, Aksay's immediate future appears relatively secure. Paradoxically, while Kazakhstan has made ambitious commitments to reduce its GHG emissions and increase the role of renewables[75], and many downstream recipients of Kazakh oil are beginning to roadmap their post-fossil fuel future, production and export continue to rise.[76]

The 2022 Russian invasion of Ukraine and the subsequent 2023 embargo on Russian oil underscore the precarious future of oil and its associated landscapes. The embargo had far-reaching effects, including the PCK refinery in Schwedt, which supplies the entire demand for crude oil in Berlin-Brandenburg, operating at only 50 % capacity.[77] In response, Germany swiftly negotiated a deal with Kaztransoil to deliver 100,000 t/m of oil to Schwedt until 2024.[78] However, from an infrastructural standpoint, almost all this oil must pass through Russia, further emphasising the historical path dependency, sunk costs, geopolitical role, and agency of fossil fuel infrastructure.

3.3.5

PCK and Schwedt

Santiago Martínez M.
Joseph Smithard

The PCK refinery in Schwedt is one of the biggest in Europe, accounting for one tenth of Germany's refining capacity.[79] Together with the Leuna refinery, it symbolises the industrial and chemical clout developed by the DDR after the Second World War. Although the town of Schwedt is now mainly known for its refinery, its history stretches back much further, with the first references to Schwedt appearing in 1265.[80] Positioned as the only crossing between Stettin and Oderberg, spanning the Oder River, Schwedt has long been a favourable site for farming and trade—and this remained the case until the advent of oil. Today, Schwedt is synonymous with petroleum production, having steadily expanded and contracted to meet the demands of this single pivotal industry.

The industrial character of the town is not a trait exclusive to modernity, however. Since the 17th century, one of the most prominent industries that shaped Schwedt's development was tobacco. Imported from France in 1686, the first factory was set up in 1787. By the end of the 19th century, public tobacco markets were held and some 13 tobacco producers were founded in Schwedt, as well as a steamboat company. Out of its 10,000 inhabitants, one third worked in either growing tobacco or in the cigar factories.[81]

Schwedt maintained a relatively steady size until the beginning of the Second World War. The town remained intact until the final months of Second World War. However, in 1945, during the defense of the Schwedt bridgehead, German troops were unable to withstand the advancing Red Army. The two-month battle left over 85 % of Schwedt's buildings in ruins. Reconstruction, now in the hands of the newly formed DDR, had a slow start but found a new lease of life through industrial development. The first paper factory, today known as LEIPA Georg Leinfelder GmbH, was founded in 1959. The year before, in 1958, the Erdölverarbeitungswerk EVW had been registered as a petroleum processing company for the first time in Schwedt, leading to subsequent construction work on a new refinery in 1960.

Fig. 17 Architectural model of the processing plant in Schwedt, 1959

The agreement for the Druzhba pipeline by the CMEA catalysed a period of continuous growth for Schwedt. Fully connected in 1963, with production starting in 1964 at an initial output of 2,000,000 t/a,[82] the pipeline marked the first time the entire Eastern Bloc was connected across the Iron Curtain. Between 1966 and 1969, the refinery expanded into natural gas processing, establishing additional facilities for gasoline and diesel. These included pipeline connections to Leuna (340 km) and to Seefeld (78 km), with the latter becoming the main supply channel for gasoline entering both East and West Berlin. The founding in 1970 of the Petrolchemisches Kombinat Schwedt PCK was followed by a period of intense modernisation and expansion. From 1972 to 1988, the refinery's provision was expanded to include, among others, an aromatic chemicals complex, a visbreaker plant, and the world's first high soaker cracking plant.

Schwedt's expansion as a relevant industrial centre in the DDR fostered migration from across the entire country. New housing developments, such as Neue Zeit, Talsand, Am Waldrand, and Kastanienallee sprung up around the city.[83] Since 1961, 13,897 apartments, 12 schools, 19 children's facilities, nine department stores, eight gymnasiums, and four medical centres were built. This culminated in a population boom that reached its peak by 1981, with around 52,500 inhabitants.[84] The town was becoming synonymous with the oil industry. By 1990, the extensive prefabricated, large panel system-buildings (*Plattenbauten*), housed over 50,000 people, highlighting Schwedt's prominence at the time.

Fig. 18 Construction of *Plattenbauten* (panel-system buildings) in Schwedt

In 1990, German reunification led to serious changes for PCK and Schwedt. The company was privatised and transferred over to Treuhand control. Its new owners included Veba Öl AG, DEA Deutsche Erdoel AG, and AET Petroleum. From 1991 to 1995 the refinery underwent substantial modernisation, becoming one of the most efficient refineries in Europe. By 1996, the Solomon Survey benchmarked PCK's refinery as having the lowest processing costs in all of Western Europe. However, ongoing economic upheaval and deindustrialisation in East Germany rendered it impossible for many small industries to adapt and survive.[85] Despite its long tradition, the tobacco industry could not be preserved. The paper industry, however, was able to endure through the founding of new companies, such as Haindl Papier Schwedt GmbH. The year 2001 brought with it the inauguration of a harbour at the Oder River, enhancing local capabilities for goods trading. In 2004, meanwhile, PCK split into two different companies: the PCK oil processing plant and the Schwedt GmbH Industrial Park.[86]

Today, the refinery has a production capacity of 12,000,000 t/a for crude oil distillation.[87] [Fig. 35] It maintains a particularly close relationship with Berlin since the city is highly reliant on its fuel. Nine in every ten vehicles in Berlin are powered with PCK fuels[88], which are distributed via the Seefeld pipeline and tanker cars to petrol stations. The Berlin-Brandenburg Airport also receives its supply of jet fuel from Schwedt via rail. Altogether, the refinery's outgoing products are dispatched by rail (66 %), pipeline (21 %), and truck (13 %).[89] [Fig. 34]

Notwithstanding the industry's survival, Schwedt's demographic dynamics could not be sustained. The town's population has been in constant decline since 1990, falling to around 30,000 inhabitants by 2021, which represents a loss of 40 %.[90] According to recent projections, the city stands to lose an additional 20 % by 2030.[91] This is owing, among other reasons, to fewer available jobs and a generally ageing population. Although the PCK refinery had 8,000 employees in 1990, by 2020 this number had decreased to 3,200.[92] This had a significant impact on the urban fabric, with vast housing vacancies leading to the demolition of complete *Plattenbauten* neighbourhoods, which have since been replaced with single-family houses. At the end of 2022, unemployment stood at 9.6 %[93] in comparison with the German national average of 5.4 %.[94]

Fig. 19 Mural of the PCK within the PCK compound in Schwedt, 2023

Currently, PCK operates with two affiliated companies in Brandenburg: Mineralölverbundleitung GmbH Schwedt MVL and PCK & elf Tanklagerbetrieb Seefeld GbR PETS. The first operates connections between the Druzhba, Rostock, and Seefeld pipelines, while the second runs fuel and oil storage facilities within the Berlin area to enable further distribution.[95]

The recent Russian invasion of Ukraine has led to significant changes for the refinery, as well as wider social and political unrest for Schwedt.[96] Shares of PCK, formerly owned by the Russian energy company Rosneft, were nationalised by the German Federal Government. The present overall ownership is split, with Rosneft Deutschland GmbH holding 37.5 %, Shell Germany GmbH with 37.5 %, and AET Raffineriebeteiligungs-Gesellschaft mbH with 25 %.[97] While the federal government has formally assured the subsistence of the local oil industry, its future is still to be determined. The suspension of oil provision through the Druzhba pipeline means that other routes—such as Rostock, Gdansk, and Kazakhstan—have now had to boost their supply.

Endnotes

1 Pyrek, “Review of Plastic Paradise”.
2 British Petroleum, Statistical Review of World Energy 2021. Authors' calculation of consumption taken from 1965–2021.
3 Blau, Rupnik, and Baan, “Baku: Oil and Urbanism”, 17.
4 See: Brenner, “The Hinterland Urbanised”.
5 See: *Hein, Space, Time and Oil.*
6 See: Yergin, *The Prize.*
7 See: *Hein, Space, Time and Oil.*
8 S&P Global Commodity Insights and International Energy Forum, “Upstream Oil and Gas Investment Outlook”.
9 International Energy Agency, “Oil 2023 Analysis and Forecast to 2028”, 8–9.
10 Chilingar, *Geology and Geochemistry of Oil and Gas,* 87.
11 See Höök et al., “Development of Oil Formation Theories and Their Importance for Peak Oil”.
12 Tissot and Welte, *Formation of Petroleum in Relation to Geological Processes. Timing of Oil and Gas Generation*.
13 Glasby, “Abiogenic Origin of Hydrocarbons”.
14 Mitchell, *Carbon Democracy,* 38.
15 Smil, *Power Density,* 108.
16 CAPP, “What Is Oil Used For | Uses for Oil and Petroleum Products”.
17 Mitchell, *Carbon Democracy,* 36.
18 Abdullah, “Oil Refining and Products”, 716.
19 Azar. “Oil and Natural Gas Drilling”.
20 International Energy Agency, “Oil and Natural Gas Logistics”.
21 Conte, “What's Made from a Barrel of Oil?”.
22 AG Energiebilanzen e. V., “Primärenergieverbrauch Jahr 2022”, 2.
23 Bundesanstalt für Geowissenschaften und Rohstoffe: “BGR Energiestudie 2023 – Daten und Entwicklungen der deutschen und globalen Energieversorgung”, 23.
24 Bundesanstalt für Geowissenschaften und Rohstoffe, “Deutschland – Rohstoffsituation 2021”. See also: Julian Wettengel, “Germany, EU Remain Heavily Dependent on Imported Fossil Fuels”.
25 Bundesanstalt für Geowissenschaften und Rohstoffe: “BGR Energiestudie 2023 – Daten und Entwicklungen der deutschen und globalen Energieversorgung”, 23.
26 Deutschlandfunk, “Erdgas, Erdöl, Kohle und Uran – Welche Rohstoffe hat Deutschland?”.
27 Bundesverband Erdgas, and Erdöl und Geoenergie e. V., “Erdölförderung Jahresbericht 2022”.
28 Destatis, “Crude Oil Imports from Russia down to 3,500 Tonnes in January 2023”.
29 Ibid.
30 Destatis. “Crude oil import volume from Kazakhstan in Germany from January 2021 to November 2024 (in 1,000 metric tons)”.
31 Druzhba is the Russian word for “friendship”.
32 Nato, “The Druzhba or ‘Friendship Pipeline’”, 2.
33 Reuters, “The Druzhba Oil Pipeline from Russia to Europe”, Reuters, 12 October 2022.
34 PCK, “Fuel for the Region: Top Refineries in Europe”.
35 Perović, “Creating a Common Energy Space: The Building of the Druzhba Oil Pipeline”, 323.
36 Perović, 324.
37 Britannica, “Soviet Union: History, Leaders, Flag, Map, & Anthem”, Encyclopædia Britannica, 2024.
38 Perović, 327.
39 Beltps, “History of Construction of the Druzhba Oil Pipelines System”, Beltps.com, 2016.
40 Perović, 329.
41 Nato, 3.
42 DW, “Nuclear Comeback? Merkel Puts Germany's Nuclear Phase-Out in Question”, DW, 1 July 2007.
43 Kuhbier, “Offshore Wind Power in Germany”, 2.
44 Kardaś, Szymon and Wojciech Konończuk, “Dirty oil: the greatest crisis in the history of the Druzhba pipeline”.
45 Yermakov, “The Domino Effect: Contaminated Oil in the Druzhba Oil Pipeline - Implications of the Incident for Russia and Europe”.
46 Warsaw Institute, “Druzhba Oil Pipeline Contamination Brings Russia's Transneft Into Disrepute”.
47 Kardaś.
48 Pandey, “Germany: How Does Its Kazakh Oil Deal Benefit Russia?”.
49 Kardaś.
50 Bealessio, Alonso, Mendes, Sande, Hascakir, “A Review of Enhanced Oil Recovery (EOR) Methods Applied in Kazakhstan”.
51 Anshool Deshmukh, “Which Countries Have the World's Largest Proven Oil Reserves?”.
52 Orizon, “Karachaganak Field”.
53 KPO, “KPO Sustainability Report”, 2021, 15.
54 International Energy Agency, “Executive Summary – Kazakhstan 2022 – Analysis”.
55 Yenikeyeff, “Kazakhstan's Gas: Export Markets and Export Routes”, 23.
56 KPO, “Export Routes”.
57 Hydrocarbons Technology, “Karachaganak Gas Condensate Field”.
58 KPO, “Environmental and Social Status of the Karachaganak Oil and Gas Condensate Field: Executive Summary”.
59 KPO, “Environmental and Social Status of the Karachaganak Oil and Gas Condensate Field: Executive Summary”, 5.
60 Ibid.
61 Yenikeyeff, “Kazakhstan's Gas: Export Markets and Export Routes”, 24.
62 KPO, “Milestones of Karachaganak Field Development”.
63 CPC, “Project Chronology”.
64 Yenikeyeff, “Kazakhstan's Gas: Export Markets and Export Routes”, 24.
65 KPO, “Milestones of Karachaganak Field Development”.
66 KPO, “KPO Sustainability Report”, 2021, 12–13.
67 Zupagrafika, "Monotowns: Soviet Landscapes of Post-Industrial Russia", Zupagrafika, 2021.
68 Aksay.kz, “Aksay”.
69 City Population, “Kazakhstan: Aqsai (Aksay)” https://www.citypopulation.de/en/kazakhstan/cities/.
70 Aksay.kz, “Aksay”.
71 Ibid.
72 Environmental Justice Atlas, “Karachaganak Oil and Gas Condensate Field, Kazakhstan”.
73 Ibid.
74 Kryukova et al., “Social-Economic Problems of Russian Mono-Towns”.
75 Kumenov, “Kazakhstan: Ambitious renewables agenda setting healthy pace”, Eurasianet.
76 Following the Russian invasion of Ukraine in 2022, Kasakhstan's oil exports rose by 10 % in 2023.
77 ZDF, “Schwedt: Raffinerie läuft ohne russisches Öl”, ZDF Heute. 2 January 2023.
78 Süddeutsche Zeitung, “Mehr Rohöllieferungen aus Kasachstan für Raffinerie Schwedt”.
79 Statista, “Crude Oil: Largest Refineries by Capacity Germany 2020”.
80 Pressestelle, “Stadtgeschichte: Stadt Schwedt/Oder”.
81 Pressestelle.
82 “Schwedt Refinery – A Barrel Full”.
83 Eddy, “The Refinery Standing Between Germany and an Oil Embargo”.
84 Landesbetrieb für Datenverarbeitung und Statistik Brandenburg, “Historisches Gemeindeverzeichnis 1875–2005”.
85 Eddy, “The Refinery Standing Between Germany and an Oil Embargo”.
86 Stadtwerke Schwedt, “10 Jahre Regionaler Wachstumskern Schwedt/Oder: Die Erfolgsgeschichte Einer Stabilen Wirtschaftsregion Mit Guter Infrastruktur”.
87 PCK, “Fuel For The Region: Top Refineries in Europe”.
88 PCK.
89 PCK.
90 Amt für Statistik Berlin-Brandenburg, “Bevölkerungsentwicklung und Flächen der kreisfreien Städte, Landkreise und Gemeinden im Land Brandenburg 2021”.
91 Eddy, “The Refinery Standing Between Germany and an Oil Embargo”.
92 Eddy.
93 “Der Arbeitsmarkt Im November 2022”.
94 Bundesregierung, “Arbeitsmarkt weiter robust”.
95 Mineralölverbundleitung GmbH Schwedt, “Geschichte: Mineralölverbundleitung GmbH Schwedt”.
96 rbb|24, “Politik und PCK-Management optimistisch über Zukunft der Raffinerie”.
97 Pressestelle, “Übernahme von PCK-Anteilen durch Rosneft | Stadt Schwedt/Oder”.

Fig. 20 Total crude oil production and exports by country, 2022 in Mt

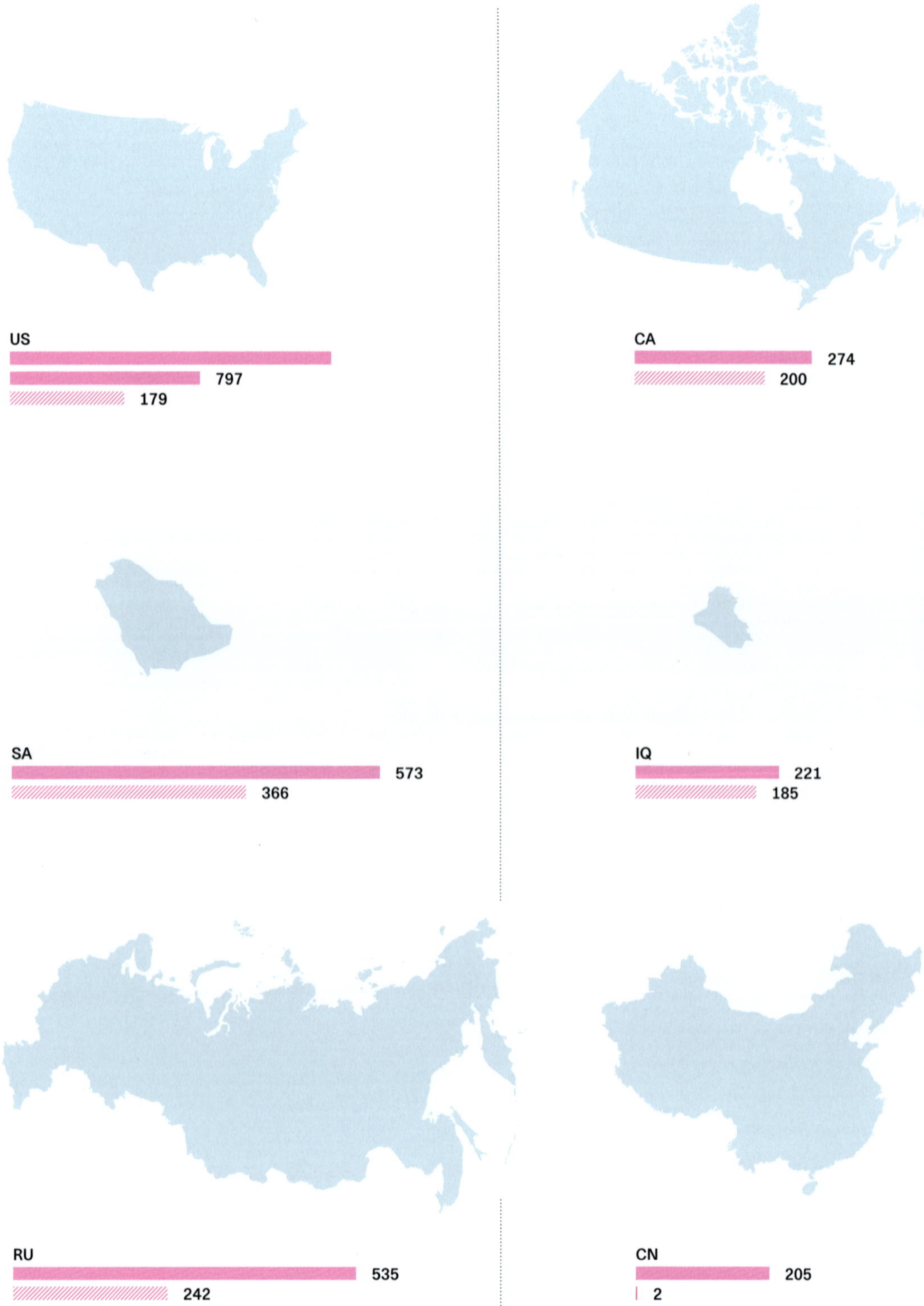

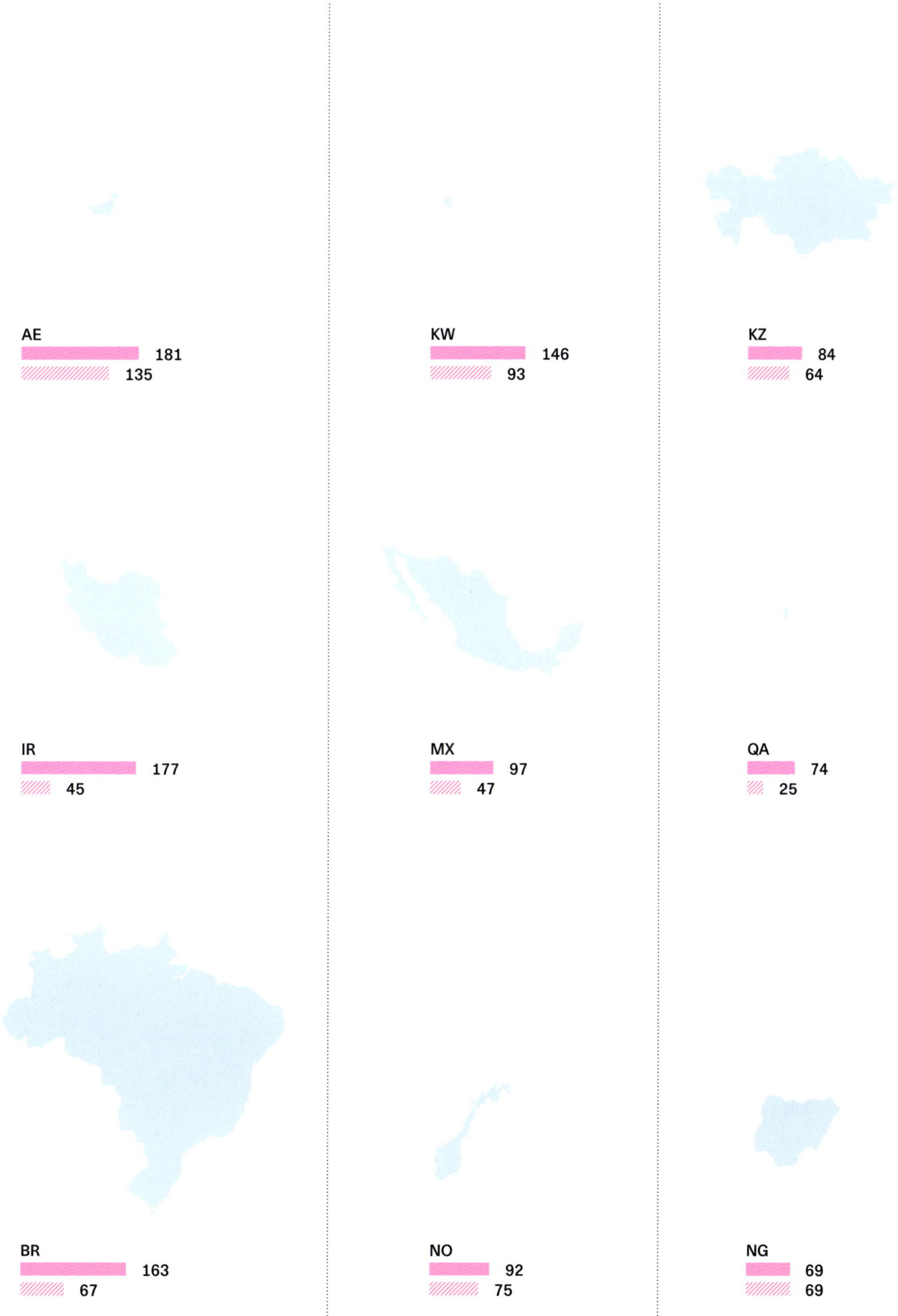
AE
181
135
KW
146
93
KZ
84
64
IR
177
45
MX
97
47
QA
74
25
BR
163
67
NO
92
75
NG
69
69

Fig. 21 Crude oil supply chain

Crude oil — Pipeline — Maritime — Railway — Road — Byproducts

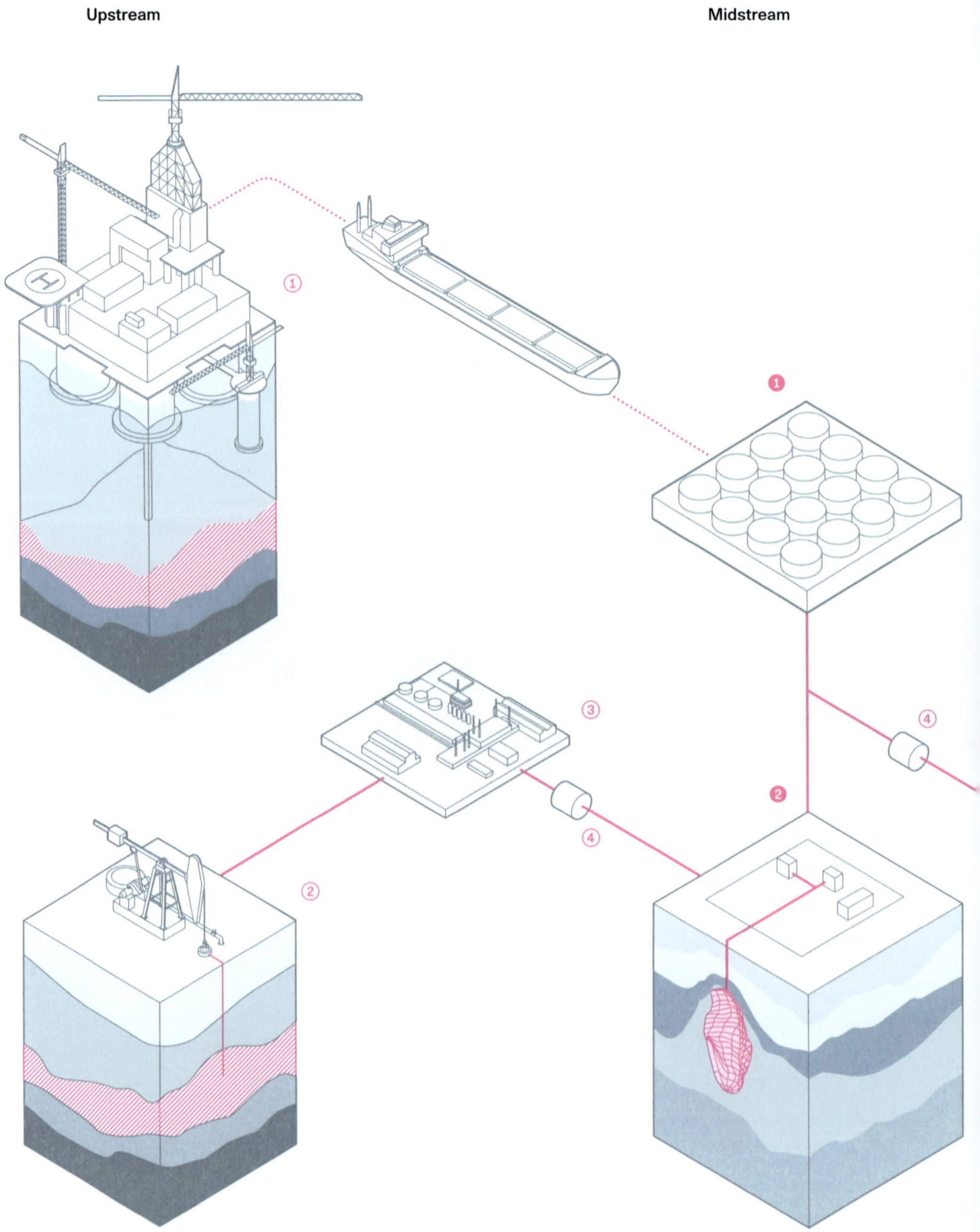

Production (NO, US, KZ, NR, LY, GB)

1. Offshore
2. Onshore
3. Processing plant
4. Pump stations

Transmission (DE)

1. Aboveground storage
2. Underground storage

Downstream

Consumption

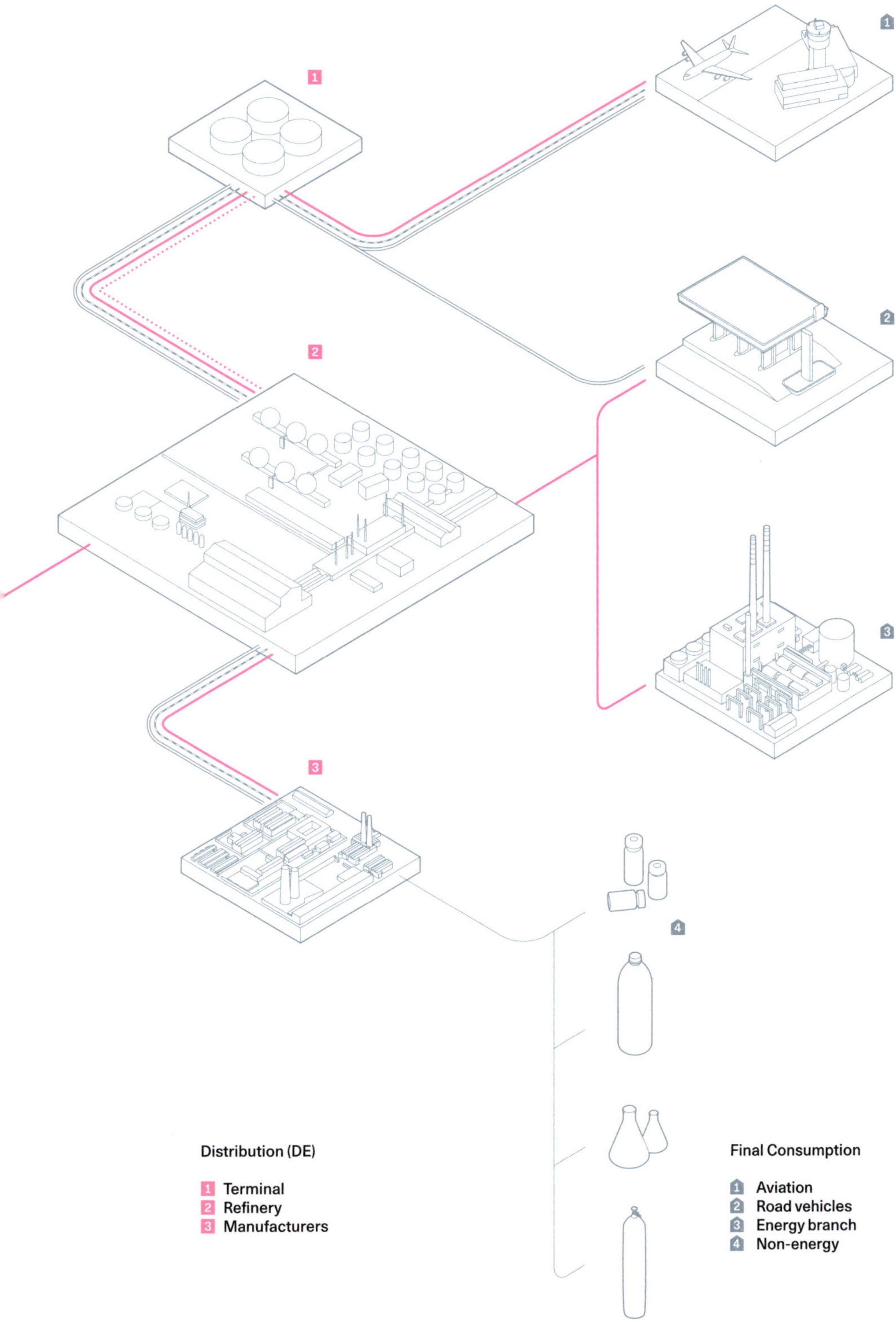

Distribution (DE)

1 Terminal
2 Refinery
3 Manufacturers

Final Consumption

1 Aviation
2 Road vehicles
3 Energy branch
4 Non-energy

Fig. 22 Global oil extraction and import routes

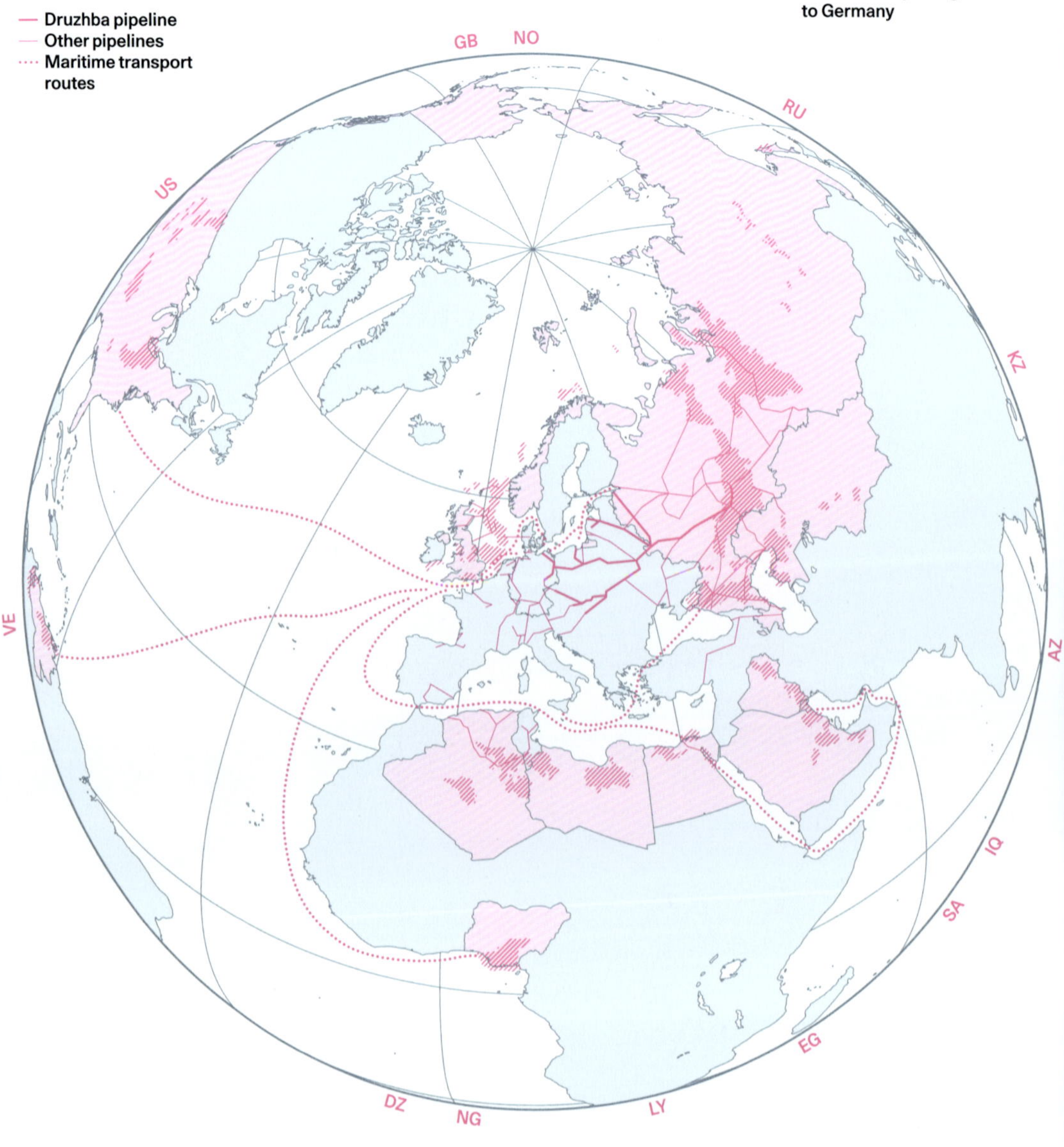

Fig. 23 Share of oil imports to Germany by selected country, 2022 and 2023 in %

	2022		2023
① NO	13.0 %	↗	18.3 %
② US	13.3 %	↗	18.1 %
③ KZ	9.8 %	↗	11.7 %
④ LY	5.8 %	↗	11.1 %
⑤ GB	7.6 %	↗	10.9 %
⑥ RU	25.5 %	↘	0.2 %
⑦ RoW	25.0 %	↗	29.7 %

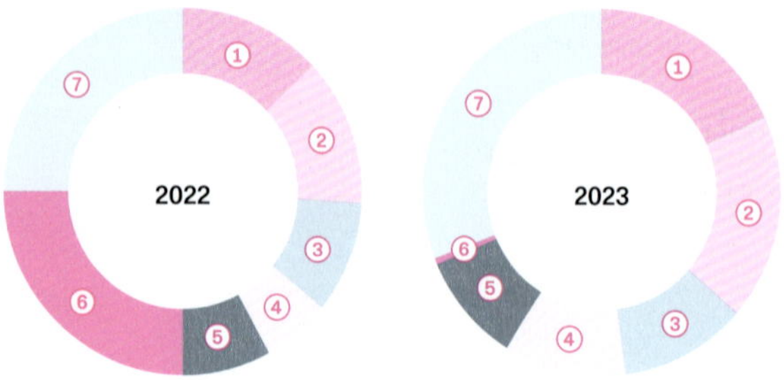

Fig. 24 Druzhba pipeline

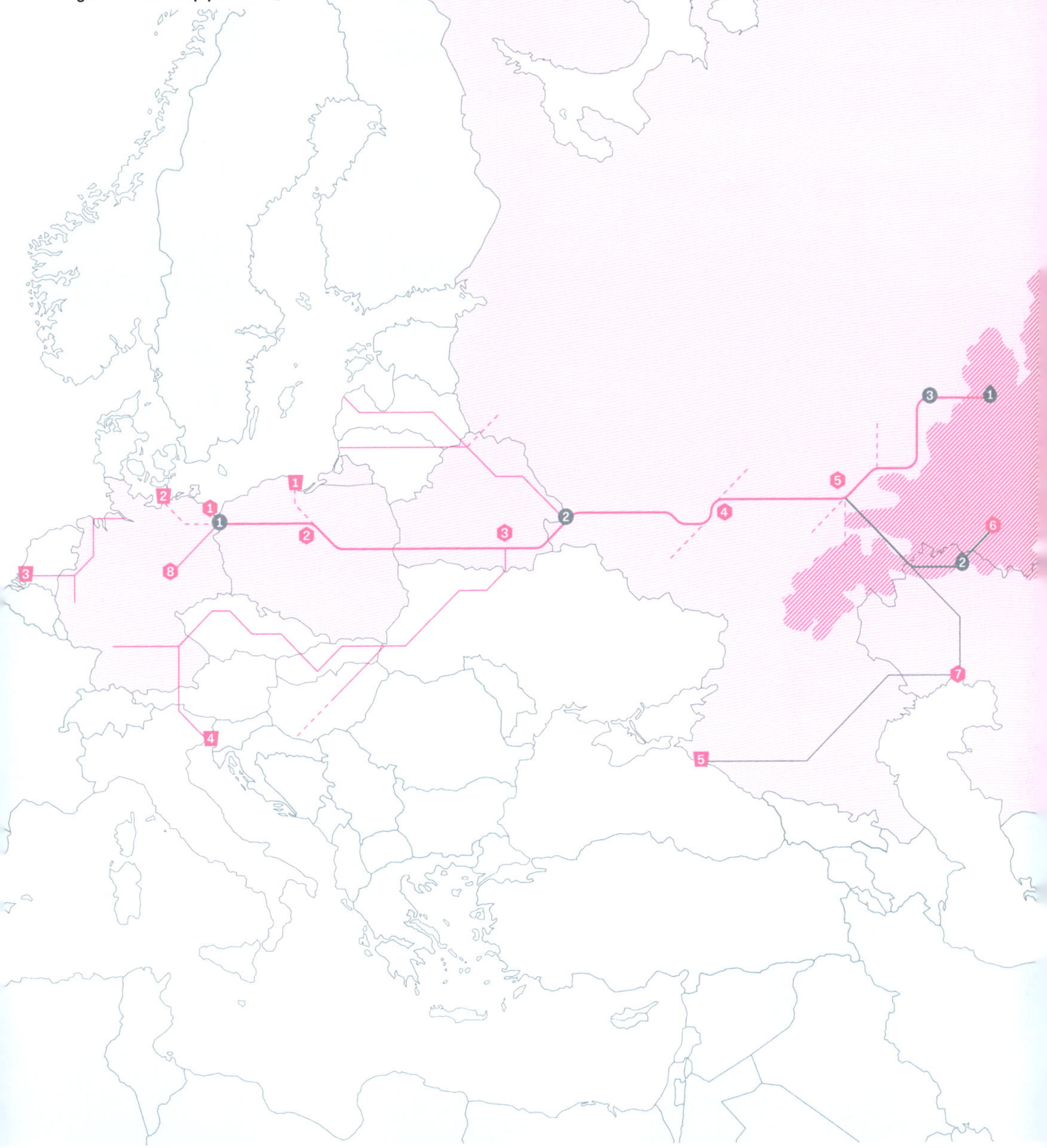

Oil and gas fields

Druzhba pipeline
- Direct Druzhba pipeline
- Other Druzhba pipelines
- Alternative routes

Pipelines from Kazakhstan
- Karachaganak–Samara pipeline
- Alternative routes

Extraction points
1. Ufa, RU
2. Karachaganak, KZ

Pipeline operations
1. Schwedt, DE
2. Unecha, RU
3. Almetyevsk, RU

Maritime oil ports
1. Gdansk, PL
2. Rostock, DE
3. Rotterdam, NL
4. Trieste, IT
5. Novorossiysk, RU

Refineries
1. Schwedt, DE
2. Plock, PL
3. Mazyr, BY
4. Syrzan, RU
5. Samara, RU
6. Orenburg, RU
7. Atyrau, KZ
8. Leuna, DE

Fig. 25 The Karachaganak extraction field, 2023

Locations
1. Aksay
2. The Karachaganak field
3. Berezovka
4. Bestau

— Karachaganak–Uralsk–Samara pipeline
— Karachaganak–Orenburg pipeline
— Power line
- - Karachaganak field Sanitary Protection Zone

Residential area
Industrial area
Extraction well
RU–KZ border
Railways

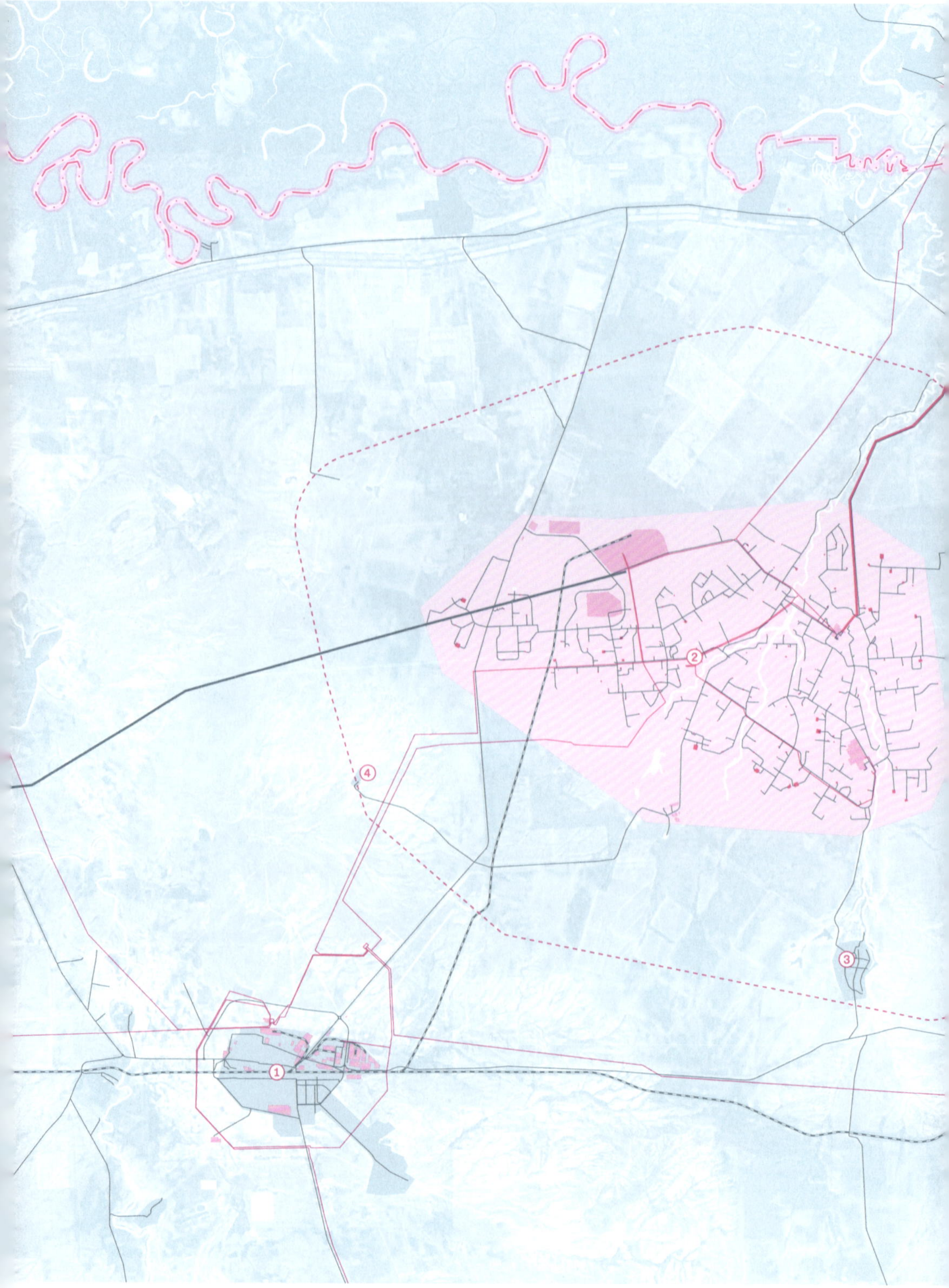

Fig. 26 Oil extraction infrastructure and facilities at Karachaganak field, 2023

Locations
1. Karachaganak Processing Complex (KPC)
2. Unit 2
3. Unit 3
4. Waste treatment plant
5. Power plant
6. Residential complex

- Karachaganak–Uralsk–Samara pipeline
- Karachaganak–Orenburg pipeline
- Power line

- Residential area
- Industrial area
- Extraction well
- Railways

Fig. 27 Aksay, 2023

Locations
1. Railway station "Kazakhstan"
2. "Czech" town
3. "GDR" town
4. Kyzyltal micro district

1 Oil storage
2 KPO headquarters
Industrial area
Railways
Power line

1 km

Fig. 28 PCK industrial complex, 2023

Industrial areas
1 Schwedt industry park
2 PCK refinery
3 Schwedt port
4 Mineralölverbundleitung Schwedt

— Pipelines
1 Pipeline from Rostock
2 Gasoline pipeline to Berlin
3 Druzhba pipeline

(1) Schwedt
Industrial area
Industrial railways
Railways
Power line

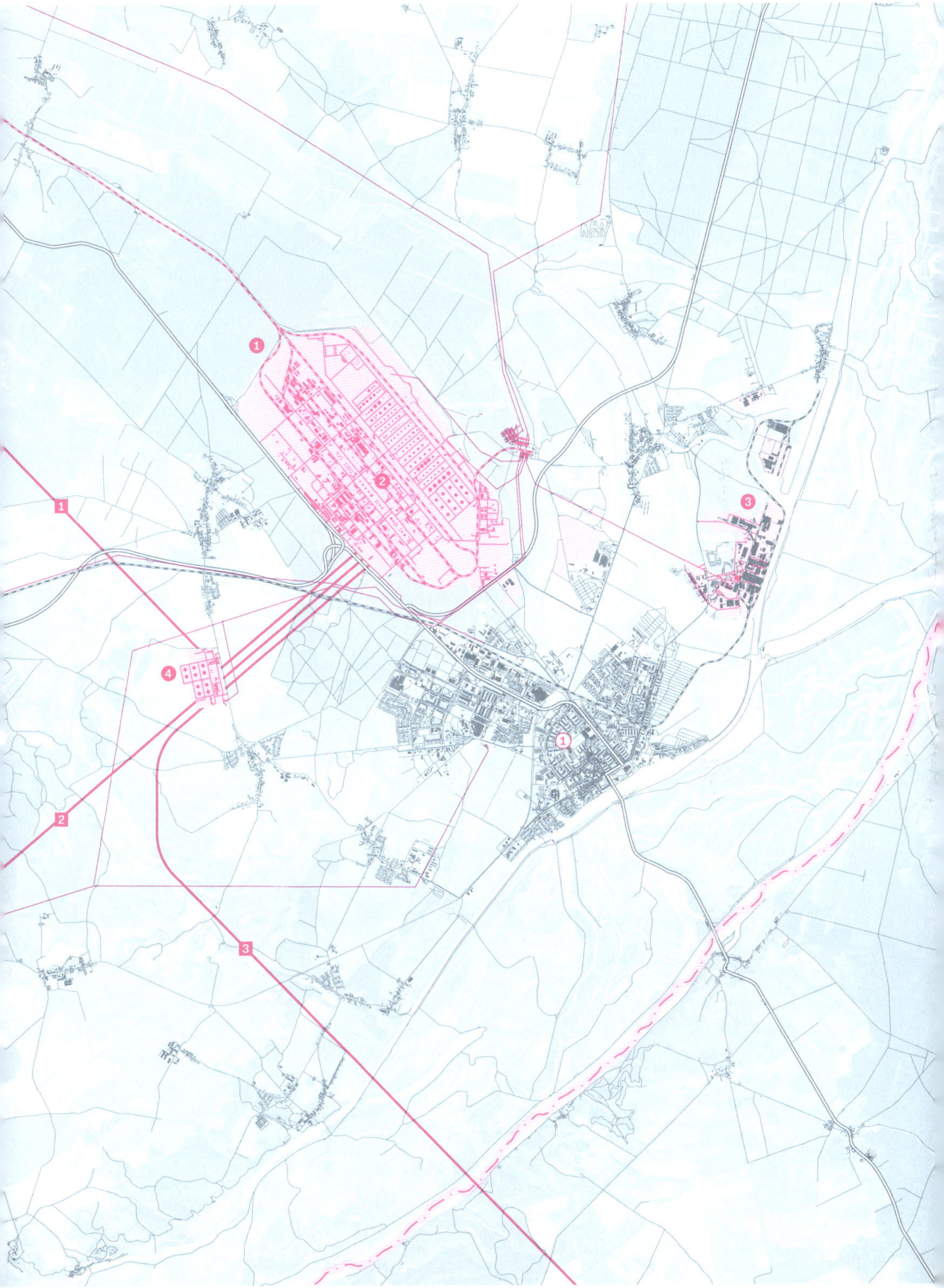

2 km

Fig. 29 Historic development of the PCK industrial complex, 1875–1945

1873 The first 25 km railway connection is established between Angermünde and Schwedt.
1875 Schwedt has a population of ca. 9,500 with one third working in the tobacco industry.
1945 During the Second World War, 85 % of Schwedt is destroyed.

Fig. 30 Historic development of the PCK industrial complex, 1946–1964

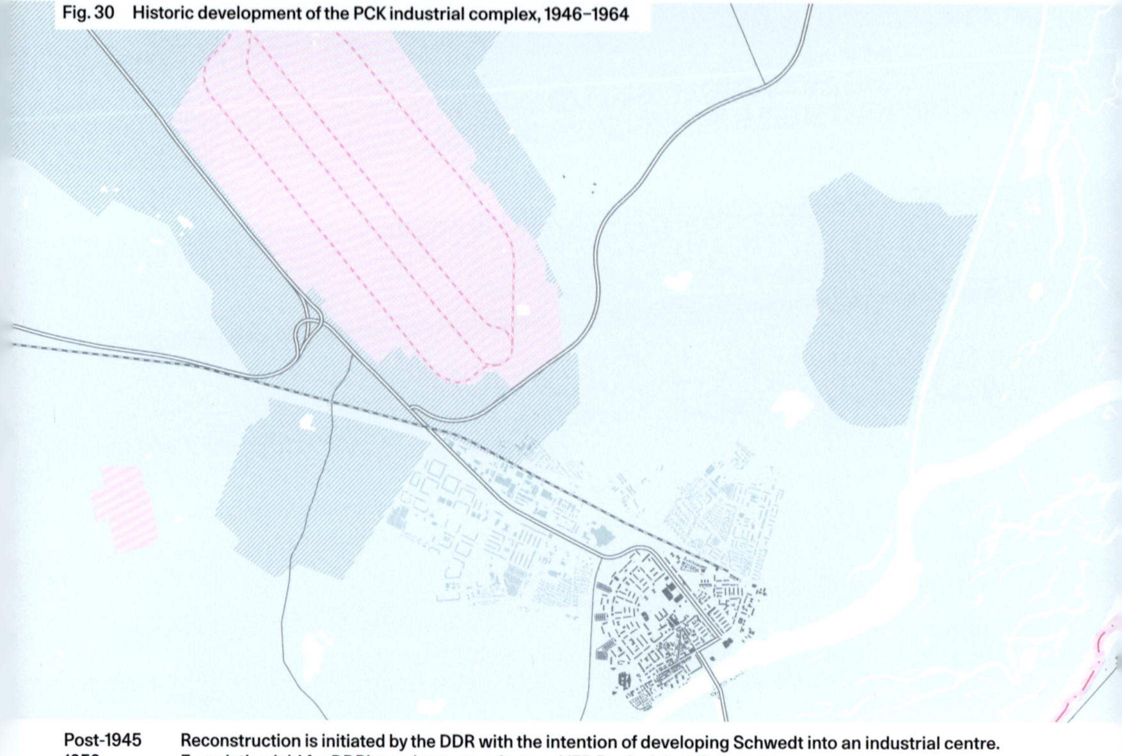

Post-1945 Reconstruction is initiated by the DDR with the intention of developing Schwedt into an industrial centre.
1959 Foundation laid for DDR's modern paper factory, VEB Papierfabrik Schwedt.
1964 The PCK is connected to Druzhba pipeline and begins operation.

Fig. 31 Historic development of the PCK industrial complex, 1970–1990

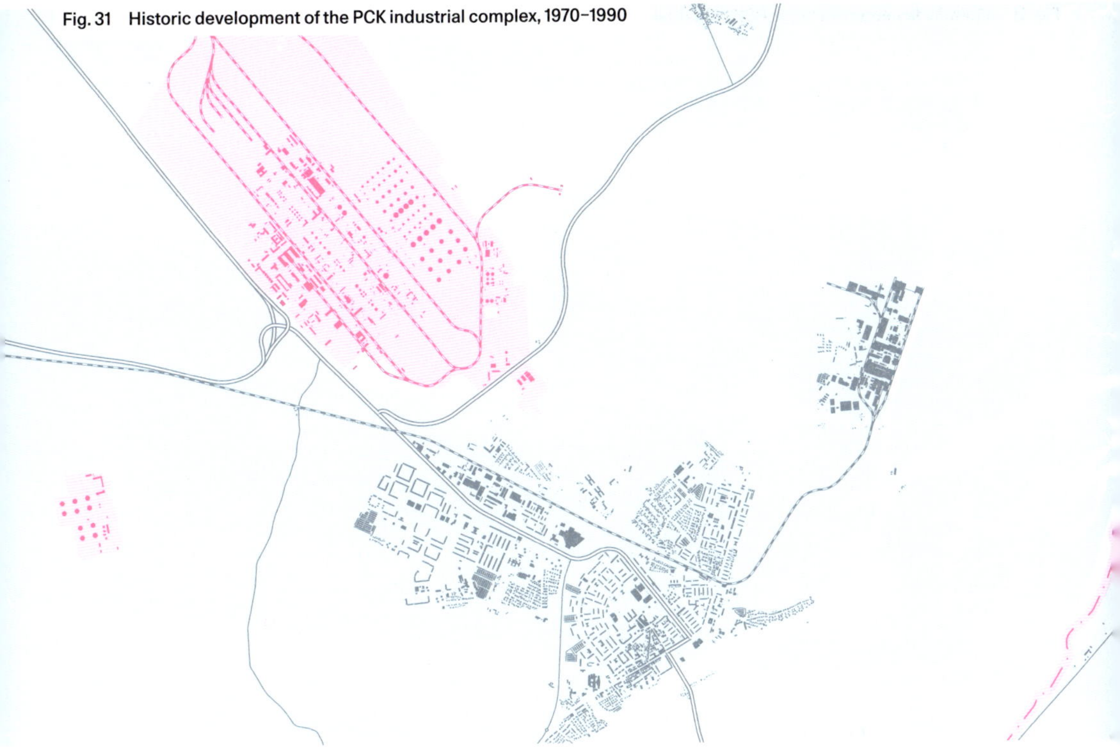

1960–90	11,000 housing units in five to eleven storey prefabricated buildings are constructed to accommodate the growing population.
1980	Schwedt reaches its population peak, with about 54,000 inhabitants.

Fig. 32 Historic development of the PCK industrial complex, 2000–2022

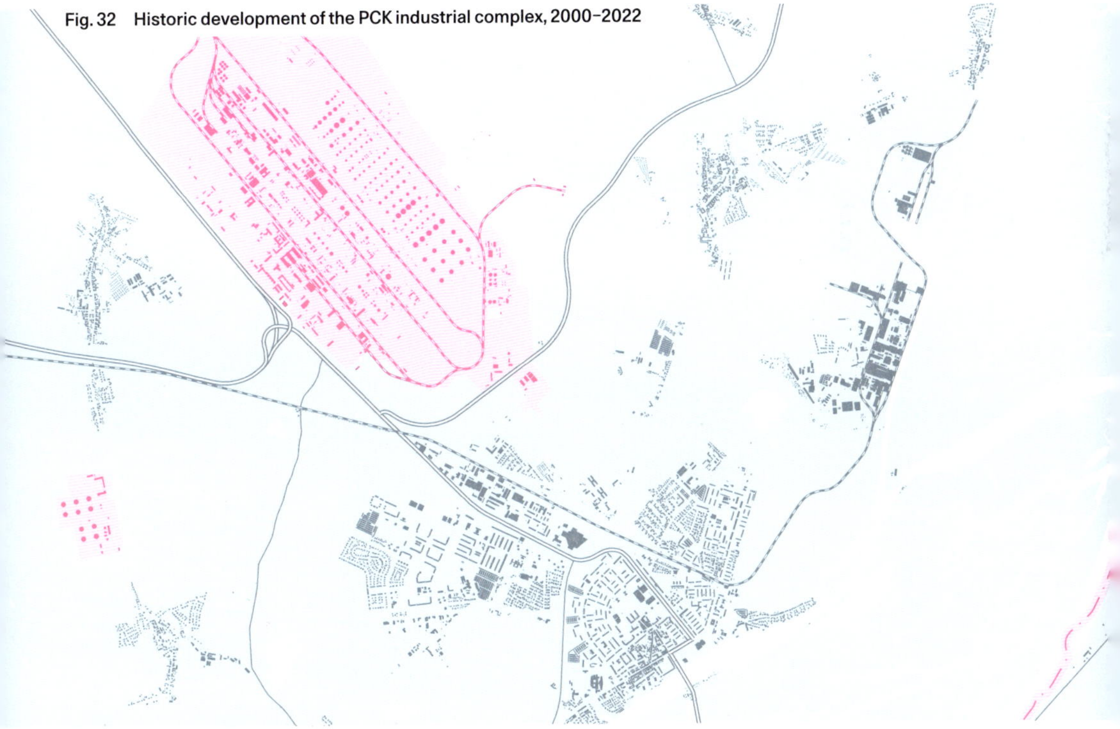

2001	The inauguration of Schwedt port marks the establishment of a tri-modal logistics hub, primarily supporting the transportation of paper products.
2000–22	Due to a 40% decrease from peak population, almost 6,000 *Plattenbau* apartments are demolished.

2 km

Fig. 33 PCK and Schwedt industrial park, 2021

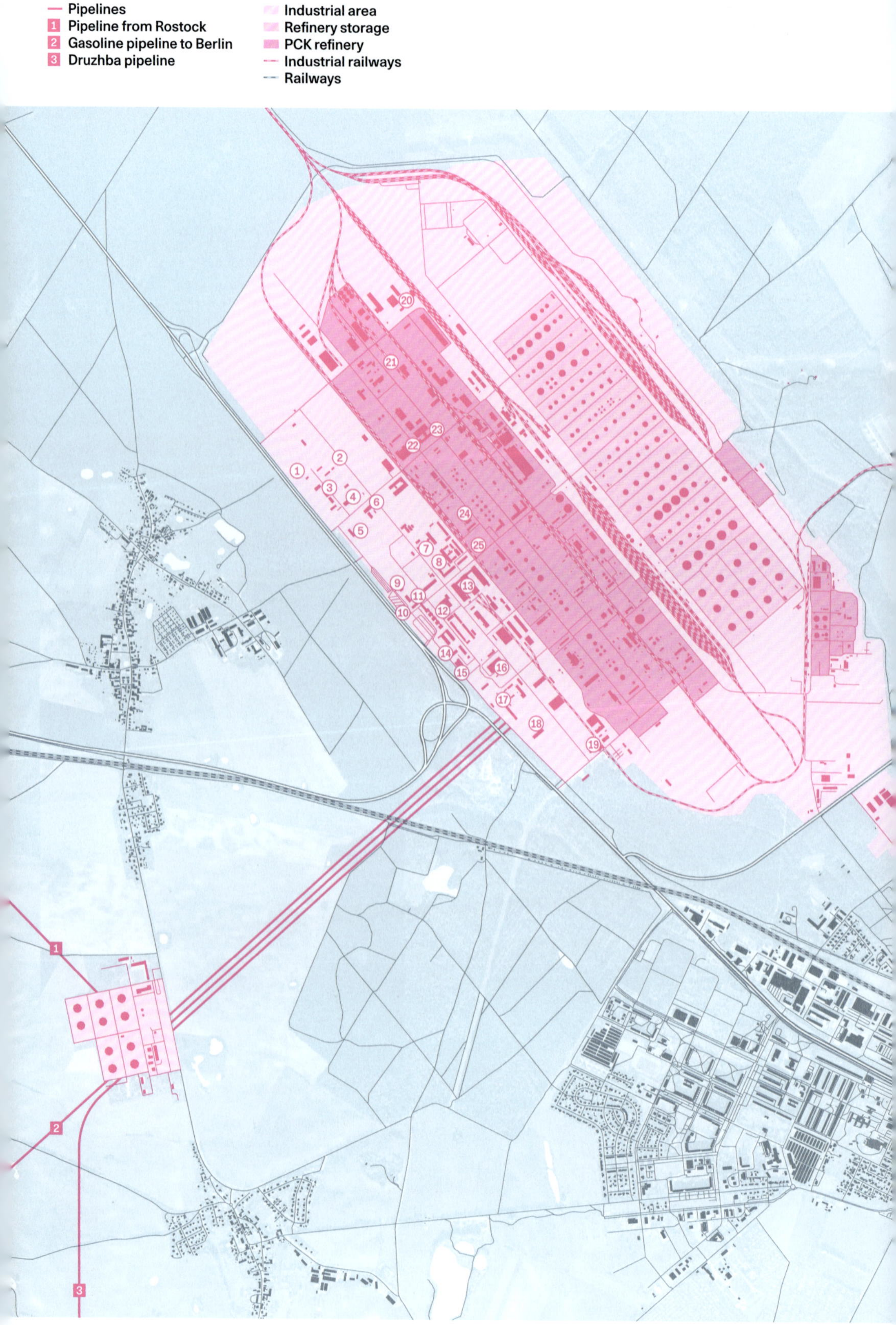

1. Märkische Montagerealisierung und Metallverarbeitung GmbH
2. Baumaschinen Martin Runge GmbH
3. Air Liquide Vertriebspartner Baumaschinen Martin Runge GmbH
4. EFG Bär & Ollenroth KG
5. M+W Central Europe GmbH
6. WISA-Laboratorium GmbH
7. Sascha Wendler & Raymond Ryll GbR W-T-F
8. John Brown Voest Schwedt GmbH
9. BARMER
10. PCK Raffinerie GmbH
11. XERVON GmbH
    VERBIO Ethanol Schwedt GmbH & Co. KG
    Velind Chemie GmbH
    TÜV Rheinland Industrie Service GmbH
12. Pedus PCK Raffinerie GmbH
13. A&W Apparate & Wärmetauscherbau GmbH
14. Oberstufenzentrum Uckermark Abt. 3
15. EPT for Storage Tanks GmbH
    World Link Industry Engineering (WLI-E) GmbH
    Varena-aer-product GmbH
16. Brandt Kran und Logistik GmbH
17. Hoyer Bitumen-Logistik GmbH Spedition
18. Lichtner Transportbeton GmbH & Co. KG – Werk Schwedt
19. ALBA Uckermark GmbH | Schrottplatz Schwedt/ Oder
20. VERBIO Logistik GmbH
21. Holzkontor und Pelletierwerk Schwedt GmbH
22. EagleBurgmann | Service-Center Schwedt
23. Bardenhagen Maschinenbau Oder GmbH
24. PCK Raffinerie GmbH
25. Technischer Industrieservice Verschleiß- und Fördertechnik GmbH

Fig. 34 Means of transportation from the PCK

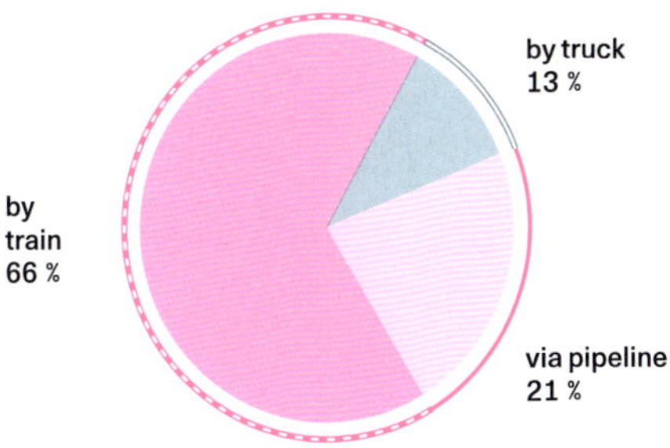

Fig. 35 Annual production of PCK, 2021 10,800 kt/a

1	Diesel fuels	4,071 kt/a
2	Petrol fuels	3,218 kt/a
3	Heating oil (extra light)	1,177 kt/a
4	Heating oil (heavy)	745 kt/a
5	Liquid gases (propane, butane, propylene)	475 kt/a
6	Aircraft turbine fuel	464 kt/a
7	Bitumen	334 kt/a
8	Others	313 kt/a

Fossil Energy Carriers

Natural Gas

3.4

3.4.1

Introduction to Natural Gas

David Bauer
Joseph Smithard

If oil is the king, then natural gas can be considered the prince of hydrocarbons. At 23 %, it ranks second only to oil in the global primary energy share.[1] Gas has gained this prominent position owing to several advantages, which render it a viable energy source despite significant handling challenges. First and foremost, it is considered a relatively "clean" fuel compared to its neighbouring fossils, as it releases lower amounts of carbon dioxide at the same level of heat output. Moreover, it is a very versatile substance with various applications, including heat and electricity production, agrochemical feedstock production, and the manufacturing of raw materials for industrial processes, such as plastics, fertilisers, and chemicals.

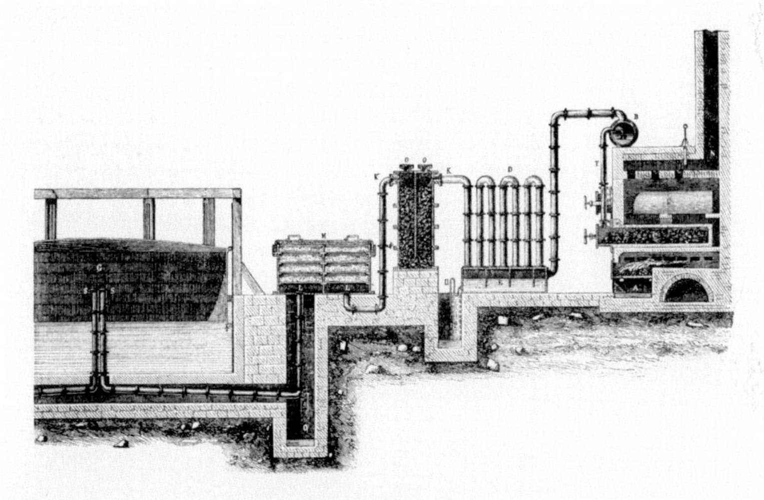

Fig. 1 Schematic section of coal gas machinery, 1886

The impacts of natural gas on urban settlements are subtle, and perhaps less obvious than the magnificent changes brought about by coal and oil. Its early cousin, manufactured coal gas, emerged in Central Europe and North America in the early 19th century, replacing whale and plant-based oils as the primary source of illumination. Before the invention of gas lamps, light was as precious as it was scarce. If needed, it had to be carried in the form of lamps, torches, and candles, moving with their bearer only where they could afford to bring them. After dusk, cities and towns were overwhelmingly dark and dangerous, with only a few places lit by dimly glowing oil lamps. The primordial, all-encompassing night that settled in the streets of towns and villages presented itself as a severe and unresolved problem for the growing factories and cities of early industrial nations. Illumination finally came with the invention of tubed coal-gas lighting systems, which were rapidly implemented in factories and urban areas, changing the faces and functions of cities profoundly. Gas pipelines were among the first elements of techno-urban infrastructure that penetrated the underground in larger cities, often earlier than canalisation.[2] [Fig. 3]

Fig. 2 Gasworks VI at Tegel, 1930

A Rough History of Natural Gas

The emergence of natural gas as a major energy player is a relatively recent phenomenon. As the last fossil fuel to be exploited, it remained a minor contributor to energy markets well into the 20th century. It started as an unwanted and hazardous by-product of petroleum extraction and was typically flared into large, ominous fires. Before modern gas-gathering and transportation systems were developed, huge amounts were simply released into the atmosphere this way, as there were no market potentials beyond the immediate surroundings of the fields themselves. To establish itself as an efficacious energy carrier necessitated the capability for distribution and storage at a considerable distance from its point of origin. This was technically challenging, as its proprietors had to rely on partially unsuitable means and technologies used for oil transportation, including pipelines, tanks, and barrels, to deliver it to consumers. While crude oil was a dense liquid easily pumped and carried in a wide range of vessels, natural gas was a light, more volatile, more explosive substance that required constant pressure and extremely tight fittings. In competition with town gas, which could be supplied through regional utilities whenever coal arrived by barge or train, it initially lacked economic incentives and advantages.

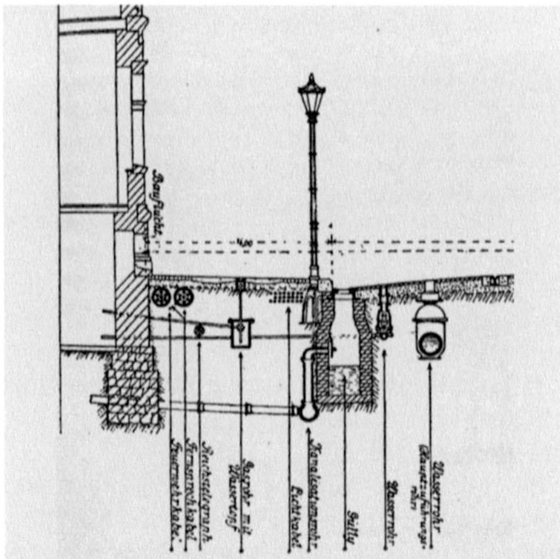

Fig. 3 Display of various piped infrastructure systems in Berlin, around 1909

Natural gas owed its ascent from a valueless by-product to several factors, including the unpredicted discovery of vast fields, significant developments in transport infrastructure, shock fluctuations in oil prices, and ongoing growth in consciousness about urban air pollution in Western industrialised cities.

The foundations for commercial adoption were laid in Pittsburgh, with the first notable catalyst being the discovery in the 1870s of large reservoirs in the northern periphery.[3] Although salt and oil drillers had already found gas within the vicinity around a decade before, the deposits were regarded as having little value and broadly flared unused due to their remote location. However, the new findings accidentally occurred in proximity to several industrial stations. A group of iron manufacturers were the first to understand the advantage of accessing the unused gas pools over purchasing expensive hard coal for their mills and began to adopt it through improvised pipelines. The successful implementation brought lower fuel costs and more consistent temperatures in the smelting process, attracting other mills to follow suit. Soon, other industrial stations inadvertently benefitted from the nearby natural gas supply, and a number of entrepreneurs began organising the industrial demand through regionally based gas firms.

However, the new utilities were reluctant to pipe natural gas into the city and connect it to the local grid due to concerns about the high investment costs for infrastructure, the risk of explosions, and competition from manufactured gas companies. Nonetheless, in 1882, two gas firms were incorporated and awarded charters to distribute fuel. The companies acquired and drilled new wells and began to supply private customers in various neighbourhoods. This led to controversy over the legal right to distribute natural gas, and a new Natural Gas Act was eventually passed in 1885, allowing for the chartering of corporations to produce, transport, store, and supply the substance.[4] The Act also contained specific requirements for sealing and plugging abandoned wells and gave gas corporations the right of eminent domain for laying pipelines, which paved the way for further proliferation. Soon, the landscape around Pittsburgh was dotted with derricks, and the city experienced the first great natural gas boom in history. Until the fields were exhausted, the widespread adoption of gas had highlighted the potential power of the substance. Not only did the smoke-plagued cities have significant increases in air quality, but questions of transportation, supply, and public consumption were now addressed through policy implementation.[5]

Fig. 4 Early gas well in Ontario, 1910

The 1920s gave rise to an advancing gas industry with a progressively viable economic model. Colossal gas fields in Texas and New Mexico attracted willing fortune seekers with a desire to invest in the industry. Accordingly, this assembled a formidable base of technological knowledge and money, expertise capable of moving unprecedented volumes of gas from holes in the ground to eager urban markets. As such, improvements in pipeline infrastructure were monumental, with new advancements in welding technology giving rise to stronger joints and seamless pipelines.[6] In spite of a series of significant incidents and explosions that underscored the volatile and hazardous nature of natural gas, the industry achieved its initial breakthrough, leading to the rapid adoption of gas wherever it was found in substantial quantities. This trend further accelerated with US wartime production and post-war industrialisation.

International gas field discoveries in the 1950s and 60s marked the beginning of a new era in the global energy landscape. The first wave coincided with explorations in the Middle East as well as North and West Africa. Evolving from the first Arab Petroleum Congress, countries such as Qatar, Iraq, Iran, and Saudi Arabia established national resource conglomerates to cement power and influence on the world stage.[7] In Europe, the first extensive gas deposits were found near Groningen in the Netherlands at the end of the 1950s. Natural gas production in the UK commenced in 1967 with the West Sole gas field, which delivered gas from the shallow waters of the southern North Sea to Bacton on the east coast of England. Around the same time, substantial discoveries were made off the coast of Norway, laying the foundation for the country's ascent as Europe's foremost fossil fuel producer.[8]

Fig. 5 Commissioning of the natural gas field in Slochteren

The availability of North Sea gas for Western Europe coincided with a period of rapid industrial and urban reconstruction in the wake of the Second World War, leading to unprecedented economic expansion and a surge in energy demand. It further rendered a notable shift from coal to gas as a primary fuel for supplying heat, thereby beginning to lift the thick veil of smoke so many cities had grown accustomed to during their industrial transformation. Along with debates over the negative impact of air pollution on public health, the transition to natural gas was seen as a pathway to improved air quality in many cities.

The Emergence of the Eastern Gas Infrastructure

The "gas boom" led to significant investment in the construction of pipelines across Western Europe. West Germany, the Netherlands, and the United Kingdom were among the first countries to adopt natural gas for household and industrial use.[9] Along with the expansion of the network, a giant on the global energy stage began rising in the east. Enormous oil and gas reserves discovered in the Volga-Ural region were propping up the Soviet Union as the most gas-rich region in the world. The abundant natural riches within the northern Eurasian landmass presented an export potential that was largely unrivalled elsewhere around the globe.[10] Despite the Soviet Union's domestic appetite for ever larger quantities of energy to support the industrial advancement of their war-beaten economy, the 1960s saw the first significant post-war outflow of energy resources into foreign markets. The expansion took place through the construction of transnational pipeline systems entering the brother states of Ukraine, Poland, Czechoslovakia, Bulgaria, and East Germany. [p. 151; p. 167] Concurrently, a long-term development plan to establish energy-intensive heavy industry, refineries, and petrochemical stations in these countries led to growing interdependencies with their allies.[11] But, beyond this, extending westwards also positioned Soviet resources right on the doorstep of other heavily industrialising and extremely energy-needy nations behind the Iron Curtain.

With its first "oil offensive", the Khrushchev leadership began to mobilise the strategic values of their infrastructural potential by flooding Western Europe with large amounts of cheap pipeline oil which could easily compete against the markets of Northern Africa and the Middle East.[12] Despite the persistent efforts by the US to impede the ascent of the Soviet Union, including the imposition of embargoes on steel pipes and pipeline technology, by the late 1960s, it had exceeded all other nations in oil exports except for the US themselves.[13]

This trajectory intensified in the wake of the 1973 global oil crisis that incurred a staggering spike in prices, escalating oil's value to previously unforeseen heights. The impact was twofold. On the one hand, this led a growing number of West European nations to consider the extensive raw material reserves of their political adversary as a reliable way to reduce their dependency on the newly formed OPEC nations and the crisis-ridden Middle East.[14] On the other hand, it boosted a surge in demand for oil alternatives. This resulted in the ultimate breakthrough for natural gas markets and stimulated the inclination to invest in extensive infrastructural projects to secure long-term energy stability for the future.

By then, gas infrastructure had become a pivotal branch of the Soviet domestic industry. While the USSR leadership sought to increase profits by liberating oil resources for export wherever possible, they gradually substituted this scarcity in the internal market with natural gas.[15] Catalysing a pivotal transformation, the discovery of hitherto unparalleled reservoirs within the bountiful terrains of Western Siberia in the 1960s and early 70s was instrumental in preparing this abundance for international departure.

By the late 1970s, the Soviet Union had commissioned three major pipeline corridors reaching far into Europe. They not only distributed their surplus gas to the allies, grouped under the CMEA, but also manifested a long-lasting connection with political adversaries, who held a relevant stake by supporting construction with vital loans, steel, and advanced technology.[16]

Fig. 6 The Brotherhood pipeline, Western Slovakia, 1956

The largest among them was the Urengoy–Pomary–Uzhgorod pipeline, also known as the Bratstvo (Brotherhood) pipeline, which extended from the Western Siberian fields to the Ukrainian-Czechoslovakian border at Uzhgorod. At this point, it connected to the Transgas pipeline, facilitating the transportation of Soviet gas to Austria and Italy via the Trans Austria Gasleitung TAG, as well as to Germany and France through the Mittel-Europäische Gasleitung MEGAL. The second pipeline corridor, known as Soyuz (Union), stretched from Russia's Orenburg hub to the same Ukrainian-Czechoslovakian border, serving as a conduit for Central Asian and Russian gas to reach Eastern and Central Europe. In addition, a third smaller pipeline was commissioned in 1974 to export a limited volume of Soviet gas directly from Russia to Finland.[17] The two consecutive decades marked a period of significant expansion for hard-wired energy relations, cementing the Soviet Union's position as Europe's key energy supplier.

The Post-Cold War Order

After the dissolution of the Soviet Union in 1991, a period of economic and political transition unfolded in Russia and other newly independent states. However, the enduring path dependency ingrained in the vast infrastructural legacy of the Soviet Union led many countries to continue relying on Russian resources. While former Soviet satellite nations in Central and Eastern Europe abandoned their planned economies and embarked on a course of political alignment with the West, many of these countries simultaneously maintained a significant dependence on Eastern gas and oil supplies for decades to come. Furthermore, while the domestic gas production of the emerging European Union and its member states was anticipated to begin a structural decline by the late 1990s, the demand was constantly rising due to an increasing share allocated to power generation and heating buildings. The substantial reserves in Siberia ensured a consistent and predictably long-term supply, and the governments in Germany, Italy, and France expressed a strong interest in enhancing Russia's integration into the Western economic system by fostering increased trade relations and the augmentation of gas supplies.[18] The immediate option involved optimising and enhancing existing pipelines, while the development of new infrastructure assumed greater importance as a medium-term objective. [Fig. 23]

In the post-Soviet era, disputes between Russia and its neighbouring nations were frequent and primarily centred around issues like transit fees, pipeline access, and ownership. Creating new trade routes that bypassed traditional transit countries like Ukraine and Poland offered a means to diversify exports and guard against potential conflicts. A series of new pipeline projects—most notably Nord Stream I, Yamal, and the dormant Nord Stream II—began to materialise throughout the first two decades of the new millennium.[19] These initiatives faced substantial opposition for several reasons, one of the most prominent being concern over developing enduring and long-term dependencies on an increasingly authoritarian state.

Although, pipeline systems had, historically speaking, epitomised a shared commitment that transitioned adversaries into trading partners, culminating in an extremely robust and stable trade relationship between Russia and its European counterparts,[20] concerns began to materialise with the Russian invasion of Ukraine and the European Union's subsequent embargo on Russian fuels. Despite the substantial media attention, it is essential to note that only oil and coal were subjected to actual import bans, while the eventual and massive decline in gas consumption ensued for myriad reasons.[21] The ripple effect of the war had a dramatic impact on the global energy landscape, with soaring prices hitting consumers hard. Germany's divorce from Russian gas amplified the need for an accelerated energy transition, with conflicting calls for rekindling outdated fuels or moving towards a future powered by low-carbon energy. Nevertheless, since the carrier plays a crucial role as a primary feedstock for heat generation across all sectors, its short-term substitution may not be feasible in many cases.[22] In numerous comprehensive decarbonisation scenarios, natural gas is often envisaged as the last remaining fossil fuel, although its long-term effects on the overall energy transition are vigorously debated and contested.[23] To address these future requirements, rapid investments in establishing Liquefied Natural Gas LNG terminals are intended to reshape the realities created by the half-century-old legacy of Eastern pipeline gas in Europe.

As the International Energy Agency IEA states, the conventional rationales supporting natural gas have centred on its role as a buffer technology in facilitating the transition towards cleaner energy sources and its capacity to fill the void resulting from the diminishing use of coal and oil. Due to the war on its eastern flank, these arguments are currently undergoing significant scrutiny—especially in Europe, where natural gas's political and economic viability have been severely compromised.[24]

3.4.2

Properties, Production, and Supply

David Bauer
Joseph Smithard

Types of Natural Gas

Natural gas shares its origin with oil, resulting from decaying layers of prehistoric organic matter, primarily made up of animals and plants. The difference is that the decomposition occurred under higher temperatures, leading to the formation of gaseous hydrocarbons.[25]

Fig. 7 Schematic geology of gas reservoirs

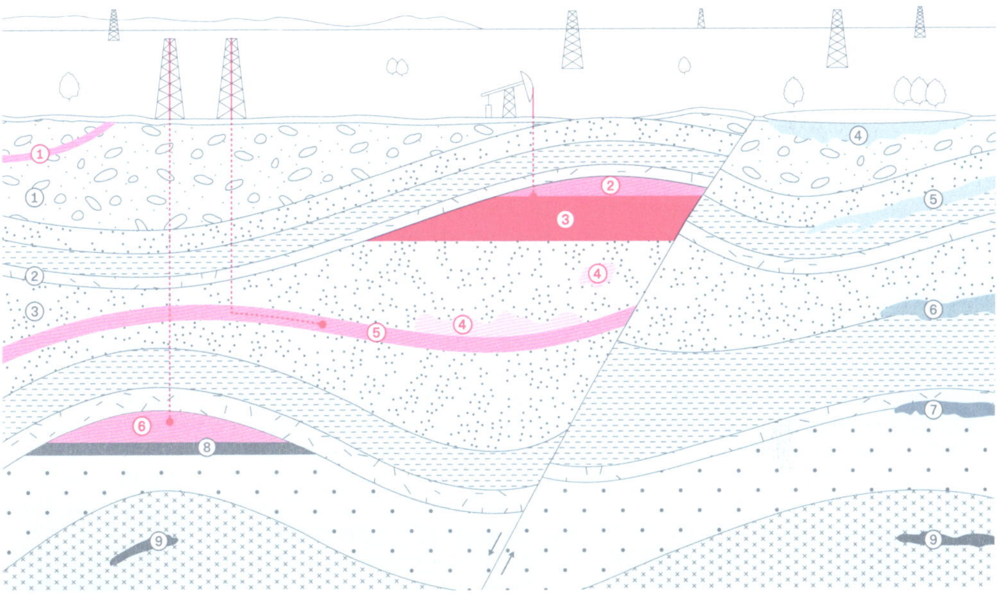

Gas reservoirs
1. Coalbed methane
2. Conventional associated gas
3. Oil
4. Tight sand gas
5. Gas-rich shale
6. Conventional non-associated gas

Other layers
1. Varying rock strata
2. Seal
3. Sandstone
4. Peat
5. Lignite
6. Bituminous coal
7. Anthracite coal
8. Asphalt
9. Graphite

There are different types of gas. When bubbling up from reservoirs and fields alongside crude oil, it is commonly referred to as "associated", "dissolved", or "wet" gas because it contains mingled liquids that must be separated directly at the wellhead. It usually comprises a high amount of methane, accompanied by a series of heavier hydrocarbons such as ethane, propane, and butane, meaning it needs heavy treatment before use.[26] [Fig. 8] Unlike oil, gas is light, transparent, odourless, and most importantly, more flammable, making it a formidable mix for handling. In the event of a fire, it can spread quickly and ignite across wide-reaching distances far away from the source. Gas does not simply spill; rather, it has a severe tendency to explode, making it difficult to contain or control. In addition, these fires can burn hotter and more intensely than oil, which makes them difficult to extinguish. The handling of gas was a seminal step in its evolution. Before the 20th century, wherever it occurred in isolated reservoirs, these were often left shut. Today, this type of source is referred to as "non-associated" or "dry" gas and is highly valuable because this form is composed primarily of a higher amount of methane, roughly 85 % on average, with a lower content of heavier hydrocarbons. The purity makes it a more sought-after energy carrier.[27]

Fig. 8 Typical composition of natural gas

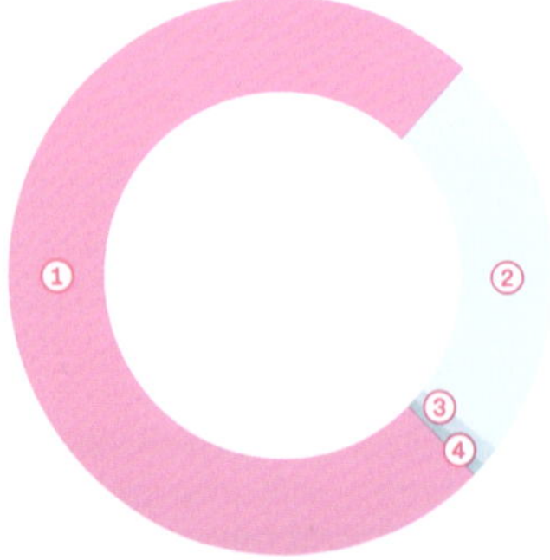

1	Carbon	74 %
2	Hydrogen	24 %
3	Oxygen	1 %
4	Nitrogen	0.75 %

Gas Fields and Reservoirs

The lifespan of a field usually depends on the underground pressure in the reservoir. After the infrastructural set-up is finished, the fields initially have an increasing production rate until finally they reach a steady plateau. [Fig. 9] As pressure begins to dwindle, the production declines significantly. The depletion can then be offset by drilling new wells or using enhanced recovery techniques—such as injecting gas or other substances into the reservoir to maintain the pressure and increase gas recovery.

During the past five decades, the intensive industrial extraction and exploitation of gas fields has led to the rapid depletion of global sources, resulting in a scarcity of pure reservoirs. The introduction of fracking, short for hydraulic fracturing, has revolutionised the oil and gas industry, and in regions where it is legally permitted, the focus of extraction has now pivoted towards accessing what is commonly referred to as "unconventional" reservoirs.[28] The technique involves injecting a high-pressure mixture of water, sand, and chemicals into deeper layers of shale, sandstone, or coal seams. Although widely used in fields within the United States, Australia, and Canada, many countries have seen widespread opposition to the application of this controversial technique. Utilising fracking to extend potential fields has become synonymous with continued environmental degradation, contamination of groundwater supplies, and the destabilisation of the subsurface geology. Fracking's potential to access unconventional deposits targets numerous regions that have never been viable options for gas extraction. These new sites shift the natural gas extraction landscapes away from the traditional oil and gas-rich reservoirs.

Needless to say, extracting natural gas through both conventional and unconventional methods comes with immense environmental impacts and deformations. When a deposit is used up or close to depletion, it often requires large sumps to recover and clean up the extraction sites. The costs for a comprehensive clean-up of massive offshore installations are so exorbitantly high that their operators may try to evade paying them, even if it causes significant environmental harm.[29]

Transport Systems

Concerning natural gas, transportation is everything. There are two ways to deliver it over long distances: either by pipeline or by ship. [Fig. 20–23] Although pipelines are seemingly the most "natural" means of transporting gas over long distances (and have consequently become the essential and unchallenged infrastructure of international and domestic distribution systems), seaborne gas shipments are increasingly an alternative to intercontinental gas transportation, even within countries operating intercontinental transmission pipelines.[30] The transportation of compressed natural gas on tankers poses significant challenges. Due to the high pressures and explosion risks involved, the gas must be

Fig. 9 Lifespan of a gas field

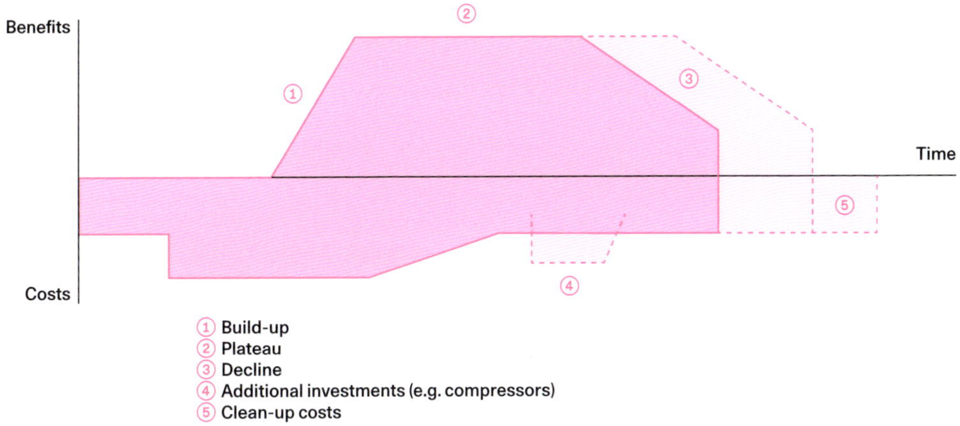

cooled and liquefied through a separate set of technologies that are not just costly but also energy-intensive. This state requires specialised LNG tankers with double hulls, enhanced insulation, and safety measures to land at specifically designed terminals. The depletion of deposits, widening geopolitical conflicts, and the elevated role of gas as a bridging technology, has led to an increased demand for LNG, as it provides a supply diversity that withstands the challenges of transit-dependent pipeline systems.

Furthermore, countries that do not have access to pipeline gas can import LNG from a wide range of global suppliers. Japan was one of the first to adopt this technology. As an island state with a high population and rapid industrial growth, it began to seek alternatives to coal and oil in the 1950s. Today, the country has the largest LNG infrastructure globally, with 30 sea terminals.[31]

The Gas Supply Chain

Like the oil industry, the gas supply chain is divided into upstream, midstream, and downstream segments.

Upstream

The first step to establishing a system that can deliver substantial amounts of gas over a prolonged period is to drill several exploratory wells across an estimated field area. Through this, an average output for the number of recoverable reserves and their quality in the field is determined so that the gas can be sold beforehand via long-term contracts and compliance agreements. The number of wells and the drilling schedule is determined based on the desired production profile, which is agreed upon by the field owners and gas buyers. Typically, the agreement calls for a consistent or increasing delivery rate over a set period before an estimated decline occurs.[32]

Once extracted from a well, natural gas must undergo a comprehensive processing procedure to standardise a natural phenomenon into an energy commodity. This process typically occurs close to the well or at a gas terminal. Here, various stages of treatment are undertaken to refine it for commercial and home use. When it leaves the wellhead, gas is collected in gathering pipelines and concentrated towards a processing plant that strips it of unwanted properties.[33] [Fig. 10]

In associated gas streams, the first step requires the separation of any oil and hydrocarbon condensates. This is accomplished through a distillation process that uses gravity, wherein the heavier oil and hydrocarbons settle at the bottom while the lighter gas rises to the top. It is then followed by the removal of any water present in the gas stream, which is typically achieved through a dehydration process. During this stage, the gas is subjected to heat and passed through a desiccant, which absorbs any moisture, leaving behind dry gas.

Fig. 10 Block diagram of major gas-producing units

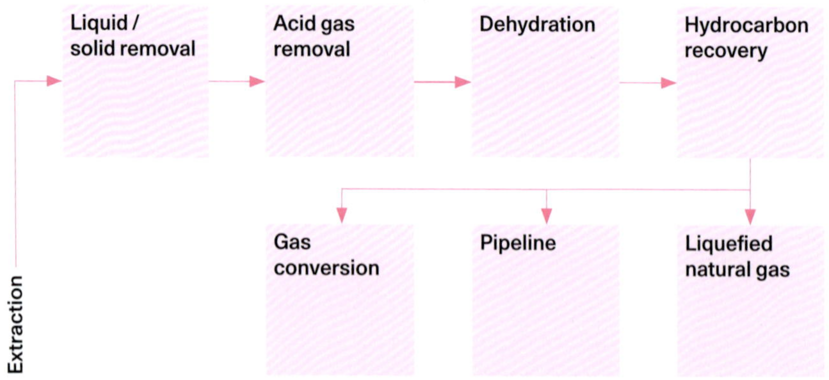

How these unwanted substances are treated and disposed of depends on the regulations of the country or region where the gas extraction occurs. Typically, the water produced undergoes treatment and is disposed of through injection wells, before being rerouted back underground. More often than not, this has heavy impacts on the local water cycle, often polluting downstream from the injection disposal facility. Although legislation is becoming stricter, records show that once pristine natural surroundings have faced long-lasting contamination, resulting in with significant transformations to existing ecosystems.

Once all contaminants have been removed, the gas is deemed to be of "pipeline quality" and can be used for chemical feedstock or injected into the high-pressure transmission system. If it is destined to be shipped, the purified gas is transported mainly via pipelines to special LNG stations where it undergoes further processing. The natural gas is cooled to a temperature of –160 °C; at this point, it becomes a clear, odourless, and non-corrosive liquid that takes up one six-hundredth of the volume occupied by natural gas in its gaseous state. The liquefaction process requires a large amount of energy, which is typically provided by natural gas itself.

Midstream

The transportation of pipeline gas is relatively straightforward. It rests on a system of large-diameter pipes that transport natural gas over long distances. Typically between 50 and 122 cm in width, these pipelines are made of steel and can operate at very high pressures.

Pipeline gas must be pressurised to create a gradient and compressed to make its volume more cost-efficient. As it travels through the system, its pressure drops due to friction, and compressor stations are placed along the pipeline route. Before it can be put to use, it must first be depressurised in special hubs located on the nodes between long-distance intermission and regional grids. [Fig. 23]

At the end of the transmission pipeline network, gas can be stored in underground facilities. Since the demand for gas is not constant and usually rises during the winter, storing gas at a time when the need and price is low is an essential factor in the gas markets. Like oil, gas pipelines offer a large storage capacity owing to their colossal size.

Due to the large quantities and set-up of the infrastructural system, the most effective way to store pipeline gas is to pump it back underground, close to where it is needed.[34] However, geology plays an important role here, as appropriate caverns are limited to specific regions. Depleted gas fields, or aquifers, provide some of the most cost-efficient methods for storage. Nonetheless, they are inflexible in that they can take a long time to fill and empty. Salt-cavern storage sites present an alternative since they can be filled and emptied in less than a month. [Fig. 30] These sites are leached underground and, as such, require significant monthly investments. Given its low temperature, storage technology for LNG differs from underground caverns. It is stored in insulated tanks at a liquefaction plant or a receiving terminal until it is ready to be transported. Floating cryogenic tankers transport the gas and simultaneously act as buffers to permanent infrastructure when necessary.

Downstream

At the end of the intercontinental transmission pipeline, gas is distributed into different systems according to its end-users, whether that's power stations, industrial facilities, or households. LNG is slightly different. Upon arrival at its destination, it is transferred to storage tanks and warmed to return it to its gaseous state. This process is known as "regasification" and requires a similar amount of energy as liquefaction.[35] After regasification, LNG is like pipeline gas and can be transferred accordingly.

After the gas reaches its destination from the reservoirs, it is commonly allocated through local networks under the management of regional gas distribution companies GDCs. These GDCs operate smaller pipeline systems that connect to individual end-users, such as households or businesses. Domestic gas enters the home and subsequently requires a tightly monitored system. Unlike oil, coal, or wood, it cannot be kept in plastic bottles or canisters but requires a constant inflow through valves.

Gas is supplied to end-users through gas meter, which measure the volume of gas consumed, and billing is typically made on a consumption-based tariff system. While pipelines play a significant role in the storage infrastructure, larger stockpile facilities are a vital safeguard against unforeseen events and fluctuations in price and availability. Firm gas, supplied to large factories and industrial hubs, is typically maintained at a relatively constant rate, primarily influenced by economic activity. On the other hand, household consumers and power stations experience fluctuations and peak demands in gas supply, not unlike the dynamics of the electricity grid.

Gas serves as the primary source of heat in Europe, making changing weather conditions the most influential factor currently impacting the timing and magnitude of gas consumption peaks.

3.4.3

Gas in the Local Context

David Bauer
Joseph Smithard

Even with a a notable decline in volume as a consequence of the geopolitical tensions between the EU and Russia, in 2022, natural gas accounted for 23 % of Germany's energy consumption, making it the country's second most important energy source.[36] With over 40 %, the heating market for households, commercial, and retail customers dominates domestic gas consumption. This is followed by the industrial sector, utilising around 37 % for production, power supply, and feedstock purposes.[37] [p. 20] Finally with a 13 % share, gas is gradually gaining significance as an energy source for electricity generation, and power stations are projected to expand by 20 to 30 GW in the next decade, effectively doubling the existing capacity.[38]

Domestic Sources

At the end of 2022, Germany possessed a confirmed domestic reserve of approximately 19,000,000,000 m³ of natural gas, supplemented by an additional 17,100,000,000 m³ from potential sources. The bulk of these reserves, comprising some 99.5 %, are concentrated in Niedersachsen, leaving the other three federal states holding gas resources only as peripheral contributors.[39] With an aggregate quantity of approximately 36,000,000,000 m³ of subterranean resources, having been assessed as either secure or probable for recovery, this figure constitutes roughly 3 % of the cumulative reserves historically contained within the geographical confines of unified Germany since initial exploitation commenced in the 1950s.[40] Owing to a substantial upswing in domestic production during

Fig. 11 Annual natural gas production (raw gas) in Germany, 1945–2023 in km³

the 1970s and 80s, the nation's indigenous gas reserves have been nearly exhausted and, against its considerable demand, Germany is simply running out of gas. [Fig. 11] Production from conventional sources has decreased since 2004 and is estimated to cease altogether throughout the decade. This depletion leaves only unconventional extraction methods, such as fracking, as viable means of accessing yet untapped future deposits. As industrial lobbyists contend, the potential for technically recoverable natural gas is enormous: in addition to 450,000,000,000 m^3 from coal seams, industrial estimates suggest reserves in shale rocks of up to 2,300,000,000,000 m^3.[41] Despite the ongoing discussions to access unconventional sources, the extraction of natural gas from shale, clay, marl, and coal seam rock is fundamentally prohibited in Germany due to the lack of experience and knowledge in this area.[42]

Imports and Exports

Due to heavy industrialisation and its heating infrastructure, Germany currently tops the European gas consumption leader board, placing it among the world's hungriest consumers of natural gas.[43] Although domestic gas reserves have a greater volume than oil, the country depends heavily on imports, with around 95 % of annual consumption being met by external sources.[44] In 2022, around 137,350,000,000 m^3 arrived at the borders through large pipeline transmission corridors.[45] Due to its central position in the continent, not all of these imports remain within its borders. Historically, the country has acted as a significant energy shed, storing and distributing gas from various ends of the geographical pipeline system. As a result, a network of intra-country connectors enables Germany, despite being a considerable importer, to rank among the top ten gas exporters by redistributing a significant portion of its imports to other European states.[46] Over the last three decades, Germany was almost exclusively served by large and small pipelines from Russia in the east, the Netherlands and the UK in the west, and Norway in the north. Until June 2022, gas imports from the eastern region constituted the largest share, accounting for nearly one-quarter of the total imports. Russia's state monopoly, Gazprom, played a significant role in supplying substantial gas volumes through three primary routes that link the vast Western Siberian reservoirs to Central Europe. The primary gas supply routes encompass the Nord Stream I undersea pipeline, the Yamal–Europe pipeline (connecting Belarus and Poland to Germany), and the extensive Ukraine gas corridor. Historically, the latter's backbone of Soviet exports includes the Bratstvo pipeline as well as the Transgas pipeline running through Slovakia and the Czech Republic. Norway contributes to the gas supply through several offshore gas fields, delivering via three main channels: Norpipe, Europipe I, and Europipe II. Additionally, Dutch gas connects to the same region through a diverse network of pipelines.[47] [Fig. 21–23]

Germany, an integral part of the Central European network, possesses one of the world's most robust and meticulous gas grids, spanning approximately 595,000 km in total, comprising 40,000 km for the long-distance transmission network and 555,000 km for the distribution network.[48] To put this into perspective, this combined length when laid out end to end would nearly encircle the Earth's equator 14 times. The German pipeline system comprises four tiers, encompassing long-distance, supra-regional, regional, and local transportation networks, all managed by various private market entities across different regions of the country. Due to the technical and economic intricacies inherent in gas management, the national gas market is subject to state regulation, which assigns distinct roles to wholesalers, storage operators, long-distance network operators, and distributors. Overseeing this comprehensive regulatory framework is the Bundesnetzagentur BNetzA, serving as the supervisory authority for the market entities, network fees, and gas flows.

Gas infrastructure requires substantial shared investments and long-term contractual commitments, to ensure stable gas flows over extended periods. Owing to the sunk costs and protracted payback periods, its construction often spans multiple decades. To mitigate the risk of unproductive investments, Germany employs a participatory approach in its expansion planning process, characterised by the periodic release of biennial network development plans. These plans encompass a mid-term ten-year horizon, grounded in trend projections, and are executed by gas transmission system operators TSOs. Given the expansive nature of the grid, there is considerable optimism and strategic planning invested in a long-term transition towards its utilisation for biogas and the emerging national and international hydrogen economy.[49]

However, the unforeseen Russian attack on Ukraine caused a significant shock to the traditionally strong reliance on West Siberian gas, leading to the sudden cessation of gas inflows through eastern corridors. [Fig. 22] As a result, there has been an urgent need for rapid reconfiguration and diversification of energy suppliers, requiring swift actions to secure alternative sources in a remarkably short timeframe.

Ramping up a previously non-existent LNG import infrastructure, while discontinuing prior stable import patterns, will significantly impact the market's composition and the entities involved in its operation for an extended duration.

Fig. 12 Geographical distribution of natural gas fields in Germany

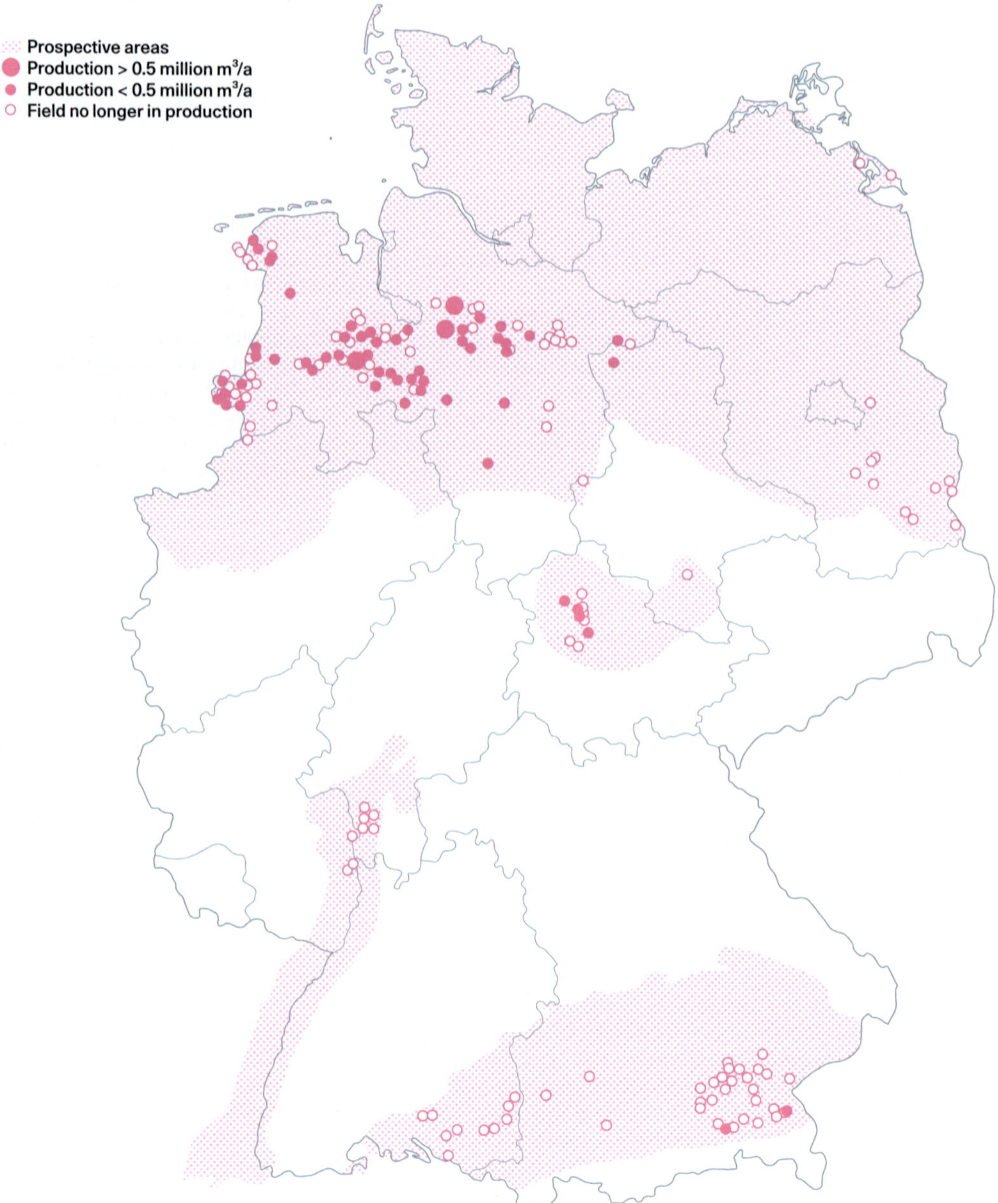

3.4.4

The Yamal Megaproject

David Bauer
Joseph Smithard

Until late March 2022, the majority of Berlin-Brandenburg's living rooms were heated with the cold riches of the perma-frosted ground in the West Siberian Arctic. Natural gas arrived via a network of pipelines that directs flows from the Yamalo-Nenets Autonomous Okrug YNAO on the Yamal Peninsula, spanning approximately 4,100 km to reach the small village of Mallnow on the German–Polish border in East Brandenburg.

Route to Europe

Natural gas departs the peninsula to the southeast, traversing the ocean floor of the ice-covered Baidarata Bay in concrete-coated pipes, ultimately reaching Ukhta—a historical focal point of Soviet oil and gas extraction with roots in the forced-labour-driven development of the resource-rich northern region during the High-Stalinist era. In Ukhta, the pipeline interconnects with a multi-string transmission system that extends southeast to Torzhok, another critical junction of the Russian Unified Gas Supply System UGSS, from which point it enters another large pipeline corridor—transporting it through Belarus and Poland to Western European markets. In its entirety, the network, aptly known as the Yamal megaproject, unites an enormously vast array of components scattered across three distinct climatic zones.[50] It includes one of the world's largest gas extraction sites at Bovanenkovo, interconnected by thousands of kilometres of multi-string trunklines and tributaries and pressurised by numerous compressor stations strategically positioned at intervals of approximately 250 km within the pipeline network.[51] Moreover, the pipeline not only functions as a transportation system but also represents a humongous artificial gas storage facility. [Fig. 21–23]

Yamal–Europe Pipeline

At its core lies the Yamal–Europe pipeline, one of the prestige projects of the post-Soviet energy infrastructure and diplomacy, forged from intergovernmental treaties between Russia, Belarus, Poland, and Germany. Commissioned in 1994 and inaugurated more than a decade later, it emerged in response to Ukraine repeatedly using critical Soviet-era transportation assets as a bargaining tool. In retaliation, Russia undertook a strategic initiative to strengthen its negotiating position and reduce dependence on Ukrainian transit by diversifying its export routes, developing alternative pathways to reach old and new friends in needy Western economies.[52]

Led by Gazprom, the Russian state-owned energy conglomerate, the construction of the pipeline was organised into sections aligned with the four participating nations, unfolding over a span of twelve years. Upon completion in 2006, the Yamal–Europe was considered the widest pipeline in the world, with a maximum diameter of 1,420 mm, enabling a carrying capacity of an incredible 33,000,000,000 m^3/a.[53]

In 2022, the gas flow came to a complete halt for the first time, as Gazprom suspended deliveries to Poland due to payment disputes, with Gazprom citing Poland's refusal to pay in roubles.[54] In response, since the winter of 2022, it has been operating in reverse mode, redirecting gas from Germany towards Poland, which, like its neighbour, relies heavily on imports. The redirection occurs through the metering and compressor stations located in Mallnow. Germany, in turn, sought alternative gas sources by relying on imports through the Nord Stream I and Transgas networks, as well as setting up additional LNG terminals at North Sea and Baltic Coast harbours. Amid evolving geopolitical dynamics, Germany's energy landscape underwent a notable transformation. By the close of 2022, Norway officially assumed the role of its primary gas supplier, with the Netherlands following suit. The unprecedented reduction in pipeline gas flows from Russia to Europe has been mitigated by a surge in LNG imports from diverse global origins with paradoxical outcomes. Despite efforts to reduce supplies, EU imports of Russian LNG have surged by 40 % since the Ukraine invasion, with Spain and Belgium serving as key marine entry points for LNG into the bloc.[55]

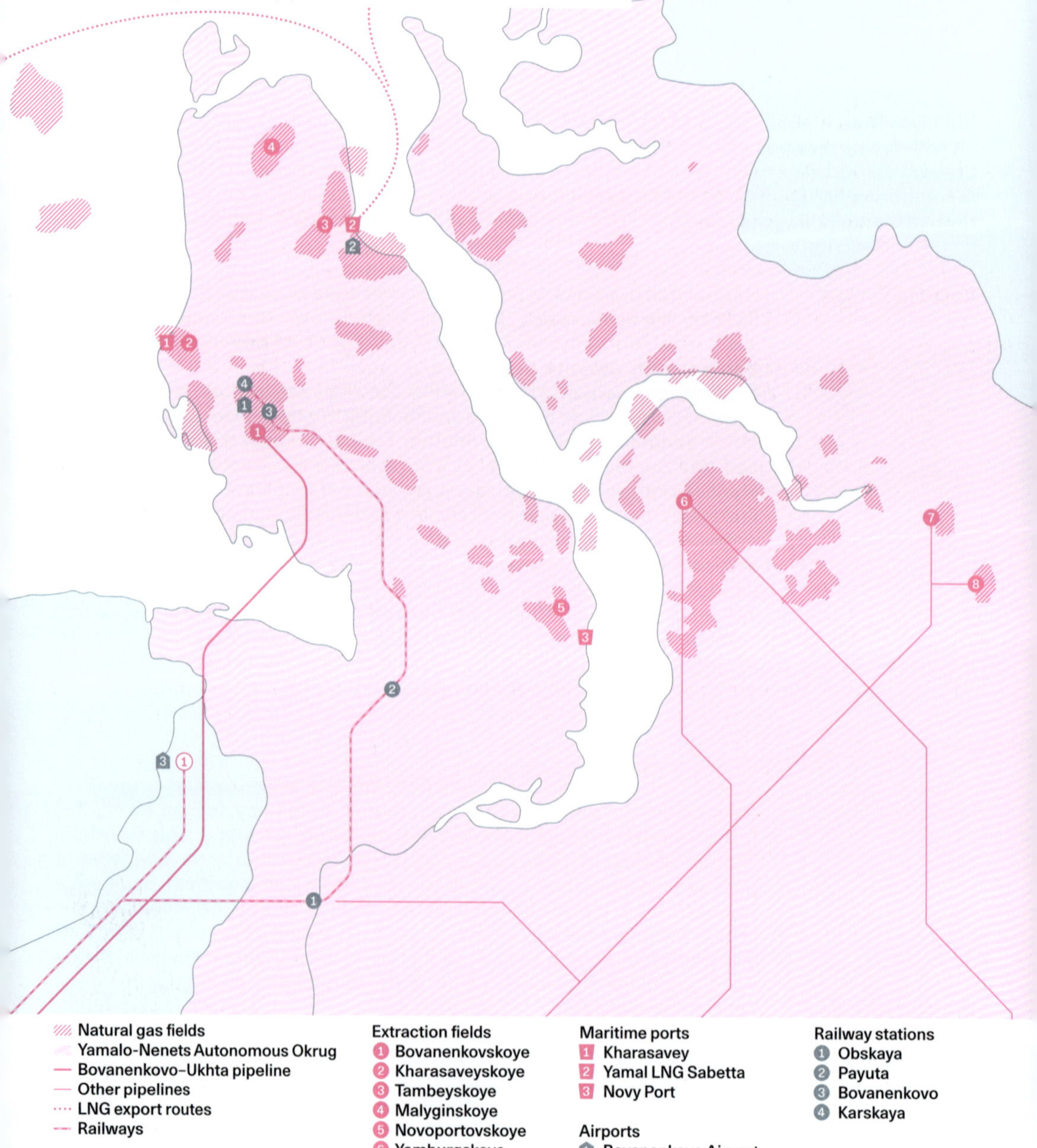

Fig. 13 Natural gas fields and pipeline infrastructure of the Yamal Peninsula

3.4.5

Extraction Field Bovanenkovo

David Bauer
Yuliya Navatskaya
Joseph Smithard

Bovanenkovo, situated in the western centre of the Yamal Peninsula, is Russia's second largest gas field, with abundant resources containing over 4,900,000,000,000 m^3 of explored gas reserves.[56] Offering tremendous potential to meet domestic and international gas demands, it is predicted that by 2030 the field will supply almost a third of Russia's internal gas consumption. Bovanenkovo has a yearly production capacity of 115,000,000,000 m^3.[57] Assuming that an average four-person household in Berlin consumes 2,000 m^3 of gas per year,[58] a production capacity of 115,000,000,000 m^3 could supply gas to over 57,500,000 households annually for the next 100 years.[59]

Located far beyond the Arctic Circle, the Bovanenkovo deposit presents a challenging climatic and logistical context, with the nearest city to the south, Vorkuta, situated almost 400 km away. Winters on the Peninsula are characterised by extended periods of darkness, heavy snowfall, and sub-zero temperatures that frequently plummet to levels below −30 °C. Conversely, during the summer, approximately 80 % of the territory is blanketed by a serene beauty of lakes, marshes, and rivers, presenting substantial hurdles for transportation, infrastructure development, and human endeavours within the region. In its pursuit to exploit the resources of the Peninsula, Gazprom relies on a comprehensive infrastructural backbone. This includes extensive road networks, the construction of gas power stations for essential energy supply, the establishment of rotational camps to accommodate workers, the creation of industrial bases for efficient operations, the implementation of a railroad system for logistics, and the construction of an airport to facilitate transportation and connectivity.[60]

Fig. 14 Russian gas field reserves, 2023 in km^3

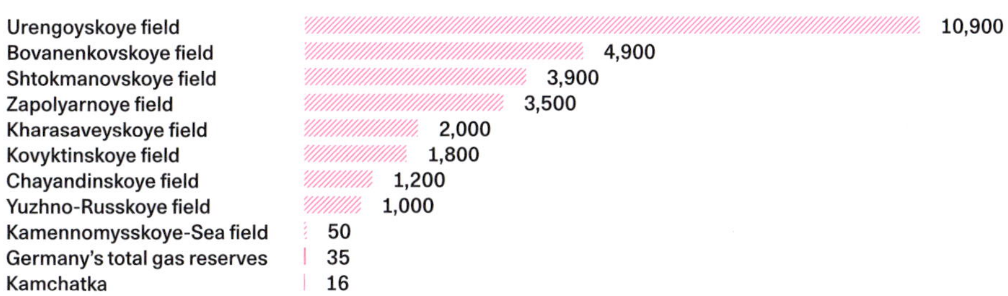

Structure of the Field

The field includes three gas production facilities consecutively brought into operation in 2012, 2014, and 2018, known as GP-1, GP-2, and GP-3. [Fig. 24] These facilities collectively employ nearly 2,400 staff members who adhere to a consistent shift schedule involving one month on and one month off, ensuring the continuous presence of 1,200 Gazprom employees on the field. While there, the employees live in a rotational residential complex, supported by a canteen, a shop, a medical outpatient clinic, and a fitness studio. Plans have been approved for the construction of a fully-fledged medical facility, a cinema, and an Orthodox church.[61]

The process of gas extraction starts with drilling using movable drilling rigs. From the wells, gas travels by pipelines to a complex treatment unit, arriving at the gathering station to be cleaned of sand and clay. Gas is then cooled to −30 °C to remove any frozen water. The final step occurs at the compressor station, where gas is pressurised and transported to the main pipeline to be fed into Russia's UGSS.

Fig. 15 Nenets people

The Nenets People

While Gazprom workers reside in their permanent city of containers, pipelines, and drill towers on one side, another group of inhabitants calls the Peninsula—roughly the size of the UK—home. For over a millennium, the Nenets nomads, akin to the Sámi and Chukchi people of Arctic Eurasia, have cultivated extensive reindeer breeding in the tundra to preserve their traditional way of life. In contrast to other regions in Arctic Russia, Yamal witnessed the persistence and even growth of reindeer husbandry following the dissolution of the Soviet Union. In fact, today, this area boasts the world's largest herds, with roughly 600,000 reindeer managed by 15,000 nomads.[62] Notably, over 60 % of the reindeer population is owned by private herders and Indigenous cooperatives, with the remaining reindeer belonging to state-owned enterprises. This intricate interplay between traditional practices and evolving economic structures characterises the unique herding landscape in this region. The Nenets' mobility—deeply ingrained in their traditional lifestyle and influenced by geographical remoteness, the vast expanse of their territory, and its impact on their values, behaviour, and economic complexity—has played a crucial role in their ability to adapt to significant climate and social changes. In turn, this adaptability has allowed them to preserve their unique culture and language, an achievement that has eluded many other Indigenous groups. However, concerns have arisen regarding the existing and potential alienation from pastures due to growing gas extraction, infrastructure, and construction development, including the 500 km-long Obskaya–Bovanenkovo railroad designed to deliver material and equipment to and from the fields. Research strongly emphasises the impact on herders' mobility, which could impede their capacity to adapt amidst growing competition for land resources and potential ecosystem degradation.[63]

More than 65 % of Russian and 18 % of world gas reserves are concentrated on the territory of the Yamalo-Nenets Autonomous Okrug.[64] Despite Gazprom's claims that they have opted for a high degree of automation in gas transmission facilities to minimise environmental impacts,[65] an operation such as the scale of the Bovanenkovo field inevitably results in significant alterations and effects on the landscape and biosphere, particularly in northern ecosystems, which are known to accumulate persistent organic pollutants due to specific climate processes and characteristic trophic chains.[66] This project, which is anticipated to span an entire century, will increasingly underscore the intricate relationship between industrialisation and environmental considerations. Moreover, it obviates the ethical and logistical difficulties inherent in attempting to preserve Indigenous cultures in a region that is now facing extensive infrastructural development, primarily in the service of sustaining energy security for far-distant lands.

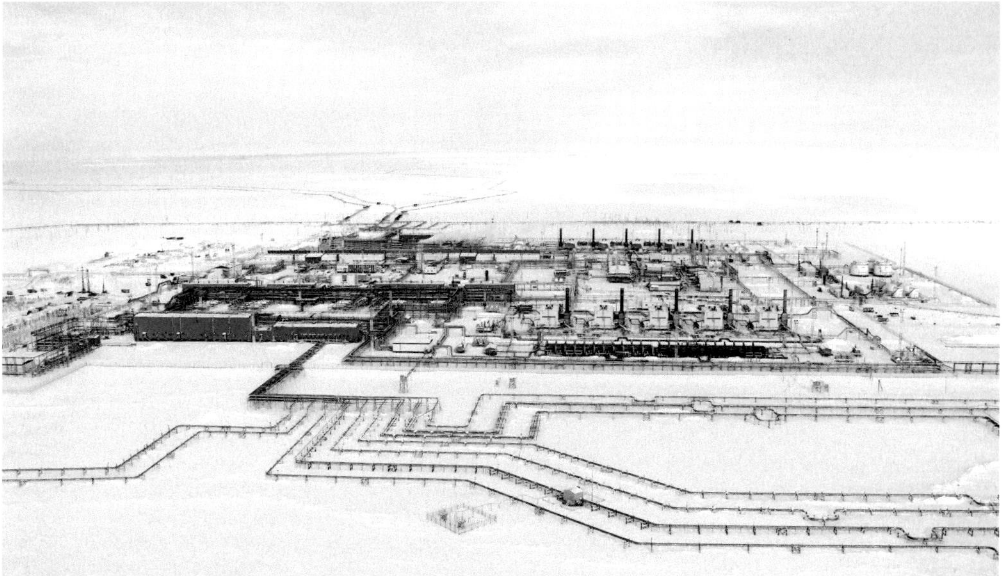

Fig. 16 Bovanenkovo field, 2013

3.4.6

Underground Gas Storage Rüdersdorf

Santiago Martínez M.
Joseph Smithard

After a decade of deliberation regarding its necessity and purpose, 2022 saw the resurgence of debates on underground gas storage as a central and extensively discussed component of energy security in Germany. A year later, fill levels were subjected to rigorous scrutiny, reported even by major news outlets on a daily basis; nonetheless, the structure, dimensions, and locations of the 46 domestic facilities remain largely unknown to the general populace.[67] [Fig. 17]

Established in 2007, the underground gas storage in Rüdersdorf sits 30 km east of Berlin and is the only operational infrastructure of its kind in Brandenburg. [Fig. 29 + 30] The facility, managed by EWE Gasspeicher GmbH, began operation in 2006 with an initial planned capacity of 300,000,000 m^3. It consists of three functional caverns. Two are designed for natural gas storage, both standing just shy of the height of the Berlin Television Tower at approximately 300 m high and 60 m in diameter. Additionally, the facility includes one cavern dedicated explicitly to experimental hydrogen storage, boasting a volume similar to that of a single-family house. According to reports, the Rüdersdorf gas storage facility had an effective working capacity of 92,000,000 m^3 by 2021.[68] However, this volume represents only a small fraction of Germany's comprehensive storage capacity, which stands at around 24,000,000,000 m^3. For comparison, the largest facility, Rehden in Niedersachsen, holds 3,900,000,000 m^3, while overall facilities in the state can store 12,425,000,000 m^3—approximately 53 % of Germany's total.[69]

Named Kalkberge-Rüdersdorf (Limestone Mountain-Rüdersdorf) until 1931, the region is known for its extensive lime deposits and stands as the most significant geological and paleontological quarry in the Berlin-Brandenburg area. The extraction of shell lime began as early as the 13th century and, over its 750-year history of limestone mining, the site has played a pivotal role in the construction of Berlin's iconic landmarks.[70] The Brandenburg Gate, Reichstag, and the Olympic Stadium, among many others, owe their structure to its limestone. The first cement factory, one of the earliest in Germany, was established in 1885. During the Second World War, the facilities experienced frequent changes in ownership and served as an expanding camp for prisoners of war. Until 1945, Preussag Rüdersdorf—now the TUI Group—retained ownership of the infrastructure, along with associated limestone mines and quarries. However, at the onset of the post-war era, authority was transferred to the Soviet Military Administration. The Soviets repurposed certain wartime infrastructure, adapting it for synthetic fertiliser production. By 1959, the newly constructed chemical factory had achieved an annual output of 21,000 t of magnesium phosphate. Nonetheless, in the post-war period, Rüdersdorf continued as a preeminent hub for limestone extraction, solidifying its position as the largest producer of building materials in the DDR, a trend that endured even after German reunification.[71] By the mid 2000s, the Rüdersdorfer Zement GmbH had established itself as one of the preeminent cement producers in Central Europe, characterised by a quarry that sprawled across an expansive territory—measuring 4 km in length, 1 km in width, and delving to depths of up to 60 m.[72]

During this period, the area witnessed the establishment of extensive subterranean facilities for the natural gas industry, taking advantage of its underground salt formations, which proved to be favourable for gas injection. Using salt caverns as storage

Fig. 17 Underground storage for natural gas and oil products, 2021 in km^3

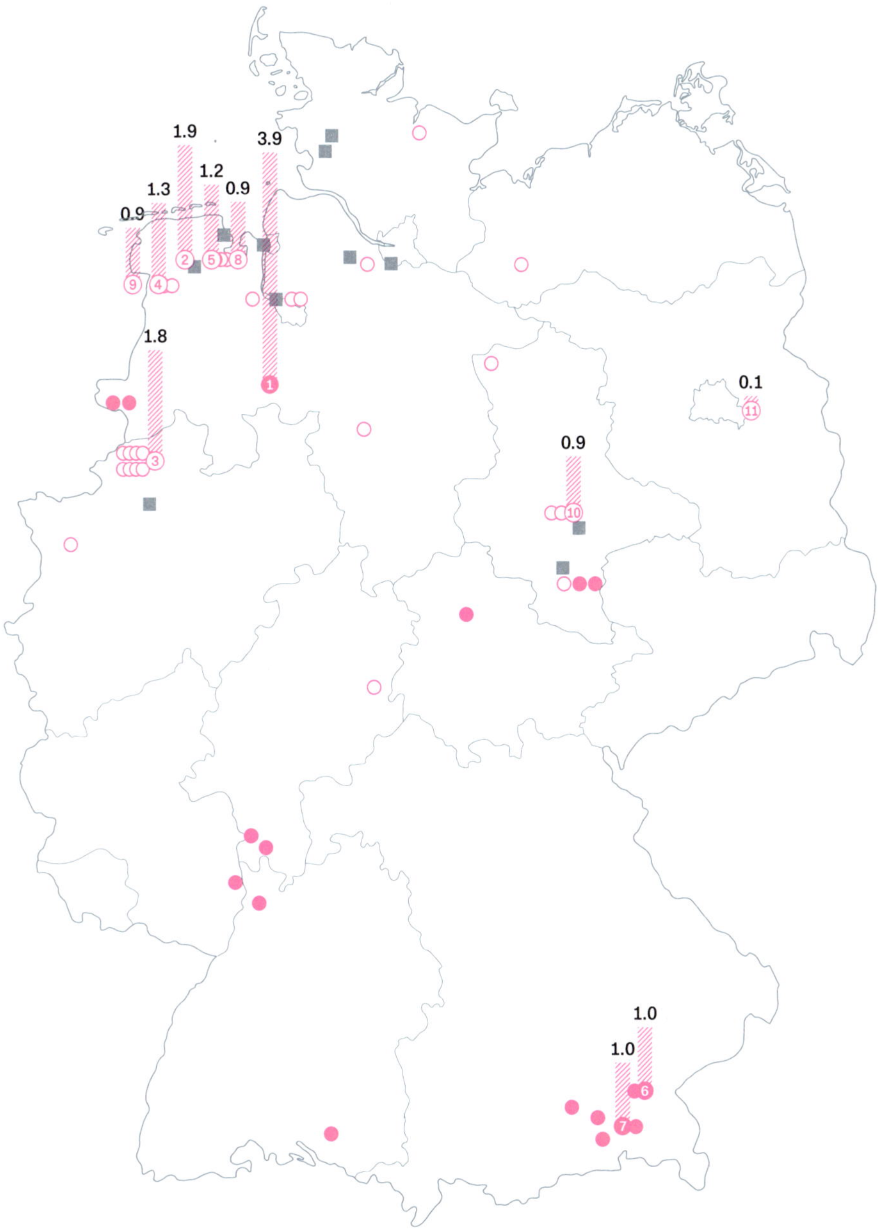

- ① Rehden (astora, WINGAS)
- ② Etzel-ESE (Uniper Energy Storage, PATRIZIA)
- ③ Epe-Uniper (Uniper Energy Storage)
- ④ Nüttermoor (EWE GASSPEICHER)
- ⑤ Etzel-EGL 1 and 2 (Equinor Storage Deutschland, PATRIZIA)
- ⑥ Bierwang (Uniper Energy Storage)
- ⑦ Breitbrunn-Eggstätt (Uniper Energy Storage, DEA, Storengy)
- ⑧ Etzel-EKB (EKB, PATRIZIA)
- ⑨ Jemgum-astora (astora, VNG, WINGAS)
- ⑩ Bernburg (VNG Gasspeicher)
- ⑪ Rüdersdorf (EWE GASSPEICHER)

- ● Storage in porous rock for natural gas
- ○ Storage in caverns for natural gas
- ■ Storage in caverns for crude oil, subproducts, and liquefied gas

solutions offered inherent advantages, since water injection into salt deposits creates large, stable chambers with natural permeability, eliminating the need for additional sealing measures. Nonetheless, these actions provoked significant concern among the local populace and the authorities, primarily due to their limited familiarity with the underlying technology. The idea of storing a substantial yet concealed "powder keg", with the potential for nearby explosions, understandably instilled fear and trepidation. However, these apprehensions gradually abated through a series of informative sessions and visits to natural gas storage facilities in other regions of the nation.[73]

Given these geological advantages, and Rüdersdorf's historical significance in the material construction of Berlin, the gas storage facility currently occupies a vital role in the region's wider energy provision. Its location, just beyond the immediate agglomeration of the city, closes the gap between natural gas and its users, a proximity that is particularly appealing in moments of supply instability or crisis.

In recent years, Germany's underground natural gas storage capacity has remained relatively stable, with only a modest increase of 22% between 2005 and 2022.[74] In contrast, between 1998 and 2022, natural gas production in Germany has seen a sharp decrease of 74%.[75] [Fig. 11] As gas usage continued to advance over the last two decades, the decline in domestic production, coupled with the relatively constant storage capacity, underscored the growing reliance on imports. However, the strategy to depend on uninterrupted daily flows primarily through eastern pipelines for gas supply, rather than expanding and maintaining sufficient local buffers, has had its drawbacks.

Fig. 18 Capacity of underground natural gas storage in Germany, 2005–2022 in km³

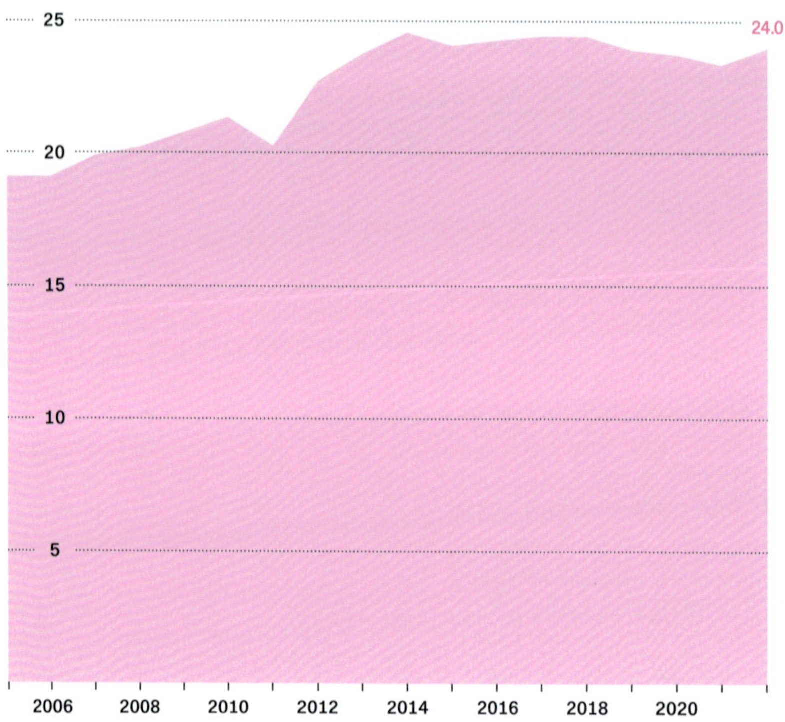

Endnotes

1 International Energy Agency, "Global Energy Review 2021 – Analysis".
2 The pioneering enterprise that initially offered manufactured gas to consumers as a utility was the Gas Light and Coke Company, headquartered in London in 1813. The technology subsequently spread from England—in the form of entrepreneurial ventures—to various European cities, including Brussels in 1818, Amsterdam and Rotterdam in 1822, and Hanover and Berlin in 1826.
3 For a detailed account see: Tarr and Clay, "Boom and Bust in Pittsburgh Natural Gas History", 324.
4 "Department of Public Utilities History | Mass.Gov".
5 Tarr and Clay, 342.
6 Castaneda, "Natural Gas, History Of", 212.
7 Banks, *Energy Economics*, 82.
8 For a compact historical account, please refer to: Craig et al., "The History of the European Oil and Gas Industry (1600s–2000s)".
9 Banks, *Energy Economics*, 82.
10 Verda, *A Link of Steel. The Western Europe-Russia Gas Pipeline Network in the Post-Soviet Era,* 37.
11 Perović, "The Soviet Union's Rise as an International Energy Power", 20.
12 Ibid., 11.
13 Jensen-Eriksen, "The Cold War in Energy Markets", 196–7.
14 Perović, 15.
15 Ibid., 22.
16 Verda, 41.
17 Ibid., 42.
18 Ibid., 45.
19 For a broader showcase of projects, please refer to: Borisocheva, *Analysis of the Oil- and Gas-Pipeline-Links between EU and Russia.*
20 Verda, 61.
21 European Council, "EU Sanctions against Russia Explained".
22 Fischer and Küper, "Die Bedeutung russischer Gaslieferungen für die deutsche Energieversorgung".
23 For a thorough analysis of the debated advantages of expanding gas supply in energy sector decarbonisation strategies, please see: Gürsan and De Gooyert, "The Systemic Impact of a Transition Fuel".
24 International Energy Agency, "World Energy Outlook 2022 – Analysis", 365.
25 Jenkins, *Energy Systems: A Very Short Introduction*, 41–42.
26 Banks, *Energy Economics*, 88.
27 Jenkins, *Energy Systems: A Very Short Introduction*, 40.
28 Kuuskraa, "Natural Gas Resources, Unconventional".
29 Banks, *Energy Economics*, 83.
30 Civan, "Natural Gas Transportation, and Storage", 275–76.
31 Weems and Howell, "Japan's Pivotal Role in the Global LNG Industry's 50-Year History".
32 Banks, *Energy Economics*, 82.
33 Mallison, "Natural Gas Processing and Products", 235–37.
34 Civan, "Natural Gas Transportation and Storage", 277.
35 Civan, 276.
36 Bundesanstalt für Geowissenschaften und Rohstoffe: "BGR Energiestudie 2023 – Daten und Entwicklungen der deutschen und globalen Energieversorgung", 20. Note that the numbers vary considerably by statistical source.
37 BDEW, "Die Energieversorgung 2022 – Jahresbericht", 11.
38 Güßgen, "RWE-Chef dringt auf Verdopplung der Gaskraft in Deutschland".
39 BVEG, "Jahresbericht Erdgasförderung". The figures vary considerably depending on the source.
40 LBEG, *Erdöl und Erdgas in der Bundesrepublik Deutschland 2021*, Apendix 13.
41 Various sources provide differing estimates of natural gas potential, with the Bundesanstalt für Geowissenschaften und Rohstoffe (BGR) indicating a conservative estimate of approximately 1,300,000,000,000 m^3. See: BGR, "Neue Studie zum Schiefergas-Potenzial in Deutschland".
42 Bundesministerium für Wirtschaft und Klimaschutz, Gesetz zur Änderung wasser- und naturschutzrechtlicher Vorschriften zur Untersagung und zur Risikominimierung bei den Verfahren der Fracking-Technologie, § 13a.
43 BGR, *Energiedaten 2022 – Daten uu Entwicklungen der Deutschen und globalen Energieversorgung*, A-19.
44 AG Energiebilanzen e. V., "Pressemitteilung: Bericht für 2022".
45 Bundesanstalt für Geowissenschaften und Rohstoffe, 20.
46 BGR, A-20.
47 Bundesministerium für Wirtschaft und Energie, "Versorgungssicherheit bei Erdgas – Monitoring-Bericht nach §51 EnWG", 11–13.
48 Bundesministerium für Wirtschaft und Klimaschutz, "Erdgasversorgung in Deutschland".
49 FNB Gas, "Netzentwicklungsplan Gas 2020–2030, Kurzfassung".
50 In accordance with the Köppen–Geiger Climate Classification.
51 Gazprom Russia, "Gazprom launches Yamal megaproject".
52 Ikonnikova, "Multilateral Bargaining and Strategic Investments in the Eurasian Gas Supply Network", 2–3.
53 Gazprom Russia, "Yamal – Europe".
54 Reuters, "Eastbound Yamal–Europe Gas Pipeline Flows Drop".
55 O'Carroll and Jones, "EU Imports of Russian Liquified Gas Leap by 40 % since Ukraine Invasion".
56 Nord Stream AG, "Die Pipeline".
57 Gazprom Russia, "Bovanenkovskoye Field's Final Gas Facility and Ukhta – Torzhok 2 Gas Pipeline Brought into Operation".
58 GASAG AG, "Gasverbrauch".
59 Author's calculation: 115,000,000,000 m^3 / 2,000 m^3 per household, which is equivalent to 57,500,000 households (annually).
60 For a comprehensive overview, please refer to: Gazprom Russia, "Power of Yamal".
61 URA, "5 Years Bovanenkovo: What You Need to Know about Yamal's Biggest Gas Project".
62 Ash, "Yamal Reindeer Herders Hemmed in by Gas Fields and Pipelines".
63 Schwalbe, *The Yamal LNG Project and the Nenets Reindeer Nomads. Impacts, Survival and Indigenous Opposition to Gas Exploitation in Russia's Arctic*, 7.
64 Alekseeva and Yashchenko, "Determination of Factors Influencing the State of Natural Environment in the Yamal-Nenets Autonomus Okrug According to Remote Data", 1.
65 Gazprom Russia 2021.
66 Kozhushkevich et al., "Temporal Dynamics of Dioxin Contamination of Reindeer Offal from Russian Far North Regions".
67 LBEG, *Erdöl und Erdgas in der Bundesrepublik Deutschland 2021*, 41.
68 Ibid., 42.
69 Ibid., 44–47.
70 Museumspark Rüdersdorf, "Industriegeschichte hautnah".
71 Ibid.
72 Wings, "The Rüdersdorf Muschelkalk Quarry".
73 Steyer, "Brandenburg".
74 BDEW, "Die Energieversorgung 2022 – Jahresbericht".
75 British Petroleum, *Statistical Review of World Energy 2021.*

Fig. 19 Total natural gas production and exports by country, 2022 in km^3

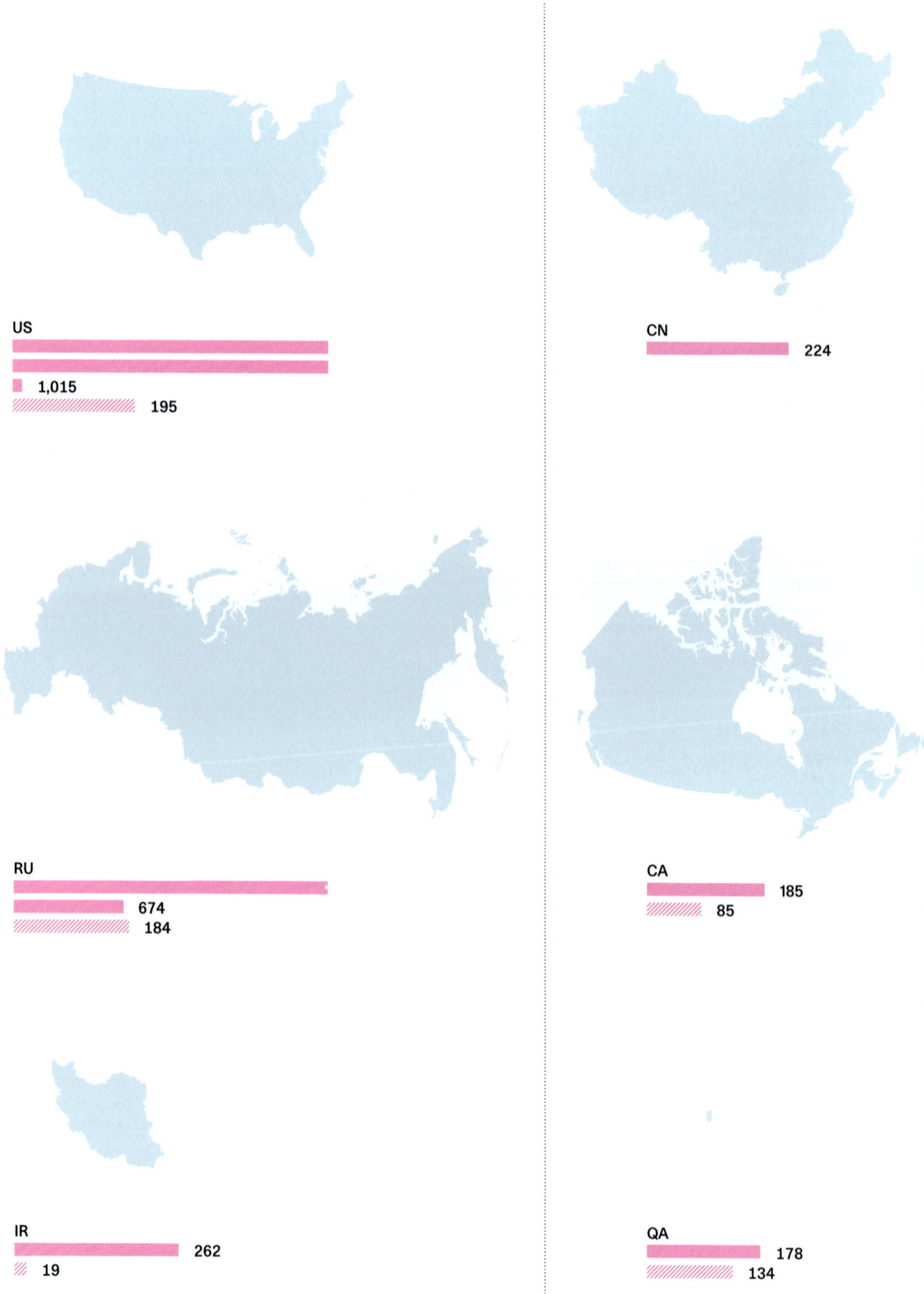

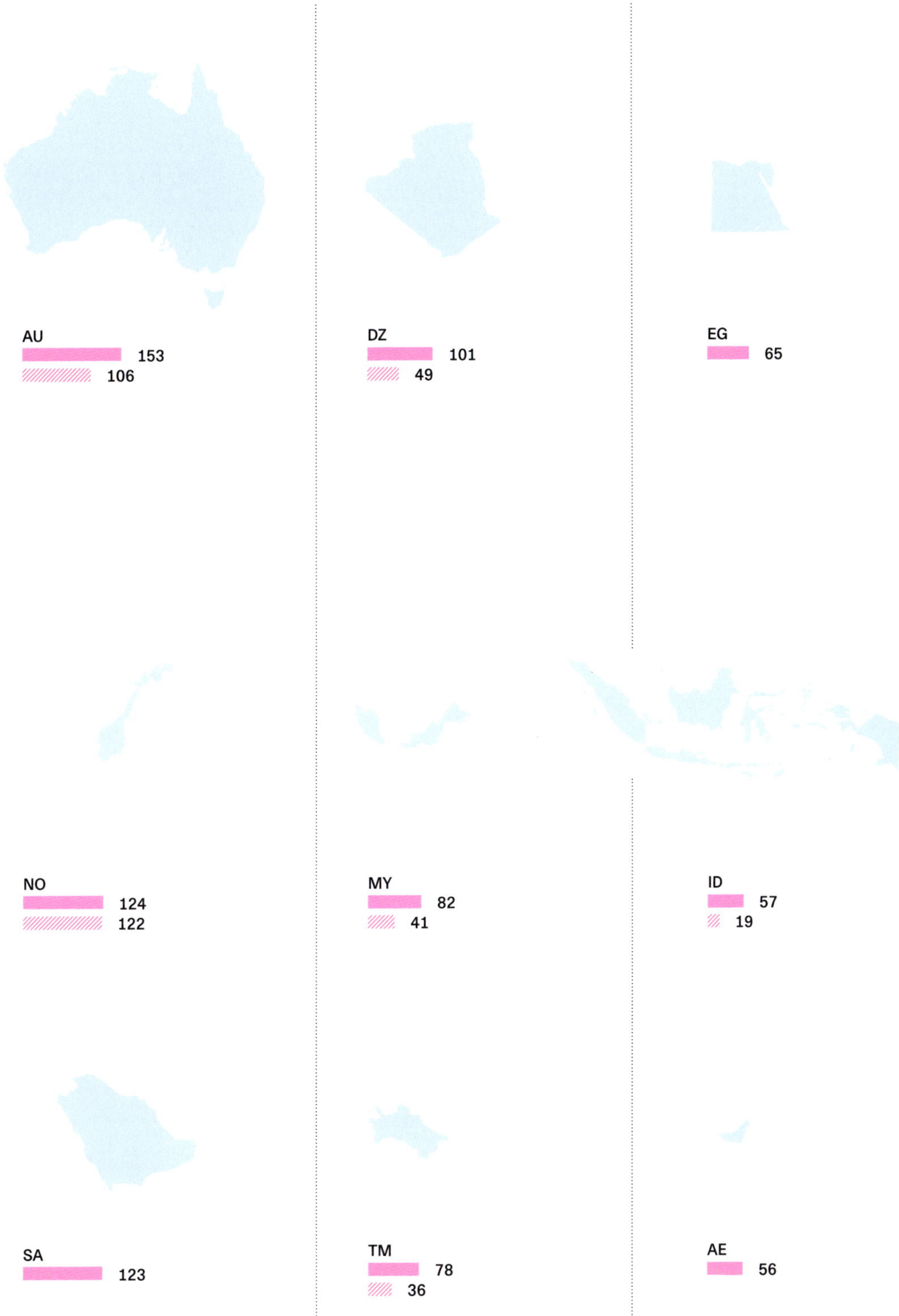
AU
153
106
DZ
101
49
EG
65
NO
124
122
MY
82
41
ID
57
19
SA
123
TM
78
36
AE
56

Fig. 20 Natural gas supply chain

Natural gas — Pipeline — Maritime — Railway — Road — Byproducts

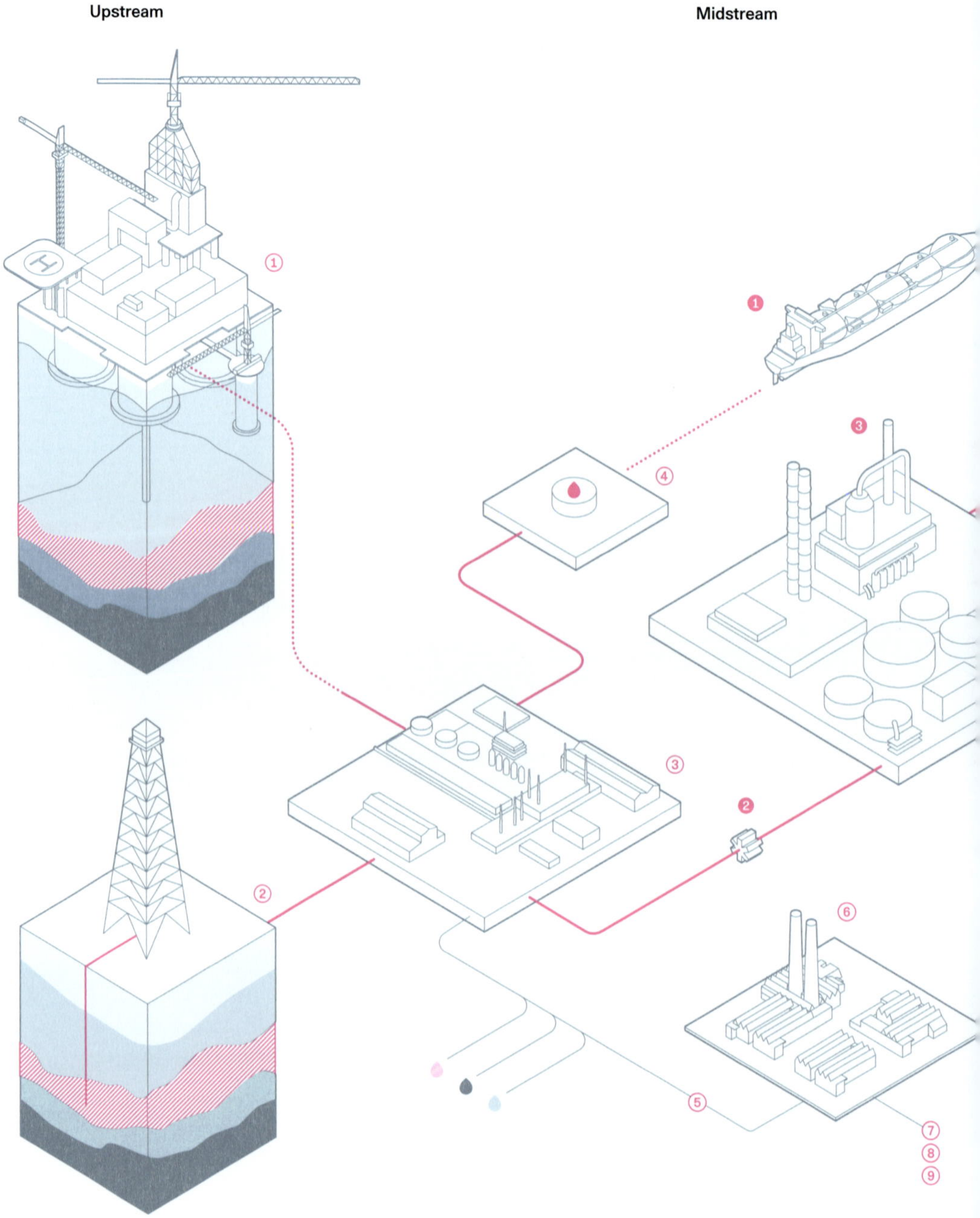

Production (RU, NO, NL, RoW)

1. Offshore
2. Onshore
3. Processing plant
4. Liquefaction plant
5. Sulphur and CO_2 removal
6. Fractionators
7. LPG
8. Refineries
9. Feedstocks

- Liquefied natural gas
- Natural gas liquids
- Water
- Oil

Transmission (various countries)

1. LNG ships
2. Pipeline inspection gauge
3. HUB
4. Storage and regasification units

Downstream

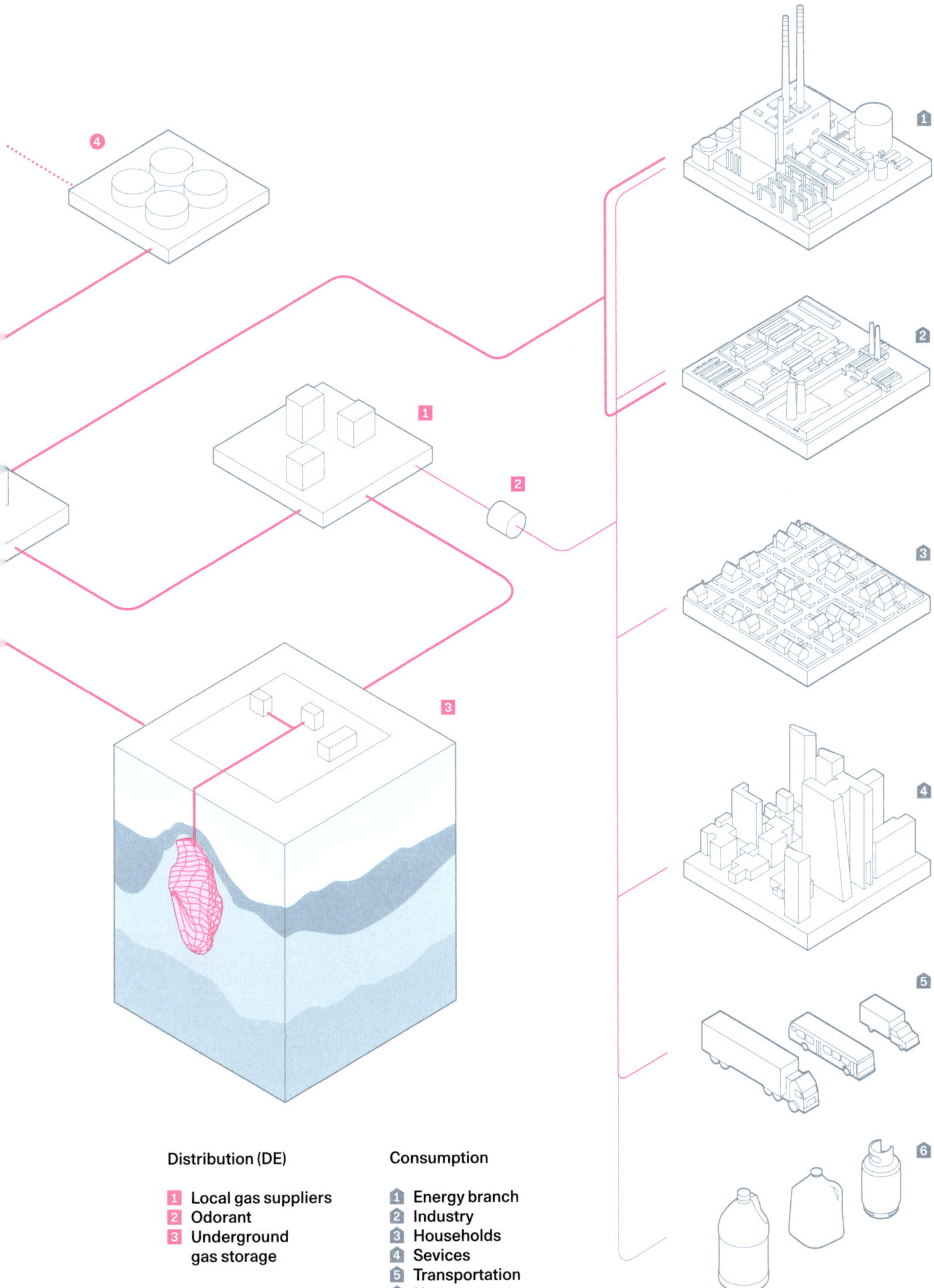

Distribution (DE)

1. Local gas suppliers
2. Odorant
3. Underground gas storage

Consumption

1. Energy branch
2. Industry
3. Households
4. Sevices
5. Transportation
6. Non-energy products

Fig. 21 Global gas extraction and import routes

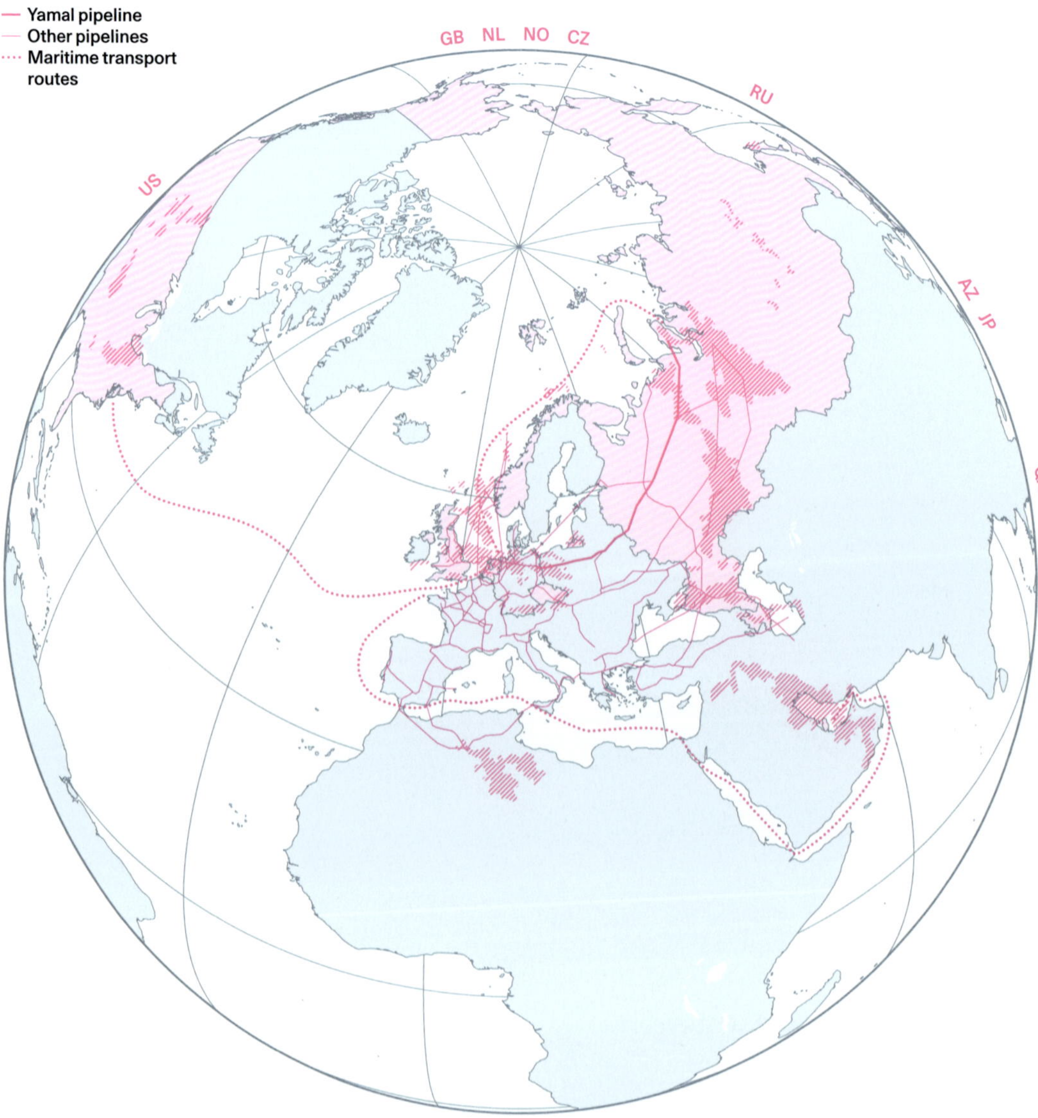

Fig. 22 Import of natural gas to Germany, 2021–24 in %

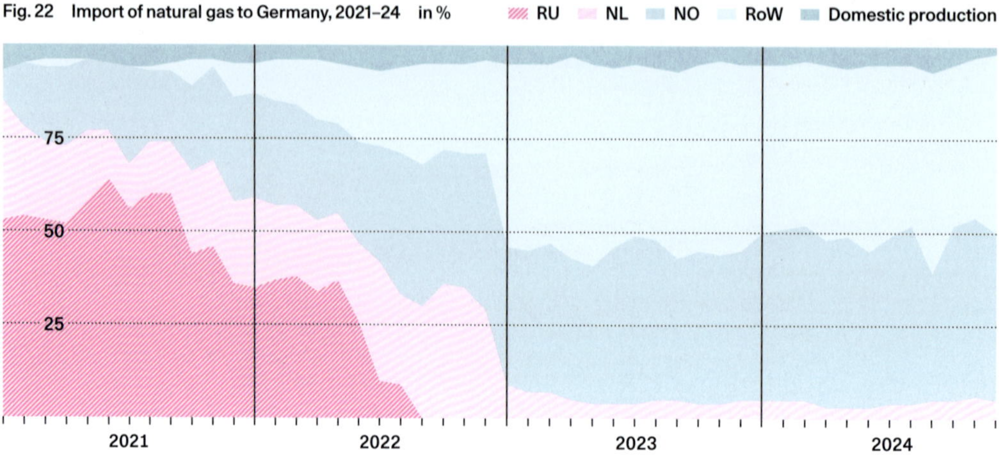

Fig. 23 Yamal–Europe pipeline

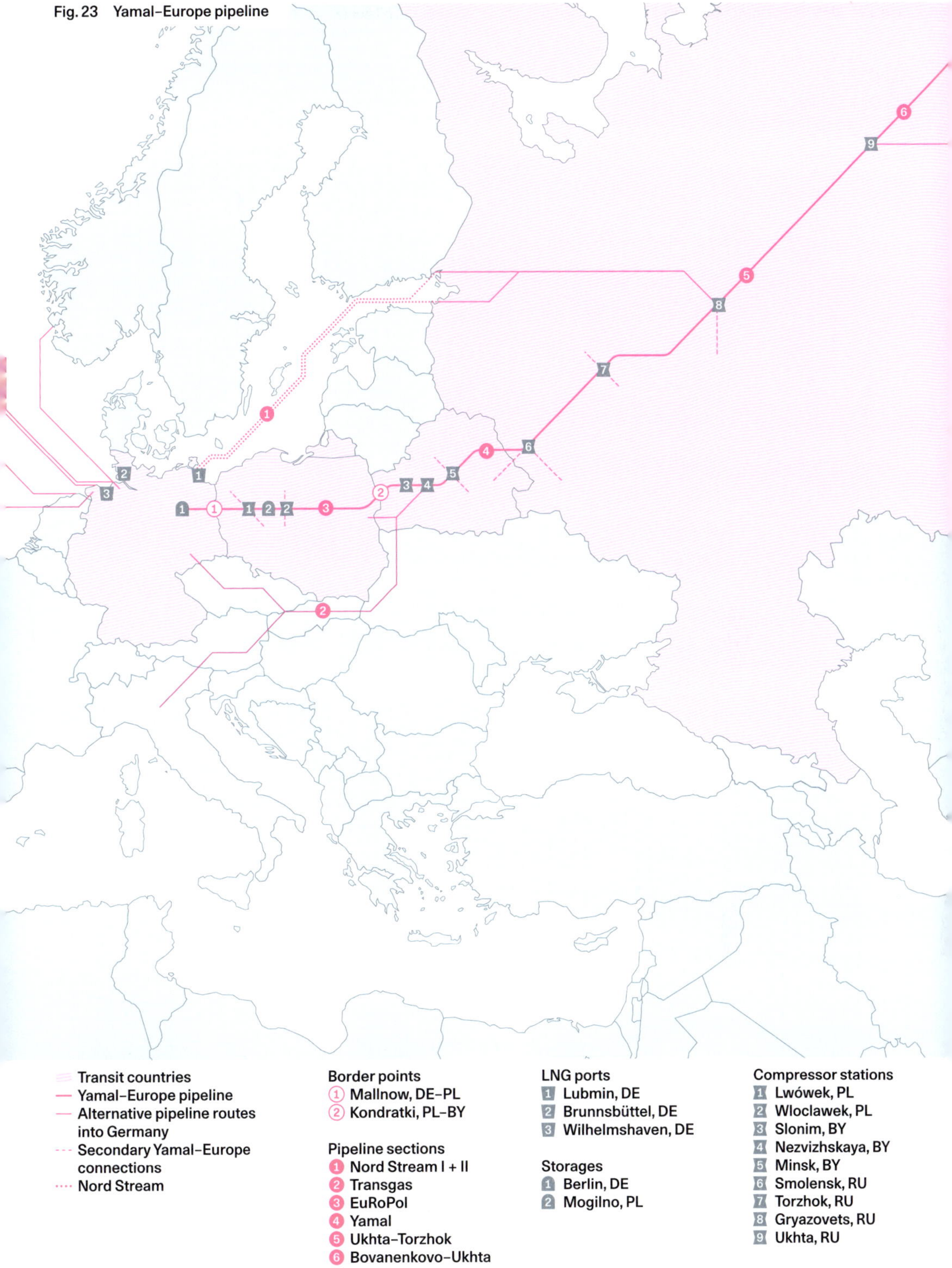

Fig. 24 Bovanenkovo gas extraction field, 2022

1 GP-1
2 GP-2
3 Substation
4 Drilling base
5 Production base for GP-2

(1) Bovanenkovo Airport
(2) Karskaya railway station
(3) Rotational residential complex
(4) Helipad

Production facility
Extraction well
Bovanenkovo–Ukhta pipeline
Other pipelines
Railways
Migration routes of reindeer

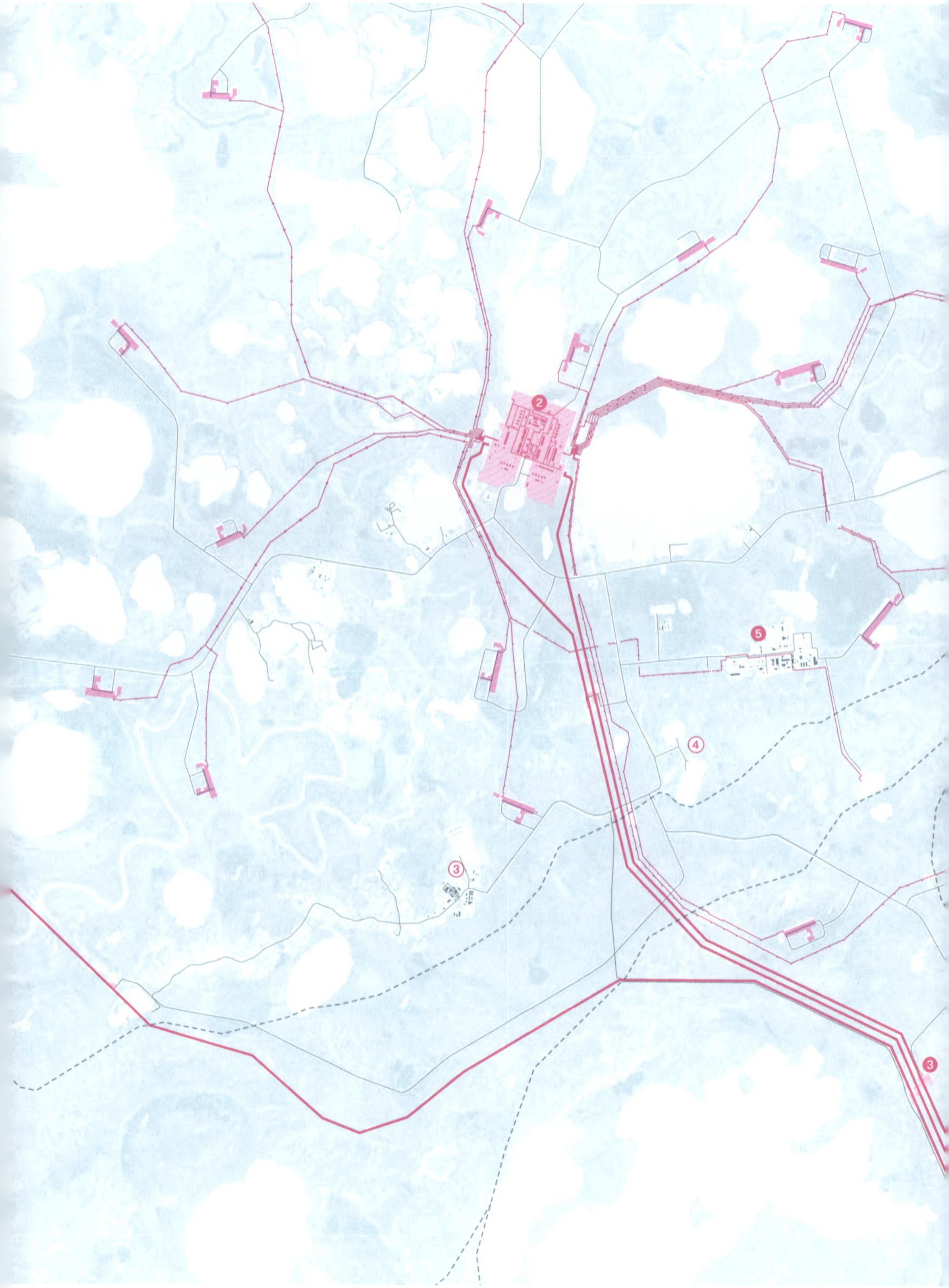

3
3
4
4
4
4
2
1
4
1
2 km

Fig. 25 Historic development of the Bovanenkovo gas extraction field, 2006

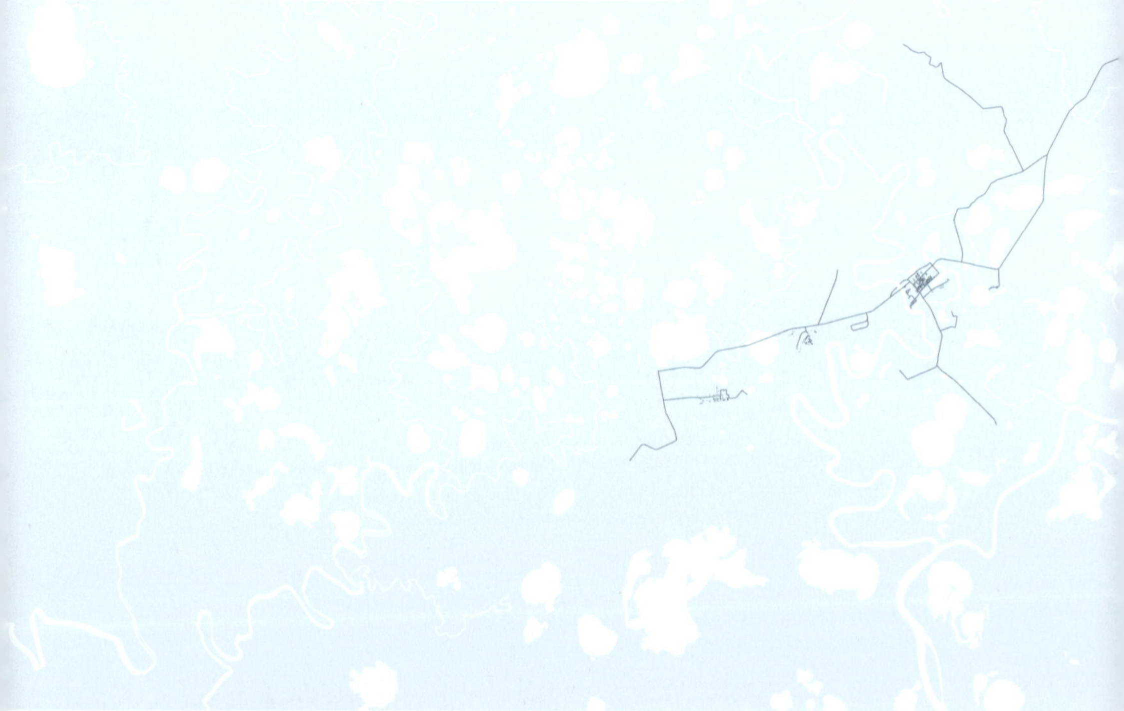

1972 The gas field is discovered.
2000s Basic civil facilities are built.

Fig. 26 Historic development of the Bovanenkovo gas extraction field, 2009

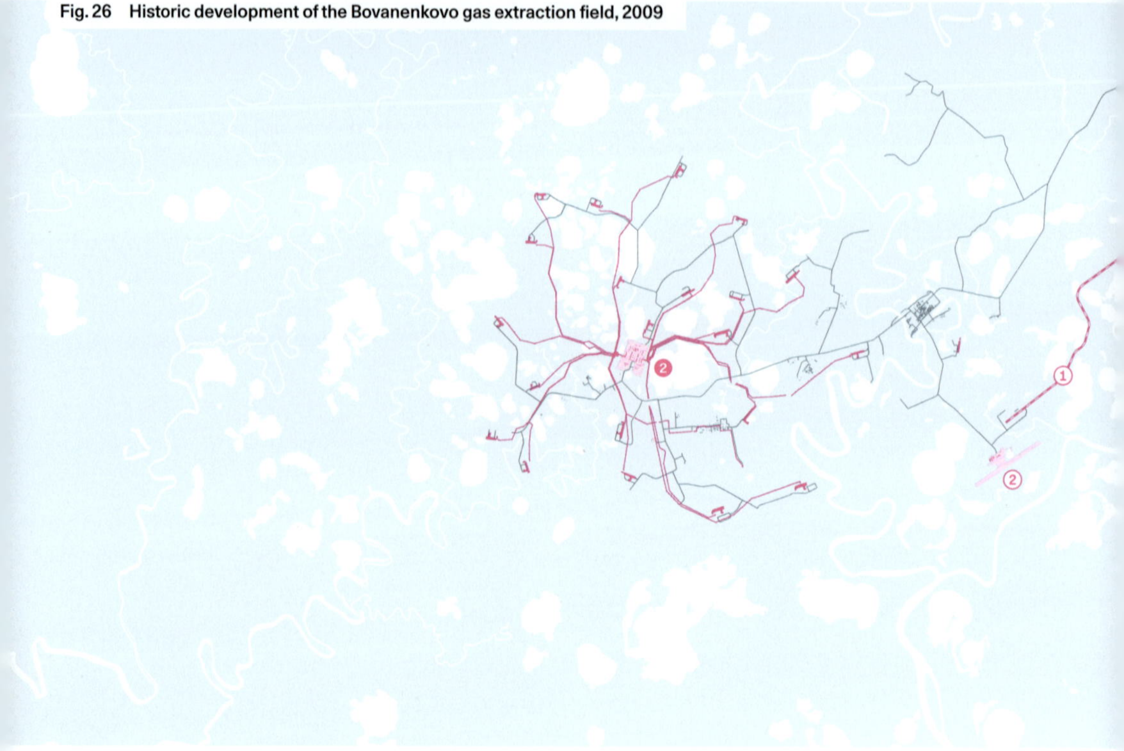

2009 Construction of the GP-2 gas field ❷, the Obskaya–Bovanenkovo–Karskaya railway ①, and the Bovanenkovo Airport ②

Fig. 27 Historic development of the Bovanenkovo gas extraction field, 2012

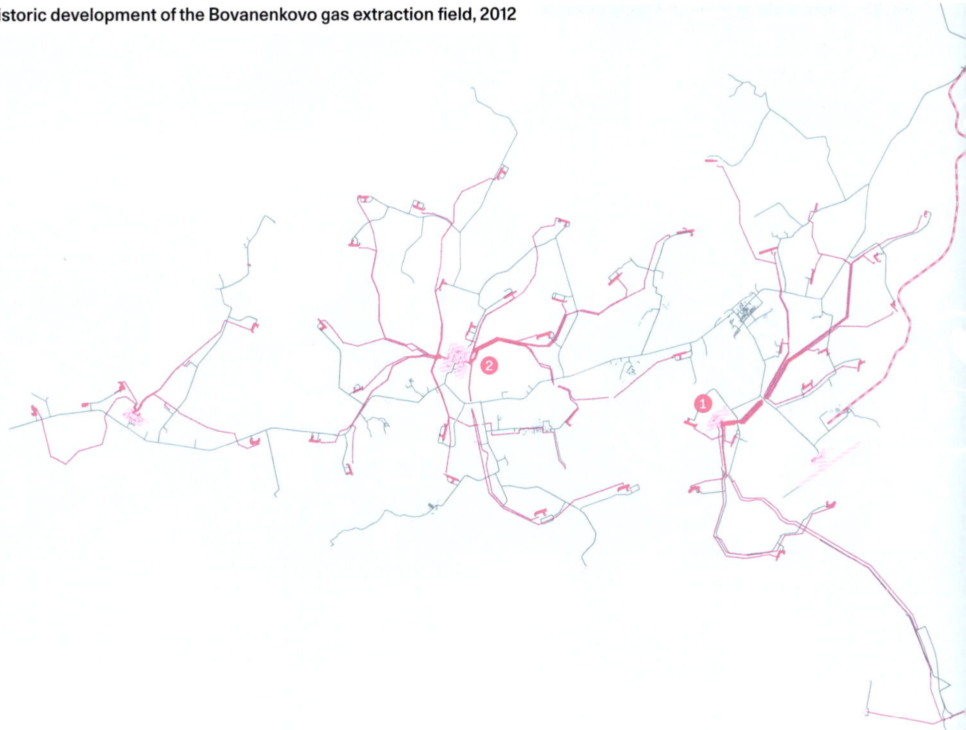

2012 GP-2 gas field ② begins to operate.
2014 GP-1 gas field ① begins to operate.

Fig. 28 Historic development of the Bovanenkovo gas extraction field, 2024

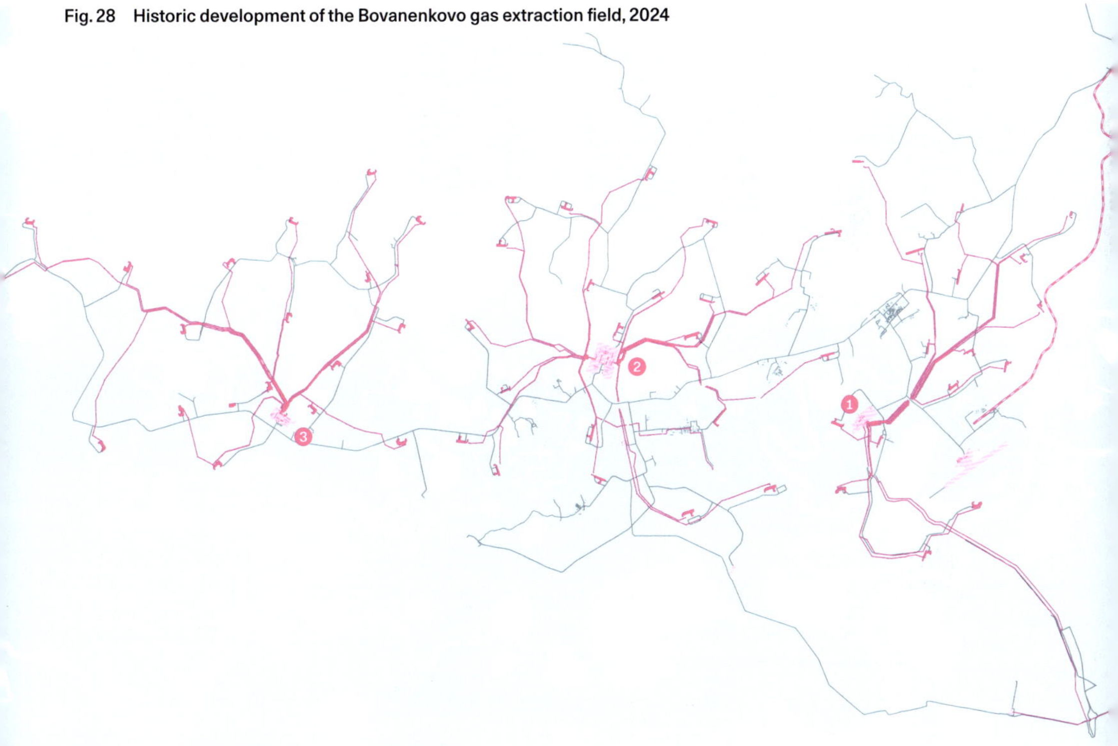

2018 GP-3 gas field ③ begins to operate.
2022 Reaches full operational capacity.

10 km

Fig. 29 Gas storage Rüdersdorf, 2022

Locations
1 EWE gas storage Rüdersdorf
2 Rüdersdorf bei Berlin
3 Alt-Rüdersdorf
4 Limestone open-pit
5 CEMEX Deutschland
6 Stienitzsee

Gas storage facility
Pipelines
Railways

1 km

Fig. 30 Schematic section of the gas storage facility in Rüdersdorf

Gas storage
① EWE gas storage Rüdersdorf
② Hydrogen cavern (experimental)
③ Natural gas caverns (~300 m high × 60 m wide)
④ Gas pipeline

Soil layers
① Ground moraine formations
② Salt rock layer
③ Anhydrite and underground water

Depths
1 300 m
2 1,000 m
3 3,000 m

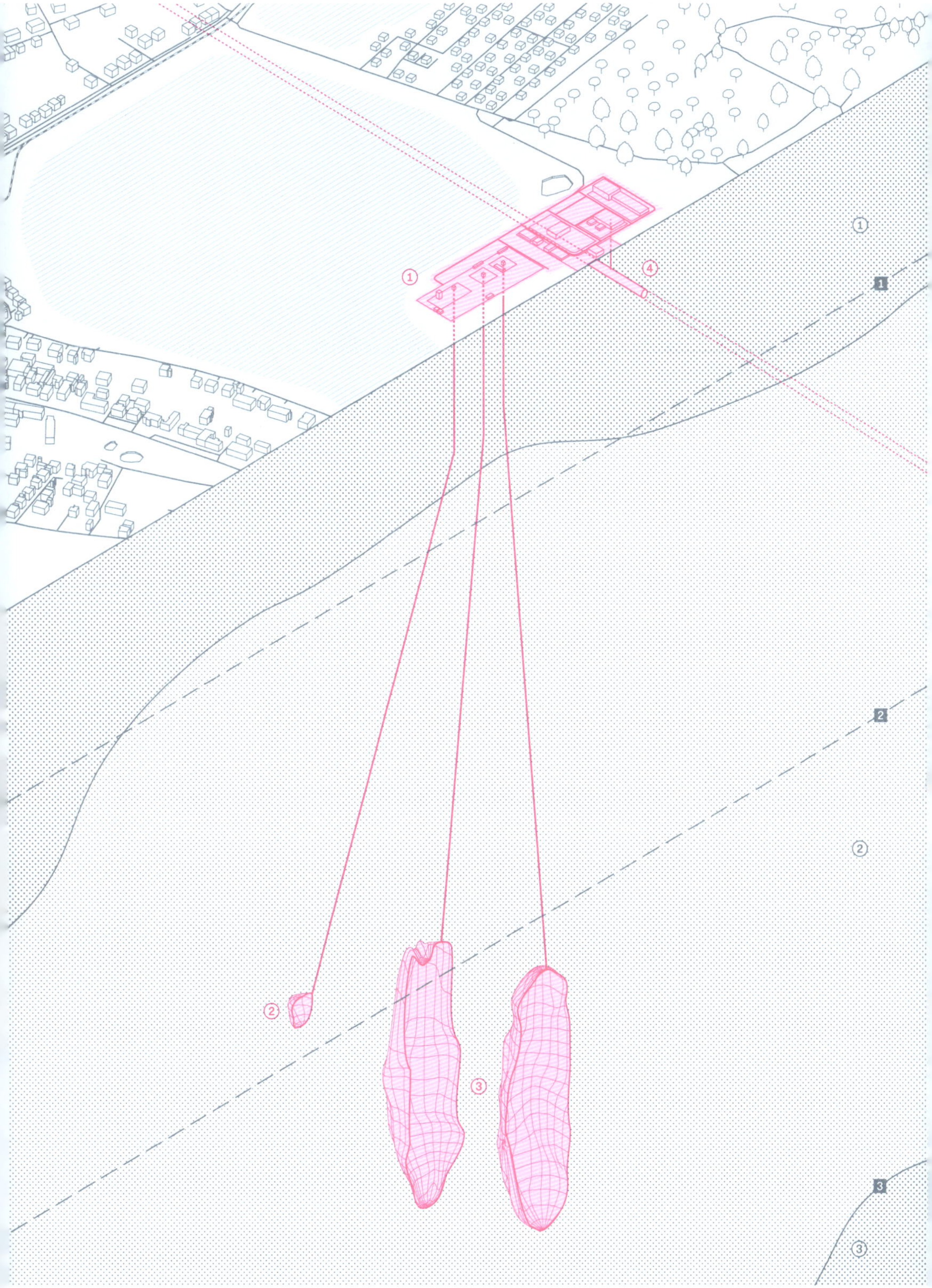

Fig. 31 Schematic construction of an underground gas storage facility

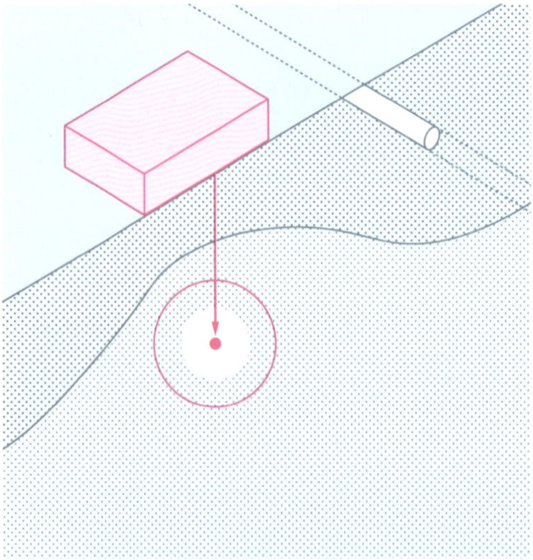

① A well is drilled in proximity to an existing gas pipeline and water is injected underground.

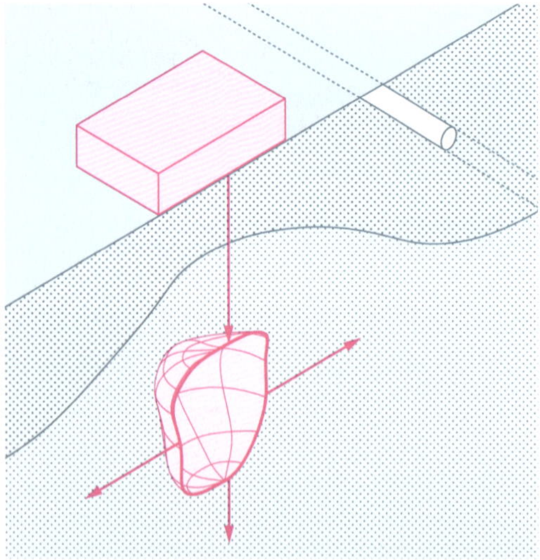

② Water dissolves salt rock and creates an airtight cavity.

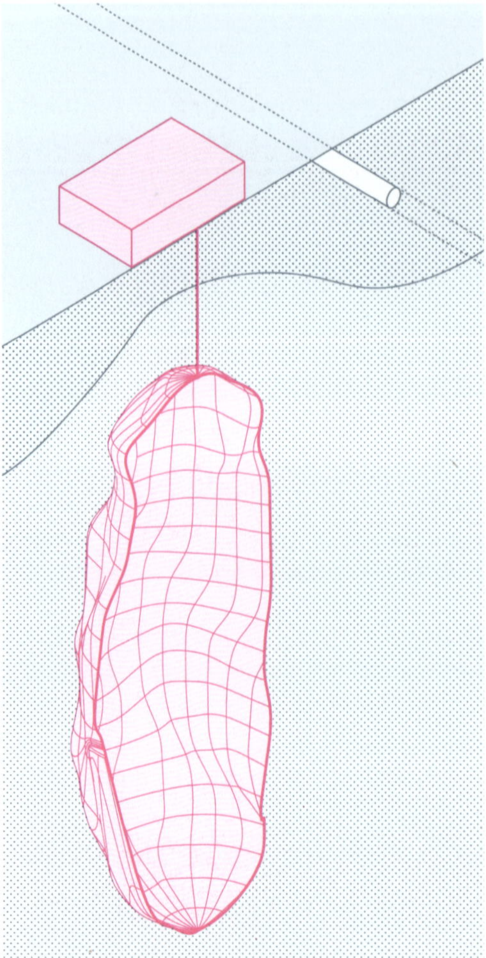

③ Cavern expands and reaches operational size, usually up to 500 m high and 100 m wide.

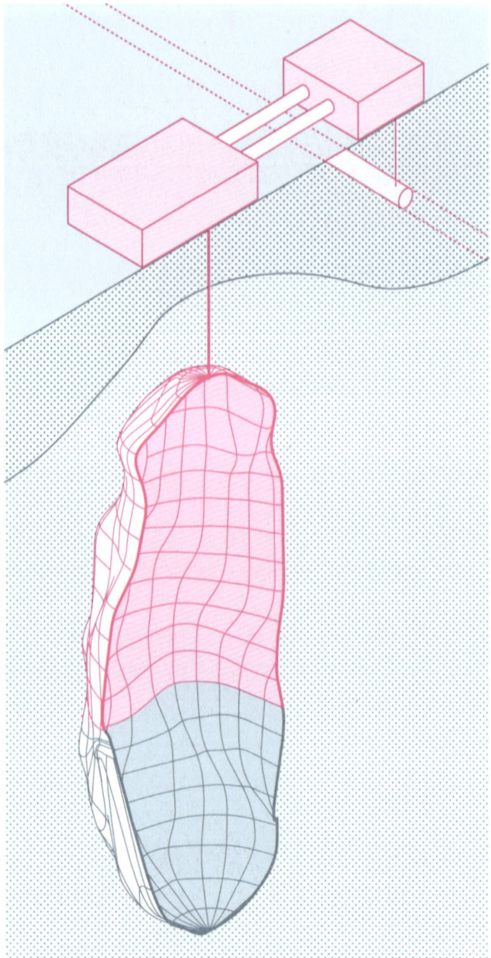

② Storage is connected to a pipeline. 70 % of volume is usable gas while 30 % is the minimum volume for structural stability.

4 Renewable Energy Carriers

16 m²

4–8 m²

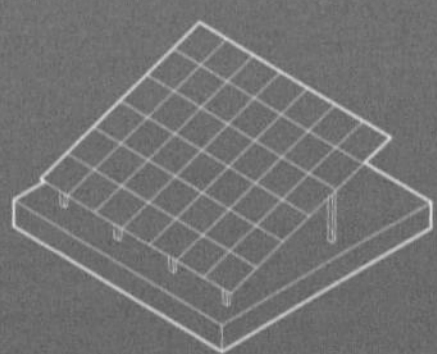

100–200 m²

Each of these units produce 1 kWh of electricity within eight hours.[1]

Introduction to Renewables

David Bauer
Philipp Deilmann
Joseph Smithard

Renewable energy [RE] has been harnessed as a technology since long before we knew what to call it. Throughout history, civilisations have ingeniously utilised the power of the environments they inhabited to meet their energy needs. Wind propelled ships across oceans, exploring new worlds and fortifying maritime trade. Water drove mills and machinery, providing food and much-needed respite from arduous heavy work. Some civilisations, where available, even harvested this technology for comfort and leisure, tapping into naturally occurring hot springs to warm their public baths.

However, it was not until the early 20th century, with writers such as the philosopher of technology Lewis Mumford, that the idea of utilising solar, wind, and water for nationwide energy supply was revisited. Mumford argued that the Industrial Revolution's dependence on fossil fuels ushered in what he called the age of "palaeotechnology"—an era defined by the interconnected exploitation of both human labour and natural resources. In his influential work *Technics and Civilization,* he suggested that this exploitative system could only be transformed through the adoption of what we now call renewable energy technologies. For Mumford, transitioning to renewables offered humanity a path to enter the age of "neotechnology", characterised by restored social and environmental harmony.[2] Even within the timeframe of modernity, solar technology is not new—evidenced by the construction of the first solar power stations in Egypt, which dates back as early as 1913. [Fig. 1]

However, before such innovations could gain any traction, the First and Second World War created an immediate need for readily available and high-energy-density fuels to power military combat machines. The pressing demands to expand industrial capacity quickly led to a prioritisation of burnable fossil fuels, and it was not until a decade peacetime that energy security brought about a new discourse around the use of renewables. Heavily influenced by M. King Hubbert's "peak oil" theory, the future-proofing potential of oil was brought into question.[3] Hubbert argued that oil production in any region would follow a bell-shaped curve, starting with steady growth before reaching a peak. Afterwards, production would begin to decline due to finite oil reserves and increased extraction costs, leading to potential economic and energy supply challenges for oil-dependent economies. Unlike today's discussions about the imperative importance of employing alternative energy sources, Hubbert's peak gained traction in the prevailing discourse primarily because it focused on resource depletion and extractive constraints as a singular concern.

The 1973 oil shock served as a wake-up call, signalling the first global energy crisis and underscoring the vulnerability of a fossil fuel-dependent Western world. In the face of a global energy shortage, the concept of scaling up renewable pilot projects—even those still in their infancy—was gaining momentum. Architect Buckminster Fuller echoed Mumford's calls for harnessing solar, wind, and water power. Fuller pioneered the concept of "Spaceship Earth", referring to the planet as a self-contained and finite system, similar to a spaceship travelling through the

THE ELECTRICAL EXPERIMENTER

H. GERNSBACK EDITOR
H. W. SECOR ASSOCIATE EDITOR

LIBRARY MAR 14 1916 U.S. PATENT OFFICE

Vol. III. Whole No. 35 MARCH, 1916 Number 11

The Utilization of the Sun's Energy

Years Ago Man Endeavored to Make Practical Use of the Energy Contained in the Sun's Rays—Even Tesla, the Electrical Wizard, Has Patented a Sun Motor, While the Shuman-Boy's Engine and Sun Boiler Has Developed 100 H. P. There Is Great Promise Held Forth to Future Engineers Who May Work on This Problem.

IT has been given to astrophysicists to measure the heat generated by the sun and calculate the force emanating from it. We know that the surface of our luminary gives out a heat estimated to be about 6,000° centigrade, and that its light equals that of 27,000,000,000 candlepower a quarter of a mile away. The heat which the were lacking, our planet, with all its thousandfold life, its thick forests and fruitful plains, would turn into a dead, rigid ball of rock, for the average annual temperature, which is now one of 13° centigradé of warmth for Europe, would, without the heat of the sun, sink to 73° centigrade of frost, it is calculated. the untaught son of nature brightens his hut, the twigs with which he stokes his fire, what are they but pieces of trees that grew in the sunlight? The gas of the city dweller, the coals with which he heats his house and from which the gas has been sucked, what are they but transformed sunbeams? The coal in the grate is the

A Successful 100 H.P. Sun Power Plant Located at Meadi, on the Nile, Egypt.

Fig. 1 World's first solar thermal power plant in Maadi, Egypt 1913

vastness of the cosmos.[4] The analogy emphasised the interconnectedness of all life on Earth as well as the need for responsible and sustainable management of its resources. Although the primary concern continued to focus on resource depletion and, as such, a demand for sufficient energy to power both technology and the economy, Fuller encouraged a shift from a mindset of unlimited resource consumption to one of mindful stewardship. Over the following decades, environmental and counterculture movements began to gather strength.

On the one hand this acceleration was propelled by the increased popularity and accessibility of texts like Rachel Carson's *Silent Spring*,[5] which fuelled global concern about the widespread, cross-boundary toxic pollution experienced across a diversity of regions, nations, and continents. Furthermore, concern about the capacity of Earth's limited resources to support a rapidly growing population—highlighted in various studies, including the prominent *Limits to Growth*[6] report—as well as matters of energy production and consumption began to capture the attention of a broader audience, arguably ranging across economic spectrums and ideologies. Elsewhere, a profound techno-pessimism emerged in response to the unfulfilled promises of "peaceful" nuclear energy, and the disturbing rationale behind the escalating nuclear arms race. In turn, this disappointment found expression through countercultural movements and off-grid groups of intentional "neo-primitives". Communities began to reimagine the world as a collaborative utopia modelled on communal ideals that were totally opposed to the greedy, alienated, and exploitive logic of the Cold War establishment. In all of this, technology regained an idealistic prospect as an essential transformative tool in leveraging and establishing autonomy—a narrative that would find its fullest expression in the emergence of the personal computer, and later by the advent of the internet. Counter-culturalists and technologists alike began jointly to reimagine computers as tools for personal liberation: platforms for constructing virtual and distinctly unconventional communities, and vehicles for venturing into unexplored social frontiers.[7]

As global protests against nuclear energy reached their peak in the final two decades of the 20th century, the term *Energiewende*—originating from a West-German ecological movement publication released in 1980—underwent a transformation, becoming a versatile loanword.[8]

Encompassing the alternative horizons envisioned by activists against nuclear power and coal usage, the term encapsulated the shifting yet persistent efforts to supplant extractive fuel-powered machinery and their metabolisms (which carried significant health risks) with renewable technologies. Presently, the worldwide recognition of the link between escalating carbon emissions and the consequences of unchecked climate change serves as the most urgent incentive to revolutionise the energy sector once and for all.

Fig. 2 Price of electricity without subsidies in $/MWh

Energy carrier	change (2010–2019)
1 Solar PV	−82 %
2 Offshore wind	−29 %
3 Onshore wind	−38 %
4 Nuclear energy	+62 %
5 Coal	−2 %

What is Renewable Energy?

The term renewable energy refers to energy sourced from natural reservoirs that undergo replenishment at a rate exceeding their consumption. Despite many potential applications and pilot projects, the electricity sector stands out as the primary domain, marked by robust growth in solar photovoltaics and wind energy in recent years, complementing the substantial contribution of the decade-old use of hydropower.
Primary energy, in the form of sunlight, weather, water, or geothermal heat can be classified as renewable since they originate from a natural cyclic process. However, the transformation of this natural energy into practically applicable forms, surpassing the millennia-old cycles of consistent energy poverty as described in previous chapters, relies on technological tools. These, like all other technological artifacts, are subject to ongoing mechanical wear. Devoid of a continual supply of care, maintenance, and essential raw materials, the solar cell lacks the means to regenerate itself and sustain the crucial task of transforming sunlight into electricity. Thus, the fuel behind renewable energy encompasses an amalgamation of solar radiation, critical minerals such as copper, lithium, nickel, cobalt, rare-earth elements REE (which will be discussed in the forthcoming chapters), as well as a often undervalued resource: space. The technical artefacts used to produce CO_2-free energy, therefore, exhibit comparable dependencies on energy and raw materials to those of their CO_2-emitting energy counterparts. The American geologist Art Berman thus speaks not of "renewable" but of "rebuildable energies".[9]

The Technological Backend

Given that the implementation of renewable energy technology is based on building and construction, the idea that its sourcing is entirely pure and free of environmental consequences may be oversimplified and partially downplaying the inherent complexity.[10] Presently, 6.2 % of the global energy demand is allocated for extracting raw materials, which relies solely on fossil energy sources.[11] Like most contemporary technologies, the energy transition necessitates an intricate interplay between a wide array of mineral elements. [Fig. 12] In Europe, particularly in Germany, the development of raw materials has assumed a secondary position. Despite the potential for domestic development of certain rare earths being deemed vital, this responsibility has predominantly been delegated to other nations. Notably, the raw materials market in China holds particular significance, revealing a comparable global monopolisation and path-dependency to that already observed among fossil energy sources. Germany relies on Chinese producers for the supply of raw materials and the manufacturing of technologies used in its renewable energy production. In turn, China has transformed the energy transition into a distinct business model. Marked by a robust concentration of resources, expertise, and domestic production, China's annual global investments in energy technology vividly underscore its status as a heavyweight in the field.

Fig. 3 Clean energy factory investment by region in %

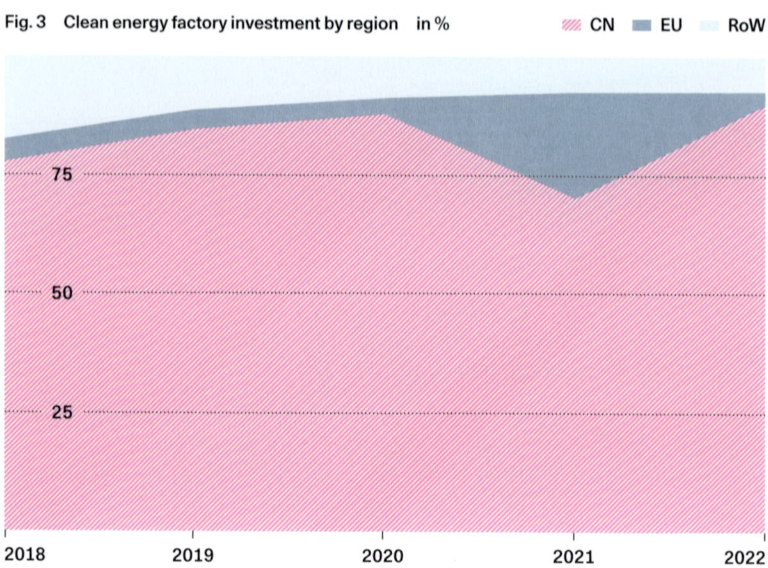

While it may seem that the primary energy source for CO_2-free electricity generation is almost endless, the respective components for producing CO_2-free energy will need periodic reconstruction.[12] The more seamlessly components can be recycled in the future, the greater their energy efficiency and environmental friendliness will become. Silicon, silver, glass reinforced plastic GRP, and carbon-fibre reinforced plastic CFRP all pose significant challenges due to the disproportionate effort of their recycling processes compared to using newly reclaimed materials. Consequently, the energy transition and its associated technical components will in the forthcoming decade not only experience a significant boost in development but will also become entangled in an ongoing journey of reconstruction and continuous advancement.

Fig. 4 Comparison of electricity demand scenarios in Germany until 2050 in TWh

1 Electricity demand 2023
2 Agora Energiewende, 2020
3 Bundesverband Erneuerbarer Energien, 2021
4 EWI Köln, 2019
5 Dena Leitstudie, 2018
6 Fraunhofer-Institut, 2021
7 BMWi, 2021

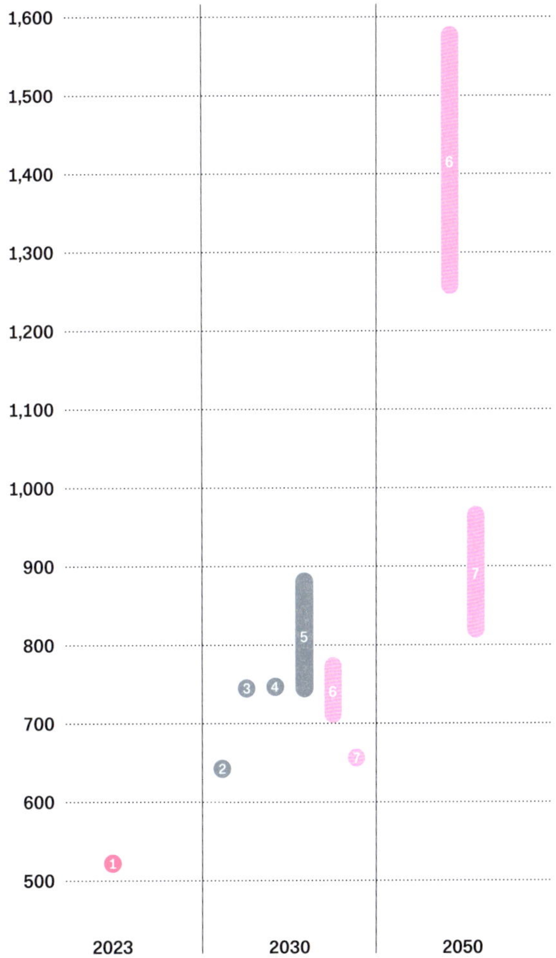

From Need to Space

Invariably, technologies display spatial dependencies. Within the framework of the energy transition, these dependencies are evident both in the global spatial frameworks of extraction and supply and in local contexts, pertaining to the selection and determination of installation locations. In the context of Germany, the evolution of the extensive electrical power system relies on economic electricity demand scenarios that are commissioned by governmental and civil society superstructures. Both private and public institutions, use these calculations.[13] The outcomes of these scenarios frequently exhibit substantial disparities; on the spatial front, they often revolve around area-specific goals for distinct technologies, expressed as percentages. These goals subsequently evolve into enforceable legal mandates at both the federal and state levels.

Fig. 5 Brandenburg's five regional planning districts

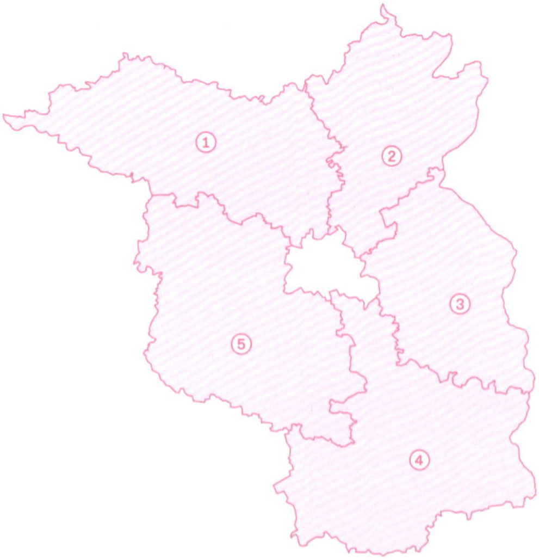

① Prignitz-Oberhavel
② Uckermark-Barnim
③ Oberland-Spree
④ Lausitz-Spreewald
⑤ Havelland-Fläming

The assumptions consistently stem from technologies that are currently predominant in the market, like wind turbines and ground-mounted solar power. This, in turn, leads to planning directives disseminated through regional planning within the respective federal states. These directives are then executed by stakeholders actively engaged in the ongoing system construction. The regional planning bodies or associations of the federal states, both composed of local representatives, are therefore pivotal in determining the sub-areas of the extensive electricity power system. These entities, comprising local politicians, are responsible for planning specific locations. For instance, in Brandenburg, five regional planning communities exist that align with the various regions in the state. Their primary function revolves around formulating regional plans and their determinations are rooted in extensive map data commissioned by the regional planning bodies. Currently, there is no comprehensive model for Germany and Brandenburg that integrates economic, ecological, engineering, and other parameters across various scales. This constellation creates a significant disparity, impeding the progress of any forthcoming electrical power systems. The interplay between intricate spatial planning, abstract economic scenarios, and pioneering technology results in varied spatial ambiences and aesthetics that are contingent upon hyper-specific contexts. Consequently, the divergent atmospheres and aesthetics can give rise to social conflicts, adding complexity to the system's conversion and ongoing construction.

Space and Law

In accordance with the expansion goals derived from electricity demand scenarios, the regional planning of federal states also evaluates suitable areas for establishing renewable energy infrastructure, and since 2022, a standardised requirement has mandated that each Federal State must allocate 2% of its total area for onshore wind energy generation by 2032, with interim goals requiring states to designate between 1.1% and 1.8% by 2027, depending on regional conditions such as size and wind potential.[14] In tandem with regional planning, the BNetzA—the regulatory federal authority responsible for overseeing the energy, telecommunications, postal, and railway sectors in Germany—is assuming a progressively significant role in site determination, a development that has garnered notable criticism from the regional planning community.[15] The BNetzA, for instance, currently holds exclusive jurisdiction over the siting of overhead power lines, a responsibility that has been removed from regional planning entities (who oversaw this placement in the past). The resulting criticisms concerning the knock-on effect of this on spatial planning are multifaceted, particularly in the context of the energy transition. On the one hand, critics lament that the absence of legal mandates at the federal level prevents the formation of a comprehensive spatial vision for Germany, which is particularly vital in the given context. On the other hand, deficiencies in personnel and expertise at the very same federal level are perceived as partial hindrances to effective planning within local contexts.

Within the political sphere, diminishing enthusiasm for planning finds expression in continuous budget cuts. This fiscal trend has led to practical ramifications, wherein infrastructure construction projects often encounter failure or substantial delays due to insufficient attention to detail. In principle, there is cross-party consensus that planning procedures should be accelerated, with conversation frequently pointing towards the reduction of bureaucracy rather than an augmentation of personnel whose expertise could fast-track planning processes.

When positioning energy infrastructure, emphasis is generally placed on areas classified as *Außenbereich,* a term in German urban planning law that encompasses all properties that are neither within the scope of a comprehensive development plan nor part of a continuously built-up urban district. In the broader public interest, these spaces are ideally intended to remain devoid of structures, as they are earmarked for agricultural production, ecosystem services, natural land utilisation, and public recreation. However, exceptions are made legally for developments termed "privileged building projects", namely projects entailing construction that serves the broader public interest. Eight categories in the BauGB (Building Code) outline various cases. Among these, Category 3 pertains to the prioritised siting of electricity infrastructure in outlying areas. With the proliferation of infrastructures dedicated to electricity generation, storage, and transportation, this passage in the legal text gains heightened importance since its aim is to keep the *Außenbereich* uncluttered by built structures, aligning with the interests of the broader public.[16] Actors intending to generate electricity in the Außenbereich necessitate a corresponding development plan from the relevant municipality, which delineates the design parameters for the installations. This planning procedure is often time-consuming and criticised as a major obstacle to the speedy proliferation of the energy transition.

Nonetheless, the logic underpinning these new technologies gives rise to distinct spatial manifestations. Unlike fossil energy sources, which embody concentrated energy units within individual spaces, renewable energy technologies are dispersed and widely fragmented across space. Building regulations also address the revisability of constructed structures. Areas that have accommodated specific building structures from across the eight categories must be reinstated to their original state after use. However, the degree to which this revisability applies to specific infrastructures—as well as the standards employed for reinstating an original condition—lack detailed definition. Once again, exceptions seem to exist, in particular for the use of nuclear energy.

Historical insights suggest that every technology eventually reaches its conclusion, potentially becoming entirely obsolete. At this juncture, myriad questions emerge regarding how best to manage the structures of the past. The cutting-edge electricity infrastructures of today will inevitably confront this phenomenon in the future, potentially sooner than anticipated.

4.2

Critical Minerals

Santiago Martínez M.
Joseph Smithard

Amid a climate of broader global intentions to phase out fossil fuels—exemplified by Germany's self-sanctioned coal phase-out by 2038—renewable energy generation and consumption technologies have emerged as a pivotal focus on numerous agendas.[17] However, these technologies, which encompass wide-ranging systems such as solar panels, wind turbines, electric cars, batteries, robotics, 3D printing, fuel cells, and traction motors, all encounter a common challenge: the procurement of minerals essential for their manufacturing. Although the production of these technologies originated at various junctures across the 20th century, the substantial surge in renewable energy investments during the 21st century skyrocketed demand and subsequent production to unprecedented heights. To illustrate, in the year 2000, the global production of solar panels amounted to approximately 0.238 GW. By 2023, in stark contrast, this figure had grown to 612 GW, representing a monumental increase of 2,571 times.[18]

Fig. 6 Annual global solar module production, 2000–2023 in GW

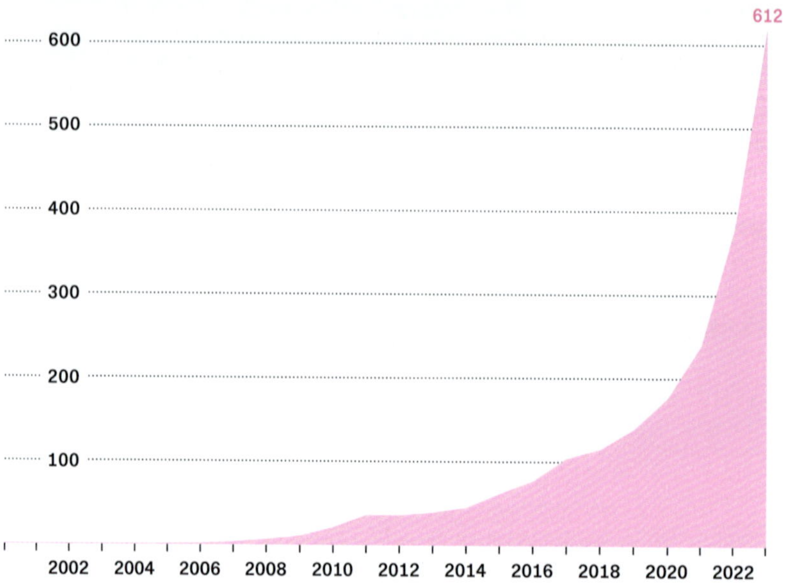

This growing rate of production comes at a cost. Clean energy technologies need a much wider range of minerals than conventional ones. An electric car uses six times more minerals than a conventional vehicle, while an onshore wind farm needs nine times the mineral content of a gas power station.[19] Put simply, these minerals must be mined, refined, produced, and distributed. Although minerals reserves are abundant, global production capacities are not uniformly distributed and this disparity has given rise to monopolies and bottlenecks in supply.

Consequently, this imbalance has led to the emergence of the term “critical minerals”.[20] Such critical minerals possess a triad of defining characteristics. Firstly, they occupy a pivotal role in fabricating present-day technologies, underscoring their indispensability. Secondly, their supply chains are susceptible to monopolisation or disruption, casting a shadow over their availability. Finally, these minerals have evolved into potent instruments often wielded as geopolitical bargaining tools, adding an intricate layer to their significance.

Fig. 7 Volume of critical minerals contained in selected energy technologies as of 2021 in kg/MW

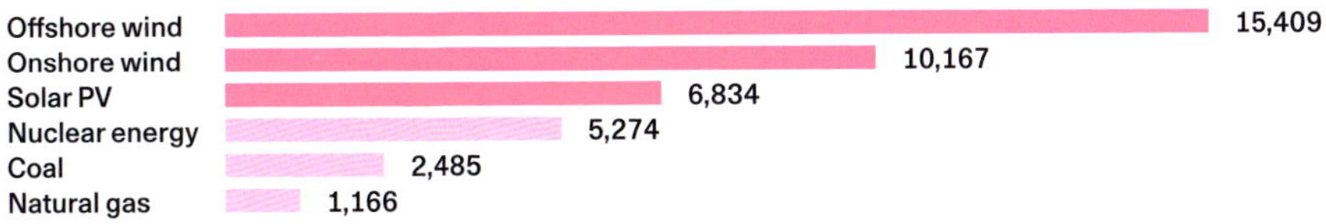

Gallium serves as a prime example here. Initially employed in semiconductors for contemporary integrated circuits, its utilisation now extends to vital components in solar panels, wind turbines, and mobile phones, as well as an array of other electronic devices. Currently China occupies a commanding position as the world’s principal gallium producer, boasting a 96.8% market share in 2021. Notably, as of July 2023, the country has enforced trade restrictions in response to the recent imposition of American sanctions on exporting cutting-edge technology to China.[21] While this could potentially impede the manufacture of numerous renewable energy technologies beyond People’s Republic’s borders, it is crucial to note that China is already the primary producer of the bulk of these technologies.

Many national agencies highlight critical minerals as pivotal in their development and national security agendas, including the US Geological Survey,[22] the European Commission,[23] the Japanese Government,[24] the British Geological Survey,[25] and the State Council of China.[26]

Fig. 8 Where are clean energy technologies manufactured? Share of China in %

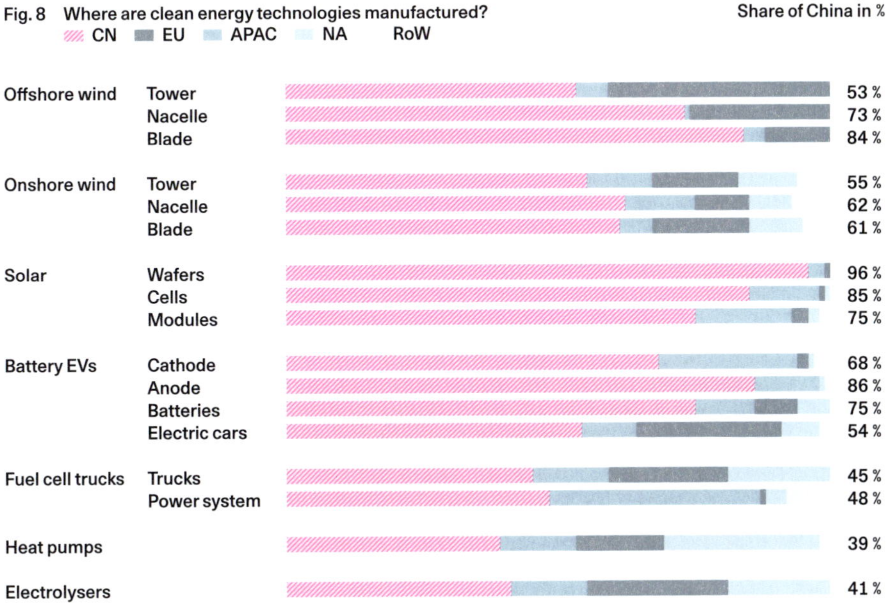

Extraction and Production: the Case of Rare Earths

The prevailing landscape of extraction and production, wherein China unmistakably holds the reins as the major player,[27] has evolved over the course of the 20th century, undergoing significant shifts in the last two decades especially. To unravel the mechanisms at play, it is necessary to delve deeper into the realm of minerals generally considered to have the highest level of risk: REE, or rare earths.

Fig. 9 Global reserves of rare earths by country, 2021 in Mt

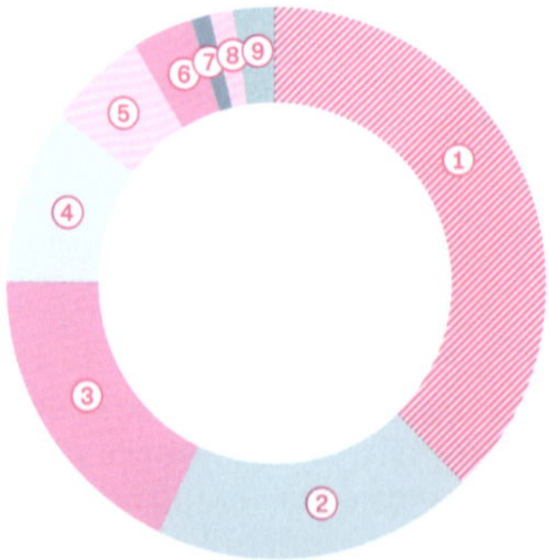

①	CN	44	38.0 %
②	VN	22	19.0 %
③	BR	21	18.1 %
④	RU	12	10.4 %
⑤	IN	6.9	6.0 %
⑥	AU	4.1	3.5 %
⑦	US	1.5	1.3 %
⑧	GL	1.5	1.3 %
⑨	Other	2.8	2.4 %
Σ	World	115.8	100 %

Rare earths, encompassing all the lanthanides along with scandium and yttrium,[28] are used in permanent magnets (38 %), catalysts (23 %), glass polishing powder and additives (13 %), battery alloys (9 %), metallurgy and alloys (8 %), ceramics (4 %), miscellaneous uses (4 %), and phosphors (3 %).[29] Abundant reserves of rare earths are mainly concentrated in China, Vietnam, and Brazil. Nonetheless, the foremost producers in 2020 were China, the US, and Myanmar. Presently, neodymium, praseodymium, and dysprosium represent around 85 % of the market value of rare earths because of their essential role in magnets.[30]

From the standpoint of the European Union, rare earths represent the pinnacle of risk, as they are indispensable for the functionality of technologies such as wind turbines, traction motors, and robotics. In the case of wind turbines, the EU contributes a mere 1 % towards the raw materials used in production but oversees over 50 % of the assembly stage. [p. 292] As for traction motors, the EU's involvement stands at a modest 8 % of the entire production process. Similarly, in robotics, the EU only contributes 2 % to the raw materials used in production yet emerges as a significant player in the processing and assembly of robotics with shares of 21 % and 41 %, respectively.[31]

The History of Industrial Extraction

The chronology of rare-earth mining can be segmented into four distinct epochs: the Steenkampskraal era, the Mountain Pass era, the Chinese Monopoly era, and the more recent phase of diversification.[32]

Between 1952 and 1963, the Steenkampskraal mine in South Africa had the world's largest rare-earth mining operation. During this period, South Africa emerged as the largest provider of newly mined minerals, including thorium and rare earths. The mine's operations were overseen by the London-based mining company, Anglo American.[33] In parallel, dating back to 1949, rare earths were discovered in the Mountain Pass mine situated in eastern San Bernardino, California. The Molybdenum Corporation of America, later known as Molycorp, acquired substantial land holdings and initiated extensive extraction efforts, primarily driven by the need for europium to meet the requirements of colour television screens. Notably, the bulk of the global rare-earth supply from 1965 to 1990 originated from this mine. However, the Mountain Pass mine met a definitive end in 2002 due to a hazardous waste incident and the competitive cost advantage of Chinese production, rendering the operation economically unsustainable.[34] In 1975, China established the "National Rare Earth Development and Application Leading Group" with the primary objective of advancing the upstream rare-earth industry, a goal it pursued until 1990. Additionally, in 1985, substantial tax deductions or reimbursements were introduced for national mining firms, resulting in a remarkable production boost that saw output double within five years.[35]

Fig. 10 Global rare-earth mineral production 1950–2023 in kt

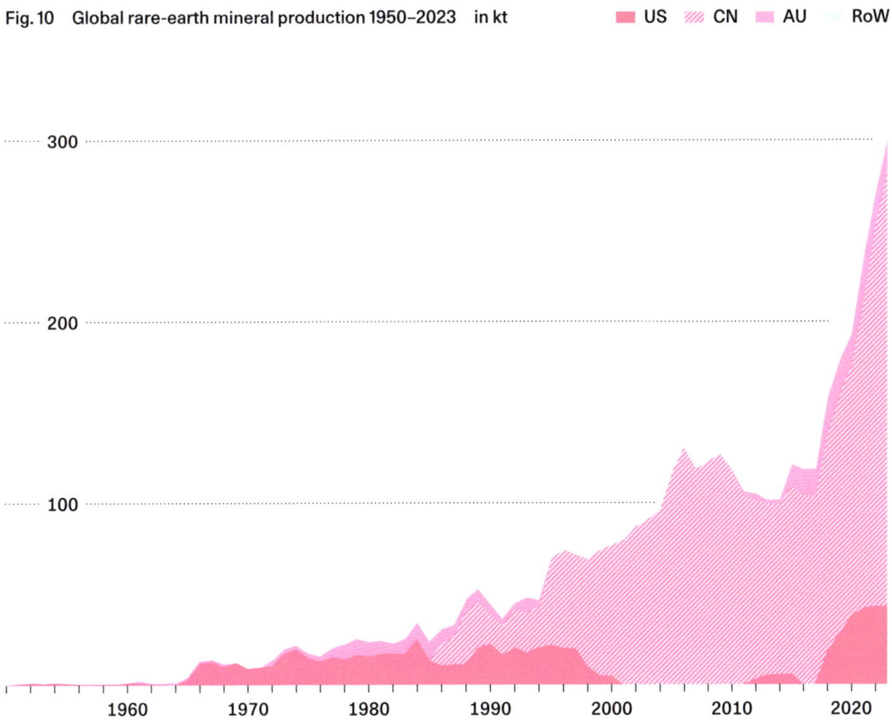

Starting in 1990, the denial of mining permits and the shutdown of plants in other countries, such as Japan and France, were the driving force behind the transfer of operations to China.[36] From this point, China's involvement extended beyond extraction to encompass processing and subsequent distribution, fostering the growth of the downstream industry. In 1992, former Chinese President Deng Xiaoping said, "The Middle East has its oil; China has rare earths". He followed this statement by emphasising, "[...] it is of extremely important strategic significance; we must be sure to handle the rare earth issue properly and make the fullest use of our country's advantage in rare earth resources".[37] China initiated restrictions on foreign investment across all stages of the rare-earth industry, encompassing exploration, mining, beneficiation, smelting, and separation. Subsequently, licenses were exclusively granted or renewed for government-affiliated entities or activities. This approach served to regulate the explosive growth of the rare-earth market in the 1990s, leading to an oversupply of inexpensive minerals and the proliferation of illicit industry. From 1995 to 2000, China's share of global rare-earth production surged from 60 % to 87 %, while in the same period the United States's contribution dwindled from 28 % to 6 %.

By 2005, despite several unsuccessful efforts to bring order to a market that had expanded somewhat unregulated, China achieved the zenith of its monopolisation. Approximately 98 % of the world's rare earths were being produced within China's borders, whereas the United States's share had plummeted to 0 % due to the closure of the Mountain Pass mine.[38] This practise transformed into a bargaining tool. In 2011, during a political dispute with Japan, China substantially curtailed the export of neodymium, a vital element for magnets. Due to the high level of monopolisation, the price per kg of neodymium surged by 1,000 %.[39] Nations with significant reserves, including the US, Russia, and Australia, responded by reactivating their production. China's export limitations prompted a dispute within the World Trade Organisation, predominantly supported by the US, Japan, and the European Union. As a result, China was compelled to remove these restrictions, leading to a price stabilisation by 2016. Since 2010, Australia has witnessed a 672 % surge in its production.[40] Myanmar has also emerged as a significant player, contributing around 30,000 t in 2020, positioning itself as the third-largest producer. The revival of the Mountain Pass mine has reinstated the US as the second-largest producer. Concurrently, other nations, such as Canada and those within the EU, are working to establish secure supply sources. Nonetheless, despite the broadening landscape of mining operations, China retains its dominance by handling 80 % of the rare-earth refining processes.

Industrial Processing

Concerning the industrial processing of rare earths, once extracted from the earth, they undergo a journey to specialised plants for separation and sorting.[41] Given that rare earths are frequently found in concentrations below 10 %, which need to be elevated to around 60 %, physical separation methods such as magnetic or electrostatic processes become imperative. Subsequently, chemical separation techniques come into play, categorised as either acid-based or base-based, facilitating the meticulous sorting of specific minerals. Many of these processes were developed during or shortly after the Second World War. By the mid-20th century, purity levels exceeding 99.99 % for individual minerals were achieved, marking the commencement of industrial-scale production.
In 2022, China emerged as the dominant player in every facet of the supply chain, encompassing up-, mid-, and downstream segments, accounting for 58 %, 89 %, and 92 %, respectively.[42] Noteworthy growth and prominence are also observed in industries across the globe, including the US, Australia, Myanmar, Russia, India, Canada, and Japan. At the time of writing, the landscape of rare-earth extraction is defined by the following five prominent mining companies:

Fig. 11 Largest rare-earth mining companies by market capitalisation, February 2025 in billion $

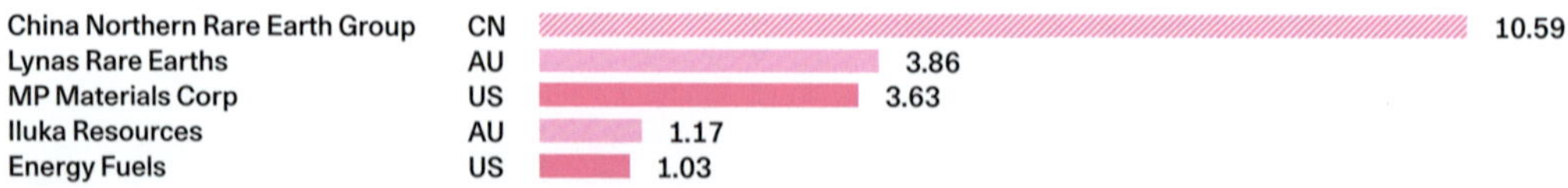

Sustainable Critical Minerals?

In light of prevailing monopolisation, geopolitical tensions, and potential future scarcity, various strategies to mitigate its effects have began to gain traction.[43] One approach involves optimising the mineral requirements for different technologies, which could alleviate strain on existing supply chains. Simultaneously, efforts are being directed towards enhancing recyclability, although this remains a complex and costly endeavour. It should also be noted that certain minerals, such as gallium and indium, simply cannot be recycled, leaving substitution as the sole viable alternative.[44] Discussions about establishing a circular economy for critical minerals, and particularly rare earths, have emerged within political spheres across the European Union, the US, and China.[45] Nonetheless, concrete recycling pathways have yet to be defined, primarily owing to the relatively recent integration of these minerals into renewable energy technologies. Given the projection of a potential quadrupling of demand for critical minerals by 2040, the need for a viable recycling strategy becomes an increasingly pressing challenge for the forthcoming decades.[46]

1 Holler, Christian, Joachim Gaukel, Harald Lesch, and Florian Lesch, *Erneuerbare Energien zum Verstehen und Mitreden,* 19, 67.
2 Mumford, *Technics and Civilization,* 154, 266–267.
3 Priest, "Hubbert's Peak".
4 See: Fuller, *Operating Manual for Spaceship Earth*.
5 See: Carson, *Rachel Carson: Silent Spring & Other Writings*.
6 See: Meadows, *The Limits to Growth: A Report for the Club of Rome's Project on the Predicament of Mankind*.
7 See: Turner, *From Counterculture to Cyberculture*.
8 The first publication using the word was: Krause, Bossel, and Müller-Reißmann, *Energie-Wende Wachstum und Wohlstand ohne Erdöl und Uran; ein Alternativ-Bericht des Öko-Instituts*.
9 Berman: *The Real Energy Paradigm*.
10 Fu et al., "Tracing Metal Footprints via Global Renewable Power Value Chains".
11 Holmberg et al., "Global Energy Consumption Due to Friction and Wear in the Mining Industry".
12 Fu et al.
13 For a comprehensive overview of some of the most relevant scenarios, see: Lübbers et al., "Vergleich der 'Big 5' Klimaneutralitätsszenarien".
14 BMWSB, "Entwurf eines Gesetzes zur sofortigen Verbesserung der Rahmenbedingungen für die erneuerbaren Energien im Städtebaurecht".
15 Bundesinstitut für Bau- stadt- und raumforschung, "Potenziale der Raumordnung Chancen erkennen, Zukunft gestalten".
16 *Baugesetzbuch*, 55. Auflage, Stand: 1. März 2023, Sonderausgabe, dtv (München: dtv, 2023), 35.
17 Wettengel, "Spelling out the Coal Exit – Germany's Phase-out Plan".
18 IEA PVPS. "Trends in Photovoltaic Applications", 55, 59
19 IEA, "Executive Summary – The Role of Critical Minerals in Clean Energy Transitions – Analysis".
20 A comprehensive list of critical minerals can be found on the "Critical Minerals Chart", on pages 228–229.
21 MIT Technology Review, "China Just Fought Back in the Semiconductor Exports War. Here's What You Need to Know".
22 U.S. Geological Survey, "U.S. Geological Survey Releases 2022 List of Critical Minerals".
23 European Commission, "European Critical Raw Materials Act".
24 Ministry of Economy, Trade, and Industry, "Signing of the Japan–U.S. Critical Minerals Agreement (CMA)".
25 British Geological Survey, "Critical Raw Materials".
26 Wang et al., "The Availability of Critical Minerals for China"s Renewable Energy Development".
27 See: "Critical Minerals Chart", on pages 228–229.
28 U.S. Geological Survey, "Rare Earths: Mineral Commodity Summaries".
29 Serpell et al., "Rare Earth Elements: A Resource Constraint of the Energy Transition".
30 Steenkampskraal Rare Earths Mine, "The History of Rare Earths".
31 European Commission, "European Critical Materials Act".
32 Jowitt, "Mineral Economics of the Rare-Earth Elements".
33 Arnoldi, "Steenkampskraal to List on LSE, JSE".
34 Hansen, "Securing U.S. Access to Rare Earth Elements".
35 Moomy, "China's Public Policies toward Rare Earths, 1975–2018".
36 Ibid.
37 Ibid.
38 Ibid.
39 Ibid.
40 Ibid.
41 Based on Processing ores in: Britannica, "Rare-Earth Element – Processing Ores".
42 Mabuni, "Breaking China's Rare Earths Monopoly".
43 DW, "Reuse and Substitutes of Critical Resources".
44 European Commission, "Critical Raw Materials Resilience: Charting a Path towards greater Security and Sustainability".
45 Geng, Sarkis, and Bleischwitz, "How to Build a Circular Economy for Rare-Earth Elements".
46 Birol, Fatih, "Critical Minerals: Responsible Supply Chains for a Sustainable Future | The OECD Forum Network".

Fig. 12 Critical minerals: production and use

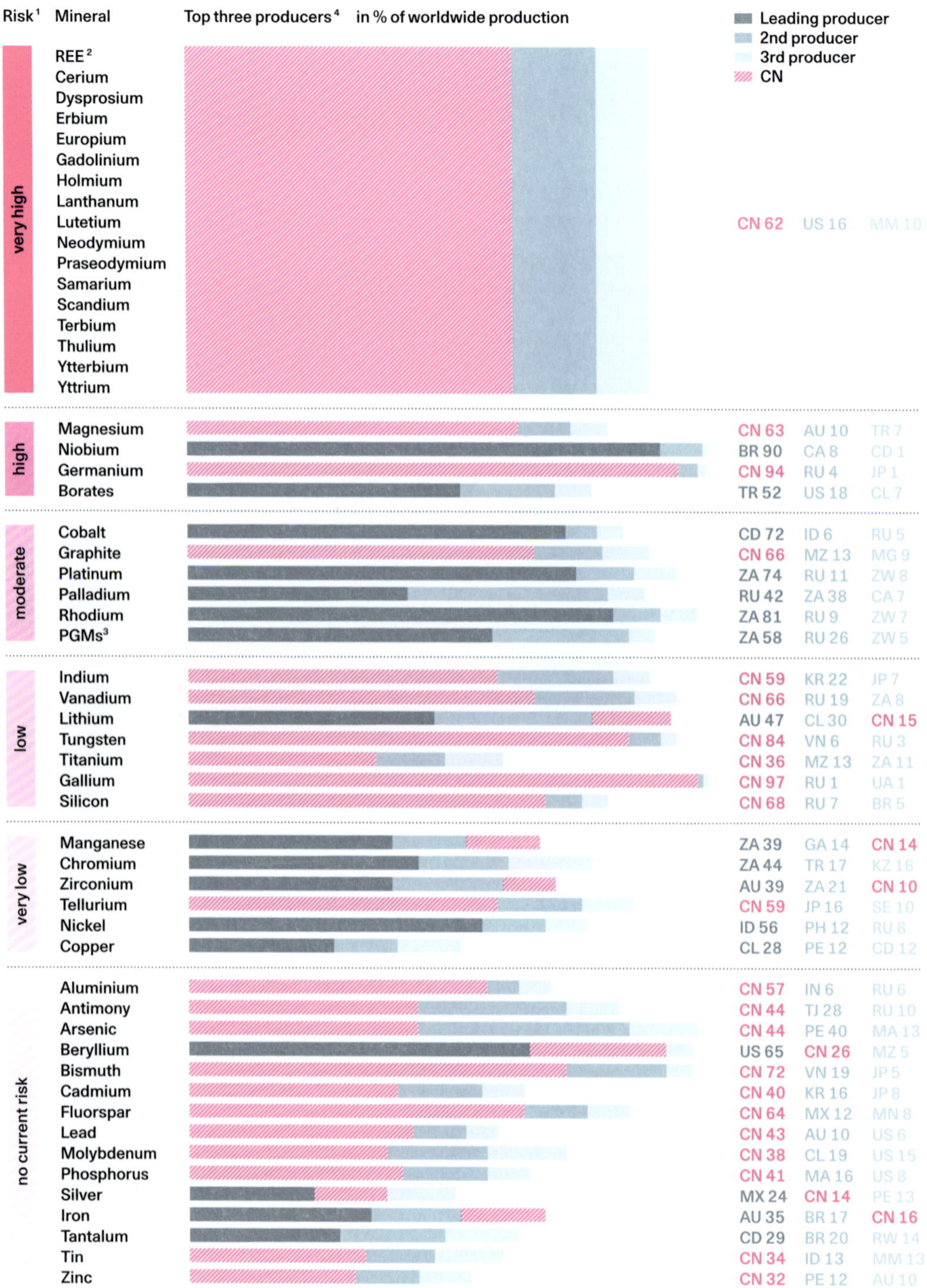

1 Level of risk in the supply chain, determined by the intersection of the criteria of the three listed entities in points 5, 6, and 7

2 Based on information from the last available year from Statista for each mineral

3 Platinum-group metals are six noble, precious metallic elements, including ruthenium, rhodium, palladium, osmium, and iridium, besides platinum

4 According to the American Geosciences Institute, REE are a set of 17 metallic elements, including the 15 lanthanides on the periodic table plus scandium and yttrium

Production in kt	Listed by: US[5]	EU[6]	IEA[7]	Used in (selected technologies)[8]: Batteries	Wind turbines	Solar panels	Robotics	Integrated circuits	General use
									Catalytic converters, oil refining
									Motors for electric vehicles
									Lasers, steel, fibre optics
									Phosphors, lasers, lamps
									Refractive glass, lasers, X-ray tubes
									Lasers, magnets
									Hydrogen storage, batteries
269	●	●			●		●	●	Emission tomographies, oil refining
									Rare-earth magnets
									Motors for electric vehicles
									Rare-earth magnets, nuclear reactors
									Aluminium alloys, tracing in refineries
									Stabiliser for fuel cells
									X-ray machines, lasers
									Stainless steel, lasers, nuclear medicine
									Superconductors, solid oxide fuel cells
27,130	●	●							Alloys with other metals
78,900	●	●		●	●		●	●	Steel and superalloys
0.14	●	●				●		●	Fibre optics
4,920		●			●	●	●	●	Magnets, lubricants
180	●	●		●				●	Rechargeable batteries
1,298	●	●		●				●	Lubricants, batteries, and fuel cells
0.19	●	●						●	Catalytic converters
0.21	●	●						●	Catalytic converters
0.02	●	●						●	Electrical components
0.40	●	●						●	Electrical contacts chip resistors
1.80	●	●	●			●	●	●	Liquid crystal display screens
106	●	●							Alloys for iron and steel
129	●	●		●				●	Rechargeable batteries
84	●	●							Wear-resistant metals
9,059	●	●		●			●	●	Metal alloys
0.43	●	●			●	●	●	●	Integrated circuits
8,793		●		●		●		●	Solar cells
49,502	●	●		●	●		●	●	Steelmaking and batteries
41,300	●	●	●		●		●	●	Stainless steel and other alloys
1,456	●	●							Corrosion-resistant alloys
0.44	●	●	●			●			Solar cells, thermoelectric devices
2,841	●	●	●	●	●	●	●	●	Steel, rechargeable batteries
18,560		●	●	●	●	●	●	●	Circuits
67,669	●		●	●	●	●	●		Structural uses and cases
94	●		●						Lead-acid batteries
55	●								Semi-conductors
6.72	●						●		Alloying agents in aerospace
11	●								Medical and atomic research
25			●			●			Solar cells
8,392	●								Cement, steel, gasoline, fluorine
4,681			●		●	●			Batteries, cables in wind turbines
268			●		●	●	●		Stainless steel and other alloys
75,371			●						Solar cells
25,939			●			●		●	Circuits in solar panels and chips
1,635,056			●		●	●	●		Production of steel
1.76	●								Electronic components
271	●		●			●			Protective coatings
12,929	●		●			●			Galvanised steel

5 U.S. Department of the Interior, U.S. Geological Survey. Mineral commodity summaries 2023
6 European Commission. Critical Raw Materials for Strategic Technologies and Sectors in the EU: A Foresight Study
7 International Energy Agency. Final List of Critical Minerals 2022
8 Selected from the European Commission, from left to right: batteries, wind turbines, solar panels, robotics, integrated circuits

Renewable Energy Carriers

Solar

4.3

4.3.1

Introduction to Solar

David Bauer
Philipp Deilmann
Joseph Smithard

Solar: Made in Germany

Despite experiencing annual sunshine hours comparable to Siberia or the Canadian North, Germany stands as one of the most relevant global players in solar energy production. As of 2022, the country achieved an installed solar capacity of 66.5 GWp through more than 2,500,000 installations.[1] This figure placed it fourth in the global ranking, third *per capita,*[2] and fifth in terms of actual electricity production.[3] In the subsequent year, the country witnessed a substantial increase in new installations, resulting in a total installed capacity of 81.7 GWp by the end of 2023.[4]

Solar photovoltaics PV have a well-established tradition and strong-standing support in the BRD, with 30 years of history closely intertwined with tremendous booms and busts. Taking off after the introduction of the Renewable Energy Source Act EEG in 2000, German solar companies swiftly became world leaders in manufacturing and developing PV panels, facilitating a massive rollout both within and outside the country before production underwent a steep decline just over a decade later. In 1990, the German state initiated a pilot programme for PV systems known as the "1,000 Roofs Programme". Under this initiative, the federal government covered 50 % of the investment costs, with an additional 20 % contribution coming from state governments (*Bundesländer*) for grid-connected PV systems installed on one and two-family houses.[5] As a result, within the following five years, approximately 2,000 rooftops were outfitted with PV modules.[6] The year 1991 also witnessed the introduction of a feed-in tariff, mandating utility companies to integrate renewable energy generators into the power grid and to purchase their generated electricity at agreed-upon rates, fixed at 80 % of the historical average retail price.[7] This paved the way for a considerable influx of solar start-ups that emerged throughout the 1990s and early 2000s, particularly in the *Neue Bundesländer* (former East Germany). Subsequently, they rapidly established themselves as world-class providers.

For example, Q-Cells, a leading German company—founded at the end of 1999 in Bitterfeld-Wolfen by a group of eco-tech entrepreneurs—began producing solar cells in 2001 with just 19 employees across a 12 MW production line.[8] By 2006 their annual capacity had expanded to 250 MW.[9] Consequently, Q-Cells ranked as the second-largest producer in the world, employing more than 2000 individuals in the heavily deindustrialised Sachsen-Anhalt. However, it was just one among many companies that contributed to Germany becoming the largest solar market[10] and the second-largest technology producer after Japan.[11] In 2007, every fourth cell was made in Germany.[12] Given the extent and the intricate nature of the supply chain, there were several niches in which new companies could thrive. In addition to research and development and panel production, there were companies responsible for purifying silicon into what is known as polysilicon, as well as those engaged in cutting this polysilicon into ingots and producing cells. Some companies turned cells into solar modules, while others specialised in electric components, such as mounting equipment, cables, wiring, and extremely valuable inverters. [Fig. 9] The exponential growth in the sector also captured the interest of established corporations like Bosch, Siemens, and Schott, as well as major energy providers, who acquired smaller enterprises to establish their own foothold in the industry.

Fig. 1 Cumulative installed capacity of solar photovoltaic systems in Germany, 2000–2023 in GW

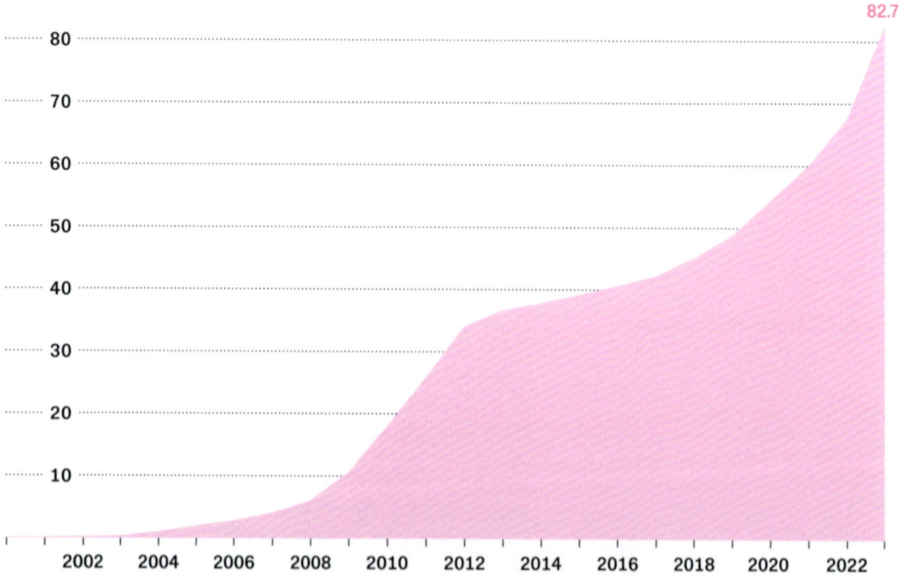

The first decade of the new millennium witnessed a remarkable surge in solar energy adoption, ramping up the installed capacity from 114 to more than 18,000 MW, representing a total increase of 1570 %.[13] By 2008, the initial 1,000 roofs had grown to hundreds of thousands (mostly private installations) nationwide. This expansion occurred even in the face of emerging global warming sceptics who tried to ridicule promoting the solar industry in a nation with sunlight levels comparable to Alaska, questioning its practicality and rationale.[14] The surge in the development and production of PV panels, however, was not entirely homegrown; it was also propelled by a pan-European wave of government support for solar energy, fuelled by growing concern about (and evidence of) climate change. Consequently, during the 2000s, several European member states adopted the model established by the German EEG and its feed-in tariff initiative.[15] Meanwhile, the world's emerging production centre, China, began to swiftly venture into the solar industry, aiming to secure a foothold in a strategically crucial sector that relied on materials abundant within their territory. China had its first serious exposure to solar cell technology in 1958 through developing the first piece of monocrystalline silicon. More than four decades passed before the first domestic PV cell production line was established, with a modest output capacity of 10 MW.[16] The Renewable Energy Law of the People's Republic of China was passed in February 2005 and implemented the following year, bolstering the advancement and application of renewable energy sources while ensuring domestic energy security.[17] Following this, China launched a state-planned expansion of solar production capacity, resulting in substantial structural changes within the industry. Within just three years, they became the world's largest producer of solar cells.[18] [Fig. 2]

The surge in solar installations also led to an unanticipated rise in its foundational material: polysilicon. Before the 2000s, the PV industry had solely lived on scrap silicon harvested from the semiconductor sector, meaning the market was ruled by an oligopoly of ten companies in Europe, Japan, and the US.[19] With the German PV market exploding around 2004, a severe polysilicon shortage led to incredible price hikes. Despite this, new plants sprouted globally, with a significant share of these in China, which began to substantially increase its polysilicon production. However, due to the complex and capital-intensive nature of the trade, the German industry not only missed out on the beginning of the polysilicon trend but it likewise failed to hit the brakes before the coming oversupply. These oversights sent prices plummeting against the wider backdrop of the global financial crisis.[20]

It was not only polysilicon prices that fell. In addition, the business models of what were (until then) the leading Western PV manufacturers were significantly impacted by declining prices triggered by the expansion of overall production capacity. This downward trend was particularly influenced by cost-effective Chinese enterprises. From 2008 until 2012, the cost of solar panels fell from $4.15 to $0.95 per watt, disrupting the established market dynamics.[21] [Fig. 3] The German solar industry, at its peak sustained by roughly 150,000 workers, soon began to feel the effects of the transitioning market, losing more and more market shares.[22] The biggest blow came in 2012 when the German government opted to dismantle the fixed pricing structure for solar power purchased by utility companies. This decision, combined with constantly falling prices, led to most PV manufacturing companies going bankrupt within several months.[23] Subsidies sparked a substantial demand for solar panels within the national and European context, which was broadly positive. However, this masked the industry's wider need to address the escalating competition from China.

Fig. 2 Market share of photovoltaics for selected countries, 1995–2023 in %
CN TW JP MY DE US RoW

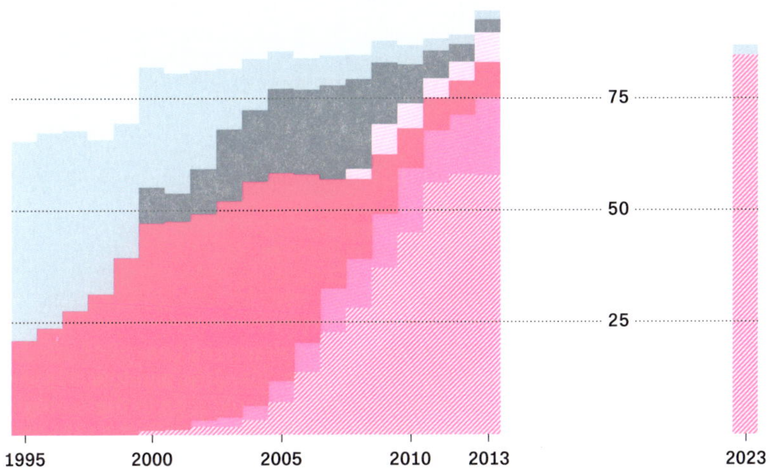

While some of the remaining companies began outsourcing their production, they nonetheless struggled to keep up. Ultimately, the global solar capacity breakthrough was achieved through the innovative efforts of companies that required consistent and supportive government policies to compete effectively against traditional fuels. These policies also facilitated ongoing investments to drive down costs over time, and they did so successfully. While in the 1970s, a solar panel was considered a luxury at $115 per watt, primarily reserved for space travel, the production cost for 1 W had plummeted as low as $0.27 by the end of 2021. However, many of those early enterprises that accelerated technological advancements and production capacity didn't have the opportunity to witness the gigantic global rollout that the world is currently on the brink of experiencing.

Fig. 3 Solar photovoltaic panel prices (adjusted for inflation), 1975–2023 in $/W

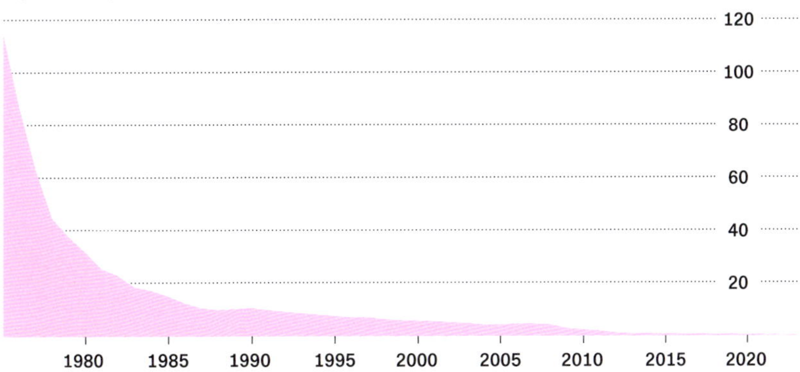

A Carbon-Free Future

In the pursuit of the European Commission's legally binding obligation to be carbon neutral by 2050,[24] varying emphasis will be placed on different carriers and technology within the German context. While the contribution of hydro and energy crops will likely remain stable in the coming years due to geographical and climatic factors, as well as food security and other environmental considerations, the primary emphasis lies in expanding solar and wind power as these technologies exhibit a notably higher energy density per unit of land compared to biomass.[25] If the envisioned carbon-neutral scenario for 2050 is to become a reality—not to mention Germany's ambitious amendment aim of 2045[26]—then the extent of solar technology's integration into the normative energy supply chain will surge far beyond what is currently imaginable.

Fig. 4 Projected scenario of future renewable energy shares

Let's embark on a journey into the future, imagining the year 2045 aboard a train on the German Intercity Express ICE. As you gaze out of the window, a tapestry unfolds before your eyes. Houses adorned with solar panels glint in the sunlight, while the train track's neighbouring strips of land are decorated with the same patchwork of technologies. Flotovoltaic platforms gracefully sway on bodies of water, and sheep graze contentedly under the shade of agrivoltaic installations.

Germany's pursuit of a carbon-free future through the integration of solar energy can be visualised as a spatial expanse resembling a square with sides spanning 95 km.[27] To put this into perspective, in 2022, the corresponding square covered just 5 km.[28] Considering Germany's desire to produce local energy, the necessary photovoltaic capacity to fill this substantial gap must increase 18-fold within its borders over the next two decades.[29]

Fig. 5 Spatial comparison of Germany's solar energy

① Germany in 2022
② Germany's intention for 2045

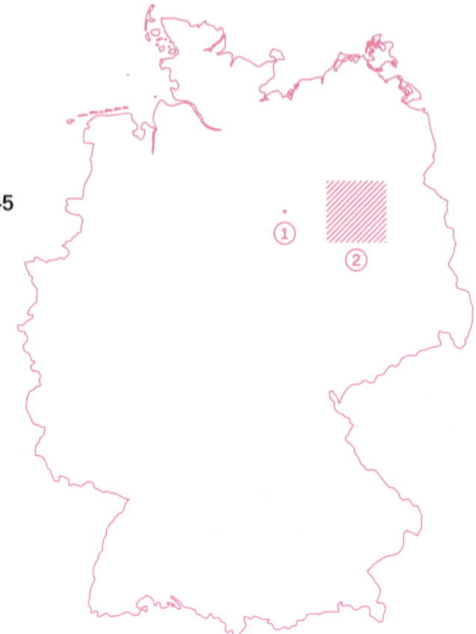

Localisation

The spatial implications of requiring 18 times more solar capacity raise questions about where this expansion will take place and how it might conflict with other land uses. In Germany, three distinct spatial approaches for advancing solar energy are currently advocated in the political arena. The first is agrivoltaics, which involves the installation of solar panels above fruit and vegetable plantations. This approach capitalises on the symbiotic relationship between solar panels and the crops underneath. Improved crop yields offset this approach's relatively high initial investment and associated costs. Additionally, these crops are shielded from intense sunlight, heavy rainfall, or hail—weather conditions that are predicted to become more frequent in the upcoming decades.

The second approach prioritises the establishment of open-space solar installations as preferred developments in landscape zones adjacent to motorways and railway lines. Ideally, these are required to sit within a 200 m corridor on either side of the linear transport infrastructure.[30] Despite its unassuming appearance, this legal adjustment is poised to accelerate the growth of open-space solar installations significantly. This is due to the anticipated reduction in planning and cost burdens for these areas in the future. However, this development introduces fresh challenges for local authorities in terms of effectively communicating upcoming projects to the public and advocating for a novel vision of infrastructure aesthetics.

The third approach revolves around the solar roof mandate, which has already been legally established in regions like Baden-Württemberg.[31] This initiative primarily focuses on commercial roof spaces and parking areas. A countrywide regulation is included in the agreement of the *Ampel* (traffic light) coalition and has the potential to be put into action by 2025.[32] The potential for harnessing solar energy in already developed areas is substantial and could alleviate the development strain on agricultural lands. For example, the automotive logistics company Mosolf owns several large parking areas in Germany. Among them is a 100 ha parking area west of Wustermark, in Brandenburg, which could potentially house a solar installation that would generate a yield of 92 MWp annually.[33] Furthermore, the adjacent wind farm showcases the potential for synergising two modes of renewable electricity generation.

Fig. 6 Spatial approaches

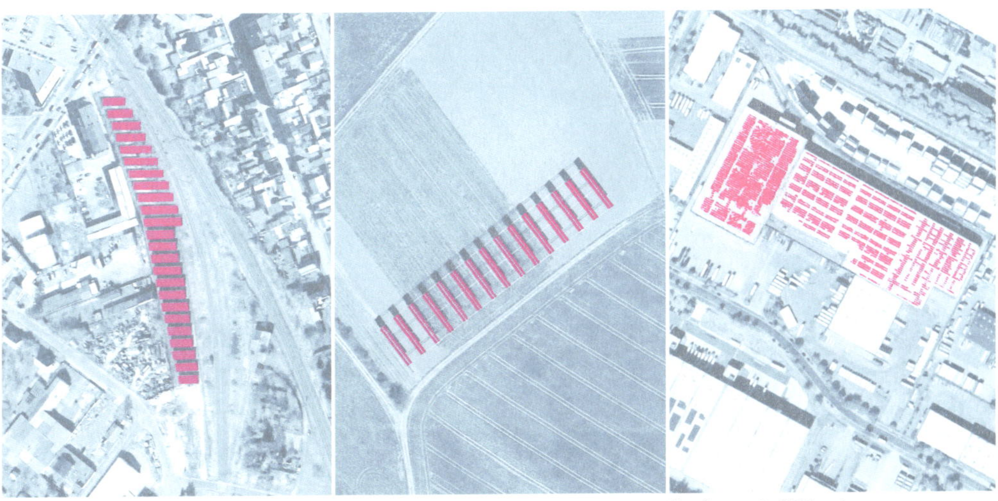

Ground-mounted PV priority zones — Agrivoltaics — Roof-mounted PV systems

For stakeholders in the private sector, both the size of the installation and its geography—in the context of establishing network nodes for feeding generated energy back into the power grid—is crucial. Currently, agricultural areas appear particularly appealing to private investors due to their relatively flexible legal regulations. Nonetheless, only time will tell whether the distributed responsibility, either through technological advancements or land-use agreements, will effectively attract the necessary investment for clean energy initiatives.

Beyond Cloud Nine

Of course, solar parks are not truly "parks" and referring to them as such is quite misleading. These installations are in fact vast built and viewing them in this way highlights their capacity to reshape land transformation. [p. 249] It is already well-known that PV panels can create shade and alter wind patterns, with potential knock-on effects impacting temperature, rainfall distribution (and hence soil moisture), as well as the rate of airflow over the land. This is notwithstanding the effect of massive structures and their security fences, which additionally block species' migration patterns, leading to the loss and fragmentation of wildlife habitats. In truth, the exact implications of large agglomerations solar panels are still uncertain. What is clear, though, is that solar energy is gaining increased momentum, with plans for enormous installations looming on the horizon. In line with this development, the construction of forthcoming solar PV parks will need to be designed to go beyond the goal of maximising energy production by incorporating collaborative land-use practices. The dimensioning of these installations will echo the visions of Buckminster Fuller and other advocates of the Biotecture movement, who envisioned vast structures and architectures seamlessly integrating ecosystems, cities, and technology into self-sustaining units.[34] However, the envisioned connection between architecture and natural energy flows in the biosphere will be apparent only at a technical level. Beyond the realm of science fiction, the habitability of these structures seems largely unachievable, let alone desirable. The future aim is to populate these technical facilities with flora and fauna, thereby offsetting the potential drawbacks of a monofunctional energy infrastructure. As a result, this has led to a growing emphasis on the concept of "CoHabitation" and the hybridisation of open-space solar installations.[35]

Fig. 7 Cloud Nine by R. Buckminster Fuller and Shoji Sadao

How is this Shift Mediated?

Currently, in Brandenburg, many large scale PV parks sit on "technical lands", or "conflict free areas", spaces that are united by their "exceptional" status—their remote location, delimited boundary, secured accessibility, and vigilant management and in most cases vacant land-use, due to either their former extractive, industrial, or military heritage.[36] Brandenburg possesses several of these disused landscapes, including former airfields, former military-restricted areas of the DDR, sand and gravel extraction areas, mines, and lignite-scarred landscapes. [p. 113] Furthermore, in the post-reunification era, ownership structures in the former DDR led to the emergence of large plots reserved for agricultural use, which has historically facilitated the siting of extensive open-space solar installations. Moreover, in 2015, Brandenburg's "disadvantaged agricultural lands"[37] were designated for establishing open-space solar installations, creating an expanse of potential landscapes. However, it's not always as easy as simply placing new solar installations on these technical lands. Take Hohensaaten in Brandenburg as an example.

Here, controversy surrounds the proposal for a 250 ha solar park in a former restricted military area, primarily due to the significant deforestation required for its installation. As of 2024, it is this point that has led the local authority to decide against the project.[38] What might be deemed a valuable habitat by some is viewed as an "unproductive" zone by others. This dichotomy vividly illustrates the contradictions between CO_2-free electricity generation technologies and their presence in our natural and cultural landscapes.

The fundamental truth is that every scenario indicates Germany's increasing requirement for more solar energy to attain carbon neutrality by 2045. However, the reality is that construction invariably comes at a cost. Prospective space is sparse, even in relatively low population regions like Brandenburg. While competition for agricultural plots presents a new market opportunity for farmers, the loss of agricultural lands poses a tangible threat if legal deregulation is pursued. Obviously, agriculture also causes significant land damage but solar could cause less. A future "CoHabitation", mediated through hybridisation and design, must just be the driving force behind Germany's next solar energy boom.

4.3.2

Properties, Production, and Supply

Santiago Martínez M.
Joseph Smithard

A solar or photovoltaic panel is an intricate assemblage of minerals carefully arranged to form a technology capable of generating electricity upon exposure to light. This phenomenon, known as the photovoltaic effect, hinges on the interaction of cells constructed from two distinct semiconductors: p-type and n-type, which coexist within a p-n junction. This unique configuration enables the generation of electron flow and, consequently, an electric current when subjected to specific electromagnetic radiation.[39] Regarding these minerals, various potential combinations are presently employed in the market for solar panel production. Silicon, for instance, can function as either a p-type or an n-type layer when combined with boron or phosphorus, respectively.[40] Another option involves the utilisation of cadmium telluride CdTe paired with cadmium sulphide CdS.[41] Consequently, the feasibility of panel production rests on the attainability of the precise mineral compositions necessary for crafting specific cell types. This gives rise to a fundamental quandary within the solar energy domain, as to whether ventures into these combinations yield substantial energy efficiency, environmental responsibility, and economic advantage.

Fig. 8 The mechanics of solar panel functionality

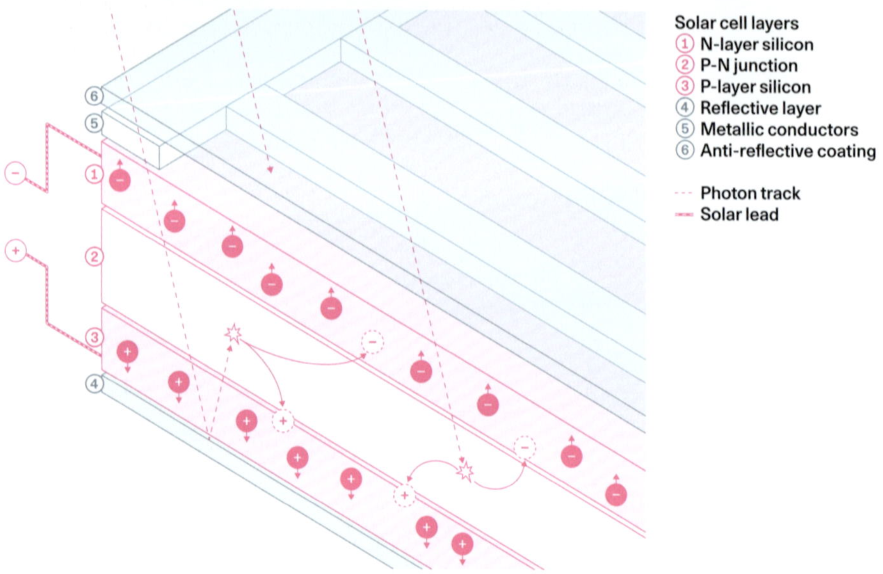

Currently, two prevalent combinations with distinct structures dominate the solar technology landscape. The first involves thin film technologies, wherein a slim compound semiconductor layer coats a flexible foil. Among the notable models in this category are CdTe-based panels and copper indium gallium diselenide CIGS.[42] The second approach centres on crystalline silicon-based panels, which captured over 95 % of the market share in 2021.[43] The prevailing dominance of silicon-based panels stems from a multifaceted interplay of factors. Firstly, silicon boasts abundant avail-

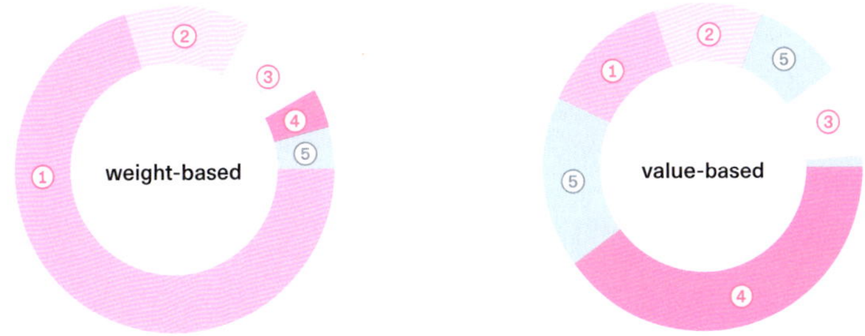

weight-based	
① Glass	68–72 %
② Aluminium	12–14 %
③ Polymers	8–10 %
④ Silicon	3–4 %
⑤ Cu, Ag, Zn, Pb, Sn	2–4 %

value-based	
④ Silicon	35–45 %
⑤ Silver (Ag)	9–23 %
① Glass	11–15 %
② Aluminium	9–12 %
⑤ Copper (Cu)	5–12 %

ability. The production of raw silicon outpaces that of raw tellurium by a staggering 18,000-fold, creating a bottleneck for CdTe-based panels. In 2020, global tellurium production amounted to a mere 444 t while silicon production reached an impressive 8,120,000 t.[44] Secondly, silicon does not possess inherent toxicity, as is the case with cadmium, a condition that significantly impacts the recyclability of glass. Lastly, the existing silicon production industry has successfully achieved economies of scale, facilitating the dispersal of initial capital expenditures across various stages of the process as well as different stakeholders.[45]

How Does the Silicon Supply Chain Work?

Silicon offers a lens through which to comprehend the operational dynamics of the solar panel industry. As a mineral pivotal to the sector's mining and production operations, its significance cannot be understated. The extraction of silicon primarily unfolds within China, which commanded a substantial 68.2 % share in 2022. Russia follows with 7.3 %, while Brazil claims a 4.6 % stake.[46] Paradoxically, despite its widespread abundance in the Earth's crust, silicon is classified as a critical mineral, namely a material with a high risk of energy supply chain disruption. This designation arises from the pronounced concentration of installed extraction capacity within China's domain. After extraction, silicon undergoes a purification process to transform from a raw material into refined ingots. This procedure takes place in facilities near the mining sites. [Fig. 11]

Fig. 10 Market shares in global polysilicon production volume, 2005–2023 in %

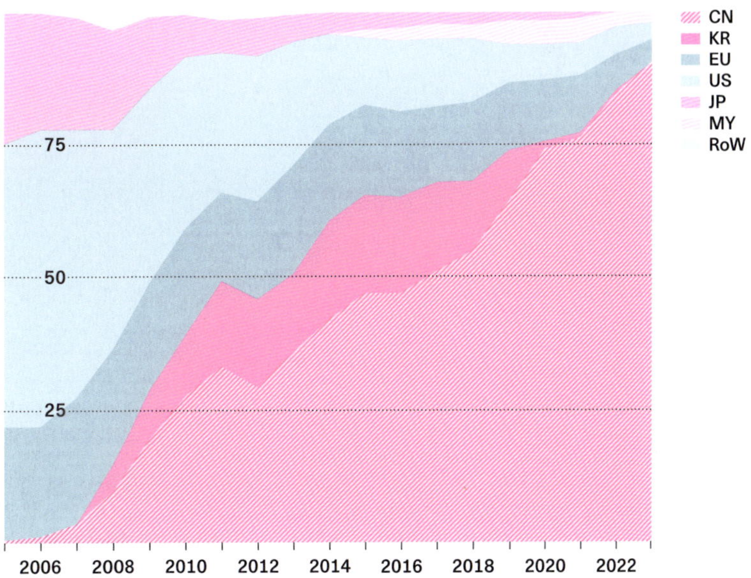

Fig. 11 Top ten polysilicon producers in 2022 in kt

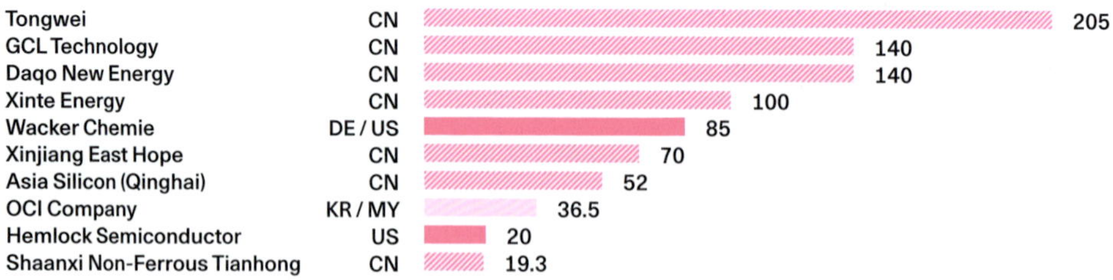

In the pursuit of ingot purification, the Siemens desalination process is the most widely adopted method due to its relatively low cost per kg.[47] The demand for exceptionally high levels of purity is paramount: ranging from 99.99999 % (7N) for solar-grade to an astounding 99.999999999 % (11N) for electronic-grade applications like integrated circuits. Once the ingots are purified, they undergo slicing to produce thin wafers. These wafers are then meticulously wired with copper on both sides to facilitate current flow, ultimately forming solar cells. Subsequently, these cells are meticulously arranged onto a supporting panel prior to their final encasement within an aluminium frame. [Fig. 33] The execution of these three critical processes can be consolidated within a single facility or distributed across different establishments, contingent on the practises of the involved companies. [Fig. 22]

Today, the majority of solar panel manufacturing is supported by fossil fuels, although this environmental impact is offset within a span of four to eight months after the panel's operation commences. Coal, which accounts for 60 % of the power for manufacturing, largely prevails due to the industry's concentration in China, particularly within the provinces of Xinjiang and Jiangsu. Notably, within these regions, coal-based energy sources supply 75 % of electricity needs, buoyed by governmental incentives.[48] In contrast to the relatively straightforward production stages of fossil fuels, the creation of a solar panel involves a complex supply chain characterised by convoluted stages, which often oscillate back and forth before culminating in a final product. Given that most production originates in East Asia, the shipping of solar panels to Europe predominantly utilises conventional cargo ships, which also transport various consumer goods. These shipments reach the continent through major ports such as Rotterdam, Hamburg, Antwerp, or Piraeus or via train connections associated with the Belt and Road Initiative, terminating in Hungary. Subsequently, the panels are distributed to wholesalers or project sites via truck or train.

Fig. 12 Solar photovoltaic manufacturing capacity by country and region, 2010 vs. 2021 in %

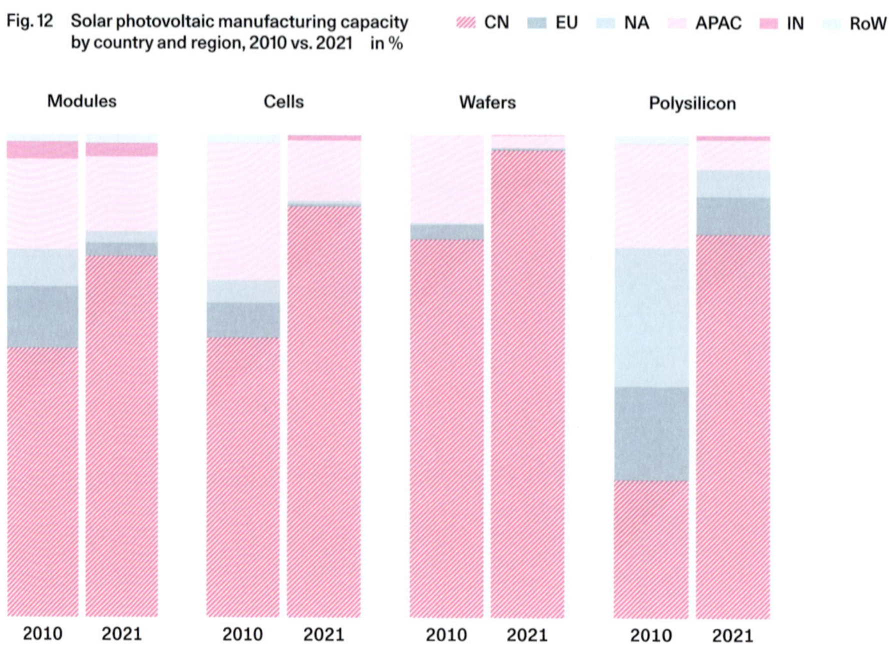

4.3.3

Solar in the Local Context

Edouard Barthen
David Bauer
Philipp Deilmann
Joseph Smithard

In 2021, PV systems in Germany produced approximately 48.4 TWh of electricity, of this 44.6 TWh was fed into the public grid and 3.8 TWh was used as a running cost.[49] Subsequently, as the sun shone in 2021, PV stations generated more electricity per month than hard coal-fired power stations from March to August and exceeded the output of gas-fired power stations from April to October. In 2023, this figure rose to an estimated 59.9 TWh, with June marking a record in solar power generation at approximately 9 TWh.[50] The available data suggests that Germany is indeed making favourable progress in the envisioned direction. Nonetheless, the complex interplay of its federal system, political ping-pong between northern and southern regions, and the juxtaposition of commitment to a low-carbon transition with resistance to crucial infrastructure significantly hinders the country's solar potential.[51]

Germany's solar capacity is concentrated within particular regions, while the heaviest electricity demands originate from metropolitan and industrial areas situated in the southern and western parts of the country. This distribution pattern—coupled with challenges like network limitations hampering efficient power transmission, grid expansion delays, and the presence of a single bidding zone for the entire country—has led to a complex energy landscape.[52] The consequences of these dynamics are particularly evident in the discrepancies between different regional geographies: the northern regions have surplus power due to increased wind and solar generation,

Fig. 13 Share of renewables and solar energy in gross power consumption in Germany, 1990–2023, and targeted path 2030 in accordance with EEG in %

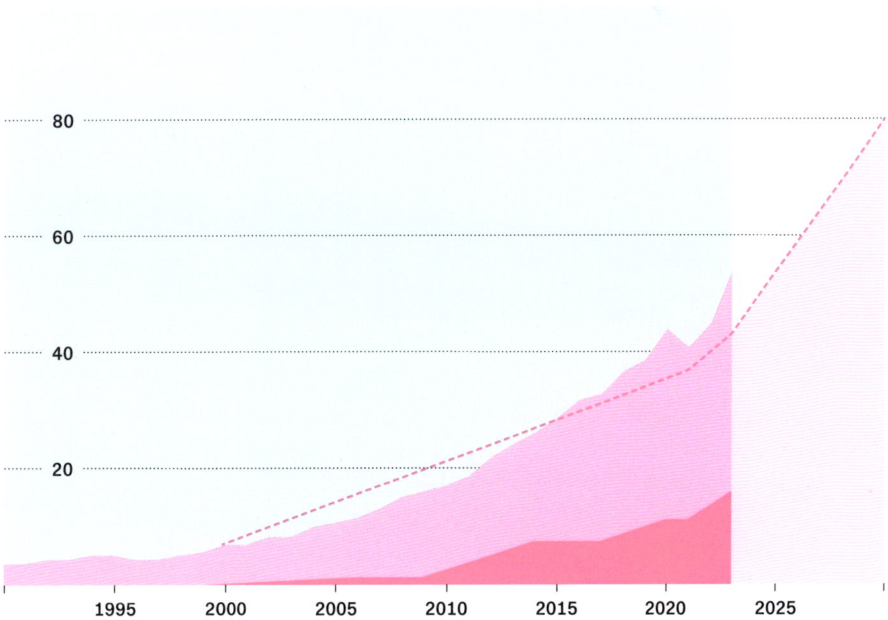

whereas the south faces clear deficits. To counter this energy imbalance, systems resort to specific measures. In the south, grid operators initiate "re-dispatch" actions, compelling power stations to escalate their output to compensate for the inadequacy of electricity reaching the southern regions. Meanwhile, in the north, grid operators enforce curtailment, mandating generators to shut down to alleviate congestion issues. These corrective measures come at a considerable cost to consumers, amounting to hundreds of millions of euros annually.[53] Infrastructurally, power transmission from the north to the south remains particularly underdeveloped. Efforts to establish high-voltage transmission lines between these regions have encountered public resistance—leading to delays and necessitating more expensive underground interconnectors.

One potential consequence that can already be anticipated is the strategic placement of new energy-intensive production facilities in regions with existing overcapacity. Regions such as Lausitz [p. 118, p. 130] in Brandenburg are currently leveraging this trend to establish themselves as new hubs for industrial development.

Berlin-Brandenburg

In its Energy Strategy for 2040, Brandenburg designates itself as an "Energy State".[54] In 2019, the state achieved the remarkable milestone of covering 95 % of its electricity consumption largely through wind and solar sources. In contrast, Berlin lags significantly behind, achieving a mere 2.7 %[55] of its consumption from renewable sources. This discrepancy hints at the need for Berlin to align with Brandenburg in order to strengthen its prospective energy collaboration and utilise Brandenburg's flatlands.[56] As of 2019, Brandenburg had achieved an absolute renewable electricity production of 19.84 TWh, positioning the state as the fifth-highest producer, trailing behind Sachsen-Anhalt, Bayern, Schleswig-Holstein, and Nordrhein-Westfalen.[57] However, the overarching objective is far more ambitious. The goal is to elevate the proportion of renewable energy consumption to a minimum of 45 TWh by 2030, followed by an even more substantial target of 75 TWh by 2040.[58]

Fig. 14 Electricity production and consumption in Berlin and Brandenburg, 2018–2021 in TWh

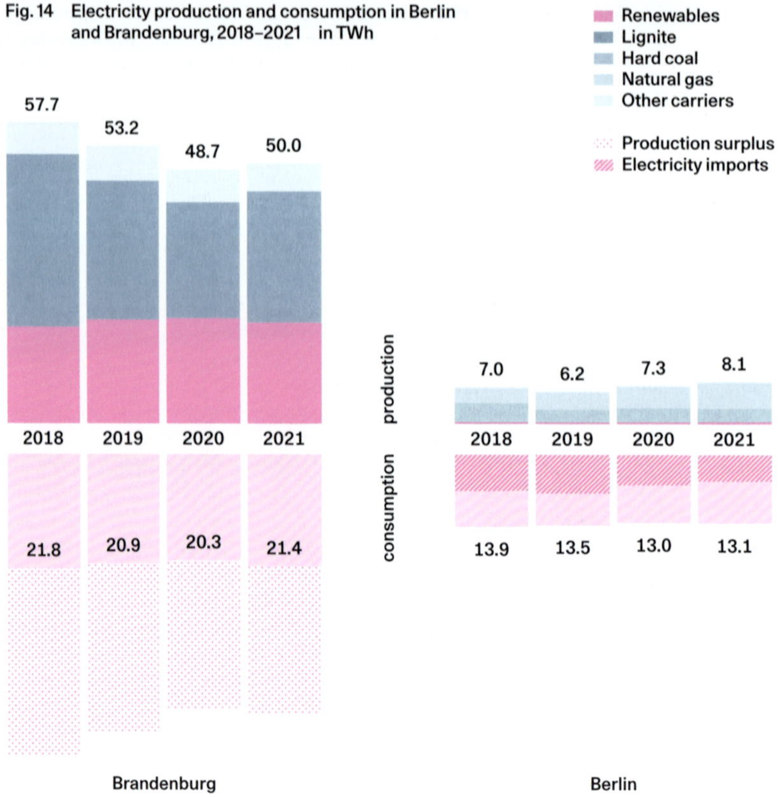

Solar Energy

Brandenburg's installed solar capacity demonstrates significant expansion, increasing from about 670 MWp in 2010 to roughly 4,500 MWp in 2021, and reaching an estimated 6,650 MWp by late 2023. Nonetheless, substantial further development will be required to meet the state's strategic targets of approximately 18,000 MWp by 2030 and 33,000 MWp by 2040.[59] An analysis of the existing installations, based on 2020 data, reveals a more nuanced composition of these capacities. From the 39,587 operational photovoltaic systems, approximately 90% consist of smaller installations (up tp 40 kWp of capacity). However, whilst these smaller systems constitute the vast majority of installations, they contribute only 4 % (326 MW) of Brandenburg's total installed capacity. Conversely, large-scale systems represent merely 2 % of installations (758 systems) yet generate 75 % (3,076 MW) of the total installed capacity, underscoring the importance of large-scale solar parks in contrast to the comparatively limited potential of rooftop systems.[60]

Fig. 15 Solar parks vs. roof outputs by capacity types in Brandenburg, 2020

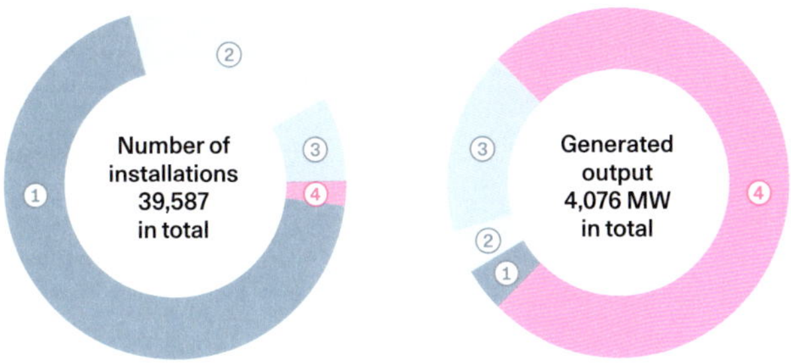

	Number of installations		Generated output
① < 10 kWp	69 %	① < 10 kWp	4 %
② 10–40 kWp	21 %	② 10–40 kWp	4 %
③ 40–750 kWp	8 %	③ 40–750 kWp	17 %
④ > 750 kWp	2 %	④ > 750 kWp	75 %

In terms of production capacity, the most extensive solar park in Germany is situated in Weesow-Willmersdorf, Brandenburg. The subject of more in-depth analysis later in this chapter [p. 249], it boasts a rated output of 187 MW. Annually, the park generates 187 GWh, which is sufficient to power approximately 50,000 households each year.[61] Assuming that Brandenburg's objective of adding 33,000 MW of solar power capacity by 2040 is to be fulfilled exclusively through ground-mounted parks such as Weesow-Willmersdorf, a further 177 solar parks would need to be established. In terms of spatial extent, these parks would occupy a combined area of 29,028 ha,[62] equivalent to more than 32 % of Berlin's total surface area (89,112 ha), and provide electricity for approximately 9,500,000 households based on today's electricity consumption patterns.[63]

In 2023, Brandenburg emerged as Germany's frontrunner in solar power output *per capita,* achieving 2,565 watts per inhabitant, with substantial potential for further expansion. Berlin's progress lags significantly behind, registering merely 73 watts per inhabitant of installed photovoltaic capacity. This figure forms a stark contrast with the national average of 974 watts per inhabitant, despite the state having the same key incentives for promoting solar energy as the rest of Germany.[64] When considering the augmentation in overall installed PV capacity per resident from 2010 to 2018, both Berlin and the entirety of Germany display an equivalent growth pattern with a factor of 2.5. This indicates that by the close of 2018, there was no observable inclination towards a more pronounced adoption of solar energy. As of 2018, the Berlin municipal utilities were in the preliminary stages of executing initiatives to harness the PV potential of properties owned by state housing companies and public institutions. Consequently, the impact of their effort is currently unrepresented in available data.[65]

Berlin's "Masterplan Solarcity" underscores the ambition to generate 25 % of its projected electricity requirements from solar energy through domestic installations by 2050—an objective which entails approximately 4,400 MW of installed capacity. This comprehensive framework, which delineates the prospects, obstacles, and strategies for amplifying solar power within the urban landscape.[66] A joint study by the Fraunhofer-Institut für Solare Energiesysteme ISE estimated that Berlin has a technical solar potential of 6,437 MW on its roofs, excluding

Fig. 16 Area comparison: Weesow-Willmersdorf solar park vs. Berlin in km^2

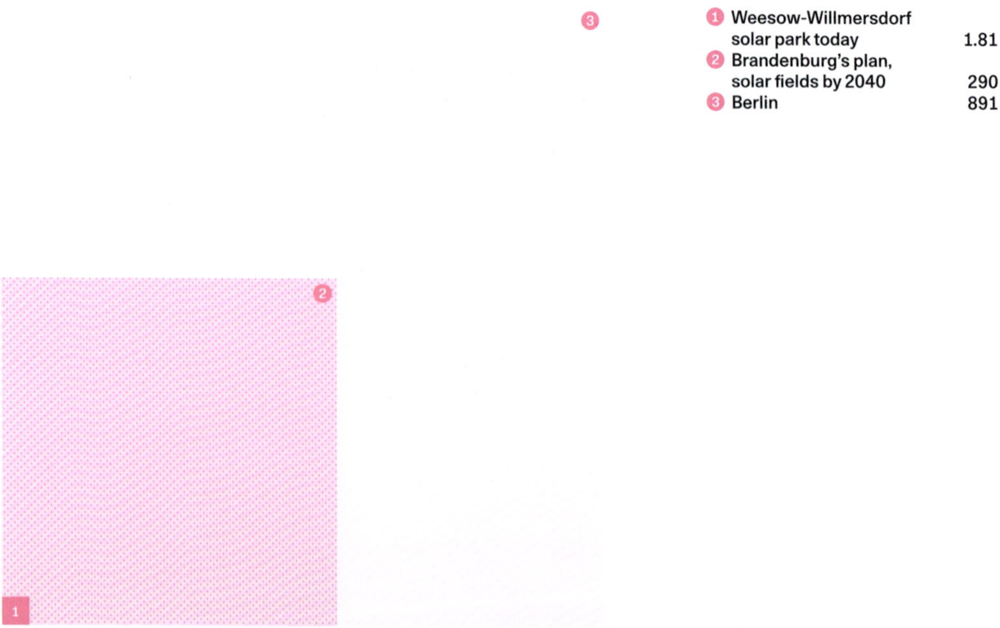

monuments and façades. Significantly, over half of this potential is located across the tenant city.[67] By equipping the rooftops of both single and two-family houses—as well as those of multi-family complexes—with existing technology, a potential of 3,744 MW could be harnessed from an existing stock of over 290,000 residential buildings.[68] Commercial and industrial sites contribute towards an additional third of this potential, with approximately 9,000 public buildings accounting for roughly the remaining 10 %. One of the most contested scenarios revolves around the building stock protected by monument preservation laws, which encompasses over 50,000 structures. These buildings could not be factored into any potential analysis, as they are governed by Berlin's monument protection law, which does not categorically preclude installation but rather subjects it to case-by-case determinations.

While Berlin undoubtedly has a role to play in the energy transition, the disparity in output between roof-based and ground-mounted systems, coupled with the potential of the neighbouring Brandenburg's land area, renders Berlin's contribution relatively modest and somewhat inefficient. At the same time, expanding renewable energies in Brandenburg triggers conflicts over land-use and strains relations with the local population. Once more, a historical pattern emerges wherein the productive landscapes beyond the city's borders are threatened with carrying the burden of resource demands.

Land-Use Conflicts

The increasing deployment of ground-mounted PV systems in Brandenburg poses a significant challenge to agricultural production, as the higher profitability of these systems potentially leads to escalating land prices that threaten the agricultural sector. Consequently, political efforts have been undertaken to direct PV to less conflictual areas, most notably to prioritise the use of marginal land. The federal government provides subsidies for establishing solar power stations on designated base areas through the EEG. These areas include marginal strips along highways and railway routes, as well as conversion areas, which are exempt from nature conservation or state planning regulations. According to a 2022 report by the MWAE, the potential for EEG base areas in Brandenburg is 25,700 MW with a total surface of 28,311 ha.[69] However, EEG base areas also face notable limitations that may dampen their appeal for potential investors. These areas often experience lower demand due to their compact size as well as the requirement to engage in a tendering process overseen by the BNetzA. Consequently, the feasibility of utilising these areas is relatively low and estimated to be at around 30 %.[70]

Beyond the EEG base areas, Brandenburg has a much larger surface potential for ground-mounted PV. The MWAE report concludes that there is considerable potential for producing solar power on agricultural land. To avoid major conflicts with agricultural production, two scenarios are imagined. One is to use land with relatively low fertility that is subsequently less attractive for agriculture.[71] The other is to have dual use of agricultural areas through PV mount systems that allow for simultaneous agricultural production, known as agrivoltaics. According to the report, agricultural areas with less than 30 soil points[72] (soils with relatively low fertility) account for an expansion potential of 117,000 MW.[73] For agrivoltaics, horizontally-mounted modules allow for an additional output of 238,000 MW on arable land and 28,000 MW on grassland. Furthermore, vertically mounted bifacial modules (two-sided sunlight receivers) allow for outputs of 105,000 MW on arable land and 12,000 MW on grassland.[74]

Solar Transition in the Region

Considering the substantial potential for ground-mounted solar power, Brandenburg's goal of reaching an expansion of 33,000 MW by 2040 could be perceived as modest, to say the least. In addition to fulfilling its own energy requirements, given its expansive landscape and relatively sparse population, Brandenburg has the potential to significantly contribute to the renewable energy supply, particularly within the framework of distributing responsibilities among federal states. A collaborative burden-sharing model could hold particular significance for the neighbouring state of Berlin, which is facing challenges in its pursuit of clean energy. However, in this classic interplay between dense metropolitan agglomerations and productive landscapes, it is essential to introduce equitable mechanisms that enhance local value creation driven by the energy transition and to establish frameworks that balances various needs, particularly concerning other ecosystem services, nature preservation, foodsecurity, and the onshoring of production capacities.

Looking at the remaining potential for wind energy in Brandenburg, the importance of ground-mounted solar plants becomes even more apparent. The state government envisions achieving a total wind power capacity of 10,500 MW by 2030, aligning with the federal government's target of 2% coverage across all states. As of 2023, 8000 MW[75] of wind power capacity is already installed, fulfilling 76.2% of the area target. The process of designating areas for wind power in Brandenburg is already well underway and has been relatively successful. Nonetheless, it is approaching its maximum efficiency. To further increase the share of wind power effectively beyond the existing 2% target, a significant expansion of its allocated surface area would be necessary. However, even with a substantial expansion, the yield potential of wind power would remain relatively limited compared to solar power. On the other hand, Brandenburg's flatlands boast an immense potential for harnessing cost-effective and comparatively straightforward solar energy. This capacity would not only provide substantial power to Brandenburg itself but would also expedite the energy transition in Berlin, and even play a role in lightening the energy load for power-hungry regions across Germany.[76]

The crucial challenge in the coming years lies in determining how this transformation's burden will be equitably distributed and how rural communities and municipalities will navigate its socio-cultural implications.

4.3.4

Suqian

Santiago Martínez M.
Joseph Smithard

Nestled within a leafy meadow 11 km northeast of Berlin stands the newly erected Weesow-Willmersdorf solar park. [Fig. 32] With its impressive capacity, the park claims its position among Germany's most substantial solar installations. However, the journey of the panels has spanned a considerable distance. Specifically, in the case of the Weesow-Willmersdorf, its solar panels were sourced from Trina Solar, a prominent Chinese corporation based in the city of Changzhou, within the province of Jiangsu.[77] As one of the world's largest solar panel manufacturers, Trina Solar has significantly expanded its operations in response to escalating demand, both domestically and on an international scale.

Fig. 17 Largest solar panel manufacturers by shipments, 2022 in GWp

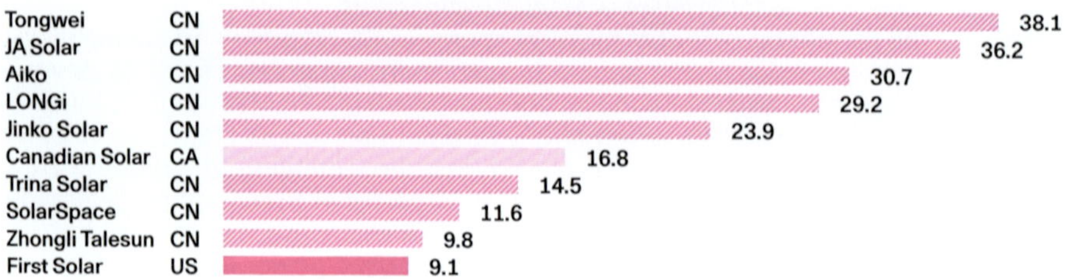

Consequently, the demand in regions like Berlin-Brandenburg could trigger territorial ramifications, encompassing not just mineral extraction but also the subsequent processing and assembly of the panels themselves. A prime instance of this can be found in Suqian, situated in the Jiangsu province of China. In 2020, Trina Solar initiated the establishment of three solar panel manufacturing facilities within the municipalities of Yiwu, in Zhejiang, and Suqian and Yancheng in Jiangsu. The strategic objective was to propel the production capacity of their 210 mm-cell panels to 22 GWp across all municipalities.[78] These state-of-the-art factories are poised to encompass the production of wafers, cells, and modules. According to Trina Solar's assertion, the Suqian plant alone was projected to achieve a module production capacity of 12 GWp annually.[79]

Establishing this factory in Suqian is not a random occurrence, as specific factors have driven the growth of this industry in the city. For instance, Suqian boasts its own Economic Development Zone, a Chinese public policy formulated to promote industrial and technological advancement within designated regions of the country.[80] These regions benefit from preferential business policies, and since their inception in the 1970s, their count has risen to over 2000. They are categorised as Provincial and National Development Zones, with the latter exhibiting a GDP growth rate nearly three-times higher than the national average in 2020. The Suqian Economic and Technological Zone, initially founded in 1998, underwent elevation to the status of National Economic Development Zone in 2012, with a pronounced focus on industries like photoelectric, food, electromechanical, and textiles.[81]

In addition to policy considerations, the city's existing infrastructure further justifies the factory's logical placement. Jiangsu is China's second-largest polysilicon-producing province after Xinjiang: in 2018 it produced 70,000 t,[82] accounting for 19 % of the global total production.[83] Moreover, the solar industry had already established a foothold in the city. In 2013, a significant development occurred when Ascent Solar entered into a collaborative agreement with the Municipal Government. This agreement paved the way for a joint venture and the subsequent establishment of a solar panel manufacturing plant.[84] Notably, other enterprises, such as Suqian Yingyan Solar Energy Co. and Triumph Group—both entities under the umbrella of the state-owned China National Building Materials Group Corporation—have also established their operational facilities within the city. More recently, in 2021, Triumph Group signed an agreement with the Municipal Government to establish a solar glass factory.[85] Beyond this, solar energy generation has also left its imprint on the city. For instance, in 2016, Zhenghui Solar erected a 20 MW solar plant within the city, which joins the ranks of numerous others adorning the roofs of industrial areas.[86]

Fig. 18 Total PV module exports by region, 2017–2021 in GW

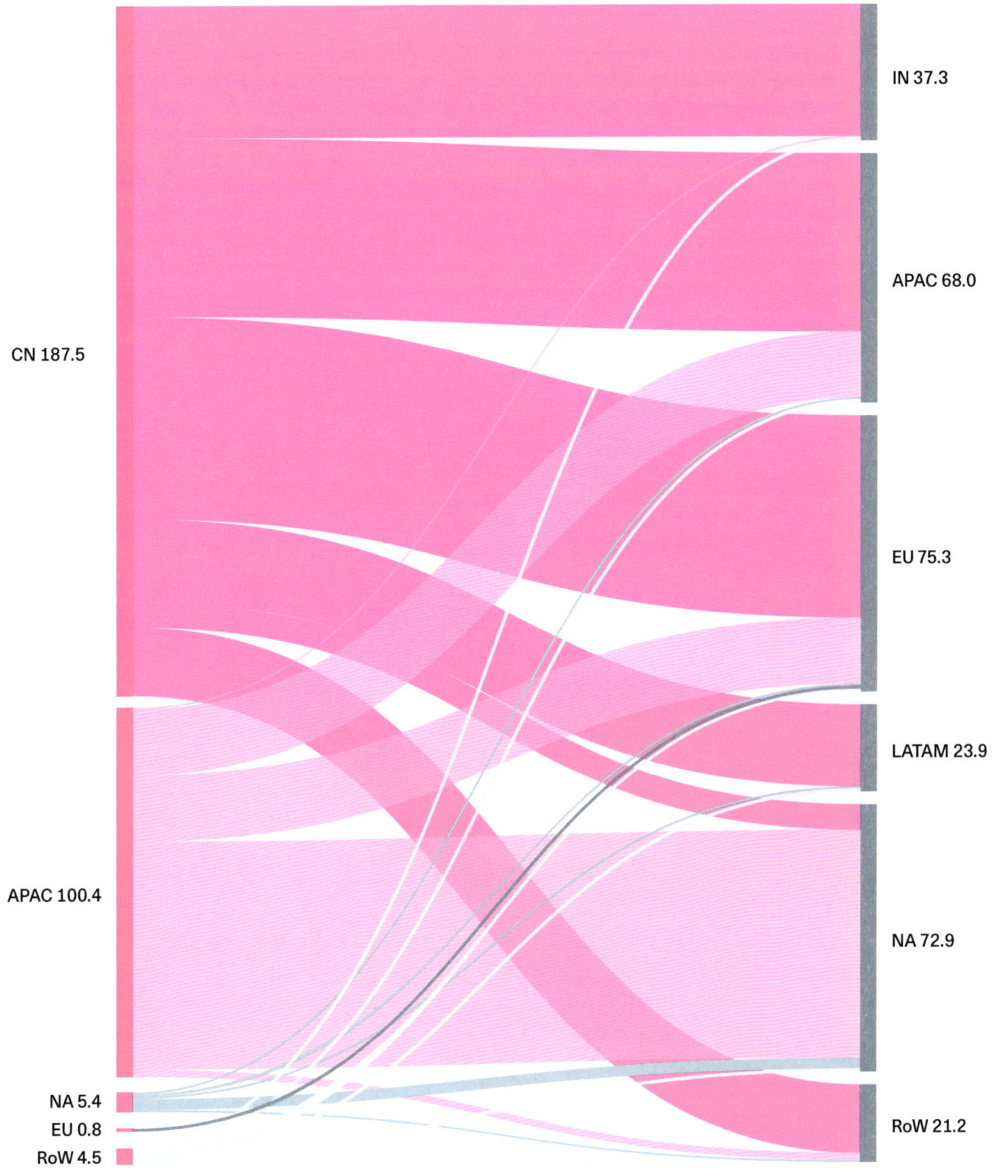

In tandem with Suqian's dramatic urban growth and expanding industrial zones, a population surge underscores its evolving role as a significant hub in the renewable energy landscape. Suqian's population has grown over ten-fold within three decades. In 1990, the population stood at around 105,000, yet by 2020, estimates fluctuate between 1,100,000 and 1,400,000.[87] [88] This unprecedented expansion is mirrored in the city's spatial expanse. Initially encompassing an urbanised area of approximately 10.5 km^2 in 1984, this figure surged to 26 km^2 by 2000, further ballooning to 132 km^2 in 2010 and currently stretching across 254 km^2. [Fig. 26–29]

Within this terrain, industrial zones span roughly 62 km^2, constituting around 24 % of the developed land. Spanning approximately 0.3 km^2, the Trina Solar factory's footprint mirrors the dimensions of the built area of Berlin-Brandenburg airport.[89] [Fig. 30] Notably, Trina Solar has embraced automation across numerous production processes, leading to a remarkable 25 % reduction in required staff per GW. Within the realm of solar panel manufacturing, automation encompasses an array of robotic applications, all contingent upon a shared resource: critical minerals. Highlighting China's prominence in this arena, the country introduced 168,400 new industrial robots in 2020, while Germany (ranking fifth globally) integrated 22,300 into its industrial landscape.[90]

In the shift towards renewable energy, precisely the magnitude of this facility's power output makes it an intriguing example compared with existing fossil fuel sources. Boasting an annual production capacity of 12 GW of solar panels, this factory's aggregate output rivals that of up to 12 nuclear power stations each year.[91] In juxtaposition with coal, Germany's operational electricity generation capacity from hard coal and lignite stood at 30.5 GW in 2022.[92] This implies that facilities like the Trina Solar factory have the potential to replace Germany's coal-based generation in just 2.54 years.

The prevailing data suggests that technological advancements, such as automation and robotics, might also lead to changes in population dynamics. However, the innovative nature of these technologies implies that historical trends may not necessarily repeat. What remains clear is the emerging need for new territorial accommodations to host facilities like Trina Solar's Suqian factory in Germany. To better grasp the scale of this transformation, considering both the panel density and the current output of the Weesow-Willmersdorf solar park, the installation of 12 GWp of solar power would necessitate an area of approximately 130.43 km^2.[93]

Fig. 19 Area comparison: Trina Solar factory vs. Berlin districts in km^2

1	Megafactory, Suqian	0.3
2	District of Friedrichshain-Kreuzberg, Berlin	20.16
3	Total ground coverage area necessary to deploy all annually produced PV panels in Suqian megafactory	130.43
4	District of Treptow-Köpenick, Berlin	168.42

4.3.5

Weesow-Willmersdorf

Santiago Martínez M.
Joseph Smithard

Pumping out around 190 MW of power annually, the Weesow-Willmersdorf solar park [Fig. 32] is not only the most powerful solar field in Berlin-Brandenburg but throughout Germany more widely.[94] The solar park—which is currently under the ownership of Energie Baden-Württemberg AG EnBW—was procured from the preceding developer, Procon Solar, in 2018. Commencing operations in 2020, the park is projected to generate energy until at least the year 2060. At peak capacity, the field can power 50,000 households and prevent 129,000 t of CO_2 emissions annually. To establish a solar field of this scale, panels are strategically organised into clusters. The generated direct current DC is then directed to inverters, that convert it into alternating current AC, which is subsequently channelled to substations. In the case of Weesow-Willmersdorf, two substations are involved in this process; these are situated in proximity to Börnicke and Blumberg, at a distance of approximately 4 and 7 km from the solar field, respectively.[95] These substations facilitate electricity distribution through three overhead lines managed by E.DIS Netz GmbH.

However, despite the proximity of the substations to the region, not all the solar energy is distributed within Berlin-Brandenburg. In 2021, EnBW and Covestro, a prominent global polymer company, entered into their first Power Purchase Agreement PPA. Within the 187 MW capacity of solar power available, Covestro secured 63 MW for a 15-year term. This energy allocation will serve Covestro's operations at their Dormagen and Krefeld-Uerdingen facilities in Nordrhein-Westfalen. The energy sourced from this agreement will be harnessed in the production of sustainable plastics.[96]

Fig. 20 Weesow-Willmersdorf solar park

Despite its significant production capacity, the solar park's actual land area is not that substantial, owing to several considerations. Firstly, the diversity of panel technologies and their corresponding capacities introduces a degree of variability in its power generation. In the case of Weesow-Willmersdorf, the panels rely on a combination of technologies, with Trina Solar supplying approximately 465,000 TSM-DEG15M.20(II) panels, each unit boasting an output of around 400 W. These panels—which are 2019 models, equipped with 144 cells each—utilise silicon-based technology and exhibit an efficiency of 20 %. [Fig. 33] This efficiency value signifies the proportion of solar energy that is effectively transformed into electricity.[97] By 2023, the efficiency percentage of these silicon-based panels had grown from 20 % to 27 %.[98] However, most commercially available panels typically offer up to 23 % efficiency. Experimental exploration is also ongoing in developing substitutes for silicon-based panels, using materials ranging from sulphides and organic compounds to dyed materials. Notably, as of 2022, the ISE in Germany achieved a significant breakthrough, developing a panel with the highest efficiency of approximately 47 %.[99]

In addition to panel efficiency, the density of panels installed per m^2 constitutes another pivotal factor in determining the overall energy output of a solar field. Deploying a higher number of panels can enhance the total power generation, yet it also necessitates a greater quantity of wiring, inverters, and supporting structures. Although the Weesow-Willmersdorf solar park boasts an efficiency typical of contemporary panels, its standout feature lies in its notably high panel density (2,229 panels per ha). For comparison, Europe's most powerful solar field, the Francisco Pizarro Solar Plant in Spain, registers 1,452 panels per ha.[100] Hence, the amalgamation of panel efficiency and planned installation density is the ultimate arbiter of a solar field's actual efficiency. Notably, Weesow-Willsmerdorf's efficiency of 103 MW/km^2 outshines that of many of the world's largest solar fields. To illustrate an example, the world's most powerful solar field, India's Bhadla solar park, records a significantly lower efficiency of 47 MW/km^2.[101] [Fig. 21] However, installing more advanced and efficient panels also requires a greater initial investment. A comparative analysis between these two solar parks underscores this financial aspect. Notably, accommodating the variations in land and installation expenses, Weesow-Willmersdorf incurs a cost per m^2 that is over twice as high as its Indian counterpart, amounting to € 47 and € 22 per m^2, respectively.

The Weesow-Willmersdorf solar park clearly illustrates that the journey towards solar technology's integration involves not only striking an intricate balance across supply chain expenditures but also carries considerable geographical implications.

Moreover, this technology is continually evolving and seems poised to improve and become more cost-effective as its utilisation expands. An especially noteworthy aspect is that EnBW undertook this project without relying on subsidies from the EEG, which marks a departure from the conventional approach taken towards solar and other renewable energy initiatives in Germany, barring hydropower. This financial independence was made possible only by the substantial reduction in the cost of solar panels, which has fallen by over 80 % since 2010.[102] Such technological progress is subsequently galvanising a paradigm shift whereby economic viability is finally catching up with environmental responsibility.

Endnotes

1 Destatis, "87 % der importierten Photovoltaikanlagen kamen im Jahr 2022 aus China".
2 International Renewable Energy Agency, "Renewable Capacity Statistics 2023", 21.
3 International Renewable Energy Agency, "Country Rankings".
4 Bundesnetzagentur, "Zubau Erneuerbarer Energien 2023".
5 Volker U. Hoffmann, "Damals War's: Ein Rückblick auf der Photovoltaik in Deutschland".
6 Ibid.
7 Bouamane and Jones, Geoffrey, *Power from Sunshine*, 47.
8 Jäger-Waldau, *PV Status Report 2007*, 98.
9 Ibid., 83.
10 Ibid., 8.
11 Bouamane and Jones, Geoffrey, *Power from Sunshine*, 69.
12 Gilles, Lepesant, "Higher Renewable Energy Targets in Germany: How Will the Industry Benefit?".
13 Bundesministerium für Wirtschaft und Energie, "Zahlen und Fakten Energiedaten".
14 See the controversial works of early climate sceptics: *Die kalte Sonne warum die Klimakatastrophe nicht stattfindet*.
15 Jäger-Waldau, *PV Status Report 2007*, 77.
16 Nengyuanjie, "History of Photovoltaic Development in China – Energy Industry".
17 Library of Congress, "China: Renewable Energy Law Amended".
18 Wikipedia, "Data on the World's Largest Solar PV Producers".
19 Bernreuter Research, "Polysilicon Manufacturers".
20 Bernreuter Research, "Polysilicon Market Analysis".
21 Our World in Data, "Solar (Photovoltaic) Panel Prices".
22 Bundesministerium für Wirtschaft und Energie, "Bruttobeschäftigung Durch Erneuerbare Energien 2000 Bis 2021".
23 Bouamane and Jones, Geoffrey, *Power from Sunshine*, 59.
24 European Commission, "European Climate Law".
25 United Nations Economic Commission for Europe, *Carbon Neutrality in the UNECE Region*, 54.
26 Bundesministerium für Wirtschaft und Energie, "BMWK – Neues Klimaschutzgesetz".
27 Calculation based on the spatial expansion calculated by Prof. Dr.-Ing. Olaf Goebel in: *Die Energiewende Zu Ende Gedacht – Was Wird Sich Für Uns Ändern?*; Another scenario by Holler, Gaukel, and Lesch suggest a square with sides of 70 km in: *Erneuerbare Energien zum Verstehen und Mitreden*.
28 Author's own calculation based on: *Erneuerbare Energien zum Verstehen und Mitreden*.
29 *Die Energiewende zu Ende gedacht—was wird sich für uns ändern?*
30 Baugesetz §35 Absatz 1: *Baugesetzbuch*.
31 Ministerium für Umwelt, Klima und Energiewirtschaft Baden-Württemberg, "Verordnung des Umweltministeriums zu den Pflichten zur Installation von Photovoltaikanlagen auf Dach- und Parkplatzflächen".
32 Koalitionsvertrag zwischen SPD, Bündnis 90/Die Grünen & FDP, "Mehr Fortschritt wagen. Bündnis für Freiheit, Gerechtigkeit und Nachhaltigkeit".
33 Calculation by author: assuming an average density of 2,300 panels per ha and 400 W per panel at peak capacity.
34 Pawley, *Theory and Design in the Second Machine Age*.
35 Oudes, Van Den Brink, and Stremke, "Towards a Typology of Solar Energy Landscapes".
36 Nesbit, Waldheim, *Technical Lands: a Critical Primer.*
37 The definition of disadvantaged lands is based on an EU legislation encompassing six criteria. (Directive 75/268/EEC)
38 Enkhard, "Bäume bleiben vorerst stehen".
39 University of Calgary, "Photovoltaic Effect – Energy Education".
40 Visual Capitalist, "How Solar Panels Work".
41 Sinha, Lilhare, and Khare, "A Review on the Improvement in Performance of CdTe/CdS Thin-Film Solar Cells through Optimization of Structural Parameters".
42 Bernreuter Research, "Solar Value Chain – Panel Supply Steps".
43 Fraunhofer-Institut für Solare Energiesysteme, "Photovoltaics Report".
44 Statista, "Global Silicon Production 2022".
45 Bernreuter Research, "Solar Value Chain – Panel Supply Steps".
46 Statista, "Silicon".
47 Bernreuter Research, "Polysilicon Production: Siemens Process".
48 International Energy Agency, "Solar PV Global Supply Chains".
49 Fraunhofer-Institut für Solare Energiesysteme, "Public Net Electricity Generation in Germany in 2021".
50 Fraunhofer-Institut für Solare Energiesysteme, "Energy-Charts 2023".
51 DW, "Germany's North-South Divide Flares up over Energy".
52 Eriksen and Clean Energy Wire, "Grid Operators Consider Splitting Germany's Single Power Market Zone".
53 International Energy Agency, "Germany 2020: Energy Policy Review", 13.
54 Ministerium für Wirtschaft, Arbeit und Energie, "Energiestrategie 2040", 17.
55 Agentur für Erneuerbare Energien, "TOP 10 – Übersicht Zur Entwicklung Erneuerbarer Energien in Allen Bundesländern – Föderal Erneuerbar".
56 Ministerium für Wirtschaft, Arbeit und Energie, "Energiestrategie 2040", 30.
57 Agentur für Erneuerbare Energien.
58 Ministerium für Wirtschaft, Arbeit und Energie, 54.
59 Energieportal Brandenburg, "Stromerzeugung Photovoltaic Installierte Leistung Absolut" and Ministerium für Wirtschaft, Arbeit und Energie, 52.
60 Ministerium für Wirtschaft, Arbeit und Energie, "Abschlussbericht: Ergebnisse der Potenzialanalyse über nutzbare Flächen für solartechnische Anlagen im Land Brandenburg", 12.
61 Wikipedia, "Solarpark Weesow-Willmersdorf".
62 Weesow-Willmersdorf has a built combined area of 164 ha.
63 Authors' calculation based on 3,500 kWh per annum.
64 Strom-Report, "Photovoltaik Deutschland".
65 See Masterplan Solarcity: Senatsverwaltung für Wirtschaft, Energie und Betriebe Berlin, "Voller Energie zur solaren Stadt: Infobroschüre zum Masterplan Solarcity Berlin".
66 Senatsverwaltung für Wirtschaft, Energie und Betriebe Berlin.
67 Stryi-Hipp et al., "Expertenempfehlung zum Masterplan Solarcity Berlin", 25.
68 Ibid., 57.
69 The suitable areas are divided into 90.8 % marginal strips of highways and train tracks, 8.6 % open areas (formerly conversion areas), and 0.6 % parking lots and landfill sites. See: Ministerium für Wirtschaft, Arbeit und Energie Brandenburg, "Ergebnisse der Potenzialanalyse über nutzbare Flächen für solartechnische Anlagen im Land Brandenburg", 25.
70 Ibid., 30.
71 On top of that, areas could be included that are currently threatened by desertification and that will become too arid for agriculture in the future.
72 Soil points determine the agricultural quality of the soil in Germany. They range from 1 (very weak fertility) to 100 points (for very rich soils).
73 Ministerium für Wirtschaft, Arbeit und Energie Brandenburg, 26.
74 Ibid.
75 As of January 2023, Ministerium für Wirtschaft, Arbeit und Energie des Landes Brandenburg, "Windenergie".
76 Hirschl, Bernd et al., "Gutachten zum Klimaplan Brandenburg – Zwischenbericht", 31.
77 Power Technology, "XXL (Weesow-Willmersdorf) Solar Park, Brandenburg, Germany".
78 Trina Solar, "Trina Solar 210 Vertex Super Factory".
79 Renewables Now, "Trina Solar Starts N-Type Cell Production at 8-GW Factory in China".
80 Invest in China, "China Economic Development Zones".
81 Municipality of Suqian, "Suqian High-Tech Industrial Development Zone".
82 Global News Wire, "Global and China Polysilicon Industry Report 2019–2023".
83 International Energy Agency, "Solar PV Global Supply Chains".
84 "Ascent Solar to Build New Manufacturing Plant in Suqian, Jiangsu, China".
85 Hall, "Chinese PV Industry Brief".
86 Global Energy Monitor, "Jiangsu Suqian Suyu Guanmiaozhen Zhenghui Solar Farm".
87 For the city, not the prefecture.
88 "Jiāngsū (China): Prefectural Division & Major Cities – Population Statistics, Maps, Charts, Weather and Web Information".
89 Pintos, Paula, "Berlin Brandenburg Airport Willy Brandt / Gmp".
90 Robotics, "IFR Presents World Robotics 2021 Reports".
91 According to data from the American Office of Nuclear Energy, the average power output per nuclear power station is 1 GW.
92 Statista, "Regional Distribution of Solar Module Production".
93 Assuming an average density of 2,300 panels per ha and 400 W per panel.
94 "Der EnBW-Solarpark in Weesow-Willmersdorf | EnBW".
95 Power Technology, "XXL (Weesow-Willmersdorf) Solar Park, Brandenburg, Germany".
96 "Solarpark Weesow-Willmersdorf größtes Solarkraftwerk Deutschlands".
97 Trina Solar, "Data Sheet: Duomax Twin, TSM-DEG15MC.20(II)".
98 National Renewable Energy Laboratory, "Champion Photovoltaic Module Efficiency Chart".
99 Fraunhofer-Institut für Solare Energiesysteme, "Fraunhofer ISE Develops the World's Most Efficient Solar Cell with 47.6 percent Efficiency".
100 Iberdrola, "Núñez de Balboa, the Largest Photovoltaic Project in Europe".
101 Square Yards, "Bhadla Solar Park: Overview of Largest Solar Park in the World".
102 BDEW, "Hier gelingt die Energiewende, Teil I".

Fig. 21 Selected solar parks across the world

Annual energy production in MW | Efficiency in MW/km²

IN

Bhadla solar park,
Rajasthan Renewable Energy
Corporation Ltd.

48 km²

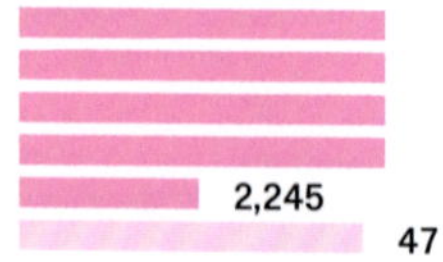

CN

Qinghai Hainan solar PV park,
Qinghai Huanghe hydro-
power plant

64 km²

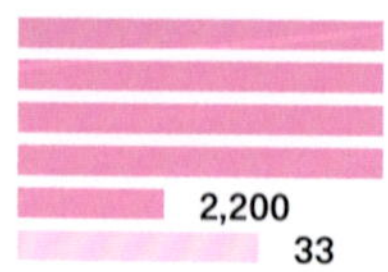

EG

Benban solar park,
New and Renewable
Energy Authority

37 km²

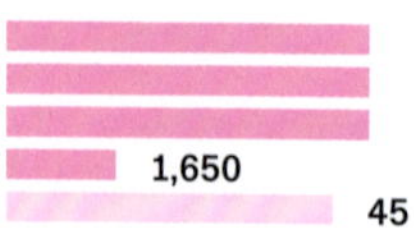

AE

Noor Abu Dhabi solar park
Emirates Water and
Electricity Company

8 km²

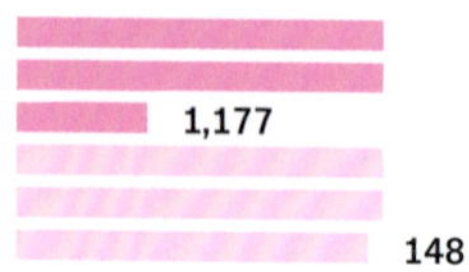

MX

Villanueva solar park, Enel Green Power

26 km²

US

Mount Signal solar farm, TerraForm Power

32 km²

ES

Francisco Pizarro solar plant, Iberdrola

10 km²

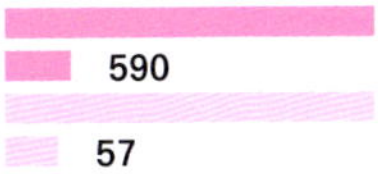

ES

Núñez de Balboa plant, Iberdrola

9 km²

DE

Weesow-Willmersdorf solar park, EnBW

2 km²

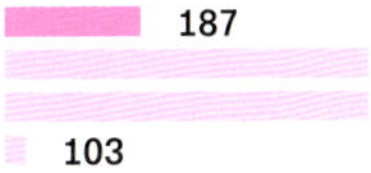

DE

Meuro solar park, GP JOULE

4 km²

Fig. 22 Solar supply chain

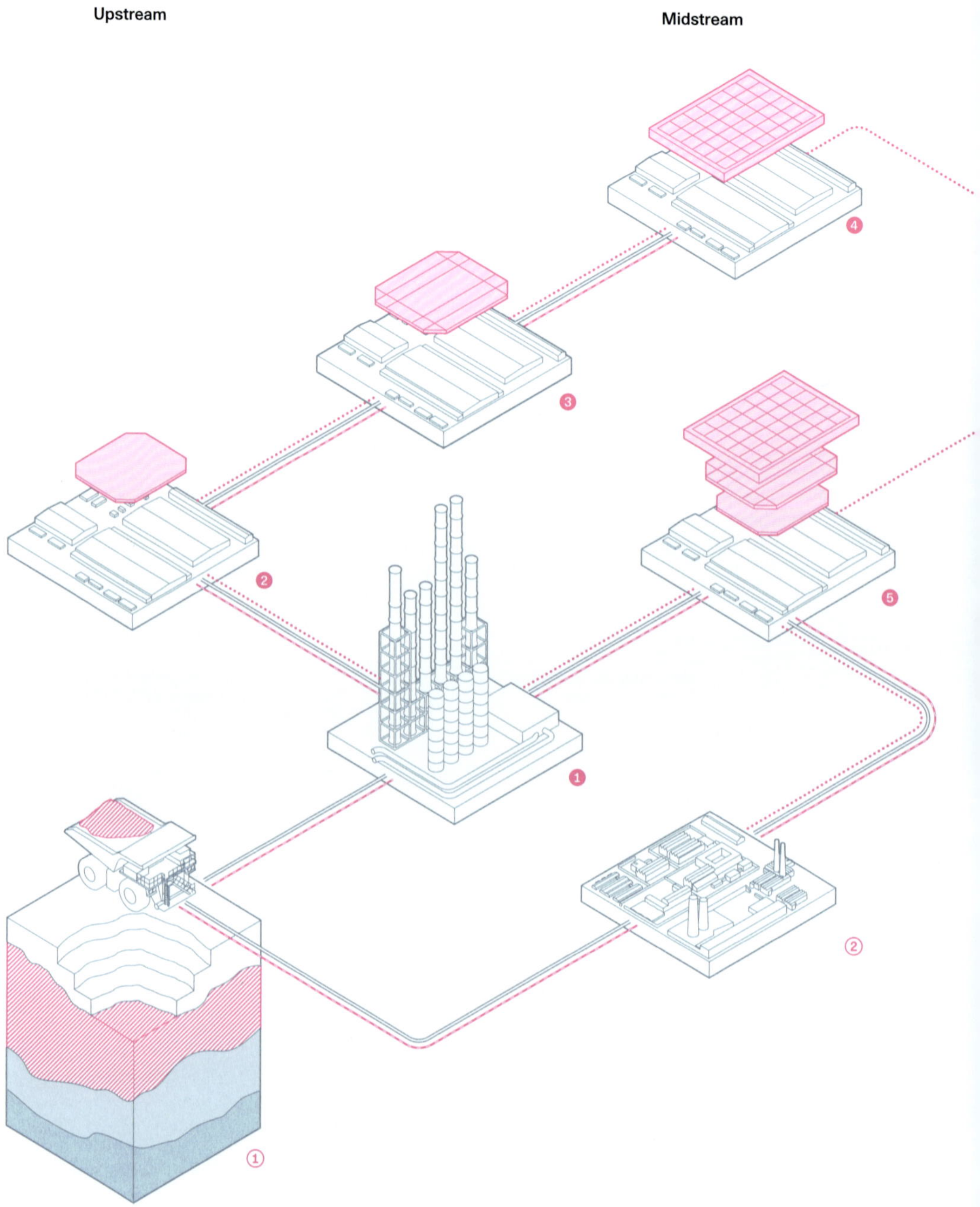

Downstream

Final Energy Consumption

1 Households

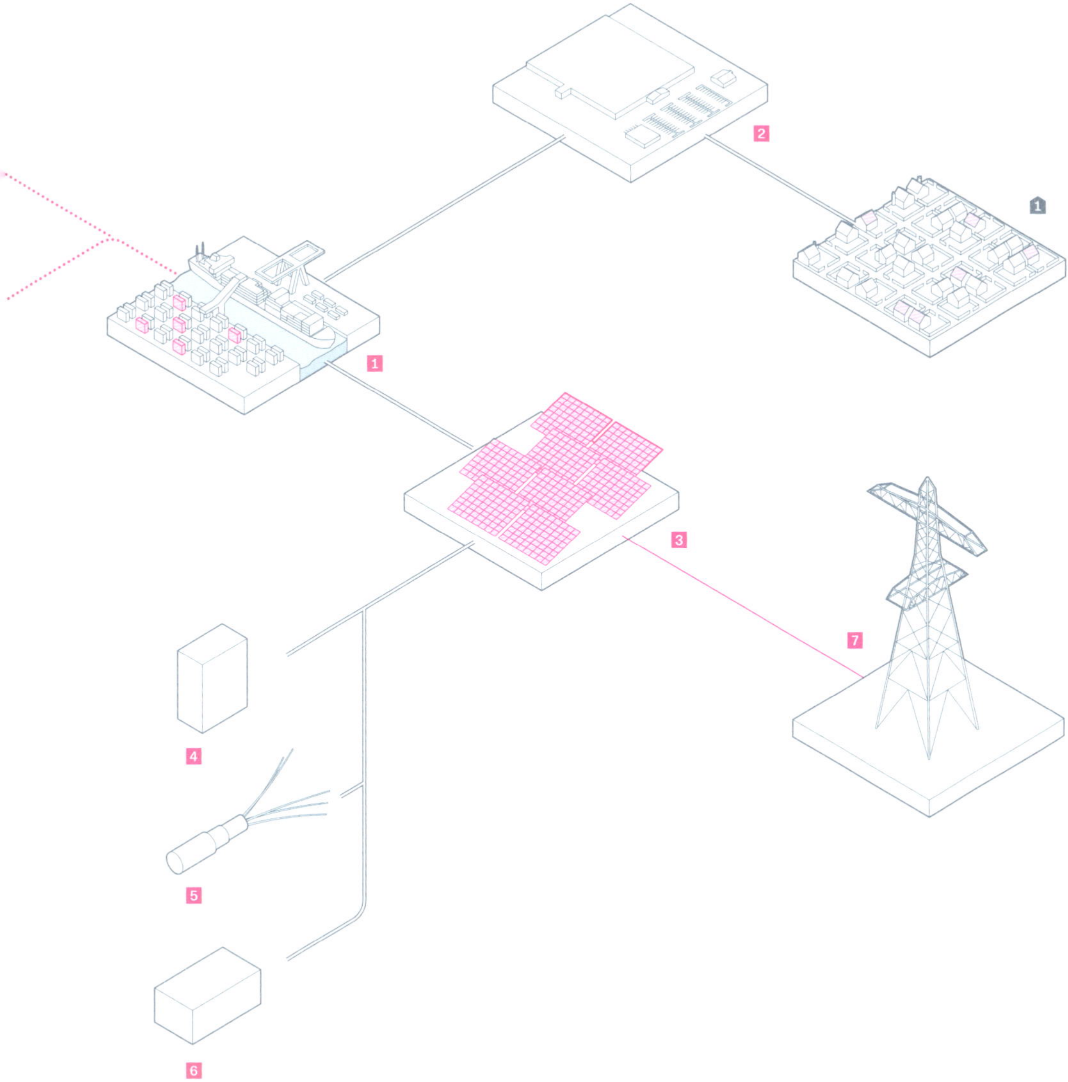

Distribution (DE)

- 1 Port
- 2 Retailers
- 3 Solar fields
- 4 Inverters
- 5 Cables
- 6 Batteries
- 7 Main electric grid

Fig. 23 Global extraction sites of raw materials used in c-Si solar PV panels

- Al Aluminium
- Sb Antimony
- Cu Copper
- In Indium
- Pb Lead
- Qz Quartz
- Ag Silver
- Sn Tin
- Zn Zinc

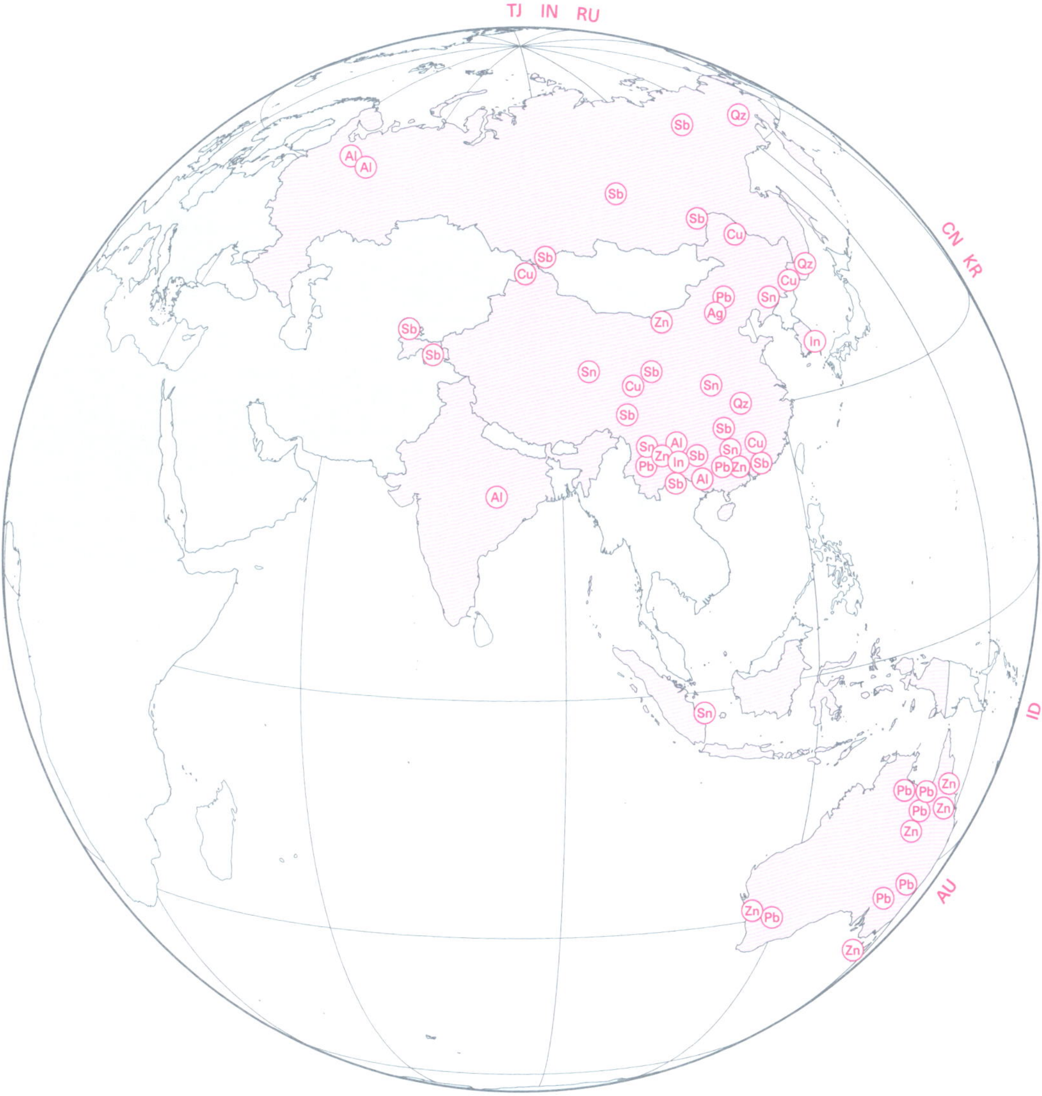

Fig. 24 Top three producing countries of selected critical minerals, 2021 in %
Leading producer 2nd producer 3rd producer CN

Mineral	Leading producer	2nd producer	3rd producer
Al	CN 57	IN 6	RU 5
Sb	CN 55	RU 23	TJ 12
Cu	CL 27	PE 10	CN 8
In	CN 57	KR 22	CA 7
Pb	CN 46	AU 12	US 7
Ag	MX 23	CN 14	PE 12
Sn	CN 30	ID 24	PE 10
Zn	CN 32	PE 12	AU 10

Fig. 25 Industrial areas in Suqian, Jiangsu, China

Locations
1 Trina Solar megafactory
2 Luoma lake
3 Liutang river

Industrial areas
New construction areas
Railways

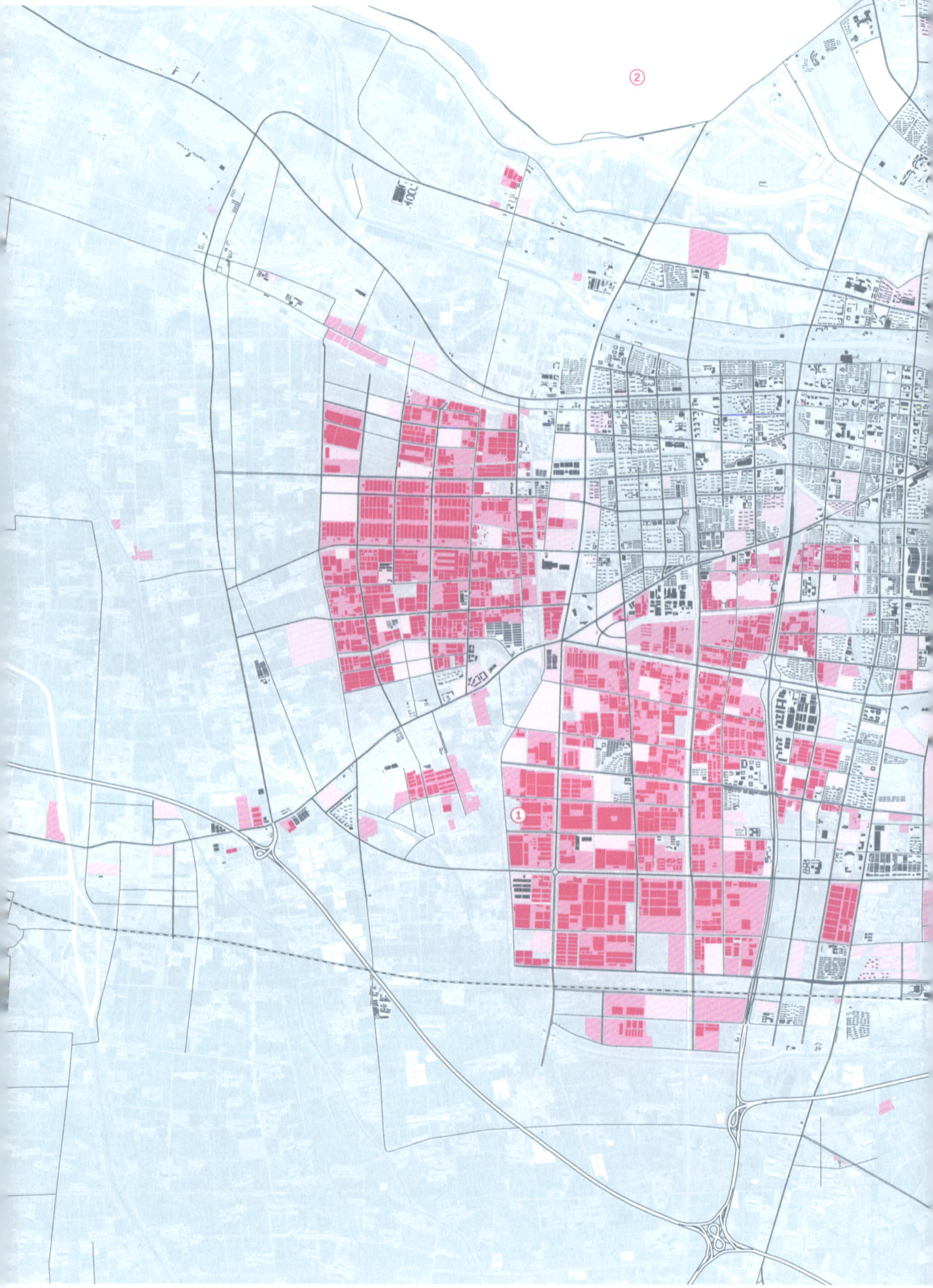

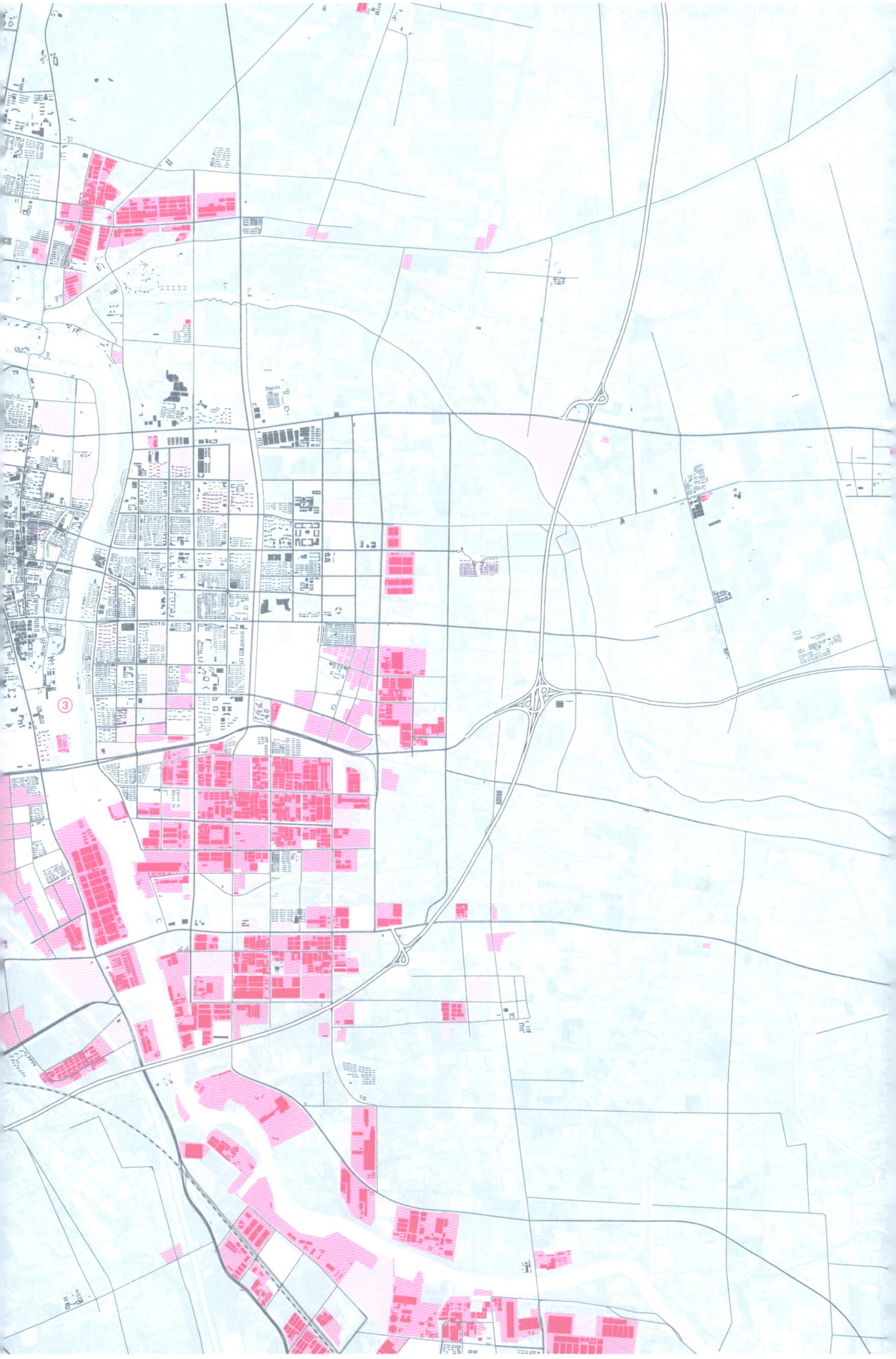

2 km

Fig. 26 Development of industrial areas in Suqian, 1985

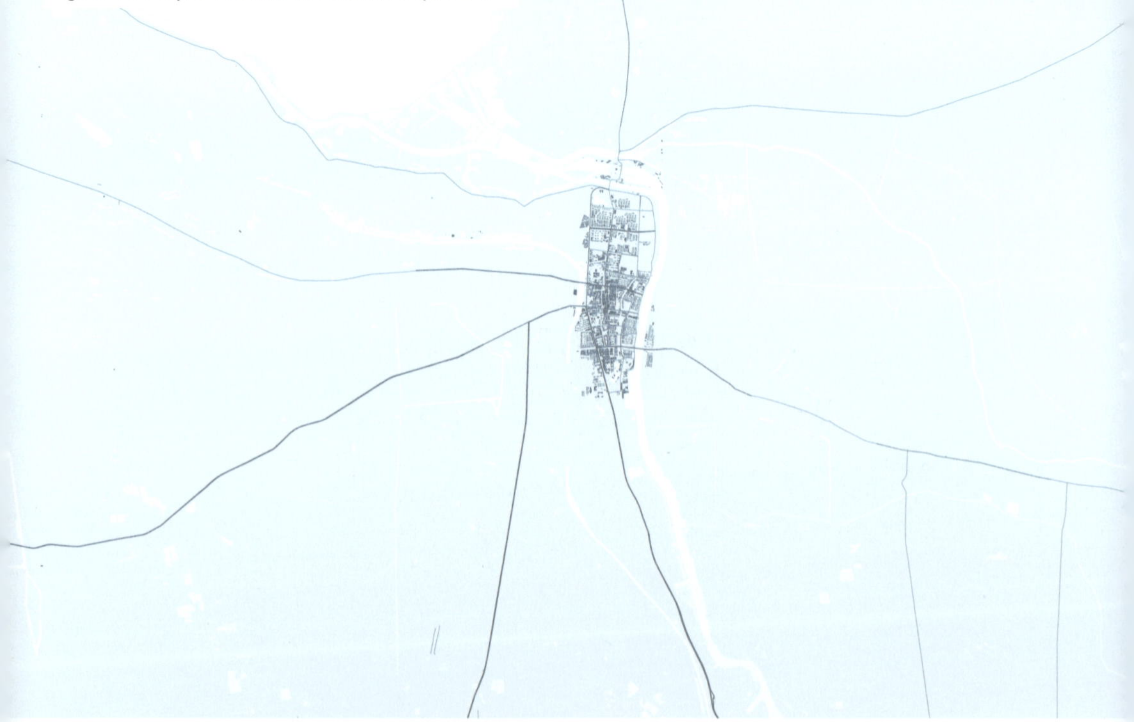

1985 Suqian has a population of 61,000 inhabitants.

Fig. 27 Development of industrial areas in Suqian, 2006

1998 Creation of the Economic Development Zone
2006 Suqian has a population of 594,000.

Fig. 28 Development of industrial areas in Suqian, 2013

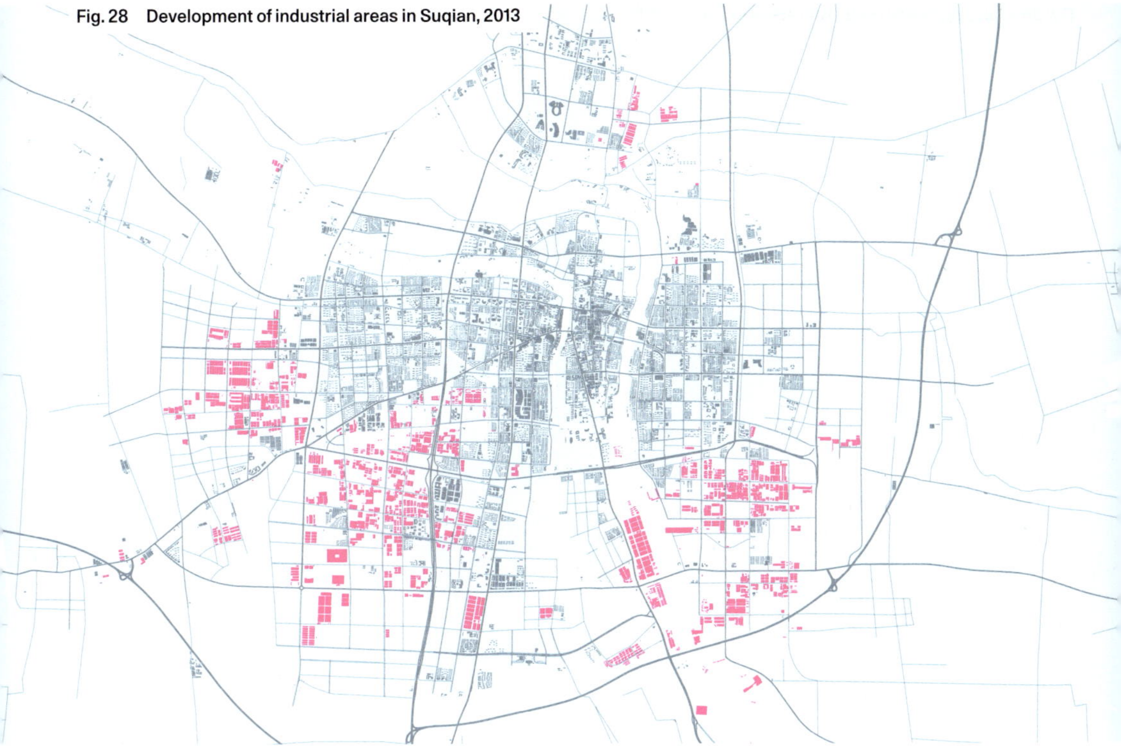

2012 Upgrade to National Economic Development Zone
2013 Suqian has a population of 928,000.

Fig. 29 Development of industrial areas in Suqian, 2023

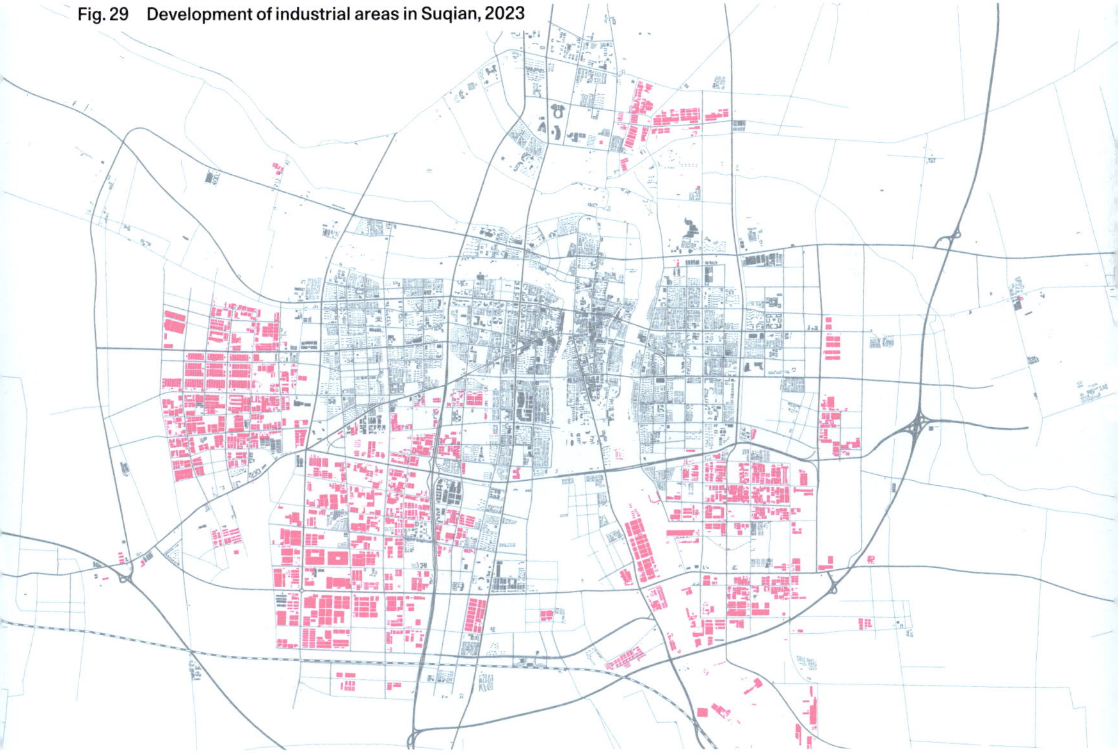

2023 Suqian has a population of 1,665,000.

4 km

Fig. 30 Trina Solar's megafactory in Suqian

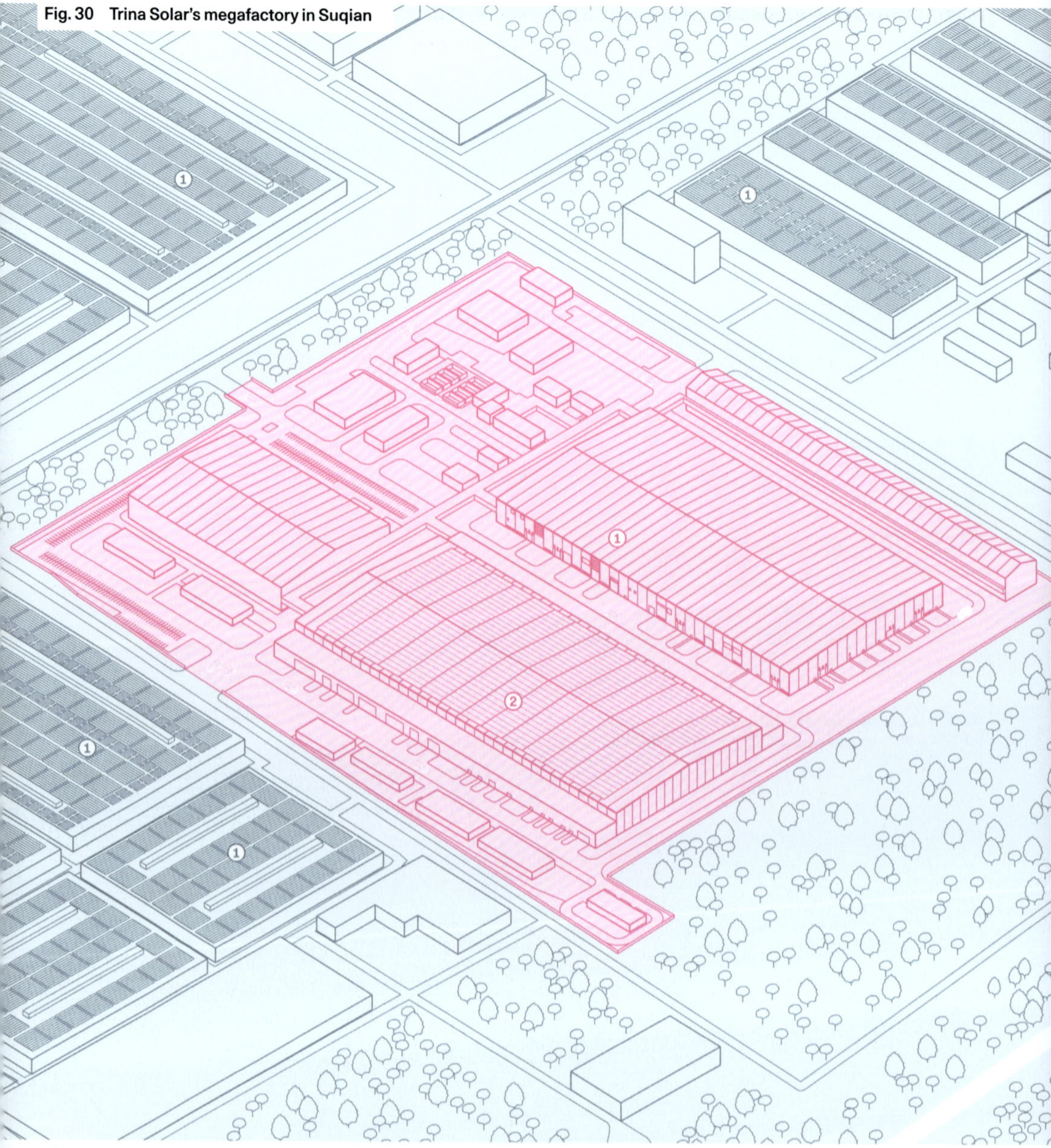

① Trina Solar megafactory
② Solar panels
① Solar panels

Fig. 31 Diagrammatic representation of automated solar panel production

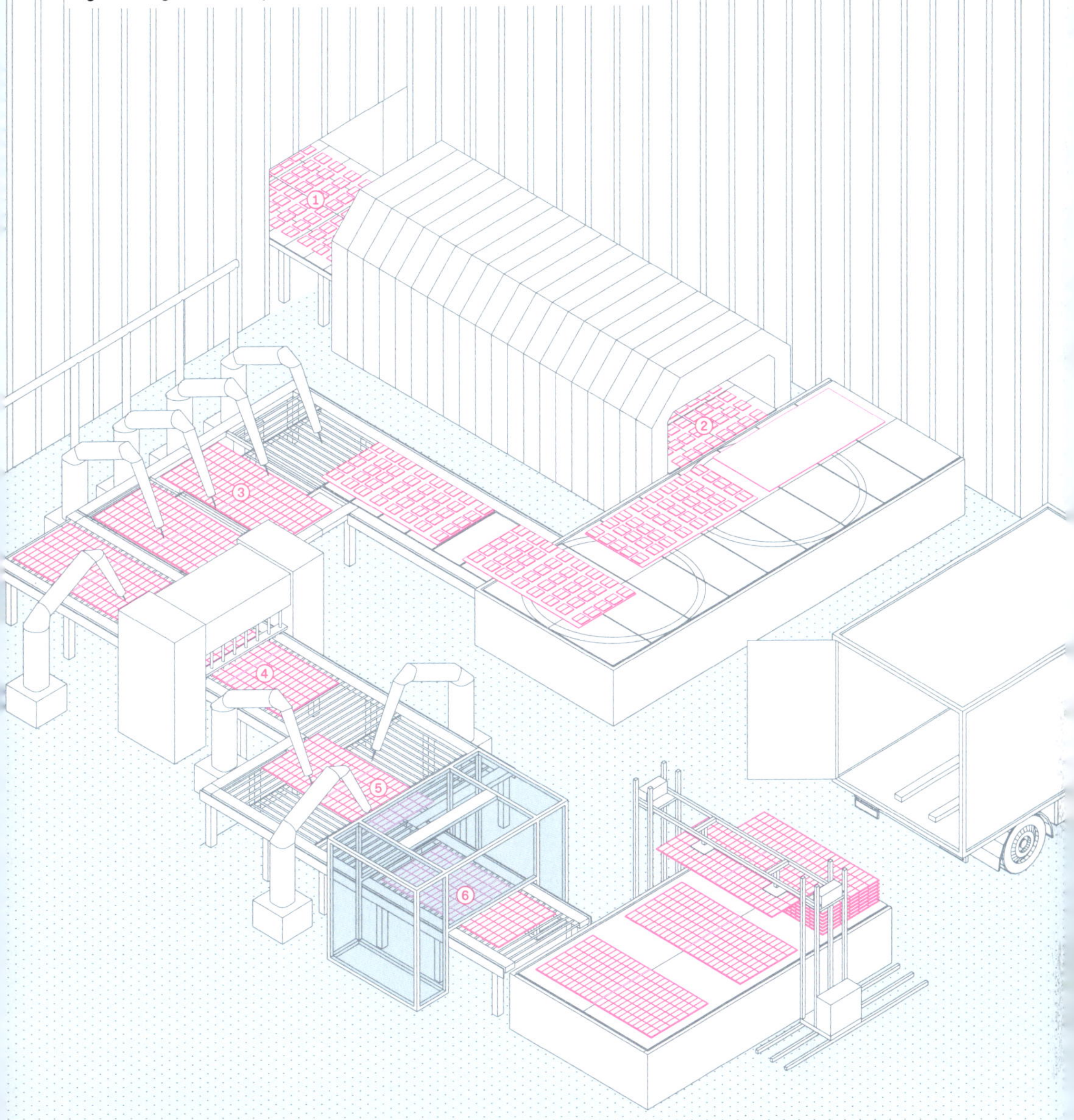

Assembly process

1. Silicon wafers are produced from ingots and joined with boron and phosphorus to produce voltage
2. Wafers are cut into cells with laser cutting
3. Cells are wired with copper circuits
4. Tempered glass is applied on top of cells
5. Cells are fixed onto the supporting base and wired together
6. Panel is insulated, sealed, and scanned for defects with light

Fig. 32 Weesow-Willmersdorf solar park

Locations
① Bernau bei Berlin
② Willmersdorf
③ Weesow

❶ Weesow-Willmersdorf solar park
❷ Börnicke substation
❸ Blumberg substation
❹ Flugplatz Werneuchen-West solar park

Railways
Power lines
Local power lines

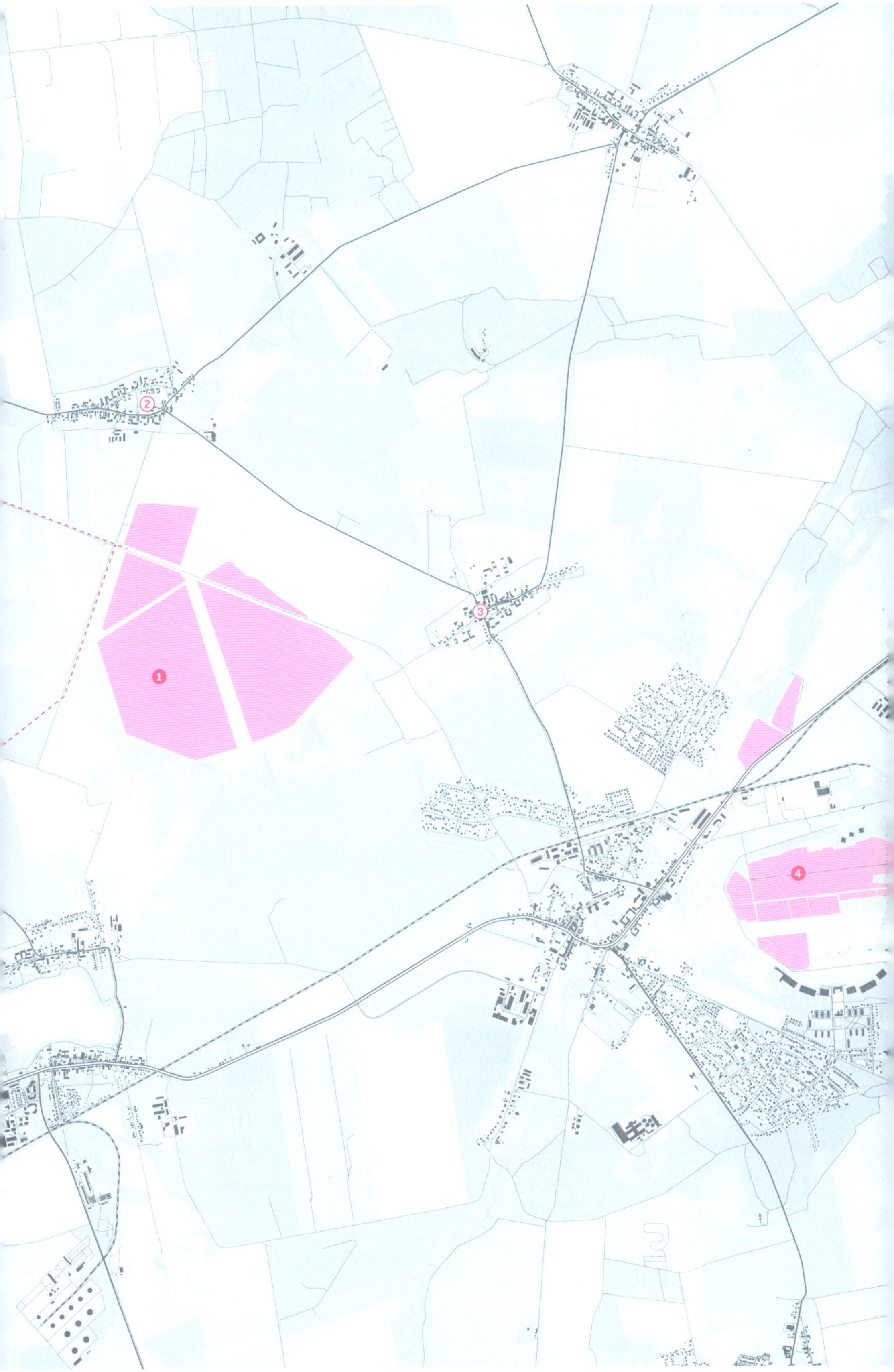

1
2
3
4
1 km

Fig. 33 Axonometric view of a typical c-Si solar panel in Weesow-Willmersdorf solar park

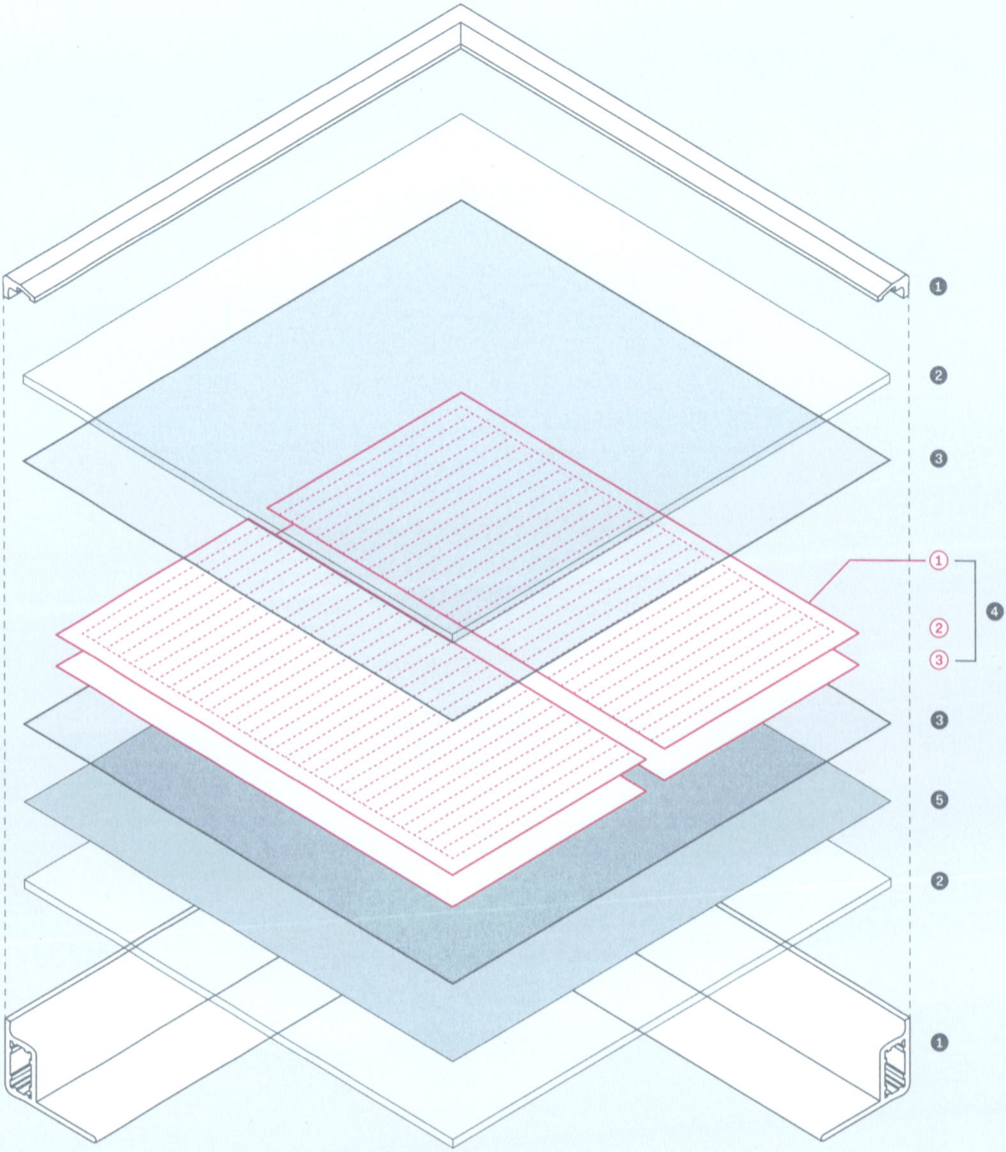

Solar panel components
❶ Anodised aluminium frame
❷ Anti-glare tempered glass
❸ Encapsulant ethylene vinyl acetate
❹ Silicon solar cell
❺ Polyvinyl fluoride film

Solar cell components
① Metallic conductors
② N-layer silicon phosphorus doped
③ P-layer silicon boron doped

Specifications

Producer	Trina Solar
Dimensions	2 m × 1 m × 3 cm
Reference	TSM-DEG15M.20(II)
Cells	144 half-cut
Output	385–410 W
Efficiency	20 %
Weight	23.6 kg
Silicon	0.9 kg

Fig. 34 Overview of technical components for electrical grid conversion

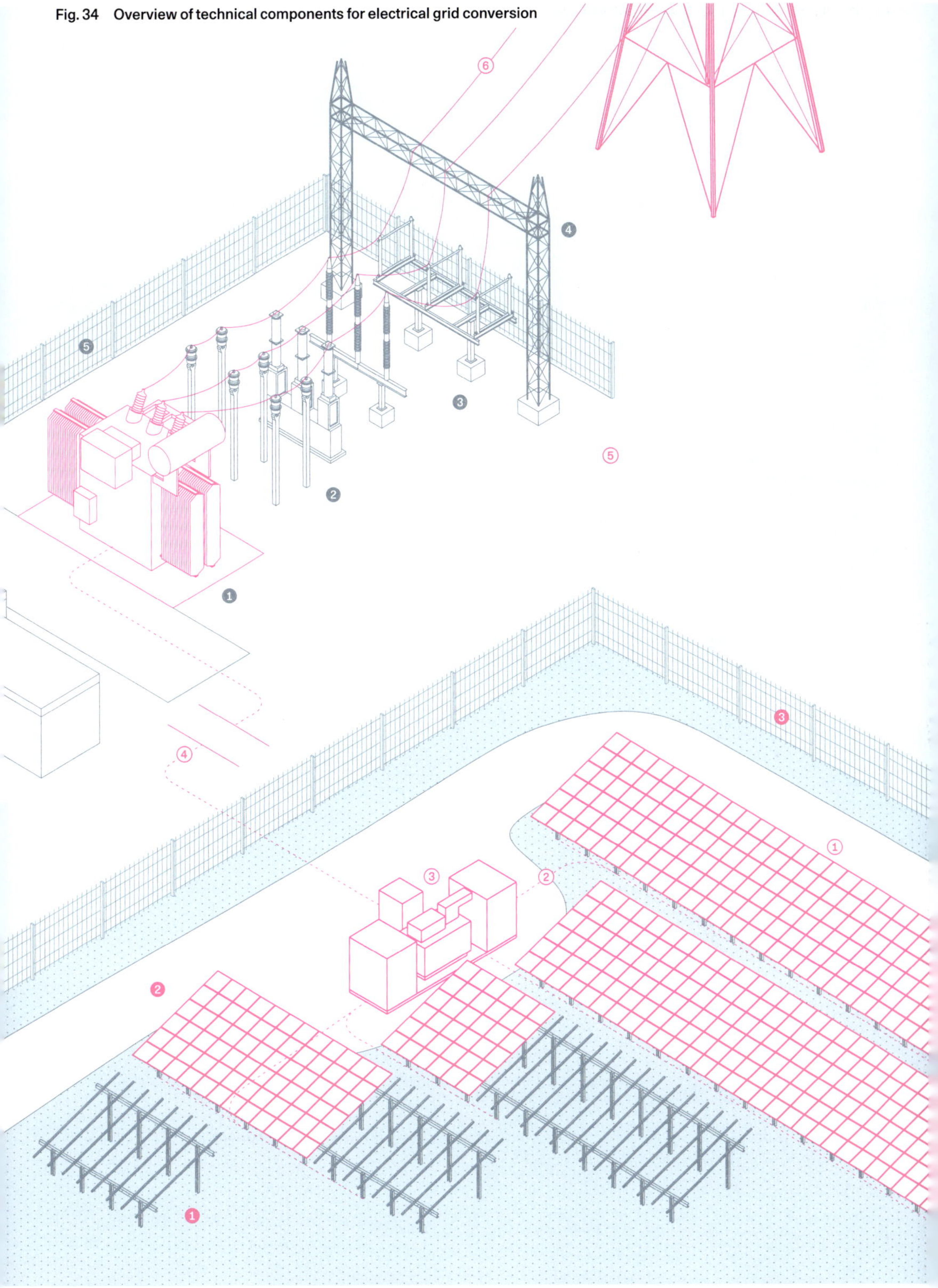

① Solar panels
② Cables (7,500 km)
③ Inverter, DC to AC
④ Underground cable (4 km)
⑤ Börnicke substation
⑥ Overhead cables (110 kV)

Solar field elements
❶ Metal profiles
❷ Interior roads
❸ Fence

Substation elements
❶ Transformer
❷ Busbar
❸ Circuit breaker
❹ Gantry
❺ Fence

Renewable Energy Carriers

Wind

4.4

4.4.1

Introduction to Wind

David Bauer
Philipp Deilmann
Joseph Smithard

Together with hydropower, wind power is among the earliest mechanisms employed for energy generation, transforming elemental flow into mechanical dynamism. Water and windmills share the same fundamental purpose: to automate repetitive and often labour-intensive physical actions, thereby liberating individual capacity while simultaneously harnessing a form of power through human ingenuity. Windmills do so by capturing aerodynamic drag forces through blades or vanes, which then spin an axis that, in turn, sets tools in motion. They are among the earliest testament to a technological evolution that went hand in hand with architectural design, optimised and tailored to the specific contexts in which they were conceived. Varied forms and typologies have emerged based on the local climate, engineering techniques, building materials, and even mythology.[1] These differences extend across a broad spectrum, encompassing not only the obvious blade orientation (horizontal or vertical) but also basic shape, intricacies of internal mechanisms, and the employment of functions such as sawing, lifting, pumping, hammering, thrashing, and grinding.

Fig. 1 A history of windmill typologies, 500–2000 AD

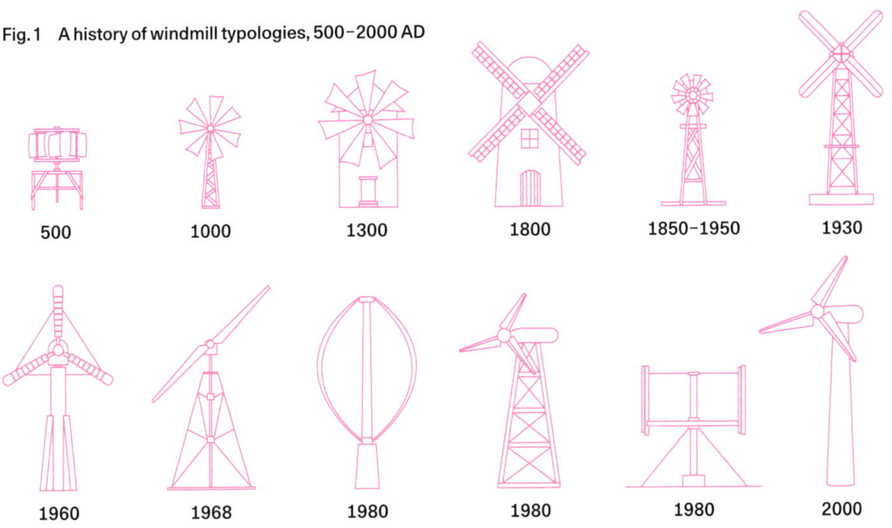

Despite their divergences, windmills epitomise a genuine architectural archetype, characterised by a universally recognised and recurring design. Until the age of the steam engine, diesel, and electric motor, they remained a consistent motif, dispersed across various continents and spanning millennia. One of the earliest examples known stems from ancient Persia, with its probable function being the pumping of water. This machine, referred to as an *Asbad* or *Panemone*[2], comprises fabric sails attached to a vertical axle and enclosed within a walled structure. This effectively embodied the essential elements: blades or sails, a power mechanism, machinery driven by the mill, and a casing (building) to integrate and protect all of these components. Throughout the centuries that followed, this basic pattern was reworked and reassembled into elaborate machines with a high level of design sophistication.

After an absence from the limelight, wind energy has re-emerged as one of the crucial cornerstones of the energy transition. In these modern and increasingly high-tech installations, however—which often tower higher than their stone or wooden predecessors and are built to brave even the fiercest storms—only certain architectural commonalities (namely the staircase and door) remain.

In 2022, Europe accumulated an installed capacity of nearly 250 GW.[3] According to the EU's Climate Target Plan Mix Scenario CPT-MIX S,[4] both onshore and offshore wind deployments will surge over the next two decades. To reach a decarbonised future, wind farm capacities must triple to produce more than 45 % of the total share of the EU's electricity generation.[5] Propelled by this trend, it is perhaps unsurprising that the wind energy sector has transformed into a global industry, boasting approximately 800 manufacturing facilities worldwide. The majority of wind factories operate in China (45 %) and Europe (31 %), followed by India (7 %), Brazil (5 %), and North America (4.5 %).[6] Offshore wind alone has an expected market potential of more than $1,000,000,000,000 in the coming decades.[7] However, the path to this achievement was far from straightforward.

Exit the Mill, Enter the Turbine

Despite the advent of the first steam machines, wind energy retained its cultural significance as a genuine prime mover and a remarkably economical energy source. Numbers continued to grow across the European continent until they peaked in the latter part of the 19th century.[8] By then, the total number of wind-powered mills in the German Empire alone reached around 18,000.[9] However, the beginning of the 20th century marked a swift decline in the number of mills, relegating them over the course of 50 years to romantic relics adorning the landscape's scenery while falling into disrepair. The emergence of new energy sources brought about a higher level of control for the industries they powered. This shift made it possible for industries to operate independently of nature's unpredictable forces, aligning their operations more closely with the rapid pace of technological innovation.

Fig. 2 The world's first wind turbine by Charles F. Brush, Cleveland, US, 1888

The revamping of wind power in a new form occurred in the late-19th century while windmills were still very much in fashion. However, this time, their purpose shifted from grinding and pumping to contributing towards one of the era's most remarkable marvels: electricity. This transformation began with inventor Charles F. Brush, who successfully used the world's first automatically operated wind turbine to illuminate his lavish Cleveland mansion. Despite its colossal size and outrageous appearance, the towering structure behind Brush's house reliably powered around 350 incandescent lights for over a decade.[10] However, its traditional mill-like design made it vulnerable to high winds due to its delicate blades—a major disadvantage inherited from its predecessors.

In the early days of aerodynamics and aviation, wind flow studies became significant on both sides of the Atlantic Ocean. Inventor and scientist Poul la Cour began systematic air foil studies in 1892 in Denmark. He was prompted by the challenge of conventional windmill designs, which could rotate in mild breezes but could not harness the substantial energy of storms without suffering severe damage. La Cour's wind turbine innovations extended beyond solving this challenge; he harboured loftier aspirations to bring electricity to rural Denmark by using experimental turbines for electrolysis, producing hydrogen to power lamps nearby.[11] For about two decades, his efforts led to a rivalry between wind-generated and coal-generated electricity in Denmark. However, by the 1920s, coal-based power became more cost-effective, causing wind power to steadily decline except for on remote islands.

The next breakthrough in the inception of modern wind turbines also arrived in the 1920s from the breezy expanse of the Montana plains, where brothers Marcellus and Joseph Jacobs began to experiment with wind-driven electricity production through the usage of surplus propellered aircraft engines from the First World War. Just as Brush before them, their initial designs bore a strong resemblance to an earlier windmill system that was commonly employed in the vast plains. These designs were modernised by the adoption of a three-blade configuration and variable pitch rotor, inspired by the emerging fighter planes, which proved effective against high winds. They started manufacturing "wind plants" for nearby farms, providing power for lights, radios, and appliances before founding a larger company in Minnesota.[12]

It was not only the exponential rise of coal, oil, gas, and their respective infrastructures and industries after 1945 that prevented developing wind conversion technologies from reaching their full potential—in terms of gaining widespread and early success in electricity production. Wind energy from small units also bucked the prevailing trend of concentrating and standardising power generation through implementing extremely large power nodes in a rapidly expanding energy grid.[13] As a result, in those countries where wind power was available, smaller experimental off-grid technologies only survived in isolated areas, such as remote islands, mountain ranges, and valleys.

Despite being a relatively niche market, expedited research and development efforts were undertaken. This drive was primarily rooted in the question of how to adapt the systems to cater to the requirements of centralised power grids. While some focused on designing large wind power stations, others concentrated on ensuring reliable alternating current generation and seamless integration into power networks.[14] Despite significant advancements, a central issue persisted: the inconsistent nature of its power generation, which stood in stark contrast to the requirements of large utilities, which instead favoured the exploration of available underground resources and, later, the prophetic calls of the emerging nuclear industries.

The latter was a substantial factor in contributing to the renewed emergence of public discourse around alternative energy technologies across many nations worldwide throughout the 1970s. In the US, Germany, and Denmark, retrieving power from wind again became an object of pursuit, with the latter installing its first modern onshore turbine in 1977.[15] With a heightened awareness of environmental degradation, airborne health risks, and the ominous nuclear peril weaving a web of toxicity across the planet, wind power—being regarded as less impactful, decentralised, and potentially DIY technology—seamlessly aligned with counterculture narratives that were increasingly sensitive to the relationship between energy crisis and environmentalism.[16] However, large utilities effectively defended their monopoly by constantly stressing wind energy's unreliability and its systemic faults.

Denmark emerged as the first testing ground for the wind industry, driven by robust financial incentives and energy-conservation policies, aiming to ensure long-term energy security in response to two preceding oil shocks. In the forthcoming decades, the latent potential of wind power emerged from two distinct directions. From the bottom up, small-scale private wind power entrepreneurs and companies provided community power from backyard workshops. Simultaneously, the state played an active role, funding research and design, implementing regulation for feed-in tariffs, and offering subsidies for each new turbine.[17] In 1980, Denmark had around 2.7 MW of wind power capacity installed. By the decade's end, this number had multiplied nearly a hundredfold, with over 2000 single units operating nationwide.[18]

Fig. 3 Installed onshore wind energy capacity in Germany by region, 2023 in MW

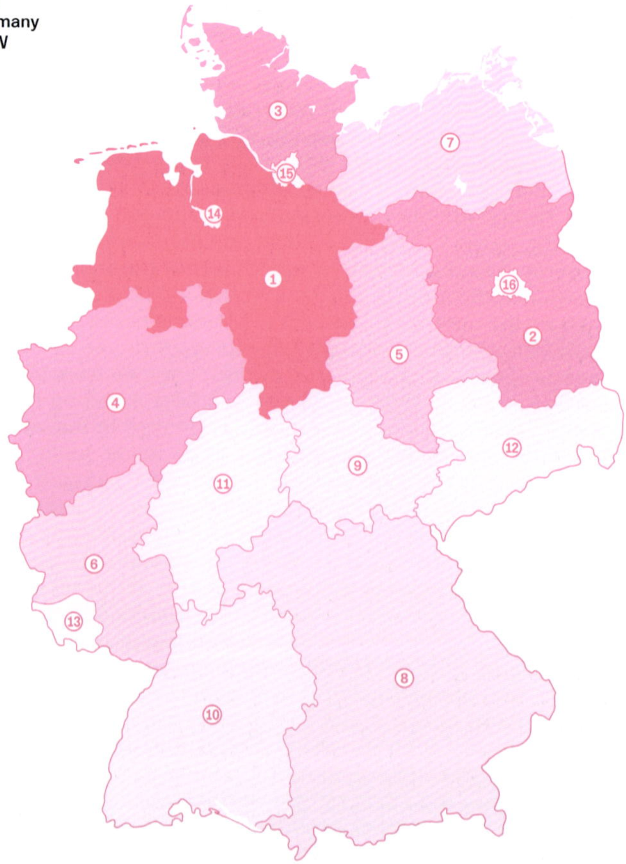

Region	MW
(1) Niedersachsen	12,547
(2) Brandenburg	8,660
(3) Schleswig-Holstein	8,541
(4) Nordrhein-Westfalen	7,188
(5) Sachsen-Anhalt	5,327
(6) Rheinland-Pfalz	4,006
(7) Mecklenburg-Vorpommern	3,735
(8) Bayern	2,633
(9) Thüringen	1,833
(10) Baden-Württemberg	1,803
(11) Hessen	1,513
(12) Sachsen	1,354
(13) Saarland	544
(14) Bremen	203
(15) Hamburg	126
(16) Berlin	17

In Germany, broad support for wind power came in 1991 with the introduction of the Stromeinspeisungsgesetz StrEG, which was focused on incentivising yield by obligating grid operators to purchase the generated electricity at predefined prices. With differences in yield becoming more pronounced, not only were more installations established, but they were also of higher quality. Investors ensured manufacturers' promises regarding performance based on wind speed and minimal downtime were contractually stipulated. The rapid expansion was further bolstered in 2001 by the EEG, which by the end of 2003 led to approximately two-thirds of European wind turbines being installed in Germany. Just as with solar, Germany achieved a leading global position in the field throughout the 2000s and early 2010s, both as a prominent market and incubator for onshore wind power, in which enthusiastic investors and guaranteed state support played a pivotal role in driving the scalability of this technology. [Fig. 4]

The Future is (Hopefully) Windy

Wind turbines have arguably emerged as the foremost representatives and conspicuously visible embodiments of a nation's dedication to transitioning away from conventional fossil fuels. Nevertheless, with each installation they have also become a subject of contention and contradiction. Despite their considerable environmental advantages, they are not exempt from inherent disadvantages and impacts. Throughout the years, matters pertaining to public planning issues have acquired paramount importance, gradually evolving through local trial-and-error phases into more structured planning protocols at the regional and national level. In the last few years, permission has become one of the central challenges.[19]

Wind farms can occupy a substantial amount of land surface area. The surrounding transport infrastructure (including roads, tracks, and paths), is intimately intertwined with each windmill for maintenance purposes, resulting in the fragmentation of agricultural acreage. Roads and pathways introduce novel boundaries and disrupt the landscape's continuity. While a solitary windmill emerges as a distinctive landmark, an aggregation of windmills forms a discrete zone within the agricultural expanse. These parameters illustrate that rural wind farms on agricultural terrain are not rural typologies per se, but rather associated with urban settlement structures that are marked by high energy consumption, owing to the urban attributes of their individual technical components. Consequently, the wind farm is not a spatial embodiment of rural demands, but rather of urban ones.

Wind turbine manufacturers currently exert substantial influence over the wind energy market. However, despite the historical advancement of wind technology, market dynamics present notable challenges to adopting non-traditional principles. While "bladeless" technologies hold the potential to enhance the acceptance of wind power—by reducing emissions and material usage without compromising efficiency—these concepts have not progressed beyond the preliminary stages of small-scale testing in Germany. Presently, in many countries encountering domestic resistance, the primary emphasis lies in the expansion of offshore wind farms in coastal waters. Despite higher construction costs, this approach not only situates the extensive wind parks beyond the reach of everyday visibility; it also possesses the capacity to generate a more substantial power output. Paradoxically, the economic landscape for offshore wind energy in Europe has suffered a substantial blow as a consequence of the 2022 Russian invasion of Ukraine, which led to the suspension of new installations—the result of escalated production costs driven by rampant inflation and global resource scarcity.[20]

As this example demonstrates, wind turbines are globally fragile configurations. Pressing geopolitical factors, combined with bottlenecks in the supply chain and material scarcities, underscore the interdependencies among different countries as they strive to achieve their respective energy transition objectives.

Fig. 4 Annual addition of onshore wind capacity in Germany, 1995–2023 in MW and — accumulated capacity in GW

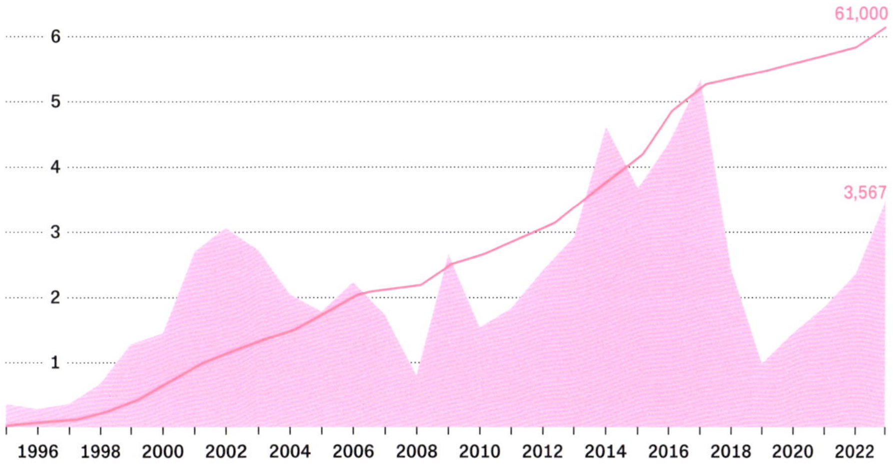

4.4.2

Properties, Production, and Supply

David Bauer
Philipp Deilmann
Joseph Smithard

Wind has no substance; you cannot see it, you cannot hold it, but you can feel it. Wind can dry your clothes in the summer while, in the cold of winter, it can chill you to the bone. Throughout history, wind has propelled nations across the ocean and violently torn trees from the ground. It is the great equaliser, carrying heat, moisture, pollutants, and dust across the globe. Winds are enshrined in folklore, bestowed with names, and even foretell fortunes. The *mistral* brings fierce storms to the Mediterranean coastline but, further inland, it clears the vines and dries the soil for the winemakers of Provence.[21]

What Is Wind?

What is wind? Put simply, wind is the movement of air. It is a motion instigated by variations in atmospheric pressure, which in turn stem from disparities in temperature.[22] Essentially, it all starts with the sun. As the sun's rays heat the Earth's surface, the atmosphere warms too. However, thanks to mountains, oceans, and modern cities that scrape the sky, the distribution of heat is uneven. Furthermore, the regions around the equator, those at 0° latitude, are heated more by the sun than the rest of the globe. Consequently, as the hot air from the equator is lighter than cold air, it rises into the sky and then spreads out to the north and south.[23] The temperature difference, combined with the Earth's rotation, generates prevailing wind patterns.

Fig. 5 Global wind patterns

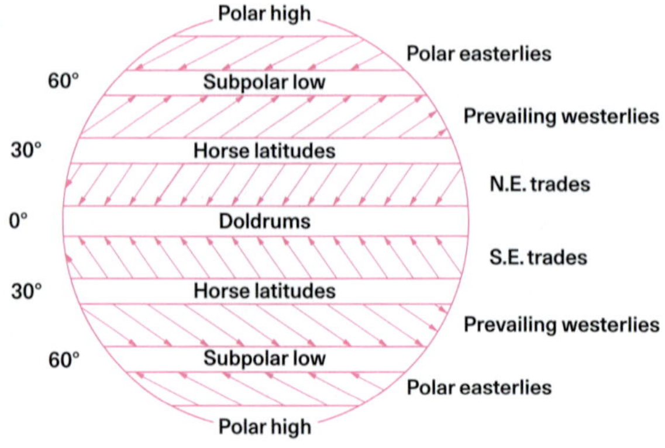

At the local scale, uneven solar heating leads to pockets of high and low pressure. As air warms, it expands and rises, leaving an area of low pressure. The surrounding air then moves to even the imbalance and the subsequent rush of air is what creates wind. The bigger the difference in pressure, the faster the air will move. Generally, the Earth's rotation produces a phenomenon known as the Coriolis effect;[24] this means that wind systems typically blow east–west rather than north–south towards the respective poles. This effect makes wind systems twist counterclockwise in the Northern Hemisphere and clockwise in the Southern Hemisphere.[25]

As such, wind energy is essentially solar energy and is fundamentally connected to the sun's radiant power. Every passing hour, the celestial powerhouse beams 174,423,000,000,000 kWh of solar energy onto the Earth's surface,[26] initiating a complex chain reaction of natural processes. Approximately 1 to 2 % of the sun's energy is transformed into the kinetic force of wind. This yield massively exceeds the renewable energy potential contained in the Earth's total biomass—generating between 50 to 100 times more power than all terrestrial plants combined.[27]

How to Harness Wind

Wind turbines are the modern iteration of the windmill. However, they do not grind or serve as alternates to prime movers; rather, they are machines that convert the wind's kinetic energy to form electricity. The turbines can stand alone, supplying a small number of houses or businesses, or can be clustered to form what is referred to as a "wind farm" or "wind park". Wind turbines, like their predecessors, the windmill, come in many shapes and sizes. Small turbines can give autonomy to someone living on a boat, while towers can power entire cities.

Wind turbine siting falls into two categories: onshore and offshore. As the name suggests, onshore turbines are situated on land, while offshore installations are located at sea. The process involves a complex intermingling of criteria. This discussion will focus on technological efficiency, although the roles of politics, stakeholders, land-use conflicts, and finances are also noteworthy (and will be further discussed within the following pages). Siting is all about surface roughness and proximity. At approximately 1 km above the ground, wind remains largely unaffected by the Earth's surface. However, closer to the ground, friction with the surface impacts wind speeds.[28] Surface roughness, such as forests and cities, can significantly decelerate wind, whereas water surfaces are smoother and less impactful. Onshore sites seek to minimise roughness-related impacts by positioning themselves close to their target areas, whereas offshore setups aim to capture unobstructed wind.[29]

Fig. 6 Wind shade wind speed in % of wind speed without obstacle
20 m obstacle 50 m wind turbine tower

height in m																					
	100	100	100	100	100	100	100	100	99	99	99	99	99	99	99	99	99	99	99	99	99
	100	100	100	100	100	100	100	99	99	99	99	99	99	99	99	99	99	99	99	99	99
60	100	100	100	100	100	100	99	99	99	99	99	99	99	98	98	98	98	98	98	98	98
	100	100	100	100	100	99	99	99	99	98	98	98	98	98	98	98	98	98	98	98	98
	100	100	100	100	100	99	99	98	98	98	98	98	98	98	98	98	98	98	98	98	98
	100	100	100	100	99	99	98	98	97	97	97	97	97	97	97	97	97	97	97	97	97
50	100	100	100	99	99	98	98	97	97	97	97	97	97	97	97	97	97	97	97	97	97
	100	100	100	99	98	98	97	96	96	96	96	96	96	96	96	96	96	97	97	97	97
	100	100	99	99	98	97	96	95	95	95	95	95	95	95	95	96	96	96	96	97	97
	100	100	99	98	96	95	94	94	93	93	94	94	94	94	95	95	95	96	96	96	96
40	100	100	98	96	95	93	93	92	92	92	92	93	93	94	94	94	95	95	95	96	96
	100	99	97	95	93	91	90	90	90	90	91	91	92	93	93	94	94	95	95	95	96
	100	98	95	92	90	88	88	87	87	88	89	90	91	92	92	93	94	94	94	95	95
	100	97	92	88	86	85	84	84	85	86	87	89	90	91	91	92	93	93	94	94	95
30	99	94	87	83	81	80	81	81	82	84	86	87	88	90	91	92	92	93	94	94	95
	99	89	91	76	75	75	76	78	79	81	84	86	87	89	90	91	92	93	93	94	94
	96	81	71	68	68	70	72	74	76	79	82	84	86	88	89	90	91	92	93	94	94
	90	68	59	58	60	63	67	70	73	77	80	83	85	87	88	90	91	92	93	93	94
20	78	48	43	46	52	57	63	67	71	75	79	82	85	87	88	90	91	92	93	94	94
	52	21	24	34	43	52	59	65	69	74	79	82	85	87	89	90	91	92	93	93	94
	4		4	22	36	48	56	63	69	74	79	82	85	87	89	90	91	92	93	94	95
				13	32	46	56	63	69	75	79	83	86	88	90	91	92	93	94	94	95
10				9	32	47	58	65	71	77	81	85	87	89	91	92	93	94	95	95	96
				14	38	53	63	70	75	80	84	87	89	91	92	93	94	95	96	96	97
				31	51	63	72	78	82	85	88	91	92	94	94	95	96	96	97	97	98
			36	60	72	80	84	88	90	92	94	95	96	97	97	98	98	98	98	99	99

distance in m 0 100 200 300 400

The Anatomy of a Wind Turbine

The anatomy of a wind turbine[30] is comprised of various crucial components. The nacelle houses the gearbox, electrical generator, and electronic controller at the centre. The rotor blades on top of the nacelle harness wind energy and transfer it to the rotor hub, which is connected to the low-speed shaft. The gearbox accelerates the rotation of the low-speed shaft to drive the high-speed shaft, which engages the electrical generator to convert rotational energy into electric power.[31] Direct-drive wind turbines skip the gearbox, using direct-drive technology to spin the generator at the same rotations per minute (rpm) as the low-speed shaft.[32] [Fig. 24]

Two prevailing technical designs of turbines concern the energy transition: gearbox, primarily used for onshore applications, and direct-drive systems, primarily used for offshore sites.[33] Gearbox turbines operate at variable speeds. Just like the Shimano gears on a decarbonised mobility device (a bicycle), the purpose of the gearbox is to increase the rotational rotor speed before feeding it into the generator. For example, to generate electricity in the case of a 1 MW wind turbine, the gearbox increases the rotation speed of the blades from 15 to 20 rpm up to 1,800 rpm.[34] Nevertheless, gearboxes introduce challenges. While rotor torque drives power generation, it concurrently subjects wheels and bearings to immense stress, resulting in gearbox defects and operational halts. The faster the wind speed, the more vulnerable gearboxes are. Consequently, this technology is more favourable for onshore setups,[35] circumventing the annoyance of repairing gear mechanisms 30 km offshore.

Manufacturers have developed wind turbines without gearboxes to eliminate the risk of gearbox failure. This type of wind turbine was introduced in 1991 and is known as the variable speed direct-drive turbine.[36] A direct-drive turbine's generator speed is equivalent to the rotor speed because the rotor is connected directly to the generator. As the rotational generator speed is low, designers place several magnetic poles in the generator to achieve a higher frequency. As well as being efficient, direct-drive turbines perform well in varying wind conditions, have fewer moving parts, lower maintenance costs, and less mechanical noise due to the lack of a gearbox, making them ideal as an offshore technology.[37] Although direct-drive technology's cost and weight has hindered its rivalry with gearboxes across all applications, recent advances in magnets and generators have led to lighter and more affordable models. This has increased the appeal of direct-drive turbines despite the thousands of gearbox turbines still in use.

Materials

In terms of materials, a wind turbine is a complex assembly encompassing around 25,000 distinct components,[38] a far cry from the humble origins of wood and stone windmills. Wind turbines continue to scale up in size, with the latest models featuring blades exceeding 100 m in length. These massive rotors sweep a circular area of 46,000 m^2 during operation, with the turbine capable of generating up to 16 MW of electrical output.[39] [Fig. 25] The bigger they are, the deeper they penetrate below ground. While a wind turbine's tower holds a substantial share in terms of both size and mass, its foundation constitutes the largest portion of mass at 75 %. Excluding the foundation, within the turbine itself, the nacelle and rotor individually contribute around 20 % of the overall weight.[40]

Fig. 7 Mass distribution of a typical turbine in %

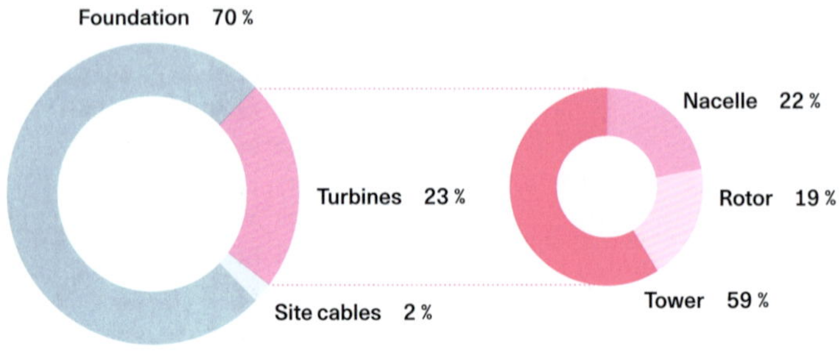

Fig. 8 Common wind turbine foundations

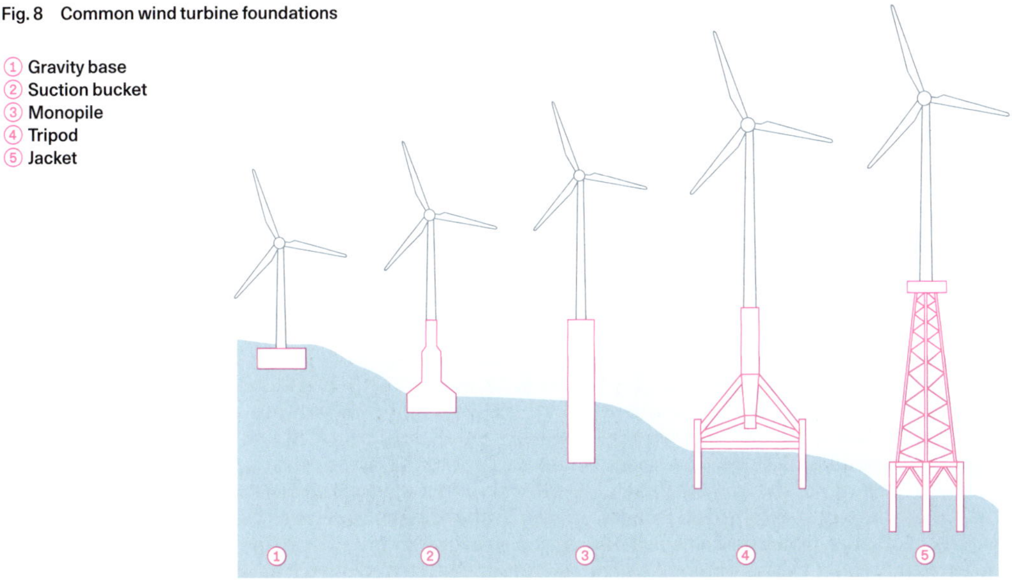

Wind turbines contain a serious amount of steel, this metal being the primary material in 85 % of turbines globally.[41] Steel is found in the tower, nacelle, rotor, gearbox, generator, turbine transformer, and in the foundation. Concrete and steel form around 95 % of onshore foundations,[42] while offshore solutions often employ thick steel monopiles anchored to the seabed. But the metals don't stop there. Aluminium contributes to lightweight tower and nacelle components, and copper is present in generator windings, cables, and transformers. REE and boron are vital for turbines using permanent magnets, with a typical magnet consisting of 28.5 % neodymium, 4.4 % dysprosium, 1 % boron, and 66 % iron, weighing up to 4 t.[43] In contrast, composite materials and polymers account for 8 to 12 % of its weight, predominantly found in the blades, nacelles, and hub covers. Finally, electronic components comprise just 1 % of the turbine's total mass.[44]

Fig. 9 Evolution of elements used in selected (energy) technology, 1700–2000 AD

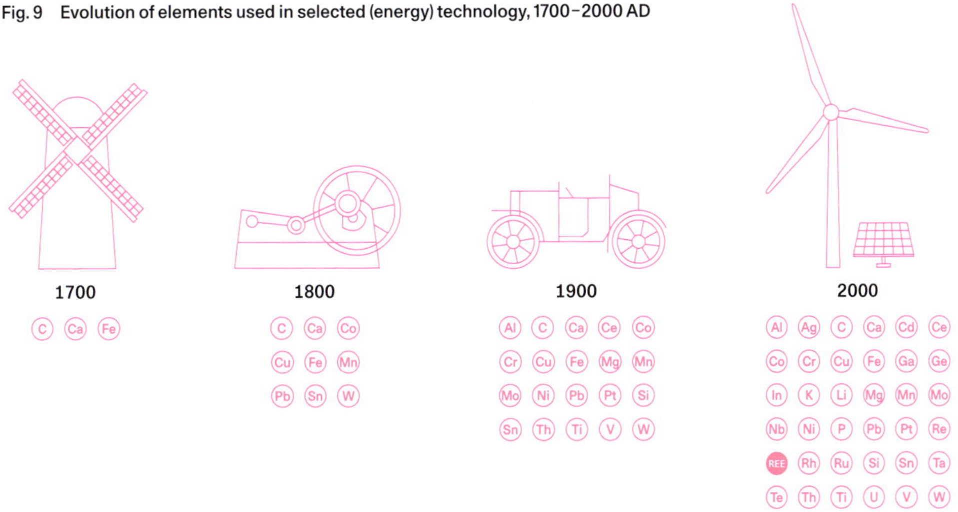

Wind Value Chains

A wind turbine is not fabricated as a singular entity but rather as a collection of components produced independently, often across various global locations, that are transported to the designated site for assembly.

The life cycle of a wind turbine begins with the mining and refining processes that yield metals like steel, aluminium, copper, and rare-earth minerals. [Fig. 21 + 22] Next comes component manufacturing, which consists of crafting turbine elements such as blades, towers, nacelles, hubs, and drivetrains. Lightweight composite materials emerge through the fusion of epoxy resin, glass fibres, or carbon fibres. Structural steel is produced in mills for key components like towers, nacelles, generators, and gearboxes, while copper and aluminium processing generates conductive materials for cables and electrical connections. Subsequently, these components are transported to the assembly site, where all the corresponding parts meet for the first time. Transporting components and turbines via trucks, ships, or other specialised means leads to onshore or offshore erection, involving foundation construction and tower assembly. Grid integration follows on from this, employing transformers, switchgear, and control systems to connect turbines to local power networks.

The typical lifespan of a wind turbine is 20 years.[45] Decommissioning involves dismantling turbines, transporting them to recycling centres, and disposing or reintegrating the materials back into the value chain. [Fig. 21] There are problems with this, however. Although 90 % of the turbine is easily recyclable (metals), the long blades—typically made from fibreglass bound together with epoxy resin—are incredibly tough and expensive to break down.[46] This, combined with a lack of legislative policy for end-of-life reuse, has led to the emergence of turbine graveyards.

Stakeholders within the turbine supply chain are notably diverse. Europe, as the birthplace of the wind industry, already boasts a well-established network encompassing turbine nacelles, key components, and raw materials. However, China has recently emerged as a dominant player, having not only risen to prominence as the foremost centre of wind turbine manufacturing but also as the world's largest production hub for essential components and raw materials.[47]

Fig. 10 Top 10 global wind turbine manufacturers, 2022 in GW

At the end of 2022, there were 153 operational turbine assembly plants globally, with 74 more under construction or in planning.[48] China leads with over 100 nacelle assembly facilities, holding 60 % of the nacelle market share and boasting 98 GW of production capacity per year. Europe is the second-largest production base, followed by the US, India, and LATAM.[49] [Fig. 11]

China's dominance extends beyond assembly processes. In late 2022, they controlled 68 % of rare-earth mining and 94 % of downstream processing, with only limited processing facilities located elsewhere, notably in Malaysia and Estonia.[50] Geopolitical tensions coupled with China's stricter export restrictions on rare-earth technologies are causing mounting global concerns. This may potentially disrupt the wind supply chain, affecting nacelle and component shortages in Europe and the US. As wind installations continue to surge, the industry faces the challenge of meeting demand with substantial investment across the global supply chain. Regional initiatives like "Made in Europe" further add to the complexity, potentially impacting the free flow of components.[51] Notably, the EU's wind turbine deployment goals for 2050 alone will demand a substantial portion of the globally available neodymium, praseodymium, dysprosium, and terbium.[52] But the question is, where will they come from?

Beyond geopolitics, the extensive environmental ramifications of these sprawling supply chains cannot be overlooked. The vast steel consumption involved in the construction of wind turbines—contributing to 7 % of global CO_2 emissions[53]—coupled with challenges in mining rare earths [p. 222] and a complex global transportation network, inevitably lead to adverse environmental effects. While wind power holds promise as a relatively clean, scalable, and cost-effective energy solution, the impact of such bottlenecks on the pace of the energy transition more broadly remains to be seen.

Fig. 11 Global wind turbine manufacturing capacity, 2023 in %

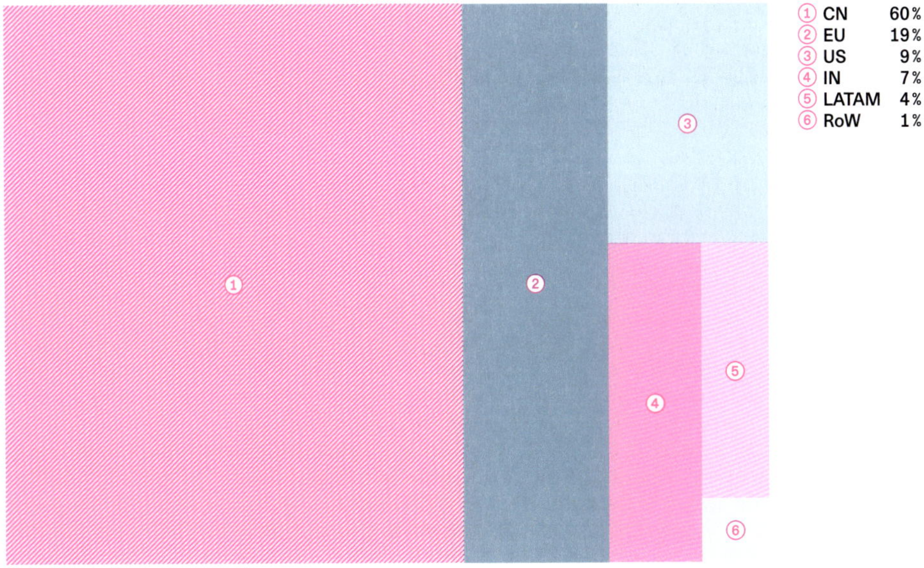

4.4.3

Wind in the Local Context

David Bauer
Philipp Deilmann
Joseph Smithard

As the world's earliest major alternative energy economy,[54] Germany's renewable share in electricity production has been steadily rising from a modest 3.4 % in 1991 to more than 10 % by 2005, reaching over 46 % in 2022.[55] At the heart of this progress is wind, the country's most important renewable energy resource. With a cumulative capacity of around 69 GW on- and offshore in 2023,[56] Germany has by far the most wind power in Europe, globally trailing only behind China and the US.[57] At the end of 2023, some 30,243 wind turbines contributed towards 32 % of the domestic electricity generated.[58] Despite the sector's modest growth in recent years and mainly average wind conditions, with an output of 123 TWh, wind energy still occupies a pivotal role as the leading electricity source in Germany today.[59]

Fig. 12 GROWIAN, Germany, 1983

The path leading towards this significant milestone was paved by GROWIAN, the first wind energy farm in the BRD, established in October 1983.[60] At the time, Germany was still divided and the farm was connected in August 1987 to the grid in Kaiser-Wilhelm-Koog, situated on the west coast of Schleswig-Holstein. When viewed in the context of today's more advanced facilities, the wind field's 30 turbines appear rather modest, yielding a total power output of just 1 KW and each with a maximum height of slightly above 20 m. In the present day, one single onshore wind turbine easily exceeds this capacity fourfold. The increase in power output for onshore installations, amounting to a factor of approximately 80, represents a technological revolution that few had anticipated.[61] An example of this evolution can be found in one of the large wind farms in Holtriem, Niedersachsen. By juxtaposing older and newer wind turbines, it forms a spatial configuration that integrates the gradual development of diverse technological approaches—not unlike the arrangement of old and new structures in cities.

Unsurprisingly, many of the largest domestic wind energy projects are located offshore. By the close of 2022, the North Sea hosted 24 fully operational offshore wind farms, with an additional four facilities situated in the Baltic Sea.[62] The most expansive of these sites encompassed an area of approximately 50 km^2. The largest onshore wind farm, located in Niedersachsen, consists of three fields, totalling 153 individual turbines.[63]

Headwinds

Despite the major production milestone, the implementation of even small increments in wind power capacity has proven more and more challenging. The cumulative impact of policy decisions—such as the introduction of auction requirements, strict annual capacity limits, reductions in tariff rates, rapidly increasing interest rates, and stringent setback rules—has led to a decline in the industry. Moreover, complicated approval processes and subsequent legal disputes have left the country in a bureaucratic corset.[64] Nationally, approximately 770 wind turbines were approved in 2020, marking a 40 % decrease compared to 2015.[65] Although there was a slight upward trend in northern Germany in 2022, the southern region reached an all-time low in approvals. These obstacles have also created an alarming situation for Germany offshore: not a single offshore turbine was built in 2021, and less than 40 were installed in 2022.[66] Based on a consistent trajectory of expansion, and even counting those projects from previous auction rounds, the offshore capacity is expected to reach only 10.8 GW by 2025, which falls 3 GW short of the national allocated target.[67]

Germany has already established a comprehensive regulatory framework to drive the expansion of onshore wind energy. The legislation mandates that 2 % of the German land area must be reserved for onshore wind generation by 2032.[68] Notably, this commitment surpasses the current designated area twofold. The larger states within Germany must allocate between 1.1 and 1.8 % of their land for onshore wind power by 2027, with a subsequent goal of achieving between 1.8 and 2.2 % by 2032.[69] [Fig. 13] In parallel, the country's three city-states—namely Berlin, Hamburg, and Bremen—are tasked with dedicating 0.5 % of their territory to wind power by 2032.[70] The contested approach of designating areas based on abstract goals to streamline the production of wind farms is reflected in the reality on the ground. Despite formally complying with the required surface strategy, the large federal states in the highly industrialised south are significantly lagging in the actual placement and inauguration of wind farms. Brandenburg produces roughly twice as much wind energy nominally as the entire southern portion of Germany. Even Berlin, with its few windmills, has half the energy output per square kilometre compared to the entire state of Bavaria.[71]

Consequently, the trajectory of Germany's energy transition sits at a crossroads. Put simply, Germany can either persist in pursuing a comprehensive allocation of its land surface to wind power—an achievement that would necessitate a collective effort from 16 federal states, each with differing attitudes. Or alternatively, it can adopt a system of burden sharing, aspiring to foster synergy between domestic partners, and potentially leveraging the inherent strengths of the wealthy industrialised south and the energy-abundant north.

Berlin-Brandenburg

With its sparse population, vast land expanse, robust infrastructure, and historical ties to energy production, Brandenburg emerges as a prominent energy centre, driven by a clear determination to position itself as a leading energy state. Once the underbelly of Germany's coal-fired industrialisation, Brandenburg is now capable of meeting its entire electricity demand using carbon-neutral technologies.[72] [p. 242] This is due in part to the two largest wind farms in the state: the first, located in the Uckermark, has a capacity of 242 MW and the other, in Ketzin, has a capacity of 175 MW.[73] Currently, the region boasts around 4,000 wind turbines, with a total capacity exceeding 8,500 MW, meaning that after Niedersachsen, Brandenburg ranks as Germany's second-largest wind energy region.[74] However, according to Brandenburg's Energy Strategy 2040, 2.2 % of the state's landmass must be designated for wind energy.[75] This constitutes an expansion target of 15,000 MW, meaning the number of wind turbines will almost need to double by 2040.

Fig. 13 Installed wind power capacity in Brandenburg, 2023 in MW

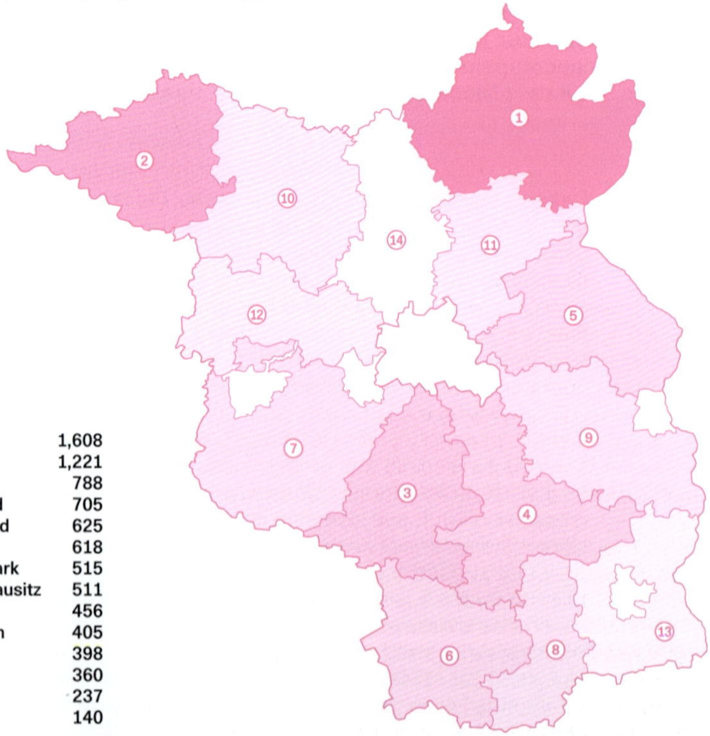

	District	MW
1	Uckermark	1,608
2	Prignitz	1,221
3	Teltow-Fläming	788
4	Dahme-Spreewald	705
5	Märkisch-Oderland	625
6	Elbe-Elster	618
7	Potsdam-Mittelmark	515
8	Oberspreewald-Lausitz	511
9	Oder-Spree	456
10	Ostprignitz-Ruppin	405
11	Barnim	398
12	Havelland	360
13	Spree-Neiße	237
14	Oberhavel	140

Hardly anything remains today of the approximately 150 mills in the former villages and communities in and around Berlin.[76] The last windmill still in active production, albeit already motor-powered, ceased operations in 1980, leaving behind roughly eight museum installations for interested visitors. Curiously, this count aligns with the relatively modest number of turbines dotting the landscape within the city-state's borders today.

In the broader context of the Berlin metropolitan region, which shares the national goal of achieving carbon neutrality, the city-state must designate 0.5 % of its area to wind power by 2032. But, like many major cities, Germany's capital has very limited space for local power generation. Nonetheless, Berlin's skyline now boasts six wind turbines with a combined capacity of 16 MW.[77] Workarounds to counteract the lack of inner-city space have also been explored, even including suggestions to utilise Berlin's two vacant airfields: Tempelhof and Tegel.[78] The Berliner Stadtwerke (Berlin's city utilities department) have expanded their renewable energy initiatives by developing wind parks on city-owned land beyond municipal boundaries. This expansion utilises the former *Rieselfelder* (sewage farms), which are now under the management of Berliner Stadtgüter GmbH. [Fig. 14] As of 2023, the areas host 57 wind turbines operated by various entities, with Berliner Stadtwerke responsible for 16 of these installations, generating a total capacity of 68 MW.[79] While fostering inter-regional collaboration is undoubtedly logical, this scenario could heighten the competition for land and potentially stimulate increased speculation concerning agricultural land in Brandenburg.

From NIMBY to PIMBY

In 2021, modifications were made to the EEG to increase public acceptance, involving local municipalities in the benefits that are derived from wind energy.[80] Community-driven energy initiatives are excluded from the competitive tendering process, and attractive feed-in tariffs are provided to incentivise further expansion. Citizen's initiatives, such as the energy-autarky achieved by the village of Feldheim in Brandenburg, have benefitted significantly from this incentivisation [p. 287]. Nonetheless, the legislation is not always aiding the drive towards renewables. Incentives do not encompass existing systems, for instance, and regional variations in grid fees can cause unfair discrepancies.[81] This issue is particularly significant in wind-rich rural regions like Brandenburg, where costs are shared among less-dense populations. The expansion of renewable power in these areas generally necessitates substantial investments in grid extensions, which can lead to significant fluctuations in domestic energy bills. In certain regions, this variation results in residents paying a smaller share; in others, it comprises nearly half of their total bill. An average family in northern Brandenburg pays grid fees of €416 for an annual power consumption of 3,500 kWh, while the average family in Bremen pays €196 for the same consumption rate.[82] Despite the positive output of renewable energy, a legislative framework that leads to immediate financial drawbacks does not typically foster increased public acceptance.

Approval rates for wind power are notably high in northern Germany, where most of the country's turbines are situated. [Fig. 3] Residents there perceive the advantages of the energy transition in their immediate vicinity, including benefits to the economy and to their social networks. However, acceptance decreases as the turbines approach residential areas. Reports reveal that while 52 % accept wind farms located at a distance of at least 5 km away, only 35 % accept those located within 500 m.[83] Compensating affected citizens could be effective in countering such NIMBYism. Proposals that promise "wind power euros" to local municipalities from wind farm profits may offer a potential solution for mitigating resistance to new projects. Clearly, the approval of wind turbines across Germany constitutes a complex back-and-forth of aesthetics, tradition, and politics. However, the Russian invasion of Ukraine has acted as a catalyst for numerous amendments made to existing laws and funding schemes, accelerating grid planning by the economics and climate ministry that is largely geared towards boosting the country's renewable capacity and approval rating. The subsequent cash-in-pocket incentives may yet be the turning point in provoking a shift in attitudes that sees the German public embrace wind power and declare, "Yes, please in my backyard".

Fig. 14 Locations of wind turbines in Berlin and on city-owned land in Brandenburg (*Stadtgüter*)

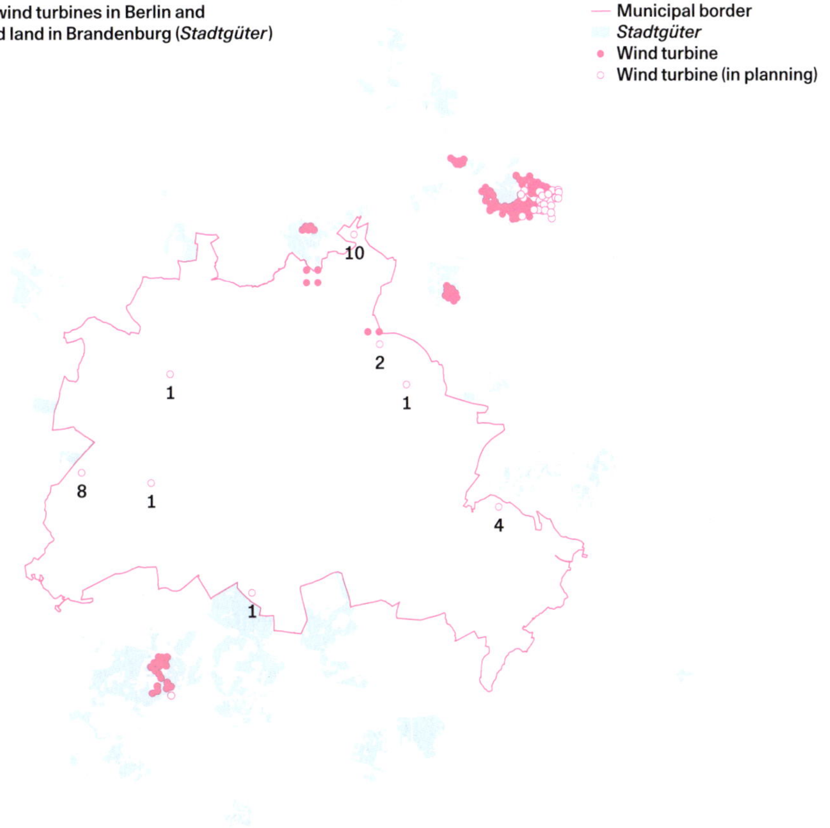

4.4.4

Bayan Obo

Santiago Martínez M.
Joseph Smithard

Fig. 15 Bayan Obo rare-earth mine

Bayan Obo currently stands as the world's largest mine dedicated to the extraction and processing of REE. [Fig. 26] These minerals, integral to all electronic technologies, play a vital role in constructing wind turbines. Located in the Inner Mongolia province, an autonomous region of China, this mine holds over 40 % of the world's known reserves of rare earths and contributes to half of all global production. Operating constantly, the mine yields a diverse array of 15 rare-earth minerals, with notable concentrations of lanthanum, cerium, and neodymium.[84] However, the scope extends far beyond this, encompassing the extraction of over 100 minerals, including iron, from its resources.

Comprising three pits—"Main", "East", and "West"—Bayan Obo operates as an open pit with further facilities for milling, tailing, storage, and dump disposal. The Main and East pit's dimensions are approximately 1.5 km in length and 1 km in width, whereas the West pit, the largest among them, stretches over 4.6 km in length and 1.2 km in width, extending to depths of more than 200 m. The expansive mine sprawls across an extensive area of 48 km^2, a surface that is roughly comparable to the Neukölln district in Berlin.[85] [Fig. 16]

The mine is under the ownership of the Chinese state-owned Baotou Iron and Steel Group, also known as Baogang Group. This conglomerate was established in 1951 with the backing of the Soviet Union during the nascent years of the Chinese communist government.[86] Iron reserves were initially discovered in 1927, followed by the discovery of rare earths in 1935. The commencement of industrial production took place in 1958 and has persisted uninterrupted until today. Initially, the goal of the Chinese-Soviet initiative was to build industrial, military, and supply capacity to Inner Mongolia. However, subsequent Chinese public policies to incentivise mining shifted away from Soviet interests and focused instead on national development.

The extracted ore is transported, for processing, to the city of Baotou, located approximately 150 km south of the mine. Baotou, the largest city in Inner Mongolia, is home to a population of 2,700,000 and is renowned as the rare-earth capital of China.[87] Benefitting from both road and rail connections to the Bayan Obo mine, within its vicinity it hosts refineries for iron and steel alongside facilities dedicated to transforming rare earths into various forms including oxides, chlorides, carbonates, and alloys. The owner and operator of these infrastructures is the China Northern Rare Earth (Group) High-Tech Co., a subsidiary of the Baogong Group. The consortium presents is the world's biggest supplier of rare earths, making this mine critical in the supply chain for an incomprehensible number of technologies. Wind turbines, in particular, rely on four rare-earth minerals for their magnets: dysprosium, neodymium, praseodymium and terbium. [Fig. 22; p. 228]

Significant controversy and concerns surround the environmental management of the mining district. Close to the expansive facilities in Baotou, which extend towards the western end of the city, there exists a waste deposit resembling an artificial lake.[88] Formed during the initial years of production on reclaimed farmland, this lake now contains the residues of the refining process, characterised by elevated concentrations of hazardous substances such as acids, sulphates, ammonia, and thorium. Consequently, crops in the surrounding villages gradually ceased to grow, and there are documented reports of health issues affecting both humans and animals in the area.[89] Put simply, the disposal of hazardous waste within the Bayan Obo and Baotou context primarily involves conspicuous storage in tailings and dams, lacking any comprehensive environmental management.[90] To provide a sense of the scale of the damage, the extraction of 1 t of rare earths results in the generation of approximately 2,000 t of toxic mining waste, 1,000 t of wastewater, 1.4 t of radioactive waste, and potentially up to 12,000 m³ of gas containing sulphur dioxide.[91]

Comparable in damage to other large mining enterprises around the world, the ecocidal outcomes of these activities arise from a political determination to disregard environmental repercussions in favor of a highly cost-effective mining and refining procedure.[92] Rare-earth minerals are abundant within the Earth's crust, yet their refining has been a subject of perpetual controversy due to the methods employed, which still closely resemble those developed during the nuclear race after the Second World War.[93] The Mountain Pass mine was specifically shut down following an

Fig. 16 Area comparison: Bayan Obo mine vs. Berlin in km²

Berlin	891
Bayan Obo mine	~48

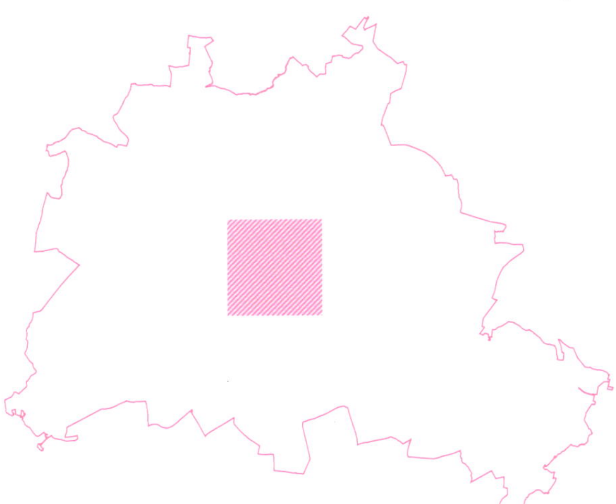

environmental debacle triggered by a toxic waste incident. Conversely, China has maintained more lenient regulations, and Western corporations and governments have collaborated to relocate production capabilities to Asia in return for cheap minerals. Similar policies have had repercussions in other countries. Madagascar, Brazil, Rwanda, the Democratic Republic of Congo, and South Africa, among others, have been cited as grappling with significant environmental conflicts linked to the extraction of critical minerals.[94]

Fig. 17 Bayan Obo solar farm

After decades of burying their heads in the sand, China has embarked on a new path by implementing public programmes and institutional initiatives to dismantle illegal mining operations and rehabilitate contaminated areas. This shift can be observed in Jiangxi province, which has been a key rare-earth producer since the 1990s.[95] Here, former mining sites have been transformed through reforestation efforts. Additionally, in the vicinity of Bayan Obo, substantial investments have been directed towards establishing approximately 470 MW of solar capacity. This renewable energy infrastructure not only powers the mine but also supports the energy needs of the surrounding mining community.[96] Countries such as the US and Australia, now in the process of expanding their rare-earth mineral production, have adopted more stringent environmental management practices within their borders. However, a paradox emerges as significant investments from China, the US, and Europe are directed towards securing supplies from other continents such as Africa and South America, most notably materials such as cobalt in Congo and niobium in Brazil. This pursuit, while aimed at resource assurance, carries the potential for neo-colonial exploitative dynamics within contexts marked by weak governance structures. In light of these circumstances, there is an increasing urgency for more transparent governance in mining agreements and a well-defined strategy for recycling. Currently, recycling efforts only manage to achieve a mere 1 % of the total demand.[97]

To break away from the extractive patterns that characterised the fossil fuel era, the manufacturing of these technologies should incorporate circular practices. This approach is crucial to avoid depleting mineral resources and prevent repeating the resource exhaustion seen during the fossil fuel era.

4.4.4

Feldheim

Santiago Martínez M.
Joseph Smithard

Approximately 80 km southwest of Berlin, the self-sufficient community of Feldheim stands as a successful embodiment of the German energy transition's ideals. This community has not only generated an ample surplus of clean energy but has also reaped positive financial benefits from its efforts. Nestled within the district of Treuenbrietzen in Brandenburg, Feldheim spans 15.7 km^2 and has a population of less than 200 people. [Fig. 27] Presently, Feldheim boasts a collection of distinct systems that, when synergised, not only render the village self-sufficient—in terms of energy—but also transform it into a net contributor to the national electricity grid. This is because only 1% of their approximated generated power is consumed locally.[98] The village attains its independence through diversification. Its facilities include a wind park, battery storage to regulate fluctuations, a solar farm, a biogas plant, a woodchip heating plant, and a locally dedicated heating grid. In essence, the village operates autonomous electricity and heating networks that are detached from the broader German grid, capitalising on their surplus energy by selling it to the market.

As of 2023, the Feldheim wind park boasts a substantial collection of over 100 wind turbines situated within its vicinity. Among these, 55 turbines, with a total capacity of 123 MW, are managed by Energiequelle GmbH.[99] Contextually, the turbines overseen by Energiequelle have the potential to provide power to as many as 65,000 households.[100] Additionally, the village's biogas plant possesses an electricity-generating capacity of 526 kW, along with a heating capacity of 560 kW. This heating system is symbiotically complemented by the woodchip plant, especially during periods of peak heating demand.[101]

Fig. 18 Biogas plant in Feldheim

The drive towards self-sufficiency began in the 1990s when Michael Raschemann, the founder of Energiequelle GmbH, sought a location for installing new wind turbines. Following discussions with Feldheim's residents, the initial four turbines were erected on land owned by the local farmers' association. Subsequent endeavours for additional turbines were realised through community investment, with backing from the city of Treuenbrietzen and the European Union via the European Regional Development Fund. The collective public investment amounts to € 12,800,000.[102]

Despite the energy diversity and robust development of energy resources, Feldheim still had one major roadblock to becoming carbon neutral. Utility company E.ON refused to sell or lease its electrical infrastructure to the village. In response, they built their own grid funded by Energiequelle, EU subsidies, capital loans, and, remarkably, contributions of € 3,000 from each villager. In 2010, the grid was switched on, and Feldheim now considers itself fully carbon neutral, with local energy prices having dropped by roughly a third.[103] Subsequently, the infrastructure model is as follows: Feldheim Energie GmbH, comprised of households, businesses, and the city of Treuenbrietzen, owns the heating grid, while the local power grid, on the other hand, is owned by Energiequelle GmbH and Co. WP Feldheim 2006 KG.

Nonetheless, it's not all smooth sailing in Feldheim, and the village is not devoid of controversies concerning adopting clean energies. The village's transportation largely depends on individual cars, almost exclusively fuelled by fossil fuels. However, it should be noted that there is a rising presence of EV charging stations, suggesting progress for the future. Furthermore, Energiequelle is in the process of constructing an electrolyser aimed at providing hydrogen for buses.[104] The proclaimed concept of carbon neutrality should also be taken with a pinch of salt. German laws stipulate that only homeowners can participate in the local electrical and heating grids. As a result, the few renters in Feldheim remain connected to the national grid and thus receive the same combination of resources as nearly all other households in Germany.[105]

While the idea of Germany achieving 100 % renewable energy by 2050 might appear a distant prospect, it has already become a reality in Feldheim. Despite its size, the village may be seen as a successful example thanks to its cohesive community, sparsely populated surroundings, and shared vision. However, the true test lies in adapting this model to larger scales and more densely populated regions with competing land strategies.

Fig. 19 First turbine in Feldheim

Endnotes

1 For a wide, detailed, and inspiring variety of windmills, please see: Notebaart, *Windmühlen. Der Stand der Forschung über das Vorkommen und den Ursprung*.
2 UNESCO World Heritage Centre, "Asbads (Windmill) of Iran".
3 Wind Europe, "Wind Energy in Europe: 2022 Statistics and the Outlook for 2023–2027".
4 See: European Commission, "Technical Note: Delivering the European Green Deal, Results of the 'Fit for 55' Core Policy Scenarios for the EU Member States".
5 Telsnig et al., "Clean Energy Technology Observatory", 21.
6 Wind Europe, "Wind Energy in Europe: 2022 Statistics and the Outlook for 2023–2027".
7 International Energy Agency, "Offshore Wind to Become a $1 Trillion Industry".
8 Heymann, "A Fight of Systems?", 115.
9 De Decker, "Wind Powered Factories: History (and Future) of Industrial Windmills".
10 A better description of the structure can be found in: Miller, *Wind Turbine Structural Dynamics*.
11 Bent Sørensen, "History of, and Recent Progress in Wind-Energy Utilization", 403.
12 See: "Beginnings | Jacobs Wind Electric".
13 Heymann, "A Fight of Systems?", 115.
14 Ibid., 116.
15 Heymann, "Signs of Hubris".
16 Heymann, "A Fight of Systems?", 121.
17 Johansen, "Blowing in the Wind", 4.
18 Wikipedia, "Wind Power in Denmark".
19 Wind Europe, "Placing Onshore Wind at the Heart of the European Green Deal: What Should Europe Do?"
20 GWEC, "Global Wind Report 2023", 24.
21 Kendall McKinnon, "Le Mistral: The Wind of Provence".
22 Kirsty McCabe, "What Is Wind? | Royal Meteorological Society".
23 Ibid.
24 Danish Wind Industry Association, "The Coriolis Force".
25 National Geographic Society, "Wind".
26 Danish Wind Industry Association, "Whence Wind: Where Does Wind Energy Come From?".
27 On average, most plants have a net primary production of about 4.95 × 106 calories per m^2/year. This is global NPP or global net primary production, i.e. the amount of energy available to all subsequent links in the food-energy chain. The Earth's surface area is 5.09 × 1014 m^2. The net power output stored by plants is thus 1.91 × 1013 W, or 0.011 % of the power emitted to Earth. See: Danish Wind Industry Association.
28 Danish Wind Industry Association, "Roughness and Wind Shear".
29 Danish Wind Industry Association, "Wind Shade".
30 Ghenai, "Life Cycle Analysis of Wind Turbine".
31 Joint Research Centre (European Commission) et al., *Raw Materials Demand for Wind and Solar PV Technologies in the Transition towards a Decarbonised Energy System*, 12.
32 For more information on turbine design see: Hau, *Wind Turbines*.
33 Van de Kaa et al., "Wind Turbine Technology Battles".
34 Shanbr, S et al., "Bearing Fault Detection within Wind Turbine Gearbox | IEEE Conference Publication | IEEE Xplore".
35 Meeschaert, A.M, "Rare Metal Supply Chains: Challenges for a Sustainable Energy Transition", 23.
36 Van de Kaa.
37 Ibid.
38 Vestas, "Vestas Sustainability Report 2021", 35.
39 As of July 2023, the most powerful wind turbine in the world is the 16 MW Mingyang MySE 16–260, with a height of 242 m and blades that are 118 m long. See: NES Fircroft, "The Biggest Wind Turbines In The World".
40 Meeschaert, "Rare Metal Supply Chains: Challenges for a Sustainable Energy Transition", 13.
41 ArcelorMittal, "Steel Solutions Provider to the Global Wind Energy Industry".
42 Meeschaert, 13.
43 Rabe, Kostka, and Smith Stegen, "China's Supply of Critical Raw Materials".
44 Meeschaert, 13.
45 Vestas, "Life Cycle Assessment of Electricity Production from an Onshore EnVentus V162-6.2 MW Wind Plant", 15.
46 Norgren, Carpenter, and Heath, "Design for Recycling Principles Applicable to Selected Clean Energy Technologies", 6.
47 Global Wind Energy Council, "Global Wind Report 2023", 24.
48 Ibid., 24.
49 Ibid., 25.
50 Ibid., 30.
51 UNFCCC, "Rapid Urbanization Increases Climate Risk for Billions of People".
52 Global Wind Energy Council, "Global Wind Report 2023", 30.
53 International Energy Agency, "Iron and Steel Technology Roadmap – Analysis".
54 International Energy Agency, "Renewable Energy Sources Act (Erneuerbare-Energien-Gesetz EEG) – Policies".
55 Umweltbundesamt, "Renewable Energies in Figures".
56 Strom-Report, "Windenergie Deutschland 2023 | Zahlen, Fakten, Charts".
57 "Renewables 2021 – Analysis", 60.
58 Strom-Report, "Windenergie Deutschland 2023 | Zahlen, Fakten, Charts".
59 Strom-Report, "Photovoltaik Deutschland".
60 Technik Museum Sinsheim, "Growian Windflügel".
61 Wirstschafts Woche, "Erster Deutscher Windpark: Vor 30 Jahren begann die Energiewende".
62 Deutsche WindGuard, "Status of Offshore Wind Energy Development in Germany", 5.
63 Hühn, "Onshore und Offshore".
64 Kerstine Appunn, "Germany Must Shed "Bureaucratic Corset" for Renewables in next Legislation Package – Wind Industry".
65 Strom-Report, "Windenergie Deutschland 2023 | Zahlen, Fakten, Charts".
66 Benjamin Wehrmann, "German Offshore Wind Power – Output, Business and Perspectives".
67 Agora Energiewende, "Germany Falls behind on Its Climate Targets in 2021".
68 Bundesregierung, "Expanding wind energy for Germany | Federal Government".
69 Bundesregierung.
70 Wind Energy Area Requirements Act v. July 20, 2022 (BGBl. I p. 1353), which is provided for by Article 5 of the Law of January 4, 2023 (BGBl. 2023 I No. 6). See: "WindBG Windenergieflächenbedarfsgesetz".
71 Deutsche Windguard, „Status des Windenergieausbaus an Land in Deutschland", 7.
72 Research Institute for Sustainability, "Sustainability in Brandenburg".
73 Wikipedia, "Liste von Windkraftanlagen in Berlin und Brandenburg".
74 Ministerium für Wirtschaft, Arbeit und Energie des Landes Brandenburg, "Windenergie".
75 Ministerium für Wirtschaft, Arbeit und Energie, "Energiestrategie 2040", 47.
76 Herzberg and Rieseberg, *Mühlen und Müller in Berlin*.
77 Senatsverwaltung Umwelt, Mobilität, Verbraucher- und Klimaschutz, "Monitoringbericht zur Umsetzung des Berliner Energie- und Klimaschutzprogramms", 20.
78 Carolina Kyllmann, "Berlin Could Use Disused Airfields for Wind Turbines, Says State Govt Official".
79 Senatsverwaltung Umwelt, Mobilität, Verbraucher- und Klimaschutz, "Monitoringbericht zur Umsetzung des Berliner Energie- und Klimaschutzprogramms", 20.
80 Appunn and Wettengel, "Germany's 2022 Renewables and Efficiency Reforms".
81 Amelang, "Power Grid Fees – Unfair and Opaque?".
82 Agora Energiewende, "Entwicklung der StromNetzentgelte 2017: Die regionalen Unterschiede nehmen zu", 4.
83 Sonnberger and Ruddat, "Die gesellschaftliche Wahrnehmung der Energiewende", 35.
84 NS Energy, "Bayan Obo Rare Earth Mine, Inner Mongolia, China".
85 Bezirksamt Neukölln, "Gebietsflächen in Neukölln".
86 Klinger, "A Historical Geography of Rare Earth Elements".
87 "Baotou Travel Guide".
88 Maughan, "The Dystopian Lake Filled by the World's Tech Lust".
89 Kaiman, "Rare Earth Mining in China".
90 Kaiman.
91 Geng, Sarkis, and Bleischwitz, "How to Build a Circular Economy for Rare-Earth Elements".
92 Standaert, "China Wrestles with the Toxic Aftermath of Rare Earth Mining".
93 Klinger, "A Historical Geography of Rare Earth Elements".
94 Penke, "The Toxic Damage from Mining Rare Elements".
95 Standaert, "China Wrestles with the Toxic Aftermath of Rare Earth Mining".
96 Wang et al., "Water Conservation and Ecological Water Requirement Prediction of Mining Area in Arid Region Based on RS-GIS and InVEST".
97 "The Global Fight for Critical Minerals Is Costly and Damaging".
98 Bowen, "Germany's Renewable Village".
99 "The Energy Self-Sufficient Village".
100 Zimmermann, "The German Village That Says It's Gone Green".
101 Neue Energien Forum Feldheim, "The Energy Self-Sufficient Village".
102 "Fünf Millionen Euro Förderung für Batteriespeicher in Feldheim".
103 Bowen.
104 Zimmermann, "The German Village That Says It's Gone Green".
105 Bowen.

Fig. 20 Selected wind parks across the world

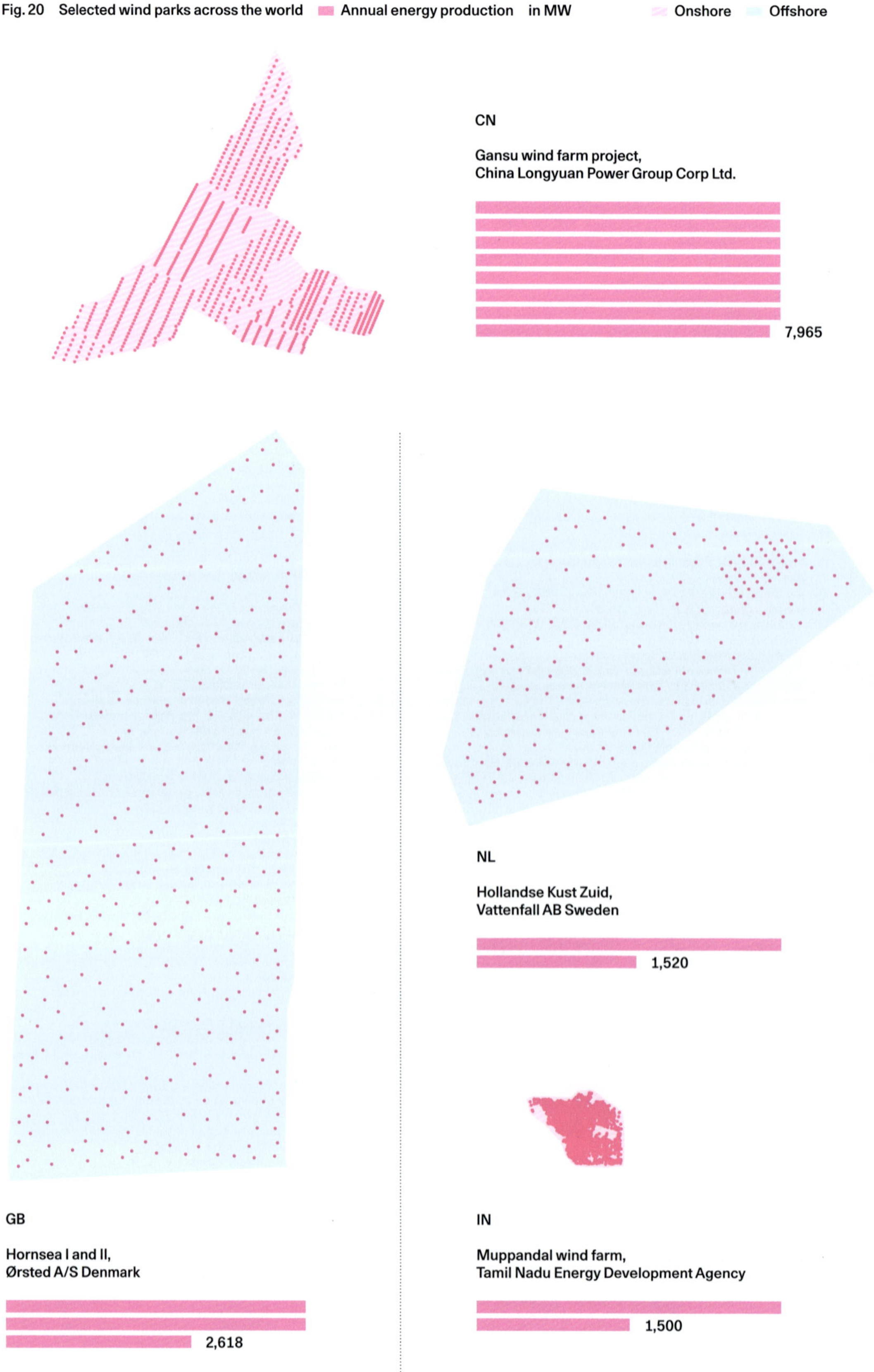

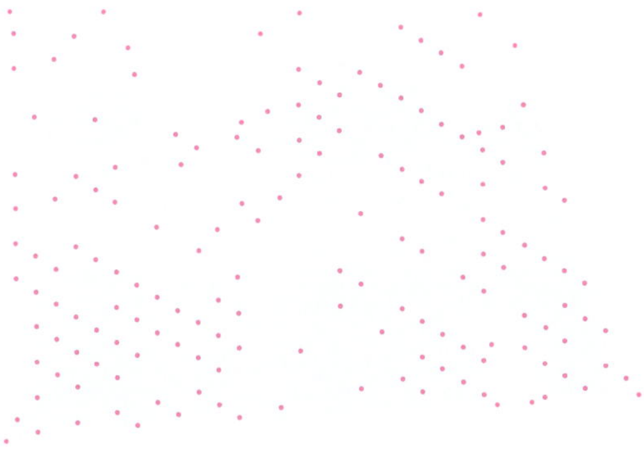

GB

Seagreen wind farm,
TotalEnergies + SSE Renewables

1,075

RO

Fântânele-Cogealac wind farm,
ČEZ Group

600

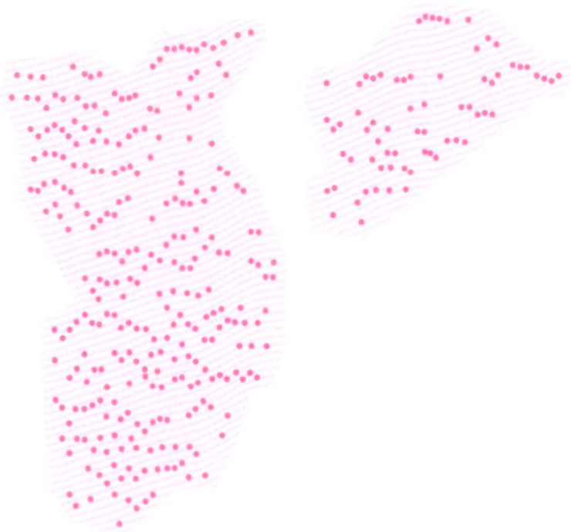

US

Traverse Wind Energy Center,
Invenergy + AEP

998

DE

Gode Wind I and II,
Ørsted A/S Denmark

582

US

Meadow Lake wind farm,
EDP Renewables North America

801

DE

Feldheim wind park,
Energiequelle GmbH & Co

254

Fig. 21 Wind turbine supply chain

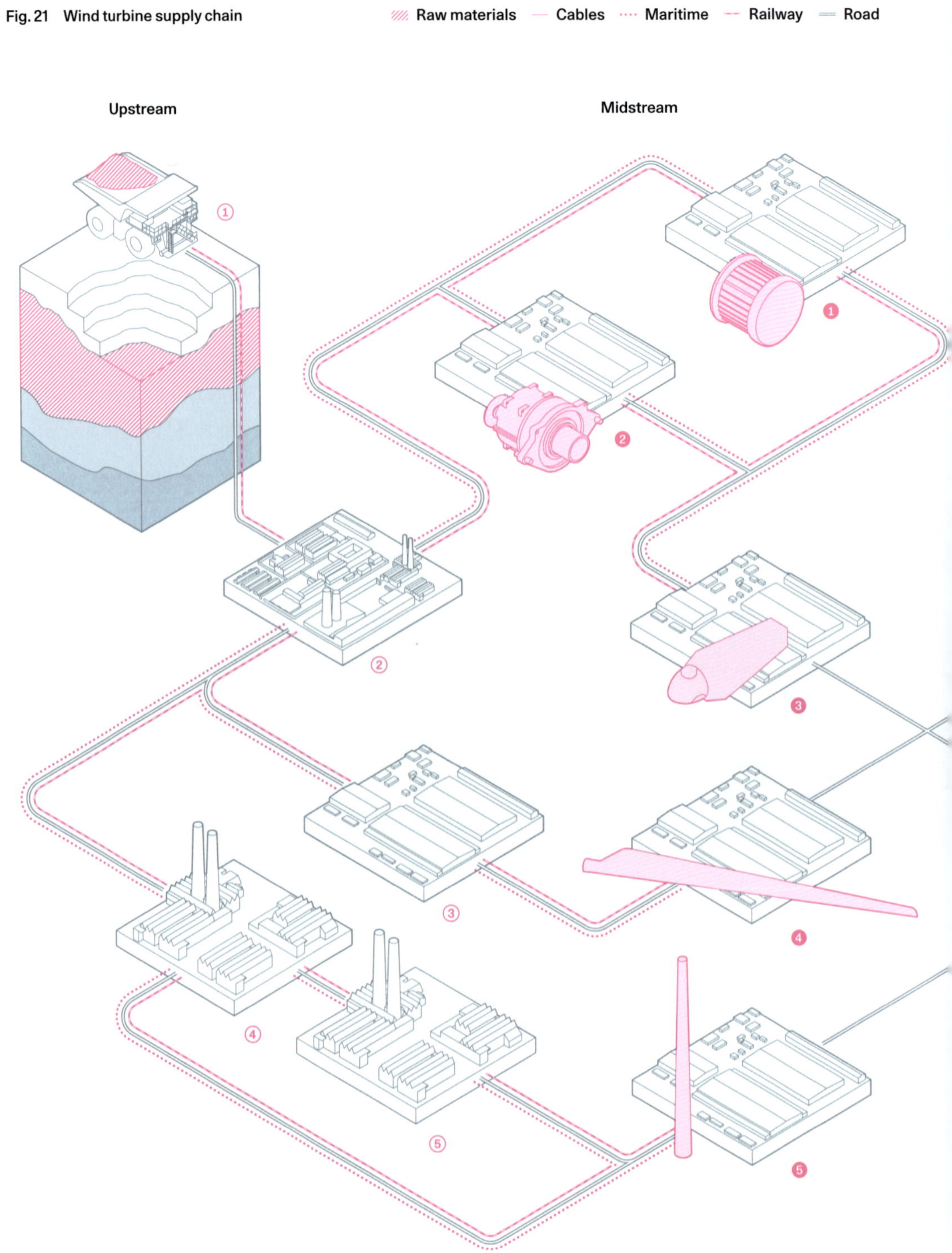

Mining and processing (CN, CL, PE, ID, PH, CD)

① Mineral mining
② Mineral processing plant
③ Carbon fibre plant
④ Steel production facility
⑤ Cement production facility (concrete towers)

Manufacturing (CN, IN, US, ES, DE)

❶ Generator manufacturing facility
❷ Gearbox manufacturing facility
❸ Nacelle assembly facility
❹ Blade manufacturing facility
❺ Tower manufacturing facility

Downstream

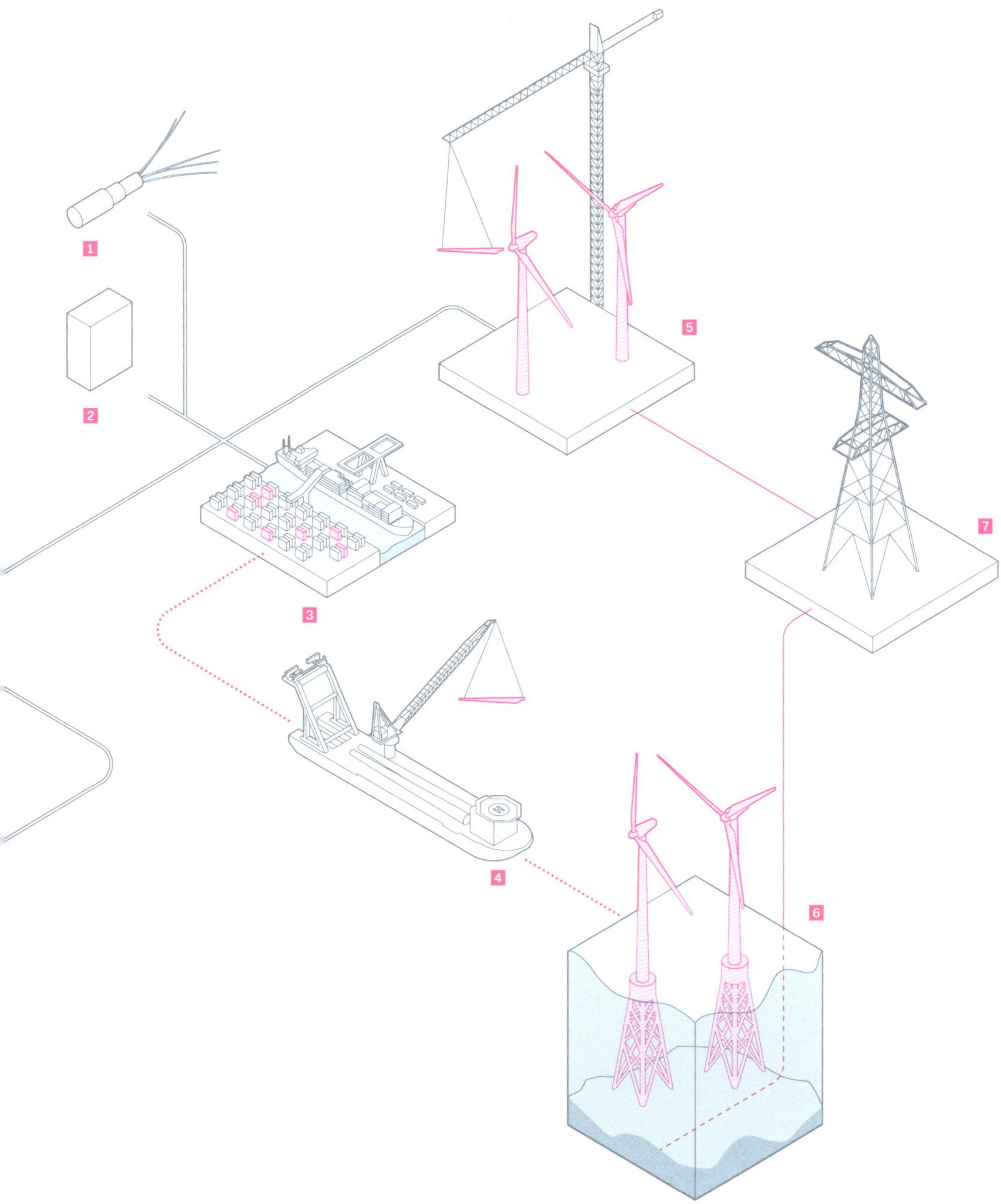

Distribution (DE)

1 Cables
2 Controller
3 Port
4 Installation vessel
5 Onshore wind park
6 Offshore wind park
7 Main electric grid

Fig. 22 Global extraction mines of raw materials used in wind turbines

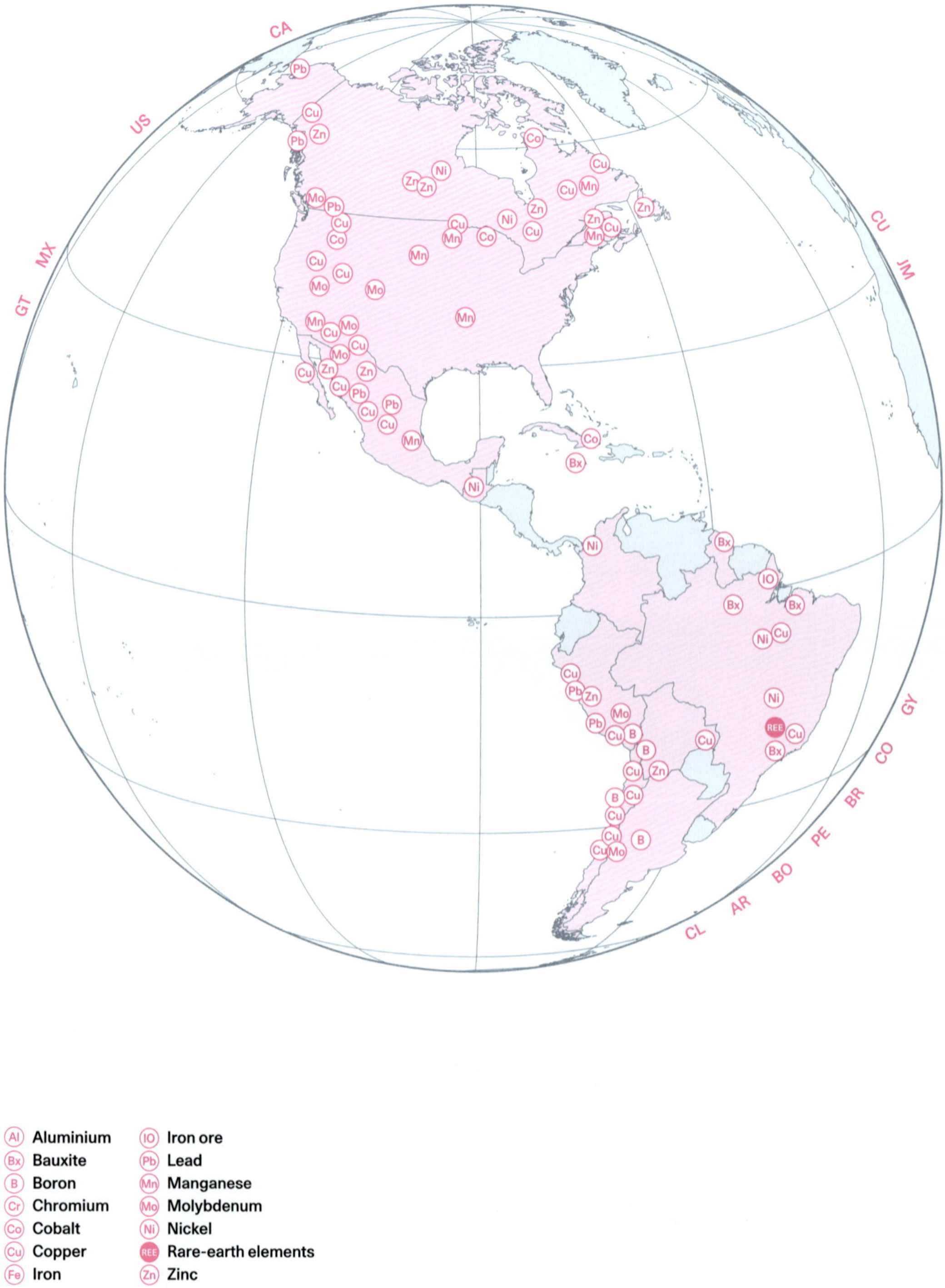

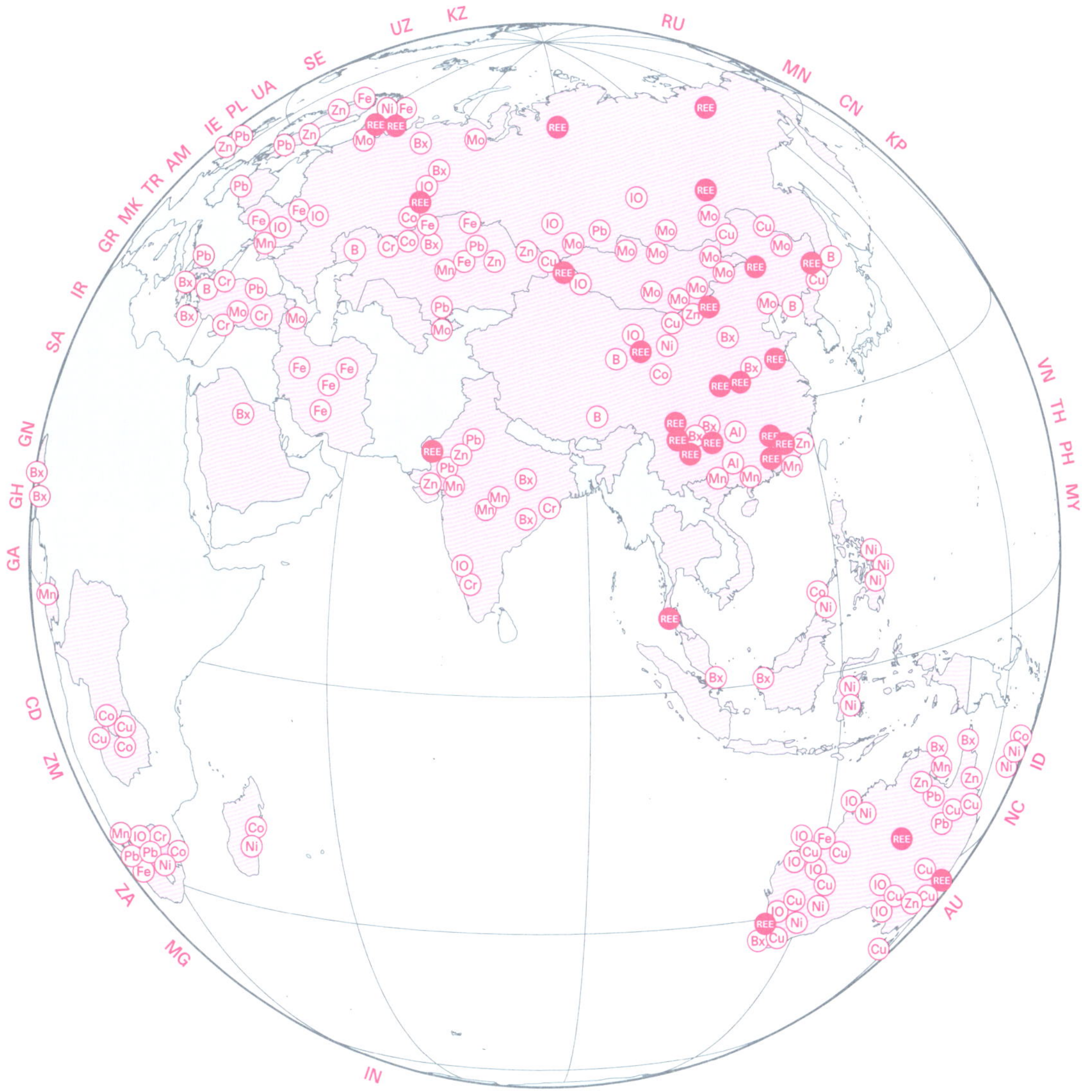

Fig. 23 Share of raw material production for wind turbines by country in %

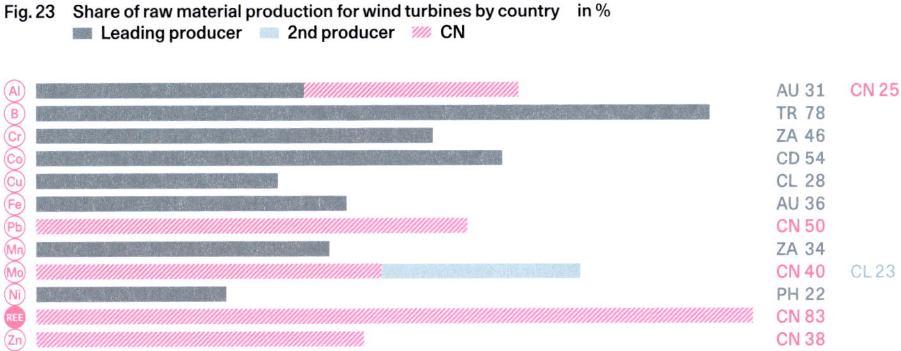

Fig. 24 Components of a wind turbine

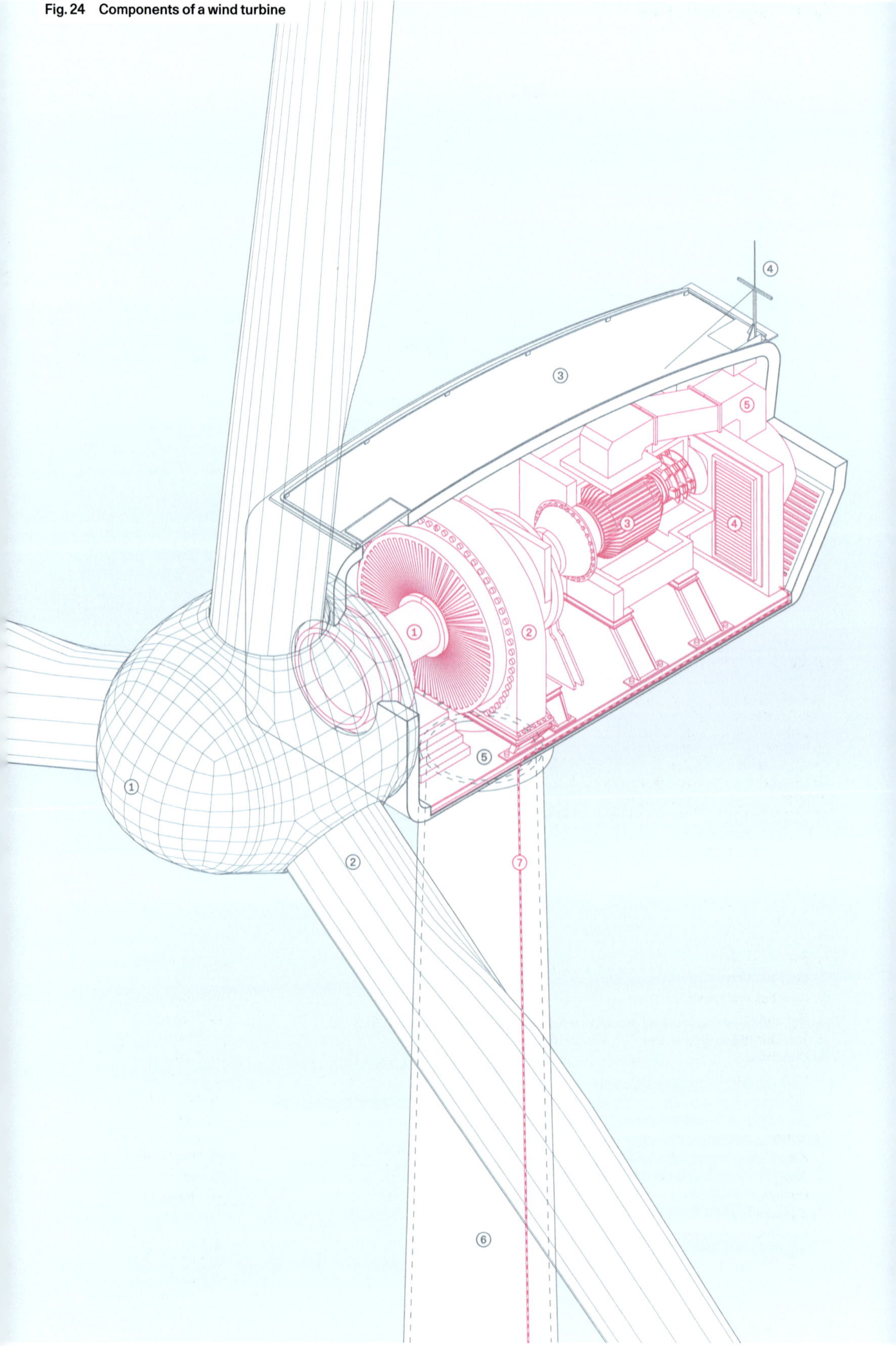

Fig. 25 Largest wind turbines

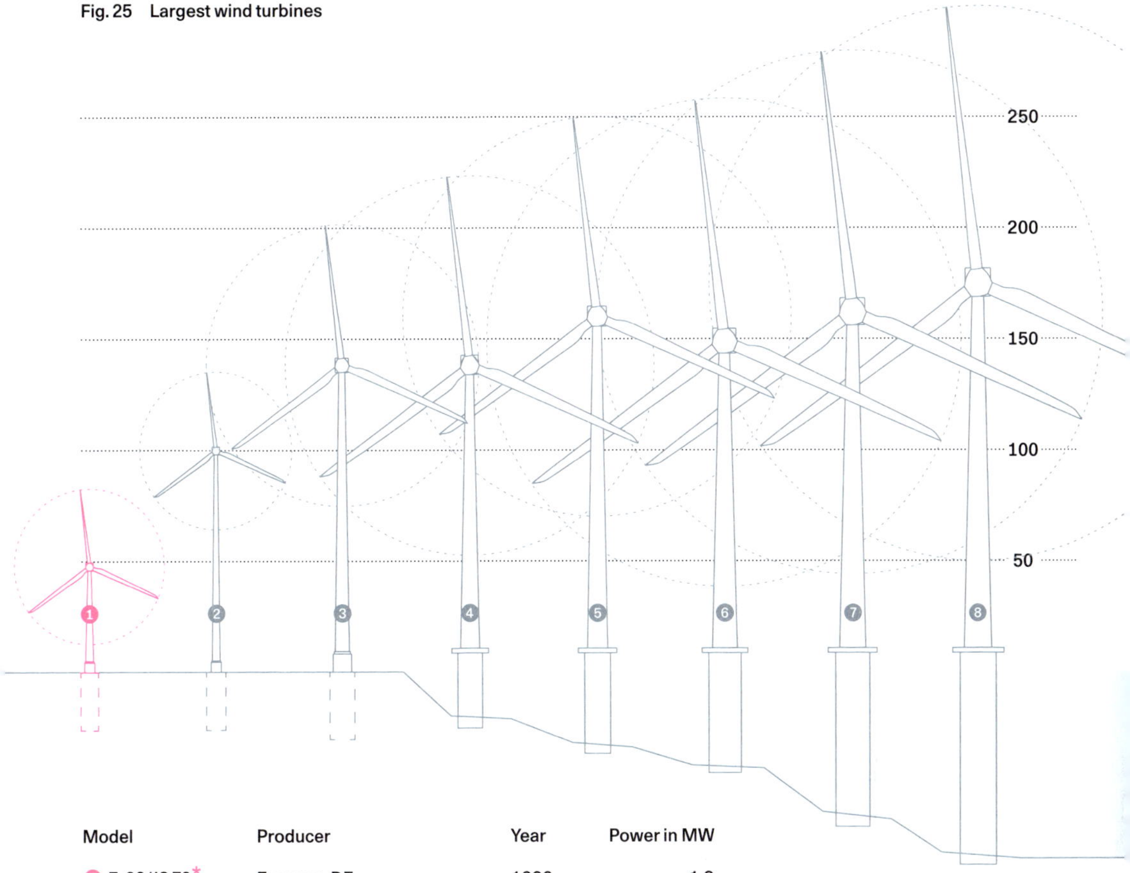

Model	Producer	Year	Power in MW
1 E-66/18.70*	Enercon, DE	1999	1.8
2 E-70 E4	Enercon, DE	2004	2.3
3 E-126	Enercon, DE	2007	7.5
4 S7.0-171	Samsung, KR	2013	8.0
5 Areva 8MW	Areva, FR	2013	8.0
6 Haliade-X	General Electric, US	2021	14.0
7 V236	Vestas, DK	2021	15.0
8 MySE 16.0-242	MingYang Smart Energy, CN	2021	16.0

* 17 units in Feldheim wind park

Engine	Materials
1 Main bearing	Al, Fe
2 Gear box and brake	Cr, Fe, Mn, Mo, Ni, Nb
3 Generator	B, Co, Cu, Fe, Dy, Nd, Pr, Tb
4 Transformer	Al, Cu
5 Controller	Al, Cu
6 Cooling system	Al, Cu
7 Cables	Al, Cu, Pb

Structure	Materials
1 Rotor	Al, C, Cr, GF, Fe, Nb
2 Blades	Al, C, Cr, GF, Fe, Nb
3 Nacelle	Al, C, GF, Fe, Nb
4 Anemometer	Al
5 Yaw drive and motor	Al, Cu, Fe, Pb
6 Tower	Al, C, Cr, GF, Fe, Mn, Mo, Ni

- Al Aluminium
- B Boron
- C Carbon-fibre
- Cr Chromium
- Co Cobalt
- Cu Copper
- GF Glass-fibre
- Fe Iron/steel
- Pb Lead
- Mn Manganese
- Mo Molybdenum
- Ni Nickel
- Nb Niobium

Rare-earth elements

- Dy Dysprosium
- Nd Neodymium
- Pr Praseodymium
- Tb Terbium

Fig. 26 Bayan Obo mine, Inner Mongolia, China

Locations
1. Main pit
2. East pit
3. West pit
4. Mining town

Production facilities
Substations
Wind turbines
Solar fields

Open pits
Tailings
Industrial railways
Power line

1
2
4
2 km

Fig. 27 Feldheim wind park, Brandenburg

Locations
1. Energy forum
2. Pig farm
3. Biogas plant
4. Control station / battery storage

Wind parks
1. Feldheim
2. Danna
3. Malterhausen-Lindow

- Feldheim
- Municipal border of Feldheim
- Windmill (Feldheim)
- Windmill (other wind park)
- Power line

1 km

Fig. 28 Feldheim, 1877

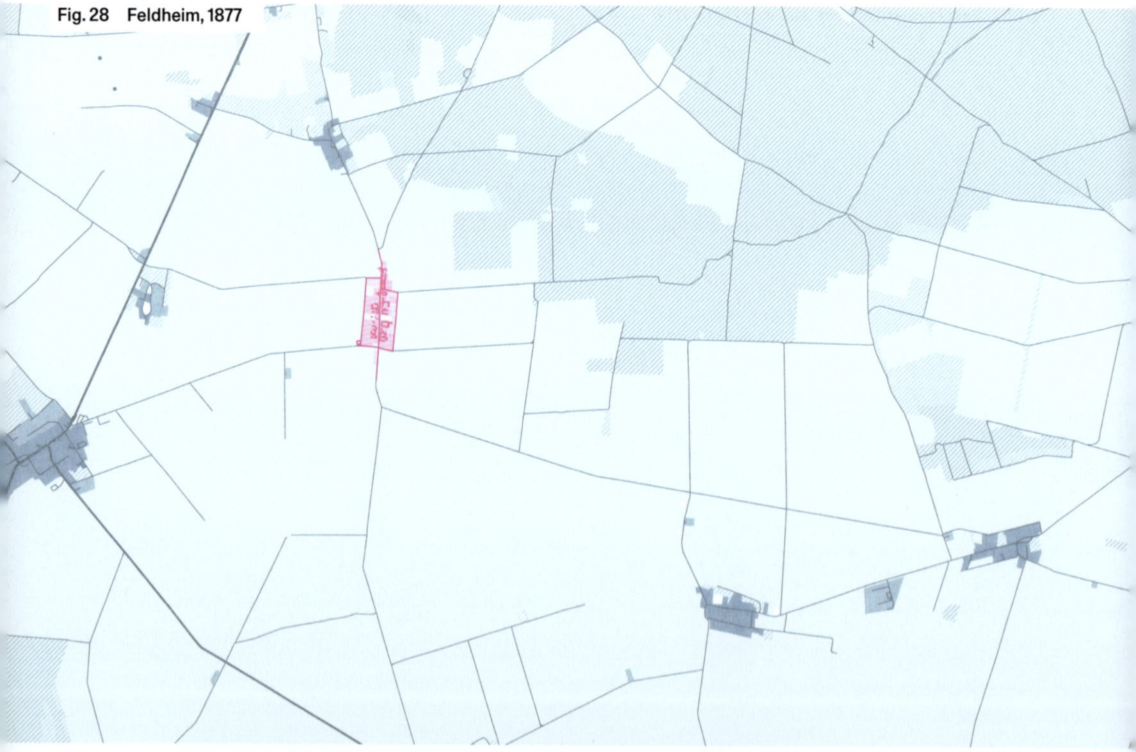

1877 Feldheim, a linear settlement (*Straßendorf*) in Prussia, features agricultural buildings including characteristic four-sided farmsteads along its main thoroughfare.

Fig. 29 Development of Windpark Feldheim, 2000

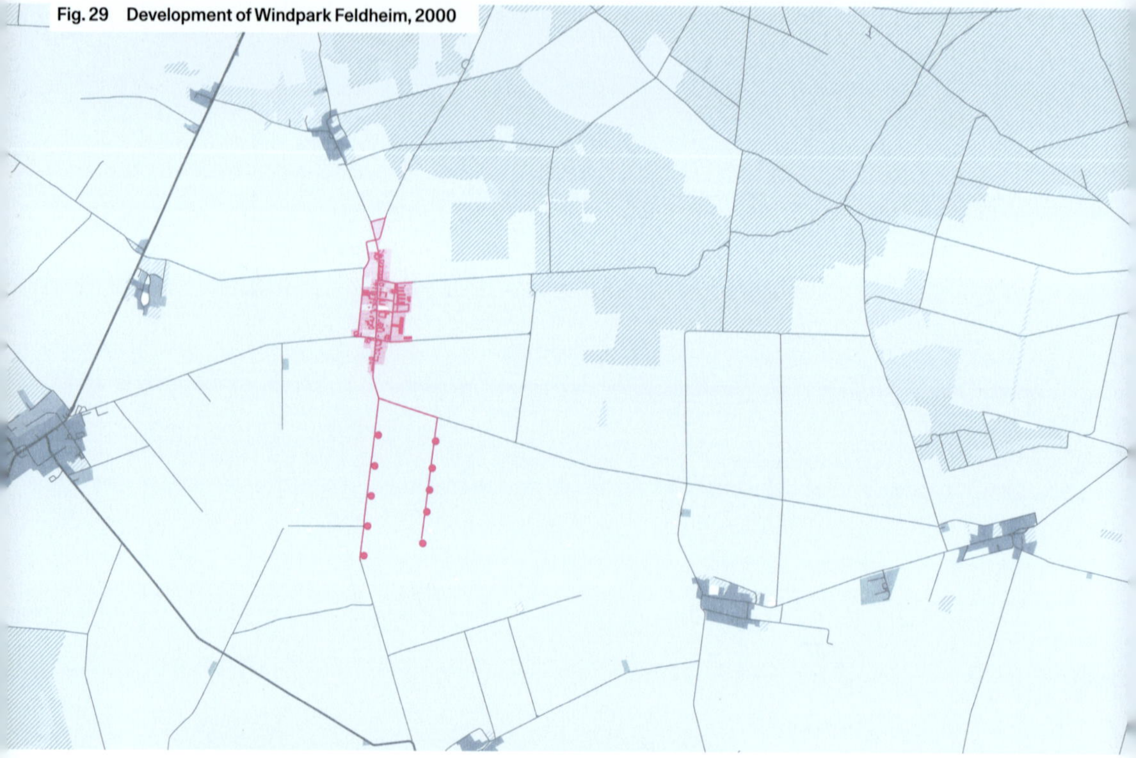

1997 Following discussions with Feldheim's residents, the initial four turbines are erected on land owned by the local farmers' association.

Fig. 30 Development of Feldheim wind park, 2010

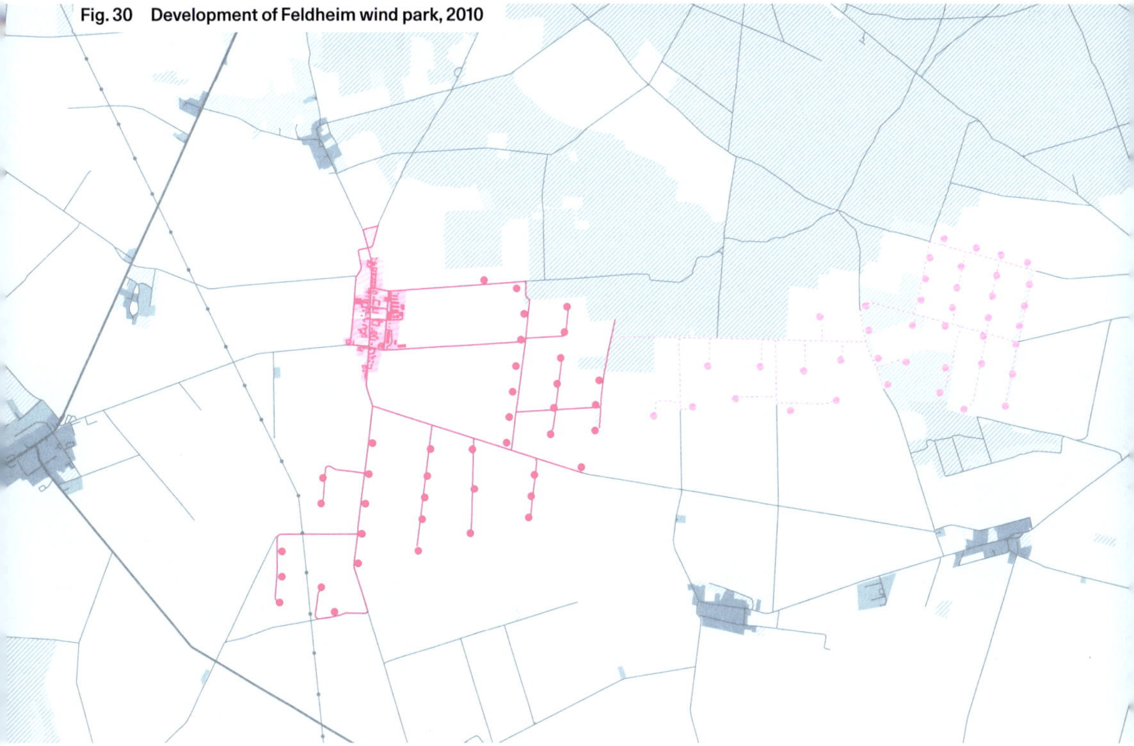

2010 Feldheim becomes the first (and only) energy self-sufficient village in Germany.

Wind turbines
- by Energiequelle GmbH
- by other operators

Access roads

Fig. 31 Development of Feldheim wind park, 2023

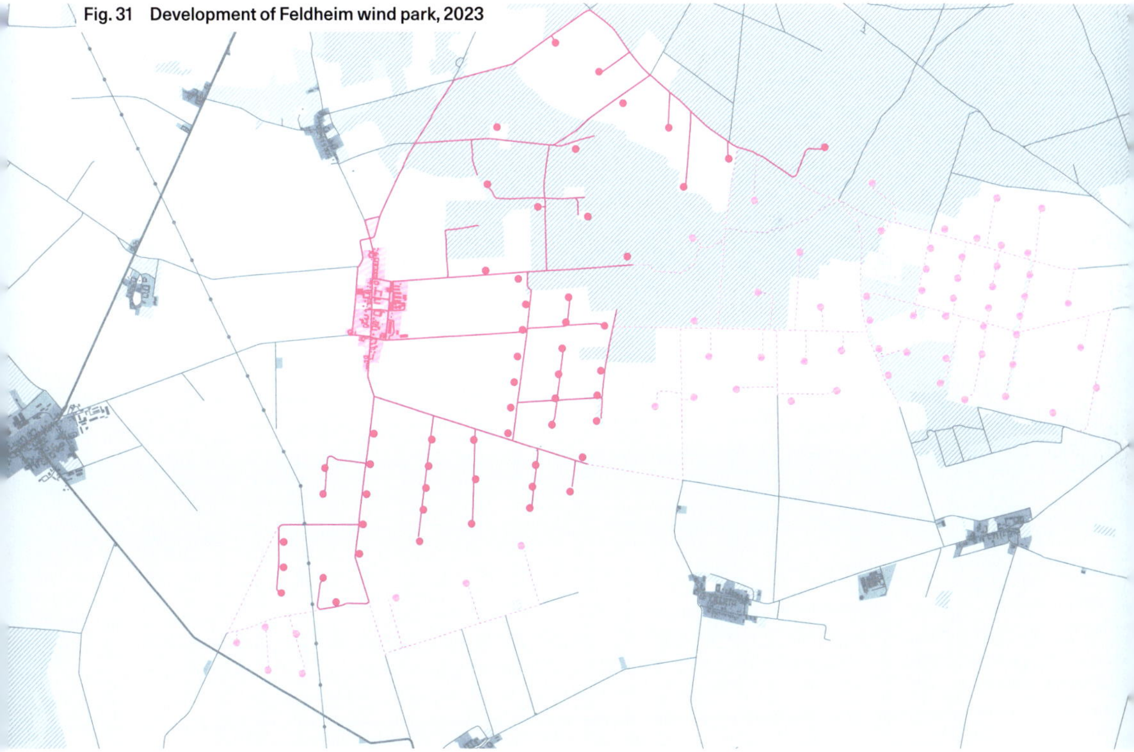

2023 Feldheim's wind energy infrastructure expands to 55 wind turbines, achieving a capacity of 123 MW. Other wind parks are also built in the surrounding area.

1 km

Nine Theses

In this final section, the authors endeavour to present nine thought-provoking conflict statements, abstracting on a higher level the cases examined throughout this book. None of these statements should be construed as predictions or scientific conclusions; instead, they offer a concise summary of themes that may remain pertinent discussion points in the coming decade. Simultaneously, these statements are intended to inspire and provoke aspirations to contemplate power, flows, and transformation with neither naïve optimism nor catastrophic denial.

1 Futures will remain extractive.

Despite their valuable reduction of atmospheric CO_2 emissions, the production of renewable energy from essentially technological devices relies upon the procurement of a broad portfolio of mineral substances obtained from various locations worldwide. In particular, the manufacture of photovoltaic panels, wind turbines, and battery storage systems necessitates sourcing materials from the extractive sector, signalling the dawn of the "all-metal Age". The strategic conflict of winding down emissions while simultaneously plunging more holes into the ground is unlikely to be resolved during the current phase of global expansion or, framed more optimistically, exponential "growth". Nonetheless, in the face of resource depletion, geopolitical shifts, and ecological repercussions associated with large-scale mining enterprises, circular practices and innovative substance compositions will ultimately become an even more significant part of the discourse.

2 The burdens and detriments will fall upon the countryside.

The proliferation of urban development unfolding under carbon-neutral imperatives is increasingly intertwined with the proliferation of large-scale energy landscapes in the countryside, supporting (especially in the Global North) the service-focused economies of contemporary cities. Wherever inexpensive, and preferably "conflict-free" land is available, solar fields and wind parks will likely emerge. However, this should not lead to the conclusion that they are merely countryside phenomena following the logic of their respective contexts; instead, they should be viewed as manifestations of urban needs and influences in rural areas. While cities are expected to undergo transformation, it is the land that is currently confronted with significant alteration and re-composition for the foreseeable future. If villages and municipalities are not supported in their autonomy, agency, and involvement in fair value creation, they will become the unwilling linchpin of a transformation unjustly superimposed by oblivious urbanites and industrial aristocracies.

3 The world is already full—turning the underground above will exacerbate this problem.

As the underground ceases to serve as a concealed reservoir of ancient energy stores on the current scale, the transition to sustainable renewable power production is likely to demand a vast amount of available land surface. Despite its seemingly boundless expanse, the countryside is imbued with human artefacts and existing land uses. Ongoing efforts to bring the underground to the surface already indicate a significant increase in land-based and sea-based energy infrastructure. However, a holistic and comprehensive transformation towards eco-social sustainability necessitates the reconciliation of energy production and security with other essential objectives, such as preserving and regenerating ecosystems, securing food production, sourcing bio-based resources, and onshoring production processes. The question that arises for successful implementation is not only whether we can find enough space but also at what cost. In opposition to trajectories of expanding endlessly into what remains, the energy transition will become a pretext to redesign, redefine, and revise the strategic goals, practices, and identities of current land-use. Anything new should repurpose the existing stock in an attempt to see if it can be partially integrated into what is already there. Through this, the energy transition may produce hybridised forms of infrastructure that simultaneously offer interfaces for multiple purposes.

4 The cities will de-function, while the countryside will re-function.

With the cessation of local coal gas manufacturing within urban perimeters, there has been a persistent trend of relocating the production of energy resources which sustain the vital metabolic functions of the city into pipelines, cables, and conduits connected to concentrated hinterlands. Consequently, the appearance of energy production has become markedly obscured and concealed from a considerable portion of its users. Due to its divided past and the insular conditions of supply in its western zone, Berlin, more than many other cities, remains replete with power stations and heat-and-power production facilities. The outsourcing of electricity generation, paired with the increasing need for space and resulting inner-city land prices, is likely to propel a continuous dismantling and relocation of CO_2-intensive practises away from a historically significant manufacturing capital, freeing up space for much sought-after socio-cultural attractions and even ecological reserves. "Kraftwerkification", or the transformation of dwindling industrial infrastructure, has become an essential aspect of the city's post-reunification identity. Former gasholders have been converted into flats and offices, while power stations and factories have become world-renowned clubs and cultural venues. Previous airports and airfields now house tech startups or provide habitats for breeding field larks. The proliferation of amenities and the increasing livability of the city as a socio-cultural hub rely on the driving expansion of highly technical and increasingly monofunctional landscapes in other locations. The ensuing polarisation of these trans-local realities is likely to intensify as the city disconnects from its underlying structural foundations, resulting in its growing vulnerability to global disruptions.

5 The energy transition is (currently) "made in China"

China is driving the energy transition globally, not just because of the dominant and absolutely indispensable role it plays in it but, additionally, because most countries and their respective industries have, whether by negligence or intention, developed an essential dependence on China's expanding production capacity. With a vertical integration of every single part of the supply chain within the country's control, this is unlikely to change in the foreseeable future. Presently, China is paving the way towards a new status quo that challenges the inertia of fossil-based regimes controlled by well-established petro- and carbo-monarchies elsewhere in the world. However, energy "made in China" nonetheless creates a complex ethical situation: although the country has set entirely new standards of scale in terms of renewable energy implementation and fabrication, this shift has been attained through an exorbitant rate of climate-change-inducing emissions. Being both a super-polluter and a proliferator of the clean (and most importantly cheap) energy revolution thus gives the country a dual role in our global future. China is increasingly evolving as a mediating power able to circumvent traditional geopolitics while, simultaneously, establishing a monopoly upon which global companies and governments—whether they approve or not—will inevitably have to rely, potentially at the expense of multilateral control.

6 Past, present, and future will stand side by side.

Unlike mineral energy carriers, which contain their power within themselves, renewable energy largely relies on technology to convert atmospheric phenomena. As the history of technology demonstrates, this is accompanied by a relentless need for updates, revolutions, disruptions, and obsolescences, which will inevitably clash with one another. The implementation of carbon neutrality will not occur as a single, organised sweep; instead, it may unfold in a messy, fragmented, though certainly pragmatic manner. This world in constant transition, where one energy landscape must coexist side by side with others, is populated by pioneers, reluctant adopters, opposition, and actors who are unable to keep pace. In this context, the communication, alignment, and (dis)connection between the various competing parts will be as important as organising consensus and finding common ground.

7 The techno-fix beats the psycho-fix—at unknown costs.

The procurement of future energy is frequently depicted as a solely technological challenge. Nonetheless, this perception is flawed. Despite ongoing efforts to improve energy efficiency, there has been no significant reduction in overall consumption rates over time. Paradoxically, the more technologically advanced societies become, the more their energy demands increase—a fact that English economist, William Stanley Jevons, already described in the 1860s using the example of resource consumption of coal. In contrast to the prevailing techno-optimism that Big Tech and Big Infrastructure are constantly massaging into the discourse, the image of achieving sufficiency through a cultural shift towards restraint and reduction leaves individuals, especially in Western economies, with the stale taste of unnecessary personal sacrifice—a hot-button issue in political debate. However, placing sole reliance on technological progress as the preferred and seemingly less contentious route to achieving carbon neutrality is a bold gamble that must be consistently challenged through public debates. For decades, Western nations have grown accustomed to stable, readily available energy at their convenience and relatively low cost—a privilege still awaited by significant segments of the population in developing nations. Recognition and acceptance of the fact that this emerging brave new world will profoundly impact daily routines and existing standards, potentially leading to intermittent scarcity and insecurities, is just as crucial as expanding the production fleet of renewable energy itself.

8 The world is fragmented and patchy; it will remain fragmented and patchy, but it should be intersectional.

Talk of a smooth and just transition to clean energy within the framework of our current economic operational system is pure fantasy. The world cannot avoid major upheaval that will fundamentally reshape the essence of the neoliberal economy with its many oppressions and interdependencies—resulting from the colonial history in which global capitalism has its roots. The departure from fossil aristocracies, therefore, should be seen not only as a commitment to getting off the needle of harmful substances that have hyper-stimulated economic growth, but as an opportunity to revise the injustices and logics propagated by the powerful energy regimes in charge. As energy procurement in 2023 cannot be thought of without considering the hegemony of its all-encompassing infrastructure, the energy transition also cannot be thought about from a localised stance of self-sufficiency. Since this is not a race to the top but rather a global effort of utopian scale, the transition made by wealthy Western economies must avoid hindering others from pursuing this goal; these nations must also concentrate their efforts on compensation, the fair distribution of resources, and opportunities for other countries. To meaningfully transform, many more voices need to be invited to sit at the table, and Kimberlé Crenshaw's concept of intersectionality—which assesses the interplay of race, gender, class, sexuality, and disability, among others, as critical factors for lifelong experiences of privilege or oppression—may serve as a tool through which to address populations whose marginalisation has been enabled by the longstanding dominance of these systems.

9 Producing a clean energy revolution from dirty fuels is a reality—and arguably one of the best ways to utilise them.

The inconvenient truth is that we need fossil fuels in order to phase out fossil fuels. Much renewable energy production is currently driven by an escalating use of coal that powers factories and by large diesel engines that ship technology all over the world, to name the most obvious examples. Until an alternative infrastructure is established, the world remains dependent on these versatile energy sources. Moreover, the concept of "Dunkelflaute"—the German term for the simultaneous absence of wind and sun—poses a challenge to energy security until large-scale storage options for renewable energy are developed. In this vulnerable transition period, unpredictable challenges will require quick adaption and room to manoeuvre. A partial redundancy in systems will most likely stay in place, especially at the domestic and community levels. However, given these circumstances, it becomes even more imperative to prioritise the allocation of resources. This entails deciding how to utilise poisonous (yet transition-relevant) mineral energy and whether the pursuit of endless Hollywood blockbusters, vacant real estate, pink Balenciaga Crocs, cryptocurrency mining, social media reels, or the development of increasingly lethal weapon systems should be included in this allocation. Every aspect must be re-evaluated based on its intrinsic value in addressing one of the critical challenges of our era: achieving carbon-emission-free energy.

Power Shift

Bui Luu Quynh Nguyen

Power Stations in Berlin and Brandenburg

SOLARPOWER
WiBau
BERLIN

MALL
EKDAY
Müller
FITX
JYSK
OPEN

SOBE
OTAS

402491
US 4310
Ladezone
Kohle
Handel

ZÜBLIN
ZÜBLIN
ZÜBLIN
ZÜBLIN
PROGAS
Ein Freund fürs Leben.

ZÜBLIN
ZÜBLIN
ZÜBLIN
ZÜBLIN
PROGAS
Ein Freund fürs Leben.

TECHNISCHE UNIVERSITÄT
Deutsche Bank
Volksentscheid am 26.03.
Der Politik
Ziele setzen!
Berlin 2030 Klimaneutral

Fun,
Forrest,
Fun.
Mach mit beim #Klima
und spar CO2!
Gute Energie.
yello

5 Appendix

Contributors

Edouard Barthen is an urban designer specialising in citizen-centred spatial development. With a background in social sciences, philosophy, and cultural studies, gained in Munich, Delhi, and Frankfurt (Oder), he navigates societal complexities and understands the dynamics of different stakeholders. Beyond academia, he is a trained design thinker with extensive experience as an innovation consultant in the corporate sector. His current work focuses on resolving land-use conflicts in rural areas by co-creating holistic landscape scenarios that integrate agriculture, climate adaptation, and environmental protection.

David Bauer is a research associate at the Habitat Unit, Institute of Architecture, TU Berlin. The Habitat Unit is a globally networked research and teaching centre that develops new approaches, expertise, and application-oriented tools relevant to global urbanisation and urban change processes. David focuses on urban design and architecture, with a strong emphasis on infrastructure regimes and system design as critical levers for the transformation towards sustainability and resilience. The methods practised underscore a robust analytical approach that captures the multi-scalar complexity of contemporary urban-rural constellations. Besides his academic work, David runs the architectural office Bauer+Pohl Projekte International (BPPI) together with his colleague Martin Pohl.

Elke Beyer is a historian and urban researcher. She holds a professorship in Architecture Theory at Hochschule Anhalt in Dessau, Germany. Previously, she taught at the Habitat Unit at TU Berlin and at ETH Zürich. Her current work focuses on commodity and material circulation, infrastructural arrangements, and questions of social reproduction and care work. Her research interests also include urban affairs in socialist and post-socialist worlds, as well as the histories of post-Second World War modern architecture and urbanism as fields of transnational practise and knowledge diffusion.

Simon Breth is an architect and space pioneer. He studied architecture and urban planning in Stuttgart, Nancy, and Valladolid before working with Polo Villacorta Arquitectos (Valladolid) and Heinle, Wischer und Partner (Berlin). He later co-founded brethdelacalle, completing projects in Berlin and Norway. In 2020, he relocated to Lausitz, transforming a disused railway station into the "Musikbahnhof Annahütte", a cultural and educational venue. He co-founded the Institute for Resilience in Rural Areas in 2022 and has been an active member of the Annahütte Volunteer Fire Brigade since 2020.

Philipp Deilmann studied architecture and urban planning at the University of Stuttgart, where he is currently pursuing a doctoral thesis on the spatial manifestation of electricity at the Chair of Urban Planning and Design. He was part of the research team for the study "Nachhaltige Transformation gestalten—Baukultur in den ländlichen Räumen Baden-Württembergs". His research interests include the influence of infrastructure on architecture and urbanism, the future of rural areas in Germany, and the role of science fiction in architecture.

Felix Frankowiak holds a bachelor's degree in architecture from the Berliner Hochschule für Technik and a master's in architecture with a focus on natural building from TU Berlin. Since 2020, he has worked as a freelance architect in various architecture and interior design offices. He has been a member of the non-profit association Haus Döschnitz e. V. since 2022.

Anke Hagemann is an urban and architectural researcher and acting professor at Habitat Unit, the Chair of International Urbanism and Design at TU Berlin. She graduated in Architecture and was a research associate in the exhibition project Shrinking Cities, Berlin. She taught at ETH Zurich and HafenCity University Hamburg before joining the Habitat Unit in 2013 as a lecturer and researcher. Between 2020 and 2021, she was interim professor of Urban Planning at BTU Cottbus-Senftenberg. Her current research topics include global commodity circulation and urban space, urban-rural metabolisms and extended urbanisation, and co-creation in strategic planning processes.

Patrick Martin is a graphic designer and co-founder of Happy Little Accidents, a studio specialising in visual communication, typography, and corporate identities. The studio's book designs have been recognized by prestigious organisations such as the Stiftung Buchkunst and the Type Directors Club New York, among others. Besides his design practise he is part of Kontextur, a digital magazine spinning around architecture.

Santiago Martínez Murillo is an architect and urban practitioner focusing on medium-scale urban operations, housing governance, transit-oriented design, and energy transition. As a curiosity-driven, socially engaged professional with experience in planning, design, and research, he works on expanding access to formal urban development and territorial equity in the Global South.

Amelia Mega has a background in architecture and urban design. She currently works at Bauhaus Earth, researching ways to advance the adoption of regenerative built environments in a transformation lab format. With experience in participatory design and research, Amelia is particularly interested in how architecture interweaves with socio-ecological issues and collaborative approaches to city-making. She is also actively involved with Architecture Sans Frontières Indonesia, where she co-designed cooperative housing with urban communities in Jakarta—a topic she also explored in depth in her master's thesis.

Yuliya Navatskaya is an architect, urban designer and GIS expert engaged in research and mapping on the strategic development of infrastructural provision and extractive practices in the former Soviet states and the Arctic region. She holds an M.Sc. in Architecture from the University of Liechtenstein.

Bui Luu Quynh Nguyen studied communication design in Berlin, specialising in documentary photography. She is currently pursuing a master's degree in social and economic communication at the University of the Arts. With a focus on urban sociology, her work explores space from both academic and artistic perspectives. She works as a freelance photographer, with published works in various books and magazines, and has participated in both group and solo exhibitions.

Cordelia Polinna is an urban planner and researcher. She studied Urban and Regional Planning in Berlin and Edinburgh, later completing a doctorate and teaching as a visiting professor at TU Berlin. In 2008, she co-founded Polinna Hauck Landscape + Urbanism and was managing director of Urban Catalyst GmbH until 2022. She now runs Forward Planung und Forschung in Berlin and co-founded the Institute for Resilience in Rural Areas in Annahütte. With extensive international experience in research and teaching, she is an expert in strategic spatial development, public good-oriented real estate development, and cooperative participation processes. Cordelia focuses on urban-rural relations, commuting between Berlin and Lausitz.

Joseph Smithard is a Berlin-based architect and urban researcher. He studied architecture (M.Arch) at the University of Manchester and urban design (M.Sc.) at TU Berlin and is currently a research associate in the InterGrad Academy EGD at Hochschule Anhalt. After completing his studies, he worked in various architecture firms in the UK and Germany on projects ranging from single-family homes to large-scale master plans. Since 2021, alongside three colleagues, he has been researching energy landscapes and infrastructure interconnections in Berlin and Brandenburg. His research focuses on trans-local urban development within the context of the European Green Deal, with an emphasis on infrastructure, climate adaptation, and storytelling.

Elif Soylu is an architect and researcher based in Rotterdam. She has contributed to exhibition design with Aslı Çiçek at BOZAR (2019) and to research and design projects with OOZE Urbanists and Architects at the IABR (2020) and the Venice Architecture Biennale (2021). She completed bachelor's degrees in Architecture and Interior Design at Istanbul Bilgi University and received a SALT research grant in 2019. Her master's thesis in Urban Design at TU Berlin explores the transformation of Istanbul's water infrastructure, reflecting her engagement with urban landscapes.

Paul Strobel is an urban planner and researcher with a Master's in Urban Design from TU Berlin. With experience in strategic planning, he currently works as a researcher at Hochschule Anhalt in Dessau in the Department of Architecture, Facility Management, and Geoinformation. His work explores the relationship between infrastructure and urbanisation processes, with a particular focus on material flows and their interaction with the built environment. Methodologically, his research centres on approaches in digital cartography.

Bibliography

Abdullah, Aitani. "Oil Refining and Products". In *Encyclopedia of Energy*, edited by Cutler J. Cleveland and Robert U. Ayres, Volume 4: 715–29. Amsterdam Boston: Elsevier Academic Press, 2004.

Academic dictionaries and encyclopaedias. "Liste von Windkraftanlagen in Berlin und Brandenburg", n.d. https://de-academic.com/dic.nsf/dewiki/2482145.

AG Energiebilanzen e. V. "Auswertungstabellen Zur Energiebilanz Deutschland Daten Für Die Jahre von 1990 Bis 2021". AGEB, September 2022. https://ag-energiebilanzen.de/wp-content/uploads/2021/09/awt_2021_d.pdf.

———. "Energieverbrauch fällt 2022 auf niedrigsten Stand seit der Wiedervereinigung". *AG Energiebilanzen e. V.* (blog), 20 December 2022. https://ag-energiebilanzen.de/energieverbrauch-faellt-2022-auf-niedrigsten-stand-seit-der-wiedervereinigung.

———. "Energieverbrauch in Deutschland Im Jahr 2022". AGEB, February 2023. https://ag-energiebilanzen.de/wp-content/uploads/2023/01/AGEB_Jahresbericht2022_20230413-02_dt-1.pdf.

———. "Pressemitteilung: Bericht für 2022". *AG Energiebilanzen e. V.* (blog), 17 April 2023. https://ag-energiebilanzen.de/ag-energiebilanzen-legt-bericht-fuer-2022-vor.

———. "Primärenergieverbrauch Jahr 2022". Excel, 17 April 2023. https://ag-energiebilanzen.de/daten-und-fakten/primaerenergieverbrauch.

Agentur für Erneuerbare Energien. "TOP 10 – Übersicht Zur Entwicklung Erneuerbarer Energien in Allen Bundesländern – Föderal Erneuerbar", n.d. https://www.foederal-erneuerbar.de/uebersicht/bundeslaender/BB/kategorie/top+10.

Agora Energiewende. "Entwicklung der StromNetzentgelte 2017: Die regionalen Unterschiede nehmen zu", November 2016. https://www.agora-energiewende.de/fileadmin/Projekte/2016/Netzentgelte_2017/Agora_Netzentgelte_2017_16112016.pdf.

———. "Germany Falls behind on Its Climate Targets in 2021", 7 January 2022. https://www.agora-energiewende.de/en/press/news-archive/germany-falls-behind-on-its-climate-targets-in-2021.

Alekseeva, M. N., and I. G. Yashchenko. "Determination of Factors Influencing the State of Natural Environment in the Yamal-Nenets Autonomus Okrug According to Remote Data". *AIP Conference Proceedings* 2310, no. 1 (14 December 2020): 020010. https://doi.org/10.1063/5.0034407.

Alexander, Jason, Michael Marnane, Travis Elsdon, Michael Bunce, Paweena Sitaworawet, Se Songploy, Sarin Chaiyakul, and Euan Harvey. "Using Environmental DNA to Better Inform Decision Making around Decommissioning Alternatives for Offshore Oil and Gas Infrastructure". *Science of The Total Environment* 901 (1 August 2023): 165991. https://doi.org/10.1016/j.scitotenv.2023.165991.

Amelang, Sören. "Power Grid Fees – Unfair and Opaque?" Clean Energy Wire, 18 January 2017. https://www.cleanenergywire.org/factsheets/power-grid-fees-unfair-and-opaque.

Amt für Statistik Berlin-Brandenburg. "Bevölkerungsentwicklung Und Flächen der Kreisfreien Städte, Landkreise Und Gemeinden Im Land Brandenburg 2021". Amt für Statistik Berlin-Brandenburg, June 2022. https://download.statistik-berlin-brandenburg.de/0449b1ed6918ad8c/d9b152f365b9/SB_A01-04-00_2021j01_BB.pdf.

———. "Güterbeförderung Auf Binnenwasserstrassen in Berlin Nach Güterabteilungen". Statistik Berlin Brandenburg, 2021.

———. "Statistischer Bericht: Energie- und CO_2-Bilanz in Berlin 2020". Potsdam: Amt für Statistik Berlin-Brandenburg, November 2022.

"Analyse des historischen Strukturwandels in der Lausitz", n.d.

Andritzky, Michael. *Oikos. Haushalt und Wohnen im Wandel: Von der Feuerstelle zur Mikrowelle*. Giessen: Anabas-Verl., 1992.

Appunn, Kerstine. "Germany Must Shed "Bureaucratic Corset" for Renewables in next Legislation Package – Wind Industry". Clean Energy Wire, 29 March 2022. https://www.cleanenergywire.org/news/germany-must-shed-bureaucratic-corset-renewables-next-legislation-package-wind-industry.

Appunn, Kerstine and Julian Wettengel. "Germany's 2022 Renewables and Efficiency Reforms". Clean Energy Wire, 21 June 2022. https://www.cleanenergywire.org/factsheets/germanys-2022-renewables-and-energy-reforms.

ArcelorMittal. "Steel Solutions Provider to the Global Wind Energy Industry", n.d. https://annual2023.windeurope.org/sites/default/files/WindenergybrochureEN.pdf.

"Archiv Verschwundener Orte – Verschwundene Orte". Accessed 28 September 2023. https://www.archiv-verschwundene-orte.de/de/verschwundene_orte/verschwundene_orte/70543.

Arnoldi, Marleny. "Steenkampskraal to List on LSE, JSE". Mining Weekly, n.d. https://www.miningweekly.com/article/steenkampskraal-to-list-on-lse-jse-2022-05-09.

Ash, Lucy. "Yamal Reindeer Herders Hemmed in by Gas Fields and Pipelines". *BBC News*, 4 May 2012, sec. Magazine. https://www.bbc.com/news/magazine-17956108.

Azar, J.J. "Oil and Natural Gas Drilling". In *Encyclopedia of Energy*, edited by Cutler J. Cleveland and Robert U. Ayres, Volume 4:521–34. Amsterdam Boston: Elsevier Academic Press, 2004.

Bahde, Curt, Claus Bürgel, and Wolfgang Hahn. "100 Jahre Stromverteilung in Berlin". In *VDE 100 Jahre Stromgeschichte. Jubiläums-Fantasie*, edited by BEWAG. Berlin: Bewag, 1984.

Banks, Ferdinand E. *Energy Economics: A Modern Introduction*. Boston, MA: Springer US, 2000. https://doi.org/10.1007/978-1-4615-4551-4.

"Baotou Travel Guide: Weather, Things to Do, Travel Tips", n.d. https://www.chinahighlights.com/baotou.

Bärthel, Hilmar and GASAG AG. *Die Geschichte der Gasversorgung in Berlin: eine Chronik*. Berlin: Nicolai, 1997.

Bauer, David. "Unboxing Urban Infrastructure: Three Methodologies for Infrastructure-Oriented Urban Design and Architecture Education". *IOP Conference Series: Earth and Environmental Science* 1078, no. 1 (September 2022): 012061. https://doi.org/10.1088/1755-1315/1078/1/012061.

Baugesetzbuch. 55. Auflage, Stand: 1. März 2023, Sonderausgabe. dtv. München: dtv, 2023. https://d-nb.info/1283691388/04.

Baxmann, Matthias, Herbert Schirmer, and Internationale Bauausstellung Fürst-Pückler-Land, eds. *Zeitmaschine Lausitz – vom "Pfützenland" zum Energiebezirk: die Geschichte der Industrialisierung in der Lausitz; [im Rahmen der Internationalen Bauausstellung Fürst-Pückler-Land 2003/04 in Grossräschen]. Vom "Pfützenland" zum Energiebezirk: die Geschichte der Industrialisierung in der Lausitz*. Husum: Verlag der Kunst, 2004.

Bayerische Staatsregierung. "Am 16. November treten die geänderten 10H-Regelungen in Kraft – Die Nachfrage nach neuen Windenergieprojekten ist bereits gestiegen – Bayerisches Landesportal", n.d. https://www.bayern.de/am-16-november-treten-die-genderten-10h-regelungen-in-kraft-die-nachfrage-nach-neuen-windenergieprojekten-ist-bereits-gestiegen.

BDEW. "Die Energieversorgung 2022 – Jahresbericht", 20 December 2022. https://www.bdew.de/media/documents/Jahresbericht_2022_Foliensatz_final_20Dez2022.pdf.

———. "Hier gelingt die Energiewende, Teil I: Solarpark Weesow-Willmersdorf", 25 October 2021. https://www.bdew.de/online-magazin-zweitausend50/schwerpunkt-aufbruch/hier-gelingt-die-energiewende-teil-1-solarpark-weesow-willmersdorf.

Bealessio, Bianca Anne, Natalia A. Blánquez Alonso, Nicholas John Mendes, Anna Vladimirovna Sande, and Berna Hascakir. "A Review of Enhanced Oil Recovery (EOR) Methods Applied in Kazakhstan". *Petroleum* 7, no. 1 (1 March 2021): 1–9. https://doi.org/10.1016/j.petlm.2020.03.003.

Berkel, Manuel and Bundeszentrale für Politische Bildung. "Die Grossen Vier". https://www.bpb.de/, 1 March 2013. https://www.bpb.de/themen/wirtschaft/energiepolitik/152780/die-grossen-vier.

Berlin.de. "Solaranlagen 2022", 14 March 2023. https://www.berlin.de/umweltatlas/energie/solaranlagen/fortlaufend-aktualisiert/kartenbeschreibung.
Berman, Art – *The Real Energy Paradigm*, 2022. https://www.youtube.com/watch?v=zVhM9F3UNZY.
Bernreuter Research. "Polysilicon Manufacturers: Global Top 10 | Bernreuter Research", n.d. https://www.bernreuter.com/polysilicon/manufacturers.
———. "Polysilicon Market Analysis: Why China Is Beginning to Dominate the Polysilicon Market?", n.d. https://www.bernreuter.com/polysilicon/market-analysis.
———. "Polysilicon Production: Siemens Process", n.d. https://www.bernreuter.com/polysilicon/production-processes.
———. "Solar Value Chain – Panel Supply Steps", n.d. https://www.bernreuter.com/solar-industry/value-chain.
BEWAG, ed. *VDE 100 Jahre Stromgeschichte. Jubiläums-Fantasie*. Berlin: Bewag, 1984.
Beyer, Elke, Lucas-Andrés Elsner, Anke Hagemann, and Philipp Misselwitz. "Industrial Infrastructure: Translocal Planning for Global Production in Ethiopia and Argentina". *Urban Planning* 6, no. 3 (23 September 2021): 444–63. https://doi.org/10.17645/up.v6i3.4211.
Beyer, Elke, Anke Hagemann, Lucas Elsner, David Bauer, Anna Steigemann, Christian Haid, Ludwig Thanhäuser, Katerina Mareckova, and Aine Ryan. "Die globale Fabrik, Räume der Logistik und die letzte in Berlin-Brandenburg". *ARCH+* 241 (1 January 2020): 194–207.
Bezirksamt Neukölln. "Gebietsflächen in Neukölln". berlin.de, 30 December 2021. https://www.berlin.de/ba-neukoelln/ueber-den-bezirk/zahlen-und-fakten/statistische-daten/gebietsflaeche.
BGR. "Neue Studie zum Schiefergas-Potenzial in Deutschland". https://www.bgr.bund.de, 2012. https://www.bgr.bund.de/DE/Gemeinsames/Oeffentlichkeitsarbeit/Pressemitteilungen/BGR/bgr-120625.html.
Bijker, Wiebe E., Thomas Parke Hughes, and Trevor Pinch, eds. *The Social Construction of Technological Systems: New Directions in the Sociology and History of Technology*. Anniversary ed. Cambridge, Mass: MIT Press, 2012.
Birol, Dr Fatih. "Key World Energy Statistics 2021", n.d.
Birol, Dr Fatih, and David Malpass. "It's Critical to Tackle Coal Emissions". IEA Paris, 8 October 2021. https://www.iea.org/commentaries/it-s-critical-to-tackle-coal-emissions.
Birol, Fatih. "Critical Minerals: Responsible Supply Chains for a Sustainable Future | The OECD Forum Network", n.d. https://www.oecd-forum.org/posts/critical-minerals-responsible-supply-chains-for-a-sustainable-future.
Bismark, Friedrich von. "Land in Bewegung". In *Bergbau Folge Landschaft: Konferenzdokumentation der Internationale Konferenz "Chance: Bergbau-Folge-Landschaft"; September 2009*, edited by Internationale Bauausstellung Fürst-Pückler-Land, Brigitte Scholz, and Oliver G. Hamm. Berlin: Jovis, 2010.
Blau, Eve, Ivan Rupnik, and Iwan Baan. *Baku: Oil and Urbanism*. Zurich: Park Books, 2018.
Borisocheva, Ksenia. *Analysis of the Oil- and Gas-Pipeline-Links between EU and Russia*. Athens: Centre for Russia and Eurasia, 2007.
Bouamane, Loubna and Jones, Geoffrey. *"Power from Sunshine": A Business History of Solar Energy*. Cambridge, Mass.: Harvard Business School, 2012.
Bowen, Andrew. "Germany's Renewable Village". dw.com, 28 May 2015. https://www.dw.com/en/feldheim-germanys-renewable-village/a-18466800.
Brenner, Neil. "The Hinterland Urbanised?" In Architectural Design, edited by Diana Periton and Timothy Brittain-Catlin, Volume 86:47-53. London: Wiley Online Library, 2016.
Brenner, Neil, and Nikos Katsikis. "Operational Landscapes: Hinterlands of the Capitalocene". *Architectural Design* 90, no. 1 (2020): 22–31. https://doi.org/10.1002/ad.2521.
Britannica. "Rare-Earth Element – Processing Ores | Britannica", n.d. https://www.britannica.com/science/rare-earth-element/Processing-ores.
British Geological Survey. "Critical Raw Materials", n.d. https://www.bgs.ac.uk/geology-projects/critical-raw-materials.
British Petroleum. *Statistical Review of World Energy 2021*. Vol. 70th edition. London: BP, Inc. London, England, 2022. https://www.bp.com/content/dam/bp/business-sites/en/global/corporate/pdfs/energy-economics/statistical-review/bp-stats-review-2021-full-report.pdf.
BSE. "Die Straßen im Kiez: Lützowplatz". *mitteNdran* (blog), 19 May 2021. https://www.mittendran.de/die-strassen-im-kiez-luetzowplatz.
Bundesanstalt für Geowissenschaften und Rohstoffe: "BGR Energiestudie 2023 – Daten und Entwicklungen der deutschen und globalen Energieversorgung". Hannover 2024; doi:10.25928/es-2023
Bundesanstalt für Geowissenschaften und Rohstoffe. "BGR Energiedaten 2022 – Daten und Entwicklungen der deutschen und globalen Energieversorgung". Excel. Hannover: Bundesanstalt für Geowissenschaften und Rohstoffe, 2023. https://www.bgr.bund.de/DE/Themen/Energie/Downloads/energiedaten_2022.html.
———. "BGR Energy Study 2021 – Data and Developments Concerning German and Global Energy Supplies". Bundesanstalt für Geowissenschaften und Rohstoffe, 2022. https://www.bgr.bund.de/EN/Themen/Energie/Downloads/energiestudie_2021_en.html.
———. "Deutschland – Rohstoffsituation 2021". BGR, 2022. https://www.bgr.bund.de/DE/Themen/Min_rohstoffe/Downloads/rohsit-2021.pdf?__blob=publicationFile&v=4.
"Bundesgesetzblatt Teil I – Gesetz Zur Sofortigen Verbesserung Der Rahmenbedingungen Für Die Erneuerbaren Energien Im Städtebaurecht – Bundesgesetzblatt". Accessed 7 October 2023. https://www.recht.bund.de/bgbl/1/2023/6/VO.html.
Bundesinstitut für Bau-, Stadt- und Raumforschung. *Potenziale der Raumordnung Chancen erkennen, Zukunft gestalten*. Redaktionsschluss: 15. Juni 2018. Informationen zur Raumentwicklung. Stuttgart: Steiner, 2018. https://www.bbsr.bund.de/BBSR/DE/Veroeffentlichungen/IzR/2018/3/Inhalt/downloads/izr-3-2018-komplett-dl.pdf?__blob=publicationFile&v=2.
Bundesministerium der Justiz. "KVBG – Gesetz zur Reduzierung und zur Beendigung der Kohleverstromung". Accessed 28 September 2023. https://www.gesetze-im-internet.de/kvbg/BJNR181810020.html.
Bundesministerium für Raumordnung, Bauwesen und Städtebau. *Leitfaden für die Instandsetzung und Modernisierung von Wohngebäuden in der Plattenbauweise: Wohnungsbauserie 70 – WBS 70, 6,3 t*. Bonn-Bad Godesberg: BMWSB, 1997.
Bundesministerium für Wirtschaft und Energie. "BMWK – Neues Klimaschutzgesetz", 2021. https://www.bmwk.de/Redaktion/DE/Schlaglichter-der-Wirtschaftspolitik/2021/10/14-neues-klimaschutzgesetz.html.
———. "Bruttobeschäftigung durch erneuerbare Energien 2000 bis 2021", May 2022. https://www.erneuerbare-energien.de/EE/Redaktion/DE/Downloads/zeitreihe-der-beschaeftigungszahlen-seit-2000.pdf?__blob=publicationFile&v=1.
———. "Integrated National Energy and Climate Plan". BMWi, 2019.
———. "Versorgungssicherheit bei Erdgas – Monitoring-Bericht nach §51 EnWG". Berlin: BMWi, 2019. https://www.bmwk.de.
———. "Zahlen und Fakten Energiedaten", September 2021. https://www.bmwi.de/Redaktion/DE/Binaer/Energiedaten/energiedaten-gesamt-xls.xlsx?__blob=publicationFile&v=131.
Bundesministerium für Wirtschaft und Energie, Prognos Institut, and Öko-Institut. "Entwicklung des Bruttostromverbrauchs bis 2030". BMWi, 15 November 2021. https://www.bmwk.de/Redaktion/DE/Downloads/E/prognos-bruttostromverbrauch-2018-2030.html.
Bundesministerium für Wirtschaft und Klimaschutz. "Erdgasversorgung in Deutschland", 2023. https://www.bmwk.de/Redaktion/DE/Artikel/Energie/gas-erdgasversorgung-in-deutschland.html.
———. Gesetz zur Änderung wasser- und naturschutzrechtlicher Vorschriften zur Untersagung und zur Risikominimierung bei den Verfahren der Fracking-Technologie (2016). https://www.bmwk.de/Redaktion/DE/Downloads/G/gesetz-aenderung-schutz-risikominimierung-fracking.html.
———. "Habeck besichtigt Projekte der Energiewende in der Lausitz", 22 February 2023. https://www.bmwk.de/Redaktion/DE/Pressemitteilungen/2023/02/20230222-habeck-besichtigt-projekte-der-energiewende-in-der-lausitz.html.
———. "Kohle", 2019. https://www.bmwk.de/Redaktion/DE/Artikel/Energie/kohlepolitik.html.
———. "Umsetzungsplan für Deutschland ("Marktreformplan") nach Art. 20 Verordnung (EU) 2019/943 über den Elektrizitätsbinnenmarkt". BMWK, 2022. https://www.bmwk.de/Redaktion/DE/Downloads/U/umsetzungsplan-fur-deutschland-marktreformplan-nach-art-20-verordnung-eu-2019-943-uber-den-elektrizitatsbinnenmarkt.pdf?__blob=publicationFile&v=6.
Bundesregierung. "Arbeitsmarkt weiter robust". Die Bundesregierung informiert | Startseite, 3 January 2023. https://www.bundesregierung.de/breg-de/themen/arbeit-und-soziales/abeitsmarkt-im-dezember-2022-2156120.
———. "Ausbau Erneuerbarer Energien Beschleunigen", 2023. https://www.bundesregierung.de/breg-de/schwerpunkte/klimaschutz/novelle-eeg-gesetz-2023-2023972.
———. "Expanding wind energy for Germany | Federal Government". Die Bundesregierung informiert | Startseite, 8 July 2022. https://www.bundesregierung.de/breg-de/schwerpunkte/klimaschutz/onshore-wind-energy-act-2060954.
———. Gesetz zur Reduzierung und zur Beendigung der Kohleverstromung und zur Änderung weiterer Gesetze (Kohleausstiegsgesetz) (2020). https://dip.bundestag.de/vorgang/.../258735.
Bundesverband Braunkohle. "Braunkohle in Deutschland – Daten und Fakten 2022", 2023. https://braunkohle.de/wp-content/uploads/2023/04/DEBRIV_Statistikflyer-de_105x210mm_Wickelfalz_20230417.pdf.
Bundesverband Erdgas, and Erdöl und Geoenergie e.V. "Erdölförderung Jahresbericht 2022". BVEG, 2023. https://jahresbericht.bveg.de/wp-content/uploads/2023/08/BVEG_Online-Jahresbericht_2022_07_RZ_B_Erdoelfoerderung.pdf.
Bundeswaltinventur. "Startseite". BMEL – Bundeswaldinventur. Accessed 5 October 2023. https://www.bundeswaldinventur.de.
Butt, Nathalie, Hawthorne Beyer, Joseph Bennett, Duan Biggs, Ramona Maggini, Morena Mills, A Renwick, Leonie Seabrook, and Hugh Possingham. "Biodiversity Risks from Fossil Fuel Extraction".

Science (New York, N.Y.) 342 (25 October 2013): 425–26. https://doi.org/10.1126/science.1237261.
Buzer. "WindBG Windenergieflächenbedarfsgesetz", n.d. https://www.buzer.de/WindBG.htm.
BVEG. "Fracking in Deutschland". *BVEG* (blog), 16 June 2023. https://www.bveg.de/die-branche/erdgas-und-erdoel-in-deutschland/fracking-in-deutschland.
———. "Jahresbericht Erdgasförderung". *BVEG Jahresbericht 2022* (blog), 2022. https://jahresbericht.bveg.de/erdgasfoerderung.
BVEG Jahresbericht 2022. "Erdgasförderung". Accessed 21 September 2023. https://jahresbericht.bveg.de/erdgasfoerderung.
Calder, Barnabas. *Architecture: From Prehistory to Climate Emergency*. A Pelican Book. UK USA Canada: Pelican, 2021.
CAPP | A Unified Voice for Canada's Upstream Oil and Gas Industry. "What Is Oil Used For | Uses for Oil and Petroleum Products". Accessed 11 October 2023. https://www.capp.ca/oil/uses-for-oil.
https://www.cleanenergywire.org/news/berlin-could-use-disused-airfields-wind-turbines-says-state-govt-official.
Carse, Asley. "Keyword: Infrastructure: How a Humble French Engineering Term Shaped the Modern World". In *Infrastructures and Social Complexity: A Companion*, edited by Penelope Harvey Morita Casper Jensen, Atsuro. London: Routledge, 2016. https://doi.org/10.4324/9781315622880.
Carson, Rachel. *Rachel Carson Silent Spring & Other Writings*. Edited by Sandra Steingraber. Library of America. New York, NY: The Library of America, 2018.
Castán Broto, Vanesa. *Urban Energy Landscapes*. Cambridge New York: Cambridge university press, 2019.
Castaneda, Christopher James. "Natural Gas, History Of". In *Encyclopedia of Energy*, edited by Cutler J. Cleveland and Robert U. Ayres, 4:207–18. Amsterdam Boston: Elsevier Academic Press, 2004.
Centre, UNESCO World Heritage. "Asbads (Windmill) of Iran". UNESCO World Heritage Centre, n.d. https://whc.unesco.org/en/tentativelists/6192.
Chen, C. Peter. "Bombing of Hamburg, Dresden, and Other Cities". WW2DB. Accessed 3 October 2023. https://ww2db.com/battle_spec.php?battle_id=55.
———. "[Photo] Reconnaissance Photo of 8th Air Force Bomb Damage to Berlin, Germany; Taken Feb 3 1945". WW2DB. Accessed 3 October 2023. https://ww2db.com/image.php?image_id=17808.
Chilingar, George V. *Geology and Geochemistry of Oil and Gas*. 1st ed. Developments in Petroleum Science 52. Amsterdam: Elsevier, 2005. http://www.gbv.de/dms/bowker/toc/9780444520531.pdf.
City Population. "Jiāngsū (China): Prefectural Division & Major Cities – Population Statistics, Maps, Charts, Weather and Web Information", n.d. https://www.citypopulation.de/en/china/cities/jiangsu/?admid=8647.
Civan, Faruk. "Natural Gas Transportation, and Storage". In *Encyclopedia of Energy*, Volume 4:273–82. Amsterdam Boston: Elsevier Academic Press, 2004.
Clean Energy Wire. "Grid Operators Consider Splitting Germany's Single Power Market Zone", 10 October 2019. https://www.cleanenergywire.org/news/grid-operators-consider-splitting-germanys-single-power-market-zone.
Clean Energy Wire. "Polls Reveal Citizen Support for Climate Action and Energy Transition", 14 August 2023. https://www.cleanenergywire.org/factsheets/polls-reveal-citizens-support-energiewende.
Clean Energy Wire. "Spelling out the Coal Exit – Germany's Phase-out Plan", 12 November 2019. https://www.cleanenergywire.org/factsheets/spelling-out-coal-phase-out-germanys-exit-law-draft.
Cleveland, Cutler J., and Robert U. Ayres, eds. *Encyclopedia of Energy*. Vol. Volume 4. Amsterdam Boston: Elsevier Academic Press, 2004.
Commonwealth of Massachusetts. "Department of Public Utilities History | Mass.Gov". Accessed 20 September 2023. https://www.mass.gov/info-details/department-of-public-utilities-history.
Conte, Niccolo. "What's Made from a Barrel of Oil?" Visual Capitalist, 14 September 2021. https://www.visualcapitalist.com/whats-made-barrel-of-oil.
Craig, Jonathan, Francesco Gerali, Fiona MacAulay, and Rasoul Sorkhabi. "The History of the European Oil and Gas Industry (1600s–2000s)". *Geological Society, London, Special Publications* 465, no. 1 (January 2018): 1–24. https://doi.org/10.1144/SP465.23.
Dame, Thorsten. *Elektropolis Berlin: Architektur- und Denkmalführer*. Petersberg: Imhof, 2014.
———. *Elektropolis Berlin: die Energie der Großstadt; Bauprogramme und Aushandlungsprozesse zur öffentlichen Elektrizitätsversorgung in Berlin*. Berlin: Mann, 2011.
Danish Wind Industry Association. "Roughness and Wind Shear". Windpower.org, June 2003. http://xn--drmstrre-64ad.dk/wp-content/wind/miller/windpower%20web/en/tour/wres/shear.htm.
———. "The Coriolis Force". Windpower.org, June 2003. http://xn--drmstrre-64ad.dk/wp-content/wind/miller/windpower%20web/en/tour/wres/coriolis.htm.
———. "Whence Wind: Where Does Wind Energy Come From?" Windpower.org, June 2003. http://xn--drmstrre-64ad.dk/wp-content/wind/miller/windpower%20web/en/tour/wres/index.htm.
———. "Wind Shade". Windpower.org, June 2003. http://xn--drmstrre-64ad.dk/wp-content/wind/miller/windpower%20web/en/tour/wres/shade.htm.
DATA, Tagesspiegel. "Berlin 1928 und Heute". Tagesspiegel. Accessed 3 October 2023. https://1928.tagesspiegel.de.
De Decker, Kris. "Wind Powered Factories: History (and Future) of Industrial Windmills". *Low Tech Magazine*, 2019. https://www.lowtechmagazine.com/2009/10/history-of-industrial-windmills.html.
de Jong, Sijbren, W.L. Auping, Willem Oosterveld, Artur Usanov, Mercedes Abdalla, Alice Van de Bovenkamp, and Christopher Frattina della Frattina. *The Geopolitical Impact of Climate Mitigation Policies: How Hydrocarbon Exporting Rentier States and Developing Nations Can Prepare for a More Sustainable Future*. The Hague Centre for Strategic Studies, 2017. http://resolver.tudelft.nl/uuid:b771f0a9-f59c-44e7-bbe9-aeb79ac100ef.
Der EnBW-Solarpark in Weesow-Willmersdorf. "Der EnBW-Solarpark in Weesow-Willmersdorf | EnBW", n.d. https://www.enbw.com/erneuerbare-energien/solarenergie/solarpark-weesow.
Deshmukh, Anshool. "Which Countries Have the World's Largest Proven Oil Reserves?" Visual Capitalist, 7 June 2021. https://www.visualcapitalist.com/ranking-the-countries-with-the-largest-proven-global-oil-reserves-in-the-world.
Destatis. "Crude Oil Imports from Russia down to 3,500 Tonnes in January 2023". Federal Statistical Office. Accessed 16 October 2023. https://www.destatis.de/EN/Press/2023/03/PE23_098_51.html.
———. "Einfuhr von Steinkohle für die Jahre 2018 bis 2022", 28 March 2023. https://www.destatis.de/DE/Themen/Branchen-Unternehmen/Energie/Verwendung/Tabellen/einfuhr-steinkohle-zeitreihe.html.
———. "Electricity Consumption of Households by Household Size", 27 September 2023. https://www.destatis.de/EN/Themes/Society-Environment/Environment/Environmental-Economic-Accounting/private-households/Tables/electricity-consumption-private-households.html.
———. "Entwicklung des Bruttoinlandsprodukts in Deutschland (Jahresdaten)". Destatis, 2023. https://service.destatis.de/DE/vgr-monitor-deutschland/bip.html.
———. "Households, by Type of Household", 30 March 2023. https://www.destatis.de/EN/Themes/Society-Environment/Population/Households-Families/Tables/households.html.
———. "Stromerzeugung 2022: Ein Drittel aus Kohle, ein Viertel aus Windkraft". Statistisches Bundesamt, 9 March 2023. https://www.destatis.de/DE/Presse/Pressemitteilungen/2023/03/PD23_090_43312.html.
———."Crude oil import volume from Kazakhstan in Germany from January 2021 to November 2024 (in 1,000 metric tons)." Statista. Accessed 10 February 2025. https://www.statista.com/statistics/1368372/german-oil-imports-from-kazakhstan/
Deutsche WindGuard. "Status of Offshore Wind Energy Development in Germany", 2022. https://bwo-offshorewind.de/wp-content/uploads/2023/01/Status-of-Offshore-Wind-Energy-Development_Year-2022.pdf.
Deutschlandfunk. "Erdgas, Erdöl, Kohle und Uran – Welche Rohstoffe hat Deutschland?" Deutschlandfunk, 11 November 2022. https://www.deutschlandfunk.de/gas-fracking-oel-kohle-uran-bodenschaetze-deutschland-energie-100.html.
Diamond, Jared M. *Collapse: How Societies Choose to Fail or Succeed*. Harmondsworth: Penguin Books, 2006.
———. *Guns, Germs, and Steel: The Fates of Human Societies*. New York: Norton, 1999.
"Die deutsche Braunkohlenwirtschaft", n.d.
Die Energiewende zu Ende gedacht — was wird sich für uns ändern?, 2022. https://www.youtube.com/watch?v=VvnmBOLuvGw.
Die kalte Sonne warum die Klimakatastrophe nicht stattfindet. 1. Aufl. Naturwissenschaft. Hamburg: Hoffmann und Campe, 2012. https://d-nb.info/1018010491/04.
DW. "Germany's North-South Divide Flares up over Energy", August 2022. https://www.dw.com/en/germanys-north-south-divide-flares-up-over-energy-crisis/a-62940864.
———. "Germany's Renewable Village – DW – 05/28/2015". Accessed 11 October 2023. https://www.dw.com/en/feldheim-germanys-renewable-village/a-18466800.
———. "Nuclear Comeback? Merkel Puts Germany's Nuclear Phase-Out in Question". dw.com, September 2007. https://www.dw.com/en/merkel-puts-germanys-nuclear-phase-out-in-question/a-2304599.
———. "Reuse and Substitutes of Critical Resources – DW – 04/13/2021", n.d. https://www.dw.com/en/rare-rocks-reuse-and-substitutes-of-critical-resources/a-57148472.
Eddy, Melissa. "The Refinery Standing Between Germany and an Oil Embargo". *The New York Times*, 23 May 2022, sec. World. https://www.nytimes.com/2022/05/23/world/europe/germany-russia-oil-embargo.html.
energie-experten. "Solarpark Weesow-Willmersdorf grösstes Solarkraftwerk Deutschlands", n.d. https://www.energie-experten.org/projekte/solarpark-weesow-willmersdorf-groesstes-solarkraftwerk-deutschlands.
Energieportal Brandenburg, "Stromerzeugung Photovoltaic Installierte Leistung Absolut". Accessed 21 September 2024. https://energieportal-brandenburg.de/cms/inhalte/ausbaustand/statistiken/photovoltaikanlagen

Energy Institute. “Statistical Review of World Energy”, 2023. https://www.energyinst.org/statistical-review/home.
———. “Statistical Review of World Energy 2023”. EI, 2023. https://www.energyinst.org/statistical-review/home.
E.N.F. “Ascent Solar to Build New Manufacturing Plant in Suqian, Jiangsu, China”, July 2013. https://www.enfsolar.com/news/3487/ascent-solar-to-build-new-manufacturing-plant-in-suqian-jiangsu-china.
Ennos, A. R. *The Age of Wood: Our Most Useful Material and the Construction of Civilization*. First Scribner hardcover edition. New York London Toronto Sydney New Delhi: Scribner, 2020.
ENTSO-E. “Mission Statement”. Accessed 2 October 2023. https://www.entsoe.eu/about/inside-entsoe/objectives.
Environmental Justice Atlas. “Karachaganak Oil and Gas Condensate Field, Kazakhstan”. EJA, n.d. https://ejatlas.org/print/karachaganak#:~:text=KPO%20and%20the%20government%20have,vision%20loss%2C%20and%20cardio%2Dvascular.
Eriksen, Freja, and Clean Energy Wire. “Grid Operators Consider Splitting Germany’s Single Power Market Zone”. *Clean Energy Wire* (blog), 10 October 2019. https://www.cleanenergywire.org/news/grid-operators-consider-splitting-germanys-single-power-market-zone.
Escher, Felix. *Berlin und sein Umland: zur Genese der Berliner Stadtlandschaft bis zum Beginn des 20. Jahrhunderts*. Berlin: Colloquium-Verl., 1985.
Euracoal. “Countryprofil Germany”, 16 February 2020. https://euracoal.eu/info/country-profiles/germany.
European Commission. “A European Green Deal”. 14 July 2021. https://commission.europa.eu/strategy-and-policy/priorities-2019-2024/european-green-deal_en.
———. “New Rules for Europe’s Electricity Market”. EC, 14 March 2023. https://energy.ec.europa.eu/system/files/2019-04/electricity_market_factsheet_0.pdf.
European Commission. Critical Raw Materials Resilience: Charting a Path towards greater Security and Sustainability (2020). https://eur-lex.europa.eu/legal-content/EN/TXT/?uri=CELEX:52020DC0474.
———. “European Climate Law”, July 2021. https://climate.ec.europa.eu/eu-action/european-climate-law_en.
———. “Technical Note: Delivering the European Green Deal, Results of the ‘Fit for 55’ Core Policy Scenarios for the EU Member States”, July 2021. https://energy.ec.europa.eu/system/files/2021-07/technical_note_on_the_ff55_core_policy_scenarios_0.pdf.
European Commission. “European Critical Raw Materials Act”. Text, n.d. https://ec.europa.eu/commission/presscorner/detail/en/ip_23_1661.
European Council. “EU Sanctions against Russia Explained”, 26 June 2023. https://www.consilium.europa.eu/en/policies/sanctions/restrictive-measures-against-russia-over-ukraine/sanctions-against-russia-explained.
European Environment Agency. “Share of Energy Consumption from Renewable Sources in Europe – 8th EAP”. Accessed 3 October 2023. https://www.eea.europa.eu/ims/share-of-energy-consumption-from.
Eurostat. “Coal Production and Consumption up in 2022 – Products Eurostat News”. *Eurostat – News Articles* (blog), 22 June 2023. https://ec.europa.eu/eurostat/web/products-eurostat-news/w/ddn-20230622-2.
———. “Energy Import Dependency by Products”. https://ec.europa.eu/eurostat/, 2023. https://ec.europa.eu/eurostat/cache/metadata/en/sdg_07_50_esmsip2.htm.
———. “Fossil Fuels in Gross Available Energy: 70% in 2020”. https://ec.europa.eu/eurostat/, 16 February 2022. https://ec.europa.eu/eurostat/web/products-eurostat-news/-/ddn-20220216-1.
———. “Industrial Production Statistics”. https://ec.europa.eu/eurostat/, June 2023. https://ec.europa.eu/eurostat/statistics-explained/index.php?title=Industrial_production_statistics.
———. “Share of Fossil Fuels in Gross Available Energy”. https://ec.europa.eu/eurostat/, 3 July 2023. https://ec.europa.eu/eurostat/cache/metadata/en/nrg_ind_ffgae_esmsip2.htm.
Federal Statistical Office. “Crude Oil Imports from Russia down to 3,500 Tonnes in January 2023”. Accessed 17 October 2023. https://www.destatis.de/EN/Press/2023/03/PE23_098_51.html.
Fischer, Andreas, and Malte Küper. “Die Bedeutung russischer Gaslieferungen für die deutsche Energieversorgung”, 23 February 2022. https://www.iwkoeln.de/studien/andreas-fischer-malte-kueper-die-bedeutung-russischer-gaslieferungen-fuer-die-deutsche-energieversorgung.html.
FNB Gas. “Netzentwicklungsplan Gas 2020-2030, Kurzfassung”. 26 May 2021.
Förster, Kim, Aleksandr Bierig, Nerea Calvillo Gonzalez, Daniel Barber, Kiel Moe, Jiat-Hwee Chang, Hannah le Roux, Isabelle Doucet, and Paulo Tavares. *Environmental Histories of Architecture*. Canadian Centre for Architecture, 2022. https://research.manchester.ac.uk/en/publications/environmental-histories-of-architecture.
Franke, Dieter, Stefan Ladage, Rüdiger Lutz, Martin Pein, Thomas Pletsch, Dorothee Rebscher, Michael Schauer, Sandro Schmidt, and Gabriela von Goerne. “BGR Energiestudie 2021 – Daten und Entwicklungen der deutschen und globalen Energieversorgung”. PDF. Bundesanstalt für Geowissenschaften und Rohstoffe, 2022. https://doi.org/10.25928/ES-2021.
Fraunhofer-Institut für Solare Energiesysteme. “Fraunhofer ISE Develops the World’s Most Efficient Solar Cell with 47.6 Percent Efficiency”. Fraunhofer Institute for Solar Energy Systems ISE, 30 May 2022. https://www.ise.fraunhofer.de/en/press-media/press-releases/2022/fraunhofer-ise-develops-the-worlds-most-efficient-solar-cell-with-47-comma-6-percent-efficiency.html.
———. “Photovoltaics Report”. Fraunhofer-Institut für Solare Energiesysteme ISE, n.d. https://www.ise.fraunhofer.de/de/veroeffentlichungen/studien/photovoltaics-report.html.
———. “Public Net Electricity Generation in Germany in 2021: Renewables Weaker Due to Weather”. Fraunhofer Institute for Solar Energy Systems ISE, 17 January 2022. https://www.ise.fraunhofer.de/en/press-media/news/2022/public-net-electricity-in-germany-in-2021-renewables-weaker-due-to-weather.html.
———. “Study: Levelized Cost of Electricity – Renewable Energy Technologies”. ISE, 2021. https://www.ise.fraunhofer.de/en/publications/studies/cost-of-electricity.html.
Fu, Rao, Kun Peng, Peng Wang, Honglin Zhong, Bin Chen, Pengfei Zhang, Yiyi Zhang, et al. “Tracing Metal Footprints via Global Renewable Power Value Chains”. *Nature Communications* 14, no. 1 (22 June 2023): 3703. https://doi.org/10.1038/s41467-023-39356-x.
Fukagawa, Naomi K., and Lewis H. Ziska. “Rice: Importance for Global Nutrition”. *Journal of Nutritional Science and Vitaminology* 65, no. Supplement (2019): S2–3. https://doi.org/10.3177/jnsv.65.S2.
Fuller, R. Buckminster. *Operating Manual for Spaceship Earth*. Edited by Jaime Snyder. New edition. Zurich, Switzerland: Lars Müller Publishers, 2019.
Ganswindt, Katrin, Sebastian Rötters, and Schücking Heffa. “Bitter Coal – Ein Dossier über Deutschlands Steinkohleimporte”. urgewald und FIAN, April 2013. https://www.en.envstudies.carsoncenter.uni-muenchen.de/student-broadcasts/blogging/clean-green-better-coal/bittercoal_mai_broschure_web.pdf.
GASAG AG. “Gasverbrauch: m3 im Jahr richtig kalkulieren”, 1 September 2021. https://www.gasag.de/magazin/neudenken/gasverbrauch-m3-im-jahr.
Gazprom Russia. “Bovanenkovskoye Field’s Final Gas Facility and Ukhta – Torzhok 2 Gas Pipeline Brought into Operation”, 5 December 2018. https://www.gazprom.com/press/news/2018/december/article469885.
———. “Gazprom launches Yamal megaproject”. https://www.gazprom.com, 3 December 2008. http://gazprom.com/eng/news/2008/12/32740.shtml.
———. “Obskaya-Bovanenkovo Railroad: A Vital Element of the Yamal Megaproject”. gazprom.com, 25 July 2021. https://www.gazprom.com/projects/bovanenkovskoye.
———. “Power of Yamal”, 30 April 2013. https://www.gazprom.com/press/news/reports/2013/power-of-yamal.
———. “Yamal – Europe”, 22 February 2018. https://www.gazprom.com/projects/yamal-europe.
Geist, Johann Friedrich, and Klaus Kürvers. *Das Berliner Mietshaus Teil 2. 1862–1945: eine dokumentarische Geschichte von “Meyer’s-Hof” in der Ackerstrasse 132–133*. München: Prestel, 1984.
Gemeinde Rüdersdorf. “Das ehemalige Chemiewerk Rüdersdorf”. Accessed 25 September 2023. https://www.ruedersdorf.de/fotos/2/101891/r%C3%BCdersdorf-bei-berlin/r%C3%BCdersdorfer-heimatfreunde-e.V./das-ehemalige-chemiewerk-r%C3%BCdersdorf/mandat/www.ruedersdorf.de/fotos/2/101891/r%C3%BCdersdorf-bei-berlin/r%C3%BCdersdorfer-heimatfreunde-e.V./das-ehemalige-chemiewerk-r%C3%BCdersdorf/mandat/57468.
Geng, Yong, Joseph Sarkis, and Raimund Bleischwitz. “How to Build a Circular Economy for Rare-Earth Elements”. *Nature* 619, no. 7969 (July 2023): 248–51. https://doi.org/10.1038/d41586-023-02153-z.
Gernsback, Hugo. “The Utilization of the Sun’s Energy”. *The Electrical Experimenter*, March 1916. https://archive.org/details/electricalexperi03gern/page/n3/mode/2up.
Ghenai, Chaouki. “Life Cycle Analysis of Wind Turbine”. In *Sustainable Development – Energy, Engineering and Technologies – Manufacturing and Environment*. IntechOpen, 2012. https://doi.org/10.5772/29184.
Gilles, Lepesant. “Higher Renewable Energy Targets in Germany: How Will the Industry Benefit?” *Briefings de l’Ifri*, January 2023. https://www.ifri.org/sites/default/files/atoms/files/lepesant_renewable-energy_germany_janv2023_4.pdf.
Glasby, Geoffrey P. “Abiogenic Origin of Hydrocarbons: An Historical Overview”. *Resource Geology* 56, no. 1 (2006): 83–96. https://doi.org/10.1111/j.1751-3928.2006.tb00271.x.
Global Energy Monitor. “Jiangsu Suqian Suyu Guanmiaozhen Zhenghui Solar Farm”. In *Global Energy Monitor*, May 2023. https://www.gem.wiki/Jiangsu_Suqian_Suyu_Guanmiaozhen_Zhenghui_solar_farm.
Global News Wire. “Global and China Polysilicon Industry Report 2019–2023”. GlobeNewswire News Room, 24 May 2019. https://www.globenewswire.com/news-release/2019/05/24/1843135/28124/en/Global-and-China-Polysilicon-Industry-Report-2019-2023.html.
Global Wind Energy Council. “Global Wind Report 2023”. https://gwec.net/wp-content/uploads/2023/04/GWEC-2023_interactive.pdf.

Goldewijk, Kees Klein, Arthur Beusen, and Peter Janssen. "Long-Term Dynamic Modeling of Global Population and Built-up Area in a Spatially Explicit Way: HYDE 3.1". *The Holocene* 20, no. 4 (2010): 565–73. https://doi.org/10.1177/0959683609356587.

Graebig, Markus, Georg Erdmann, Niko Rogler, Ingo Uhlig, and Ellery Studio for Creative Strategy, eds. *Strom, Netz, Fluss: ein Atlas unserer Stromwelt und ihres Wandels*. Erste Auflage. Berlin: Ellery Studio, 2021.

Gürsan, C., and V. De Gooyert. "The Systemic Impact of a Transition Fuel: Does Natural Gas Help or Hinder the Energy Transition?" *Renewable and Sustainable Energy Reviews* 138 (March 2021): 110552. https://doi.org/10.1016/j.rser.2020.110552.

Güßgen, Florian. "RWE-Chef Dringt Auf Verdopplung der Gaskraft in Deutschland". *Wirtschaftswoche*, 8 October 2021. https://www.wiwo.de/unternehmen/energie/versorgungssicherheit-warum-energieriese-rwe-den-ausbau-der-gaskraft-in-deutschland-fordert/27688336.html.

Gemeinsamer Verbundkatalog. "GVK – Gemeinsamer Verbundkatalog – 2.1". Accessed 28 September 2023. https://gvk.k10plus.de/SET=10/TTL=1/SHW?FRST=2/PRS=HOL.

Hagemann, Anke, and Elke Beyer. "Globalizing Urban Research, Grounding Global Production Networks: Transnational Clothing Production and the Built Environment". *Articulo – Revue de Sciences Humaines*, no. 21 (31 January 2020). https://doi.org/10.4000/articulo.4622.

Hagemann, Anke, and Natacha Quintero González, eds. *Feeding the City: Lebensmittelkreisläufe und die Produktion städtischer Räume*. Cottbus: Brandenburgische Technische Universität Cottbus-Senftenberg, IKMZ—Universitätsbibliothek, 2021. https://opus4.kobv.de/opus4-btu/frontdoor/index/index/docId/5505.

Hahn, Hans-Werner. *Die Industrielle Revolution in Deutschland*. 3., Durchgesehene und um einen Nachtrag erw. Aufl. Enzyklopädie Deutscher Geschichte 49. München: Oldenbourg Verlag, 2011.

Hall, Vincent and Max Shaw. "Chinese PV Industry Brief: New Solar Glass Factory in Jiangsu, Longi Maintains Wafer Prices Unchanged". pv magazine International, 25 June 2021. https://www.pv-magazine.com/2021/06/25/chinese-pv-industry-brief-new-solar-glass-factory-in-jiangsu-longi-maintains-wafer-prices-unchanged.

Hannemann, Christine. "Schrumpfende Städte in Ostdeutschland: Ursachen und Folgen einer Stadtentwicklung ohne Wirtschaftswachstum". *Aus Politik und Zeitgeschichte: APuZ / Bundeszentrale für Politische Bildung* 53, no. 28 (2003): 16–24.

Hansen, Tobin. "Securing U.S. Access to Rare Earth Elements". *Defense 360*, March 2020. https://defense360.csis.org/wp-content/uploads/2020/03/Hansen_Rare-Earth_v1.pdf.

Hau, Erich. "Basic Concepts of Wind Energy Converters". In *Wind Turbines: Fundamentals, Technologies, Application, Economics*, edited by Erich Hau, 65–78. Berlin, Heidelberg: Springer, 2013. https://doi.org/10.1007/978-3-642-27151-9_3.

———. "Commercial Applications of Wind Turbines". In *Wind Turbines: Fundamentals, Technologies, Application, Economics*, edited by Erich Hau, 637–76. Berlin, Heidelberg: Springer, 2013. https://doi.org/10.1007/978-3-642-27151-9_16.

———. "Control Systems and Operational Sequence". In *Wind Turbines: Fundamentals, Technologies, Application, Economics*, edited by Erich Hau, 429–65. Berlin, Heidelberg: Springer, 2013. https://doi.org/10.1007/978-3-642-27151-9_11.

———. "Electrical Power from the Wind – The First Attempts". In *Wind Turbines: Fundamentals, Technologies, Application, Economics*, edited by Erich Hau, 23–64. Berlin, Heidelberg: Springer, 2013. https://doi.org/10.1007/978-3-642-27151-9_2.

———. "Electrical System". In *Wind Turbines: Fundamentals, Technologies, Application, Economics*, edited by Erich Hau, 385–428. Berlin, Heidelberg: Springer, 2013. https://doi.org/10.1007/978-3-642-27151-9_10.

———. "Environmental Impact". In *Wind Turbines: Fundamentals, Technologies, Application, Economics*, edited by Erich Hau, 605–36. Berlin, Heidelberg: Springer, 2013. https://doi.org/10.1007/978-3-642-27151-9_15.

———. "Loads and Structural Stresses". In *Wind Turbines: Fundamentals, Technologies, Application, Economics*, edited by Erich Hau, 167–231. Berlin, Heidelberg: Springer, 2013. https://doi.org/10.1007/978-3-642-27151-9_6.

———. "Mechanical Drive Train and Nacelle". In *Wind Turbines: Fundamentals, Technologies, Application, Economics*, edited by Erich Hau, 305–83. Berlin, Heidelberg: Springer, 2013. https://doi.org/10.1007/978-3-642-27151-9_9.

———. "Offshore Wind Energy Utilisation". In *Wind Turbines: Fundamentals, Technologies, Application, Economics*, edited by Erich Hau, 677–718. Berlin, Heidelberg: Springer, 2013. https://doi.org/10.1007/978-3-642-27151-9_17.

———. "Physical Principles of Wind Energy Conversion". In *Wind Turbines: Fundamentals, Technologies, Application, Economics*, edited by Erich Hau, 79–87. Berlin, Heidelberg: Springer, 2013. https://doi.org/10.1007/978-3-642-27151-9_4.

———. "Power Output and Energy Yield". In *Wind Turbines: Fundamentals, Technologies, Application, Economics*, edited by Erich Hau, 549–603. Berlin, Heidelberg: Springer, 2013. https://doi.org/10.1007/978-3-642-27151-9_14.

———. "Rotor Aerodynamics". In *Wind Turbines: Fundamentals, Technologies, Application, Economics*, edited by Erich Hau, 89–166. Berlin, Heidelberg: Springer, 2013. https://doi.org/10.1007/978-3-642-27151-9_5.

———. "Rotor Blades". In *Wind Turbines: Fundamentals, Technologies, Application, Economics*, edited by Erich Hau, 269–304. Berlin, Heidelberg: Springer, 2013. https://doi.org/10.1007/978-3-642-27151-9_8.

———. "The Tower". In *Wind Turbines: Fundamentals, Technologies, Application, Economics*, edited by Erich Hau, 467–503. Berlin, Heidelberg: Springer, 2013. https://doi.org/10.1007/978-3-642-27151-9_12.

———. "The Wind Resource". In *Wind Turbines: Fundamentals, Technologies, Application, Economics*, edited by Erich Hau, 505–47. Berlin, Heidelberg: Springer, 2013. https://doi.org/10.1007/978-3-642-27151-9_13.

———. "Vibration Characteristics". In *Wind Turbines: Fundamentals, Technologies, Application, Economics*, edited by Erich Hau, 233–68. Berlin, Heidelberg: Springer, 2013. https://doi.org/10.1007/978-3-642-27151-9_7.

———. "Wind Turbine Costs". In *Wind Turbines: Fundamentals, Technologies, Application, Economics*, edited by Erich Hau, 789–843. Berlin, Heidelberg: Springer, 2013. https://doi.org/10.1007/978-3-642-27151-9_19.

———. "Wind Turbine Installation and Operation". In *Wind Turbines: Fundamentals, Technologies, Application, Economics*, edited by Erich Hau, 719–87. Berlin, Heidelberg: Springer, 2013. https://doi.org/10.1007/978-3-642-27151-9_18.

———. *Wind Turbines: Fundamentals, Technologies, Application, Economics*. Berlin, Heidelberg: Springer, 2013. https://doi.org/10.1007/978-3-642-27151-9.

———. "Windmills and Windwheels". In *Wind Turbines: Fundamentals, Technologies, Application, Economics*, edited by Erich Hau, 1–21. Berlin, Heidelberg: Springer, 2013. https://doi.org/10.1007/978-3-642-27151-9_1.

Hauptstadtregion Berlin-Brandenburg. "Hauptstadtregion Berlin-Brandenburg". Accessed 4 October 2023. https://www.berlin-brandenburg.de/hauptstadtregion-berlin-brandenburg.

Hein, Carola. "Space, Time, and Oil". In *Oil Spaces: Exploring the Global Petroleumscape*, edited by Carola Hein, 1 Edition. New York; London: Routledge, Taylor & Francis Group, 2022.

Hermann, Hauke, Katja Schumacher, Hannah Förster, and Öko-Institut Berlin. "Beschäftigungsentwicklung in der Braunkohleindustrie: Status quo und Projektion". Umweltbundesamt, July 2018.

Herzberg, Heinrich, and Hans Joachim Rieseberg. *Mühlen und Müller in Berlin*. Lizenzausg. Düsseldorf: Werner, 1987.

Heymann, Matthias. "A Fight of Systems? Wind Power and Electric Power Systems in Denmark, Germany, and the USA". *Centaurus* 41, no. 1–2 (1999): 112–36. https://doi.org/10.1111/j.1600-0498.1999.tb00277.x.

———. "Signs of Hubris: The Shaping of Wind Technology Styles in Germany, Denmark, and the United States, 1940–1990". *Technology and Culture* 39, no. 4 (1998): 641–70. https://doi.org/10.2307/1215843.

Hirschl, Bernd, Torliene, Lukas, Schwarz, Uwe, Dunkelberg, Elisa, Weiss, Julika, Lenk, Clara, Hirschberg, Raoul, et al. "Gutachten zum Klimaplan Brandenburg – Zwischenbericht". Auftrag des Ministeriums für Landwirtschaft, Umwelt und Klimaschutz des Landes Brandenburg, 2021. https://mluk.brandenburg.de/sixcms/media.php/9/Zwischenbericht-Gutachten-Klimaplan-BB.pdf.

Hoffmann, Volker U. "Damals War's: Ein Rückblick auf der Photovoltaik in Deutschland". *Deutsche Gesellschaft für Sonnenenergie e. V.*, November 2008, 38–39.

Holler, Christian, Joachim Gaukel, Harald Lesch, and Florian Lesch. *Erneuerbare Energien zum Verstehen und Mitreden*. Sonderausgabe für die Bundeszentrale für Politische Bildung. Bundeszentrale für Politische Bildung. Bonn: Bundeszentrale für Politische Bildung, 2022. https://d-nb.info/1276202369/04.

Holmberg, Kenneth, Päivi Kivikytö-Reponen, Pirita Härkisaari, Kati Valtonen, and Ali Erdemir. "Global Energy Consumption Due to Friction and Wear in the Mining Industry". *Tribology International* 115 (November 2017): 116–39. https://doi.org/10.1016/j.triboint.2017.05.010.

Höök, Mikael, Ugo Bardi, Lianyong Feng, and Xiongqi Pang. "Development of Oil Formation Theories and Their Importance for Peak Oil". *Marine and Petroleum Geology* 27, no. 9 (1 October 2010): 1995–2004. https://doi.org/10.1016/j.marpetgeo.2010.06.005.

Hughes, Thomas P. "The Evolution of Large Technological Systems". In *The Social Construction of Technological Systems: New Directions in the Sociology and History of Technology*, edited by Wiebe E. Bijker, Thomas Parke Hughes, and Trevor Pinch, Anniversary ed., 45–76. Cambridge, Mass: MIT Press, 2012.

Hughes, Thomas Parke. *Networks of Power: Electrification in Western Society, 1880-1930*. Baltimore: Johns Hopkins University Press, 1983.

Hühn, Silvia. "Onshore und Offshore: Die grössten Windparks in Deutschland – ingenieur.de". ingenieur.de – Jobbörse und Nachrichtenportal für Ingenieure, 25 October 2021. https://www.ingenieur.de/technik/fachbereiche/energie/onshore-und-offshore-die-groessten-windparks-in-deutschland.

Iberdrola. “Núñez de Balboa, the Largest Photovoltaic Project in Europe”. Iberdrola, n.d. https://www.iberdrola.com/about-us/what-we-do/solar-photovoltaic-energy/francisco-pizarro-photovoltaic-plant.

Ibert, Oliver, Martin Hess, Jana Kleibert, Felix Müller, and Dominic Power. “Geographies of Dissociation: Value Creation, “Dark” Places, and “Missing” Links”. *Dialogues in Human Geography* 9, no. 1 (March 2019): 43–63. https://doi.org/10.1177/2043820619831114.

IEA. “Executive Summary – The Role of Critical Minerals in Clean Energy Transitions – Analysis”. Accessed 4 October 2023. https://www.iea.org/reports/the-role-of-critical-minerals-in-clean-energy-transitions/executive-summary.

IEA. “Global Investments in Oil and Gas Upstream in Nominal Terms and Percentage Change from Previous Year, 2010-2020 – Charts – Data & Statistics”. Accessed 11 October 2023. https://www.iea.org/data-and-statistics/charts/global-investments-in-oil-and-gas-upstream-in-nominal-terms-and-percentage-change-from-previous-year-2010-2020.

IEA. “Renewables 2021 – Analysis”, December 2021. https://www.iea.org/reports/renewables-2021.

IEA PVPS. “Trends in Photovoltaic Applications 2024”. 2024. https://doi.org/10.69766/JNEW6916

IKEM. “Region of the future: Economic potential of renewable energies in Brandenburg”, 2024. https://www.ikem.de/en/zukunftsregion-brandenburg-economic-potential-of-renewable-energies/ Invest in China. “China Economic Development Zones”, n.d. https://govt.chinadaily.com.cn/chinaedzs.

Ikonnikova, Svetlana. “Multilateral Bargaining and Strategic Investments in the Eurasian Gas Supply Network”, 2008.

Industrie- und Handelskammer Cottbus. “Konjunkturreport Lausitz”, 2022. https://www.cottbus.ihk.de/konjunkturreport-lausitz.html.

International Association of Oil Transporters. “Druzhba Pipeline”. www.simopt.cz, 2015. https://www.iaot.eu/en/oil-transport/druzhba-pipeline.

International Energy Agency. *Coal in Net Zero Transitions: Strategies for Rapid, Secure and People-Centred Change*. OECD, 2022. https://doi.org/10.1787/5873f7bb-en.

———. “Energy Technology Perspectives 2023 – Analysis”. IEA. Accessed 27 October 2023. https://www.iea.org/reports/energy-technology-perspectives-2023.

———. “Executive Summary – Kazakhstan 2022 – Analysis”. IEA, n.d. https://www.iea.org/reports/kazakhstan-2022/executive-summary.

———. “Executive Summary – Solar PV Global Supply Chains – Analysis”. IEA, n.d. https://www.iea.org/reports/solar-pv-global-supply-chains/executive-summary.

———. “Germany 2020: Energy Policy Review”, 2020. https://www.iea.org/reports/germany-2020.

———. “Global Energy and Climate Model”. IEA, Paris, 2022. https://www.iea.org/reports/global-energy-and-climate-model/net-zero-emissions-by-2050-scenario-nze.

———. “Global Energy Review 2021 – Analysis”. IEA, Paris, 2021. https://www.iea.org/reports/global-energy-review-2021.

———. “Iron and Steel Technology Roadmap – Analysis”, October 2020. https://www.iea.org/reports/iron-and-steel-technology-roadmap.

———. “Offshore Wind to Become a $1 Trillion Industry”, October 2019. https://www.iea.org/news/offshore-wind-to-become-a-1-trillion-industry.

———. “Oil 2023 Analysis and Forecast to 2028”. IEA, Paris, 2023. https://iea.blob.core.windows.net/assets/6ff5beb7-a9f9-489f-9d71-fd221b88c66e/Oil2023.pdf.

———. “Oil and Natural Gas Logistics”. IEA ETSA, 2011.

———. “Renewable Energy Sources Act (Erneuerbare-Energien-Gesetz EEG) – Policies”. IEA, 2000. https://www.iea.org/policies/3858-renewable-energy-sources-act-erneuerbare-energien-gesetz-eeg.

———. “Solar PV Global Supply Chains”, July 2022. https://www.iea.org/reports/solar-pv-global-supply-chains.

———. “Solar PV Module Shipments by Country of Origin, 2012-2019 – Charts – Data & Statistics”. IEA, n.d. https://www.iea.org/data-and-statistics/charts/solar-pv-module-shipments-by-country-of-origin-2012-2019.

———. *Sustainable Recovery: World Energy Outlook Special Report*. OECD, 2020. https://doi.org/10.1787/3f36f587-en.

———. “World Energy Outlook 2022 – Analysis”. IEA, Paris, 2022. https://www.iea.org/reports/world-energy-outlook-2022.

International Renewable Energy Agency. “Country Rankings”, n.d. https://www.irena.org/Data/View-data-by-topic/Capacity-and-Generation/Country-Rankings.

———. “Renewable Capacity Statistics 2023”, 21 March 2023. https://www.irena.org/Publications/2023/Mar/Renewable-capacity-statistics-2023.

Jacobs Wind Electric. “Beginnings | Jacobs Wind Electric”, n.d. Accessed 10 October 2023 https://www.jacobswind.net/history/beginnings.

———. “History | Jacobs Wind Electric”. Accessed 10 October 2023. https://www.jacobswind.net/history.

Jäger-Waldau, Arnulf. *PV Status Report 2007*. Institute for Environment and Sustainability, Renewable Energies Unit: Office for Official Publications of the European Communities, 2007.

Jenkins, Nicholas. *Energy Systems: A Very Short Introduction*. Oxford: Oxford University Press, 2019.

Jensen-Eriksen, Niklas. “The Cold War in Energy Markets: British Efforts to Contain Soviet Oil Exports to Non-Communist Countries, 1950–1965”. In *Le Pétrole et La Guerre – Oil and War*, edited by Alain Beltran, 191–208. Bruxelles: Peter Lang, 2012.

Johansen, Katinka. “Blowing in the Wind: A Brief History of Wind Energy and Wind Power Technologies in Denmark”. *Energy Policy* 152, 2021. https://ideas.repec.org//a/eee/enepol/v152y2021ics0301421521000082.html.

Joint Research Centre (European Commission), P. Alves Dias, C. Pavel, B. Plazzotta, and S. Carrara. *Raw Materials Demand for Wind and Solar PV Technologies in the Transition towards a Decarbonised Energy System*. LU: Publications Office of the European Union, 2020. https://data.europa.eu/doi/10.2760/160859.

Jowitt, Simon M. “Mineral Economics of the Rare-Earth Elements”. *MRS Bulletin* 47, no. 3 (1 March 2022): 276–82. https://doi.org/10.1557/s43577-022-00289-3.

Julian Wettengel. “Germany, EU Remain Heavily Dependent on Imported Fossil Fuels”. Clean Energy Wire, 10 January 2023. https://www.cleanenergywire.org/factsheets/germanys-dependence-imported-fossil-fuels.

Kaa, Geerten van de, Martijn van Ek, Linda M. Kamp, and Jafar Rezaei. “Wind Turbine Technology Battles: Gearbox versus Direct Drive – Opening up the Black Box of Technology Characteristics”. *Technological Forecasting and Social Change* 153 (1 April 2020): 119933. https://doi.org/10.1016/j.techfore.2020.119933.

Kabus, Petra. “The History of an Industrial Region”. In *Redesigning Wounded Landscape: The IBA-Workshop in Lusatia*, edited by Katja Sophia Wolf and Internationale Bauausstellung Fürst-Pückler-Land, 37–52. Berlin: Jovis-Verl, 2012.

Kahlert, Joachim. *Die Energiepolitik der DDR: Mängelverwaltung zwischen Kernkraft und Braunkohle*. Edited by Friedrich-Ebert Stiftung. Bonn: Verl. Neue Gesellschaft, 1988.

Kaiman, Jonathan. “Rare Earth Mining in China: The Bleak Social and Environmental Costs”. *The Guardian*, 20 March 2014, sec. Guardian Sustainable Business. https://www.theguardian.com/sustainable-business/rare-earth-mining-china-social-environmental-costs.

Karachaganak Petroleum Operating. “Karachaganak Export Routes”. KPOBV, n.d. https://www.kpo.kz/en/operations/export-routes.

Kardaś, Szymon and Wojciech Konończuk. “Dirty Oil: The Greatest Crisis in the History of the Druzhba Pipeline”. OSW Centre for Eastern Studies, 8 May 2019. https://www.osw.waw.pl/en/publikacje/analyses/2019-05-08/dirty-oil-greatest-crisis-history-druzhba-pipeline.

Kemmler, Andreas. “Entwicklung des Bruttostromverbrauchs bis 2030”, n.d.

Kenessaryiev, U. I., A. E. Yerzhanova, D. U. Kenessary, and A. U. Kenessary. “[Trends of change in demographic indices of population in the area of oil and gas deposits of the republic of Kazakhstan]”. *Gigiena I Sanitariia* 95, no. 10 (2016): 946–49.

Kil, Wolfgang, Gerhard Zwickert, Herbert Schirmer, and Internationale Bauausstellung Fürst-Pückler-Land, eds. *Zeitmaschine Lausitz – Werksiedlungen: Wohnform des Industriezeitalters; [im Rahmen der Internationalen Bauausstellung Fürst-Pückler-Land 2003/04 in Grossräschen]. Werksiedlungen – Wohnform des Industriezeitalters: [Internationale Bauausstellung Fürst-Pückler-Land, 2003/04 in Grossräschen]*. Dresden: Verl. der Kunst, 2003.

Klinger, Julie Michelle. “A Historical Geography of Rare Earth Elements: From Discovery to the Atomic Age”. *The Extractive Industries and Society* 2, no. 3 (1 August 2015): 572–80. https://doi.org/10.1016/j.exis.2015.05.006.

Kloos, R. “Der Wasserverkehr”. In *Berlin und seine Bauten. Teil X, Band B Anlagen und Bauten für den Verkehr ; 2, Fernverkehr*, edited by Architekten- und Ingenieur-Verein zu Berlin. Berlin: Ernst & Sohn, 1984.

Koalitionsvertrag zwischen SPD, Bündnis 90/Die Grünen & FDP. “Mehr Fortschritt wagen. Bündnis für Freiheit, Gerechtigkeit und Nachhaltigkeit”. Sozialdemokratische Partei Deutschlands (SPD), 2021. https://www.spd.de/koalitionsvertrag2021.

Kohler, E. “The History of Lime Production at Rudersdorf”. *ZKG INTERNATIONAL* 55 (1 January 2002).

Koolhaas, Rem, Irma Boom, and James Westcott. *Elements of Architecture: A Series of 15 Books Accompanying the Exhibition Elements of Architecture at the 2014 Venice Architecture Biennale. Fireplace*. Venezia: Marsilio, 2014.

Kost, Christof. “Studie zu Stromgestehungskosten: Photovoltaik und Onshore-Wind sind günstigste Technologien in Deutschland – Fraunhofer ISE”. *Fraunhofer-Institut für Solare Energiesysteme ISE* (blog), 20 March 2018. https://www.ise.fraunhofer.de/de/presse-und-medien/presseinformationen/2018/studie-zu-stromgestehungskosten-photovoltaik-und-onshore-wind-sind-guenstigste-technologien-in-deutschland.html.

Köstering, S., and A. Schleicher. “Berlins ist keine Hafenstadt. Kleinschiffahrt 1850–1920”. In *Landgang in Berlin: Stadtgeschichte an Landwehrkanal u. Spree*, edited by C. Carsten. Berliner Geschichtswerkstatt: Berliner Geschichtswerkstatt. Berlin: Nishen, 1987.

Kozhushkevich, A., V.V. Ovcharenko, A. Kalantaenko, K. Turbabina, A. Lebedev, and Alexander Komarov. "Temporal Dynamics of Dioxin Contamination of Reindeer Offal from Russian Far North Regions". *IOP Conference Series: Earth and Environmental Science* 263 (13 May 2019). https://doi.org/10.1088/1755-1315/263/1/012053.

KPO Karatschaganak. "Operations and Development Projects – KPO Sustainability Report 2021". Accessed 22 October 2023. https://www.kpo.kz/docs/sustainability_report_2022/en/005-proizvodstvo_proekty_razvitiya.php.

Krause, Florentin, Hartmut Bossel, and Karl-Friedrich Müller-Reißmann. *Energie-Wende Wachstum und Wohlstand ohne Erdöl und Uran; ein Alternativ-Bericht des Öko-Instituts, Freiburg*. 2. Aufl. Frankfurt am Main: Fischer, 1980.

Kryukova, E. M., E. A. Vetrova, A. N. Maloletko, O. V. Kaurova, and S. V. Dusenko. "Social-Economic Problems of Russian Mono-Towns". *Asian Social Science* 11, no. 1 (2 December 2014): 258. https://doi.org/10.5539/ass.v11n1p258.

Kuuskraa, Vello. "Natural Gas Resources, Unconventional". In *Encyclopedia of Energy*, edited by Cutler J. Cleveland and Robert U. Ayres, 4:257–72. Amsterdam Boston: Elsevier Academic Press, 2004.

Kyllmann, Carolina. "Berlin Could Use Disused Airfields for Wind Turbines, Says State Govt Official". Clean Energy Wire, 21 August 2023.

Landesbetrieb für Datenverarbeitung und Statistik Brandenburg. "Historisches Gemeindeverzeichnis 1875–2005", December 2006. https://download.statistik-berlin-brandenburg.de/4438563dcbb21294/dbc9bf84f9f6/SB_A01-99-01_2006u00_BB.pdf.

Landesvermessung und Geoinformation Brandenburg. "Luftbilder Historisch". Accessed 3 October 2023. https://geobasis-bb.de/lgb/de/geodaten/luftbilder/luftbilder-historisch.

Laudel, Katja. "Der Typenwandel des ländlichen Wohnhauses im Oderbruch zwischen 1753 und 1850 – Der Einfluss von Friderizianischer Kolonisation und Preussischer Obrigkeit auf die Hausformen der ländlichen Untertanen". Bauhaus-Universität Weimar, 2005. https://doi.org/10.25643/bauhaus-universitaet.634.

Lausitz Energie Bergbau AG. "Tagebau Lausitz | Geschäftsfeld Bergbau | LEAG". Accessed 28 September 2023. https://www.leag.de/de/geschaeftsfelder/bergbau.

Lausitzer und Mitteldeutsche Bergbau-Verwaltungsgesellschaft mbH. "Werkbahnen im Lausitzer Braunkohlenbergbau". LMBV: Senftenberg, 2014. https://www.lmbv.de/wp-content/uploads/2021/04/doku-25_Werkbahnen_Bergbau_Lausitz.pdf.

———. "Wassermanagement –LMBV", 5 March 2021. https://www.lmbv.de/aufgaben/wassermanagement.

LBEG. *Erdöl Und Erdgas in Der Bundesrepublik Deutschland 2021*. Geobericht 49. Landesamt für Bergbau, Energie und Geologie, 2022. https://www.lbeg.niedersachsen.de/erdoel-erdgas-jahresbericht/jahresbericht-erdoel-und-erdgas-in-der-bundesrepublik-deutschland-936.html.

LEAG. "Letzte Lausitzer Kohle für Kraftwerk Klingenberg in Berlin", 11 May 2017. https://www.leag.de/de/news/details/letzte-lausitzer-kohle-fuer-klingenberg-in-berlin.

LePan, Nicholas. "Rare Earth Elements: Where in the World Are They?" Visual Capitalist, 23 November 2021. https://www.visualcapitalist.com/rare-earth-elements-where-in-the-world-are-they.

Levi, Isaac. "2023 – Monthly Analysis on Russian Fossil Fuel Exports and Sanctions". Centre for Research on Energy and Clean Air, 22 August 2023. https://energyandcleanair.org/july-2023-monthly-snapshot-on-russian-fossil-fuel-exports-and-sanctions.

Lewis, Simon L., and Mark Maslin. *The Human Planet: How We Created the Anthropocene*. New Haven; London: Yale University Press, 2018.

Library of Congress, Washington, D.C. 20540 USA. "China: Renewable Energy Law Amended". Web page, n.d. https://www.loc.gov/item/global-legal-monitor/2009-12-31/china-renewable-energy-law-amended.

Lien, L. "Advances in Coal Mining Technology". In *The Coal Handbook: Towards Cleaner Production*, 193–225. Elsevier, 2013. https://doi.org/10.1533/9780857097309.2.193.

Lintz, Gerd, and Peter Wirth. "Sanierung Alter Industrieregionen in Ostdeutschland". In *Regionalentwicklung in Ostdeutschland: Dynamiken, Perspektiven und der Beitrag der Humangeographie*, edited by Sören Becker and Matthias Naumann, 467–80. Berlin, Heidelberg: Springer Berlin Heidelberg, 2020. https://doi.org/10.1007/978-3-662-60901-9_36.

London Online. "London Population". Accessed 10 October 2023. https://www.londononline.co.uk/factfile/historical.

Lübbers, Sebastian, Marco Wünsch, Miriam Lovis, Johannes Wagner, Frank Sensfuss, Gunnar Luderer, and Frederike Bartels. "Vergleich der 'Big 5' Klimaneutralitätsszenarien". *Energiewirtschaftliches Institut an der Universität zu Köln (EWI)*, April 2022. https://www.ewi.uni-koeln.de/de/publikationen/vergleich-big-5.

Luczak, Andreas. *Forschungbericht zum Energiesystem x.0 – Nr. 1: Intelligente und effiziente Vernetzung von Energieerzeugern und -verbrauchern auf Quartiersebene*. Edited by Dr Jan-Hendrik Meier, Dr Stephan Schneider, Holm Voss, Anna-Katharina Dhungel, and Fachhochschule Kiel. Gesellschaft für Energie und Klimaschutz Schleswig-Holstein GmbH, 2021.

Mabuni, Brandt. "Breaking China's Rare Earths Monopoly". *Asia Times*, 15 March 2023. http://asiatimes.com/2023/03/breaking-chinas-rare-earths-monopoly.

Mallison, Richard. "Natural Gas Processing, and Products". Edited by Cutler J. Cleveland and Robert U. Ayres, 4:235–47. Encyclopedia of Energy. Amsterdam Boston: Elsevier Academic Press, 2004.

Malvadkar, Shreekant B., Sarah Forbes, and Gilbert V. Mcgurl. "Coal Resources, Formation Of". In *Encyclopedia of Energy*, edited by Cutler J. Cleveland and Robert U. Ayres, Volume 4:529–50. Amsterdam Boston: Elsevier Academic Press, 2004.

Marot, Sebastien. "Fireplace". In *Elements of Architecture: A Series of 15 Books Accompanying the Exhibition Elements of Architecture at the 2014 Venice Architecture Biennale*, by Rem Koolhaas and Irma Boom, 156. Venezia: Marsilio, 2014.

Maughan, Tim. "The Dystopian Lake Filled by the World's Tech Lust". BBC, n.d. https://www.bbc.com/future/article/20150402-the-worst-place-on-earth.

McCabe, Kirsty. "What Is Wind? | Royal Meteorological Society", January 2023. https://www.rmets.org/metmatters/what-wind.

McGhee, George R. *Carboniferous Giants and Mass Extinction: The Late Paleozoic Ice Age World*. New York: Columbia University Press, 2018.

McKinnon, Kendall. "Le Mistral: The Wind of Provence". France Today, 17 May 2021. https://francetoday.com/culture/le-mistral-the-wind-of-provence.

McPhee, John. *Basin and Range*. In Annals of the Former World, edited by William Shawn and Robert Gottlieb, Volume 1:23-219. New York: Farrar, Straus and Giroux, 1998.

McWilliams, Ben, Georg Zachmann, and Giovanni Sgaravatti. "European Natural Gas Imports". Bruegel | The Brussels-based economic think tank, 18 September 2023. https://www.bruegel.org/dataset/european-natural-gas-imports.

Meadows, Donella H. *The Limits to Growth: A Report for the Club of Rome's Project on the Predicament of Mankind*. New York: University Books, 1972.

Meeschaert, A.M. "Rare Metal Supply Chains: Challenges for a Sustainable Energy Transition", 2019. https://www.shareholdersforchange.eu/wp-content/uploads/2019/07/2019-07-SFC-Rare-metals-report.pdf.

Miller, D. R. *Wind Turbine Structural Dynamics*. NASA Lewis Research Center, 1978. https://ntrs.nasa.gov/citations/19780011673.

Mineralölverbundleitung GmbH Schwedt. "Geschichte: Mineralölverbundleitung GmbH Schwedt", n.d. https://www.mvl-schwedt.de/ueber-uns/geschichte.

Ministerium für Infrastruktur und and Landwirtschaft des Landes Brandenburg. "Facts on Forests and Forestry in Brandenburg". MIL, 2013. https://mluk.brandenburg.de/sixcms/media.php/9/Daten-Forst.pdf.

Ministerium für Umwelt, Klima und Energiewirtschaft Baden-Württemberg. "Verordnung des Umweltministeriums zu den Pflichten zur Installation von Photovoltaikanlagen auf Dach- und Parkplatzflächen", 2021. https://um.baden-wuerttemberg.de/fileadmin/redaktion/m-um/intern/Dateien/Dokumente/4_Klima/Klimaschutz/Klimaschutzgesetz/Photovoltaikpflicht-Verordnung-Baden-Wuerttemberg-barrierefrei.pdf.

Ministerium für Wirtschaft, Arbeit und Energie. "Energiestrategie 2040". Land Brandenburg, 2022. https://mwae.brandenburg.de/media/bb1.a.3814.de/Energiestrategie2040.pdf.

Ministerium für Wirtschaft, Arbeit und Energie Brandenburg. "Energie Strategie 2040", n.d. https://mwae.brandenburg.de/media/bb1.a.3814.de/Energiestrategie2040.pdf.

———. "Ergebnisse der Potenzialanalyse über nutzbare Flächen für solartechnische Anlagen im Land Brandenburg", March 2022. https://energieportal-brandenburg.de/cms/fileadmin/medien/dokumente/solaratlas/abschlussbericht_solarpotenzialanalyse_endfassung.pdf.

Ministerium für Wirtschaft, Arbeit und Energie des Landes Brandenburg. "Windenergie". Ministerium für Wirtschaft, Arbeit und Energie (MWE), n.d. http://brandenburg.de/de/bb1.c.478387.de.

Ministerium für Wirtschaft, Arbeit und Energie (MWE). "Fünf Millionen Euro Förderung für Batteriespeicher in Feldheim", n.d. http://brandenburg.de/de/bb1.c.372166.de.

Ministry of Economy, Trade, and Industry. "Signing of the Japan–U.S. Critical Minerals Agreement (CMA)", n.d. https://www.meti.go.jp/english/press/2023/0328_001.html.

MIT Technology Review. "China Just Fought Back in the Semiconductor Exports War. Here's What You Need to Know". Accessed 4 October 2023. https://www.technologyreview.com/2023/07/10/1076025/china-export-control-semiconductor-material.

Mitchell, Timothy. *Carbon Democracy: Political Power in the Age of Oil*. London: Verso, 2013.

Moomy, Ruthann. "China's Public Policies toward Rare Earths, 1975–2018". *Mineral Economics: Raw Materials Report* 33, no. 1 (2020): 127–51.

Morita, Penelope Harvey, Casper Jensen, Atsuro, ed. *Infrastructures and Social Complexity: A Companion*. London: Routledge, 2016. https://doi.org/10.4324/9781315622880.

Moss, Timothy. *Remaking Berlin: A History of the City through Infrastructure, 1920–2020*. Infrastructures Series. Cambridge, Massachusetts; London, England: The MIT Press, 2020.

Mühlen und Müller in Berlin: ein Beitrag zur Geschichte der Produktivkräfte. Berlin: VEB Verlag für Bauwesen, 1986.
Müller, Adriaan von. *Museumsdorf Düppel: lebendiges Mittelalter in Berlin*. 4., Überarb. Aufl. Berliner Sehenswürdigkeiten BV000010455 2. Berlin: Haude und Spener, 1986.
Müller, Winfried, and Swen Steinberg. “Region Im Wandel: Eine Kurze Geschichte Der Lausitz (En)”. *Aus Politik und Zeitgeschichte: APuZ / Bundeszentrale für Politische Bildung* 70, no. 6 (2020): 15–22.
Mumford, Lewis. *Technics and Civilization*. University of Chicago Press ed. Chicago, Ill.: The University of Chicago Press, 2010.
———. *The City in History*. [1st ed.]. Power and Morality Collection at Harvard Business School. New York: Harcourt, Brace & World, 1961.
Municipality of Suqian. “Suqian High-Tech Industrial Development Zone”, n.d. http://www.sqgxq.cn.
Museumspark Rüdersdorf. “Industriegeschichte hautnah”. https://www.museumspark.de/industriegeschichte. Accessed 25 September 2023. https://www.museumspark.de/industriegeschichte.
National Geographic Society. “Wind”. National Geographic, n.d. https://education.nationalgeographic.org/resource/wind.
National Renewable Energy Laboratory. “Champion Photovoltaic Module Efficiency Chart”. nrel, n.d. https://www.nrel.gov/pv/module-efficiency.html.
Nato. “The Druzhba or ‘Friendship Pipeline”, Ministry of Foreign Affairs Bulgaria, 1973. https://www.mfa.bg/upload/77157/AC_127-D_443_ENG_NHQL11897.pdf
Nature. “The Global Fight for Critical Minerals Is Costly and Damaging”, 19 July 2023. https://www.nature.com/articles/d41586-023-02330-0.
Natzschka, Werner. *Berlin und seine Wasserstrassen*. Berlin: Duncker & Humblot, 1971.
Nengyuanjie. “History of Photovoltaic Development in China – Energy Industry”, January 2020. http://www.nengyuanjie.net/article/33815.html.
NES Fircroft. “The Biggest Wind Turbines in The World”, 21 December 2021. https://www.nesfircroft.com/resources/blog/the-biggest-wind-turbines-in-the-world.
Nesbit, Jeffrey S. and Waldheim, Charles. *Technical Lands a Critical*. Berlin: Jovis, 2022.
Neue Energien Forum Feldheim. “The Energy Self-Sufficient Village”, n.d. https://nef-feldheim.info/the-energy-self-sufficient-village/?lang=en.
Newell, Elizabeth A., Stephanie Hanus, Stevie Monteiro, Destiny Harbison, and James McTighe. “Film Review: Plastic Paradise: The Great Pacific Garbage Patch”. *Teaching Sociology* 48, no. 3 (1 July 2020): 259–61. https://doi.org/10.1177/0092055X20931523.
Niagara Park. “Niagara Falls Facts | Geology Facts & Figures”, 6 November 2021. https://www.niagaraparks.com/visit-niagara-parks/plan-your-visit/niagara-falls-geology-facts-figures.
Nord Stream AG. “Die Pipeline”. Nord Stream AG. Accessed 25 September 2023. https://www.nord-stream.com/de/das-projekt/die-pipeline.
Norgren, Alex, Alberta Carpenter, and Garvin Heath. “Design for Recycling Principles Applicable to Selected Clean Energy Technologies: Crystalline-Silicon Photovoltaic Modules, Electric Vehicle Batteries, and Wind Turbine Blades”. *Journal of Sustainable Metallurgy* 6, no. 4 (1 December 2020): 761–74. https://doi.org/10.1007/s40831-020-00313-3.
Norwegianpetroleum.no. “Norway’s Petroleum History”. Accessed 11 October 2023. https://www.norskpetroleum.no/en/framework/norways-petroleum-history.
Notebaart, J. C. *Windmühlen. Der Stand der Forschung über das Vorkommen und den Ursprung [von] Jannis C. Notebaart*, 1972.
NS Energy. “Bayan Obo Rare Earth Mine, Inner Mongolia, China”, n.d. https://www.nsenergybusiness.com/projects/bayan-obo-rare-earth-mine/#.
Oberhollenzer, Ines. “Öffentliche Elektrizitätsversorgung”. In *Elektropolis Berlin: Architektur- und Denkmalführer*, edited by Thorsten Dame and Jörg Haspel. Petersberg: Imhof, 2014.
O’Carroll, Lisa, and Sam Jones. “EU Imports of Russian Liquified Gas Leap by 40% since Ukraine Invasion”. *The Guardian*, 30 August 2023, sec. Business. https://www.theguardian.com/business/2023/aug/30/eu-imports-of-russian-liquified-gas-leap-by-40-since-ukraine-invasion.
Office of Nuclear Energy. “INFOGRAPHIC: How Much Power Does a Nuclear Reactor Produce?” Energy.gov, n.d. https://www.energy.gov/ne/articles/infographic-how-much-power-does-nuclear-reactor-produce.
Öko-Institut. “Die Deutsche Braunkohlen Wirtschaft. Historische Entwicklungen, Ressourcen, Technik, Wirtschaftliche Strukturen und Umweltauswirkungen. Studie im Auftrag von Agora Energiewende und der European Climate Foundation.”, 2017.
O’Rourke, Dara, and Sarah Connolly. “Just Oil? The Distribution of Environmental and Social Impacts of Oil Production and Consumption”. *Annual Review of Environment and Resources* 28, no. 1 (November 2003): 587–617. https://doi.org/10.1146/annurev.energy.28.050302.105617.
Oswald, B.R. “Vorlesung Elektrische Energieversorgung – Vorlesungsskript”. Universität Hannover Institut für Energieversorgung und Hochspannungstechnik, 2005. https://www.repo.uni-hannover.de/bitstream/handle/123456789/9971/Oswald_2005_Skript_Elektrische_Energieversorgung.pdf?sequence=10.
Oudes, D., A. Van Den Brink, and S. Stremke. “Towards a Typology of Solar Energy Landscapes: Mixed-Production, Nature Based and Landscape Inclusive Solar Power Transitions”. *Energy Research & Social Science* 91 (September 2022): 102742. https://doi.org/10.1016/j.erss.2022.102742.
Our World in Data. “Solar (Photovoltaic) Panel Prices”, n.d. https://ourworldindata.org/grapher/solar-pv-prices.
Pandey, Ashutosh. “Germany: How Does Its Kazakh Oil Deal Benefit Russia?” dw.com, January 2023. https://www.dw.com/en/germany-how-does-its-kazakh-oil-deal-benefit-russia/a-64849621.
Patel, Raj, and Jason W. Moore. *A History of the World in Seven Cheap Things: A Guide to Capitalism, Nature, and the Future of the Planet*, 2018.
Paul, Anton Dilo. “Coal, Fuel and Non-Fuel Uses”. In *Encyclopedia of Energy*, edited by Cutler J. Cleveland and Robert U. Ayres, 435–44. Amsterdam Boston: Elsevier, 2004. https://doi.org/10.1016/B0-12-176480-X/00290-4.
Pawley, Martin. *Theory and Design in the Second Machine Age*. Oxford: Blackwell, 1990.
PCK. “Fuel For the Region: Top Refineries in Europe”, n.d. https://www.pck.de/en.
PCK Schwedt. “PCK – Wir bewegen Berlin und Brandenburg!”, 17 October 2023. https://www.pck.de.
Penke, Michel. “The Toxic Damage from Mining Rare Elements”. dw.com, 13 April 2021. https://www.dw.com/en/toxic-and-radioactive-the-damage-from-mining-rare-elements/a-57148185.
Perović, Jeronim, ed. *Cold War Energy: A Transnational History of Soviet Oil and Gas*. Cham: Springer International Publishing, 2017. https://doi.org/10.1007/978-3-319-49532-3_1.
———, ed. “Creating a Common Energy Space: The Building of the Druzhba Oil Pipeline”. In *Cold War Energy: A Transnational History of Soviet Oil and Gas*, 323–33. Champaign, Ill.: Springer International Publishing, 2017. https://doi.org/10.1007/978-3-319-49532-3_1.
———. “The Soviet Union’s Rise as an International Energy Power: A Short History”. In *Cold War Energy*, edited by Jeronim Perović, 1–43. Champaign, Ill.: Springer International Publishing, 2017. https://doi.org/10.1007/978-3-319-49532-3_1.
Peters, Deike. “Rail City Berlin: Rail Infrastructure Development and Intermodality in the Reunified German Capital”. *Transportation Research Record: Journal of the Transportation Research Board* 2146, no. 1 (January 2010): 60–68. https://doi.org/10.3141/2146-08.
Pintos, Paula. “Berlin Brandenburg Airport Willy Brandt / Gmp”. ArchDaily, 31 October 2020. https://www.archdaily.com/950522/berlin-brandenburg-airport-willy-brandt-gmp.
Pipelines International. “Druzhba Pipeline”. *The international pipeline magazine*, 27 September 2009. https://web.archive.org/web/20090927135650/http://pipelinesinternational.com/news/druzhba_pipeline/008045.
Porsch, A.R., and W. Schossig. *Die Wiedervereinigung der Netze in Europa, Deutschland und Thüringen (Strom, Bahn, Gas und Telekommunikation)*. Erfurt: TEAG, 2021.
Power Technology. “XXL (Weesow-Willmersdorf) Solar Park, Brandenburg, Germany”, October 2020. https://www.power-technology.com/projects/xxl-weesow-willmersdorf-solar-park.
Pressestelle, Stadt Schwedt/Oder-. “Stadtgeschichte: Stadt Schwedt/Oder”. schwedt.eu, 30 December 2022. https://www.schwedt.eu/de/25004.
———. “Übernahme von PCK-Anteilen durch Rosneft | Stadt Schwedt/Oder”, 30 December 2022. https://www.schwedt.eu/de/29926.
Priebs, Axel. *Stadt-Umland- Beziehungen*. Hannover: Akademie für Raumforschung und Landesplanung, 2018. https://www.arl-net.de/system/files/media-shop/pdf/HWB%202018/Stadt-Umland-Beziehungen.pdf.
Priest, Tyler. “Hubbert’s Peak: The Great Debate over the End of Oil”. *Historical Studies in the Natural Sciences* 44 (1 February 2014): 37–79. https://doi.org/10.1525/hsns.2014.44.1.37.
Prognos Institut, Öko-Institut, and Wuppertal-Institut. “Klimaneutrales Deutschland 2045 Wie Deutschland seine Klimaziele schon vor 2050 erreichen kann, Zusammenfassung”. Agora Energiewende, 14 June 2021. https://static.agora-energiewende.de/fileadmin/Projekte/2021/2021_04_KNDE45/A-EW_209_KNDE2045_Zusammenfassung_DE_WEB.pdf.
Pyrek, Cathy. *Review of Plastic Paradise: The Great Pacific Garbage Patch [Documentary]*, 2016. http://hdl.handle.net/10125/43735.
Rabe, Wiebke, Genia Kostka, and Karen Smith Stegen. “China’s Supply of Critical Raw Materials: Risks for Europe’s Solar and Wind Industries?” *Energy Policy* 101 (1 February 2017): 692–99. https://doi.org/10.1016/j.enpol.2016.09.019.
Radkau, Joachim. “Wood and Forestry in German History: In Quest of an Environmental Approach”. *Environment and History* 2, no. 1 (1 February 1996): 63–76. https://doi.org/10.3197/096734096779522482.
rbb. “Politik und PCK-Management optimistisch über Zukunft der Raffinerie”, 5 May 2023. https://www.rbb24.de/studiofrankfurt/wirtschaft/2023/05/pck-raffinerie-politik-management-optimistisch-zukunft.html.

Renewables Now. "Trina Solar Starts N-Type Cell Production at 8-GW Factory in China", January 2023. https://renewablesnow.com/news/trina-solar-starts-n-type-cell-production-at-8-gw-factory-in-china-810718.

Research Institute for Sustainability. "Sustainability in Brandenburg", 16 November 2023. https://www.rifs-potsdam.de/en/output/dossiers/sustainability-in-brandenburg.

Reuters. "Eastbound Yamal-Europe Gas Pipeline Flows Drop". *Reuters*, 1 September 2022, sec. Energy. https://www.reuters.com/business/energy/eastbound-yamal-europe-gas-pipeline-flows-drop-2022-09-01.

———. "The Druzhba Oil Pipeline from Russia to Europe", n.d. https://www.reuters.com/business/energy/druzhba-oil-pipeline-russia-europe-2022-10-12.

Rhodes, Richard. *Energy: A Human History*. First Simon & Schuster trade paperback edition. New York: Simon & Schuster Paperbacks, 2019.

Ritchie, Hannah, and Max Roser. "Sector by Sector: Where Do Global Greenhouse Gas Emissions Come From?" *Our World in Data*, 27 September 2023. https://ourworldindata.org/ghg-emissions-by-sector.

———. "What Are the Safest and Cleanest Sources of Energy?" *Our World in Data*, 1 September 2023. https://ourworldindata.org/safest-sources-of-energy.

Ritchie, Hannah, Max Roser, and Pablo Rosado. "Energy". *Our World in Data*, 27 October 2022. https://ourworldindata.org/electricity-mix.

Rittel, Horst W. J., and Melvin M. Webber. "Dilemmas in a General Theory of Planning". *Policy Sciences* 4, no. 2 (1 June 1973): 155–69. https://doi.org/10.1007/BF01405730.

Robinson, Kim Stanley. *The Ministry for the Future*. First paperback edition. New York, NY: Orbit, 2021.

Robotics, IFR International Federation of. "IFR Presents World Robotics 2021 Reports". IFR International Federation of Robotics, n.d. https://ifr.org/ifr-press-releases/news/robot-sales-rise-again.

Röck, Sabine, and Hilmar Bärthel. *Berlin und seine Bauten. 10, A,2, Teil X, Bd. A Anlagen und Bauten für Versorgung; Teil 2, Stadttechnik*, 2006.

Roesler, Sascha. *City, Climate, and Architecture: A Theory of Collective Practice*. KLIMA POLIS, vol. 1. Basel: Birkhäuser, 2022.

Rosenberg, Joel. *Electrify Everything in Your Home – A Guide to Comfy, Healthy, Carbon-Free Living*. Rewiring America, 2021. https://www.rewiringamerica.org/electrify-home-guide.

Schissler, Andrew P. "Coal Mining, Design and Methods Of". In *Encyclopedia of Energy*, edited by Cutler J. Cleveland and Robert U. Ayres, 4:485–94. Amsterdam Boston: Elsevier Academic Press, 2004.

Schott, Dieter. "Energizing European Cities: From Wood Provision to Solar Panels: Providing Energy for Urban Demand, 1800–2000". In *Urbanizing Nature: Actors and Agency (Dis)Connecting Cities and Nature Since 1500*, edited by Tim Soens, Michael Toyka-Seid, and Bert De Munck, 1st ed., 135–56. New York: Taylor & Francis, 2018; Routledge, 2019. https://doi.org/10.4324/9780429024726.

Schulz, Sabrina, and Julian Schwartzkopff. "Europäische Braunkohleregionen im Wandel". Heinrich-Böll-Stiftung, 2018.

Schwalbe, Daria. *The Yamal LNG Project and the Nenets Reindeer Nomads. Impacts, Survival and Indigenous Opposition to Gas Exploitation in Russia's Arctic*. Köln: GegenStrömung – CounterCurrent c/o Institut für Ökologie und Aktions-Ethnologie (INFOE) e. V., 2017.

Schwarz, Gabriele. *Die Ländlichen Siedlungen, die zwischen Land und Stadt stehenden Siedlungen*. Edited by Erich Obst and Josef Schmithüsen. 4th ed. Berlin: de Gruyter, 1989. http://www.gbv.de/dms/ilmenau/toc/124617492.PDF.

Senatsverwaltung für Mobilität, Verkehr, Klimaschutz und Umwelt. "Bericht Zur Umsetzung Des Berliner Energie- und Klimaschutzprogramms (BEK 2030) – Berichtjahr 2022". SenMVKU, January 2023. https://www.berlin.de/sen/uvk.

Senatsverwaltung für Umwelt, Verkehr und Klimaschutz. "Berliner Energie- und Klimaschutzprogramm 2030 Umsetzungskonzept Für Den Zeitraum Bis 2021". SenUVK, 2023.

Senatsverwaltung für Wirtschaft, Energie und Betriebe. "Berlin – Länderbericht zum Stand des Ausbaus der Erneuerbaren Energien sowie zu Flächen, Planungen und Genehmigungen für die Windenergienutzung an Land". BMWK, 31 May 2022.

———. "Masterplan Solarcity Berlin Monitoringbericht 2022". Sen WEB, 05.23. https://www.solarwende-berlin.de.

———. "Voller Energie zur solaren Stadt: Infobroschüre zum Masterplan Solarcity Berlin", April 2021.

Senatsverwaltung für Wirtschaft, Energie und Betriebe Berlin. "Voller Energie zur solaren Stadt: Infobroschüre zum Masterplan Solarcity Berlin", April 2021. https://www.solarwende-berlin.de/fileadmin/user_upload/Solarwende/Grafiken_Contentseiten/0_Material_extern_fuer_upload/Infobroschu__re_Solarcity_RZ_deutsch_digital.pdf.

Senatsverwaltung Umwelt, Mobilität, Verbraucher- und Klimaschutz. "Monitoringbericht zur Umsetzung des Berliner Energie- und Klimaschutzprogramms", February 2022. file:///Users/jsmithard/Downloads/broschuere_bek_monitoring-2021.pdf.

Serpell, Oscar, Benjamin Paren and Wan-Yi Chu. "Rare Earth Elements: A Resource Constraint of the Energy Transition". *Kleinman Center For Energy Policy*, May 2021. https://kleinmanenergy.upenn.edu/wp-content/uploads/2021/05/KCEP-Rare-Earth-Elements.pdf.

Shanbr, S, Elasha, F, Elforjani, M, and Teixeira, J.A. "Bearing Fault Detection within Wind Turbine Gearbox | IEEE Conference Publication | IEEE Xplore". In *Institue of El*, 565–70. Shanghai, China, 2017. https://ieeexplore.ieee.org/document/8186568.

Shaw, Scott Richard. *Planet of the Bugs: Evolution and the Rise of Insects*. Chicago, IL: University of Chicago Press, 2015.

Sieferle, Rolf Peter. *The Subterranean Forest: Energy Systems and the Industrial Revolution*. Cambridge: White Horse Press, 2001.

Smil, Vaclav. *Grand Transitions: How the Modern World Was Made*. New York, NY: Oxford University Press, 2021.

———. *How the World Really Works: A Scientist's Guide to Our Past, Present and Future*. Gurugram: Penguin Random House India, 2023.

Sobek, Werner. "The Term 'Renewable' Energy Is Misleading", 21 July 2022. https://www.wernersobek.com/news/renewable-energy-is-a-misleading-term.

Sonnberger, Marco, and Michael Ruddat. "Die gesellschaftliche Wahrnehmung der Energiewende: Ergebnisse einer deutschlandweiten Repräsentativbefragung". workingPaper. Stuttgart: Institut für Sozialwissenschaften, Abt. für Technik- und Umweltsoziologie, Universität Stuttgart, 2016. https://doi.org/10.18419/opus-8894.

Sørensen, Bent Erik. "History of, and Recent Progress in Wind-Energy Utilization". *Annual Review of Energy and the Environment*, 1995. https://www.annualreviews.org/doi/pdf/10.1146/annurev.eg.20.110195.002131.

S&P Global Commodity Insights, and International Energy Forum. "Upstream Oil and Gas Investment Outlook". IEF, February 2023.

Square Yards. "Bhadla Solar Park: Overview of Largest Solar Park in the World", August 2022. https://www.squareyards.com/blog/bhadla-solar-park-gvi.

Stadtwerke Schwedt. "10 Jahre Regionaler Wachstumskern Schwedt/Oder: Die Erfolgsgeschichte Einer Stabilen Wirtschaftsregion Mit Guter Infrastruktur", n.d. https://www.schwedt.eu/media_fast/4/SCH-Broschuere-10-Jahre_final-Mail.pdf.

Standaert, Michael. "China Wrestles with the Toxic Aftermath of Rare Earth Mining". Yale E360, 2 July 2019. https://e360.yale.edu/features/china-wrestles-with-the-toxic-aftermath-of-rare-earth-mining.

Statista. "Crude Oil: Largest Refineries by Capacity Germany 2020". Statista, n.d. https://www.statista.com/statistics/1330217/largest-crude-oil-refineries-by-refined-volume-germany.

———. "Electric Vehicle Market Share in Germany", 2023. https://www.statista.com/statistics/1166826/electric-vehicles-market-share-germany.

Statista. "German Crude Oil Imports from Kazakhstan Monthly 2023". Accessed 16 October 2023. https://www.statista.com/statistics/1368372/german-oil-imports-from-kazakhstan.

———. "Germany: Fossil Fuel Power Capacity in Reserve", n.d. https://www.statista.com/statistics/1322352/fossil-fuel-power-capacity-in-reserve-in-germany.

———. "Global Silicon Production 2022", 2023. https://www.statista.com/statistics/573585/global-silicon-production.

———. "Regional Distribution of Solar Module Production". Statista, October 2022. https://www.statista.com/statistics/668749/regional-distribution-of-solar-pv-module-manufacturing.

———. "Silicon: Leading Producing Countries Ranking 2022". Statista, n.d. https://www.statista.com/statistics/268108/world-silicon-production-by-country.

Statistik der Kohlewirtschaft e. V. "Ausfuhr von Braunkohle nach Empfängerländern ab 1979", March 2023. https://kohlenstatistik.de/downloads/braunkohle.

———. "Beschäftigte nach Revieren ab 1929", 2022. https://kohlenstatistik.de/downloads/braunkohle.

———. "Braunkohleförderung Deutschland gesamt, ab 1840, nach Revieren ab 1930", 2022. https://kohlenstatistik.de/downloads/braunkohle.

Statistisches Bundesamt. "2,2 Millionen Photovoltaik-Anlagen in Deutschland installiert". Accessed 4 October 2023. https://www.destatis.de/DE/Presse/Pressemitteilungen/2022/06/PD22_N037_43.html.

Statistisches Bundesamt. "87 % der importierten Photovoltaikanlagen kamen im Jahr 2022 aus China", n.d. https://www.destatis.de/DE/Presse/Pressemitteilungen/2023/03/PD23_N012_43.html.

Steenkampskraal Rare Earths Mine. "The History of Rare Earths | Steenkampskraal Rare Earth Mine", 3 May 2016. https://www.steenkampskraal.com/rare-earths-history.

Steffen, Will, Wendy Broadgate, Lisa Deutsch, Owen Gaffney, and Cornelia Ludwig. "The Trajectory of the Anthropocene: The Great Acceleration". *The Anthropocene Review* 2, no. 1 (2015): 81–98. https://doi.org/10.1177/2053019614564785.

Steinhuber, Uwe. "Einhundert Jahre bergbauliche Rekultivierung in der Lausitz. Ein historischer Abriss der Rekultivierung, Wiederurbarmachung und Sanierung im Lausitzer Braunkohlenrevier". Philosophische Fakultät der Palacký-Universität Olomouc, 2005.

Sterchele, Philip, Julian Brandes, Judith Heilig, Daniel Wrede, Christoph Kost, Thomas Schlegl, Andreas Bett, and Hans-Martin Henning. *Studie: Wege zu einem klimaneutralen Energiesystem – Die deutsche Energiewende im Kontext gesellschaftlicher Verhaltensweisen*. Freiburg: Fraunhofer-Institut für Solare Energiesysteme ISE, 2020. https://www.ise.fraunhofer.de/content/dam/ise/de/documents/publications/studies/Fraunhofer-ISE-Studie-Wege-zu-einem-klimaneutralen-Energiesystem.pdf.

Steyer, Claus-Dieter. "Brandenburg: Hohlräume – so gross wie der Fernsehturm in Rüdersdorf beginnt der Bau riesiger unterirdischer Gasspeicher". *Der Tagesspiegel Online*, 24 March 2004. https://www.tagesspiegel.de/potsdam/brandenburg/hohlraume-so-gross-wie-der-fernsehturm-in-rudersdorf-beginnt-der-bau-riesiger-unterirdischer-gasspeicher-1103884.html.

Stierand, Rainer. "Transformationsprozesse in der Lausitzer Braunkohleregion". In *Räumliche Auswirkungen des Transformationsprozesses in Deutschland und bei den östlichen Nachbarn*, edited by Jiří Musil and Wendelin Strubelt. KSPW Transformationsprozesse, Bd. 25. Opladen: Leske + Budrich, 1997.

Stiftung – Das Deutsches Historisches Museum. "Gerade auf LeMO gesehen: LeMO Zeitzeuge". Accessed 3 October 2023. https://www.dhm.de/lemo/zeitzeugen/karl-deutmann-berlin-im-bombensturm.html.

Stromnetz Berlin. "Zahlen, Daten, Fakten". Accessed 2 October 2023. https://www.stromnetz.berlin/uber-uns/zahlen-daten-fakten.

Strom-Report. "Photovoltaik Deutschland: Aktuelle Zahlen & Charts". STROM-REPORT, n.d. https://strom-report.com/photovoltaik.

———. "Windenergie Deutschland 2023 | Zahlen, Fakten, Charts". STROM-REPORT, 2023. https://strom-report.com/windenergie.

Stroms, Peter, and Stefan Siedentop. *Stadt und Land: Gleichwertig, Polarisiert, Vielfältig: Eine Metastudie zu Stadt-Land-Beziehungen*. Hamburg: Zeit-Stiftung Ebelin und Gerd Bucerius, 2021.

Tang, Liang, and Tim T. Werner. "Global Mining Footprint Mapped from High-Resolution Satellite Imagery". *Communications Earth & Environment* 4, no. 1 (22 April 2023): 1–12. https://doi.org/10.1038/s43247-023-00805-6.

Tarr, Joel A., and Karen Clay. "Boom and Bust in Pittsburgh Natural Gas History". In *Making Industrial Pittsburgh Modern*, edited by Edward K. Muller and Joel A. Tarr, 250–68. Environment, Landscape, Transportation, and Planning. University of Pittsburgh Press, 2019. https://doi.org/10.2307/j.ctvr43hhj.16.

Technik Museum Sinsheim. "Growian Windflügel", 1 April 2023. https://sinsheim.technik-museum.de/de/growian-windfluegel.

Technische Universität Cottbus. "Entwerfen Im System – Der Architekt Wilfried Stallknecht". BTU, n.d.

Telsnig, Thomas, Aliki Georgakaki, Simon Letout, Anna Kuokkanen, Aikaterini Mountraki, Ela Ince, Drilona Shtjefni, Ordonez Geraldine Joanny, Olivier Eulaerts, and Marcelina Grabowska. "Clean Energy Technology Observatory: Wind Energy in the European Union – 2022 Status Report on Technology Development, Trends, Value Chains and Markets". JRC Publications Repository, 7 October 2022. https://doi.org/10.2760/855840.

Tepasse, Heinrich. *Stadttechnik im Städtebau Berlins – 19. Jahrhundert: Kompendium Stadttechnikgeschichte: Wasser und Abwasser, Gas und Strom*. Berlin: Mann Berlin, 2001.

Tillmann, Hans-Bernd. "Die Entwicklung des Verbundbetriebes in Deutschland und in Europa. 25 Jahre elektrische Wiedervereinigung Deutschlands". VDE. Accessed 2 September 2023. https://www.vde.com.

Tissot, Bernard P., and Dietrich H. Welte. "Formation of Petroleum in Relation to Geological Processes. Timing of Oil and Gas Generation". In *Petroleum Formation and Occurrence*, edited by Bernard P. Tissot and Dietrich H. Welte, 215–28. Berlin, Heidelberg: Springer, 1984. https://doi.org/10.1007/978-3-642-87813-8_12.

Tourismusverband Lausitzer Seenland e. V. "Lausitzer Seenland". Accessed 28 September 2023. https://www.lausitzerseenland.de/de.html.

Trina Solar. "Data Sheet: Duomax Twin, TSM-DEG15MC.20(II)". Trina Solar, 2019. https://static.trinasolar.com/sites/default/files/EU_TSM_DEG15MC.20%28II%29_FF_datasheet_A_2019_Web.pdf.

———. "Trina Solar 210 Vertex Super Factory", n.d. https://www.trinasolar.com/en-apac/SuperFactory.

Tsing, Anna. "Supply Chains and the Human Condition". *Rethinking Marxism* 21, no. 2 (1 April 2009): 148–76. https://doi.org/10.1080/08935690902743088.

———. "What Is Emerging? Supply Chains and the Remaking of Asia". *The Professional Geographer* 68, no. 2 (2 April 2016): 330–37. https://doi.org/10.1080/00330124.2015.1099186.

Turner, Fred. *From Counterculture to Cyberculture: Stewart Brand, the Whole Earth Network, and the Rise of Digital Utopianism*. Chicago, IL: University of Chicago Press, 2006. http://catdir.loc.gov/catdir/toc/ecip064/2005034149.html.

Uhlemann, Hans-Joachim. *Berlin und die Märkischen Wasserstrassen*. 1. Aufl. Hamburg, [Herford]: DSV-Verl. Busse-Seewald, 1994.

Umweltbundesamt. *Analyse Des Historischen Strukturwandels in Der Lausitz (Fallstudie)*. Dessau: UBA, 2021. www.umweltbundesamt.de/sites/default/files/medien/1410/publikationen/2021-12-28_cc_31-2021_fallstudie_analyse_historischer_strukturwandel_lausitz.pdf.

———. "Energieverbrauch nach Energieträgern und Sektoren". Text. Umweltbundesamt. Umweltbundesamt, 17 March 2023. https://www.umweltbundesamt.de/daten/energie/energieverbrauch-nach-energietraegern-sektoren.

———. "Primärenergieverbrauch". Text. UBA. Umweltbundesamt, 22 March 2023. https://www.umweltbundesamt.de/daten/energie/primaerenergieverbrauch.

———. "Renewable Energies in Figures". Text. *UBA* (blog). Umweltbundesamt, 15 March 2023. https://www.umweltbundesamt.de/en/topics/climate-energy/renewable-energies/renewable-energies-in-figures.

Umweltbundesamt, Sibylle. "Indicator: Primary Energy Consumption". Text. Umweltbundesamt. Umweltbundesamt, 24 March 2023. https://www.umweltbundesamt.de/en/data/environmental-indicators/indicator-primary-energy-consumption.

UN Department of Economic and Social Affairs. "The World Cities in 2018 – Data Booklet". United Nations, 2018. https://population.un.org/wup/?_gl=1*13pncix*_ga*Nzc3Nzc4NzI4LjE2OTY3MDAxNTA.*_ga_TK9BQL5X7Z*MTY5NjcwMDE0OS4xLjAuMTY5NjcwMDE0OS4wLjAuMA..

UNFCCC. "Rapid Urbanization Increases Climate Risk for Billions of People", July 2017. https://unfccc.int/news/rapid-urbanization-increases-climate-risk-for-billions-of-people.

United Nations. "The Paris Agreement | UNFCCC". Accessed 3 October 2023. https://unfccc.int/process-and-meetings/the-paris-agreement.

United Nations Economic Commission for Europe. *Carbon Neutrality in the UNECE Region: Integrated Life-Cycle Assessment of Electricity Sources*. ECE Energy Series. United Nations, 2022. https://doi.org/10.18356/9789210014854.

University of Calgary. "Photovoltaic Effect – Energy Education", n.d. https://energyeducation.ca/encyclopedia/Photovoltaic_effect.

URA. "5 Years Bovanenkovo: What You Need to Know about Yamal's Biggest Gas Project". ura.ru. Accessed 25 September 2023. https://ura.news/specials/bovanenkovo.

Urban Catalyst, Studio Amore, and brethdelacalle Architekten. "Von Der Lausitz Zur WOWsitz: Planungslabor Raumbild 2050". Leibniz-Institut für ökologische Raumentwicklung, 2021. https://transformation-lausitz.ioer.eu/fileadmin/user_upload/transformation-lausitz/files/raumlabor_dokumente/wowsitz_A3_plaene_ml.pdf.

U.S. Geological Survey. "Rare Earths: Mineral Commodity Summaries", January 2023. https://pubs.usgs.gov/periodicals/mcs2023/mcs2023-rare-earths.pdf.

———. "U.S. Geological Survey Releases 2022 List of Critical Minerals | U.S. Geological Survey". Accessed 4 October 2023. https://www.usgs.gov/news/national-news-release/us-geological-survey-releases-2022-list-critical-minerals.

VDE Verband der Elektrotechnik Elektronik Informationstechnik e. V. "Hochspannungsleitung Teufelsbruch – Werderstraße". VDE Geschichte. Accessed 29 September 2023. https://www.vde.com/geschichte.

Verda, Matteo. "A Link of Steel. The Western Europe-Russia Gas Pipeline Network in the Post-Soviet Era". In *European Energy and Climate Security: Public Policies, Energy Sources, and Eastern Partners*, edited by Rossella Bardazzi, Maria Grazia Pazienza, and Alberto Tonini, 37–63. Champaign, IL: Springer International Publishing, 2016. https://doi.org/10.1007/978-3-319-21302-6_3.

Vereingung Deutscher Wirtschaftsarchivare e. V., Clemens Heitmann, Matthias Fiedler, and Sebastian Müller, eds. "Entstehung, Entwicklung und Bedeutung der Lausitzer und mitteldeutschen Braunkohlenindustrie im Spiegel ihrer Überlieferung im Bergarchiv Freiberg". In *Archiv und Wirtschaft*, Heft 1:11–23. 43. Jahrgang. Berlin: VDW, 2010.

Vestas. "Life Cycle Assessment of Electricity Production from an Onshore EnVentus V162-6.2 MW Wind Plant", 2023. https://www.vestas.com/content/dam/vestas-com/global/en/sustainability/reports-and-ratings/lcas/LCA%20of%20Electricity%20Production%20from%20an%20onshore%20EnVentus%20V162-6.2.pdf.coredownload.inline.pdf.

———. "Reports & Ratings", 9 October 2023. https://www.vestas.de/de-de/Nachhaltigkeit/reports-and-ratings.

———. "Vestas Sustainability Report 2021", 2021. https://www.vestas.de/content/dam/vestas-com/global/en/sustainability/reports-and-ratings/sustainability-reports/Sustainability%20Report%202021.pdf.coredownload.inline.pdf.

Visual Capitalist. "Animated Infographic: How Solar Panels Work", n.d. https://www.visualcapitalist.com/animation-how-solar-panels-work.

Wang, Jianliang, Lifang Yang, Jingli Lin, and Yongmei Bentley. "The Availability of Critical Minerals for China's Renewable Energy Development: An Analysis of Physical Supply". *Natural Resources Research* 29, no. 4 (1 August 2020): 2291–2306. https://doi.org/10.1007/s11053-020-09615-5.

Wang, Qian-Qian, Cheng-Xin Geng, Lu Wang, Ting-Ting Zheng, Qing-Hong Jiang, Tong Yang, Yong-Qi Liu, and Zhe Wang. "Water Conservation and Ecological Water Requirement Prediction of Mining Area in Arid Region Based on RS-GIS and InVEST: A Case Study of Bayan Obo Mine in Baotou, China". *Sustainability* 15, no. 5 (January 2023): 4238. https://doi.org/10.3390/su15054238.

Waterhouse, Alan. *Boundaries of the City: The Architecture of Western Urbanism*. Toronto [u.a.]: University of Toronto Press, 1993.
Weems, Philip, and Nina Howell. "Japan's Pivotal Role in the Global LNG Industry's 50-Year History". *King & Spalding Energy Newsletter*, 2014.
Wehrmann, Benjamin. "German Offshore Wind Power – Output, Business and Perspectives". Clean Energy Wire, January 2023. https://www.cleanenergywire.org/factsheets/german-offshore-wind-power-output-business-and-perspectives.
Westphal, Kirsten, Maria Pastukhova, and Jacopo Maria Pepe. "Geopolitics of Electricity: Grids, Space and (Political) Power", 2022. https://doi.org/10.18449/2022RP06.
Wettengel, Florian. "Spelling out the Coal Exit – Germany's Phase-out Plan." In Clean Energy Wire, edited by Sven Egenter. Berlin: Clean Energy Wire CLEW, 2024. https://www.cleanenergywire.org/factsheets/spelling-out-coal-phase-out-germanys-exit-law-draft.
Wikipedia. "Data on the World's Largest Solar PV Producers, Including China, Taiwan, US, Japan, and Germany: Solar Power in China". In *Wikipedia*, 26 September 2023.https://en.wikipedia.org/w/index.php?title=Solar_power_in_China&oldid=1177117254.
———. "Solarpark Weesow-Willmersdorf", n.d. In *Wikipedia*, 26 September 2023. https://de.wikipedia.org/wiki/Solarpark_Weesow-Willmersdorf.
———. "Wind Power in Denmark". In *Wikipedia*, 28 August 2023. https://en.wikipedia.org/w/index.php?title=Wind_power_in_Denmark&oldid=1172671628#Statistics.
———. "Liste von Windkraftanlagen in Berlin und Brandenburg". https://de.wikipedia.org/wiki/Liste_von_Windkraftanlagen_in_Berlin_und_Brandenburg.
Wind Europe. "Placing Onshore Wind at the Heart of the European Green Deal: What Should Europe Do?", 2020. https://windeurope.org/wp-content/uploads/files/policy/position-papers/Power-ONshore-Policy-Recommendations.pdf.
———. "Wind Energy in Europe: 2022 Statistics and the Outlook for 2023–2027". Wind Europe, February 2023. https://windeurope.org/intelligence-platform/product/wind-energy-in-europe-2022-statistics-and-the-outlook-for-2023-2027/#.
———. "Wind Supply Chain Map". WindEurope. Accessed 27 October 2023. https://windeurope.org/about-wind/campaigns/local-impact-global-leadership.
Wings, Oliver. "The Rüdersdorf Muschelkalk Quarry", 7th Annual EAVP Meeting 2009, 24 June 2009.
Wirstschafts Woche. "Erster Deutscher Windpark: Vor 30 Jahren Begann Die Energiewende", 17 August 2017. https://www.wiwo.de/technologie/green/deutschlands-erster-windpark-als-vor-30-jahren-die-energiewende-begann/20202770.html.
World Bank. "World Development Indicators". World Bank Data Catalog. Accessed 4 October 2023. https://datacatalog.worldbank.org/search/dataset/0037712/about:blank.
Xie, Mian, and Susana Lopez-Querol. "Numerical Simulations of the Monotonic and Cyclic Behaviour of Offshore Wind Turbine Monopile Foundations in Clayey Soils". *Journal of Marine Science and Engineering* 9, no. 9 (September 2021): 1036. https://doi.org/10.3390/jmse9091036.
Yahoo Finance. "10 Largest Rare Earth Companies in the World", 23 June 2023. https://finance.yahoo.com/news/10-largest-rare-earth-companies-105755371.html.
Yergin, Daniel. *The Prize: The Epic Quest for Oil, Money, and Power*. Paperback ed. New York, NY: Free Press, 2009.
Yermakov, Vitaly. "The Domino Effect: Contaminated Oil in the Druzhba Oil Pipeline – Implications of the Incident for Russia and Europe". Oxford Institute for Energy Studies, 2019. https://www.oxfordenergy.org/publications/domino-effect-contaminated-oil-druzhba-oil-pipeline-implications-incident-russia-europe.
Zimmermann, Antonia. "The German Village That Says It's Gone Green". politico, 27 April 2023. https://www.politico.eu/article/germany-energy-village-feldheim-sustainability-sort-of-self-sufficient-energy-village.
Zupagrafika. *Monotowns: Soviet Landscapes of Post-Industrial Russia*. Zupagrafika, 2021. https://www.zupagrafika.com/shop/monotowns.

Image Credits

1 Introduction

1.2 Power, Flows, and Transformation

Fig. 1 Eurostat. "nrg_ind_id". Eurostat, 2022. https://doi.org/10.2908/SDG_07_50. Eurostat. "nrg_ind_ffgae". Eurostat, 2022. https://doi.org/10.2908/NRG_IND_FFGAE.
Fig. 2 Eurostat. "nrg_ind_ffgae". Eurostat, 2022. https://doi.org/10.2908/NRG_IND_FFGAE.
Fig. 3 Our World in Data. "Primary energy consumption by source". Accessed 22 July 2024. https://ourworldindata.org/grapher/primary-energy-source-bar?country=SWE~ITA~FRA~GRC~POL~DEU~CZE~AUT~BEL~BGR~HRV~CYP~DNK~EST~LVA~FIN~HUN~IRL~LTU~LUX~PRT~ESP~ROU~SVK.
Fig. 4 AG Energiebilanzen. "Auswertungstabellen zur Energiebilanz Deutschland Daten für die Jahre von 1990 bis 2023". Accessed 1 November 2024. https://ag-energiebilanzen.de/wp-content/uploads/2024/01/quartalsbericht_q4_2023.pdf.
Fig. 5 Ibid.
Fig. 6 BGR – Bundesanstalt für Geowissenschaften und Rohstoffe. "BGR Energiestudie 2023 – Daten und Entwicklungen der deutschen und globalen Energieversorgung, 2024, 16. https://doi.org/10.25928/es-2023.
Fig. 7 Ritchie, Hannah and Max Roser. "How Does the Land Use of Different Electricity Sources Compare?" Our World in Data, 18 March 2024. https://ourworldindata.org/land-use-per-energy-source.
Fig. 8 LAEG. "Zusammenstellung der Tabelle – Länderarbeitskreis Energiebilanzen". Accessed 24 July 2024. https://www.lak-energiebilanzen.de/energiebilanzen.
Fig. 9 Umweltbundesamt. "Komponentenzerlegung: Treiber energiebedingter THG-Emissionen". Accessed 24 July 2024. https://www.umweltbundesamt.de/themen/klima-energie/treibhausgas-emissionen/komponentenzerlegung-treiber-energiebedingter-thg#komponentenzerlegung. Prognos, Öko-Institut, Wuppertal-Institut. "Klimaneutrales Deutschland 2045. Wie Deutschland seine Klimaziele schon vor 2050 erreichen kann". Zusammenfassung im Auftrag von Stiftung Klimaneutralität, Agora Energiewende und Agora Verkehrswende, 2021.
Fig.10 Drawing by Patrick Martin. Eurostat. "Energy balance flow diagram". Accessed 24 January 2025. https://ec.europa.eu/eurostat/cache/sankey/energy/sankey.html.

2. Transmission, Transition, Transformation

Fig. 1 Left: drawing by Amelia Mega and Yuliya Navatskaya. Geist, Johann Friedrich and Klaus Kürvers. *Das Berliner Mietshaus Teil 2. 1862–1945: eine dokumentarische Geschichte von „Meyer's-Hof" in der Ackerstrasse 132–133.* München: Prestel, 1984, p. 501. Right: drawing by Amelia Mega and Yuliya Navatskaya. Von Müller, Adriaan. *Museumsdorf Düppel: lebendiges Mittelalter in Berlin.* 4, Überarb. Aufl. Berliner Sehenswürdigkeiten BV000010455 2. Berlin: Haude und Spener, 1986.
Fig. 2 Drawing by Amelia Mega and Yuliya Navatskaya. Laudel, Katja. *Der Typenwandel des ländlichen Wohnhauses im Oderbruch zwischen 1753 und 1850 – Der Einfluss von Friderizianischer Kolonisation und preußischer Obrigkeit auf die Hausformen der ländlichen Untertanen.* Bauhaus-Universität Weimar, 2005.
Fig. 3 Drawing by Amelia Mega and Yuliya Navatskaya. Geist, Johann Friedrich and Klaus Kürvers. *Das Berliner Mietshaus Teil 2. 1862–1945: eine dokumentarische Geschichte von „Meyer's-Hof" in der Ackerstrasse 132–133.* München: Prestel, 1984.
Fig. 4 Drawing by Amelia Mega and Yuliya Navatskaya. Bundesministerium für Raumordnung, Bauwesen und Städtebau. *Leitfaden Für Die Instandsetzung und Modernisierung von Wohngebäuden in Der Plattenbauweise: Wohnungsbauserie 70 – WBS 70, 6,3 t.* Bonn-Bad Godesberg: BMWSB, 1997.
Fig. 5 Drawing by Amelia Mega and Yuliya Navatskaya. Rosenberg, Joel. *Electrify Everything in Your Home: A Guide to Comfy, Healthy, Carbon-Free Living.* Rewiring America, 2021. Accessed 13 February, 2025. https://www.rewiringamerica.org/electrify-home-guide.
Fig. 6 Amt für Statistik Berlin-Brandenburg. Accessed 24 July, 2024. https://www.statistik-berlin-brandenburg.de.
Fig. 7 Drawing by Paul Strobel. Basemap: 1685/1890 Plan von Berlin mit Umgebung, https://www.berliner-stadtplansammlung.de/index.php/karten/1685-1890-plan-von-berlin-mit-umgebung
Fig. 8 Drawing by Paul Strobel. Herzberg, Heinrich and Rieseberg, Hans Joachim. *Mühlen und Müller in Berlin.* Berlin: VEB Verlag für Bauwesen, 1987.
Fig. 9 Drawing by Paul Strobel Basemap: Situationsplan der Haupt- und Residenzstadt Berlin. Accessed 13 February, 2025. https://digital.zlb.de/viewer/image/34765711/
Fig. 10 Drawing by Paul Strobel. Natzschka, Werner. *Berlin und seine Wasserstraßen.* Berlin: Duncker & Humblot, 1971. Uhlemann, Hans-Joachim. *Berlin und die Märkischen Wasserstraßen.* Berlin: Transpress VEB Verlag für Verkehrswesen, 1987.
Fig. 11 Drawing by Paul Strobel. Basemap: Sineck Situations-Plan von Berlin 1882. Accessed 13 February, 2025. https://de.m.wikipedia.org/wiki/Datei:Sineck_Situations-Plan_von_Berlin_1882.jpg.
Fig. 12 Drawing by Paul Strobel. Kloos, R. "Der Wasserverkehr". In Architekten- und Ingenieurverein zu Berlin-Brandenburg e.V. (ed.) *Berlin und seine Bauten. Anlagen und Bauten für den Verkehr.* Berlin: Ernst & Sohn, 1984.
Fig. 13 Drawing by Paul Strobel. Basemap: 1937 Pharus-Plan Berlin. Accessed 13 February, 2025. https://www.berliner-stadtplansammlung.de/index.php/karten/1937-pharus-plan-berlin.
Fig. 14 Drawing by Paul Strobel. Bärthel, Hilmar. Anlagen und Bauten der Elektrizitätserzeugung. In Architekten- und Ingenieurverein zu Berlin-Brandenburg e.V. (ed.) *Berlin und seine Bauten.* Stadttechnik. Ernst & Sohn, 2006.
Fig. 15 "Chronik Der Elektrotechnik – Kraftwerke". Accessed 24 July, 2024. https://www2.vde.com/wiki/chronik_2016/Wiki-Seiten/Kraftwerke.aspx. (AI-optimised)
Fig. 16 Drawing by Felix Frankowiak and Yuliya Navatskaya. Bahde, Curt, Bürgel Claus, and Hahn, Wolfgang. "100 Jahre Stromverteilung in Berlin". In BEWAG (ed.) *VDE 100 Jahre Stromgeschichte. Jubiläums-Fantasie.* Berlin: Bewag, 1984, p. 51.
Fig. 17 Drawing by Felix Frankowiak and Yuliya Navatskaya. Bahde, Curt, Bürgel Claus, and Hahn, Wolfgang. "100 Jahre Stromverteilung in Berlin". In BEWAG (ed.) *VDE 100 Jahre Stromgeschichte. Jubiläums-Fantasie.* Berlin: Bewag, 1984, p. 52.

Fig. 18 Drawing by Katerina Tzouvala, Elif Soylu and Yuliya Navatskaya. Open Street Map, authors
Fig. 19 Drawing by Katerina Tzouvala, Elif Soylu and Yuliya Navatskaya. Open Street Map, authors
Fig. 20 Drawing by Felix Frankowiak and Yuliya Navatskaya. Bahde et al., 1984, p. 56.
Fig. 21 Drawing by Felix Frankowiak and Yuliya Navatskaya. Bahde et al., 1984, p. 57.
Fig. 22 Drawing by Katerina Tzouvala, Elif Soylu and Yuliya Navatskaya. Open Street Map, authors
Fig. 23 Drawing by Katerina Tzouvala, Elif Soylu and Yuliya Navatskaya. Open Street Map, authors
Fig. 24 Drawing by Felix Frankowiak and Yuliya Navatskaya. "Historische Orte der Elektrotechnik". Accessed 24 July, 2024. https://www.vde.com/de/geschichte/karte.
Fig. 25 Drawing by Felix Frankowiak and Yuliya Navatskaya. "Stromnetz Berlin | Berlins zuverlässiger Netzbetreiber". Accessed 22 August, 2023. https://www.stromnetz.berlin.
Fig. 26 Drawing by Joseph Smithard. SlideShare. "380kV-Freileitung in Birkenwerder Und Hohen Neuendorf", 4 December, 2014. Accessed 13 February, 2025. https://de.slideshare.net/slideshow/380kvfreileitung-in-birkenwerder-und-hohen-neuendorf/42369547.
Fig. 27 Drawing by Patrick Martin. Stromnetz Berlin "Faktenblatt". Accessed 14 January, 2024. https://www.stromnetz.berlin/uber-uns/zahlen-daten-fakten.
Fig. 28 By Dilara Uçar and Elif Soylu. "NKT". Accessed 14 March, 2023. https://www.nkt.de. "ZMS-Kabel – Xiangyun International". Accessed 14 March, 2023. https://www.zmscables.com.

3. Fossil Energy Carriers

3.1 Spatial Consequences of Fossil Fuel Utilisation

Fig. 1 Authors.
Fig. 2 Smil, Vaclav. *Grand Transitions: How the Modern World Was Made.* New York, NY: Oxford University Press, 2021. p. 121.
Fig. 3 Will, Steffen, Broadgate, Wendy, Deutsch, Lisa, Gaffney, Owen, and Ludwig, Cornelia. "The Trajectory of the Anthropocene: The Great Acceleration". *The Anthropocene Review 2,* no. 1 (April 2015): 81–98. https://doi.org/10.1177/2053019614564785.
Fig. 4 Nadar. Catacombes de Paris. 1861. Accessed 13 February, 2025. https://commons.wikimedia.org/wiki/File:Nadar_-_Catacombes_de_Paris_-_NPS_10.jpg.
Fig. 5 "Geological History of Earth". *Wikipedia,* 8 July, 2024. https://en.wikipedia.org/w/index.php?title=Geological_history_of_Earth&oldid=1233412792.
Fig. 6 @ArthurHidden. "Free Photo | The Top View on Dubai". Accessed 25 July, 2024. https://www.freepik.com/free-photo/top-view-dubai_6525921.htm.
Fig. 7 ENERGY.GOV. *Tender-Platform Rig. Offshore, Louisiana. c. Undated.* 7 February, 2014. HD.11B.160. Accessed 13 February, 2025. https://commons.wikimedia.org/wiki/File:Tender_and_offshore_oil_rig_platform,_Louisiana.jpg.
Fig. 8 Gazprom.
Fig. 9 Photo by Simon Breth.

3.2 Coal

Fig. 1 Von Hohberg, Wolf Helmhardt. *Georgica Curiosa Aucta.* In Verlegung Martin Endters, 1716.
Fig. 2 Unknown photographer on behalf of A. Borsig, *Borsig Catalogue,* 1898. Accessed 13 February, 2025. https://commons.wikimedia.org/wiki/File:A._Borsig,_Berlin_-_3-3_gek._Tender-Locomotive_f%C3%BCr_500_mm_Spurweite,_gebaut_1895_-_Katalog_1898.jpg?uselang=de.
Fig. 3 Meyers Großes Konversations-Lexikon, Volume 5. Leipzig, 1906. Accessed 13 February, 2025. http://www.zeno.org/Meyers-1905/B/Elektrische+Maschinen.
Fig. 4 Eurostat. "nrg_bal_c". Eurostat, 2024. https://doi.org/10.2908/NRG_BAL_C.
Fig. 5 Our World in Data. "Coal Consumption". Accessed 25 July, 2024. https://ourworldindata.org/grapher/coal-consumption-by-country-terawatt-hours-twh?tab=chart&facet=none&country=Lower-middle-income+countries~Upper-middle-income+countries~High-income+countries~OWID_WRL.
Fig. 6 Krämer, Hans. *Der Mensch und die Erde. Die Entstehung, Gewinnung und Verwertung der Schätze der Erde als Grundlage der Kultur.* Vol. 7. Deutsches Verlagshaus Bong & Co, 1911.
Fig. 7 Jenkins, Nicholas. *Energy Systems: A Very Short Introduction.* Oxford: Oxford University Press, 2019.
Fig. 8 Photo by David Bauer.
Fig. 9 Meyers Großes Konversations-Lexikon, Volume 5. Leipzig, 1906. Accessed 13 February, 2025. http://www.zeno.org/Meyers-1905/B/Bergbau?hl=bergbau+1.
Fig. 10 BGR – Bundesanstalt für Geowissenschaften und Rohstoffe. "BGR Energiestudie 2023 – Daten und Entwicklungen der deutschen und globalen Energieversorgung". Hannover, 2024, p. 30. https://doi.org/10.25928/ES-2023.
Fig. 11 Ibid, p. 109.
Fig. 12 Ibid, p. 29.
Fig. 13 Sammlung Matthias Gleisner, Senftenberg.
Fig. 14 Photo by Simon Breth.
Fig. 15 Drawing by Santiago Martínez Murillo, David Bauer and Elif Soylu. BGR – Bundesanstalt für Geowissenschaften und Rohstoffe. "BGR Energiestudie 2023 – Daten und Entwicklungen der deutschen und globalen Energieversorgung". Hannover, 2024, pp. 101–103. https://doi.org/10.25928/ES-2023.
Fig. 16 Drawing by Elif Soylu and Yuliya Navatskaya.
Fig. 17 Drawing by Yuliya Navatskaya. Global Energy Monitor. "Tracker Map". Accessed 26 July, 2024. https://globalenergymonitor.org/projects/global-coal-terminals-tracker/tracker-map.
Fig. 18 Statistisches Bundesamt. "Einfuhr von Steinkohle für die Jahre 2018 bis 2023". Accessed 25 July, 2024. https://www.destatis.de/DE/Themen/Branchen-Unternehmen/Energie/Verwendung/Tabellen/einfuhr-steinkohle-zeitreihe.html.
Fig. 19 Drawing by Yuliya Navatskaya. Open Street Map, authors Global Energy Monitor. "Tracker Map". Accessed 26 July, 2024. https://globalenergymonitor.org/projects/global-coal-terminals-tracker/tracker-map.
Fig. 20 Statistik der Kohlenwirtschaft e. V. "Braunkohle". *Statistiken Braunkohleausfuhr.* Accessed 26 July, 2024. https://kohlenstatistik.de/downloads/braunkohle.
Fig. 21 Drawing by Yuliya Navatskaya. Open Street Map. Archiv der Verschwundenen Orte. "Interaktive Karte". Accessed 26 July, 2024. https://archiv-verschwundene-orte.de/kartenteppich/karte.html.
Fig. 22 Drawing by Yuliya Navatskaya. Open Street Map. Internationale Bauausstellung Fürst-Pückler-Land, Scholz, Brigitte, and Hamm, Oliver G., eds. *Bergbau Folge Landschaft.* Berlin: JOVIS Verlag, 2010.
Fig. 23–26 Drawing by Santiago Martínez Murillo. Open Street Map; Google Earth; authors.
Fig. 27 Drawing by Yuliya Navatskaya. "F60 | Im Detail". Accessed 1 August, 2024. https://www.f60.de/de/die-bruecke/im-detail.html.
Fig. 28 Drawing by Yuliya Navatskaya, Elif Soylu and Oded Yatzkan. Open Street Map, reconstructed from model photos from the Energie Museum, Berlin.
Fig. 29 Drawing by Elif Soylu and Yuliya Navatskaya. Open Street Map

3.3 Oil

Fig. 1 Our World in Data. "Oil Consumption". Accessed 30 July, 2024. https://ourworldindata.org/grapher/oil-consumption-by-country?tab=chart&country=USA~NOR~CHN~DEU~OWID_EUR.
Fig. 2 University of Calgary. "In a Barrel of Oil: Energy Education". Accessed 30 July, 2024. https://energyeducation.ca/encyclopedia/In_a_barrel_of_oil.
Fig. 3 Investopedia. "10 Biggest Oil Companies". Accessed 30 July, 2024. https://www.investopedia.com/articles/personal-finance/010715/worlds-top-10-oil-companies.asp.
Fig. 4 Jenkins, Nicholas. *Energy Systems: A Very Short Introduction.* Oxford: Oxford University Press, 2019.
Fig. 5 Wikimedia Commons. Accessed 30 July, 2024. https://commons.wikimedia.org/wiki/File:Pump_Jack.jpg.
Fig. 6 Authors. Krohne. "Distillation in the oil & gas industry" Accessed 30 July, 2024. https://co.krohne.com/en/industries/oil-gas-industry/refining-oil-gas-industry/distillation-in-the-oil-and-gas-industry.
Fig. 7 Bundesverband Erdgas, Erdöl und Geoenergie e.V. "Jahrensbericht 2023". Accessed 30 August, 2024. https://jahresbericht.bveg.de/erdoelfoerderung. BGR – Bundesanstalt für Geowissenschaften und Rohstoffe. "BGR Energiestudie 2023 – Daten und Entwicklungen der deutschen und globalen Energieversorgung". Hannover, 2024, pp. 79–84. https://doi.org/10.25928/ES-2023.
Fig. 8 Destatis. "Erdölimporte aus Russland im Januar 2023 auf 3,500 Tonnen gesunken". Statistisches Bundesamt. Accessed 30 July, 2024. https://www.destatis.de/DE/Presse/Pressemitteilungen/2023/03/PD23_098_51.html.
Fig. 9 Statista. "Crude Oil: Largest Refineries by Capacity Germany 2020". Accessed 30 July, 2024. https://www.statista.com/statistics/1330217/largest-crude-oil-refineries-by-refined-volume-germany.
Fig. 10 Nies, Susanne and. *Oil and Gas Delivery to Europe: An Overview of Existing and Planned Infrastructures.* Ifri, 2011. p. 34.
Fig. 11 Stolp. *Erdölförderung Der UdSSR.* 6 September 1962. Deutsches Bundesarchiv. https://commons.wikimedia.org/wiki/File:Bundesarchiv_Bild_183-A0906-0008-001,_Erd%C3%B6lf%C3%B6rderung_der_UdSSR.jpg.

Fig. 12 No author. "Erdölleitung Freundschaft, Briefmarke DDR-Jahrgang 1966" https://www.suche-briefmarken.de/marken/ddr/ddr66078.html
Fig. 13 Wikimedia. "Magyar: Zsámbok, A Barátság II. kőolajvezeték építése". Accessed 30 July, 2024.
Fig. 14 "КПО Завершила Проект Снятия Производственных Ограничений По Газу На Карачаганаке". Accessed 31 July, 2024. https://kaztag.kz/ru/news/kpo-zavershila-proekt-snyatiya-proizvodstvennykh-ogranicheniy-po-gazu-na-karachaganake.
Fig. 15 "Kazakhstan 2022 – Analysis – IEA". Accessed 1 August, 2024. p. 38. https://www.iea.org/reports/kazakhstan-2022.
Fig. 16 "Cities & Towns of Kazakhstan". Accessed 31 July, 2024. http://pop-stat.mashke.org/kazakhstan-cities.htm.
Fig. 17 Bundesarchiv. Wikimedia Commons. Accessed 30 July, 2024.
Fig. 18 Bundesarchiv. Wikimedia Commons. Accessed 30 July, 2024.
Fig. 19 Photo by Elif Soylu.
Fig. 20 Drawing by Elif Soylu and Santiago Martínez Murillo. BGR – Bundesanstalt für Geowissenschaften und Rohstoffe. "BGR Energiestudie 2023 – Daten und Entwicklungen der deutschen und globalen Energieversorgung, 2024, pp. 81–83. https://doi.org/10.25928/es-2023.
Fig. 21 Drawing by Elif Soylu.
Fig. 22 Drawing by Yuliya Navatskaya. Nies, Susanne and. *Oil and Gas Delivery to Europe: An Overview of Existing and Planned Infrastructures.* Ifri, 2011. https://www.ifri.org/en/publications/ouvrages-de-lifri/oil-and-gas-delivery-europe-overview-existing-and-planned. "Global Oil Infrastructure Tracker – Global Energy Monitor". Accessed 1 August, 2024. https://globalenergymonitor.org/projects/global-oil-infrastructure-tracker.
Fig. 23 Destatis. "Erdölimporte aus Russland im Januar 2023 auf 3 500 Tonnen gesunken". Statistisches Bundesamt. Accessed 30 July, 2024. https://www.destatis.de/DE/Presse/Pressemitteilungen/2023/03/PD23_098_51.html. Statista. "Anteile ausgewählter Länder an der deutschen Importmenge von Erdöl in den Jahren 2022 und 2023". Accessed 30 July, 2024. https://de.statista.com/statistik/daten/studie/1346532/umfrage/verteilung-der-deutschen-importmenge-von-erdoel-nach-laendern.
Fig. 24 Drawing by Yuliya Navatskaya. Petroleum Economist Cartographic. "Pipeline Infrastructure of Europe and the CIS". Penspen Group, 2008. https://iiif-cloud.princeton.edu/iiif/2/b1%2F3e%2Fb6%2Fb13eb69d3cbc4f92bdb8bcbbb812ec45%2Fintermediate_file/full/full/0/default.jpg.
Fig. 25–27 Drawing by Yuliya Navatskaya. Open Street Map.
Fig. 28 Drawing by Santiago Martínez Murillo. Open Street Map.
Fig. 29–32 Drawing by Santiago Martínez Murillo. Open Street Map; Google Earth, https://www.oldmapsonline.org/de.
Fig. 33 A Barrel Full Oil & Gas Wiki. Accessed 30 July, 2024. http://abarrelfull.wikidot.com/schwedt-refinery.
Fig. 34 PCK. "Unsere PCK Spitzen-Raffinerie in Europa". Accessed 30 July, 2024.https://www.pck.de/unternehmen.
Fig. 35 Drawing by Santiago Martínez Murillo. Open Street Map.

3.3 Gas

Fig. 1 Delahaye, Philibert. Herstellung von Steinkohlengas (schematisch) nach Delahaye, Philibert, *L'éclairage dans la ville et dans la maison historique et considérations générales, l'éclairage chez soi, l'industrie de l'éclairage, applications diverses.* Paris 1886. Accessed 13 February, 2025. https://commons.wikimedia.org/wiki/File:Steinkohlengas_schematisch.jpg.
Fig. 2 Architekturforum Architectura Pro Homine. "Gaswerk VI Tegel". Accessed 1 August, 2024. https://www.stadtbild-deutschland.org/forum/gallery/index.php?image/31588-gaswerk-vi-tegel.
Fig. 3 Tepasse, Heinrich. *Stadttechnik im Städtebau Berlins – 19. Jahrhundert: Kompendium Stadttechnikgeschichte: Wasser und Abwasser, Gas und Strom.* Berlin: Mann Berlin, 2001.
Fig. 4 Wikipedia Commons. "Westinghouse Gas Derrick No. 1". Accessed 1 April, 2024. https://commons.wikimedia.org/wiki/File:Westinghouse_Gas_Derrick_No1.jpg.
Fig. 5 Anefo, Joop van Bilsen. *Nederlands: Collectie/Archief: Fotocollectie Anefo.* 25 July, 1963. Accessed 13 February, 2025. http://proxy.handle.net/10648/aa3fc91c-d0b4-102d-bcf8-003048976d84. https://commons.wikimedia.org/wiki/File:Aardgasveld_te_Slochteren_officieel_in_gebruik_gesteld_mr_Fock_en_drs_de_Pous_,_Bestanddeelnr_915-3823.jpg.
Fig. 6 Teraz.sk. "plynovod Bratstvo". TERAZ.sk, 2 December, 2014. Accessed 13 February, 2025. https://www.teraz.sk/fotodennik/vystavba-plynovodu-bratstvo-v-retrospek/115867-fotografia.html.
Fig. 7 Drawing by Yuliya Navatskaya. Jenkins, Nicholas. *Energy Systems: A Very Short Introduction.* Oxford: Oxford University Press, 2019.
Fig. 8 Jenkins. 2019.
Fig. 9 Banks, Ferdinand E. *Energy Economics: A Modern Introduction.* Boston, MA: Springer US, 2000. https://doi.org/10.1007/978-1-4615-4551-4.
Fig. 10 Mallison, Richard. "Natural Gas Processing, and Products". Cutler J. Cleveland and Robert U. Ayres (eds.), 4:235–47. *Encyclopaedia of Energy.* Amsterdam/Boston: Elsevier Academic Press, 2004.
Fig. 11 LBEG. *Erdöl Und Erdgas in Der Bundesrepublik Deutschland 2023.* Geobericht 49. Landesamt für Bergbau, Energie und Geologie, Hannover, 2024. doi.org/10.48476/geober_49_2024, p. 47.
Fig. 12 LBEG. 2024, p. 54.
Fig. 13 Drawing by Yuliya Navatskaya. Open Street Map. Gazprom.ru. Accessed December, 2021. https://www.gazprom.ru/projects/bovanenkovskoye.
Fig. 14 Gazprom.ru. Accessed December, 2021.
Fig. 15 Ibid.
Fig. 16 Ibid.
Fig. 17 LBEG. 2024, p. 54.
Fig. 18 LBEG. 2021, p. 55.
Fig. 19 Drawing by Elif Soylu. BGR – Bundesanstalt für Geowissenschaften und Rohstoffe. "BGR Energiestudie 2023 – Daten und Entwicklungen der deutschen und globalen Energieversorgung, 2024, p. 91–93. https://doi.org/10.25928/es-2023.
Fig. 20 Drawing by Elif Soylu.
Fig. 21 Drawing by Yuliya Navatskaya. Global Energy Monitor. "Global Oil and Gas Extraction Tracker". Global Energy Monitor (blog). Accessed 1 August, 2024. https://globalenergymonitor.org/projects/global-oil-gas-extraction-tracker.
Fig. 22 Bundesverbands der Energie- und Wasserwirtschaft e. V. "Energieversorgung 2022: Foliensatz". 2022. https://www.bdew.de/media/documents/Jahresbericht_2022_Foliensatz_final_20Dez2022.pdf, p. 15. Bundesverbands der Energie- und Wasserwirtschaft e. V. "Energieversorgung 2024: Jahresbericht". 2024, p. 18. Accessed 13 February, 2025. https://www.bdew.de/service/publikationen/jahresbericht-energieversorgung.
Fig. 23 Drawing by Yuliya Navatskaya. Entso-G. "Gas Infrastructure Europe: System Capacity Map 2024". Accessed 13 February, 2025. https://www.entsog.eu/sites/default/files/2024-01/ENTSOG_GIE_SYSCAP_2024_1600x1200_168L.pdf.
Fig. 24 Drawing by Yuliya Navatskaya. Open Street Map, Social Media
Fig. 25–28 Drawing by Santiago Martínez Murillo. Open Street Map, Google Earth.
Fig. 29 Drawing by Santiago Martínez Murillo. "Rüdersdorf I EWE Gasspeicher". Accessed 1 August, 2024. https://www.ewe-gasspeicher.de/standorte/ruedersdorf.
Fig. 31 Drawings by Santiago Martínez Murillo.

4. Renewable Energy Carriers

4.1 Introduction to Renewables

Fig. 1 Gernsback, Hugo. *The Electrical Experimenter.* New York: [s.n.], 1913. Accessed 13 February, 2025. http://archive.org/details/electricalexperi03gern.
Fig. 2 Roser, Max. "Why Did Renewables Become so Cheap so Fast?" Our World in Data, 18 March 2024. Accessed 13 February, 2025. https://ourworldindata.org/cheap-renewables-growth.
Fig. 3 Bloomberg NEF. 'Global Low-Carbon Energy Technology Investment Surges Past $1 Trillion for the First Time', 26 January 2023. https://about.bnef.com/blog/global-low-carbon-energy-technology-investment-surges-past-1-trillion-for-the-first-time.
Fig. 4 Photo by Philipp Deilmann.
Fig. 5 Gemeinsame Landesplanung Berlin-Brandenburg. "Regionen". Accessed 30 July, 2024. https://gl.berlin-brandenburg.de/regionalplanung-im-land-brandenburg/regionale-planungsgemeinschaften.

4.2 Critical Minerals

Fig. 6 Statista. "Annual solar module production globally from 2000 to 2023". Accessed 28 July, 2024. https://www.statista.com/statistics/668764/annual-solar-module-manufacturing-globally.
Fig. 7 Statista. "Critical Minerals in Energy Technologies". Accessed 28 July, 2024. https://www.statista.com/statistics/1317385/global-volume-critical-minerals-in-power-generation-technologies.
Fig.8 IEA. "Executive Summary – Energy Technology Perspectives 2023 – Analysis". Accessed 28 July, 2024. https://www.iea.org/reports/energy-technology-perspectives-2023/executive-summary.
Fig. 9 Chen, P., Ilton, E. S., Wang, Z., Rosso, K. M., & Zhang, X.. Global rare earth element resources: A concise review. *Applied Geochemistry, 175,* 106158, 2024. https://doi.org/10.1016/j.apgeochem.2024.106158.
Fig. 10 Ibid.

Fig. 11 Yahoo Finance. "10 Largest Rare Earth Companies in the World", 23 June, 2023. Accessed 13 February, 2025. https://finance.yahoo.com/news/10-largest-rare-earth-companies-105755371.html.
Fig. 12 European Commission. "Critical Raw Materials for Strategic Technologies and Sectors in the EU: A Foresight Study", 2 September, 2020. Accessed 13 February, 2025. https://ec.europa.eu/docsroom/documents/42881.
"Final List of Critical Minerals 2022: Policies – IEA". Accessed 1 August, 2024. https://www.iea.org/policies/15271-final-list-of-critical-minerals-2022.
"Mineral Commodity Summaries | U.S. Geological Survey". Accessed 1 August, 2024. https://www.usgs.gov/centers/national-minerals-information-center/mineral-commodity-summaries.
Fig. 23 Drawing by Yuliya Navatskaya.
Maus, V., Giljum, S., Gutschlhofer, J. et al. A global-scale data set of mining areas. *Sci Data* 7, 289 (2020). https://doi.org/10.1038/s41597-020-00624-w.
"Mineral Resources Online Spatial Data". Accessed 1 August, 2024. https://mrdata.usgs.gov/general/map-global.html#home.
Fig. 24 IEA. "Special Report on Solar PV Global Supply Chains". 2022, p. 60. https://www.oecd.org/en/publications/special-report-on-solar-pv-global-supply-chains_9e8b0121-en.html.
Fig. 25 Drawing by Santiago Martínez Murillo.
Fig. 26–29 Drawing by Santiago Martínez Murillo. Open Street Map, Google Earth.
Fig. 30–32 Drawing by Santiago Martínez Murillo. Open Street Maps, Google Earth.
Fig. 33–34 Drawing by Santiago Martínez Murillo.

4.3 Solar

Fig. 1 Fraunhofer ISE: Energy-Charts. "Installierte Netto-Leistung zur Stromerzeugung in Deutschland in 2023". Accessed 28 November, 2024. https://www.energy-charts.info/charts/installed_power/chart.htm?c=DE&year=2023&timeslider=0.
Fig. 2 Earth Policy Institute. "Annual Solar Photovoltaics Production by Country, 1995–2012", 2013. http://www.earth-policy.org/data_center/C23.
PVPS, IEA. "Distribution of solar photovoltaic module production worldwide in 2023, by country". Statista. Statista Inc. Accessed 4 February, 2025. https://www.statista.com/statistics/668749/regional-distribution-of-solar-pv-module-manufacturing.
Fig. 3 Our World in Data. "Solar (Photovoltaic) Panel Prices". Accessed 28 July, 2024. https://ourworldindata.org/grapher/solar-pv-prices.
Fig. 4 Agora Energiewende. "Towards a Climate-Neutral Germany by 2045", 6 May, 2021. Accessed 13 February, 2025. https://www.agora-energiewende.org/publications/towards-a-climate-neutral-germany-by-2045.
Fig. 5 Holler, Christian, Gaukel, Joachim, Lesch, Harald, and Lesch, Florian. *Erneuerbare Energien zum verstehen und mitreden.* C. Bertelsmann, 2021, p. 43.
Fig. 6 Google Maps.
Fig. 7 "On Air – Cloud Nine (Tensegrity Sphere)". Accessed 1 August, 2024. https://on-air.caricomassimo.org/en/airchive/cloud-nine-tensegrity-sphere.
Fig. 8 Drawing by Yuliya Navatskaya.
Fig. 9 IEA. "Solar PV Global Supply Chains: Analysis", 7 July, 2022, p. 21 https://www.iea.org/reports/solar-pv-global-supply-chains.
Fig. 10 "Polysilicon Market – Free Info on Size, Shares, Trends & China". Accessed 29 July, 2024. https://www.bernreuter.com/polysilicon/market-analysis.
Fig. 11 "Polysilicon Manufacturers: Global Top 10 | Bernreuter Research". Accessed 29 July, 2024. https://www.bernreuter.com/polysilicon/manufacturers.
Fig. 12 IEA. "Solar PV Global Supply Chains: Analysis", 7 July, 2022, p. 18. https://www.iea.org/reports/solar-pv-global-supply-chains.
Fig. 13 Bundesverbands der Energie- und Wasserwirtschaft e.V. "Energieversorgung 2023: Foliensatz". 2023. p.28; p. 40. https://www.bdew.de/media/documents.
Fig. 14 "Energie- und CO_2-Bilanz für Berlin und Brandenburg". Accessed 29 July, 2024. https://www.statistik-berlin-brandenburg.de/e-iv-4-j.
Fig. 15 Wirtschaftsförderung Land Brandenburg GmbH. "Abschlussbericht – Ergebnisse der Potenzialanalyse über nutzbare Flächen für solartechnische Anlagen im Land Brandenburg nach EEG 2021", Energieportal Brandenburg 2022, p. 12. https://energieportal-brandenburg.de/cms/inhalte/tools/solaratlas-brandenburg/abschlussbericht-solarpotenzialanalyse.
Fig. 16 Drawing by Santiago Martínez Murillo.
Fig. 17 NREL. "Leading solar PV manufacturers worldwide in 2023, based on shipments (in gigawatts)". Statista. Statista Inc. Accessed: 4 February 2025. https://www.statista.com/statistics/269741/the-biggest-solar-module-manufacturers-worldwide-based-on-production.
Fig. 18 IEA. "Special Report on Solar PV Global Supply Chains". 2022, p. 31. https://www.oecd.org/en/publications/special-report-on-solar-pv-global-supply-chains_9e8b0121-en.html.
Fig. 19 Trina Solar. "AP/Super Factory", 17 December, 2020. https://www.trinasolar.com/en-apac/SuperFactory.
Fig. 20 Photo by Philipp Deilmann.
Fig. 21 Drawing by Santiago Martínez Murillo.
Fig. 22 Drawing by Yuliya Navatskaya and Santiago Martínez Murillo.
Carrara, Samuel, Alves Dias, Patrícia, Plazzotta, Beatrice, and Pavel, Claudiu. *Raw Materials Demand for Wind and Solar PV Technologies in the Transition towards a Decarbonised Energy System,* 2020. https://doi.org/10.2760/160859.
IEA. "Special Report on Solar PV Global Supply Chains". 2022. https://www.oecd.org/en/publications/special-report-on-solar-pv-global-supply-chains_9e8b0121-en.html.

4.4 Wind

Fig. 1 Drawing by Joseph Smithard.
"Wind Power Lesson Starter: Answer". Accessed 30 July, 2024. https://technologystudent.com/energy1/wind11.htm.
Fig. 2 "Brush-Wind-Dynamo-F07e3438dc210438.jpg (2048×1632)". Accessed 30 July, 2024. https://media.cleveland.com/metro/photo/brush-wind-dynamo-f07e3438dc210438.jpg.
Fig. 3 Strom-Report. "Windenergie Deutschland | Zahlen, Fakten, Charts". Accessed 30 July, 2024. https://strom-report.com/windenergie.
Fig. 4 Bundesverband Windenergie. "Windenergie in Deutschland – Zahlen und Fakten". Accessed 30 July, 2024. https://www.wind-energie.de/themen/zahlen-und-fakten/deutschland.
Fig. 5 Bouzekri, Amina and Tayeb, Allaoui. (2018). *Hybrid algorithms for the intelligent management of a renewable production system: Power Quality Enhancement and service continuity contribution.* https://doi.org/10.13140/RG.2.2.28826.57288.
Fig. 6 Danish Wind Industry Association. "Wind Shade". Windpower.org, June 2003. Accessed 13 February, 2025. http://xn--drmstrre-64ad.dk/wp-content/wind/miller/windpower%20web/en/tour/wres/shade.htm.
Fig. 7 Carrara, Samuel, Alves Dias, Patrícia, Plazzotta, Beatrice, and Pavel, Claudiu. *Raw Materials Demand for Wind and Solar PV Technologies in the Transition towards a Decarbonised Energy System,* 2020. https://doi.org/10.2760/160859.
Fig. 8 Xie, Mian and Lopez-Querol, Susana. "Numerical Simulations of the Monotonic and Cyclic Behaviour of Offshore Wind Turbine Monopile Foundations in Clayey Soils". *Journal of Marine Science and Engineering* 9, no. 9 (September 2021): 1036. https://doi.org/10.3390/jmse9091036. https://www.mdpi.com/2077-1312/9/9/1036.
Fig. 9 "Development of Element Use in Energy Generation over Time". Accessed 30 July, 2024. https://www.cleanenergywire.org/sites/default/files/styles/gallery_image/public/paragraphs/images/esys-elementuse-en.jpg?itok=Qc0-Rygb.
Fig. 10 "Top 10 Wind Turbine Manufacturers in the World 2022 – BizVibe". Accessed 30 July, 2024. https://blog.bizvibe.com/blog/energy-and-fuels/top-10-wind-turbine-manufacturers-world.
Fig. 11 Global Wind Energy Council. "Global Wind Report 2023". 2023, p. 25. https://gwec.net/globalwindreport2023.
Fig. 12 Weller, Thygge "Growian in the summer of 1984, at the Kaiser-Wilhelm-Koog near Marne, Schleswig-Holstein, Germany". 1984. Wikimedia Commons. Accessed 14 December, 2023. https://commons.wikimedia.org/wiki/File:Growian001.png.
Fig. 13 Energieportal Brandenburg. "Windkraftanlagen (Stromerzeugung)". Accessed 30 July, 2024. https://energieportal-brandenburg.de/cms/inhalte/ausbaustand/statistiken/windkraftanlagen.
Fig. 14 "Die Stadtgüter: Berliner Stadtgüter". Accessed 30 July, 2024. https://www.berlinerstadtgueter.de/unternehmen/die-stadtgueter.
Fisbroker Berlin. "Standorte der Windkraftanlagen (Windkraft)". Accessed 30 July, 2024. Energieportal Brandenburg.
Fig. 15 Baidu. "Bayan Obo Mine". Accessed 30 July,2024. https://mbd.baidu.com/newspage/data/dtlandingsuper?nid=dt_4941113124785621493.
Fig. 16 Drawing by Santiago Martínez Murillo.
Fig. 17 Baidu. "Bayan Obo Mine". Accessed 30 July, 2024. https://mbd.baidu.com/newspage/data/dtlandingsuper?nid=dt_4941113124785621493.
Fig. 18 Photo by Elif Soylu.
Fig. 19 Photo by Elif Soylu.
Fig. 20 Drawing by Santiago Martínez Murillo.
Fig. 21 Drawing by Yuliya Navatskaya.
Fig. 22–23 Drawing by Yuliya Navatskaya.
Carrara, Samuel, Alves Dias, Patrícia, Plazzotta, Beatrice, and Pavel, Claudiu. *Raw Materials Demand for Wind and Solar PV Technologies in the Transition towards a Decarbonised Energy System,* 2020, p.7. https://doi.org/10.2760/160859.

"Mineral Resources Online Spatial Data". Accessed 1 August, 2024. https://mrdata.usgs.gov/general/map-global.html#home.
Shareholders for Change. "Rare Metal Supply Chains: Challenges for a Sustainable Energy Transition". 2019. Accessed 13 February, 2025. https://www.shareholdersforchange.eu/wp-content/uploads/2019/07/2019-07-SFC-Rare-metals-report.pdf.

Fig. 24–25 Drawing by Santiago Martínez Murillo.
Hetyei, Csaba. 'Review of Wind Turbine Failures, Highlighting Fire Accidents.' In Műszaki Katonai Közlöny. 2021, pp. 43–56. https://doi.org/10.32562/mkk.2020.2.4.
Carrara, Samuel, Alves Dias, Patrícia, Plazzotta, Beatrice, and Pavel, Claudiu. *Raw Materials Demand for Wind and Solar PV Technologies in the Transition towards a Decarbonised Energy System,* 2020, p. 14. https://doi.org/10.2760/160859.

Fig. 26 Drawing by Santiago Martínez Murillo. Open Street Map, Baidu.

Fig. 27 Drawing by Santiago Martínez Murillo. Open Street Map, site visit 2023.

Fig. 28–31 Drawing by Santiago Martínez Murillo. Open Street Map, Google Earth.

Fig. 32 Drawing by Yuliya Navatskaya. Open Street Map, "Bioenergiedorf Feldheim – Stadt Treuenbrietzen". Accessed 1 August, 2024. https://www.treuenbrietzen.de/seite/370570/bioenergiedorf-und-nef.html.

Imprint

Editors: David Bauer, Santiago Martínez Murillo, Philipp Misselwitz, Yuliya Navatskaya, and Joseph Smithard
Editorial Assistance: Elif Soylu
Copy editing and proofreading: Joseph Smithard and Cecilia Tricker
Book and information design, layout, and lithography: Patrick Martin, hla.studio
Printing and binding: Grafisches Centrum Cuno, Calbe (Ultra HD® Print)

For questions about the General Product Safety Regulation please contact productsafety@degruyterbrill.com.

Bibliographic information published by the Deutsche Nationalbibliothek: The Deutsche Nationalbibliothek lists this publication in the Deutsche Nationalbibliografie; detailed bibliographic data are available on the Internet at http://dnb.d-nb.de

jovis Verlag
Genthiner Straße 13
10785 Berlin

www.jovis.de

jovis books are available worldwide in select bookstores. Please contact your nearest bookseller or visit www.jovis.de for information concerning your local distribution.

ISBN 978-3-98612-020-7

Habitat Unit

This publication has been made possible by the generous support of the Robert Bosch Stiftung.

Robert Bosch Stiftung

Country and territorial codes

AE United Arab Emirates
AM Armenia
AR Argentina
AT Austria
AU Australia
AZ Azerbaijan
BA Bosnia and Herzegovina
BE Belgium
BG Bulgaria
BO Bolivia
BR Brazil
BY Belarus
CA Canada
CD Democratic Republic of the Congo
CH Switzerland
CL Chile
CN China
CO Colombia
CR Costa Rica
CU Cuba
CY Cyprus
CZ Czech Republic
DE Germany
DK Denmark
DZ Algeria
EE Estonia
EG Egypt
ES Spain
FI Finland
FR France
GA Gabon
GB Great Britain
GH Ghana
GL Greenland
GN Guinea
GR Greece
GT Guatemala
GY Guyana
HR Croatia
HU Hungary
ID Indonesia
IE Ireland
IN India
IQ Iraq
IR Iran
IS Iceland
IT Italy
JM Jamaica
JP Japan
KP North Korea
KR South Korea
KW Kuwait
KZ Kazakhstan
LT Lithuania
LU Luxembourg
LV Latvia
LY Libya
MA Morocco
MG Madagascar
MK Macedonia
MM Myanmar
MN Mongolia
MT Malta
MX Mexico
MY Malaysia
MZ Mozambique
NC New Caledonia
NG Nigeria
NL Netherlands
NO Norway
NZ New Zealand
PE Peru
PH Philippines
PL Poland
PT Portugal
QA Qatar
RO Romania
RU Russia
RW Rwanda
SA Saudi Arabia
SE Sweden
SI Slovenia
SK Slovakia
TH Thailand
TJ Tajikistan
TM Turkmenistan
TR Turkey
TW Taiwan
UA Ukraine
UK United Kingdom
US United States
UZ Uzbekistan
VE Venezuela
VN Vietnam
ZA South Africa
ZM Zambia
ZW Zimbabwe

Regions:
EU European Union
APAC Asia Pacific
LATAM Latin America
NA North America
RoW Rest of World

Units

Spatial units:
mm Millimetres
cm Centimetres
m Metres
km Kilometres
ha Hectares
m^2 Square metres
km^2 Square kilometres

Weight:
g Grammes
kg Kilogrammes
t Metric tons
kt Kilotons
Mt Million metric tons
Bt Billion metric tons

Volume:
ℓ Litres
m^3 Cubic metres
km^3 Cubic kilometres
Mm^3 Million cubic metres
Bm^3 Billion cubic metres

Voltage:
V Volts
kV Kilovolts
MV Megavolts
GV Gigavolts
TV Teravolts

Energy:
J Joules
kJ Kilojoules
MJ Megajoules
GJ Gigajoules
TJ Terajoules
PJ Petajoules
EJ Exajoule
MJ/kg Megajoules per kilogram

Currencies:
$ US dollars
€ Euros
к Kopeck (0.01 rouble)
£ Pound sterling

Quantities:
nmol/kg Nanomoles per kilogram
ppm Parts-per-million
ppb Parts-per-billion
ppt Parts-per-trillion
rpm Rotations per minute

Power:
W Watts
W/pc Watts *per capita*
kW Kilowatts
MW Megawatts
GW Gigawatts
TW Terawatts
kW/h Kilowatts per hour
MW/h Megawatts per hour
GW/h Gigawatts per hour
TW/h Terawatts per hour
kWh/m^2 Kilowatt-hours per square metre
MW/km^2 Megawatts per square kilometre
kWp Kilowatts (peak)
MWp Megawatts (peak)
GWp Gigawatts (peak)

Production:
b/d Barrels per day
b/a Barrels per annum
Mb/a Million barrels per annum
t/d Metric tons per day
t/m Metric tons per month
t/a Metric tons per annum
kt/m Kilotons per month
Mt/a Million metric tons per anum
Mt CO_2e Million metric tons CO_2 equivalent
m^3/a Cubic metres per annum
Mm^3/a Million cubic metres per annum
kg/MW Kilogrammes per megawatt
m^2/MWh Square metres per megawatt-hour
$/W US dollars per watt
$/MWh US dollars per megawatt hour

Renewable energy infrastructure in Brandenburg

Solar parks (selected)	performance in MWp
1 Weesow-Willmersdorf	187
2 Meuro	166
3 Templin	128
4 Jocksdorf	104
5 Briest	91
6 Finow	85
7 Senftenberg	82
8 Schipkau	81
9 Neuhardenberg	77

Wind parks (selected)	performance in MWp
1 Feldheim	254
2 Prenzlau-Schenkenberg-Dauer	249
3 Dahme-Görsdorf-Falkenberg	203
4 Karstädt-Premslin	197
5 Ketzin	175
6 Klettwitz	169
7 Jacobsdorf-Petersdorf	155
8 Duben	153
9 Willmersdorf	122

Substations

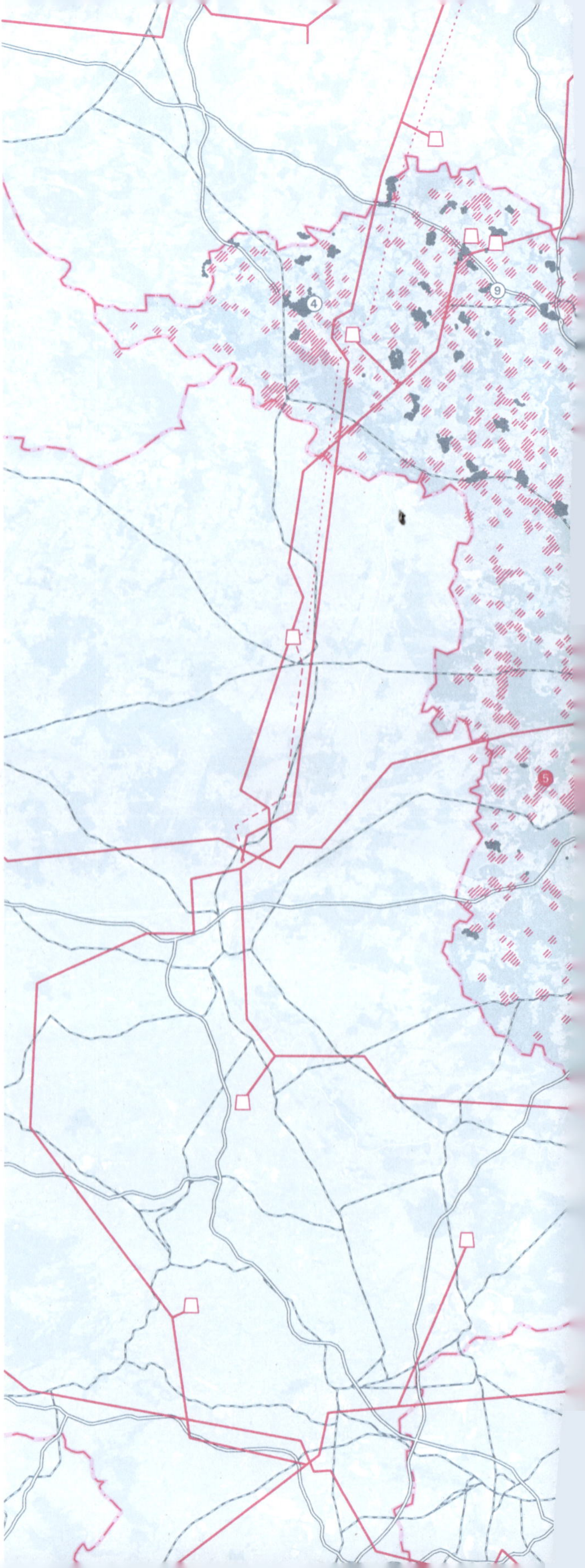

Highway
Railway
National border
Regional border

Solar parks
Wind turbines

High-voltage lines
In operation
Under construction
In planning

25 km